Contents

Introduction

This is yet another inn book. But it's far more, too.

We enjoy reading others, but they rarely tell us what we *really* want to know – which inns and B&Bs are especially good and what they are like, where to get a good meal and what there is to do in the area. No inn is an island – they are part of their locale. With their neighbors, they share a sense of place.

These insights are what we now share with you. We start not with the inn but with the area (of course, the existence of inns or lack thereof determine the 35 special destination areas to be included). Then we tour each area, with the eyes and ears of the first-time visitor and the perspective of seasoned travelers and journalists. We visit the inns, the restaurants and the attractions. We *work* these areas as roving journalists, always seeking out the best and most interesting. We also *live* them – staying in, eating in, and experiencing as many places as time and budget allow.

The result is this book. It's a selective compendium of what we think are the best and most interesting places to stay, eat and enjoy in these 35 special destinations, some of them New England's best-known and some not widely known at all.

The book reflects our tastes. We want creature comforts like private bathrooms and comfortable reading areas in our rooms. We like to meet other inn guests, but we also cherish privacy. We seek interesing and creative food and pleasant settings for meals. We enjoy unusual, enlightening things to do and places to see. We expect to receive value for our time and money.

While touring the past year to research this book as well as the third edition of its companion, *Inn Spots & Special Places / Mid-Atlantic,* we continue to be surprised by how many innkeepers say we are among the few guidebook writers who actually visit their facility and do not expect them merely to fill out a questionnaire and forward it with a considerable fee.

We also were struck by how many inns report, quite suddenly, an impact from the Internet. They say increasing numbers of travelers find places to stay and book reservations via the Net. The prospective guest likes the immediacy, the ability to see pictures and get detailed descriptions, the instant gratification of a quick, visual reservation. And yet, the realists among both innkeepers and browsers worry that the Web traveler finds only what the Web site wants them to know. They miss the insights offered by well traveled observers who have been there.

The inn experience is highly personal, both for the innkeeper and the inn-goer. The listing services, the advertising and the Web site hype do not have an objective perspective. Nor can they convey the personality of the place.

That's the role of experienced guidebook writers who make the rounds year after year and report things as they see them. Yes, the schedule is hectic and we do keep busy on these, our working trips that everyone thinks must be nothing but fun. One of us says she never again wants to get up in the middle of the night and cope with a strange bathroom. The other doesn't care if he never eats another bedside chocolate.

Nonetheless, it's rewarding both to experience a great inn and to discover a promising B&B. We also enjoy savoring a good meal, touring a choice musuem, poking through an unusual store and meeting so many interesting people along the way.

And that's what this book is about. We hope that you enjoy its findings as much as we did the finding.

Nancy and Richard Woodworth

About the Authors

Nancy Webster Woodworth began her travel and dining experiences in her native Montreal and as a waitress in summer resorts across Canada during her McGill University years. She worked in London and hitchhiked through Europe on $3 a day before her marriage to Richard Woodworth, whom she met while skiing at Mont Tremblant. She started writing her "Roaming the Restaurants" column for the West Hartford (Conn.) News in 1972. That led to half of the book, *Daytripping & Dining in Southern New England,* written in collaboration with Betsy Wittemann in 1978. She since has co-authored *Inn Spots & Special Places / Mid-Atlantic, Weekending in New England, Getaways for Gourmets in the Northeast, Waterside Escapes in the Northeast,* and *The Restaurants of New England.* She and her husband have two grown sons and live in West Hartford.

Richard Woodworth has been an inveterate traveler since his youth in suburban Syracuse, N.Y., where his birthday outings often involved train trips with friends for the day to nearby Utica or Rochester. After graduation from Middlebury College, he was a reporter for newspapers in Syracuse, Jamestown, Geneva and Rochester before moving to Connecticut to become editor of the West Hartford News and eventually executive editor of Imprint Newspapers. With his wife and their sons, he has traveled to the four corners of this country, Canada and portions of Europe, writing their findings for newspapers and magazines. He has co-authored *Getaways for Gourmets in the Northeast* and *The Restaurants of New England* as well as *Inn Spots & Special Places / Mid-Atlantic.* Between travels and duties as publisher of Wood Pond Press, he tries to find time to ski in the winter and weed the garden in summer.

Excerpts from the authors' books are on line at **www.getawayguides.com**

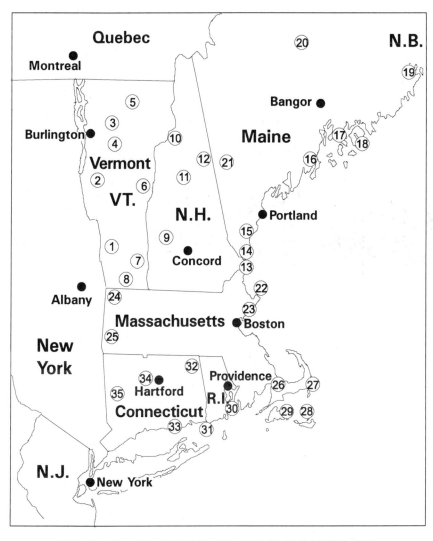

INN SPOTS AND SPECIAL PLACES IN NEW ENGLAND

1. Dorset
2. Middlebury
3. Stowe
4. Waitsfield/Warren
5. Craftsbury/Burke
6. Woodstock/Quechee
7. Newfane/Grafton
8. West Dover
9. Sunapee
10. Franconia/Sugar Hill
11. Squam Lakes
12. Jackson
13. Portsmouth
14. The Yorks
15. Kennebunkport
16. Camden
17. Blue Hill/Deer Isle
18. Mt. Desert Island
19. Eastport/St. Andrews
20. Greenville/Moosehead
21. Oxford Hills and Lakes
22. Rockport
23. Marblehead
24. Williamstown
25. Lenox
26. Sandwich
27. Chatham
28. Nantucket
29. Edgartown
30. Newport
31. Watch Hill/Stonington
32. Northeast Connecticut
33. Essex/Old Lyme
34. Farmington Valley
35. Litchfield

Historical marker tells about Dorset outside Dovetail Inn.

Dorset, Vt.

The Town that Marble Built

There is marble almost everywhere in Dorset, a town that marble helped build and upon which it has long prospered.

You see it on the sidewalks all around the picturesque green, on the porch at the historic Dorset Inn and on the terrace at the newer Barrows House, on the side of the turreted United Church of Christ and on the pillars of the Marble West Inn. The sight of an entire mansion built of marble stuns passersby along Dorset West Road.

It seems as if all Dorset has been paved with marble – and with good intentions. Here is what residents and writers alike have called the perfect village. Merchant Jay Hathaway phrased it well in a Dorset Historical Society lecture: What could be better than running "a small country store nestled in the mountains of Vermont in a town that is as close to perfect as Dorset?"

A village of perhaps 1,800 (about two-thirds of its population during the height of its marble-producing days a century ago), it's a mix of charm and culture in perfect proportion.

Dorset is unspoiled, from its rustic Dorset Playhouse (the oldest summer playhouse in the state) to its handsomely restored inn (the oldest in the state) to its Dorset Field Club (the oldest nine-hole golf course in the state) to its lovely white, green-shuttered homes (many among the oldest in the state) to its two general stores, both of them curiously different relics of 19th-century life. Here is a peaceful place in which to cherish the past.

Barely six miles away is Manchester, one of the more sophisticated tourist destinations around. Some of its visitors, who come to shop until they drop, don't know about nor are they particularly interested in Dorset. But people in Dorset can take advantage of all Manchester's urbane attractions as desired.

So the Dorset visitor has the best of both worlds – a tranquil respite amid a myriad of activities and attractions. What could be more copacetic?

Inn Spots

Cornucopia of Dorset, Route 30, Dorset 05251.

One of the more inviting and elegant B&Bs anywhere is offered by Bill and Linda Ley, who left Ipswich, Mass., to realize a goal of running a country inn. That they ultimately found Cornucopia of Dorset was as pleasing to them as it was to the guests who have been entertained there since. Their B&B lives up to its name, offering an abundance of warmth, comfort and personality.

Cornucopia has only four guest rooms and a cottage suite, but what accommodations they are! All air-conditioned and with large, modern baths, they contain poster or canopy beds ranging in size from queen to king, afluff with down comforters or colorful quilts and pillows and merino wool mattress pads. All but one have fireplaces. Upholstered chairs flank three-way reading lamps. Terrycloth robes, bowls of fresh fruit, telephones and Crabtree & Evelyn toiletries are the norm. Bill painted the walls in the rear Dorset Hill Room in two kinds of white stripes that look like wallpaper. We found the Mother Myrick Room especially comfortable with a kingsize bed against a wall of shelves containing books and family photos, and a full bath with a double vanity. The rear cottage with a cathedral-ceilinged living room, fireplace, eat-in kitchen and a queensize loft bedroom has a stereo and a private sundeck.

The common rooms are more than an adjunct – they are the focal point of Cornucopia. Off a small, cozy library is an inviting living room with overstuffed sofas. Both have fireplaces. Beyond is an enormous dining room opening into a sunroom, a contemporary area that's cool and shaded in the summer, warm and bright in

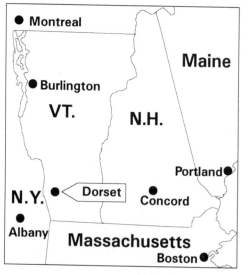

winter. It is here that we like to gravitate to study the leather scrapbooks of restaurant menus and area attractions, browse through a cornucopia of magazines or pore through a hardbound book called "At the Movies," listing all the video tapes the Leys offer on their VCR. But there's little inclination to read or watch, given the innkeepers' hospitality and propensity for lively conversation.

Outside are a marble patio and a covered porch. Enough bird feeders are attached to the sunroom windows to accommodate a flock.

Innkeepers Bill and Linda Ley welcome guests to Cornucopia of Dorset.

Breakfast is served by candlelight at the formal table in the airy dining room. Our latest repast, detailed on a personalized card left in the room the night before, started with fresh orange juice and a colorful dish of honeydew melon, nicely presliced into bite-size pieces and topped with raspberries, strawberries, kiwi and banana slices, and vanilla yogurt. The pièce de résistance was a baked croissant à l'orange with crème fraîche. Colombian coffee with a hint of cinnamon and Twining's English tea accompanied. The baked raspberry pancake served on another occasion was so good that we asked Linda for the recipe. Other specialties include bread pudding with warm berry sauce, quiche lorraine, baked ham and egg cup with Vermont cheddar cheese, and baked cinnamon french toast with sausage patties.

The goodies don't end there. Complimentary champagne is served at check-in (wines and champagnes are available for purchase as well), and help-yourself coffee, tea and hot chocolate are at hand 24 hours a day. Upon returning from dinner, you'll find your bedroom lights turned off, an oil lamp flickering, and candy – perhaps a Lindt truffle or a slice of buttercrunch from our favorite Mother Myrick's confectionery store in Manchester – on the pillow of a bed turned down ever so artistically. In the room are stationery and stamped envelopes and postcards upon which we'd spread the word, "great place – you ought to be here."

(802) 867-5751 or (800) 566-5751. Fax (802) 867-5753. www.cornucopiaofdorset.com. Four rooms and one cottage with private baths. Doubles, $125 to $155 weekends and foliage, $115 to $140 midweek. Cottage, $200 and $225. Two-night minimum weekends and foliage. Children over 16. No smoking.

Marble West Inn, Dorset West Road, Dorset 05251.

The thank-you note penned to June and Wayne Erla and displayed in the Marble West scrapbook says it well: "Every detail that could enhance your guests' comfort has been thought of: beautifully appointed rooms, superb food, a comfortable sitting room, beautiful grounds,...wonderful hospitality." High praise, coming from a fellow innkeeper from Marblehead, Mass. And accurate. The Erlas took early retirement from their IBM positions in Burlington and started enhancing the historic Holley-West house two miles southwest of Dorset. The stately Greek Revival, built in the 1840s by the owner of a marble quarry, is graced with seven marble columns in front. A marble sign has identified its status as an inn since 1985.

The Erlas have redecorated and furnished with great style and taste. They retained the extraordinary stenciling (done by Honey West, one of the quarry owner's daughters) in the front entry and upstairs hall, and several other unusual decorative and architectural features, such as the low stairway banisters installed for a woman in the West family who was less than five feet tall. Swagged draperies, fine oriental rugs, a grand piano and furniture upholstered in Waverly fabrics and chintz welcome guests into the main parlor. It's open to the dining room, where ten Queen Anne chairs flank a solid mahogany table. The adjacent library has a marble fireplace, comfortable furniture, a nifty window seat and a coffee table covered with the latest magazines vying for attention with shelves of century-old books.

The main floor also contains the West Suite with a working fireplace, a queensize bed topped with a Ralph Lauren comforter, a sitting room with sofa and wing chairs, and a small sunroom just big enough for two. Off the library at the other end of the house is the Birch Suite with a kingsize bed, sitting area, a shower tucked into the small, ingenious bathroom space and a private patio. Upstairs off two stairways are six other attractive guest rooms with private baths. Each is amply furnished with oriental rugs and Laura Ashley or Ralph Lauren fabrics, and chocolates await on the night stands. We're partial to the rear-corner Dorset Room with a canopied queensize bed, lots of floral chintzes and windows on three sides. The windows were opened wide on a warm autumn evening for cross-ventilation, and we didn't hear a sound all night.

Breakfast was by candlelight in a serene dining room with gray walls, floral swags, colorful oriental rugs on a polished dark wood floor and a ficus tree in one corner. Wayne does the cooking and June plays the piano for a musical accompaniment to the meal. Ours started with orange juice, a half grapefruit enhanced by just enough maple syrup and coconut to sweeten the tartness, and June's piping-hot morning glory muffins. The main course was walnut pancakes, half a dozen "medallions" garnished with cranberries and served with delicious mild sausages that Wayne imports by the case from Pennsylvania.

Fed by a passing creek, a two-tiered pond out back provides a home for 27-inch rainbow trout. Around the grounds, Adirondack chairs face the pond as well as a croquet lawn.

(802) 867-4155 or (800) 453-7629. www.marblewestinn.com. Six rooms and two suites with private baths. Doubles, $90 to $155; foliage, $100 to $165. Children over 12. No smoking.

Dovetail Inn, Main Street, Box 976, Dorset 05251.
Nicely located facing the green in the heart of town just across from the Dorset Inn (in fact it was once an inn annex and housed chauffeurs and staff in the posh old days) is the two-building Dovetail. Jim and Jean Kingston, he a marine engineer and now a local property manager, moved from Connecticut and, as they say, picked a thriving area.

They have refurbished the nine guest rooms and a two-room suite in one Federal-style structure, and added a sitting room with a TV and butler's pantry stocked with hot and cold beverages. The other building houses their quarters and a cheery "keeping room" for guests' use. On the second floor landing is a nook with a window seat and many books for borrowing.

Rooms vary in size and all have private baths and air conditioning. All but one double come with queensize or king/twin beds. Each has a sitting area with a couple of easy chairs (ours had a sofa) and pretty new wallpaper and curtains. The Village Suite in front can accommodate four, what with a queensize bed with a handpainted headboard in the bedroom, an adjoining sitting room with queen sofabed, new corner gas fireplace and TV, and two bathrooms. The prized Hearthside Room in back offers a fireplace and kitchenette-wet bar, a queensize poster bed, loveseat, TV, a private deck and easy access to the gardens. Jim, a woodworker of note, built the pencil-post queen bed in one room, and refers to the "magic headboards" in another – "I move them to make the beds twins or kingsize," he quips.

In the back yard, the Kingstons tired of the upkeep of the swimming pool they inherited from the Dorset Inn and filled it in with a terrace and gardens "so we finally have a back yard," Jean said. They also have a front porch with rocking chairs for viewing the Dorset green. Friendly hosts, they have a beer and wine license and serve outside or in the keeping room. They also offer tea and cookies in the afternoon.

The continental buffet breakfast consists of juice, fresh fruits or compotes, muffins (the orange ones were delicious), breads and coffee cakes. You may have it brought to your room in a basket, if you wish.

Why the name Dovetail? "I like quality building and furniture," says Jim, "and a cutesy name didn't fit Dorset."

(802) 867-5747 or (800) 436-8382. Fax (802) 867-0246. www.dovetailinn.com. Nine rooms and one suite with private baths. Doubles, $80 to $99 weekends, $65 to $85 midweek; $85 to $135 in foliage, $65 to $95 in spring. Suite, $165 weekends, $120 midweek, $195 foliage, $165 spring. No smoking.

Barrows House, Main Street, Dorset 05251.

We don't know what is more appealing about the Barrows House: the comfortable rooms and cottages amid eleven acres of park-like grounds with a swimming pool, two tennis courts and an intricate gazebo, or the meals in the greenhouse addition that extends the dining room to the outdoors.

Black wicker rockers are at the ready behind the columns that front the 200-year-old main house, which has a fireplaced living room, the expansive dining room (see Dining Spots), six upstairs guest rooms and, beside a canopied outdoor patio, a charming tavern notable for its trompe-l'oeil walls of books so real you feel you're in a library.

There are eight rooms upstairs in the main inn. Most popular, however, are twenty scattered in eight outbuildings converted into sophisticated lodging. Each house has its own sitting room, porch or terrace. All rooms have private baths. Five suites have fireplaces and sitting rooms. Wallpapers, draperies and quilts are coordinated, and all are filled with nice touches like ruffled pillows and patchcraft hangings.

Since taking over in 1993, innkeepers Jim and Linda McGinnis have sponsored the annual "Littlest Music Festival," a series of four free Sunday afternoon concerts on the inn's lawn each June. Attendees contribute food items and cash for the Manchester Area Food Cupboard.

The inn also has found a niche in welcoming children and pets. "We're family-friendly and dog-friendly," says Jim. Dogs can stay in one of three separate accommodations for families with dogs for $10 a day.

(802) 867-4455 or (800) 639-1620. Fax (802) 867-0132. Eighteen rooms and ten suites with private baths. B&B: doubles, $130 to $165; off-season $125 to $140; suites, $160 to $200, off-season $135 to $170. MAP: doubles $180 to $215, off-season $155 to $170; suites, $210 to $250, off-season $165 to $200 in off-season. Two-night minimum most weekends. Children and pets welcome.

The Dorset Inn, Route 30, Dorset 05251.

Vermont's oldest continuously operated country inn, with a history dating back to 1796, was nicely renovated in 1984 and 1985 by what chef-owner Sissy Hicks bills as "the inspired revival of an historic site."

Overnight guests are greeted by a stunning collection of blue glass displayed in lighted cases at the top of the stairway on the second floor. All 24 rooms on the two upper floors have been redone with wall-to-wall carpeting, modern baths with wood washstands, print wallpapers and antique furnishings. Two of the nicest are the third-floor front corner rooms, one with twin sleigh beds, two rockers, Audubon prints and floral wallpaper, and the other with a canopy bed, marble table and wallpaper of exotic animals and birds. A second-floor corner suite overlooking the green includes a sitting room with TV, telephone and refrigerator and a bedroom with double brass bed. Three of seven rooms at the rear of the ground floor also have TVs and telephones. Beds are about equally split between queens, doubles and two twins.

On the ground floor, stuffed bears in little chairs welcome guests in the reception area. The main sitting room appeals with comfortable furniture around a fireplace, a collection of blue and white china on the mantel, scrubbed wide-plank floors and a small television set. Beyond is a cheery, porch-like breakfast room with Vermont-woven mats atop wood tables and green floral curtains against small-paned windows that extend to the floor.

The inn serves a hearty breakfast (sourdough or fruit pancakes, all kinds of eggs, bacon, ham and sausage). Out back are an attractive, country-style dining room (see Dining Spots) and a pleasant tap room with a big oak bar.

(802) 867-5500 or (800) 835-5284. Fax (802) 867-5542. Thirty-one rooms with private baths. Doubles, MAP $210, $230 in foliage, $175 in winter and spring, $125 winter midweek. Suite, $300 in summer, $325 in fall, $225 in winter-spring. Two-night minimum peak weekends. Children over 10. No smoking.

The Little Lodge at Dorset, Main Street, Box 673, Dorset 05251.

"We have more places to sit per guest than any inn we've seen," says Allan Norris of the appealing, five-room B&B he and wife Nancy run with TLC.

Guests in those five rooms have access to a formal dining room with oriental rugs, shining silver and bone china for breakfast service, a living room with wood stove and large hooked rug, a large and luxurious den with barnwood walls, blue leather sofa, fireplace and shelves of books and games, an attached five-sided gazebo that has black garden furniture cushioned with yellow and green pads, a wet bar with refrigerator and a hallway with separate entrance for stashing skis and boots. Outside are a rope hammock and a garden sitting area overlooking a trout pond, the verdant fairways of the Dorset Field Club and the mountainside beyond.

Stone wall opens onto path to Little Lodge at Dorset.

Given all these inviting public areas, one might expect the Norrises, transplanted Baltimoreans, to have skimped on their upstairs guest rooms. Not so. All have private baths and are furnished with twin beds usually made up as kings. They contain paintings by Nancy's great-uncle (one of the Boston School of Impressionists) and quilts made by Nancy or bedspreads crocheted by Allan's sister. They exude an air of lived-in comfort.

Breakfast is continental-plus, Nancy supplementing juices and cereals with her homemade strawberry-pecan, orange-coriander and pear-walnut breads or muffins. She and her guests are fond of exchanging recipes. Tea and coffee are available anytime, and Vermont cheese and crackers are put out in the late afternoon.

The grounds yield trails for cross-country skiing and hiking in the rear, a stocked trout pond (no fishing, but you can feed them) dug by the home's former owner who runs the Orvis sporting goods company in Manchester, and a view of an oriental garden with colorful red bridges in front of the house next door. Enjoying all this with the guests is Azalea, an unusually friendly Doberman pinscher who nuzzles up to one and all. "More people write in our guest book about our dog than anything else," Allan reports.

(802) 867-4040 or (800) 378-7505. Five rooms with private baths. Doubles, $85 to $95.

Inn at West View Farm, Main Street, Dorset 05251.

The accommodations have been upgraded, the bar and waiting area expanded, and a comfy parlor and sun porch added since Helmut and Dorothy Stein took over the old Village Auberge. The dining room, made famous by former chef-owner Alex Koks, remains familiar to guests who predate the Steins' arrival, and the food has improved lately after a few years of ups and downs.

The inn's addition has created a new entry and reception area and a welcoming common area that was lacking earlier. No longer must arriving overnight guests share a small parlor with waiting dining patrons. Everyone can enjoy the expanded lounge, a large sitting room with a fireplace and two sofas, and an exceptionally nice enclosed porch full of white wicker sofas and chairs.

The four original guest rooms upstairs have been redecorated, and six more tidy rooms with full baths have been added. All but one have queensize beds. They are nicely furnished with country antiques.

Breakfast is served to inn guests in the cheery, plant-filled bay-window end of the dining room. Eggs any style, pancakes, croissants and pain perdu with various fillings are among the offerings.

(802) 867-5715 or (800) 769-4903. Fax (802) 867-0468. Ten rooms with private baths. Doubles, $98; foliage, $140. Two-night minimum weekends. No smoking. Closed early November and April.

Dining Spots

Chantecleer, Route 7A, East Dorset.

As far as area residents are concerned, there's near unanimity as to the best restaurant around: the Chantecleer in East Dorset. The food is consistent, the service professional and the atmosphere rustically elegant.

Swiss chef Michel Baumann features Swiss and French provincial cuisine in the contemporary-style restaurant fashioned from an old dairy barn.

Our party of four sampled a number of the autumn offerings, starting with a classic baked onion soup, penne with smoked salmon, potato pancakes with sautéed crabmeat and a heavenly lime butter sauce, and bundnerfleisch fanned out in little coronets with pearl onions, cornichons and melba rounds. For main courses, we savored the rack of lamb, veal sweetbreads morel, sautéed quail stuffed with mushrooms duxelle and the night's special of boneless pheasant from a local farm, served with smoked bacon and grapes, among other things. Fabulous roesti potatoes upstaged the other accompaniments, puree of winter squash, snow peas and strands of celery.

Bananas foster, grand marnier layer cake, crème brûlée and trifle were worthy endings for a rich, expensive meal. A number of Swiss wines are included on the reasonably priced wine list, and Swiss yodeling music may be heard on tape as background music.

In 1994, Chantecleer opened a neat little offshoot, **The Little Rooster Cafe,** an innovative place for breakfast and lunch in Manchester Center. In 1996, Michel and partners added a nearby restaurant called **Jasper's Cafe,** a casual establishment offering a mix of Southwest and eclectic American fare for lunch and dinner.

(802) 362-1616. Entrées, $21 to $28. Dinner by reservation, nightly except Tuesday from 6.

Barrows House, Main Street, Dorset.

Innkeepers Jim and Linda McGinnis preside over a dining operation that's long been known for good food in pleasant surroundings. The focal point for many is the sunken greenhouse on the side, where you almost feel you're dining under the stars. The main dining room has been made darker and more intimate with the introduction of dimmer switches, Pierre Deux wallpaper, swag curtains and white woven mats over rust and white patterned cloths. The cozy tavern, with its trompe-l'oeil walls of books, also is a pleasant spot for dining.

The menu features contemporary New England cuisine, and includes an appealing "lighter side menu" at lighter prices, such treats as Maine crab cakes, sautéed calves liver and grilled duck breast with spicy peanut sauce.

At one visit, we started with smoked tuna with caper and red onion crème fraîche and a tartlet of smoked scallops and mussels with scallions and red peppers, both excellent. A small loaf of bread and a garden salad with a honey-mustard dressing came next. Main courses were grilled chicken with fresh berries, mint and grand marnier and pan-roasted veal tenderloin with pancetta, tomatoes and shiitake mushrooms. They were accompanied by a platter of vegetables served family style, on this night spaghetti squash creole, lemon-scented broccoli, carrot puree with maple syrup, and risotto with fennel and red peppers. Vegetables have always been a Barrows House strong point; one summer dinner brought carrots glazed with raisins and ginger, asparagus with hollandaise, squash and spinach with dill, and warm potato salad.

A huckleberry tart and cappuccino ice cream tempted from the dessert list.

(802) 867-4455 or (800) 639-1620. Entrées, $15.95 to $24.95; light entrées, $10.25 to $13.95. Dinner nightly, 6 to 9.

The Dorset Inn, Church and Main Streets, Dorset.

Interesting, creative food has been emanating from the kitchen of this venerable inn since Sissy Hicks took over the chef's chores in 1984.

The main dining room has been redecorated in hunter green with white trim and wainscoting. A focal point is a spotlit glass cabinet displaying cups and horse figurines along one wall. Out back are a tavern with dining tables and a large oak bar, and in front, a dining porch that's especially pleasant for lunch.

A practitioner of the new American cuisine, Sissy Hicks changes her menu seasonally. She also has changed the previously separate tavern and dining room menus into one that serves both areas. Now you'll find a turkey burger on the same menu as loin lamb chops with roasted shallots and garlic confit. Not to mention the spicy chicken wings and crisp potato skins alongside the "original warm chicken tenderloin salad." At least five vegetarian items – including baked eggplant crêpes and grilled polenta with sautéed portobello mushrooms – also are offered.

Among appetizers, we found the crabmeat mousse with a cucumber-mustard dill sauce and a few slices of melba toast enough for two to share. Crusty French bread with sweet butter and green salads with excellent stilton or basil-vinaigrette dressings accompanied. Having been advised that the calves liver was the best anywhere, we had to try it. Served rare as requested with crisp bacon and slightly underdone slices of onion, it was superb. The fresh trout, deboned but served with its skin still on, was laden with sautéed leeks and mushrooms. A Wente chardonnay, golden and oaky, was a good choice from the reasonably priced wine list.

Pies, bread pudding with whiskey sauce and chocolate terrine with raspberry sauce are on the dessert menu. We chose a kiwi sorbet, wonderfully deep flavored, accompanied by a big sugar cookie. One of the favorite fall desserts is Sissy's cider sorbet with spiced wine sauce.

(802) 867-5500 or (800) 835-5284. Entrées, $8.50 to $18.50. Lunch daily in summer and fall, 11:30 to 2. Dinner nightly, 5 to 9.

Auberge at The Inn at West View Farm, Route 30, Dorset.

Former chef-owner Alex Koks was a tough act to follow, and a procession of chefs has had varying degrees of success since. The latest is owner Helmut Stein, who had been host and back-up sous chef. When his last chef gave notice in 1996,

Helmut moved into the kitchen. "I cooked the same menu and nobody knew the difference," he said. He's been cooking since.

The handsome Auberge dining room with its striking built-in china cabinets and a large bay window at the far end is about the only vestige of its former life as the Village Auberge. An addition houses Clancy's Tavern, an attractive room with dark green wainscoting and beams, where the polished wooden tables are topped with English placemats.

A piping-hot cheese fritter is delivered to each diner with the menu. Among starters are a stellar black bean and ginger soup with curried crème fraîche, oysters rockefeller and venison pâté with brandy and maple-mustard sauce. Excellent sourdough bread and house salads with zesty roquefort or vinaigrette dressings precede the main course. We savored the veal sweetbreads with pink peppercorns and a whole grain mustard jus and the pan-roasted breast of duck with rhubarb, ginger and risotto cake. Desserts included apple tart, plum cake and a refreshing assortment of ice creams and sorbets.

The tavern menu adds items like grilled bratwurst, crab cakes and garlic shrimp with red pepper linguini.

(802) 867-5715 or (800) 769-4903. Entrées, $18.50 to $23.95; tavern, $9.75 to $12.95. Dinner, Tuesday-Sunday 6 to 9. Also closed Tuesday in winter and early November and April.

The Artist's Palate Cafe, West Road, Manchester.

This nifty cafe, halfway up a mountain at the Southern Vermont Art Center, was run for years by people associated with noted area restaurateur Alex Koks, formerly of the Village Auberge in Dorset. Now run by The Equinox resort in Manchester, it's a great place for lunch with a view of the sculpture garden as well as birch trees, valleys and hills.

Dine inside or on the outdoor terrace on ice-cream parlor chairs. At our visit, the changing menu, attached to an artist's palette, offered choices like crab and asparagus melt over a toasted English muffin, warm ham and cheese croissant, seafood caesar salad (with smoked shrimp and scallops), poached salmon and vermicelli, and a burger topped with Vermont cheddar. We remember a fantastic tomato-orange soup and a good chicken salad with snow peas. Dessert could be a crispy apple tart or melon with berries.

(802) 362-5223. Entrées, $7 to $9.50. Lunch, Tuesday-Saturday 11:30 to 3, Sunday noon to 3, June to early October.

Diversions

Marble. It's everywhere, and hard to miss around Dorset. Take a gander at the large marble mansion on Dorset West Road, set back in the trees south of Marble West Inn. Although none of the six quarries that once made Dorset the most extensive quarrying center in Vermont still operates, you can swim in an abandoned marble quarry on the east side of Route 30 just south of the village. You'll know you're there when you see **Cat's Dogs,** the outdoor hot-dog stand run daily in season by Catherine (Cat) Ferenc across from the quarry

Back Roads. They're all around, but a few are special. Dorset West Road and adjacent West Road in Manchester take you past some interesting and impressive country homes. Dorset Hollow Road makes "an absolutely gorgeous circle that takes about ten minutes," in the words of innkeeper Bill Ley of Cornucopia. The

Danby Mountain Road winds through secluded forests and, if you keep bearing right at every intersection, you eventually come to a dead-end with a spectacular wide-open view across the hillsides toward mountain peaks 50 miles away. The sight at fall foliage's height actually produced a few "wows" out of us and lived up to Dovetail innkeeper Jim Kingston's promise of one of the best foliage trips in Vermont.

Local Lore. During Vermont's Bicentennial, the **Dorset Historical Society** moved to a new house donated as its headquarters, open Saturday mornings and by appointment. Take a recorded village walking tour, learn about the local marble and cheese-making industries or trace the genealogy of a Vermont ancestor here. Another local gem is the **Dorset Village Public Library** with its McIntyre Art Gallery, located in the restored Gray's Tavern building at Church and Main Streets, open daily except Sunday.

Dorset Playhouse, Cheney Road, Dorset.
Tucked away in the trees just off Church Street, the rustic, all-wood barn with the red and white awning on the side was the first summer theater in Vermont. Since 1975, it has been home to the Dorset Theater Festival, a non-profit professional theater company committed to the revival of plays from the past and the development of new plays and playwrights. Its rediscovery of Cole Porter's 1938 musical "You Never Know" went on national tour. Other new plays have gone on to New York and Washington.
(802) 867-5777. Performances nightly except Monday, June-September. Tickets, $16 to $26.

Merck Forest & Farmland Center, (802) 394-7836. These days it's rare to find so large and unspoiled an area so available for public use as this 2,820-acre preserve northwest of Dorset off Route 315 in Rupert. Twenty-six miles of roads and trails are accessible for hiking in the forests, meadows and mountains. Established by George Merck of chemical-company fame, it is a non-profit outdoor education center open to the public year-round. Scholars study the organic garden, the maple sugaring and forest management. Hikers, campers and cross-country skiers enjoy the trails to Birch and Beebe ponds and the vista of the Adirondacks from the Viewpoint. The forest is a New England treasure.

General Stores. Peltier's General Store has been the center of Dorset life since 1816, the more so since it was acquired in 1976 by Jay Hathaway and his wife Terri, who have augmented its everyday goods with exotica like balsamic vinegars, cheddar cheese from Shelburne Farms, aromatic coffee beans and fine wines. Just back from New York with an array of new items, Jay said his store "is ever-changing because we don't want to be routine." Peltier's celebrated its 175th anniversary during Vermont's Bicentennial and abounds with every need from champagne to newspapers.

Equally historic but thoroughly unchanging is the **H.M. Williams Department Store,** two attached barns identified by a small sign at the south edge of town and an incredible jumble of merchandise placed helter-skelter (foodstuffs amidst the hardware, boxes of ladies' shoes identified with a cardboard sign: "With this quality and these prices, let the big boys compete"). Prices are marked by crayon and the cash register is a pouch worn around his waist by proprietor Dennis Brownlee. While we waited for 50 pounds of sunflower bird seed for a bargain $13.10, the woman ahead of us bought 50 pounds of rabbit pellets and was told where she could find a bale of hay.

A few other Dorset stores like the new **Flower Brook Pottery** and **Stonewalls Antiques, Green Gate Antiques** and **Carlson Antiques** are of interest. More than 200 heirloom quilts are offered by **Marie Miller American Quilts,** and **Wild Birds** stocks everything related to birds. Plans were in the works for a high-style antiques co-op on the green. South of town is the **J.K. Adams Co.** factory store, which stocks woodware and housewares made from native hardwoods. Butcher blocks, knife racks, bowls, cutlery and homespun tablecloths are for sale at substantial savings. Much smaller but equally rewarding is **Wardies Woodies,** where the owners make all kinds of wood things from racks to beds to whirlagigs.

More Shopping. Since adjacent Manchester offers such fine shopping opportunities, we suggest a few favorites. Silk-screened greeting cards from the **Crockett Collection** are available at discount prices at the showroom on Route 7 north of Manchester. Fishermen gravitate to the **Orvis Retail Store** in Manchester Center, where fishing rods are produced (and can be tried out at the adjacent trout pond). **Northshire Bookstore** is one of the best of its genre. **The Jelly Mill,** a three-story barn, is crammed with gifts, cards, gourmet foods, kitchenware and much more; the **Buttery Restaurant** on the second floor serves lunch and snacks. **Anne Klein, Polo-Ralph Lauren, Brooks Brothers, Giorgio Armani, Burberry's, Calvin Klein, Coach, Cole-Haan, Crabtree & Evelyn. Hickey Freeman** and **Baccarat** are among the growing number of fashionable outlet stores.

Southern Vermont Art Center, West Road, Manchester.

High up a mountainside along the back road to Dorset is this special place not to be missed. The oldest cultural institution in Vermont, it was started in 1929 when five local artists banded together to display their works at the Dorset Town Hall. Inside the 28-room Georgian Colonial mansion are changing exhibits staged year-round, plus the Garden Cafe for lunch. Plays and concerts by such groups as the U.S. Military Academy Band, the New England Brass Consort and the Southern Vermont Chamber Orchestra are always well attended. The Manchester Garden Club restored the Boswell Botany Trail, a three-quarter-mile walk past hundreds of wildflowers and 67 varieties of Vermont ferns, all identified by club members. An hour's hike through the woods is another attraction, and the sculpture garden featuring a 250-year-old sugar maple is bordered by amazing vistas.

(802) 362-1405. Open Tuesday-Saturday 10 to 5, Sunday noon to 5.

Extra-Special

Mother Myrick's Confectionery & Ice Cream Parlor, Route 7A, Manchester Center.

We can't ever seem to get through this area without stopping at Mother Myrick's, the ultimate ice-cream parlor and confectionery shop. One of the things that lures us is the fudge sauce – so good that a friend to whom we give it hides her jar in a cupboard and eats it with a spoon. Here you can buy the most extraordinary home-made chocolates, get a croissant and cappuccino in the morning, tea and a slice of Vermont maple cheesecake in the afternoon, or a piece of grand marnier truffle cake and espresso at night. Ice-cream sodas, milkshakes, floats, sundaes and pastries are served in a fantastic art-deco setting with etched-glass panels, bentwood cases, light columns and the like done by gifted Vermont craftsmen.

(802) 362-1560. Open weekdays, 10 to 10 in summer; weekdays to 6, weekends and holiday weeks to 9 in off-season.

Mountains provide backdrop for Middlebury College's picturesque campus.

Middlebury, Vt.
Robert Frost Country

The great poet Robert Frost spent the last 23 summers of his life in the mountains outside Middlebury. Little wonder. This gently rugged area enlivened by a college town is mountain country, Frost country, an area of rambling white houses, red barns and green fields – the essence of Vermont, if you will.

The poet who adopted New England and made it his own also adopted the Middlebury area. The small cabin where he slept is not open to the public, but there's a nearby interpretive trail where you can get a taste of his enduring poetry and the sights that inspired him. The Middlebury College library houses many of his first editions. The founder of the town's Vermont Book Shop knew the poet well and the store stocks many of his works. And the college's Bread Loaf mountain campus carries on his tradition with its annual summer writers' conference.

Middlebury is, for us, the epitome of the New England college town. The campus of the "college on the hill" on the west side of town is unusually picturesque, its newer gray limestone buildings complementing the older ones dating back to the college's founding in 1800. One of us first saw the campus on a snowy April day in the 1950s and decided then and there that this was to be the college for him. In summer, when the regular college is not in session, its famed Summer Language Schools turn the area into a rural United Nations as graduate students chat in almost every language except English.

The college gives the town its solid heritage and vibrant character. ("The strength of the hills is His also" are the words etched above the portals of the striking college chapel in which Robert Frost lectured to turnaway student audiences every few years.) And a returning alumnus is struck by a new dynamic – an array of restaurants and shops that is remarkable for a town its size (8,000). Except for eight annoying new traffic lights along main Route 7, Middlebury remains a tranquil college town.

To the east are East Middlebury and Ripton, quiet mountain hamlets, Middlebury's bucolic Bread Loaf campus and the college's impressive Snow Bowl ski area. To the west lies the Champlain Valley, a surprisingly vast and undeveloped expanse sidling up to Lake Champlain. To the north is Vergennes, which claims to be the nation's smallest city. The vistas of water and mountains are stunning, thanks to the Green Mountains on the east, the Adirondacks to the west and Lake Champlain shimmering in the middle.

Inn Spots

Swift House Inn, 25 Stewart Lane, Middlebury 05753.

A rambling white clapboard manse, built in 1814 and once the home of a Vermont governor, is the focal point of this exceptional, elegant inn and restaurant run by John Nelson and his daughter, Karla Nelson-Loura. John and his late wife Andy started with ten rooms, added five more in the Gatehouse Annex and restored the side carriage house as the crowning touch: six deluxe rooms with fireplaces, double jacuzzis, kingsize beds, TVs and telephones. Rooms are handsomely outfitted with poster beds and handmade quilts, and the bathrooms are knockouts. One in the Gatehouse, done up with white wicker and purple walls, has bath pillows "so you can lie in the whirlpool tub with a good book," our guide explained.

Rooms come with the amenities like telephones and terrycloth robes that help give the inn its four-diamond AAA rating. We first enjoyed the Governor's Room, upstairs in the front corner of the main house, elegantly traditional in blue florals, with a kingsize bed, antique armoire, fireplace, two wing chairs and a writing desk. Bedside chocolates accompanied a note of welcome from the innkeeper. A subsequent stay was in the prized Mansfield suite on the lower level of the carriage house. It is large, light and airy in bleached pine with an abundance of windows screened by Indian shutters. We stepped up into a kingsize bed, watched the TV news on a sofa and wing chair (each flanked by good reading lamps) in the ample sitting area, and enjoyed cocktails on our own patio beside a rose garden. The front foyer had a closet with an ironing board, the dressing area was equipped with a coffee-maker, and the lavish bathroom with double jacuzzi positively shone with solid brass fixtures.

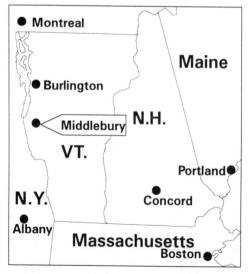

Public rooms in the inn include a wide hall used as a parlor with one of the inn's many fireplaces and a comfortable little cocktail lounge with five seats at the bar. A steam room and sauna are available in the carriage house. The expansive grounds are dotted with Adirondack chairs and private hideaways for two.

Candlelight dinners are served in the inn's gracious dining rooms (see Where to Eat). A continental breakfast with fresh fruit, cereal, muffins and popovers is

Rural Federal-style building is home of Strong House Inn.

included in the rates; more elaborate fare can be ordered from a menu. After breakfast, settle on the front porch for a look down the wide lawns toward the Adirondack mountains in the distance.

(802) 388-9925. Fax (802) 388-9927. Twenty-one rooms with private baths. Doubles, $80 to $160. Carriage house, $185 to $195.

Strong House Inn, 82 West Main St., Vergennes 05491.

The vitality and enthusiasm of its owners pervades this 1834 Federal-style B&B, listed on the National Register of Historic Places and nicely located on six acres on the crest of a hill at the western edge of town.

Mary and Hugh Bargiel, transplants from Florida where both were with the Burger King headquarters, have upgraded the property and marketed their offerings with a flair that won Mary the Vermont Lodging and Restaurant Association's B&B operator of the year award in 1997.

The substantial residence, built by the local bank president for whom it is named, offers eight rooms and suites, all with private baths. They vary widely in size and style, from the double-bedded English Garden Room with its own bath down the hall to Samuel's Suite. The latter takes up one entire section of the main floor and includes an impressive English country library with a queen sofabed, fireplace and TV, a small bedroom with a queen poster bed and a sun porch with Adirondack views. The Empire Room, the original master bedroom, takes its name from its Empire chest, and has a queen canopy bed, a day bed and two leather wing chairs facing the fireplace. We'd be quite content in the new Vermont Room, a hideaway added above the garage, with a beamed ceiling, sturdy queen country pine bed, pine armoire, writing desk, plump settee and chair, and french doors opening onto a small balcony. The chairs and the handmade quilt match the colors of the flow blue plates hung above the bed.

Mary, a stickler for detail, stenciled the ivy in one room, made the bed quilts and provides bathrobes in all rooms. She also cooks up a storm, offering afternoon snacks and a breakfast to remember in the large and fancy dining room, where the china is color-coordinated with the teal and burgundy decor. The morning fare the day of our visit included yogurt with blueberries and bananas, and fruit crêpes with strawberry topping. Other treats are a four-cheese and herb quiche, frittatas and eggs in puff pastry. Mary says that french toast made with real french bread is her claim to fame.

Another claim to fame is her elaborate English tea, offered by reservation ($15) one Sunday a month from November to May. A harpist plays as upwards of 50 people are seated throughout the house – living room, dining room, library and hallways – for champagne, salmon pâté with crackers, crumpets with honey and butter, and a tiered plate with tea sandwiches, scones with clotted cream and jam, and a dessert buffet.

Although Mary no longer cooks dinner for house guests, she has arranged for a nearby restaurant, Roland's Place, to provide four kinds of "dinner picnics" for $22.50 each. With a bottle of wine from the inn's little tavern, guests can enjoy a feast in the back-yard gazebo as the sun sets over the Adirondacks.

The grounds also contain a goldfish pond, skating pond, snowshoeing and walking trails, and two sled runs.

(802) 877-3337. Fax (802) 877-2599. Six rooms and two suites with private baths. Doubles, $75 to $150. Suites, $120 and $175. Add $20 for foliage and special-event weekends. Children over 8. No smoking.

Whitford House, Grandey Road, Addison (RR 1, Box 1490, Vergennes 05491).

Their daughter attended Middlebury College and they fell in love with the area, so Midwesterners Bruce and Barbara Carson decided to retire here after 30 years in California. "We wanted an old house, off the beaten path, with a mountain vista," Barbara said. They got their wish in spades.

They restored a 1790s house located along a gravel road on 37 acres in the back of beyond, with a panoramic view of the Adirondack Mountains across nearby Lake Champlain. Near a wild bird preserve, they lie under a snow geese flyway. Six sheep share the back yard with a stunning sculpture of a horse, made by a friend from vines and sticks found on the property.

The prize accommodation here is a guest cottage. It harbors a large bedroom with twin beds that are usually joined as a king, a full bath with a radiant-heated floor, a comfortable sitting room, a kitchenette and big windows all around to take in the views.

The pale yellow house is no slouch. Guests enter through the rear and a great room with slate floor, fieldstone fireplace, baby grand piano and tall windows onto the mountains. You'd never guess it once was the buggy barn, occupied by swallows and hornets when the Carsons arrived in 1992. Next comes a pantry as big as some kitchens. Here is where the Carsons offer wine, beer and hors d'oeuvres for guests in the afternoon. The pantry adjoins an open kitchen, which obviously is the heart of the house. Orange juide and coffee are put out in the morning in the side library, which opens onto a rear deck. Another favorite spot for lounging is a front porch furnished with rockers. In the front of the house is a corner dining room, where the table is set for a candlelit breakfast for eight. Across the hall is a guest bedroom with a double bed and a private bath with an old five-seater (which they found cantilevered off the back of the house) incorporated into the top of the barnwood wall for decorative – and conversational – purposes.

Wraparound porch at Whitford House looks onto verdant countryside.

Upstairs are two more guest rooms, for which the Carsons were adding private baths, plus the owners' kingsize suite, which they occasionally vacate for guests.

The entire place is furnished with family heirlooms, antiques and unexpected finds, including an old milk chest from a dairy barn that was converted into a corner china cabinet in the dining room. The room is lit entirely by candles for breakfast, a hearty affair that brings fresh fruit, zucchini bread, croissants and perhaps vegetable frittatas, baked eggs florentine or belgian waffles. "I love to cook," says Barbara in an understatement.

Many guests find the Carsons' welcome so warm and the surroundings so relaxing that they scarcely leave the property.

(802) 758-2704 or (800) 746-2704. Fax (802) 758-2089. Three rooms and a cottage with private baths. Doubles, $110. Cottage, $150. Add $15 each for foliage and special weekends. Children and pets accepted. No smoking. No credit cards.

Cornwall Orchards Bed & Breakfast, Route 30, Cornwall (RD 4, Box 428, Middlebury 05753).

Sturdy Adirondack-style chairs on the idyllic rear deck here overlook what remains of Cornwall Orchards, once the town's biggest employer, and the distant Adirondacks. Some of the apple trees still dot the property, but the original 1783 farmhouse on fourteen rural acres has been turned into a stylish B&B by Robert and Juliet Gerlin.

Former Connecticut residents where he was a lawyer, they were smitten with the area when their children attended Middlebury College. They spent a year renovating, adding dormers and six bathrooms before opening in 1995. The rambling, pale yellow structure lent itself to the purpose, what with a comfortable living room with fireplace, a dining room and a substantial country kitchen, which opens onto that great rear deck.

Three guest rooms with full baths occupy wings on the ends of the main floor. The largest is typical with a down duvet on the queensize bed, shiny hardwood floors and navaho white walls. Two upstairs bedrooms have bathrooms with tiled showers. One has a queen bed and the other twins. Décor is crisp yet simple.

Zinnias enhance side yard of restored Inn on the Green.

Juliet prepares a full breakfast incorporating ingredients from nearby farms. Expect fresh fruit, homemade granola and perhaps organic blueberry pancakes with bacon from Pork Chop Farm or scrambled eggs from eggs supplied by the free-range chickens next door.

Juliet grew up in England and worked as assistant to a well-known musician and composer for many years. Here she is a part-time assistant to a professor at Middlebury.

(802) 462-2272. Five rooms with private baths. Doubles, $80. Children welcome. No smoking. No credit cards.

The Inn on the Green, 19 South Pleasant St., Middlebury 05753.

The Middlebury green gained a new hostelry in 1997 with the opening of this 1803 landmark listed on the National Register. Steve and Micki Paddock, owners of the Blue Spruce Motel south of town, fulfilled a dream from the days when they managed a coastal inn.

The stately house, painted gray-blue with yellow trim, has been restored with great care and with guests' privacy in mind. The main floor holds a small common room that doubles as an office and two suites. The rear Bristol has two bedrooms, one with queen bed and one with twins, plus a sitting room. The Addison in front has an antique day bed in the sitting room, a queen bed topped with a quilt and nine pillows in the bedroom, and two chairs in a bay window. As is the case throughout, the walls are painted interesting colors (the sitting room dark blue, the bedroom pale yellow) and are decorated with quilts, plates and paintings for sale.

Other guest rooms, all with queen beds and private baths, are located upstairs in the house and on two floors of a carriage house to the side and rear, next to a Baptist church. Those on the upper level of the carriage house are cozy with slanted ceilings.

All of the rooms, true to their period, are curtain-less. Instead, the windows may be screened with louvered blinds. The TV set rests atop a table on wheels. Amenities are one monogrammed robe in the bathroom, a basket of Haversham and Holt toiletries, and bottles of Poland Spring water.

There being no appropriate common space, the staff delivers continental breakfast to the guest rooms. Orange juice, fruit and pastries are the fare.

(802) 388-7512 or (888) 244-7512. Nine rooms and two suites with private baths. Doubles, $125 to $175, foliage $155 to $195, midweek in winter $90. Two-night minimum peak weekends. Children welcome. No smoking.

Brookside Meadows, Painter Road, RD 3, Box 2460, Middlebury 05753.

A gaggle of geese noisily announced our arrival at this strikingly contemporary farmhouse built in 1979 from a 19th-century design. Colorful in blue-green with a red shingled room, it's located in the rolling countryside three miles east of Middlebury, with the Green Mountains looming in the background.

Linda and Roger Cole share their rambling home with guests in four rooms with private baths, plus a detached two-bedroom suite. Each has king/twin or queensize beds, upholstered reading chairs and coordinated comforters with dust ruffles. The main floor holds two bedrooms, one with whitewashed pine paneling and a queen bed and the other with twin beds.

The other accommodations are on the second floor. One is a large room, paneled in native basswood, with a kingsize bed and two skylights that open. The largest is a master bedroom with queen bed, TV and full bath with a double vanity. A detached, pine-paneled apartment suite with private entrance has a queen-bedded room and another bedroom with two twins, plus a living room with TV and gas fireplace, small dining area and kitchenette.

A guest living room with a wood stove is furnished with comfortable chairs and loveseats. It opens onto a shady brick patio and a lawn sloping to a pond. Complimentary soft drinks and wine are offered here in the afternoon.

Pancakes, waffles or french toast are served for breakfast at a communal table in the dining room.

(802) 388-6429 or (800) 442-9887. Four rooms and a two-bedroom suite with private baths. Doubles, $95 to $125. Children over 10. Two-night minimum in summer and fall and all weekends.

Middlebury Inn, Court House Square, Middlebury 05753.

Since 1827, this mellow red-brick inn has dominated the village square. The obligatory (but seemingly seldom used) rockers are lined up on the marble floor of the side porch near the entry.

The 45 rooms in the rambling main building have been renovated, upgraded and redecorated under innkeepers Frank and Jane Emanuel. So have five in the attached Hubbard House and ten more in the adjacent Porter House Mansion. Varying in shape and size, all have high ceilings, brass fixtures and intricate moldings as well as private baths, cable TV and two telephones. The twenty rooms in a rear motel annex are large and modern. Each contains two double beds or a double and twin bed plus a queensize sofabed for family use. They also have hair dryers and coffee makers.

The inn's spacious lobby, where complimentary afternoon tea is served, has nooks for reading or playing checkers and lots to look at. The Country Peddler gift shop offers everything from books to maple syrup. You can order cocktails and sandwiches on the screened porch in summer, or a full range of luncheon entrées in the Rose Room. More formal is the pillared, blue and white Founders Room. Traditional New England cuisine takes on contemporary accents in a dinner menu ranging from stuffed sole to venison with bourbon chutney glaze. Light fare, desserts and coffee are among the evening offerings in the pleasant Morgan Tavern.

(802) 388-4961 or (800) 842-4666. Fax (802) 388-4563. Eighty rooms with private baths. Doubles, $90 to $156 weekends, foliage and holiday periods; $78 to $146 midweek. Entrées, $10.95 to $17.95. Lunch, 11:30 to 2. Dinner, 5:30 to 9.

Linens & Lace, 29 Seminary St., Middlebury 05753.

The name bespeaks the theme at this elegant and ornate Victorian along a residential side street in Middlebury. Peter Newburg, a builder from Atlanta, and his wife, Mary Botter, gutted the former private home-turned-apartment-house to the frame and rebuilt to the original specifications. "We did this as our home," explained Peter, "but I was bored silly in retirement at age 45. So I said let's do a B&B."

They furnished their home with family antiques, mainly Victorian and Chinese. The front of the house dates to 1823 and the middle from 1840-50, which accounts for the French Empire look of the living room. A smaller parlor is done in Victoriana. The windows throughout are swagged in fabric above sheer lace curtains.

Peter serves a full breakfast on century-old china and silver in a formal dining room notable for beautiful carved oriental screens. The fare might be wild blueberry pancakes, scrambled eggs with cream cheese, brandied peach waffles or Dutch baked apples. Tea, lemonade, cookies and scones are offered in the afternoon.

Upstairs in the handsome yellow house with a wraparound veranda are four bedrooms, two with private baths. Beds range from twins to double and queen. A room in the rear carriage house comes with twin beds, oriental carpets and private bath.

Besides the veranda, there's seating amid gardens on the long side lawn.

(802) 388-0832. Three bedrooms with private baths and two with shared bath. Doubles, $99 with private bath, $89 shared. No smoking.

By the Way B&B, 407 Main St. (Route 125), Box 264, East Middlebury 05740.

Her artworks and those of her late husband adorn the walls of this homey B&B run with TLC by artist Nancy Simoes. The art, the country antiques, the colorful new garden in front of the wide wraparound veranda and the spacious rear lawn with a swimming pool set this place apart.

Guests enjoy a comfortable, book-filled living room with TV and a dining room with a pine harvest table in the middle and a schoolmaster's desk in a bay window. Upstairs are a front bedroom with a double bed, game table, small TV and built-in desk, and a larger rear bedroom with twin beds and some of the five generations of family antiques with which the house abounds.

A hammock and lounge chairs await beside the swimming pool in the long back yard hedged for privacy. An ancient maple shades Adirondack chairs.

Nancy serves a continental breakfast in summer and more substantial fare, such as eggs or french toast, the rest of the year.

(802) 388-6291 or (800) 769-6145. Two rooms with private baths. Doubles, $75; $85 major weekends; $65 most of winter. Children over 8. No smoking. No credit cards.

Waybury Inn, Route 125, East Middlebury 05740.

"The Bob Newhart Show made us famous,'" advertises this establishment, whose

Exterior of Waybury Inn served as fictional inn on Bob Newhart TV show.

facade served as the fictional New England inn on the TV sitcom. But the inn has been attracting travelers since 1810, lately under the auspices of Middlebury restaurateurs Marty and Marcia Schuppert of Mr. Up's fame.

Marcia grew up in the inn when her parents owned it, and two of her sisters have worked here since they were youngsters. She and her husband took over the inn after it had suffered through four owners in ten years.

Away from the mainstream, the Waybury is quiet and peaceful, with a wide, shaded front porch and a side deck upon which to while away the hours. You can swim in a river gorge almost across the street, or stroll up the road into the mountains. The fourteen guest rooms with private baths have been upgraded, many with king poster and queen sleigh beds. They are simply furnished in homey Vermont style. Our large room had comfy twin beds, a red velvet rocking chair, a sofa and fresh white curtains. The old-fashioned parlor harbors books, games and, the only modern touch, a small TV.

Meals are served in the dining room and porch (see Dining Spots) or in the rear pub, which sports some of the signs and props that were used when the Newhart show was filmed here. A full country breakfast is included in the rates.

(802) 388-4015 or (800) 348-1810. Fax (802) 388-1248. Fourteen rooms with private baths. Doubles, $80 to $115.

Elizabeth's October Pumpkin, Route 125, Box 226, East Middlebury 05740.
This cheery, orange and rust-colored 1850 Greek Revival house lives up to its name, but never more so than in the autumn when it's surrounded by pumpkins and cornstalks. The deep rear yard backs up to an orange gazebo.

Elizabeth and Bill Wells took over in 1994 from the original owners whose pumpkin theme was carried out in stenciling in the front hall and up the stairs. They added a glassed-in solarium in place of the back porch and upgraded the decor with Laura Ashley fabrics and country quilts.

The premier guest room is one on the main floor off the dining room with a queensize poster bed, full bath, sitting area and bow window onto the pleasant back yard. Upstairs are three bedrooms, one with a queen canopy bed and private bath in front. Another room with a queen bed and one with twins share a bathroom with a large, sit-down shower.

The living room has a TV set. A full country breakfast is served in the typical New England dining room or in the new solarium. Elizabeth's signature dish is an egg soufflé; her husband's is homemade waffles.

(802) 388-9525 or (800) 237-2007. Two rooms with private baths and two rooms with shared bath. Doubles, $60 to $80. Children over 6. No credit cards. Closed mid-November to May.

The Chipman Inn, Route 125, Ripton 05766.

In a real country hamlet in the heart of Robert Frost country, this small, informal inn dating from 1828 is operated by Bill Pierce and his wife, Joyce Henderson. There's lots of space to spread out – in the comfy parlor with a big fireplace by the little bar, in a lounge full of hooked rugs, in a sitting area with magazines in the upstairs hall, and in the stenciled dining room where prix-fixe dinners are served by reservation at 7:30 for $25.

The day's menu is posted with appropriate wine suggestions. The meal begins with hors d'oeuvres at 7 in the lounge; salmon mousse, marinated mushrooms and prosciutto could be the fare. Lentil or asparagus soup and salad precede the single-entrée main course, perhaps loin of pork roast with rosemary and garlic or wiener schnitzel with vegetables of the day. Maple-walnut pie or chocolate pâté with raspberry sauce could be the dessert.

All eight guest rooms have private baths. One has a sitting room and another a skylight, and all are pleasantly furnished with antiques. There's no television, Joyce is quick to point out, but there are plenty of books for amusement. And there's no pool, "but mountain lakes and streams abound."

Bill makes granola for the hearty breakfast, which includes a choice of egg dishes.

(802) 388-2390 or (800) 890-2390. Eight rooms with private baths. Doubles, $85 to $105; foliage, $96 to $115. Children over 12. Smoking restricted.

Where to Eat

Swift House Inn, 25 Stewart Lane, Middlebury.

One of the legacies of the inn's late co-founder, Andrea Nelson, is the dining operation that was her pride and joy. Lately, the Swift House has expanded its hours to serve nightly and has broadened its offerings with an enticing café menu as well as making entrées available in half portions.

Dining is by candlelight in three small and serene dining rooms – one a library – appointed in hunt green. The entire menu is available in each. A complimentary hors d'oeuvre, goat cheese and mango salsa on crostini, garnished with an edible flower, and superior crusty sliced breads got our dinner off to a good start. One of us enjoyed an appetizer of sautéed mushrooms ragoût in puff pastry and a café entrée, a sensational duck confit napoleon with local chèvre and field greens. The other loved the house salad and a generous half portion of herb-crusted rack of lamb with rosemary and madeira sauce. Choices ranged from sesame seared tuna steak drizzled with a warm ginger soy vinaigrette to local venison with homemade mango-ginger chutney.

Swift House Inn is known for fine lodging and dining.

Dessert was a house specialty, Andy Nelson's original coffee-toffee pecan torte, a dessert that any chocoholic woud love.

(802) 388-9925. Entrées, $15.95 to $21.95; café menu, $8.95 to $10.95. Dinner nightly, 6 to 9:30.

Christophe's on the Green, 5 North Green St., Vergennes.

Taking over the small restaurant in the landmark 1793 Stevens House facing the village green, French chef Christophe Lissarrague quickly gained a reputation for offering the most exciting dining in the area. Tables are on two levels in a simple, pale yellow room with dark green trim. Christophe is in the kitchen and his wife Alice, a native of nearby Shelburne, is out front.

The with-it menu is available à la carte (with all choices for each course the same price) or prix-fixe, $28 for three courses. It starts with such exotica as anaheim peppers filled with cod brandade, accompanied by a tomato and red pepper coulis, and sardines poached in white wine with cold boiled potatoes and pickled cucumbers. The half-dozen main courses range from sautéed sea scallops with a hard cider sauce, ruby chard and zucchini puree to roasted free-range poussin and rabbit with fettuccine in a sauce of sundried tomatoes and pearl onions.

A cheese tray is offered following the entrée. Masterful desserts are thyme ice cream with langue de chat cookies, espresso crème caramel with cardamom chantilly, and dark chocolate tart flavored with smoked tea and served with a coffee sauce.

Christophe returns to Pays Basque with his family in the winter.

(802) 877-3413. Prix-fixe, $28; entrées, $19.50. Dinner, Tuesday-Saturday 5:30 to 9:30. Open mid-May to mid-October.

Woody's, 5 Bakery Lane, Middlebury.

The interior of this contemporary, multi-level restaurant with enormous windows looks like a cross between a diner and an ocean liner, its decks overlooking Otter Creek. Decor is art deco in burnt orange, black and stainless steel, the colors repeated on the covers of the various menus.

Run by Woody Danforth, formerly of Mary's in nearby Bristol and the Ritz-Carlton in Boston, the place is California casual and the innovative international cuisine consistently good. Eating outside on the curved wraparound deck, right above the creek, is likened to being on a ship. This was the setting for a good summer lunch: seafood quiche with salad, and gazpacho with a chicken tenderloin pita melt.

At night, start with Woody's country pâté with pommery sauce or his seafood sausage, sliced and sautéed with fresh salsa beurre blanc. Proceed to a main course like the signature bourbon shrimp over linguini, cajun grilled salmon with sweet roasted corn salsa or grilled peppercorn-crusted loin of lamb with tahini-yogurt sauce. The homemade desserts are ever-changing.

(802) 388-4182. Entrées, $13.95 to $16.95. Lunch, Monday-Saturday 11:30 to 3. Dinner, 5 to 10. Sunday brunch, 10:30 to 3.

Roland's Place, Route 7, New Haven.

A handsome yellow farmhouse five miles north of Middlebury has been transformed into a restaurant of distinction. Chef-owner Roland Gaujac, a graduate of the Grenoble Hotelry School, specializes in the provençal cuisine of his native France. His American wife Lisa runs the front of the house.

Villeroy & Boch china in the Beaulieu pattern graces the white-clothed tables spaced well apart in several salmon-colored dining rooms. The best bet for appetizers may be Roland's sampler, yielding perhaps crab cakes with corn relish, home-cured salmon and salmon soufflé with basil oil and a roasted portobello mushroom topped with goat cheese. Expect main courses like poached rainbow trout with champagne sauce, potato-crusted chicken with Vermont cheddar and dijon sauce, smoked pork tenderloin with sour cherry sauce, and grilled beef tenderloin with bourbon and shallot sauce. There's a Vermont game sampler with mushroom risotto, as well as four vegetarian entrées.

In the French style, Roland makes the rounds of the dining room after dinner. He and his wife offer two simple guest rooms, one a two-bedroom suite, upstairs in the front of their restored 1796 House (doubles, $75).

(802) 453-6309. Entrées, $11.50 to $17.95. Lunch, Monday-Saturday 11:30 to 2:30. Dinner nightly, 5 to 9. Sunday brunch, 9 to 2.

Dog Team Tavern, Dog Team Road, Middlebury.

Generations of starving Middlebury students have filled their little tummies here, including one of us who used to O.D. on the sticky buns when his visiting parents treated him to a meal out. Built in the early 1920s by Sir Wilfred and Lady Grenfell, the rambling, atmospheric structure was operated by the Grenfell Mission as a teahouse and outlet for handicrafts from Labrador. New ownership has maintained the tradition of the Joy family, who turned it into a restaurant in the 1940s.

It's a wonder how they can still serve such huge amounts of food for the price, starting at $7.95 for fried chicken with fritters and topping off at $12.95 for prime rib. The tab includes soups, salads, buckets of relishes and vegetables served family style).

After 50 years, the Dog Team finally has reversed its policy of not taking reservations. But if there's a wait, you can enjoy the living room with its collections of memorabilia, read a magazine on one of the stuffed sofas, browse through the craft and gift shop in the newly restored 1859 church next door, or wander into the large cocktail lounge where dips and chips are served with drinks. Off the bar is a pleasant, two-level deck overlooking the ubiquitous Otter Creek.

You order your entrée from the blackboard menu as you enter. Then when you're called into the charming dining room or porches, you eat (and eat and eat). One of us feels that far too much food is served, but the other generally is up to the challenge. *(802) 388-7651 or (800) 472-7651. Entrées, $7.95 to $12.95. Dinner nightly, Monday-Saturday 5 to 9, Sunday noon to 9.*

Waybury Inn, Route 125, East Middlebury 05740.
Dinner and Sunday brunch are served in the maroon and white dining room or on the enclosed side porch of the inn pictured on the Bob Newhart Show. A pub menu is served in the Pub and Club Room out back, dark and cozy as can be. The food here is widely considered better these days than at Mister Up's, the large and popular creekside restaurant run by owners Marty and Marcia Schuppert in Middlebury.

We went here for years just for the London broil with the best mushroom sauce ever, but that specialty has been missing from the recent repertoire. The extensive menu focuses instead on such entrées as sautéed brook trout with saffron, rock cornish game hen encrusted with sesame seeds, pan-seared pork medallions with West Indies spices and rack of lamb with rosemary sauce. The Waybury version of surf and turf teams gulf shrimp with Kentucky bourbon steak.

Typical appetizers are prosciutto timbale, seafood ravioli and pecan-fried calamari with a ginger-soy sauce. The Waybury rum parfait, assorted mousses and chocolate crêpes are popular desserts. *(802) 388-4015. Entrées, $12.50 to $21.95. Dinner nightly, 5 to 9. Sunday brunch, 11 to 2. No smoking.*

Fire & Ice, 26 Seymour St., Middlebury.
Opened by Middlebury graduates in 1974 and greatly expanded over the years, this is a sight to behold. A 1997 renovation doubled the footprint and expanded the kitchen, salad bar and lobby. The result is a ramble of rooms highlighted by Tiffany or fringed lamps, brass chandeliers, boating and sport fishing memorabilia. One room has a copper-dome ceiling and there's an upside-down canoe on the ceiling of the lounge.

Co-owner Dale Goddard's restored 22-foot Philippine mahogany runabout is moored majestically in a lobby surrounded by salad bars. "I had fun with this," says Dale, who calls the décor eclectic but notes recurring themes of college, fishing, skiing, family, dungeon and bordello. A total of 215 people can be seated at booths and tables, in nooks and crannies – some off by themselves in lofts for two and others in the midst of the action around the massive copper bar.

The food is consistently first-rate and the staff obliging. The stir-fries are famous, as is the shrimp and seafood salad bar, which includes all the shrimp and crab salad you can eat. The Sunday salad bar adds soup and crab legs, and the event is billed as "just like Sunday dinner at grandma's."

Prime rib and steaks are featured, anything from blackened rib to châteaubriand and steak au poivre. Roast duckling, chicken boursin and cashew chicken stir-fry are specialties. A light fare menu also includes the salad and bread bars.

The restaurant's name comes from the title of a Robert Frost poem. The fire reflects the cooking and the ice the drink mixing that goes on here. *(802) 388-7166 or (800) 367-7166. Entrées, $13.50 to $18.95. Lunch daily except Monday, 11:30 to 4. Dinner nightly, 5 to 9 or 9:30, Sunday from 1.*

The Storm Café, Frog Hollow Mill, Middlebury.

This is the successor to the late Otter Creek Cafe, which had provided one of our best dinners ever, and a couple of more recent incarnations. Dinner is no longer served, but the continental breakfasts, lunches and weekend brunches are among the best in town, and the homemade soups are unsurpassed. Chef-owner Erika Albinson makes her tortillas, focaccia and baguettes from scratch.

The setting is perfect for a leisurely lunch, outside on a tight little deck overlook the Otter Creek falls and inside in the lower level of an 1840 mill building. Local organic produce, vegetarian fare, interesting salads and sandwiches, espresso and modest wines are featured.

(802) 388-1063. Entrées, $6 to $7. Light breakfast and lunch daily. Weekend brunch.

The Otter Creek Bakery, 1 College St., Middlebury.

Ben and Sarah Wood patterned their original cafe and bakery in Frog Hollow Mill on the models they know in San Francisco. Problem was that Sarah's bakery became the tail that wagged the dog and Ben closed the cafe (the space since taken over by the Storm Cafe) to concentrate on the growing bakery business up the street.

Here the baked goods are sensational as ever, and the Woods have garnered quite a following for their mail-order cookies and dough (chunky peanut butter, maple-oatmeal-raisin and lemon-pecan among them). Now they're doing a land-office takeout business with sandwiches (we liked the Otter Creek pâté and the Norwegian smoked salmon) in the $4.50 to $5.25 range. They also have a few soups, salads and pizzettes to go. And, of course, the requisite fancy coffees.

(802) 388-3371. Open Monday-Saturday 7 to 6 (to 8 in summer), Sunday 7 to 3.

Diversions

Middlebury College, Route 125, occupies a 1,200-acre campus on the southwest edge of Middlebury. It is notable for the consistent use of gray limestone in its buildings as well as for its summer foreign language schools. Founded in 1800, the college has evolved from the lower Old Chapel-Painter Hall row to the hillside beside Le Chateau. Now about 2,000 undergraduates are enrolled at one of the top-ranked liberal-arts colleges in the country. Hundreds of graduate students flock to the eight Summer Language Schools and the Bread Loaf School of English, where 250 writers attend the annual Bread Loaf Writers Conference, the oldest and largest in the country (Robert Frost is remembered as "the godfather of Bread Loaf"). The college library has excellent collections in its Robert Frost Room. Middlebury's $16 million Center for the Arts is a state-of-the-art showplace for the performing arts, five galleries housing the Middlebury Museum of Art, the college's top-flight concert series and even a cafe.

Vermont State Craft Center/Frog Hollow, 1 Mill St., Middlebury.

Just off Main Street in the center of Middlebury, this is one of our favorite crafty places anywhere, and 150,000 visitors a year agree. With windows onto the Otter Creek falls, it's a fine showplace for sculpture and pottery. Inside the renovated mill is a 3,000-square-foot treasure trove of pottery, stained glass, pewter, quilts, pillows, wall hangings, jewelry and stuffed and wooden toys, all by Vermont artists. We managed to resist some great sculptures of dogs and bunnies ($450 to $675). We could not resist a woodcut print by artist Sabra Field, a Middlebury grad with a wonderful sense of design, and for years now her "Apple Tree Winter" with snowy chickadee has been ensconced in our dining room. The nation's first state craft center has expanded to locations in the Church Street Marketplace in Burlington and the Equinox shops in Manchester. *(802) 388-3177. Open Monday-Saturday 9:30 to 5, also Sundays 11 to 4, spring through fall. Free.*

Vermont Folklife Center, 2 Court St., Middlebury.

Founded in 1984 to display the folk art and traditions of Vermont, this small but rewarding educational venture occupies the downstairs of Middlebury's historic Gamaliel Painter House, the oldest mansion in town (1802). Of particular appeal to specialists, video shows and changing exhibits portray the people and places that make Vermont's folk traditions and multi-cultural heritage distinctive. The works of Franco-American wood carvers were displayed front and center at one visit and 200 years of handweaving at another. Traditional crafts from Vermont are featured in the annual Arts Showcase and Sale in December. *(802) 388-4964. Open Monday-Friday 9 to 5; also Saturday noon to 4, late May to late October.*

The Sheldon Museum, 1 Park St., Middlebury

Bachelor Henry Sheldon bought the brick 1829 Judd-Harris House opposite Cannon Park and opened it as a museum in 1882, advertising it with a twenty-foot sign that read "Sheldon's Art and Archeological Museum." It was the first village museum in the country, said our guide.

The place is a find, filled with all sorts of odd but interesting items like a mousetrap that kills a rodent by drowning it in a cylinder of water, a pair of shoes worn by Calvin Coolidge as a child, newspapers from the 1800s and a collection of old dentist's tools, including a primitive ether bottle. There's even a stuffed cat – it seems that Sheldon, the town clerk, saved everything.

The highlights of one of the most exemplary museum collections in Vermont are exhibited in room settings in the elegant Federal house built by local marble merchants. Middlebury's garden clubs have created an early Victorian garden next door. The Fletcher Community History Center, a wing connecting the museum and the Stewart-Swift Research Center, replaced the old summer kitchen and woodshed. *(802) 388-2117. Open Monday-Friday 10 to 5, Saturday 10 to 4, late May to mid-October; hours vary rest of year. Adults, $3.50.*

Robert Frost Interpretive Trail, off Route 125 between Ripton and Middlebury's Breadloaf campus. "Please take your time and leave nothing but your footprints," urges the sign at the start of this easy-to-walk, three-quarter-mile trail blazed in 1976 by the U.S. Youth Conservation Corps. Several benches are strategically placed for creative contemplation. This is a thoroughly delightful way to spend an hour or two, reading some of Frost's poems mounted on plaques en route. Meadows, woods, groves of birches and streams are traversed and identified. Frost lived and worked within a mile of here; the fields and forests were the inspiration for his poems and mentioned in many. Nearby is the Robert Frost Wayside Area with picnic tables and grills in a grove of red pines that Frost pruned himself. Up a dirt road is the Homer Noble Farm, site of the log cabin where Frost spent his last 23 summers.

Vermont Rail Excursions, Marble Works, Middlebury.

The new **Sugarbush Express** takes passengers in vintage passenger cars, a dining car and a bar car through the Champlain Valley and near Lake Champlain from the old rail yard in Middlebury to the Burlington waterfront. The round trip, with stops in Vergenes and Shelburne, takes three hours (at speeds up to 55 miles anhour). Narration outlines the history, folklore and attractions along the way. New Tuesday trips go from Middlebury to Rutland, with stops in Brandon and Proctor.

(802) 388-0193 or (800) 707-3530. Trains run Memorial Day to late October, twice daily in summer, three times daily on weekends in fall. Adults, $12. hour).

Shopping. The compact center of Middlebury is still a downtown, claiming a Ben Franklin variety store and a movie theater. The biggest store in town, appropriately, is the **Skihaus** at the corner of Main and Merchants Row. Two Rossignol skis are the handles on the doors to this institution run by two couples, all of whom are Middlebury graduates. Inside in a ramble of rooms on two floors you'll find summer and winter clothes, Hawaiian dresses, Austrian boiled wool jackets, cuddly Lanz nightgowns, boots for all reasons, jewelry, gifts and, of course, skiwear. They even have Lederhosen. Skihaus is the biggest single customer of Geiger of Austria, whose factory is located off Route 7 on Exchange Street north of town.

One of our favorite bookstores anywhere is the neatly jumbled **Vermont Book Store,** whose former owner knew Robert Frost. It has one of the country's largest collections of Robert Frost works, including out-of-print collector's items. Also along Main Street you'll find funky women's clothes at **Wild Mountain Thyme,** antique jewelry and vintage apparel at **Bejewelled,** and kitchenware and housewares at **Dada. Greenfields Mercantile** is a showcase for the clothing, bags and accessories of American designers working in hemp and other sustainable and recycled fibers. Aromas of soaps emerge from **Teasel,** a good lingerie and bath store.

Most of the rest of the shopping action is in restored mill buildings around Frog Hollow, site of the Vermont State Craft Center. **Great Falls Collection** (up a staircase beside the Otter Creek falls) has unusual jewelry, home accessories and nature and garden items. In the Star Mill, **Charlotte's Collections** carries quilts, fabrics and yarns. **Sweet Cecily** stocks great cow pottery, cow placemats and painted cabinets among its folk art and fine crafts. **Natural Selections** features natural, recycled and organic products, clothing and designs by Vermont artist Dee Sprague. From here a 276-foot pedestrian bridge across Otter Creek yields a view of the falls and connects with the **Marble Works,** a collection of businesses, offices and specialty stores in old white marble factory buildings. Local producers back up their trucks and tailgates to the parking lot for the small farmer's market (where we bought some delicious bread, corn and salsa) beside the falls on Wednesday and Saturday mornings. Here also is the showroom for **Danforth Pewterers,** where we ogled all the pewter products from thousands of buttons for $1 to dinner plates for $72. A dolphin on a corded necklace for $12 caught our eye.

Extra-Special ――――――――――――――――――――

Woody Jackson's Holy Cow Store, Frog Hollow Mill, Middlebury.

The cows and colors of Vermont, as depicted by local artist Woody Jackson, are on display in this whimsical shop. The Middlebury graduate's trademark cows are the motif on everything from golf balls to light switch plates, pocket knives to tablecloths. Here are many of the items available in his clever "cowtalogue" and then some. The gift shop was relocated in 1997 into the center of town from the main floor of his production facility at 52 Seymour St.

(802) 388-3582. Open daily, 10 to 5, weekends to 4.

Village of Stowe nestles in valley beneath Mount Mansfield.

Stowe, Vt.

A Resort for All Seasons

When former Olympic skier Phil Mahre first saw Stowe clad in summer's green rather than winter's white, he was struck by its beauty. So were many in the Eastern Ski Writers audience he addressed that August day.

Most downhill skiers haven't been to Stowe in what for them is the off-season. But the undisputed Ski Capital of the East is a year-round destination resort, more than its newer, less endowed competitors can hope to be.

For one thing, Stowe *is* Stowe, a legendary village unto itself about eight miles from Mount Mansfield, a legendary ski area unto itself. The twain meets all along the Mountain Road, which links village and mountain. Such a marriage between town and ski area is unrivaled in New England and rich in history – a history unequaled by any other ski town in the country, according to Mount Mansfield Company officials.

The ski resort was led for years by Sepp Ruschp, who left Austria in 1936 to be ski instructor for the fledgling Mount Mansfield Ski Club. The alpine mystique of the area was enhanced by Baroness Maria von Trapp and her family, whose story was immortalized by "The Sound of Music," when they founded the Trapp Family Lodge.

The rolling valley between broad Mount Mansfield on the west and the Worcester Mountains on the east creates an open feeling that is unusual for northern New England mountain regions. In Stowe's exhilarating air, recreation and cultural endeavors thrive.

Cross-country skiing complements downhill in winter. Other seasons bring golf, tennis, polo, horseback riding, hiking, performing arts, art exhibits and enough sights to see and things to do to make credible the area's claim to being a world-class resort. The first International Food & Wine Expo in July 1997 attracted national bigwigs. Although a financial failure, local organizers hoped to make it an annual event rivaling one in Aspen.

Foremost a ski center, Stowe is somewhat lacking in inns of the classic New England variety. Instead, it has resorts, motels, ski dorms, condominiums and more Alpine/Bavarian chalets and lodges than you'll find just about anywhere this side of the Atlantic.

Still, Stowe is Stowe, a storybook New England ski town dominated by Vermont's highest peak. It's a place to be treasured, by skier and non-skier alike.

Inn Spots

Edson Hill Manor, 1500 Edson Hill Road, Stowe 05672.

A French Provincial-style manor with old English charm, built in 1940 as a gentleman's estate, became a country inn in 1954. It obtained a new role in life after it was purchased in 1991 by Eric and Jane Lande, well-traveled ex-Montrealers of the fabled Bronfman family, who had set up a thriving maple-syrup business at their Vermont farm in nearby Johnson.

The Landes hired a talented chef and lured veteran local hotelier Billy O'Neill to be their fulltime manager. They since acquired one of Stowe's other best-known small inns, Ten Acres Lodge, and brought in noted chefs to enhance its already acclaimed dining room. Continually perfecting these two premier places to eat and stay, the Landes have a corner on the high-end market. Many of their ideas and aspirations came from having lived in France for ten years while Eric was working on a doctorate in economics.

A mile-long country lane leads from the white post gates to the manor, which a loyal following considers one of the few true country inns in the Stowe area. It retains its original private-home flavor except in the four newer carriage houses with modern accommodations.

Set high amidst 225 secluded acres, it has a spectacular terrace beside a spring-fed, kidney-shaped swimming pool, a pond stocked for trout fishing, an upgraded cross-country ski center and stables for horseback riding.

The manor was a prime location in 1980 for the filming of winter scenes for Alan Alda's movie, "The Four Seasons." The famous Mercedes scene took place on the pond.

Inside the manor are nine guest rooms, a pine-paneled parlor with oriental rugs and Delft tiles around the fireplace, a library with more books and magazines than anyone could possibly read, a refurbished downstairs lounge, plus a renovated dining room

Edson Hill Manor occupies hillside property high above village of Stowe.

where meals are available to the public (see Dining Spots). The beams in the large parlor are said to have come from Ethan Allen's barn. Many of the striking artworks are by Canadian artist Lillian Freeman.

The Landes are gradually upgrading the accommodations, starting with handpainting some of the bathrooms with floral and bird scenes.

Each of four carriage houses, up a hill beyond the inn, has four spacious guest rooms done in the decor of the original manor with beamed ceilings, pine-paneled walls, brick fireplaces and private baths. Billed as the inn's luxury units, they accommodate two to four people.

All told, five rooms in the manor plus those in the carriage houses contain working fireplaces – a great attraction for winter visitors. We'd happily settle any time in the manor's large Studio, which has queensize bed, fireplace, skylight (this was formerly an artist's studio) and an exceptionally nice sitting area with picture windows overlooking the pool, pond and gardens.

Breakfasts are a treat. The buffet table contains several hot entrées – on one winter morning, scrambled eggs with spinach and goat cheese, blackberry waffles and polenta. Fresh juices, fruit platters, homemade breads and muffins, and maple syrup from the Landes' farm accompany.

(802) 253-7371 or (800) 621-0284. Fax (802) 635-2694. Twenty-five rooms and suites with private baths. Most of year: doubles, $110 to $170 B&B, $150 to $210 MAP. Spring and late fall: $75 to $85 B&B. Foliage and Christmas week: $190 to $250 MAP. Two-night minimum weekends. No smoking.

Ten Acres Lodge, 14 Barrows Road, Stowe 05672.

Built as a farmhouse in 1826 with several later additions, this rambling and picturesque red frame house with white trim on a quiet hillside is best known for its restaurant (see Dining Spots). Owners Eric and Jane Lande of Edson Hill Manor have upgraded the overnight accommodations as well.

The dining rooms and the small, slate-floored tavern are altogether appealing, and the plush parlor and front library could not be more comfortable. The striking

Tree trunks support porte cochere at entrance of Stowehof Inn.

wing chairs and couches piled with pillows in the parlor are popular with houseguests. Large bay windows look out onto ever-changing vistas of valley and mountains.

All eight guest rooms on two floors of the main lodge have private baths. One is rather small; the rest are quite spacious and more luxurious. One with kingsize bed has a bathroom in two parts, one containing the tub and the other the w.c. and wash basin. The Landes have redecorated every room with a mix of country furniture and antiques.

Two renovated cottages offer two or three bedrooms, kitchens, working fireplaces and terraces with great views in every direction.

Worth the extra tab are eight luxury rooms with fireplaces in the newer Hill House. Each has a large sitting area, private deck, cable TV and phone. Guests here share an outdoor hot tub open to the stars.

A buffet breakfast includes fresh fruit, granola, yogurt, an egg dish, ham and Vermont cheese.

The grounds contain a small pool, tennis court, and flower and herb gardens that beckon white rabbits. Beyond, cows graze on neighboring farmlands. Who could ask for a more tranquil setting?

(802) 253-7638 or (800) 327-7357. Fax (802) 253-4036. Sixteen rooms and two cottages with private baths. Most of year: doubles, $110 to $140 B&B, $150 to $180 MAP. Spring and late fall: $75 to $85 B&B. Foliage and Christmas Week: $160 to $220 MAP. Two-night minimum weekends. No smoking.

Stowehof Inn, 434 Edson Hill Road, Box 1108, Stowe 05672.

"Slow – Deer Crossing," warns the sign as you drive up the steep road to the Stowehof, whose soaring Alpine exterior is a hilltop landmark hereabouts. "No parking – sleigh only," reads the sign at the door.

Such touches reflect the character of this unusual, thoroughly charming place that grew from a private ski house into one of Stowe's larger inns.

At the front entrance, the trunks of two maple trees support the enormous porte cochere above the small purple door. More tree trunks are inside the huge living room, nicely broken up into intimate nooks and crannies, the two-level dining room, the downstairs game room and the Tyrolean Tap Room. The bell tower, the sod roof laced with field flowers and the architecture are reminiscent of the Tyrolean Alps. The upstairs library and game room is a replica of the interior of an old Vermont covered bridge. Little white lights twinkle all around.

You'd never suspect that the owners are from Hawaii, but their decorating flair is apparent in most of the 46 guest rooms, some of them unusually large and sumptuous. Queen Anne chairs and Chippendale desks add elegance. Terrycloth robes and Godiva chocolates are put out at nightly turndown. All rooms have balconies or patios with views in summer of lovely clumps of birches, a swimming pool, a trout pond, lawns and the mountains. Three guest rooms are available in a farmhouse on the adjacent working farm within walking distance.

Three meals a day are served in the well-appointed **Seasons** dining room with beamed ceiling, fireplaces and windows looking onto pool and mountains. There's also dining in summer on the terrace, site of a popular Sunday buffet brunch. The regional American dinner menu changes several times weekly. Specialties on the dinner menu are wiener schnitzel and beef wellington. Lighter fare is available in the Tyrolean Tap Room.

Locals advise going to Stowehof just to see it. We think it's an equally appealing place in which to stay.

(802) 253-9722 or (800) 932-7136. Fax (802) 253-7513. Forty-nine rooms with private baths. Rates B&B. Summer and winter: doubles, $110 to $230. Foliage: $175 to $275. Spring and late fall: $70 to $120.

Entrées, $16.95 to $21.95. Lunch, 11:30 to 2. Dinner, 6 to 9 or 9:30.

Ye Olde England Inn, 433 Mountain Road, Stowe 05672.

Stowe seems an unlikely spot for an English coaching inn, but this restored and expanded inn is British all the way from the bright red phone booth out front to the menu in the pub and the "Anglo" and "Saxon" on the license plates of the owners' cars.

Transplanted Brits Chris and Lyn Francis, skiers both, are more in evidence at their inn than are many innkeepers in the area. Chris and two friends have formed the Stowe Polo Club and have gotten the community involved. He also spearheaded Stowe's annual British Invasion in mid-September, a four-day celebration of classic cars and "all manner of other things British."

All seventeen of the inn's original guest rooms have private baths and seven have jacuzzis. They are spacious, decorated in Laura Ashley style, contain Gilchrist & Soames amenities and, on the third floor, are notable for interesting shapes and views of the mountains. Three luxury two-bedroom English "cottages" in a building out back beside the swimming pool each contain a fireplace, jacuzzi, cable TV, lounge-dining area and kitchen facilities. The newest are ten "super-luxurious suites" in the Bluff House, perched atop a granite bluff with spectacular views of the Worcester Mountain range. Each has a queensize four-poster in the bedroom, a bath with jacuzzi and separate shower, a private deck and a "lounge" with fireplace, sofabed, wet bar, refrigerator and microwave.

English-style tea is offered in the afternoon. An English breakfast and fancy dinners are served in the beamed **Copperfields** dining room in season. Here the fare includes sautéed pheasant, broiled venison, beef wellington, salmon oscar and tournedos rossini. The all-Australian wine list has been cited by Wine Spectator as one of the world's best.

A pub-type menu is available all day in **Mr. Pickwick's Pub & Restaurant** with a hearthstone fireplace or on canopied decks, lined with umbrellas advertising British ale and presenting a scene straight from the English countryside. We enjoyed a lunch of spinach salad in a tostada shell and a good steak and kidney pie served inexplicably with a side bowl of gravy (could it have been for dipping the french fries in?), all washed down with pints of Whitbread and Watneys ales, presented in proper pub glasses. The list of more than 150 foreign beers and ales is extraordinary, and one can even get ale by the yard. In the evening, live entertainment is enjoyed by the laid-back crowd.

(802) 253-7558 or (800) 477-3771. Fax (802) 253-8944. Seventeen rooms, ten suites and three cottages, all with private baths. Rates, B&B. Doubles, $118 to $158; cottages, $165 to $220; suites, $165 to $295. Foliage: doubles, $150 to $190; cottages, $250 to $300; suites, $275 to $400. Two-night minimum weekends.
Entrées, $15.95 to $19.95. Lunch daily, 11:30 to 4; dinner, 4 to 11.

Green Mountain Inn, Main Street, Box 60, Stowe 05672.
Its deep red facade a landmark in the center of the village since 1833, this inn has been carefully restored and upgraded in the last few years.

The complex includes the formal Main Street Dining Room for breakfast and the legendary Whip Bar & Grill downstairs (see Dining Spots). The latter is where the action is, in the cozy bar as well as in the cafeteria-style grill and on the outdoor deck by the pool. A couple of parlors in front retain the New England inn charm.

Most of the 72 guest rooms and suites are behind the inn in a motel-type configuration, albeit with an antique look. The modern baths, color TVs and phones are combined with twin or queensize canopy beds, floral quilts, custom-designed reproduction furniture manufactured specially for the inn, period wallpapers and stenciling. Fifteen rooms in the annex were nicely renovated; many have balconies overlooking the outdoor pool, brook and gardens. Two clubhouse suites come with kitchen, living room, dining area, fireplace, jacuzzi and queen canopy bed.

The latest additions are eight luxury suites in the new Mill House, adjacent to the clubhouse building on the site of a former lumber mill. Each has a queen canopy bed, fireplace, sitting area, VCR and a large bathroom with oversize jacuzzi opening into the bedroom.

The health center in the clubhouse offers a spa program. An enclosed walkway connects the inn to the Depot Building shopping complex next door.

(802) 253-7301 or (800) 253-7302. Fax (802) 253-5096. Seventy-two rooms and suites. Rates, EP. Summer and winter: doubles, $113 to $125; suites $139 to $150. Foliage and Christmas: doubles $134 to $165, suites $174 to $204. Rest of year: doubles $89 to $115, suites $109 to $139. Children and pets welcome.

Butternut Inn, 2309 Mountain Road, Stowe 05672.
The doorbell may play "The Eyes of Texas Are Upon You," and that's just the start at this transformation of the old Skimore Lodge. Texan owners Jim and Deborah Wimberly advertise theirs as "an award-winning, non-smoking, exclusive inn – a romantic couples' retreat" and have a hallway wall of letters and thank-you notes to prove it.

The eighteen guest rooms, all with private baths and most air-conditioned, vary widely in size and remain true to their ski-lodge heritage, although each is furnished with antique dressers, country crafts, and black and white TVs. Most have king or queensize beds and one of the nicer on the third-floor corner has a balcony.

There's a small living room on the main floor, but most of the action is on the lower floor: a parlor with a piano handmade from one large walnut tree, a billiards room with a 1905 pool table, a small sitting area and a large-screen TV (the room's walls are covered with photos that Jim has taken of inn guests), a sunroom with a bay window to show off the inn's flowers, and a large dining room. Christmas decor is on display all year, from the lights out front on the spruce tree to the sleigh filled with teddy bears to the twinkling Christmas village in the dining room.

Looking up toward Mount Mansfield, the eight-acre back yard is a showplace of flower and herb gardens, a terrace, a flagstone courtyard, a grape arbor, a gazebo by the swimming pool, a fountain and a little park area for picnics by the river. Folks sit in red Adirondack chairs and feed the goldfish and koi in the pond at the side. Depending on the season, they can walk or ski on illuminated trails through five acres of woods to a secret tree house. There's plenty of room for eighteen romantic couples to be alone or sociable, as they wish.

Breakfast is bountiful enough that most don't eat lunch, according to Jim. A favorite is eggs Butternut – poached eggs on pork chops with sautéed onions and cajun peppers. The inn makes its own corned beef hash. On summer afternoons, tea and homemade chocolate-chip cookies are served. In winter, there's an after-ski "grazing board" that might include soup of the day, pheasant pâté, barbecued ribs, sirloin-blackened roast with horseradish sauce, pork roast with barbecue sauce, and Deborah's chocolate desserts and cheesecake. With that for cocktail-party fare, it's no wonder that some guests decide against going out for dinner.

(802) 253-4277 or (800) 328-8837. Eighteen rooms with private baths. Spring to mid-September: doubles, $90 to $130. Foliage: $110 to $150. December to spring: $110 to $160. Two-night minimum foliage. No smoking.

The Gables Inn, 1457 Mountain Road, Stowe 05672.

What many consider to be the best breakfast in town is served at the Gables, either under yellow umbrellas on the front lawn (facing a spectacular view of Mount Mansfield), on the front porch or on tables inside.

Guests are not only well fed but well housed here. Thirteen guest rooms in the main inn and four in a renovated carriage house sport charming country furniture and antiques, homemade wreaths and – an unusual touch – all rooms (and even a couple of bathrooms) are decorated with a few fine china plates from the extensive collection of owners Sol and Lynn Baumrind. All have private baths, most gleaming white and modern. Some are in what Sol laughingly calls a "toilet tower" he added just for the purpose. The inn's prized master room offers a lace-canopy queensize bed, fireplace, sofa, TV and a modern bathroom with skylight.

Much in demand are four spacious rooms in the air-conditioned Carriage House, which shows no trace of its motel-annex heritage. These come with cathedral ceilings, woodburning fireplaces, jacuzzi tubs, queensize canopy beds and television, and more room than we could possibly put to use between a swim in the pool, reading on the lawn and a sensational breakfast the next morning. The occupants before us on a cool summer night had obviously used the fireplace; Sol says he goes through at least ten cords of wood a year.

Top of the line are two Riverview Suites converted from a neighboring homestead. Each has a kingsize bed made of cedar fence posts with a split-rail fence for
a headboard, a dual woodburning fireplace shared by bedroom and living room, a
convenience center with refrigerator and microwave, and a double jacuzzi tub.
The upstairs suite with cathedral ceiling has a balcony off the bedroom and a deck
off the living room. The wraparound porch off the main-floor suite faces the pool area.

An outdoor hot tub, a plant-filled solarium and a large, comfortably furnished
den and living room with TV are other attractions in this homey place. In winter
the downstairs den is used for après-ski. The owners put out crockpots full of
steaming hot soup, hot hors d'oeuvres and cheese and crackers after 4 p.m. for
hungry skiers, who BYOB.

As for that breakfast, it's open to the public, and some days the Baumrinds serve
as many as 300. Says Sol with a smile, "service is leisurely – that's a code word for
slow." Aside from all the old standbys, one can feast on eggs Portuguese, kippers
or chicken livers with onions and scrambled eggs, matzoh brei, and eggs in a
basket, poached eggs in puff pastry with crumbled bacon, artichoke hearts and
mornay sauce. We were impressed with the new portobello mushroom benedict
and a special of sautéed vidalia onions with poached eggs, roasted peppers, and
hollandaise sauce on English muffins.

A staffer grills chicken and ribs on the front lawn for a garden lunch and barbecue
in summer – a popular break for strollers and cyclists on the Stowe Recreation
Path across the street. In ski season, dinner is served in the Gables Tables dining
rooms amid a collection of Royal Copenhagen plates. The tables are covered with
cloths, and candles glow.

In 1997, The Gables received the 1997 Golden Fork Award from the Gourmet
Dining Society of North America.

*(802) 253-7730 or (800) 422-5371. Fax (802) 253-8989. www.gablesinn.com. Seven-
teen rooms and two suites with private baths. Summer and winter: doubles, $90 to $130;
Carriage House and suites, $135 to $185. Foliage: $95 to $140 peak; suites $145 to $200.
Off-season: $65 to $75; suites $90 to $140. No smoking.*

*Entrées, $9.95 to $15.95. Breakfast daily, 8 to noon, weekends and holidays to 12:30.
Lunch in summer, noon to 2. Dinner nightly in winter, 6 to 9.*

Timberhölm Inn, 452 Cottage Club Road, Stowe 05672.

The rustic, weathered cedar facade trimmed in Wedgwood blue hints that this
1949 house along a quiet road is more than just another ski lodge. Inside, the Great
Room confirms it. This really is a great room – a huge, sunny space containing lots
of sofas in two comfy sitting areas, a fieldstone fireplace, TV, shelves of books
and, at the near end, an open dining area. Beyond are two walls of picture windows
onto a wide deck – perfect for relaxing in summer – and a tree-framed view of the
golf course and the Worcester Mountain range. Downstairs is a game room with a
guest refrigerator and TV/VCR, and outside is a whirlpool spa. We'd gladly curl
up with a book in the Great Room or on the deck and spend the day.

Overnight accommodations are in a lodge-style wing with eight rooms and two
suites. Four rooms are small and have bathrooms with showers. Four that are a bit
larger add full baths. The largest are part of two-bedroom suites with living rooms
that seem superfluous, given all the public space.

Innkeepers Louise and Pete Hunter serve lemonade and banana bread on summer
afternoons, changing to soup by the fire in winter. Breakfast is a buffet with fresh

Breakfast on the lawn is a summer tradition at The Gables Inn.

fruit, homemade granola, yogurt, banana-bran muffins and perhaps quiche, french toast or eggs florentine.

(802) 253-7603 or (800) 753-7603. Fax (802) 253-8559. Ten rooms with private baths. Summer: doubles $80 to $110. Foliage: $90 to $140 foliage. Rest of year: $70 to $120. No smoking.

Brass Lantern Inn, 717 Maple St. (Route 100), Stowe 05672.

This 1800 farmhouse and carriage barn that housed the old Charda restaurant building was in sad shape when it was acquired in 1988 by Andy Aldrich, a home builder. "I could look at the property and see the potential," he said. Doing most of the work himself, he undertook a total restoration, "doing all the things people think about doing when they're upgrading."

The result is a comfortable, air-conditioned B&B with a pleasant mix of old and new and an award from the Vermont Builders Association for restoration. The walls are stenciled and baskets hang from the beamed ceiling in the dining room. Modern baths, six with whirlpool tubs, adjoin the nine soundproofed bedrooms. Three have fireplaces and queensize beds. Each has stenciled walls, planked floors, brass or canopy beds with handmade quilts, and one or two wing chairs. The honeymoon room has a heart-shaped headboard and footboard on the queensize iron bed and a couple of "frolic pillows" on the floor near the fireplace.

Guests gather around the fireplace in the living room or on a large rear deck overlooking the mountains. A native Vermonter, Andy features Vermont products on his breakfast menu, which changes daily. The guest book is full of raves about the apple crêpes, and his breakfasts won an award from the Gourmet Dining Society of North America. Sourdough french toast was the entrée at our visit. Broccoli-mushroom quiche, vegetable omelets, blueberry pancakes or scrambled eggs with Cabot cheese and bacon are other possibilities. Tea and baked goods are offered in the afternoon.

(802) 253-2229 or (800) 729-2980. Fax (802) 253-7425. Nine rooms with private baths. Doubles, $80 to $150, foliage and Christmas week $100 to $200. No smoking.

The Plum Door, School Street, Box 606, Stowe 05672.

Both their families had run cottage colonies on Cape Cod, so Herb and Fran Greenhalgh had the hospitality business in their blood. Their opportunity came when their grown children moved out of their century-old Vermont farmhouse in a residential area of Stowe. They gutted the front of the house, raised the roof and put in new windows and private baths.

The result is a low-key B&B. Three comfortable guest rooms contain vaulted ceilings and queensize beds. Each bears a family name and unusual colored walls – raspberry in the Spaulding, blue-green in the Earle. The premier Dunbar Room comes with a franklin stove.

Guests share a downstairs common room with TV and an upstairs guest kitchen. The latter is stocked with everything folks need for continental breakfast, including homemade breads and cereals. "They help themselves and we come in afterward to clean up," says Herb. There's a little table for partaking on the balcony outside.

The name derives from the color of the door. "My wife and a friend mixed the paint and when they finished we had a plum door," says Herb. He had skied at Stowe since the late 1930s, which explains the old skis and poles displayed across the front of the house.

(802) 253-9995 or (800) 258-7586. Fax (802) 253-9977. Three rooms with private baths. Spring through fall: doubles, $55 to $65. Foliage and winter: $65 to $75. No young children. No smoking.

Dining Spots

Blue Moon Cafe, 35 School St., Stowe.

Well-known local chef Jack Pickett, whose food we enjoyed during his ten-year tenure at Ten Acres Lodge, finally got the chance to do his own thing, opening his own restaurant along a side street in Stowe. It's amazingly small, a main room with a dining bar and five tables plus two enclosed front porches, each with three tables for two. A side patio nearly doubles the size in summer – one record night Jack served 95 dinners, which doesn't sound like much until you consider the size of the place.

He's in his element here, serving exciting food in a simple bistro atmosphere. We could not have been happier with our lunchtime choices: a grilled lamb sandwich with sautéed sweet peppers and onions, and grilled flatbread with sundried tomato pesto, grilled onion, sardo cheese and chorizo. Lunch has been discontinued lately.

The changing menu lists about seven starters and entrées. The meal could begin with French lentil soup with Vermont feta cheese, Maine crab cakes with tomatillo sauce and chipotle cream, or cured Atlantic salmon with sweet potato pancake and maple whiskey sauce. For main courses, how about seared peppered yellowfin tuna with tomatillo sauce and avocado salsa, pan-roasted Atlantic salmon with sundried tomato vinaigrette and garlic potato crust, or braised Craftsbury rabbit with foraged mushrooms and wild leeks? Often on the menu are butterflied leg of lamb with grilled leeks and rosemary and chargrilled cornish game hen with tomato, basil and crème fraîche, both of which we sampled when Jack was at Ten Acres and found outstanding.

Among desserts are an acclaimed crème brûlée, chocolate ganache with hot caramel sauce, a deep-fried cheesecake and a mascarpone tart drizzled with chocolate sauce and fresh fruit.

Although Jack has downscaled his cuisine a bit from his Ten Acres days, he's

hardly lost his touch, nor has he lost his reverence for regional ingredients. He's been getting his produce from the same farmer for fifteen years.
(802) 253-7006. Entrées, $13.75 to $17.25. Dinner nightly, 6 to 9:30; fewer days off-season. No smoking.

Edson Hill Manor, 1500 Edson Hill Road, Stowe.
Another "in" spot for dining lately in Stowe is the reborn dining room at Edson Hill – reborn in both decor and cuisine.
Owners Eric and Jane Lande transformed the inn's formerly rustic dining room into an airy, garden-like setting that's exceptionally pretty. Tables with wrought-iron bases and chairs with deep green seats are spaced about a multi-colored slate floor. Stunning Martstone china rests atop pale pink tablecloths. A local artist painted flowers and birds on the walls and ivy on the ceiling; the sky shows through handpainted lattices. Even the walk-out lounge downstairs is graced with handpainted quails and partridges on the walls and a squirrel at the bar. A handpainted cat with its tail draped across a shelf graces the ladies' room.
The contemporary fare with a continental accent is highly acclaimed. The short dinner menu might start with crayfish and andouille sausage gumbo, smoked trout with tobikko caviar and wasabi crème fraîche, and red curry crab cakes with mango ginger drizzle. For a main course, how about one night's choices of sesame-crusted striped bass with citrus plum vinaigrette, ale-braised rabbit with carrots and fennel, rosemary-crusted pork loin with caramelized mustard juice, and grilled New York steak with black bean ginger broth? Accompaniments change with the entrée, ranging from stir-fried bok choy and a medley of red, gold and chiogga beets to garlic mashed potatoes and golden chanterelle-barley ragoût.
Desserts could be cocoa dacquoise with espresso ganache, vanilla bean and grand marnier crème brûlée or gingerbread cake with cranberry-orange compote and cider ice cream. The 80 or so wines are pricey but as well chosen as the rest of the fare.
(802) 253-7371 or (800) 621-0284. Entrées, $18.50 to $21.50. Dinner nightly, 6 to 9:30; Tuesday-Saturday in summer and weekends only in off-season.

Asiago, 284 Mountain Road, Stowe.
This new wood grill and noodle bar bistro provided one of our more enjoyable – and affordable – dinners in a long time. Chef-owner Matt Buckels, a Rhode Islander who trained at Cioppino's in Nantucket, and his wife Joyce opened their first restaurant in 1997 to immediate acclaim. Two cozy dining rooms and a small marble bar are rag-rolled in salmon colors. One has a wall of wine racks and dark navy tables.
Our choice on a summer evening was the front porch outlined with little white lights. A little dish of mushrooms arrived with the menu, and exceptional asiago biscuits and foccacia rolls quickly followed. The warm spinach and grilled portobello salad with maple-pecan dressing and gorgonzola was a masterpiece. It preceded one of the day's selections from the noodle bar, fire-roasted chicken teamed with hand-cut corn thyme pasta and alfredo sauce, grated with asiago cheese so assertive it almost bit. Two tasty appetizers – timbale of jonah crab with a cool cucumber relish and chile-seared beef sirloin with a smoked bacon corn relish and chipotle mayonnaise – made a memorable meal. Stellar desserts were raspberry key lime pie and cantaloupe ice cream in puff pastry.
Asiago's is a menu made for grazing. Those with the heartiest of appetites can

select from such main courses as fire-roasted whole trout with sesame grilled asparagus and ginger red cabbage slaw, smoky jerk duck with a banana chutney and limey sweet potato salad, and wood-grilled veal T-bone steak.

Joyce calls the friendly atmosphere "casual cosmopolitan." We call the food dynamite.

(802) 253-2125. Entrées, $12 to $19. Dinner nightly except Tuesday, 5 to 9.

Ten Acres Lodge, 14 Barrows Road, Stowe.

After putting Edson Hill Manor on the list of Vermont's top culinary destinations, Eric and Jane Lande acquired Ten Acres Lodge and maintained its highly rated dining operation.

The dining room and airy summer porch where we've enjoyed a couple of meals are classically pretty. Mint-linened tables are set with Villeroy & Boch service plates and classical music plays softly in the background. The changing menu might feature Thai bouillabaisse, herb-crusted salmon with lemon-dill nage, seared duck breast on orange plum sauce with fried confit ravioli, and rack of lamb with bordelaise sauce.

Among starters are lobster and corn tamale with a spicy tomato coulis, roast stuffed quail and triple squash ravioli in curry pasta. Great desserts include profiteroles, vanilla crème brûlée and three chocolate mousse cake. The huge wine list has a page of old and rare vintages.

(802) 253-7638 or (800) 327-7357. Entrées, $18 to $23. Dinner nightly, 6 to 9:30; Thursday-Monday in summer and weekends only in off-season. No smoking.

The Cliff House Restaurant, Atop Mount Mansfield, Stowe Mountain Resort, Stowe.

For a change of pace, try this summit ski-lodge cafeteria gone fancy. Others have tried – in fact, Stowe experimented unsuccessfully with it for years – but this one seems to be succeeding. The management is committed to providing haute dining on high, an environment fraught with challenges.

You reach the restaurant via a ten-minute airborne ride in one of Stowe's new eight-passenger gondolas ($9 for sightseers, but free for diners). At the summit, pause for a drink on the outdoor deck or proceed into the 70-seat dining room. The tables bear linens, fresh flowers and candles, and the view from windows on three sides speaks for itself. In winter, you can watch skiers on the Gondolier, Stowe's lighted trail below.

The fare is as lofty as the elevation. The four-course, prix-fixe dinner might start with a triple fish terrine served with cucumber-dill salad and maple-mustard vinaigrette, rabbit pâté with tomato-golden raisin chutney or pan-fried crab cake on Boston brown bread with light curry sauce. A mixed green or caesar salad precedes the main course. Look for choices like grilled yellowfin tuna with a tomatillo salsa, sautéed pork tenderloin with caramelized shallot sauce, roast duck with fruit chutney and grilled filet mignon with shiitake mushroom sauce. Dessert could be chocolate-chip cheesecake, chocolate linzer torte or hazelnut torte.

Lunch is à la carte, $3.95 to $8.95. A Sunday brunch that packs in the throngs costs $9.95.

(802) 253-3665. Prix-fixe, $39. Lunch, Wednesday-Saturday 11:30 to 2:30. Dinner, Thursday-Saturday 5:30 to 9. Sunday brunch, 11:30 to 2:30. Closed for a month in spring and fall. No smoking.

Ten Acres Lodge is known for fine dining as well as lodging.

The Whip Bar and Grill, Green Mountain Inn, Main Street, Stowe.

The Whip is a casual and creative focal point of the Green Mountain Inn. Downstairs, it's smartly decorated and striking for the antique buggy whips in the wall divider separating bar from dining room and over the fireplace. Just outside is a most attractive deck, where the garden furniture is navy and white and tables are shaded by white umbrellas.

The day's specials are chalked on blackboards above cases where the food is displayed. Some of the dishes are calorie-counted for those who are there for the inn's spa facilities. Country pâté with cornichons on toast points, smoked salmon with capers, Mexican vegetable soup, salads with dressings devised by the Canyon Ranch in Arizona, crabmeat on a croissant with melted cheddar, open-face veggie melt (184 calories) – this is perfect grazing fare.

At lunchtime, you might find a chargrilled turkey burger, black pepper fettuccine alfredo, lobster ravioli on greens with mint vinaigrette or a flatbread pizza. Or try an overstuffed sandwich on thick slices of homemade oatmeal-honey bread, a trademark as well known as the Whip's riding paraphernalia.

Main dishes like grilled yellowfin tuna with smoked jalapeño beurre blanc, maple-marinated duck breast with orange ginger jus and roasted pheasant with lingonberries are posted starting at 6 at night.

Blueberry-apple crumb pie, raspberry bash, lemon cream carrot cake and a sac de bon bon for two are some of the ever-changing desserts.

(802) 253-7301. Entrées, $13.95 to $17.95. Lunch daily, 11:30 to 6. Dinner, 6 to 9:30 or 10.

The Shed, Mountain Road, Stowe.

An institution among skiers for years, the Shed has grown from its original shed to include a wraparound solarium filled with Caribbean-style furnishings, trees and plants, plus a menu offering something for everyone. Following a disastrous 1994 fire, owner Ken Strong rebuilt it bigger and better than ever, and added a microbrewery and Brewery Pub featuring European-style ales brewed on site.

Rebuilt to look old, the expansive main dining room has bright red walls, a beamed ceiling, a stone fireplace in the center and green woven mats on wood tables flanked by high-back chairs. Also popular is the outdoor deck brightened by planters full of petunias in summer.

The food is with-it, from nachos to bruschetta to onion flowers to chalupa taco salad to Asian stir-fry noodles. You can get shrimp and scallop scampi, seafood strudel, Caribbean mango duck, lamb bourbon, cajun flank steak, prime rib and goodness knows what else from the extensive menu.

The omelet and belgian waffle buffet had people lined up outside for Sunday brunch on the holiday weekend we tried to get in.

(802) 253-4364. Entrées, $11.95 to $15.95. Lunch daily, noon to 4:30. Dinner, 5 to 10, late menu to midnight. Sunday brunch, 10 to 2.

Restaurant Swisspot, Main Street, Stowe.

Skiers have always been partial to fondues. They're the specialty at this small and enduring place, brought to Stowe in 1968 after its incarnation as the restaurant in the Swiss Pavilion at Expo 67 in Montreal.

The classic Swiss cheese fondue with a dash of kirsch, $22.95 for two, made a fun meal for our skiing family. Also good is the beef fondue oriental, served with four sauces. There are six quiches and a handful of entrées like bratwurst, chicken florentine and sirloin steak.

Onion soup, eleven variations of burgers and many sandwiches are featured at lunch. The dessert accent is on Swiss chocolate, including a chocolate fondue with marshmallows and fruits for dunking.

(802) 253-4622. Entrées, $10.95 to $16.95. Open daily, noon to 10 p.m. Closed spring and late fall.

Austrian Tea Room, Trapp Family Lodge, Luce Hill Road, Stowe.

In summer or foliage season, we know of no more charming place for lunch or a snack than the rear deck of the Austrian Tea Room, with planters of geraniums and petunias enhancing the view across the countryside and horses grazing nearby. Surely you can feel the spirit of the late Maria von Trapp (who lived at the lodge until her death in 1987) and the Trapp Family Singers. It's a majestic setting where you feel on top of the world.

The broccoli, ham and swiss quiche and the grilled shrimp caesar salad looked great, as did the curried chicken and rice salad in a pineapple shell. We opted for a bratwurst with German potato salad and sauerkraut (the latter two surprisingly mild – better for tourist tastes?) and the cold pineapple-walnut soup with a smoked salmon plate. There are open-face sandwiches, fancy drinks, cafe Viennoise and Austrian wines by the glass or liter.

Those Austrian desserts we all know and love – sacher torte, linzer torte, apfelstrudel and the like – as well as Bavarian chocolate pie, peach torte and jailhouse pie, are in the $4 range. With a cup of cafe mocha, they make a delightful afternoon pick-me-up.

The trip up Luce Hill Road gives you a chance to see the rebuilt, exotic Trapp Family Lodge, which the locals consider the closest thing to Disneyland in Vermont. The tea room remains true to the lodge's heritage.

(802) 253-8511. Entrées, $5.50 to $9.50. Open daily, 10:30 to 5:30. Dinner on Friday and Saturday. No smoking.

Diversions

Mount Mansfield. Skiing is what made Stowe famous, legions of skiers having been attracted to New England's most storied mountain since the East's first chairlift was installed in 1940 (the Mount Mansfield Company is its official name, but everyone from near and far calls the ski area simply Stowe). Today, Mount Mansfield has sleek new eight-passenger gondola cars among its seven lifts and vastly expanded snowmaking. Nearly one-third of its slopes are for expert skiers, including the awesome "Front Four" – the precipitous National, Goat, Starr and Liftline trails, so steep that on the Starr you cannot see the bottom from the ledge on top. They almost make the Nosedive seem tame. There's easier terrain, of course, and the related Spruce Peak ski area across the way has four more lifts, a sunny southeast exposure and a special section for new skiers. Combined with accommodations and nightlife, the total skiing experience ranks Stowe among the top ski resorts in the world.

Summer at Mount Mansfield. The **Stowe Gondola** takes visitors 7,000 feet up to the Cliff House, just below Vermont's highest summit (adults $9, Memorial Day to late October). Cars can drive up the 4.5-mile **Stowe Auto Road,** known to skiers who ease down it in winter as the Toll Road (cars $12, daily late May to mid-October). The **Alpine Slide at Spruce Peak** appeals especially to children; you take a chairlift up and slide down (single rides, $7.50; daily in summer, weekends in late spring and early fall).

Smugglers' Notch. Up the Mountain Road past the ski area you enter the Mount Mansfield State Park, passing picnic areas and the Long Trail. A couple of hairpin turns take you into Smugglers' Notch, a narrow pass with 1,000-foot cliffs looming on either side. It's a quiet, awe-inspiring place to pause and gawk at such rock formations as Elephant Head, King Rock and the Hunter and His Dog. Stop at Smugglers' Cave and, farther on, hike into Bingham Falls. The road is not for the faint-hearted (it's closed in winter, for good reason). We drove back from Jeffersonville after a summer thunderstorm and found waterfalls that had been trickles on the way over suddenly gushing down the rocks beside the lonely road.

The Arts. The hills are alive with the sound of music as the Stowe Performing Arts series offers Sunday evening concerts in the concert meadow near the Trapp Family Lodge. The Vermont Mozart Festival also presents concerts there. More concerts are staged at the Stowe Mountain Performing Arts Center, a 12,000-seat amphitheater at the base of Spruce Peak. The **Stowe Theatre Guild** presents its summer season at the Town Hall Theater. The **Helen Day Art Center** hosts rotating exhibits in a restored 1863 Greek Revival structure that once was the high school on School Street.

The **Stowe Recreation Path** is the pride of the community. Opened in 1984 with an extension in 1989, the much-used, nationally recognized 5.3-mile walking and biking greenway starts in the village behind the Community Church and roughly parallels the Mountain Road up to Brook Road. Also in the recreation category is the **Stowe Polo Club,** another community-based effort, which stages polo events throughout the season.

The **Cold Hollow Cider Mill,** south of town along Route 100, is a large and intriguing red barn where you can watch cider being made (and drink the sweet and delicious free samples). For more than twenty years the Chittenden family also have sold tart cider jelly, cider donuts and other apple products as well as cookbooks, wooden toys, gourmet foods and about every kind of Vermont jam, jelly or preserve imaginable.

Nearby, all kinds of cheeses and dips may be sampled (and purchased) at the large **Cabot Creamery Annex Store.** Also part of the complex is a branch of famed pastry chef Albert Kumin's **Green Mountain Chocolate Company,** headquartered down Route 100 below Waterbury, which caters to Stowe's sweet tooth.

Shopping. Shops are concentrated in Stowe and scattered along Route 100 and the Mountain Road. Along Main Street in the village, **Shaw's General Store** considers itself 90 years young and carries most everything, especially sporting goods, sportswear, gifts and oddities. Nearby are the **Old Depot Shops,** an open, meandering mall of a place containing the **Green Mountain Pantry, Vermont Furniture Works, The Craft Sampler, Stuffed in Stowe** with thousands of stuffed animals and **Bear Pond Books.** Tread the creaky floorboards of **Val's Country Shop** for T-shirts, maple syrup, candy and such. **Gracie's Gourmutt Shop** features dog-emblazoned clothes and gifts as well as specialty foods from Gracie's restaurant. For a different experience, head to **Everything Cows.** It's a bovine boutique where cows prevail in socks, mugs, stained glass and even Christmas decorations. Upstairs is **The Udder End,** a gallery of cow country collectibles including cow-famed Woody Jackson serigraphs and custom-made quilts.

Up the Mountain Road at the Straw Corner Shops are the **Stowe Craft Gallery** and the **Stowe Coffee House.** Farther along at 108 West are the **Stowe Kitchen Co.,** with practical cookware and gadgets; **Ivy Brooks** for men's clothing and **Stowe Bath & Linens.** The gourmet-to-go **Harvest Market** is the place for specialty foods, wine and espresso. At the Red Barn Shops, **Mountain Cheese and Wine** carries an impressive selection, **Samara** features works of Vermont craftsmen and **The Yellow Turtle** offers "classy clothes for classy kids," the kind that well-heeled grandparents like to buy. We were impressed with all the sophisticated handicrafts, the MacKenzie-Childs pottery, the Claire Murray rugs and the whimsical, even wild furniture at Constance Rasmussen's suave **Emotional Outlet Gallery.**

Extra-Special _____

Ben & Jerry's Ice Cream Factory, Route 100, Waterbury.

Just south of Stowe, this factory producing 130,000 pints daily of the ice cream that transplanted Vermont characters Ben Cohen and Jerry Greenfield made famous is one of Vermont's busiest tourist attractions. And with good reason. During half-hour guided tours, you see a humorous slide show, watch the ice cream being made, learn some of the history of this intriguing outfit that donates one percent of its profits to peace and, of course, savor a tiny sample, obtained by lowering a bucket on a rope to the production area below. At busy times, the place is a madhouse – with live music outside, lineups of people waiting to buy cones, a gift shop filled with Vermont cow-related items, and every bit of publicity Ben and Jerry ever got decorating the walls. If you can't get inside, at least buy a dish or cone of ice cream from the outdoor windows.

(802) 244-8687. Tours daily 9 to 8 in summer, to 6 in fall, 10 to 5 rest of year. Adults $1.50, under 13 free.

Skiers enjoy fresh powder conditions on a sunny day at Sugarbush.

Waitsfield and Warren, Vt.
The Spirit of the Valley

Even more than most Vermont areas best known for skiing, the Mad River Valley is a year-round paradise for sports enthusiasts.

The focus, of course, is on skiing – at the venerable and spartan Mad River Glen, a challenging area for hardy, serious skiers, and at Sugarbush, the tony resort spawned by and for jet-setters. Both are very much "in" with skiers, for vastly differing reasons.

In the off-season, which extends from May into November, there are the conventional athletic pursuits associated with other destination ski resorts, such as golf and tennis. There also are the more unusual: mountaineering, polo, rugby, cricket, Icelandic horse trekking and soaring.

Off-mountain, activity centers along Route 100, which links the villages of Waitsfield and Warren. Ironically, Waitsfield (the home of Mad River Glen) is busier and more hip in the Sugarbush style. Warren (the address for Sugarbush) is in the Mad River Glen tradition, remote and seemingly bypassed by the times. The skiing spirit extends to the entrepreneurial. An uncommon number of crafts ventures thrive here, as do unusual businesses. Two unassuming enterprises that ship fresh or frozen pizzas to connoisseurs around the East have suddenly turned Waitsfield into the pizza capital of northern New England.

The spirit of the valley – considered unique by its adherents – emerges from its rugged terrain as well as from the contrasting mix attracted by its two skiing faces.

Unlike other ski resorts where one big mountain crowns a plateau, here mountains crowd the valley on all sides, forging several narrow valleys that leave some visitors feeling hemmed in. To understand, you have only to stay in summer in a remote chalet at Mad River Glen, the mountains rising in silence all around, or descend the back road from Roxbury Gap, one of Vermont's more heart-stopping drives, which rewards the persevering with awesome close-ups of some of the state's highest peaks.

The chic of Sugarbush joins with the rusticity of Mad River to present choices from racquetball to backpacking, from boutiques to country stores, from nightclubbing to roadhouses. For fine dining, the valley is in the vanguard among Eastern ski resorts.

Although the valley is at its best and busiest in the winter, its spirit spans all seasons.

Inn Spots

The Inn at the Round Barn Farm, East Warren Road, RR 1, Box 247, Waitsfield 05673.

The Joslin Round Barn – a National Historic Landmark and one of the last remaining of its kind in Vermont – is a focal point of this deluxe and animated B&B. Its three vast floors have been renovated into a cultural center, a theater, a space for meetings and weddings, and the headquarters of the Round Barn Farm Cross-Country Ski Center. There's even a 60-foot-long lap pool on the lower level.

The inn is not in the Round Barn as one might think, however. Rather, it occupies a gracious farmhouse and connecting carriage house next door, has six comfortable bedrooms and five extravagant suites, luxurious common rooms and a terraced, 215-acre back yard that rolls down a hill to a couple of ponds and meanders uphill past cows grazing in the distance. It's an idyllic setting, and an exciting B&B.

Owners Jack and Doreen Simko, longtime skiers in the valley, retired from the family floral business in New Jersey to open the inn with daughter Anne Marie in 1987. Their background prompts all the flowers and greenery throughout the house, pots of flowering hibiscus on the terrace, and flowers sprouting from piles of rocks beneath a giant apple tree. Relaxing on the back terraces is a treat, what with animals grazing, a few barns scattered up the hill, whimsical things like a cow made out of iron and, at our first visit, a pen with Jack's three pet pigs – gifts for his 50th birthday. There's only one pig now, and a new attraction is an undulating, fourteen-foot-deep spring-fed pond for swimming, canoeing and fishing.

Our original stay coming at the end of one of the hottest summers ever, we passed up the two largest rooms with jacuzzi tubs in the main house in favor of the breezy Palmer Room at the rear corner. It had a highback Victorian queen bed sporting a crazy quilt made in 1915, lovely lace curtains and a framed fan on the wall.

Raspberry-cranberry walls enhance the refurbished Joslin Room, with its kingsize canopy

Joslin Round Barn and landscaped lawns are focal points of Inn at the Round Barn Farm.

bed, new fireplace and a huge bathroom complete with wing chair, oriental rug, steam shower and corner jacuzzi tub for two. Three people can sleep comfortably in the spacious, ground-level Terrace Room, which has a queensize bed and a sitting area with sofabed.

Other than the Joslin, the prime accommodations are now in four mini-suites with queen or kingsize beds, steam showers, gas fireplaces and separate sitting areas beneath twenty-foot beamed ceilings in the rear loft area of the original carriage house. The top-of-the-line Richardson contains a sunken bathroom with an oversize jacuzzi (you can watch the farm animals outside the window as you soak), a separate shower, and his and her vanities. Relax on the chintz loveseat or chaise lounge beside the marble fireplace and you may never leave.

Striking fabrics on canopies and window treatments provide colorful accents against the barnwood walls in each mini-suite. Even the custom-designed Kleenex boxes match the decor. Although not as splashy as some, the pristinely white Dana at the end is favored by honeymooners for its Schumacher wall coverings and its crown-canopied black iron queensize bed draped in chiffon. Besides fine oriental and Claire Murray rugs, burgundy terrycloth robes, stenciling and other interesting decorative touches, the inn has nightly turndown service with chocolates as well as toiletries like Neutrogena bath conditioners and moisturizers.

The main floor offers a large, elegant library with walls of books, a fireplace and a fancy stereo system issuing forth perhaps Mozart or Vivaldi. A less formal game room downstairs contains a pool table, TV and VCR.

At cocktail time, Anne Marie gets creative with nibbles, usually putting out something like guacamole or a hot shrimp dip.

Breakfast is served in an expansive dining area fashioned from the original milking barn. Vines trail around the beams and the colorful tables are set with fresh flowers and striking ceramic napkin rings. We feasted on raspberries and bananas in cream, followed by a fantastic omelet blending bacon, cottage cheese, onions, red peppers and basil from the garden. Anne Marie's cinnamon-raisin belgian waffles with maple cream is another favorite, and her pumpkin soufflés are a hit during foliage season.

Based on requests of guests, the Simkos began bottling the raspberry sauce they serve with their cottage-cheese pancakes. Said a California friend who was enjoying a reunion with the Simkos and joined us all at the breakfast table: "These are high-energy people with 85 irons in the fire. Staying with them is like being part of the family." The Simkos have retired nearby, but Anne Marie, now married and the mother of two, and her resident innkeepers continue e family tradition.

(802) 496-2276. Fax (802) 496-8832. www.innatroundbarn.com. Six rooms and five mini-suites with private baths. Weekends: doubles $125 to $150, suites $175 to $205. Midweek: doubles $115 to $140, suites $165 to $195. Holidays and foliage season: $15 surcharge. Children over 15. No smoking.

The Pitcher Inn, Main Street, Warren 05674.

The old Pitcher Inn, which burned to the ground in 1993, was rebuilt in 1997. The loggers who frequented the rustic place in the 1800s wouldn't recognize its reincarnation, nor would any of the folks who might have breakfasted here over the years, including Heather Carino, who occasionally started the day here with her parents on ski trips from their home in Greenwich, Conn.

Winthrop Smith of the founding Merrill Lynch family financed the rebuilding and installed newlywed daughter Heather and her husband John as resident inn-keepers. Reborn like a phoenix, the three-story, pristine white building is a beauty with upstairs balconies overlooking the village and the rear porches looking onto the rushing Mad River.

The ten striking guest accommodations contain all the creature comforts, and all but two have fireplaces. Jacuzzi tubs, telephones, computer-fax hookups and hidden TV/VCRs are standard issue. Each incorporates a Vermont theme in its furnishings. The least expensive School Room comes with a kingsize bed, private porch, and old slate chalk boards on the walls and a school desk reminiscent of a one-room school house. The Mallard adds a bed shaped like a duck, a sofabed, antique duck decoys and antique guns in a display case; its ceiling is domed to give the illusion of a duck blind. Other rooms have woodburning fireplaces and steam showers. The Trout room with separate seating area and private porch is unusual with cut trees used as bedposts and columns, looking as if they're growing out of the floor. The adjacent barn holds a couple of two-bedroom suites, each with a fireplaced living room. The saddles in the main-floor suite carry out a stables theme, while the Hayloft is outfitted with antique barn supplies.

Two large common rooms in the main inn offer comfy seating around the fire-places. There also are a library and a billiards/game room.

The inn's elegant dining room is open to the public for breakfast and dinner. Overnight guests have their choice of the full menu, served in a sunny breakfast room off the dining room overlooking the river.

(802) 496-6350 or (888) 867-4824. Fax (802) 496-6354. Eight rooms and two suites with private baths. Doubles, $165 to $300. Suites, $325. Two-night minimum weekends.

Hamilton House, German Flats Road, RR 1, Box 74, Warren 05674.

There are those who would think Joyce and James Plumpton have it all: an aristocratic British background, a successful business career, world travels, three grown sons, a huge retirement home in the midst of 25 forested acres between golf

Grounds of Hamilton House are blanketed in winter's white.

course and ski mountain. So why would they want to open their home as a B&B? "We like to entertain," say the Plumptons, whose house lends itself to entertaining and is frequently the site of large parties for local groups and causes with which they are affiliated. "We love people, looking after them and making them feel good."

That they do to perfection, with great taste and jolly good British humor. The Plumptons first started thinking of doing a B&B when they were living in a substantial stone manor house in northern England in the 1970s. But James's business took them to New Jersey, and they also acquired a ski house at Sugarbush. In 1988, they purchased the 30-year-old home of the man who developed the Sugarbush Inn and golf course. They transformed the 8,000-square-foot structure from a ski lodge into an English manor house to accommodate friends and family gatherings. They named it Hamilton House in memory of Florence Hamilton, Joyce's mother, a member of one of Scotland's leading families and related by marriage to the Royal Family. "The crest we use is that of the Duke of Hamilton," advises the inn's detailed and informative welcome letter.

Some might think staying here would be intimidating – "I'm very pickity," Joyce said the first time she showed us the Maiden Cross Rooms, a suite named for their last home in England. "I won't put the twin beds together because I think a kingsize bed would spoil the effect of the room." (She later relented, replacing the twins with a queen bed and pronouncing the effect "just as lovely, if not nicer.") And only one suite, the College Rooms, has a TV because Joyce could not fathom people "coming to Vermont to watch TV." But the Plumptons' welcome is down-to-earth and heartfelt. We selected the Garden Room for its kingsize bed, and quietly repaired after dinner to the empty College Rooms' living room to catch up on the evening news on TV.

Two spacious bedrooms and two suites are available for guests on the second floor. All have full private baths. Largest is the College Rooms, a living room and queensize bedroom with paraphernalia from the hosts' college days in England, including a stash of tennis and squash racquets displayed ever so smartly in a basket. The family's chappals (similar to sandals) are lined up beneath a side table in the India Room, which is dressed in rich fabrics and rattans reminiscent of the family's residence in India. The Garden Room overlooking a clump of rhododendrons and azaleas reflects the "great pleasure" that the Plumptons have derived from creating gardens in different parts of the world. Floral fabrics on the headboard matched the swagged curtains and wallpaper border along the top of the pale yellow walls. Three rows of framed floral prints traced the months of the year, two garden books were on a side table and a cement turtle served as the door stop. A basket of apples and grapes was in the room upon our arrival. A small gold box of chocolates was presented at turndown.

On the main floor, guests enjoy their own large drawing room, full of comfortable seating and shelves of books; a long, plant-filled conservatory that's a joy year-round, and a magnificent formal dining room centered by an oval mahogany table for eight. "Obviously my furniture came with me from England," Joyce points out. Off the long front hall are a wet bar, stocked with bottles of wines to which guests may help themselves, beers and James's favorite Long Trail ales, and a laundry room where skis and boots may be stashed and where the family cats Riley and Ophelia sleep in baskets atop the washer and dryer.

The conservatory was the setting for a "proper English breakfast," as described by Joyce and cooked by James. Orange juice and a glass dish rimmed with sugar and bearing raspberries, grapes and melon balls with mint and a sour cream sauce began the repast. Next came a plate of small harvest muffins and croissants. The main event was scrambled eggs, served with mushroom caps, link sausages and delicious grilled tomatoes on toasted bread rounds spread with a zesty pesto sauce.

This is "very much our home and we intend to keep it that way," says James, who was building a game room in the basement with a dartboard near the fireplace at our latest visit. They bought twenty acres of spruce forest adjacent for "a wood garden" and to prevent unwanted development.

(802) 583-1066 or (800) 760-1066. Fax (802) 583-1776. Two rooms and two suites with private baths. Doubles, $140 and $160. Suites, $180 and $200. No smoking.

West Hill House, West Hill Road, RR 1, Box 292, Warren 05674.

A wonderfully secluded setting on fifteen acres next to the Sugarbush Golf Course and Ski Touring Center, a quaint Vermont farmhouse dating to 1862 and welcoming hosts commend this seven-room B&B. Not to be overlooked are luxury amenities, gourmet breakfasts, occasional dinners and charming common rooms.

The place reflects the talents of owners Dotty Kyle and Eric Brattstrom, originally from Maplewood, N.J. Dotty, an artist and accomplished cook, painted the beautiful border of flowers that winds around the living room, stairway and cathedral ceiling. She also painted the floral borders that match the prized wildflower quilt on the queen bed in the upstairs Wildflower Room. Her husband, a construction project manager, built the wall of shelves in the living room to house part of their huge book collection. He remodeled a shared bath upstairs to make private baths for two bedrooms. Lately he added a rear wing to provide a skiers' entry, powder room and a huge great room with a stone fireplace and a large sunroom with a vaulted ceiling and a wood stove. The sunroom opens through french doors onto a side deck overlooking rock gardens. Look there for the birdbath that Eric carved with a shallow end for chickadees and a deep end for blue jays.

Front veranda of West Hill House overlooks gardens and valley.

The dormer windows and sloping ceilings in the main house yield nooks and crannies, which the artist in Dotty has turned to good advantage. She sponge-painted the walls light green in one bedroom and added a king/twin bed configuration to the main-floor Stetson Suite, where we enjoyed the extra space of a sitting room with a TV. Other premier accommodations are the Wildflower with a double jacuzzi tub and fireplace, and the beamed Fireplace Room up its own spiral staircase above the great room, also with a queen bed, fireplace and jacuzzi tub.

All rooms have queen or king/twin beds. Two have fireplaces and some have TVs. Thick towels, down pillows and comforters, attractive quilts and assorted toiletries are the norm. Arrangements of fresh or dried flowers and bowls of seasonal candies are placed about.

Guests relax on the new side deck or the wicker-filled front porch facing bird feeders, tiny red squirrels and prolific gardens. Other haunts are the cozy barnwood-paneled living room with its treasury of books, vaulted ceiling, wide-board floors and a large recessed fireplace at one end and the rear great room which, Dotty thinks, sounds pretentious "but everybody says 'what a great room!'" A pantry holds a refrigerator and wet bar, where guests help themselves to cookies, soft drinks, cider and wine.

Breakfast in the beamed English antique dining room begins with a fresh fruit bowl ("we have a blueberry patch that won't quit," Dotty advised) or, in our case, bananas West Hill (like bananas foster, spiked with rum) and scones. An herbed cheese omelet and bacon followed. Other treats include "the best sticky buns in the world – I've always loved them and worked very hard to get them the way I want them." Among main courses are baked apple pancakes, banana-nut waffles and vegetable soufflés.

On Saturday nights or by reservation, Dotty prepares optional candlelight dinners with soup, salad, entrée and dessert. Favorites include roast chicken basted with maple syrup over roasted vegetables, braised pork chops with onions and apples, and steak diane.

Her newly renovated kitchen includes a wood-burning bake oven in which Dotty bakes flatbreads and other treats for guests.

The architect who helped design the renovations was so impressed with Eric's work at the inn that he brought a group of his students here to meet "a builder who makes his new work look as if it has always been here."

(802) 496-7162 or (800) 898-1427. Fax (802) 496-6443. www.westhillhouse.com. Six rooms and one suite with private baths. Winter and weekends: doubles, $100 to $145. Summer and midweek: $90 to $125. Two-night minimum weekends. Children over 10. No smoking.

The Sugartree Inn, Sugarbush Access Road, RR1, Box 38, Warren 05674.

Energetic new owners are leaving their mark on the Sugartree, an inviting inn transformed from what essentially had been a ski chalet for 30 years. Frank and Kathy Partsch traded corporate life in Boston for new roles as jack-of-all-trades innkeepers. Besides their hospitality roles, Frank has put his handyman/carpentry talents to good use and Kathy has taken up sewing. Her job description lists cook, decorator, part-time work at Mad River Canoe and volunteer stints at the local Chamber of Commerce.

Guests arriving at the homey, nine-bedroom inn see evidence of Frank's talents immediately. He renovated the office/reception area at the entry to make it seem less like an office. It opens into a new fireplaced suite he created with a small wicker sitting room, a queensize bedroom and a renovated bath with a vanity he made himself in a workshop rapidly taking over the garage.

More of Frank's handiwork is evident in the spacious living room. He built the tall clock as well as the wood-carved folk art Santa Clauses lined up along the fireplace mantel. The figures often reflect local activities, from skiing Santas to one with a tennis racquet. Kathy's new-found sewing talent has revealed itself in the quilts she is making for the guest bedrooms. "I couldn't sew before I got here," she confessed. Now she has dressed up several bedrooms with quilts, one made of 800 pieces. She made curtains for the sitting room in the suite, and found an antique pump organ for the living room. The bedrooms, all with private baths, are furnished in country style with puffy curtains, shams, dust ruffles, crocheted bed canopies, samplers, needlework wall hangings and wreaths on the doors. All but two have queensize beds, and two were completely renovated with new carpeting, furniture and paint jobs in peach and teal. The bathrooms have glycerin soaps, herbal bath grains and built-in hair dryers.

The rooms are named for birds that frequent the inn's feeders. Each has the appropriate painting by a local artist on the door and on the key chain.

Kathy serves a full country breakfast in the dining room. The menu, posted on a blackboard, included juices, apple crisp, bacon and french toast with orange sauce or maple syrup at a recent visit. Baked eggs with three cheeses, sour cream coffee cake and assorted berry pancakes are other specialties, nicely detailed in a new cookbook sold at the inn. In the afternoon, Kathy puts out cookies and perhaps chocolate fondue.

Outside, summer's trees, incredible gardens and window boxes envelop the inn in its own delightful island of color and greenery. There's a gazebo, and Frank has put in a rock garden and an herb garden. In winter, when the trees are bare, the landscape opens onto the mountains and guests can see skiers at Sugarbush across the way.

(802) 583-3211 or (800) 666-8907. Fax (802) 583-3203. www.sugartree.com. Eight rooms and one suite with private baths. Winter: doubles $90, suite $125. Foliage and holidays: doubles $110, suite $135. Rest of year: doubles $80, suite $100. Three-night minimum peak weekends. Children over 7. No smoking.

Rear deck is favorite gathering spot for guests at Beaver Pond Farm Inn.

Beaver Pond Farm Inn, Golf Course Road, RD Box 306, Warren 05674.

A farmhouse this may be, but an elegant one it is indeed. Located off a quiet country road overlooking several beaver ponds and the Sugarbush Golf Club fairways, the light green house with green roof has candles lighted in the windows even on a summer afternoon. The back yard has a driving range with two tees, such is the interest of owners Betty and Bob Hansen (she's been golf club champion and president of the Vermont Women's Golf Association).

They share their gorgeous property and home with guests, who enjoy a stylish fireplaced living room done in rusts and navy, a small bar where setups and hors d'oeuvres are provided in the late afternoon, a beamed dining room with a long harvest table on an oriental rug and decanters of brandy and sherry at the ready, and a small library with TV and telephone, furnished in contemporary style in red and gray. Best of all, perhaps, is a fabulous rear deck that runs the length of the house, where the Hansens and guests like to have cocktails and watch the beavers in the pond.

Betty, a French-trained chef and onetime New Jersey caterer, is considered the best cook in the valley by fellow innkeepers. Her country breakfast starts with fresh juice, fruit and cereal. Orders are taken for choices among four main courses, always a special egg dish (eggs florentine at one visit), eggs any way, grand marnier french toast and perhaps apple-walnut pancakes.

The Hansens offer dinners in winter on Tuesday, Thursday and Saturday for $20 to $22. She cooks and he serves the meal, which starts at 7:30. A typical dinner could be soup or smoked trout mousse topped with caviar, salad, butterflied lamb and floating island. French wines accompany.

Upstairs are five well furnished guest rooms, three with private baths. Three have queensize beds and two are twins. Those in the older section dating to 1840 have sloping "coffin windows." Explains Bob: "everything slopes, there are no straight angles in a Vermont farmhouse." The Hansens now offer a sixth queensize bedroom with private bath adjoining the rear deck downstairs. Cheery in pink and yellow, it became available when they moved to a new apartment in the barn. *(802) 583-2861. Fax (802) 583-2860. www.beaverpondfarminn.com. Four rooms with private baths and two with shared bath. Doubles, $72 to $104.*

The Lareau Farm Country Inn, Route 100, Box 563, Waitsfield 05673.

This really is a farm with gardens, two dogs, four cats, seven horses and occasionally chickens and pigs, the whole menagerie dubbed the Lareau Zoo and the name delightfully emblazoned on sweatshirts, aprons, T-shirts and the like. The 1852 farmhouse with a barn, woodshed and appropriate 67-acre country setting on flatlands that were farmed until a few years ago by the Lareau family was converted into an inn in 1984 by Pennsylvanians Sue and Dan Easley, who have been expanding and upgrading ever since.

In the Mad River on the property, a ten-foot-deep swimming hole is flanked by rocks. "The water is so clear you can see the brown trout," according to Sue. Actually, there are three swimming holes: one for the public and families, one for house guests and one for skinny-dipping ("we send one couple at a time," advises Dan). The flora and fauna on the property are so interesting that Sue has published a detailed walking trail guide for guests.

Since she pieced together the squares for ten bed quilts in their first summer, the Easleys have added bathrooms and expanded to thirteen guest rooms. In the former woodshed, the dirt floors have given way to carpeting, but the four rooms retain some of the original posts and beams amid such modern conveniences as private baths. Brass bedsteads and rockers are mixed with a profusion of hanging plants.

An addition to the rear of the main house holds four guest rooms, all with full baths and queensize beds, a much-enlarged dining room and a sitting room around the fireplace in the former kitchen. A new jacuzzi suite is among the other five rooms in the oldest part of the house, built in the 1700s. The main structure was added to it, and has a parlor full of Victorian furniture and stuffed animals. Guests like to laze on the assortment of porches that wrap all the way around the house.

The main gathering place has turned out to be the huge rear dining room and back porch with six columns obtained at auction. Pretty in beige and blue, the dining room has four big tables, oriental rugs and windows on three sides. "It's changed our orientation," says Sue, "bringing the focus out back." Adirondack chairs are gathered on the back lawn for gazing across the farmlands up against the mountains.

Dan, the breakfast chef, whips up homemade muffins or breads and perhaps an egg soufflé casserole and blueberry or banana-oatbran pancakes. The inn has a beer and wine license, and provides hors d'oeuvres and setups for guests in the winter.

The old slaughterhouse has been turned into the home of the locally famous American Flatbread business and restaurant (see Dining Spots).

The Easleys offer sleigh rides and cider parties. They donate their food leftovers to Meals on Wheels and give a percentage of the room rates to the Nature Conservancy ("our way of trying to protect Vermont's future," says Dan). One year every guest received a cookie cutter in the shape of a maple leaf for use as a napkin ring. It symbolized their theme to be "a cut above."

(802) 496-4949 or (800) 833-0766. Eleven rooms with private baths and two with shared bath. Doubles, $80 to $110 weekends, $70 to $95 midweek. Two-night minimum weekends.

The Featherbed Inn, Route 100, RD 1, Box 19, Waitsfield 05673.

There are plump featherbeds on the beds, naturally, and featherbed eggs are the breakfast specialty at this historic and stylish B&B opened by New Jersey transplants Clive and Tracey Coutts. After three years of painstaking renovations, the place bears faint resemblance to its background as the area's first B&B/ski lodge in the 1950s. The result is the more remarkable in that the couple did most of the work themselves. He handled the construction, even putting 3,000 of the original bricks into the foundation and the living-room fireplace. She did the decorating, window treatments and some spectacular stenciling.

Two pleasant guest rooms are at one end of the main floor and share a den with television. Upstairs are three more bedrooms and two suites, all with private baths. The Ilse Suite at the north end has a skylit, beamed cathedral ceiling with a loveseat in the corner, a hooked rug on the original softwood flooring and an antique quilt on the queensize sleigh bed. The prized Beatrice Suite in the middle of the house holds a queensize canopy bed whose quilt coordinates with the floral swags draped across three windows and the fabric on the rare spindle bench beneath. The suite is also notable for fancy stenciling along the chair rails, a wet bar with refrigerator, and a small bedroom equipped with a day bed and trundle bed. The Alexandra Room at the south end has a queensize iron bed and two wing chairs. The sprinkling of antiques and period memorabilia produces a simple but cheery look, one in keeping with the early 19th-century origin of the house.

Under construction in 1997 in a rear cottage were two garden-level rooms and an upstairs suite with the original beams. All with queensize featherbeds, the two downstairs rooms have gas fireplaces.

Tracey's stenciling, evident in most rooms, reaches its zenith in the informal, main-floor lodge room. Here, beneath a beamed ceiling, stenciled geese and ducks fly up and around the windows and french doors in random procession. The room is sunny in wicker, the doors open onto an outdoor deck and an open fireplace is ablaze in winter. Guests also enjoy a handsome living room, where Clive may play for singalongs around the grand piano. Teal wainscoting and a lace-covered table enhance the formal dining room.

Tracey often serves featherbed eggs in individual ramekins, eirkuchen (German pancakes stuffed with apples or peaches), or french toast stuffed with creamed cottage cheese sweetened with maple syrup and fruit. These treats follow a fancy fruit course (perhaps baked pineapple or a pear compote with cider and spices) and homemade apricot or strawberry breads. Fruit and cheese, cookies, tea and hot cider are put out in the afternoon.

(802) 496-7151. Seven rooms and three suites with private baths. Doubles, $85 to $115. Suites, $115 to $125. Children over 10. No smoking.

1824 House Inn, Route 100, Box 159, Waitsfield 05673.

Susan and Lawrence McKay moved back East from Washington state in 1994 to take over Newtons' 1824 House Inn. Moving from Vashon Island and high-level careers, she said, there was only one other state in which they would choose to raise their young children and that was Vermont.

They spiffed up the inn, "letting in the light," in Susan's words. They replaced dark curtains with sheers, took up the carpets to show the oak flooring and added antiques from the West Coast. The result is a clean, fresh and elegant look in keeping with the house's designation on the National Register of Historic Places.

These ex-Pennsylvanians are nothing if not versatile. Lawrence, a film and TV writer, was about to publish his second children's book at our latest visit. A gourmet cook, he handles the breakfast duties, when fresh blueberries and raspberries (even in winter) are the rule. Next might come blueberry or raspberry muffins. The main event could be Dutch babies, Mexican quiche with salsa, yellow cornmeal pancakes with blueberries or a chile rellenos soufflé. Espresso or latte accompany. In the winter, pâté and cheese are offered with wine in the afternoon. The host, a folk music buff, might play some bluegrass or jazz.

Susan, an educator and psychologist, went to work with a decorator's eye in the common rooms and six guest rooms, all with private baths. Enter the house through a foyer/parlor with a baby grand piano. On one side is a full-length living room with a fireplace and a couple of spectacular Larson chairs. On the other side is the dining room with two tables and some of the McKays' newer Scandinavian pieces. The walls are enhanced by artworks given by an artist-friend, the late Russell Twiggs. Bedrooms, named for poets and artists, contain king, queen or double featherbeds. The largest is the side William Yeats Room, stately with a king bed and armoire. The rear Boris Pasternak Room has a king bed, while the Robert Frost Room holds the McKays' Edwardian wedding bed.

Susan, a dressage rider, stables two Morgan horses in the barn. She created a dressage arena with white fencing facing the road. The 22-acre property includes trails, an organic garden and a swimming hole in the Mad River.

(802) 496-7555 or (800) 426-3986. Fax (802) 496-7559. Six rooms with private baths. Doubles, $110 to $165; off-season $85 to $125. No smoking.

Tucker Hill Lodge, Route 17, RD 1, Box 147, Waitsfield 05673.

New owners Susan Francheschini Noaro and her husband Giorgio from Ottawa are trying to restore this establishment of wide renown to its former glory and finding a niche that balances simple guest rooms with a reputation for high-end dining.

This has always been one of the more lavishly landscaped inns we have seen. In summer, the spectacular flower gardens contain hanging clematis, flowering kale and decorative mullen.

The 21 guest rooms vary in size and decor. Fourteen have private baths. They are homey and rustic, with handmade quilts, bouquets of flowers and what the inn's brochure calls "a mountain cabin feeling." One of the nicest is the Innkeepers' Suite (home of the former innkeepers) with a fireplace, kingsize feather bed and connecting twin-bedded room. Also popular is the Catamount Suite in the former cross-country building across the way. The Eastman House, an 1810 farmhouse across from the pool, is historic as can be but accommodates up to six people in modern comfort.

In the main inn, a paneled living room has TV and a fieldstone fireplace. The main dining room is known as Giorgio's Cafe (see Dining Spots). The downstairs barnwood cafe/lounge section, which Suzie planned to convert into more of a game room, is where the renowned American Flatbread country pizzas got their start. Tennis courts, the pool and a large outdoor deck ringed with cedar trees are attractions.

Breakfasts are hearty: seasonal fresh fruit, followed perhaps by cottage-cheese pancakes with peaches, a broccoli, tomato and mushroom omelet, or Vermont toast, which is french toast with shredded cheddar cheese between the layers.

The Noaros recommend hiking the local trails (the Long Trail is not far away). You'll need to after one of their breakfasts or dinners.

(802) 496-3983 or (800) 543-7841. Fax (802) 496-3203. www.tuckerhill.com. Twelve rooms and two suites with private baths and seven rooms with shared baths. Summer and winter: B&B, doubles $70 to $90 weekends, $60 to $80 midweek; suites $115 weekends, $100 midweek; Eastman House, $300, two-night, four-person minimum. Spring and late fall: doubles $60, suite $80, Eastman House $200. Add $60 for MAP in summer and winter, $50 rest of year.

Dining Spots

The Common Man, German Flats Road, Warren.

Here is the ultimate incongruity: a soaring, century-old timbered barn with floral carpets on the walls to cut down the noise and keep out wintry drafts. Crystal chandeliers hang from beamed ceilings over bare wood tables set simply with red napkins and pewter candlesticks. A table headed by a regal Henry VIII chair occupies a prime position in front of a massive, open fieldstone fireplace.

The whole mix works, and thrivingly so since its establishment in 1972 in the site we first knew as Orsini's. Destroyed by fire in 1987, it was replaced by a barn dismantled in Moretown and rebuilt here by English-born owner Mike Ware.

The extensive wine list comes in two picture frames, hinged together to open like a book, and contains good values. Ingenious, custom-made brackets hold wine buckets at the edge of the tables.

The escargots maison "served with our famous (and secret) garlic butter sauce" leads off the French/continental menu. Other appetizers include a daily charcuterie, gravlax and Vermont goat cheese baked in puff pastry. We can vouch for the Vietnamese shrimp with chilled oriental noodles and a peanut sesame sauce, and a classic caesar salad.

Main courses like monkfish grenobloise, roast duck with a sauce of Belgian cherries and cherry heering liqueur, and sautéed Vermont veal with local mushrooms represent uncommon fare – not to mention value – for common folk. At one visit, the fresh Vermont rabbit braised with marjoram and rosemary was distinctive, and the Vermont sweetbreads normande with apples and apple brandy were some of the best we've tasted. Our latest dinner produced a stellar special of penne with smoked chicken and asparagus and a plump cornish game hen glazed with mustard and honey.

Desserts include kirschen strudel, marquise au chocolat and meringue glacé. The mandarin orange sherbet bearing slivers of rind and a kirsch parfait were refreshing endings to an uncommon meal.

(802) 583-2800. Entrées, $12 to $19. Dinner nightly from 6 or 6:30 (from 5:30 or 6 on Saturdays and holidays). Closed Monday, Easter through Christmas.

Bass, Sugarbush Access Road, Warren.

Highly rated new American cuisine is the hallmark of this newish restaurant in a contemporary-looking alpine lodge of a building. Which should come as little surprise, until you learn – from their chatty little newspaper flyer/menu – that owner Stratis Bass is a Greek perfectionist and his wife Beth, the chef from Zambabwe is a self-styled African gypsy. Somehow their marriage translated into a sharing of American cuisine, which they think is "the best."

We'd have to agree, after sampling selections from their appetizer tray, which that night included samosas, smoked trout, crab salad and antipasti. Main courses ranged widely from seared scallops with ginger and garlic shrimp over crushed tomato and feta with herb-tossed orzo to grilled filet mignon with whole-grain mustard sauce. We were quite satisfied with the roast duckling with raspberry-kumquat sauce and the braised lamb shanks, accompanied by house salads and a Australian shiraz from a good, reasonably priced wine list. Desserts, again from the tray, included kahlua cheesecake, white chocolate mousse, hot fudge sundae and passionfruit sorbet.

Dining is on several levels, with soaring windows, angled ceilings and interesting art on the walls of wood and fieldstone.

(802) 583-3100. Entrées, $10.75 to $17.50. Dinner from 5. Closed in April and November.

The Pitcher Inn, Main Street, Warren.

Reborn after a disastrous fire, this glamorous new hostelry is "committed to filling not only the footprint of the old Pitcher Inn but its boots as well," according to innkeeper Heather Carino.

Chef Tom Bivens moved from the acclaimed Inn at Shelburne Farms to head the dining operation here. The 40-seat restaurant is traditional with white table-cloths, silver candlesticks, a large fireplace and an antique piano. A breakfast room overlooking the Mad River to the side is used for overflow.

The fare is new American. The initial winter 1998 menu opened with such exotica as pumpkin and Vermont hard cider bisque with an apple-sage fritter, confit of duck with hot winter slaw, and a warm lobster and potato salad with fennel and smoked bacon. Main courses included salmon en papillote, grilled sea scallops with saffron tagliatelle, pan-fried rabbit with cranberry-vodka sauce, pan-roasted filet of beef tenderloin with scotch whiskey sauce and medallions of leg of lamb with maple glaze.

Typical dessert choices are chocolate mousse torte with a walnut crust and a trio of sauces, apple-frangipane tart with maple cream sauce and crème caramel with ginger snaps.

A café menu offers light fare, including half portions of some dinner entrées. wine cellar is distinguished, specializing in American boutique wineries.

(802) 496-6350 or (888) 867-4824. Entrées, $18 to $21.50. Breakfast, 7:30 to 11:30. Dinner, 5 to 9. Closed Tuesday.

Millbrook Inn & Restaurant, Route 17, Waitsfield.

Everyone considers this small inn on the road to Mad River Glen one of the better places to eat in the valley. It's run by chef Thom Gorman, innkeeper with his wife Joan.

The restaurant seats 40 in two small dining rooms (one with a fireplace) at tables covered with paisley cloths. Anadama bread, a specialty, is made in house, as are pastas and acclaimed desserts, from scratch. Start with mushrooms à la Millbrook, filled with a secret blend of ground veal and herbs, if it's offered. Entrées include a daily roast, shrimp scampi or curry, five-peppercorn beef, garden vegetarian lasagna, cheese cannelloni made with Vermont cheddar and fresh basil, and three-cheese fettuccine tossed with Cabot cheddar, parmesan, Vermont mascarpone and sundried tomatoes. There are also four dishes from the Bombay region, where Thom lived for two years while in the Peace Corps. The badami rogan josh, local

Reborn like a phoenix, The Pitcher Inn offers dining and lodging.

lamb simmered in all kinds of spices and yogurt and served with homemade tomato chutney, is a longtime favorite.

Millbrook has a wine and beer license. As for those famous desserts, ice creams like chocolate chip and brickle candy are made here, as are a signature apple brown betty and a coffee-crunch pie filled with coffee mousse in a nut crust. In summer, open berry pies (maybe a raspberry and blackberry combination) are gobbled up.

Upstairs are seven guest rooms, four with private baths, decorated with stenciling and interesting handmade quilts and comforters. A full breakfast with choice of menu is served. Doubles are $100 to $140, MAP.

(802) 496-2405 or (800) 477-2809. Entrées, $9.95 to $16.95. Dinner nightly, 6 to 9. Closed Tuesday in summer, April-May and most of November. No smoking.

China Moon, Sugarbush Village, Warren.

The much esteemed Phoenix restaurant gave way to this upscale Oriental restaurant, run by Haddon Blair, longtime maître-d' and sommelier at the Phoenix. His wife Jodie oversees **Bella Luna,** an all-day pizzeria-trattoria, downstairs in what had been the Phoenix-owned Odyssey.

Like the setting, the menu is rather sophisticated for a Chinese restaurant. The food, which covers an enormous range, is highly regarded and considered good value. Some 75 items represent a mix of Szechuan, Mandarin, Cantonese and Hunan cuisines. The chef, for whom Chinese cooking has been a passion for more than 25 years, marks his dishes with one, two or three red peppers to indicate hotness. You could start with scallion pancakes, steamed vegetable dumplings with sesame sauce, steak kew or beijing spicy cabbage. Main dishes include shrimp with sweet walnuts and broccoli, Taiwanese crispy shrimp, Cantonese ginger lobster, kung pao chicken, red crispy duck and Hunan spiced beef with black bean sauce.

Fruits and fortune cookies are about it for desserts. But you could go downstairs for crème caramel, fruit tarts, gelato or tirami su. Bella Luna also features New York-style pizzas and pastas at earthy prices.

(802) 583-6666. Entrées, $9.95 to $16.95. Lunch, Saturday and Sunday noon to 3. Dinner nightly, 5:30 to 9:30. Open winter only.

Chez Henri, Sugarbush Village, Warren.

The longest-running of the valley's long runners, Chez Henri is into its fourth decade as a French bistro and an after-dinner disco. It's tiny, intimate and very French, as you might expect from a former food executive for Air France.

Henri Borel offers lunch, brunch, après-ski, early dinner, dinner and dancing – inside in winter by a warming stone fireplace and a marble bar and outside in summer on a small terrace bordered by a babbling mountain brook.

The dinner menu, served from 4 p.m., starts with changing soups and pâtés "as made in a French country kitchen," a classic French onion soup or fish broth, and perhaps mussels marinière, a trio of smoked seafood with greens or steak tartare "knived to order."

Entrées, served with good French bread and seasonal vegetables, often include bouillabaisse, coq au vin, calves liver with onion-turnip puree, rabbit in red wine sauce, veal normande, filet au poivre and rack of lamb. A shorter bistro menu is available as well at peak periods.

Crème caramel, coupe marron and chocolate mousse are among the dessert standbys. The wines are all French.

(802) 583-2600. Entrées, $13.50 to $21.50. Open from noon to 2 a.m. in winter. Weekends in summer, hours vary.

Giorgio's Cafe at Tucker Hill Lodge, Route 17, Waitsfield.

Tucker Hill innkeepers Suzie and Giorgio Noaro have turned their entire restaurant into Giorgio's Cafe, which had started in the basement lounge. The cafe menu has been expanded into what Suzie calls an amalgamation of northern Italian fare from Giorgio's and specialties of the more traditional main dining room. The upstairs, which used to be fairly plain and formal, now is warmer and more colorful, with a Mediterranean theme. The inner dining room is paneled and beamed; the outer addition is greenhouse-style, with skylights and brick floors.

Stone-oven pizzas are baked in an outdoor beehive oven like that in which the famed American Flatbreads got their start here. An outdoor wood grill is used to prepare such entrées as grilled swordfish with arugula pesto and chicken with oyster mushrooms and a white wine cream sauce. Vermont venison with dried cherry and merlot sauce is a favorite. Stone-seared scallops in a raisin-pinenut sauce reflects a recipe from Giorgio's mother in Italy.

Desserts could be maple crème brûlée, frangelico cheesecake, frozen lime mousse with raspberry and mango sauce, and an orange genoise layered with apples, maple syrup and blueberry butter cream (deceptively called Vermont apple pie torte). A good finale is flaming grolla – a grappa-laced coffee that is the Italian version of a peace pipe, says Suzie. It's passed around the table amid much toasting and fanfare.

(802) 496-3983. Entrées, $9.75 to $16.95. Dinner nightly, 5 or 5:30 to 9:30. Sunday brunch in summer, 11-2.

John Egan's Big World Pub & Grill, Route 100, Warren.

Ensconced at the front of the Madbush Falls Country Motel is this casual, 50-seat place with a mouthful of a name and a skier's spirit. It was opened by two well-known local restaurateurs who met at Tucker Hill Lodge and the Sugarbush Inn. Chef Jerry Nooney and maître-d' Bernie Isabelle named it for John Egan, a world-renowned "extreme team" skier from Sugarbush who is a local contractor (he built Jerry's house) when he's not jumping off cliffs for moviemaker Warren

Miller. The "big world" refers to Egan's worldwide connections and the theme is carried out on the restaurant's wallpaper.

Jerry mans the wood grill in the semi-open kitchen, from which he can chat with patrons. George Schenk of the nearby American Flatbreads, with whom Jerry started at Tucker Hill, built a dome-shaped bread oven outside the restaurant in which to bake the small flatbreads he furnishes.

The menu is simple but with-it. The corn and crab stew comes in a mug. Appetizers include big world nachos, roasted garlic and hummus, duck wontons, and "dog bones," a revival of Tucker Hill days: Polish sausage in puff pastry with kraut and mustard on the side. There are a few burgers and sandwiches, salads (one of fancy greens with lots of roasted garlic cloves, grated asiago cheese and croutons) and pastas (perhaps grilled shrimp and asiago cheese over fettuccine).

Among the entrées are sea scallops with sundried tomato pesto, grilled chicken with cider and ginger, Hungarian goulash, grilled leg of lamb and New York sirloin. *(802) 496-3033. Entrées, $9.50 to $16.25. Dinner, Tuesday-Sunday 5 to 9:30.*

Flatbread Kitchen, Lareau Farm Country Inn, Route 100, Waitsfield.

The American Flatbread pizzas that got their start in the outdoor wood-burning oven at Tucker Hill Lodge are now produced for the gourmet trade in the old slaughterhouse at Lareau Farm. Here, in an 800-degree wood-fired earthen oven with a clay dome, founder George Schenk and staff create the remarkable pizzas that are frozen and sold at the rate of more than 2,000 a week to grocery stores as far south as Florida in a phenomenon that is making Waitsfield the pizza capital of northern New England.

We were among their first on-site customers the first time we stopped by for a tour and a snack. They since have opened a wildly popular weekend restaurant, serving pizzas, great little salads dressed with homemade ginger-tamari vinaigrette, wine and beer to upwards of 250 people a night at tables set up around the production facility's oven room and kitchens and outside on the inn's west lawn. The delicious flatbreads with asiago and mozzarella cheeses and sundried tomatoes have made many a convert of pizza skeptics. The bakers use organically grown flour with restored wheat germ, "good Vermont mountain water" and as many Vermont products as they can.

Each night's dinner is dedicated to an employee, a friend or maybe the people of Bosnia. George's heart-felt "dedications," posted around the facility, make for mighty interesting reading.

(802) 496-8856. Flatbreads, $10.25 to $14.50. Dinner, Friday and Saturday 5:30 to 9:30; Fridays only in off-season.

R.S.V.P., Bridge Street, Waitsfield.

The initials stand for Richard's Special Vermont Pizza in this mega-funky place near the covered bridge. Its old chrome, naugahyde chairs and strange lamps transport one back to the '50s, as does the loud music. The oblong, thin-crust pizza is indeed special. It's made with unbleached white and stone-ground whole wheat flours and topped with exotica like cob-smoked bacon, roasted garlic, hot salsa, Basque chorizo, cilantro pesto and even fiddlehead ferns. Thirteen flavors of fresh pizzas (which they market to fine stores across the East to the tune of 2,500 a week) are available here for takeout or mail order (overnight by Federal Express).

We lunched on a couple of sensational focaccia sandwiches ($5.95 to $6.95) – a

Vermont classic club and a summer sandwich (with all kinds of veggies) – and each was enough for four. Addictive garlic fennel pita chips come on the side. The salad bar, decorated with autumn leaves and green onions at our October visit, is filled with goodies – some from owner Richard Denby's garden. Among its treats were roasted red peppers with goat cheese and fresh rosemary, three-cheese tortellini, Thai calamari, poached salmon with aioli and house-cured gravlax. Over it is a sign saying "do not steal food off the salad bar – public humiliation will result. If you are hungry and have no money, we will feed you at no charge." *(802) 496-7787. Pizzas, $9.99. Open daily from 11:30 to 9, 10 or 11.*

The Warren Store Deli, Warren.
At the rear of the Warren Store is a delightful place for breakfast or lunch. You can get a three-egg omelet or breakfast burrito for $2 to $3. For lunch, how about turkey à la king on buttered linguini with tossed salad and French bread, or any number of possibilities from the gorgeous array of gourmet salads and sandwiches in the $4 to $6 range? Finish with a huge chocolate-chip cookie or one of the treats from the ice-cream stand. Take it all outside to tables on a deck under a green striped canopy beside the roaring falls of the Mad River, where our tomato-dill soup and a pesto-provolone sandwich tasted extra good on a summer day. The store also has a fine selection of rare wines.
(802) 496-3864. Open daily, 8 to 7, Sunday to 6.

Diversions

Downhill skiing reigns supreme and gives the valley its character.
Mad River Glen, Waitsfield. Billed as a serious place for serious skiers, Mad River has been challenging hardy types since 1947 ("ski it if you can," is its motto). There are no frills here: little snowmaking, a few lifts including the original single chairlift (with blanket wraps provided to ward off the chill) to the summit, hair-raising trails like Paradise and the Fall Line, plenty of moguls and not much grooming, and a "Practice Slope" steep enough to scare the daylights out of beginners. The Birdland area is fine for intermediates. There's a Mad River mystique (blue jeans and milk runs) that you sense immediately and attracts you back. Former Owner Betsey Pratt, who bought the area in 1972 with her late husband, still skis it every day, but the place is now owned by a cooperative of loyal skiers.
Sugarbush, Warren. Founded in 1958 and among the first of Vermont's destination ski resorts, Sugarbush with its own "village" at its base appealed immediately to the jet set and fashion models and became known as "Mascara Mountain." From its original gondola lift to its expert Castle Rock area, from its clusters of condos and boutiques to its indoor Sports Center, Sugarbush draws those who appreciate their creature comforts – and good skiing as well (the Glades offer the best glade skiing in the East). Recently the fastest-growing destination ski resort in New England, Sugarbush was acquired by Les Otten and his American Ski Co. which launched further expansion, including seven new lifts and a hotel. The home of famed extreme skiing brothers John and Dan Egan, Sugarbush offers the first guided backcountry skiing in the East. The new Slide Brook Express connects Sugarbush and neighboring Sugarbush North (which has the valley's greatest vertical drop, 2,600 feet).
Other sports. This is a four-season sports area with a difference. Yes, there is

golf, at the Robert Trent Jones-designed **Sugarbush Golf Club** par-72 course with water hazards (pond or brook) affecting eight consecutive holes. Yes, the **Sugarbush Sports Center** has indoor and outdoor tennis courts, racquetball and squash courts, indoor and outdoor pools, whirlpools and an exercise facility.

But there's much more: this is something of an equestrian center with a number of stables offering trail rides. Among them are the **Vermont Icelandic Horse Farm,** which specializes in horse trekking on one of the oldest and purest breeds in the world – anything from half-day rides to four-day inn-to-inn rides to six-day mountain expeditions. The **Sugarbush Polo Club,** started in 1962 by skiers using ski poles and a volleyball, now has four polo fields for games and tournaments, staged Thursday, Saturday and Sunday afternoons June through September. Also for horse fanciers are the annual Valley Classic and Sugarbush horse shows in late July and early August.

The **Mad River Valley Cricket Club** sprang out of a chance conversation between two resident Brits, innkeeper James Plumpton and restaurateur Mike Ware. Now 100 members strong, it stages weekend cricket matches, an annual cricket festival and a summer garden party with a cherry-pit spitting contest and a cow pat frisbee contest (BYOCP). James Plumpton is president, player, newsletter editor and frequent party host. He says his club is the only one whose membership includes a choir master and a poet laureate. Fellow innkeepers are taking up the sport.

Soaring via gliders and sailplanes is at its best from the Warren-Sugarbush Airport, where instruction and rentals are available. Biplane rides for one or two persons also go from the airport, which hosts an annual air show early in late June.

For hiking and backpacking, the Long Trail is just overhead; innumerable mountain peaks and guided tours beckon. Sugarbush has a mountain biking center at Lincoln Peak. The Mad River and Blueberry Lake are ready for swimming, canoeing and fishing. The Mad River rugby team plays throughout the summer and fall at the Waitsfield Recreation Field. Finally, a round-robin English croquet tournament is staged in mid-summer.

Scenic drives. The Lincoln Gap Road, the McCullogh Turnpike (Route 17) beyond Mad River Glen and the steep Roxbury Gap Road each have their rewards. For the most open vistas and overall feeling for the area, traverse Brook Road and Waitsfield Common Road out of Warren, past the landmark Joslin Round Barn and Blueberry Lake, Sugarloaf Airport and come the back way into Waitsfield.

Shopping. Waitsfield has three shopping complexes, each worthy of exploration: the Mad River Green and the Village Square along Route 100 and the Bridge Street Marketplace beside Vermont's second oldest covered bridge. Our first stop at every visit is **The Store** in the red 1834 Methodist Meeting House along Route 100. Owner Jackie Rose, dean of the area's merchants (hers was the first store at Sugarbush Village), has an exceptional and vast array of Vermont foods, books, accessories, gifts, Christmas things, and a lovely collection of handmade quilts and pillows. A rear children's room resembles a giant toy box, while the second floor is stocked with antique furniture. The well-known **Green Mountain Coffee Roasters,** founded in Waitsfield with a retail store in Mad River Green, roasts 30 varieties of coffees and decafs, including founder Jamie Balne's special blend, and offers teas, coffee grinders and accessories, plus a cafe and espresso bar that's good for breakfast and lunch. **The Collection** features high-quality American arts and crafts, antiques and accessories. In Village Square, the **Blue Toad** gift shop specializes in particularly nice, inexpensive baskets from twenty countries and good greeting cards, as well as English tin boxes and jelly beans. **Tulip Tree** shows Vermont crafts and art, including lots of cows and many of the prints by Sabra Field, our favorite Vermont artist.

The **Bridge Street Bakery** offers great Portuguese breads, baked goods and snacks (cranberry buns with orange crème, gorgeous fresh fruit Danish pastries, ham and Vermont cheddar croissants, and maybe even a hearty sausage stew with French bread ($3). **Baked Beads** is a factory outlet store for some of its jewelry – dig through the bead bird bath to create your own. Upstairs, Elisabeth von Trapp sells the custom clothing she designs at **von Trapp Design.**

Along Route 100 are **Luminosity** stained glass and **Cabin Fever Quilts,** stocking a wondrous array of handmade quilts in the Old Church. **A Schoolhouse Garden** offers dried floral designs, Vermont-made furniture and accents for home and garden. **Waitsfield Pottery** sells nice lamps and vases, mostly in greens and blues, produced in the basement of an 1845 house.

The **Artisans' Gallery** offers wooden salad bowls painted in luminous colors as well as fantastic jewelry, one-of-a-kind bird houses, unusual children's attire and elegant women's clothing.

Gargoyles are everywhere at the offbeat **Gargoyle Cafe & Shop,** a magical place where you can select from a fantastic array of angels, statues and concrete animals for the garden as you sip an ambrosia latte. .

In tiny Warren, everything you need and a lot you don't expect is found at the **Warren Store,** an old-fashioned general store with provisions, fine wines and a deli (see Dining Spots), plus upstairs, the **More Store,** with handicrafts from around the world, kitchenware, jewelry, apparel and cards. Lots of the things here are from India. **The Bradley House** shows some whimsical crafts and furnishings among its sophisticated stock. We were struck by the unusual candles, bowls painted with Vermont scenes, and "Memories of Skiing," a box of old skis for a cool $500.

The von Trapp Greenhouse, run by Maria von Trapp's grandson Toby, off a dirt road east of Waitsfield Common, is worth a visit (open May-July, limited hours). Beautiful flower gardens surround the family's alpine-style house. There's a retail shop in front of one of the two greenhouses, which furnish lavish floral displays and produce for the valley's inns and restaurants.

Extra-Special

All Things Bright and Beautiful, Bridge Street, Waitsfield.

In two houses next to the covered bridge is the ultimate collection of stuffed animals – mainly bears, outfitted in everything from a London bobby's uniform or a wedding dress to ski vests that proclaim "Save the Bear." Twin sisters Bonnie and Gaelic McTigue preside over an enterprise that "started with Christmas and teddies" and just keeps expanding. A cheery "hello" emanated from Gael hidden behind a Christmas tree at a desk painting Christmas ornaments one summer day when we entered the new **Tree Top Christmas Shop.** In the other house, Bonnie is assisted by Bridgit the cat atop the cash register and Megan the dog on a wicker loveseat in front of one of twelve rooms chock full of character. We picked up a few of Gael's remarkable handpainted birds for Christmas presents. It's a bit overwhelming, but the twins are both characters and their shops are not to be missed.

(802) 496-3997. Open daily, 9 to 6.

United Church is on view from gazebo on Craftsbury Common.

Craftsbury/Burke, Vt.
The Look and Lifestyle of a Century Ago

Picture the picture-perfect Vermont town: a white-spired church and public buildings facing the village green, pristine clapboard houses on shady lawns, cows grazing against a hilly landscape, youngsters picking wildflowers along the road.

The town is Craftsbury, population 1,000. And the picture is of Craftsbury Common, a hilltop village of perhaps 200 souls in the middle of nowhere – the west-central section of Vermont's most remote region, the Northeast Kingdom.

Craftsbury Common indeed has a common, which is nearly as big as the rest of the village. It's a serene two acres or so flanked by a few houses (one turns out to be an annex of an inn) and institutional buildings. Among them are the nation's smallest accredited college, the state's smallest public high school, a rickety post office, a wonderful little library and a funeral home, the village's only commercial enterprise besides the inn. North of the village is a sports/education center believed to be unique in the world.

A few miles downhill from Craftsbury Common's perch astride a ridge is the village of Craftsbury, site of the town hall, the Catholic church, two general stores and another inn. From here an unnumbered road leads to East Craftsbury, home of a British woolens store and an English-style B&B.

That's about it for Craftsbury, the most prosperous part of a Northeast Kingdom that reflects the Vermont of old, uncondoed and uncutesied. Nearby is Greensboro, a lakeside summer colony of academics and the "metropolis" of the immediate area, the place where the flatlanders go to pick up the New York Times. Beyond are the Burkes – East Burke, Burke Hollow et al – at the foot of Burke Mountain, a growing ski center and a center of sophistication in the Northeast Kingdom.

A bit farther afield but worth the trip is Lake Willoughby, the "Lucerne of America." It's a sight to behold from a couple of inns on its sharply rising shores.

Vermont's most rural region is an area of tranquility, scenic beauty, little-traveled byways, country stores and, somewhat unexpectedly, considerable summer music and exotic garden enterprises. Time spent here celebrates the look, the landscape and the lifestyle of a century ago.

Inn Spots

The Inn on the Common, Craftsbury Common 05827.

Greensboro summer cottagers Penny and Michael Schmitt chucked their New York corporate jobs in 1973 and, on a whim, bought a house in Craftsbury that they proceeded to turn into a small inn. "We started with four small bedrooms with shared baths and were too naive to know better," Penny recalls. "As we traveled more and became more demanding, we became more demanding of ourselves." In the next eight years, they turned two more houses into inn annexes, created a dining room of renown, added a pool and a tennis court, upgraded the gardens, helped found a sports center and, in effect, turned tiny Craftsbury Common into a destination area. They have spent the last seventeen years at the inn upgrading everything in sight, fussing over details to make everything as perfect as possible.

Theirs is a class act, far classier than one would expect in out-of-the-way Craftsbury and more intimate than its size would suggest. Spread out in three houses, the sixteen guest rooms are the ultimate in comfort. All have sitting areas made for relaxing instead of show and are stylishly furnished with vivid, color-coordinated prints and fine wallpapers, good artworks and antiques. We're partial to the South Annex across from the main inn. Here, besides an office and a lounge with TV/VCR and a video library of 300 cassettes, is our favorite Room 12, main floor rear. It contains a kingsize bed, a sofa, a reclining chair custom-designed for a frequent guest, an enormous bathroom that doubles as a dressing area and plenty of room to spread out. Many like the upstairs Room 10 with its wood stove, a queensize canopy bed covered with a blue-starred quilt, a sofa and two side chairs,

and an old butter churn in the bathroom. Another favorite is Room 3, The Porch, upstairs and rear in the main inn with a great view of the spectacular specimen rose garden and the perennial gardens and mountains to the rear. For what once was a porch it has what Penny calls serious furniture (meaning antiques), plus two leather chairs that are so soft you think you'll never get up. Penny's latest favorite is Room 5 in the main inn, totally redecorated in red wisteria and "so glamorous it's uncanny."

These are among the eight deluxe rooms, which cost $20 more than the others but are worth it.

Picket fence surrounds main building at The Inn on the Common.

Every room is a treasury of caring touches, however. Penny favors those in the North Annex, the Schmitts' latest acquisition, where they were able to do everything they wanted to. It's a couple of blocks removed from the main inn and the only one actually facing the serene, expansive common. The main inn has a parlor, a library and a gorgeous dining room looking onto the rose garden. Its five guest rooms are up a steep, tightly curved staircase.

Meals are an integral part of the inn experience here, although the Schmitts – blessed with a talented young staff – no longer preside at the dinner hour as they used to. Their restaurant is now open to the public (see Dining Spots) and is a local favorite for special-occasion meals.

Breakfast is a culinary treat as well. An extensive menu offers many choices. Juice, a platter of fresh fruit and cranberry-lemon muffins came first at our visit. The herbed-cheddar quiche with Canadian bacon was a succulent special. Shirred eggs and Vermont-made sausage were accompanied by thick toasted bread.

Play English croquet on the course laid out between perennial gardens behind the main inn or tennis on the clay court beyond the perennial gardens behind the main inn. Swim in the natural-looking, free-form gunite pool sequestered behind the South Annex. Read a book in your room or watch a movie in the lounge. Almost every creature comfort you could want is at the uncommon Inn on the Common, and all the area's rural pleasures are close at hand.

(802) 586-9619 or (800) 521-2233. Fax (802) 586-2249. www.innonthecommon.com. Sixteen guest rooms with private baths. Doubles, MAP, $230 to $250; foliage $270 to $290. Children and pets accepted.

The Craftsbury Inn, Craftsbury 05826.

A white-columned building across from the general store houses ten guest rooms and a restaurant of note (see Dining Spots). Blake Gleason, a chef with Sheraton experience, and his wife Rebecca have been the innkeepers since 1988.

The long front parlor offers a small fireplace (from the original post office in

Montpelier) and a piano beneath an embossed pressed-tin ceiling. Adjacent is a game room with a TV. Guests also enjoy wraparound verandas on two floors.

Six of the upstairs guest rooms have private baths. One called the honeymoon room possesses a canopied double bed and the inn's only combination bath-shower. Two front bedrooms are summery in wicker. One room has a 1750 Quaker bed so high that the occupants may need a ladder to climb into it. Four rooms in the oldest section of the house share a large hall bath. Mini-print wallpapers, sheer curtains, pretty quilts made by Rebecca's great-grandmother and the inn's own toiletries are the rule.

The Gleasons offer a full breakfast in the sunny dining room overlooking the garden and a rear yard bordered by the Black River, which winds around the property. The choice might be eggs any style, an omelet or french toast.

(802) 586-2848 or (800) 336-2848. Six rooms with private baths, four rooms with shared bath. Doubles, $90 to $110 B&B, $140 to $160 MAP. Children welcome. Closed mid-October through November and April through mid-May.

Highland Lodge, RR1, Box 1290, Greensboro 05841.

On a hillside across the East Craftsbury Road from Caspian Lake is a country inn of the old school. "A real refuge from the busyness of modern life" is how its brochure describes it. Families comprise the bulk of the devoted clientele. Built in the 1860s as a farmhouse, it was converted into an inn in the 1920s. It's now run by David and Wilhelmina Smith, the second generation of an innkeeping family.

Accommodations are basic in eleven guest rooms, reached by three separate staircases from the main floor. Each has private bath, an assortment of beds with white Bates spreads, Ethan Allen furniture and sheer white curtains. Amenities consist of a small bar of Ivory soap and a box of Kleenex. The rooms are clean, but not the kind in which to linger.

That's okay, because much of the downstairs is given over to three side-by-side common rooms. One is a cozy library with a corner fireplace, another has a TV and a wood stove, and one in the middle contains a grand piano with a sign regulating the hours of play. Out back, behind the gift shop and office, is a children's library and game room where the ping-pong table was getting a good workout the rainy day we visited. On summer mornings, youngsters aged 4 to 9 link up with the "Play Lady," who devises crafts programs and nature hikes.

Across the street are a clay tennis court and, down a path, the lodge's private beach and "bathhouse," which looked to us like a boathouse. Rowboats, paddleboats and canoes may be borrowed to explore Caspian Lake.

Three meals a day are served in the restaurant, which is open to the public (see Dining Spots), except on summer Mondays when lunch is a picnic at the beach.

Just behind the lodge is a lineup of eleven white cottages, each with one to three bedrooms. Four are winterized and some have kitchenettes.

(802) 533-2647. Fax (802) 533-7494. Eleven rooms with private baths and ten cottages. Rates MAP, service charges included. Doubles, $180. Cottages, $220 to $230. Smoking restricted. Closed mid-October to Christmas and mid-March to Memorial Day.

The Village House Inn, Route 14, Box 212, Albany 05820.

A glider and tall rockers on the wraparound veranda greet visitors at this new in-town inn fashioned from a big white extended house that is typical of Vermont. Former owners spent ten years renovating the old house and adding a new section behind, with bedrooms above the new dining room and kitchen. But it was left to John and Kate Fletcher to turn this into a destination for dining.

After many years at the Heermansmith Farm (see below), the Fletchers had been seeking a place of their own. Now besides an excellent restaurant, the Fletchers offer eight cozy guest rooms with private baths, appointed in light Victorian florals, country curtains and star quilts. Bed configurations vary from twins to queen, and several have a double and a twin. Furnishings are simple, a bureau here and a canvas deck chair there.

Guests share a homey living room outfitted with a wood stove, TV and rocking chairs. Breakfast and dinner are served at sturdy wood tables in the dining room, or on the back porch where three white tables overlook the fields. A cupboard at the entrance to the dining room is stocked with local crafts for sale.

John offers a choice of two entrées for breakfast. They range from buttermilk pancakes and eggs any style to belgian waffles and eggs benedict.

The hard-working Fletchers, parents of an infant son, are a two-person operation. Kate had just finished moving the lawn when we arrived. She was about to change for dinner, when she becomes hostess and waitress. Amazingly, they offer dinner every day (see Dining Spots). In their first year, they were only closed two days – to install new carpeting and to have a baby.

(802) 755-6722. Eight rooms with private baths. Doubles, $75. No smoking.

WilloughVale Inn & Restaurant, Route 5A, Westmore 05860.

Overlooking the length of beautiful Lake Willoughby from its more built-up, less picturesque north end, this is a restaurant (see Dining Spots), an inn with lodging facilities and – the prize, we think – four cottages across the road and right on the lake. The owners of the Green Mountain Inn in Stowe, who acquired the inn in 1997, have breathed new life into an establishment that had grown tired. The former owners had razed the old WilloughVale Inn and put up a new, weathered-gray clapboard building with front and side verandas in 1988.

The eight upstairs rooms with private baths in the main inn vary in size and layout. We liked Room 1, fairly large with a table and chair against the wall, a sofa, a queensize bed with a woven coverlet, pictures of birds on the walls and two windows overlooking the lake. Room 3 is a deluxe room with a queensize four-poster, sofa and upholstered chair, and a bathroom with a double jacuzzi, a separate shower and a double sink. If we had enough time, we'd splurge for one of the four fireplaced cottages, especially No. 2 with a queen bed, a sunken living room, kitchen, a screened porch and a deck with lounge chairs, right at lake's edge. Each of the other cottages has two bedrooms and either a dining area or eat-in kitchen. All but one two-bedroom are rented by the week in July and August.

There are gathering spots on the front porches and in the inn's library, which has antique books and games. A continental breakfast is served. Expect fresh fruit, homemade granola, Vermont cheddar cheese, muffins or sweet breads (peach and raspberry muffins and banana bread at our visit).

(802) 525-4123 or (800) 594-9102. Fax (802) 525-4514. Eight rooms and four cottages with private baths. Mid-June to mid-October and fall midweek: doubles $109 to $134. Fall weekends: $139 to $159. Mid-October to mid-June: $79 to $109. Two-night minimum weekends in summer and foliage. Children and pets accepted. No smoking.

Cottages, EP: $1,074 to $1,170 weekly in summer, $179 to $195 nightly late spring and early fall, $99 to $119 rest of year.

Heermansmith Farm Inn, Heermansmith Farm Road, Coventry 05825.

A bit hard to find along a dirt road west of Coventry, this is the family home of Jack and Louise Smith, part of the Heerman family who have been dairy farmers here for five generations. The Smiths began serving ice cream to people who came to pick the strawberries in their fields. When someone suggested they should offer cross-country skiing in winter, they found that skiers wanted something to eat. So in 1982 the Smiths opened their 1860 home to guests in a homey yet elegant dining room (see Dining Spots) and then began putting up guests overnight.

Upstairs are six guest rooms, all with private baths, in the old farmhouse and a new addition above a private dining room. The newer ones contain beds with colorful quilts and interesting built-in sinks with wood all around. Except for an end room with a sofa, rooms here are smaller than in the older section.

Jack cooks breakfast, a hearty affair served in the main dining room. Guests might have scrambled eggs with bacon and muffins or pancakes with strawberries and maple syrup.

The Black River skirts the surrounding strawberry fields and pasture lands, providing a place for wildlife, fishing, canoeing and swimming at the base of a waterfall. A covered bridge crosses the river nearby.

(802) 754-8866. Six rooms with private baths. Doubles, $75 in peak season and holidays, $65 rest of year.

The Wildflower Inn, Darling Hill Road, Lyndonville 05851.

If you're among those inn-goers who feel the children should go with you, here's the place. Mary and Jim O'Reilly have eight of their own – the number changes annually, a staffer advised as she counted up on her fingers – and think families should vacation together.

And what a place they have for family vacations: Twenty-two rooms and suites (some with bunk beds), a full-service restaurant and lunch snack bar, a swimming pool, a petting barn with farm animals, horse-drawn hay and sleigh rides, indoor and outdoor play areas, a skating pond, tennis court, batting cage, soccer field, hiking and nature trails, flower gardens, an indoor sauna and hot tub, a supervised children's program. Little wonder the barn up the street is the home of the Children's Theater.

And what a location: Atop a ridge with a view that won't quit, revealing undulating mountains and valleys to the west. The place is paradise on earth for families of young children, who were everywhere in evidence at our latest visit. Some were cavorting in the pool as their mother camcorded the event for posterity and their father relaxed in an Adirondack chair to enjoy the vista with the day's newspaper. Others were climbing aboard the horse-drawn wagon for a hay ride. Still others were snacking on afternoon lemonade and cookies in the inn's living room.

Accommodations are a suite and two rooms upstairs in the main house, nine rooms and three suites in the rambling carriage house across the way, six more rooms and suites in the Meadows complex (the first of the O'Reillys' homes here, long since outgrown – they moved to a new hilltop house nearby in 1997). There's also a School House Cottage with queen bed, double jacuzzi, kitchenette and deck down the road, a bit removed from the hubbub and billed as the honeymoon suite.

Rooms come with varying bed configurations, from a few with single queen or king beds to the more common double beds and doubles with bunks. Two in the main inn share a bath. The Grand Meadow Suite in the O'Reillys' former quarters

Terrace tables outside Wildflower Inn provide panoramic view.

includes a queen bedroom with hot tub, living/dining area, full kitchen and a second bedroom with double bed and bath. Four more rooms and suites in the Meadows Complex have kitchenettes and patios or decks sharing the awesome view. All are comfortably furnished and appointed with stenciling, hooked rugs, quilted comforters and country effects – no antiques to be broken and no television. Supervised morning activities and nightly movies keep the children occupied.

When he's not cooking some mighty good meals, chef Joshua Farrington leads back-woods trail rides. "Most of the staff are multi-faceted," Mary O'Reilly advised. "They have to be when they're dealing with families."

A full country breakfast is included in the rates. Dinner is available to guests and the public in a pleasant dining room open onto an enclosed sunporch over-looking the mountains. In addition to a children's menu and early serving hours, a more sophisticated menu allows parents to eat well and in peace while youngsters are entertained. About ten entrées, including one or two for vegetarians, are offered nightly. Typical are spicy grilled yellowfin tuna with tomato compote, ginger-glazed chicken with mango chutney and sirloin steak sautéed with mushrooms or onions.

A new deck off the game room is the setting for snacks and lunch from an outdoor snack bar near the pool area.

(802) 626-8310 or (800) 627-8310. Fax (802) 626-3039. Fourteen rooms and six suites with private baths; two rooms with shared bath. Doubles, $110 with private bath, $95 with shared bath. Suites, $135 to $220. Cottage, $155. Add $10 for fall foliage season. Two-night minimum weekends. No smoking. Children welcome.

Entrées, $14.95 to $16.95. Dinner nightly, 5:30 to 8:30.

The Inn at Mountain View Creamery, Darling Hill Road, Box 355, East Burke 05832.

Set on 440 pastoral acres with views of the Willoughby Gap and Burke Mountain, the only intact turn-of-the-century stock farm in Vermont is now home to a small country inn and gourmet restaurant.

Marilyn and John Pastore operate a ten-room inn in the former creamery, which

Inn at Mountain View Creamery is part of attractive farm complex.

still holds the boiler and engine that powered the churns in the architecturally grand creamery. Local philanthropist Elmer Darling raised prize-winning Jersey cattle on the farm, which is notable for a farmhouse, monumental barns, outbuildings, perennial gardens and a sylvan landscape that constitute the last gentleman's farm remaining in the Northeast Kingdom. The Pastores say that most have been destroyed or converted to other uses or modernized, as is the case with the well-known Shelburne and Billings farms, while Mountain View remains virtually the same as is in the early 20th century.

The classic red-brick, Georgian-style creamery with a butter churn cupola has been refurbished as an inn. Across the courtyard is the main house, with several larger units for overnight guests. The periphery of the courtyard is framed with striking red barns that hold farm animals and invite exploration. The perennial gardens behind the barns and afternoon horse-drawn wagon rides are attractions.

Upstairs in the creamery are nine bedrooms and a family suite named for towns in the area. Two have queen beds, three have doubles and the rest are twins, which appeal to the touring bicycle groups that make this a frequent stop. Each is furnished with handmade quilts, antiques and coordinated fabrics.

The spacious downstairs common room with fireplace is dressed in traditional and contemporary furnishings in what the Pastores call an English country manor style. Here is where watermelon slices and cranberry spritzers were set out the afternoon of our visit.

A black iron stove serves as a buffet table in the dining room. The day starts with a hearty breakfast of fresh fruit from the farm, cereals, yogurt, homemade sweet breads and a main dish, perhaps vegetable frittata, apple or blueberry pancakes, or french toast.

On certain evenings, the dining room turns into **Darling's,** featuring elegant country cuisine. An innovative menu offers stuffed rainbow trout, Moroccan lemon chicken, broiled tenderloin with portobello mushrooms and roasted rack of lamb with an apricot-mint glaze. The meal could start with chipotle shrimp, bruschetta or mesclun salad with sundried tomatoes. Worthy endings include strawberry shortcake and fresh ginger frozen yogurt.

(802) 626-9924 or (800) 572-4509. Nine rooms and a family suite with private baths. Doubles, $105 to $140. No smoking.

Entrées, $13.95 to $18.95. Dinner, Thursday-Saturday 5 to 9.

The Garrison Inn, Burke Hollow Road, East Burke 05832.

A lineup of white molded chairs on the back lawn faced the gazebo and took in the view of Burke Mountain. It's typical of the relaxed, casual atmosphere offered by owner Nancy Anastasia in her secluded, brown clapboard house down a little hill off Burke Hollow Road.

Built in the garrison style, the house offers six bedrooms with private baths off a central corridor on the second floor. The spacious rooms we saw had a king or two double beds, floral comforters and hooked rugs on the wide-planked floors.

The main floor has a couple of common and game rooms plus a skiers' work and hot-wax room, which makes the Garrison attractive to ski racers.

Nancy serves a full breakfast, starting with juice, fruit, cereals and hot oatmeal (in winter). The entrée is cook's choice, perhaps corned-beef hash, vegetable omelet with baked tomatoes or belgian waffles with strawberries or bananas.

(802) 626-8329 or (800) 773-1914. Six rooms with private baths. Doubles, $75. Children over 4. No smoking.

Dining Spots

The Inn on the Common, Craftsbury.

Dinner at this sophisticated inn is prix-fixe, available at one or two seatings outside on the side patio or in the dining room. It's served in a dinner-party atmosphere, following cocktails and hors d'oeuvres in the library. Chef Gene Kote, an upstate New Yorker who arrived in Craftsbury via the Shed in Stowe, explains the night's choices posted on a blackboard. Our table of ten sampled the entire menu and was impressed with both the food and service.

Superior appetizers were rabbit pâté and homemade fettuccine with mushrooms stuffed with sausage and leeks. Homemade bread and a spicy cucumber-dill soup with slivered carrots followed. Main courses were chicken with creamy thyme sauce, grilled local partridge with pommery mustard glaze and swordfish with herbed aioli, accompanied by small yellow beans, broccoli and baked potatoes. A green salad with a cracked peppercorn dressing preceded desserts, an ethereal pear strudel with homemade buttermilk sorbet and a light chocolate pecan torte with vanilla ice cream.

Michael Schmidt's carefully chosen wine list is pricey, but a low markup produces great values. Coffee and chocolates are served after dinner in the library, where guests like to linger over cordials.

(802) 586-9619 or (800) 521-2233. Prix-fixe, $35. Dinner nightly, seatings at 7 or 6:30 and 8, Memorial Day through October, also Christmas through March. No smoking.

The Craftsbury Inn, Craftsbury.

A pretty dining room overlooking spotlit gardens and a talented young chef commend this restaurant that's open to the public by reservation. Dining is at round tables set with white linens, candles and fresh flowers in a cheery room with yellow floral wallpaper above white wainscoting and big windows onto the back yard.

Dinner is à la carte, with entrées ranging from cheese-filled tri-colored tortellini to rack of lamb with roquefort sauce. Chef-owner Blake Gleason changes his four-course menu seasonally. You might start with gazpacho, butternut squash and apple soup or smoked trout and spinach fettuccine with an alfredo sauce. Entrées could be cajun catfish, poached salmon with cucumber-caper sauce, sautéed pork medallions with an apricot-brandy sauce or New York sirloin with wine-rosemary sauce. Plates are garnished with edible nasturtiums and fresh herbs, and three or four vegetables accompany.

Dessert choices could be raspberry mousse roulade, chocolate truffle torte and black raspberry ice cream. There's a short but serviceable wine list. A small bar contains a couple of high round tables and chairs.

(802) 586-2848 or (800) 336-2848. Entrées, $13 to $18. Lunch in season, Wednesday-Sunday 11:30 to 2. Dinner by reservation, Wednesday-Sunday, 6:30 to 8. Closed mid-October through November and April through mid-May.

The Village House Inn, Route 14, Albany.

The founding chef for the Heermansmith Farm's acclaimed dining room, John Fletcher spent fifteen years there before striking out on his own in 1996. Joined by his wife Kate, the dining room manager at Heermansmith, he set about leaving his considerable culinary imprint on this small country inn. Some of his fans followed, making this a culinary destination for knowledgeable diners throughout northern Vermont.

The dining room, pretty in cream and Wedgwood blue, has frilly curtains on the windows and print wallpaper above the wainscoting. It seats 26 people, plus a few more outside on the porch in season.

The contemporary/continental menu is sophisticated for the area. Expect main courses like grilled salmon on a bed of spinach with saffron beurre blanc, pork marsala, veal oscar and a Fletcher specialty, crisp roast duck with a strawberry-merlot sauce. Starters could be locally smoked salmon, cajun fried shrimp with a ginger citrus sauce or sherried mushrooms in puff pastry. A pasta and two chicken dishes are offered under lighter fare.

Desserts include a stellar hazelnut-caramel cheesecake, profiteroles and puff pastry with bananas and caramel sauce. There's a short, affordable wine list.

(802) 755-6722. Entrées, $13.95 to $17.95. Dinner nightly, 5 to 9.

Highland Lodge, Greensboro.

Lunch on the front porch with a distant view of Caspian Lake is a summertime treat here, and we were surprised how many were enjoying it on a raw, dank day. The menu covers the basics, but the daily specials can get interesting: a warm spinach salad with grilled duck breast and a rabbit and ham stew with buttermilk biscuits and rainbow cole slaw at our visit. The problem was they'd run out of the spinach-duck salad and one special was sort of lacking: the borscht with Ma Smith's beets didn't seem like the real thing and its accompaniment, half a beer cheese and tomato sandwich on wheat bread, was rather strange-tasting. The sautéed sea scallops with snow peas on rice was much more successful.

Nightly specials are the heart of the dinner menu as well. Grilled blank angus sirloin steak is a staple, but other entrées could be coho salmon with mushrooms and white wine, grilled mustard-glazed chicken breast and maple-cured Vermont ham with apple chutney. Starters include corn and green chile soup, grilled mushroom salad, herbed Vermont chèvre or fresh fruit cup. For dessert, try the blueberry-lemon cream cake or chocolate cream pie.

Some people come here just for the lodge's special dessert hour, starting nightly at 7:30. In addition to the specials, they go for things like chocolate mousse parfait, ishkabibble (brownie à la mode with hot fudge sauce) and something called for-gotten dessert, a meringue with ice cream and strawberries. The lodge also has a

Side porch at WilloughVale Inn yields full-length view of Lake Willoughby.

short menu of lighter dinner fare. The L-shaped dining room with a wood stove is rustic and pretty in pink, but we'd choose the porch any time we could.

(802) 533-2647. Entrées, $14.25 to $16.75; light fare, $8 to $8.75. Lunch, Tuesday-Sunday noon to 2; dinner nightly by reservation, 6 to 8.

WilloughVale Inn & Restaurant, Route 5A, Westmore.
Seasonal American and vegetarian cuisine is offered at this restaurant with a striking view down Lake Willoughby.

Chef René Hodgkins, a New England Culinary Institute graduate, oversees the fare in two dining rooms and a taproom menu in the lounge. Windows onto the water, shiny wood tables with fanned moss green napkins and matching mats, heavy cutlery, windsor chairs and area rugs on the floors create a crisp country setting. The ceilings of both dining rooms are painted like a quilt. There's quite a display of antique fly rods in a glass case in the taproom, which features Vermont microbrews on tap.

The fare has been toned down since the heady early days, when the menu changed daily. We heard an elderly gent complaining to the waiter that the chef had put too much pepper in the spicy clam and red pepper chowder that began one dinner. Now the menu is changed seasonally, and the starters are more apt to be a safe soup of the day, shrimp cocktail, steamed mussels and baked artichoke dip "with a hint of garlic," served with roasted pita wedges.

Main courses range from pan-seared sesame-crusted Canadian salmon with herb beurre blanc to black angus T-bone steak with a wild mushroom ragoût. Roast Vermont turkey dinner is a house specialty. Those with more adventurous palates can try the Bar Harbor crab cakes with sweet red pepper aioli or the mixed grill of the day. The inn's pastry chef offers a changing selection of desserts.

The taproom menu includes the aforementioned starters along with nachos, baby back ribs, flatbread pizzas and a grilled sirloin steak.

In the off-season, the taproom menu is available for dinner, augmented by nightly specials.

(802) 525-4123 or (800) 594-9102. Entrées, $9.95 to $18.95. Lunch daily in summer, 11:30 to 5:30. Dinner, 5:30 to 9. Sunday, brunch 11 to 2, dinner 6 to 9. November-April: dinner, Wednesday-Sunday 3 to 9.

Heermansmith Farm Inn, Heermansmith Farm Road, Coventry.

There is something immensely appealing about the dining experience at Heermansmith Farm. Perhaps it is the setting: glamorous, white-linened tables scattered about an open living room and dining room centered by a huge slate fireplace amid antiques and the glow of candles and kerosene lamps. Perhaps it is the food served up by Bob Karg, a cooking instructor at the high school. Perhaps it is the good little wine list, amazingly priced from yesteryear.

Probably it is everything put together. The food is certainly the match for the stylish living-room setting. The short menu might start with haddock chowder, crab cakes on a bed of shallot cream or mushrooms stuffed with lobster and lump crabmeat and topped with béarnaise sauce.

For main courses, how about the house specialty, roast duck with a strawberry and chambord sauce? Choices include grilled salmon with cucumber-dill beurre blanc, baked stuffed shrimp, raspberry pecan chicken, pork tenderloin madeira or grilled delmonico steak. Desserts could be blueberry buckle, amaretto cheesecake with hazelnuts, french bread pudding with whiskey sauce, and puff pastry with lemon cream and fresh raspberries.

(802) 754-8866. Entrées, $15.95 to $18.95. Dinner nightly, 5 to 9. Closed Monday and Tuesday in off-season.

Old Cutter Inn, Mountain Access Road, East Burke.

Swiss chef Fritz Walther is known for continental cuisine of the old school at this vintage 1845, barn-red farmhouse on the approach to Burke Mountain ski area. The dining room with exposed beams and fireplace is popular with skiers from Burke Mountain; so is the adjacent rustic tavern with semicircular bar and round tables, where light fare and sandwiches are available.

The kitchen is on view from the check-in area, so that Fritz can greet arriving guests. His extensive restaurant background ensures consistency in such standards as veal piccata, rahmschnitzel, baked stuffed shrimp, salmon duglère, coq au vin and tournedos of beef served on a crouton with a piquant béarnaise sauce. Rack of lamb and beef wellington can be ordered in advance; the dinner menu also offers an omelet, served with potato and vegetable of the day. Roesti potatoes are extra, but salad comes with. Appetizers range from smoked trout to escargots provençal.

A Sunday champagne brunch featuring eggs benedict, crêpes and homemade pastries is one of the area's more popular.

The inn and rear carriage house also have nine simple guest rooms, five with private bath, plus a two-bedroom apartment with fireplace, TV and kitchen. Doubles are $52 to $64 EP.

(802) 626-5152 or (800) 295-1943. Entrées, $13.25 to $18.95. Dinner nightly except Wednesday, 5:30 to 9. Sunday brunch, 11 to 1:30. Closed November and April.

River Garden Café, Main Street (Route 114), East Burke.

Robert Baker, who owned a restaurant called Sofi in New York City, had been coming to the Northeast Kingdom on vacations for over twenty years. New York got to be too much and he headed to East Burke in 1992 to open this cafe with gardens leading to the East Branch of the Sutton River in back. With the staff (including the owner) often in green striped shirts, a window seat full of pillows in the cozy front bar, a long screened back porch, a collection of kitschy salts and pepper shakers, and "jadeite" tables from the '30s, it's quite offbeat and charming.

The international menu is fairly sophisticated for the area and the prices are right. You can snack on anything from bruschetta to grilled shrimp caesar salad or a Jamaican jerk chicken salad with a spicy lime vinaigrette. Or go for filet mignon with a roquefort cream sauce, by far the most expensive entrée on the menu that ranges from pesto salmon to Singapore beef and fajitas . Salads, burgers, vegetarian dishes and specials like warm duck salad with apricot-curry dressing and mango chutney often have the place full shortly after 5 o'clock.

Tirami su is a house specialty. Or you might find triple chocolate torte, warm apple tart or a chipwich, two cookies centered with ice cream and topped with chocolate sauce and whipped cream.

(802) 626-3514. Entrées, $9.95 to $13.95. Lunch, Tuesday-Saturday 11:30 to 2. Dinner, Tuesday-Sunday 5 to 9. Sunday brunch, 11:30 to 2. Closed November and April.

The Pub Outback, Route 114, East Burke.
Housed in a barn behind Bailey's Country Store, this is a lively, casual place beloved by skiers. Focal points on the main floor are a long, rectangular bar in the center and two solariums used as non-smoking dining areas. Above the bar is a free-standing dining loft, open on all sides with beams overhead and barn artifacts here and there. Tables are custom-inlaid with local memorabilia, and it's all unexpectedly airy and contemporary.

Bowls of homemade popcorn stave off hunger as diners select from an all-day international menu of appetizers, salads, sandwiches and vegetarian dishes. West Indian roti (curried chicken and potato in a pastry with mango chutney), black bean cakes with cilantro salsa and sour cream, bruschetta, wontons, oriental chicken salad and a chef's salad topped with grilled chicken, steak and ham are among the possibilities. Main courses include garlic sesame stir-fries, scampi primavera, chargrilled angus sirloin, and skewered chicken, beef and shrimp Thai sticks, served on rice with a spicy peanut sauce.

(802) 626-5187. Entrées, $8.95 to $15.95. Lunch daily from 11. Dinner, 5 to 9 or 9:30.

Diversions

There's a lot to see and do – or nothing to see and do – in the Northeast Kingdom, depending on your point of view. The scenery varies from low-key to spectacular. This remains an essentially rural, old-fashioned area where folks meet at the general stores, and church suppers and band concerts are the social gatherings of importance.

All kinds of sports and educational pursuits are offered on the property and under the auspices of the **Craftsbury Outdoor Center,** (802) 586-7767 or (800) 729-7751. Walking, running, hiking, bicycling, sculling, cross-country skiing, horseback riding – you name it, they've got it. There's also a state-of-the-art fitness center, **The Wellness Barn at CoachWorks Farm,** Page Pond Road, Albany, (802) 755-6342. Owners Bill and Judy Bevans offer an indoor swimming pool, spa, sauna, steam bath, massage, weight machines, aerobics and more.

Craftsbury Common is a wonderful hilltop town with a serene common and an institutional presence lent by Craftsbury Academy, the state's smallest public high school and one of the town's drawing cards for newcomers, and Sterling College, the nation's smallest degree-granting, accredited college with 70 students involved in environmental studies.

Another must-see spot is scenic **Darling Hill Road** in Lyndonville and East Burke. With views of Burke Mountain on one side and Willoughby Gap on the other, the ridge is lined with stately farms and manicured estates. Elmer Darling's former mansion once served as a men's dormitory for Lyndon State College. He was a benefactor of the college on Vail Hill, along with friend Theodore N. Vail, the first president of AT&T.

Music. The **Craftsbury Chamber Players** are in such demand that they cross the state on a pre-season tour and share their talents with audiences in Burlington and Burke Mountain each summer. They're in residence at the Town House in Hardwick from mid-July to mid-August, playing Thursday evenings at 8 and moving on to the Burke Mountain base lodge Fridays at 8. They also give free afternoon mini-concerts "for children and their friends" in Hardwick, at the Craftsbury Town Hall, the Greensboro Fellowship Hall and the Burke base lodge. The annual **Summer Music from Greensboro** series takes place in the Church of Christ sanctuary and the Greensboro Fellowship Hall. The Greensboro Association has sponsored concerts on a dock at Caspian Lake every summer Sunday at 7:30 for nearly 50 years. The signature scene in Craftsbury Common is the summer band concerts in the bandshell on the common Sunday nights at 7 in July and August. Those who remain in their vehicles honk their horns if they like what they hear.

Gardens. Gardeners in the know flock to **Perennial Pleasures Nursery** in East Hardwick, where two acres of perennial and herb gardens are on display and English cream tea is served by reservation on the lawns outside the Brick House, a quirky Victorian B&B, Tuesday-Sunday from noon to 4:30. Old-fashioned, hardy perennial flowers and herbs from the 17th to 19th centuries are the specialties. Gardeners also seek out places like **Stone's Throw Gardens** in East Craftsbury for hardy perennials, including heritage roses and lilies, displayed on several levels around a restored 1795 farmhouse, against stone walls and in fields strewn with flowers. Other favorites for rare varieties are **Vermont Day Lilies** on Barr Hill in North Greensboro, where retired Colgate University administrator David Perham and his wife Andrea also run the Greensboro House, a homey B&B (two bedrooms with shared bath) and a collectibles and sports card business, and **Dooryard Lilacs** in Greensboro.

Shopping. There's not much of it, but what there is is interesting. **Willey's** in the center of Greensboro is a general store to end all general stores. Celebrating its 100th birthday in 2000, this local institution is a ramble of rooms, with three levels of hardware and housewares, a rear meat market and grocery and an upstairs for clothing. It's the kind of place where you'll find an open box of dog biscuits sandwiched between a display case of Timex watches and a crate of fresh peaches. Across the aisle are shelves of chewing tobacco. Bulletin boards on either side of the entry dispense fascinating information. One poster announced a public forum on the future of Greensboro, "Condos or Cupolas?" Across the street is **The Miller's Thumb,** two levels of gifts built around a chute opening onto the basement mill and waterfall. The Old Forge in East Craftsbury has Scottish and Irish woolens, including tams, deerstalkers and perfectly beautiful sweaters from $100 to $200-plus. Arts and crafts by Vermont artisans are featured at the **South Albany Store** on the East Craftsbury Road. Want Vermont game birds? Visit the **Wylie Hill Farm** in Craftsbury Common, where pheasant, partridge, quail, turkeys and more are raised naturally and sold by mail-order.

The center of East Burke has several shops of interest. Penny candy, Vermont specialty foods, country clothing, crafts and more are offered at the with-it **Bailey's Country Store.** Across the street, mountain bikes, canoes, kayaks, clothing and sports accessories are available at **East Burke Sports.** Eclectic crafts, gifts and collectibles are the forte of **Lasso the Moon.** Three styles of beers and tours are offered nearby at the **Trout River Brewing Company.**

Cabot Creamery, 128 Main St., Cabot.

If this area has a real, live tourist attraction, this is it. Upwards of 350 people on busy days visit the Cabot Farmers' Cooperative Creamery, begun in 1919 when 94 dairy farmers founded the original creamery plant to churn butter. Today, nearly 500 Vermont farmers sell milk to the creamery, which produces twenty to thirty tons of cheese daily. Its sharp Vermont cheddar won top honors in the U.S. Championship Cheese Contest in Wisconsin, which considers itself the home of American cheddar, and it is sold at Harrods in London. Following a video presentation, visitors leave on guided tours of the manufacturing plant. Through windows into the production areas you can watch many of the 250 employees as they separate the curds from the whey, mold the cheese into 42-pound blocks and package it for aging in the huge uphill warehouse. The half-hour tour tells you all you want to know about cheese. At tour's end, you get to sample low-fat, jalapeño, sharp and extra-sharp varieties to spur sales in the gift shop. The visitor center is dedicated to the unheralded role of farm women everywhere.

(802) 563-2231. Open Monday-Saturday 9 to 5, Sunday in summer, 11 to 4. No cheese production on Sunday and one day at midweek. Adults, $1.

Extra-Special

The Old Stone House Museum, Brownington.

This charming place is part of the out-of-the-way Brownington Village Historic District, a time warp listed on the National Register. The impressive structure lives up to its billing as "the rarest kind of museum: a building as fascinating as the collection it houses." The four-story structure was built stone by stone in the 1830s by the Rev. Alexander Twilight, who is believed to have been America's first black college graduate (Middlebury) and its first black legislator, and his neighbors. The school in which he taught the region's school children for two decades is history, but the 30-room monument still instructs and inspires. It's filled with antiques and memorabilia displayed by the Orleans County Historical Society. You can see Alexander Twilight's desk and Bible there.

(802) 754-2022. Open daily in summer, 11 to 5; Friday-Tuesday in off-season. Closed mid-October to mid-May. Adults, $5.

Woodstock/Quechee, Vt.
A Chic Blend of Old and New

Picture the perfect Vermont place and you're likely to picture Woodstock, the historic shire town portrayed by the media as the picture-perfect New England village.

Picture an old river town with handsome 19th-century houses, red brick mill, waterfall and covered bridge and you have Quechee, the hamlet being restored to reflect Vermont as it used to be.

Join them with Rockefellers, Billingses, Pearces and other old names and new entrepreneurs, and you have an unusual combination for a chic, changing dynamic.

Carefully preserved and protected, Woodstock has such an impressive concentration of architecture from the late 17th and 18th centuries that National Geographic magazine termed it one of the most beautiful villages in America. That it is, thanks to its role as a prosperous county seat following its settlement in 1765 and to early popularity as both a summer and winter resort. Vermont's first golf course was established south of town around the turn of the century and the nation's first ski tow was installed on a cow pasture north of town in 1934.

That also was the year when Laurance S. Rockefeller married localite Mary Billings French, granddaughter of railroad magnate Frederick Billings. The Rockefeller interests now are Woodstock's largest landowner and employer. They buried the utility poles underground, provided a home and much of the stimulus for the Woodstock Historical Society, bought and rebuilt the Woodstock Inn, acquired and redesigned the golf course, bought and upgraded the Suicide Six ski area, opened the Billings Farm Museum, and built a multi-million-dollar indoor sports and fitness center.

Entrepreneur Simon Pearce, the Irish glass blower, has provided some of the same impetus for neighboring Quechee. He purchased an abandoned mill as a site for his glass-blowing enterprise, powered it with a 50-year-old turbine using water

from the river outside, added more craftspeople and a restaurant, and sparked a crafts and business revival that has enlivened a sleepy hamlet heretofore known mainly for its scenic gorge.

In this inspirational setting of old and new, entrepreneurs are supported, and arts and crafts are appreciated.

Inn Spots

Twin Farms, Barnard 05031.

A dozen miles north of Woodstock at the edge of the unlikely hamlet of Barnard lies the ultimate in small, luxury

Extravagant Studio with its soaring living room ceiling is biggest cottage at Twin Farms.

country resorts, one attracting jet-setters from across the world. The secluded farm once owned by writers Sinclair Lewis and Dorothy Thompson was converted to the tune of $11 million into the East's most sumptuous inn in 1993. One of a kind, it offers six suites and eight cottages, superb dining and a full-time staff of 30 to pamper up to 28 guests. The rates – $700 to $1,500 a night for two – includes meals, drinks and recreational activities, but not tax or service charge.

Twin Farms is deluxe, of course, but understated and not at all ostentatious – not nearly as drop-dead showy as one might expect. "The idea is you're a guest at somebody's country estate for the weekend," says Beverley Matthews, innkeeper with her husband Shaun, both of whom are British and who come with impeccable resort-management credentials. "For our guests, money is not an object. Time is."

The idea evolved after the Twigg-Smith family of Honolulu acquired the estate's main Sonnenberg Haus and ski area as a vacation home in 1974 when chef Sepp Schenker left to open his nearby Barnard Inn. In 1989, Laila and Thurston Twigg-Smith acquired the other half of Twin Farms from Sinclair Lewis's grandchildren, returning the estate to its original 235 acres. Son Thurston (Koke) Twigg-Smith Jr. and his wife Andrea, twenty-year residents of Barnard, managed the development phase of Twin Farms.

Their resources and taste show throughout the property, from the electronically operated gates at the entrance to the fully equipped fitness center and separate

Japanese furo soaking tubs beneath a creekside pub reached by a covered bridge. In the main house, three living rooms, each bigger than the last, unfold as the innkeepers welcome guests. One with a vaulted ceiling opens onto a library loft and soaring windows gazing onto a 30-mile view toward Mount Ascutney. Decor is elegantly rustic and utterly comfortable.

Upstairs are four bedrooms bearing some of the Twin Farms trademarks: plump kingsize feather beds, tiled fireplaces, comfortable sitting areas, fabulous folk art and contemporary paintings, TV/VCR/stereos, tea trays with a coffee press and Kona coffees from the family-owned corporation, twin sinks in the bathrooms, baskets of all-natural toiletries, terrycloth robes, and unbleached and undyed cotton towels. They impart a feeling of elegant rusticity, but come with every convenience of the ultimate home away from home.

Less antiquity and even more convenience are found in the newly built stone and wood guest cottages, each with at least one fireplace, a screened porch or terrace, an incredible twig-sided carport and its own private place in the landscape. The Perch, for instance, is situated above a small stream and beaver pond. It harbors luxuriant seating around the fireplace, a desk, a dining area, a refrigerator with ice maker, a bed recessed in an alcove and shielded by a hand-carved arch of wooden roping, a wicker-filled porch where a wood sculpture of a shark hangs overhead, and a bathroom with a copper tub the size of a small pool and a separate shower stall, both with windows to the outdoors.

The largest cottage – the contemporary Studio with a two-story window and loft bedroom – fulfills an artist's dream. The soaring Treehouse is furnished in Adirondack twig. The Japanese-style contemporary motif of the Orchard Cottage is striking, from its split-ash herringbone woven ceiling and white ash floors to the bamboo-framed marquetry breakfast table. Even more stunning is the Moroccan theme in the Meadow Cottage, likened to a desert king's traveling palace. The bed chamber is beneath a tented ceiling holding a chandelier of colored glass, and an inglenook fireplace of intricate mosaic tiles is framed by multi-colored banquettes and terra cotta floors. After these, the Log Cabin offers a Vermont-like respite.

Good food and drink (from help-yourself bars) are among Twin Farms strong points. Guests meet at 7 o'clock for cocktails in a changing venue – perhaps the wine cellar, one of the living rooms or, the night before our visit, in the Studio, the largest cottage. A set, four-course dinner is served at 8 at tables for two in a baronial dining hall with chandeliers hanging from the vaulted ceiling and fieldstone fireplaces at either end.

Talented chef Neil Wigglesworth came here from The Point on Saranac Lake in the Adirondacks, a smaller but similarly grand inn that has been upstaged by Twin Farms. A typical dinner might start with medallions of lobster with avocado relish and angel-hair pasta, followed by warm red-cabbage salad with slices of smoked chicken. The main course could be veal mignon with timbales of wild rice and xeres sauce or five-spiced duck with nut-brown cabbage and golden beets. For dessert? Perhaps fresh figs with beummes de venese ice cream and peach-caramel sauce. Coffee, cheeses and a glass of aged port might round out the evening.

Breakfast is continental if taken in the guest rooms and cooked to order in the dining room from a small menu – raspberry pancakes or eggs benedict with lobster the day we visited.

Lunch is a movable feast, depending on the day and guests' inclinations. It could be a sit-down meal in the dining room, a picnic anywhere, or a barbecue beside the

New rear dining room looks onto landscaped back yard at The Jackson House Inn.

inn's seven-acre Copper Pond or at its own ski area, where there's never a lineup for the pomalift. Afternoon tea is a presentation worthy of the Ritz, complete, perhaps, with little gold leaves on one of the five kinds of tea pastries.

The creekside pub, incidentally, is nearly a museum piece with its collection of beer bottles from around the world. Beer-bottle caps cover the light shades over the billiards table, outline the mirror and sconces above the fireplace, and cover the candlesticks on the mantel. Even a pub chair is dressed in beer caps – a dramatic piece of pop art from the Twigg-Smiths' renowned art collection. Such are some of the delights and surprises encountered by guests at Twin Farms.

(802) 234-9999 or (800) 894-6327. Fax (802) 234-9990. Six suites and eight cottages with private baths. Doubles, $800 and $950. Cottages, $1,150. Studio $1,500. All-inclusive, except for 15 percent service charge and 8 percent state tax. Two-night minimum weekends, three nights on holidays. Children over 18. No smoking.

The Jackson House Inn, 37 Old Route 4 West, Woodstock 05091.

We didn't think a B&B could get much better than this three-story Victorian house on four acres of beautiful grounds west of the village. But new owners Juan and Gloria Florin, former Argentineans by way of Connecticut, had plans. Taking over in 1997, they made it a true inn – adding four luxury suites, an acclaimed dining room open to the public, and a level of service for potential affiliation with Relais & Chateaux.

"We didn't change the inn," Juan stressed to the legions of steady customers. "We just added to it."

The nine guest rooms and two suites in the original inn merited coverage in antiques and decorator magazines. Each is different and eclectically furnished with such things as antique brass lamps on either side of the bathroom mirror, a marble-topped bedside table, an 1860 sleigh bed, an 1840 English mahogany pedestal desk, a prized Casablanca ceiling fan, Chinese carved rugs, handmade afghans coordinated to each room's colors, bamboo and cane furniture, a blanket box made of tiger maple, an antique three-drawer sideboard with its faded original green paint and much more.

Room decor varies from French Empire to British Oriental to old New England. Each bathroom has a glassed-in shower and a hair dryer. Most choice are two third-floor beauties, considered suites because they're about twice the size of most other rooms. Both have queensize cherry sleigh beds, gas fireplaces, Italian marble baths and french doors onto a rear deck overlooking an English garden. We found plenty of room in the Francesca suite to spread out on an upholstered sofa, a wing chair and, on the deck beyond, two lounge chairs. The mirrored bathroom was so sparkling it looked as if we were the first ever to use it. Upon our return from dinner, a couple of Godiva chocolates were on our pillows.

Lately in demand are the four luxury suites in a new wing off the east side of the inn. Here are large rooms with sitting areas, gas fireplaces and modern bathrooms with cherry floors, whirlpool jetted tubs, separate showers and towel warmers. They're elegantly appointed with Italian fabrics by Anichini.

Another showplace is the cathedral-ceilinged dining room in a rear addition with soaring open-hearth granite fireplace in the center and tall windows onto four acres of landscaped grounds and gardens. The chef presents inspired modern American fare (see Dining Spots).

Guests gather with innkeepers Matt and Jennifer Barba in the elegant parlor and intimate library for complimentary champagne and wine and an elaborate buffet of hors d'oeuvres before dinner. And we mean elaborate: perhaps California rolls, curried grilled chicken with diced green apple on a chickpea flour crisp, crab salad on corn bread and prosciutto-wrapped black mission figs.

The treats continue the next morning. The first breakfast course might be a plate of honeydew, cantaloupe and kiwi, bananas in cream or, in winter, baked apple with mincemeat in rum and wine. Juices, croissants and muffins come next. Poached eggs on dill biscuits with poached salmon and hollandaise sauce highlighted one of the best breakfasts we've had. The next day produced a plate of fresh fettuccine with homemade pesto and a poached egg with béarnaise sauce in the center, teamed with salmon poached in court bouillon with a sprig of dill and a stuffed mushroom cap.

After all this, settle into a deep wing chair in the library or retire to a lounge chair around the pond in the remarkably landscaped back yard for a morning nap. Or work it off in a spa located on the lower level. It includes exercise equipment, steam room, large-screen TV and a juice bar.

(802) 457-2065 or (800) 448-1890. Fax (802) 457-9290. www.jacksonhouse.com. Nine rooms and six suites with private baths. Doubles, $170. Suites, $240. Children over 14. No smoking.

Woodstock Inn and Resort, 14 The Green, Woodstock 05091.

The biggest institution in town, the Woodstock Inn is solid. Solid, as in the 1823 Paul Revere bell weighing 1,463 pounds standing guard outside its newish 18th-century-style wing or the expanses of rich hardwoods comprising floor, walls and ceiling of the elegant Richardson's Tavern.

The inn sits majestically back from the green, its front facing a covered bridge and mountains, the rear looking across the pool and putting green and down the valley toward its golf course and ski touring center. The resort's other leisure facilities include the Suicide Six ski area, ten tennis courts and two lighted paddle tennis courts, an indoor sports and fitness center, and such attractions as sleigh rides, dogsledding and horseback riding.

The interior of the inn is impressive as well. Built by Rockresorts in 1969 after Laurance Rockefeller found the original Woodstock Inn beyond salvation, it contains a lobby warmed by a ten-foot-high stone fireplace around which people always seem to be gathered, a large and glamorous dining room, a cafe, a wicker sunroom and lounge where afternoon tea is served, an always-busy gift shop and a smashing barnwood library outfitted with books and the day's Boston and New York newspapers.

The main inn has three stories in front and four in the rear, the lowest downstairs from the lobby. The 144 guest accommodations are among the more luxurious in which we've stayed: spacious rooms with handmade quilts on the beds, upholstered chairs, three-way reading lights, television, telephones, and large bathrooms and closets. Walls are hung with paintings and photographs of local scenes.

The most prized rooms now seem to be 34 in the newer rear brick tavern wing, 23 with fireplaces and three with sitting-room porches overlooking the putting green. They are notable for graceful reading alcoves, dark blue and burgundy bed coverings matching the carpets, TVs on wheels hidden in cupboards, mini-refrigerators, and double marble vanities in the bathrooms. Interestingly, except for four suites, they seem smaller and more intimate than many of the rooms in the main inn. Covered parking is provided in a garage below.

The long main dining room, lately doubled in size, has large windows onto a spacious outdoor terrace overlooking the pool, putting green and gardens. The contemporary fare ranges from Atlantic salmon or roasted chicken to Vermont rack of lamb. The elaborate Sunday buffet brunch is enormously popular.

The stylish **Eagle Cafe** offers a more casual lunch or dinner. We've enjoyed interesting salads and, most recently, smoked chicken and green onion quesadillas and a grilled chicken sandwich with melted jack, roasted peppers and herbed mayonnaise on toasted focaccia. Linger with an after-dinner drink in the sophisticated **Richardson's Tavern,** as urbane a night spot as you'll find in Vermont.

(802) 457-1100 or (800) 448-7900. Fax (802) 457-6699. One hundred thirty-seven rooms and seven suites with private baths. Doubles, $159 to $325 EP. Suites, $419 to $525 EP. Add $106 for MAP.

Entrées, $19.95 to $26.95. Lunch, 11:30 to 2. Dinner, 6 to 9, jackets requested. Sunday brunch, 11 to 1:30.

The Maple Leaf Inn, Route 12, Box 273, Barnard 05031.

The would-be innkeepers from Texas could not find the perfect old New England inn in their search among existing buildings. So they built it – a brand new, meant-to-look-old Victorian structure with the requisite gingerbread and gazebo – in a clearing amid sixteen acres of maples and birches at the end of a long driveway in tiny Barnard.

For their 1994 opening, Gary and Janet Robison from Houston engraved their names and the date – as they would for a cornerstone – at the beginning of the sidewalk leading to their impressive Victorian manse. "We couldn't resist," said Gary. "It's the child in all of us."

Up the long sidewalk, guests head to the wraparound front porch with its corner gazebo and authentic Tennessee oak rockers. Enter the front door, its window engraved with a maple leaf. On the right is an intimate library, full of foreign

Maple Leaf Inn is new. built-to-look old Victorian structure set back in woods.

travel books and artifacts from the days when the Robisons lived abroad. On the left is a parlor with a corner fireplace, one of seven woodburning fireplaces in the house and all topped with different antique mantelpieces. The traditional furniture here blends nicely with the occasional antique. Beyond and still farther out in this undulating house that seems to have a surfeit of windows everywhere is a fireplaced dining room, its five tables for two set for breakfasts by candlelight. "We cater to the getaway couples market," explains Gary.

Couples get away in seven comfortable bedrooms, most positioned to have windows on three sides. Five have fireplaces. All have modern baths (four with whirlpool tubs), kingsize beds, sitting areas, TV/VCRs secreted in the armoires, ceiling fans and closets. An unusual picket fence affair replaces the usual head-board behind the kingsize bed in the main-floor Country Garden Room because the Robisons preferred not to block the window against which the bed rests. The pickets also continue the theme of the fences and gardens just outside. This room is typical with its swivel club chair/rockers, colorful bed quilt, gray carpeting and walls, and sheer lace curtains. Each mantelpiece holds what Gary calls an antique doodad. The four upstairs corner rooms are named and decorated for each season. Janet spent a week in each room creating the remarkable stenciling. She stenciled an elaborate winter village over the fireplace and around the doors and windows in the Winter Haven Room in which we stayed.

In 1997, the Robisons added two more rooms on the third floor, each with king bed, sitting area and two-person soaking tubs. They are value-priced so those on tighter budgets may enjoy the hosts' hospitality and amenities that merit AAA's four-diamond award.

The candlelight breakfast is a highlight of one's stay. Ours began with buttermilk scones garnished with flowers. The accompanying orange and cranberry-apple butters were shaped like maple leaves, and the preserves were presented in leaf dishes. Next came a fruit course of sautéed bananas with Ben & Jerry's ice cream. The main course was stuffed french toast with peach preserves and cream cheese, garnished with nasturtiums.

In the afternoon, the Robisons serve tea and wine with crackers and cheese. They also offer light suppers of soup, bread, salad and dessert by request in winter.

Two chocolates are placed at bedside at nightly turndown. You may find a jar of maple syrup wrapped in a ribbon or a personalized wood Christmas ornament in the shape of a maple leaf hung on the door knob. Hospitable Janet could send you home with a farewell package of pumpkin bread or muffins.

(802) 234-5342 or (800) 516-2753. www.mapleleafinn.com. Seven rooms with private baths. Doubles, $110 to $175. Two-night minimum holidays and foliage season. No children. No smoking.

The Charleston House, 21 Pleasant St., Woodstock 05091.

When we first saw the Charleston House, it was festooned for Christmas, inside and out, and looked like a spread for House Beautiful.

But the red brick 1835 Greek revival house is gorgeous at any time of year. Named for the hometown of the original innkeeper, it remains the epitome of Southern charm and hospitality under new owners Dixi and Willa Nohl. They spent a weekend here in 1997, learned the place was for sale and started the purchase process on the spot. "It was serendipitous," said retiring owners Bill and Barbara Hough, ready to rest after eleven years. Dixi was general manager of Burke Mountain ski area and grew up in the lodging business in St. Anton in his native Austria.

Listed in the National Register of Historic Places, the house is elegantly furnished with period antiques and an extensive selection of art and oriental rugs.

The retiring innkeepers recently built a substantial addition – nicely secluded in back – to produce two deluxe guest rooms with jacuzzi tubs, fireplaces, TVs and porches. One has a queen bed and the other a kingsize four-poster. As the sale was closed in early 1998, the finishing touches were being put on two more deluxe guest rooms upstairs in the addition. The newest is the largest, the Henry Hatch Suite with queen bed, jacuzzi, sitting room, fireplace and porch.

Five other rooms upstairs in the main house have queen beds and private baths.

Stunning floral arrangements and lovely needlepoint pillows adorn the dining room and the comfortable living room.

Breakfasts here are such an attraction that the owners put together a cookbook of recipes, called *Breakfast at Charleston House.* Among specialties are puffed pancakes filled with fruit;" a cheese and grits soufflé, macadamia-nut waffles with papaya and strawberries, and Charleston strata, an egg dish with sausage and apples.

(802) 457-3843 or (888) 475-3800. Eight rooms and one suite with private baths. Doubles, $110 to $175. Suite, $200. Two-night minimum weekends. Children over 10. No smoking.

Ardmore Inn, 23 Pleasant St., Woodstock 05091.

A structure that looks like a covered bridge stands beside this white Georgian Greek Revival house that for years was the home of the well-known F.H. Gillingham family. The look was created by opening the rear of what had been a garage – it was the only way for cars to get through to park in the back yard, explained owner Bill Gallagher.

He bought the impressive house with distinguished palladian windows as "a nice place for my aunts and me" when he retires from Our Lady of Snows church across the street. Meanwhile, he and resident innkeeper Giorgio Ortiz restored the original woodwork, added new bathrooms, brought in family furnishings and opened it as a B&B. They named it Ardmore, which means "Great House" in the Irish tradition.

In his booming baritone voice, the ebullient host likes to show prized features of the house, such as the etched glass in the solid mahogany front door, the circular moldings around the original light fixtures on the ceilings and the recessed pocket windows screened with Irish lace curtains in the fireplaced living room. The five bedrooms, all with private baths, are painted in light pastel colors. "That's my grandmother's bed," says Bill of the carved black walnut headboard in the mint-green Sheridan bedroom, main-floor front, which is accented with Waverly fabrics and oriental rugs. The bathroom here has a walk-in Vermont marble shower and jacuzzi. "My father was in the marble business," Bill explains, so the bathroom floors are enhanced with marble. The biggest bedroom is in the upstairs rear. Called Tarma, Irish for sanctuary, it lives up to its name with a kingsize bed, a new fireplace, a loveseat facing a marble coffee table, and guardian angels as night lights. The inn's own toiletries are placed in little white baskets.

Breakfast is served for ten at an English mahogany banquet table inlaid with rosewood. Giorgio, the chef, gets creative with things like pumpkin pancakes, stuffed french toast and vegetable frittatas. His masterpiece is the "Woodstock Sunrise," Vermont flatbread bearing baked spiced eggs, Vermont cheddar, smoked apple sausage and asparagus with béarnaise sauce and put together to look like a sunrise. Tea biscuits and cheesecake are offered with tea and cider on the rear screened veranda on summer afternoons.

(802) 457-3887 or (802) 497-9652. Fax (802) 457-9006. www.ardmoreinn.com. Doubles, $110 to $150; $85 to $135 in March and April. Two-night minimum in foliage season. No children. No smoking.

The Carriage House of Woodstock, 15 Route 4 West, Woodstock 05091.

Mike and Shirley Wagner traded their jobs in medicine in Baltimore for a new lifestyle. "We were in businesses where people always were sick and we wanted to be where people were happy," explains Shirley. They took over a bankrupt B&B with a wraparound veranda up against the highway, did a total renovation and put on a rear addition.

The Wagners offer seven carpeted bedrooms on the second and third floors, all with private baths (one with a whirlpool tub) and queensize beds. They're furnished in a fresh, flouncy style that Shirley calls "relaxed Victorian."

In 1997, they added two more rooms in the walkout basement beneath the rear carriage house. Each comes with a whirlpool tub, TV and french doors to the outside. One with a kingsize bed has a fireplace.

The game room that previously occupied part of the basement was moved upstairs in the carriage house.

Shirley's prized antique glass collection is housed in custom-made glass cases separating the living room and dining room in the main structure. From her spectacular cathedral-ceilinged kitchen come daily breakfasts involving a choice of eggs any style with bacon or sausage, pancakes, waffles or french toast. Fruit cup, juice and homemade muffins accompany. Cookies and tea or hot cider are offered in the afternoon.

(802) 457-4322 or (800) 791-8045. Nine rooms with private baths. Doubles, $95 to $155; foliage, $125 to $165. Two-night minimum in foliage season. Children welcome. No smoking.

Ardmore Inn wears its Christmas finery.

Deer Brook Inn, Route 4, HCR Box 443, Woodstock 05091.

A year's hands-on restoration by Rosemary and Brian McGinty turned this 1820 farmhouse west of town into an attractive B&B. Their sweat equity, decorating talents and personal touches produced five guest rooms with private baths, in-room vanities and king or queensize beds. One is a two-room suite.

Country pretty in Colonial style, they're painted in cream colors with Colonial trim and have wide-board floors and the odd exposed beam. Magazines are spread out on an old sewing machine in one room.

Good art hangs on the walls of the living room, where there's a TV, and in a large dining room. The McGintys, who have young children, serve a full breakfast. It includes fresh fruit, homemade breads and an entrée like featherbed eggs or baked apple pancakes. The food, good as it is, is almost upstaged by an unusual built-in bird feeder in the back window of the dining room. It attracts a bevy of birds that seem to be right in the room, where they can be observed pecking away at breakfast as guests enjoy theirs.

Beyond the bird feeder is a pleasant back yard. Wicker seats on the front porch are good for watching the Ottauquechee River meander by.

(802) 672-3713. Five rooms with private baths. Doubles, $70 to $95. Suite, $125. Children welcome.

Quechee Bed & Breakfast, 753 Woodstock Road (Route 4), Quechee 05059.

The waters of the Ottauquechee River can be seen from the back yard and rear upstairs guest rooms of this large 1795 house perched on a cliff not far from Quechee Gorge. It was converted into a luxury B&B by Susan and Ken Kaduboski, transplanted Boston accountants, who have restored eight spacious, air-conditioned bedrooms with private baths.

Guests enter a large living/dining area with sofas gathered around a huge fireplace. A cactus stands in one corner, and an interesting art collection is on display.

A smaller parlor has been converted into a breakfast area with four tables for two. It leads through heavy doors into the original house and the guest quarters, nicely secluded and private with a separate entry hall and staircase. Three rooms are on the first floor and five on the second, including two with beamed, half-cathedral ceilings. Each is suavely furnished with king or queensize beds (four of them rice-carved four-posters) or, in one case, twin mahogany sleigh beds that can be joined as a king, antique dressers, two wing chairs, sprightly wallpapers and decorative touches like swags and stenciled lamp shades, and large bathrooms with beige towels. Sheets and pillow cases are beige and cream and lavishly trimmed with lace. One bathroom is all in pink and pretty as can be.

The Kaduboskis serve a full breakfast of juices, broiled grapefruit or apple-cinnamon custard and homemade breads with different jams. Main dishes could be scrambled eggs with chives and Vermont cheddar, apple pancakes, buttermilk waffles with fresh fruit or french toast stuffed with cream cheese and walnuts.

(802) 295-1776. Eight rooms with private baths. Doubles, $109 to $139. Children over 13. No smoking.

The Quechee Inn at Marshland Farm, Clubhouse Road, Quechee 05059.

This venerable establishment – a beautifully restored 1793 farmstead built by Vermont's first lieutenant governor – is every Hollywood set designer's idea of what a New England country inn should look like: a pure white rambling Vermont farmhouse, red barns out back against a backdrop of green mountains and, across the quiet road, the Ottauquechee River heading into Quechee Gorge.

The interior lives up to expectations as well: a welcoming beamed and barnwood living room, lately expanded and so carefully integrated with the older section that many don't notice the change. There's a rustic, stenciled restaurant and 24 comfortable guest rooms and suites. All come with private baths, Queen Anne-style furnishings, brass and four-poster canopy beds, wing chairs, braided and Chinese rugs on wide-plank floors and, a surprise for the purists, cable TV.

With fourteen rooms in the original farmhouse and ten more on the second floor of a wing that houses the expanded common rooms and restaurant, the inn is large enough to be a focal point for activity – a Christmas Eve open house for inn guests, cocktails before a crackling fire in the lounge, summer get-togethers on the canopied patio, the Wilderness Trails Nordic Ski School in a small barn. The Vermont Fly Fishing School is based here, and guests have golf, tennis, swimming and skiing privileges at the private Quechee Club.

A full breakfast buffet – from fruits and yogurts to scrambled eggs and sausages – is set out in the dining room. Coffee, tea and fruit breads are offered in the afternoon.

Most people enjoy drinks by the fire in the living room/lounge before adjourning for dinner in the antiques-filled dining room called the **Meadows Restaurant.** Beamed ceilings, wide-plank floors and lovely pink and blue stenciled borders on the walls are the setting for interesting fare. Recent choices included seafood gumbo, Moroccan spiced duckling and sliced Vermont lamb drizzled with balsamic syrup.

(802) 295-3133 or (800) 235-3133. Fax (802) 295-6587. Twenty-two rooms and two suites with private baths. Doubles, $140 to $240, MAP. Suites, $200 to $260 MAP. Deduct $40 for B&B. No smoking.

Entrées, $19 to $22. Dinner nightly, 6 to 9.

Parker House Inn, 16 Main St., Quechee 05059.

Guests have filled the room diaries with comments about the food and hospitality since Walt and Barbara Forrester left Chicago with their teenaged sons to become innkeepers here. The lively couple look at their inn as a continuing house party. "Schmoozing is my calling," says Walt, and cooking is his new profession.

Walt was selling medical equipment for Toshiba when he decided to enroll in the Culinary Institute of America with the idea of buying an inn in the East. Barbara had been a pastry chef and the couple had operated a pub near Wrigley Field.

It was love at first sight when they came across the Parker House, an elegant red brick and white frame Victorian mansion with a steep mansard roof crowned with an ornamental wrought-iron railing. A Vermont state senator and mill owner, Joseph C. Parker, built the mansion in 1857 next to his mill on the Ottauquechee River. It was converted into an inn by Frank Parker, no relation to the original owner but – by amazing coincidence – Walt's onetime boss at Toshiba. The two had lost track of each other; in the interim, Frank had started and sold the Parker House and Walt had come along unknowingly eight years later.

Long known for its restaurant (see Dining Spots), the accommodations have been upgraded with three cheery and fresh guest rooms with queensize beds and modern baths on the third floor and a second-floor TV/sitting room. The new rooms join four large, high-ceilinged guest rooms with private baths on the second floor. Emily's huge room in front, named for the original Mrs. Parker, has twin white enamel and brass poster bedsteads joined by a kingsize mattress, a dressing room with an enormous modern bathroom and an antique desk that Walt calls an early Murphy bed – it opens up, the sides go down and voilà, a futon. Even larger is another kingbedded room running along most of the back of the house with a fine view of the river. We chose Joseph's Room in the rear corner with a queen brass bed, chest, armoire and writing desk and a large bathroom with double vanity and thick towels. The only drawbacks were only one chair and a lack of reading lights, but we simply adjourned to the small sitting room across the hall.

Breakfast the next morning was a treat in the sunny bar area (it's served outside on an awninged deck in the summer). Juice and half a grapefruit preceded an ample platter of bagels with smoked salmon, cream cheese and all the fixings. On other occasions you might have scrambled eggs with cream cheese and dill and homemade sausage, pancakes with maple syrup or frittata.

(802) 295-6077. www.pbpub.com/quechee/parkherhouse.htm. Seven rooms with private baths. Doubles, $100 to $125. Smoking restricted.

Country Garden Inn, 37 Main St., Quechee, Vt. 05059.

From the floral stenciling in the guest rooms to a landscaped swimming area fashioned from a dammed-up creek, a garden theme prevails at this showy new B&B. Shelly and Don Gardner say they've never worked so hard as since they took it on as "a retirement project."

Blessed with ostensibly deep pockets but doing almost everything themselves, they have given new dimension to the innkeepers' lexicon, transforming five rather ordinary bedrooms into refuges of hand-crocheted bed quilts and hand-starched pillows, prized oriental rugs, floral stenciling and museum-piece artworks. Amenity is a word that Shelly employs freely, pointing out the deadbolt door locks, room diaries, terrycloth robes, scented candles, hair dryers, electric blankets, six-position shower heads, liquid soap dispensers, curling irons, disposable razors ("we replace them whether used or not") and note cards and letterheads in each room. Room configurations range from cozy with twin mahogany sleigh beds to spacious with queen brass bed and sleep sofa.

Common areas include a Victorian parlor with a collection of Russian art (said to be the only such pieces outside Russia) and a lounge with cable TV, hundreds of videos and a refrigerator in an old safe. There's a greenhouse atrium in which English tea and scones are served to guests (and the public by reservation, December-April). Out back in a former glassmaker's shed is a recreation room with a cherry pool table, a card and game table and a mini-exercise area including computerized treadmill and stationary bike. The rippling creek traversing the property has what Shelly calls an antique pool that swimmers share with sizable rainbow trout. The woodsy pool area is flanked by a pleasant stone patio, picnic areas and lounge furniture. Guests also enjoy full sports privileges at the Quechee Club, to which the Gardners belong.

Breakfast is a three-course affair. Fresh orange juice and assorted fruits are served with cereals and homemade blueberry muffins shaped like flowers to convey the garden theme. The main dish could be french toast sprinkled with cinnamon, nutmeg and crushed walnuts, served with country ham.

All the amenities helped earn this B&B the AAA's four-diamond rating.

(802) 295-3023 or (800) 859-4191. Fax (802) 295-3121. Five rooms with private baths. May to mid-September: doubles, $130 to $180. Foliage: $150 to $200. November-April: $110 to $160. No smoking.

Dining Spots

Simon Pearce Restaurant, The Mill, Quechee.

The restaurant beside the Ottauquechee River has as much integrity as the rest of Irish glass blower Simon Pearce's mill complex. The chefs train at Ballymaloe in Ireland, and they import flour from Ireland to make Irish soda and brown breads.

You sit on sturdy ash chairs at bare wood tables (dressed with white linens at night). The heavy Simon Pearce glassware and the deep brown china are made at the mill. Irish or classical music plays in the background. Through large windows you have a view of the river, hills rising beyond. A large dining addition looks through a handsome arched window out onto the falls and, in season, an enclosed deck that can be opened to the outside is almost over the falls. (Indeed, a couple of interior tables could give one vertigo, being right over the falls).

Several wines from the Wine Spectator award-winning list are available by the glass. At lunches we've tried both the house white and red ($4 a glass) as well as spicy bloody marys with a real kick, while nibbling the sensational Ballymaloe bread.

The menu changes frequently but there are always specialties like the delicious beef and Guinness stew, a generous lunch serving of fork-tender beef and vegetables, served with a small salad of julienned vegetables. Other midday entrées include lamb and rosemary pie, warm goat cheese salad, sesame-seared salmon with wasabi and pickled ginger, and brochettes of beef tenderloin with crispy sweet potatoes. The pasta salad, a huge heap of spirals, featured many vegetables and a splendid dressing of oil, vinegar, basil and parmesan cheese. Hickory-smoked coho salmon with potato salad and a skewer of grilled chicken with a spicy peanut sauce and a green salad with vinaigrette also were extra-good.

The walnut meringue cake with strawberry sauce, a menu fixture, is crisp and crunchy and melts in the mouth. Cappuccino cheesecake, chocolate rum cake, Irish apple cake and pecan pie are other possibilities, but when we go back, which we seem to do often, nothing but the walnut meringue cake will do.

At night, a candlelight dinner might start with some of the luncheon entrées as appetizers, say Maine crab cakes with rouille or grilled Cavendish quail with apple cider glaze and cranberry compote. Main courses could be grilled swordfish with lime hollandaise, poached salmon with white wine sauce, crisp roast duck with mango chutney sauce, scallops of veal with sundried tomatoes, and black angus sirloin flamed with Irish whiskey and served with caramelized onions.

Naturally, you can get beers and ales from the British Isles. You also can buy loaves of the restaurant's wonderful bread and flavored vinaigrettes.

Here's a restaurant that's so unpretentious but so appealing that we're not surprised that several of the traveling friends we've directed there for lunch liked it so much they returned for an encore the next day.

(802) 295-1470. Entrées, $15.50 to $22. Lunch daily, 11.30 to 2:45. Dinner nightly, 6 to 9. No smoking.

Barnard Inn, Route 12, Barnard. (802) 234-9961.
Ever since Swiss chef Sepp Schenker left the old Sonnenberg Haus (now part of Twin Farms) to open the Barnard Inn, this serene, sophisticated restaurant has

been considered one of the best in Vermont. Marie-France and Philip Filipovic from Quebec knew they had a lot to live up to when they purchased the restaurant in 1994. But they came with impeccable credentials. Self-taught Yugoslav chef Philip, who started as a waiter in Montreal's Ritz-Carlton Hotel, and his wife owned a four-star restaurant called simply Marie Philip in the Laurentian resort town of St. Sauveur. It had been rated the best in the province by the Quebec government in its annual awards competition.

Moving to Vermont for "quality of life," Marie said, they took over a going concern and began adding their imprimatur. They hung their favorite paintings, added more French wines, and planned to add oriental rugs and upholstered chairs. They also started smoking their own salmon.

Fireside dining at Barnard Inn.

From the kitchen comes the inn's longtime specialty, roast crisp duck, done as in the past and teamed with the inn's trademark potatoes, shaped and coated to look like a pear with a clove at the bottom and a pear stem on top. Philip has added more chicken dishes (one is stuffed with small vegetables and served with pickled ginger and turmeric sauce). Lamb is his trademark – we loved the noisettes wrapped in spinach mousse, as well as the rabbit tenderloin with wild mushrooms, everything beautifully garnished and served on dramatic square plates.

Although dinner is à la carte, a good value is the five-course tasting menu we sampled for $33 each. Besides the aforementioned entrées, the smoked salmon napoleon, a zucchini blossom with lobster and shrimp mousse, a salad dressed with balsamic and peanut oil, and the artist's palette of six intense sorbets made for one of the better meals of our travels.

Service is friendly yet impeccable in four cozy dining rooms (one with a wood-burning fireplace) of the elegant, late-Colonial inn. The owners occupy the upstairs with their young family.

(802) 234-9961. Entrées, $19 to $28. Dinner, Tuesday-Sunday from 6; nightly in fall. Closed Sunday and Monday in winter.

Jackson House Inn, 37 Old Route 4 West, Woodstock.

New owners elevated this B&B to a higher level with the opening in late 1997 of a handsome new dining room with cathedral ceiling, a stunning granite open-hearth fireplace and big windows onto four acres of gardens. Nicely spaced tables are flanked by chairs handcrafted by Charles Shackleton, a local furniture maker.

New American cuisine is prepared by executive chef Brendan Nolan, who was previously with the acclaimed Aujourd'hui at the Four Seasons Hotel in Boston. His food quickly attracted the attention of the national media and earned him invitations to cook at the James Beard House and an American Institute of Food and Wine dinner in New York in the winter of 1998.

Dinner is prix-fixe, with several choices for each of three courses. The chef's tasting menu ($49) adds a second appetizer, a palate-cleansing mango-lime sorbet and a plate of cheeses with dried fruits and spiced nuts before dessert.

A typical winter night's menu starts with a choice of lobster bisque, a salad of baby field greens with chèvre and a feuilletée of veal sweetbreads and asparagus with madeira cream, among others. Main courses could be grilled Atlantic salmon with charred tomato bouillon, pan-seared muscovy duck breast with figs, quince and red currants, herb-roasted veal loin with roasted red pepper sauce, and grilled filet of beef with red wine sauce. Desserts include banana napoleon, warm chocolate cake with raspberry ice cream profiteroles, chestnut soufflé with cognac crème anglaise and crème brûlée.

(802) 457-2065 or (800) 448-1890. Prix-fixe, $42. Dinner by reservation, nightly except Wednesday and some Tuesdays, 6 to 9.

The Prince and the Pauper, 34 Elm St., Woodstock.

A cocktail lounge with the shiniest wood bar you ever saw is at the entry of what many consider to be Woodstock's best restaurant. Tables in the intimate, L-shaped dining room (many flanked by dark wood booths) are covered with linens, oil lamps and flowers in small carafes. The lamps cast flickering shadows on dark beamed ceilings, and old prints adorn the white walls, one of which has a shelf of old books.

Chef-owner Chris J. Balcer refers to his cuisine as "creative contemporary" with French, continental and international accents.

Meals are prix-fixe for appetizer, salad and main course. The soup of the day could be billi-bi or Moroccan lentil, the pasta perhaps basil fettuccine with a concasse of tomatoes and garnished with goat cheese, and the pâté Vermont pheasant teamed with orange chutney. There's a choice of six entrées, perhaps grilled swordfish with mango-horseradish sauce, roast duckling with a sauce of kiwi and

Walt and Barbara Forrester create house party atmosphere at Parker House Inn.

rum, and filet mignon au poivre. The specialty is boneless rack of lamb in puff pastry with spinach and duxelles.

Homemade bread, house salad and seasonal vegetables accompany. The interesting wine list, honored by Wine Spectator, is strong on Californias.

Desserts might be a fabulous raspberry tart with white chocolate mousse served with raspberry cabernet wine sauce, strawberry sabayon with triple sec or homemade Jack Daniels chocolate-chip sorbet. Top them off with espresso, cappuccino or an international coffee.

A bistro menu is available in the lounge. Hearth-baked pizzas, crab cakes with tomato mayonnaise, sautéed chicken with calvados and Indonesian lamb curry are typical offerings.

(802) 457-1818. Prix-fixe, $34. Dinner nightly, 6 to 9 or 9:30. Bistro, entrées, $11.95 to $15.95, nightly 5 to 10 or 11.

Parker House Inn, 16 Main St., Quechee.

After fourteen years in sales in Chicago, Walt Forrester decided to attend the Culinary Institute of America and team up with his wife Barbara, a sometime pastry chef, in the hospitality business. The Parker House Inn is the fortuitous result. Moving here with their teenagers, who sometimes help in the dining room, they have changed the restaurant's focus from haute French to what Barbara calls "American comfort food," presented with style. One look at the choice wine list harboring five prized pinot noirs from Oregon hints of treats to come.

The atmosphere is elegant in two dining rooms and a rear cocktail lounge opening onto the river balcony. Dinner begins with an amuse-gueule, in our case roasted eggplant, red peppers and garlic pickled with fennel. A sampler of three appetizers produced a stellar grilled portobello mushroom with warm Vermont goat cheese on a spinach salad, a mushroom cap stuffed with an escargot and a country pâté. An extraordinary house salad of California mesclun with mustard vinaigrette and goat cheese followed.

Among main courses, the pork normandy sauced with apples, leeks, cider and applejack, and roasted Hudson Valley moulard duck breast marinated with soy sauce, garlic and ginger lived up to advance billing. Other possibilities ranged from Maine crab cakes atop a roasted red pepper coulis to rack of lamb with rosemary-wine sauce. After a couple of Barbara's desserts, apple crisp with vanilla ice cream and chocolate-almond torte, we lingered over cappuccino and savored the memory of an unforgettable meal.

(802) 295-6077. Entrées, $16.95 to $21.95. Dinner nightly except Tuesday, 5:30 to 9.

Wild Grass, Gallery Place, Route 4, Woodstock, Vt.

Multi-regional cuisine – from Pacific Rim to island jerk – is offered by Steve and Gail Buckley at this establishment fashioned from the former Rachel's Deli on the lower level of a gallery/office complex. Chef Paul "Shultz" Langhans attracted a wide local following at Simon Pearce and The Prince and the Pauper before leaving for the Pacific Northwest, only to be enticed back for this venture.

The cream-colored decor with hunter green and mauve accents is sleek yet simple. Bare pine tables seat 85 people inside an open dining room and bar, with more seating outside on a seasonal terrace beside Route 4.

The short dinner menu ranges widely from jerk chicken with sweet potato puree and wilted greens to cioppino served over linguini with garlic-rubbed crostini. Possibilities include peppered grilled ahi tuna on spicy buckwheat soba noodles, roasted pork loin marinated in juniper berries and cumin, and grilled adobo-rubbed lamb with black bean cakes and plantain fritters.

Starters might be crispy sage leaves with assorted dipping sauces, carpaccio with arugula, parmesan and roasted shallot vinaigrette, and scallops wrapped in smoked salmon with wasabi cream sauce. Among desserts are pear galette with crème anglaise, chocolate ganache with espresso sauce and locally made sorbets.

(802) 457-1917. Entrées, $10.75 to $14.25. Dinner nightly, 5:30 to 9:30.

Bentleys Restaurant, 3 Elm St., Woodstock.

Entrepreneurs David Creech and Bill Deckelbaum Jr. started with a greenhouse and plant store in 1974, installed a soda fountain, expanded with a restaurant catering to every taste at every hour, added a specialty-foods shop, and then developed the colorful Waterman Place with retail stores and a restaurant called FireStones with a wood-fired oven in a 100-year-old house along Route 4 in Quechee.

The flagship of it all is the original Bentleys, a casual, engaging and often noisy spot at the prime corner in Woodstock. Close-together tables are on several levels. Old floor lamps sport fringed shades, windows are framed by lace curtains, the plants are large potted palms, and walls are covered with English prints and an enormous bas-relief.

The menu is interesting as well. For lunch, we enjoyed the specialty French tart, a hot puff pastry filled with vegetables in an egg and cheese custard, and a fluffy quiche with turkey, mushrooms and snow peas, both accompanied by side salads. From the dessert tray came a delicate chocolate mousse cake with layers of meringue, like a torte, served with the good Green Mountain coffee in clear glass cups.

Appetizers, salads, sandwiches and light entrées such as sausage crespolini and cold sliced marinated flank steak make up half the dinner menu. The other side offers more hearty fare from maple-mustard chicken to Jack Daniels steak. With options like these, it's little wonder that Bentleys is always crowded and bustling.

(802) 457-3232. Entrées, $15.95 to $19.50. Lunch daily, 11:30 to 3. Late lunch, 3 to 5. Dinner, 5:30 to 9:30 or 10. Sunday brunch, noon to 3.

Diversions

The sportsman and the sightseer have plenty to do in the Woodstock-Quechee area. You can ski at Suicide Six, not far from Gilbert's farm where Woodstockers installed the nation's first rope tow in 1934, or you can ski at nearby Killington, the East's largest ski area. You can golf at the historic Woodstock Country Club, site of Vermont's first golf course and home also of the fine Woodstock Ski Touring Center, or at a newer golf course in Quechee. You can hike through the Quechee Gorge area or the hundreds of acres of forests maintained by the Woodstock Inn. You can climb a switchback trail up Mount Tom for a bird's-eye view of the area. You can walk around the village green and center, marveling in the architectural variety and browsing through the Dana House Museum of the Woodstock Historical Society. But it is arts, crafts and shopping that make Woodstock so appealing for many.

Arts and Crafts. A sculpture of a man walking five dogs, taken out to the sidewalk every morning, attracts visitors into the spectacular **Stephen Huneck Gallery** at 49 Central St., where the sign says "dogs welcome" on the door. Animals (especially dogs and cats) are the theme of Vermont resident Huneck, one of America's hottest artists, who's known for playful hand-carved furniture, jewelry and sculpture. The smallest pins start at $10 but you could spend up to $30,000. You'll come out of here chuckling and feeling that the world isn't such a bad place, after all.

The Vermont Workshop, 73 Central St., is said to be the oldest gallery in Woodstock, having evolved from a summer workshop established in 1949. Everything from woven mats and interesting lamp shades to wall hangings and cookware is for sale in room after room of great appeal. **North Wind Artisans Gallery** is rather avant garde – we were struck by a papier-mâché flamingo, a mirror shaped like a face with hair on top and big earrings, and a torso of a nude male made of mesh. **Gallery on the Green** shows the works of more than 40 New England artists in six galleries.

Shopping. Check out the pottery depicting fish by Giovanni DeSimone, a student of Picasso, at **Aubergine,** a kitchenware shop, where you might find a thermos full of chocolate-raspberry coffee to sample and some dips to spread on crackers. The **Unicorn** stocks handicrafts and jewelry by New England artisans and some clever games and toys.

The children dressed in flannel shirts sitting outside **The Vermont Flannel Co.** looked so real that we almost spoke to them. You can barely get through the aisles at **Primrose Garden,** there are so many silk flowers spilling from the shelves. We found several nice presents for gardeners here. One of us admired the jewelry and the mini-birch-bark canoes at **Arjuna,** an international store "bearing antiques and adornments from as far away as Sumatra and as near as the Adirondacks." Across Elm Street from each other, **House of Walsh** and **Morgan-Ballou** offer classic apparel for the well-dressed Woodstock woman.

F.H. Gillingham & Co. at 16 Elm St. is the most versatile store of all. Run by the Billings family for over 100 years, it's a general store, but a highly sophisti-cated one – offering everything from specialty foods and wines to hardware – and so popular that it does a land-office mail-order business. Here you'll probably find every Vermont-made dressing, candy, condiment and more. Owner Jireh Swift

Billings's young son represents the ninth generation of the Swift family, dating to the 1600s.

The **Taftsville Country Store,** 155 years old, is an institution in tiny Taftsville, a blip in the road between Woodstock and Quechee. The things most people expect to find in a general store are in back. Up front are all kinds of upscale Vermont foodstuffs, from chutneys to cheddars.

Shops seem to come and go on the three levels of **Waterman Place,** a 100-year-old restored house with a new glass atrium and elevator above Quechee village off Route 4.

Billings Farm & Museum, Route 12 north of Woodstock.

This dairy farm and agricultural museum is an artfully presented display of life-like exhibits portraying the Vermont farm year of 1890. Housed in four interconnected 19th-century buildings on the working Billings Farm, it shows how crops were planted and harvested. Farm life also meant making butter and cider, cutting ice and firewood, sugaring and darning socks, as well as going to school and the general store and participating in community life; such activities are imaginatively shown. Down a path the modern farm is evident. Visitors can see the Jersey herd, calves, sheep, oxen and two teams of Belgian horses, and the milking barn is open. Historic varieties of vegetables and herbs grow in the heirloom kitchen garden.

(802) 457-2355. Open daily 10 to 5, May to late October, Saturday-Sunday 10 to 4 in November and December. Adults, $6.50.

Extra-Special

Simon Pearce, The Mill at Quechee.

Every time we're in the area, we stop at Simon Pearce's magnificent mill, partly because it's all so fascinating and partly because there's always something new. Simon Pearce is the glass blower who left Ireland in 1981 to set up business in the abandoned flannel mill beside the Ottauquechee. The site is inspiring: thundering waterfalls, covered bridge, beautifully restored mill and classic white Vermont houses all around. The interior has a fine restaurant (see Dining Spots) and a handsome shop offering glass, pottery and Irish woolens, all beautifully displayed, plus a second floor with seconds at 30 to 40 percent off, although even then, everything is expensive. Downstairs is a glass-blowing area where you can watch Simon Pearce and eight associates turn out 120 pieces a day, a working pottery, the hydro station with enormous pipes from the river and a steam turbine that provides enough power to light the town of Quechee as well as serve the mill's energy needs (melting sand into glass, firing clay into porcelain and stoneware). "The whole idea was to become self-sufficient and provide an economic model for small business in Vermont," says Simon. The mill is zoned utility in the sub-basement, manufacturing in the basement, retail in the restaurant and shop, office-retail on the second floor and residential on the third, where Simon once lived with his family. The enterprise is growing all the time, opening retail stores (two locations in New York and one in Boston), expanding its production capability with a facility in nearby Windsor and adding ventures (furniture, wooden bowls and brother Stephen Pearce's Irish pottery). We defy anyone not to enjoy, learn – and probably buy.

(802) 295-2711. Open daily, 9 a.m. to 9 p.m. Glass-blowers work weekdays.

The Old Tavern in Grafton is a classic of its genre.

Newfane/Grafton, Vt.

The Essence of Vermont

There's not much to do in Newfane, Grafton and Vermont's surrounding West River Valley. And that's the way the inhabitants like it.

The interstates, the ski areas, the tony four-season destination resorts are some distance away. This is the essence of old Vermont, unspoiled by tourism and contemporary commercial trappings.

The meandering West River creates a narrow valley between the mountains as it descends toward Brattleboro. Along the way are covered bridges (one is the longest in Vermont), country stores, flea markets and a couple of picture-book villages.

The heart of the valley is Newfane, the shire town of Windham County, without so much as a brochure to publicize it. In 1824, Newfane "moved" to the valley from its original site two miles up Newfane hill and now has fewer residents than it had then. The Newfane green is said to be Vermont's most-photographed. Clustered around the green are the white-columned courthouse, the matching Congregational church, the town hall, two famed inns, two country stores and, nearby, some houses – and that's about it.

Upriver is Townshend ("Historic Townshend," one of the area's few tourist brochures calls it), with a larger green and more business activity, though that's relative. Beyond is Jamaica, an up-and-coming hamlet with some good art galleries and gift shops.

And out in the middle of nowhere to the north is Grafton. Preserved by the Windham Foundation, it's the quintessential 19th-century Vermont hamlet where the utility wires have been buried underground and the sophistication of better-known Vermont towns considered quintessential is noticeably absent. Here is a piece of yesteryear, forever preserved for posterity.

There are back roads and country stores to explore, but for many visitors this quiet area's chief blessing is its collection of fine inns and restaurants amidst a setting of Vermont as it used to be.

Guest rooms are in front and restaurant at rear of Four Columns Inn.

Inn Spots

The Four Columns Inn, 230 West St., Box 278, Newfane 05345.

Ever since French chef René Chardain left the Old Newfane Inn to open the Four Columns, this spot has been widely known for outstanding cuisine (see Dining Spots). Under the auspices of subsequent innkeepers, it has become known for comfortable overnight accommodations as well.

Five guest rooms and four suites, all with private baths and most with king or queensize beds, are located in the main columned inn, built in 1830 by General Pardon Kimball for his Southern-born wife as a replica of her girlhood home. Another five rooms and a suite are in the main restaurant building.

All rooms are colorfully decorated with antiques, hooked rugs, handmade afghans and quilts. An 84-year-old craftsman made the canopied four-poster bed in one.

We're especially fond of the third-floor hideaway suite in the front building. Centered by a chimney that divides the room into unusual spaces, it has a canopied bed set into an alcove, a sitting room with a private front porch overlooking the Newfane green, thick beige carpeting and Laura Ashley fabrics.

New owners Gorty and Pam Baldwin from Manhattan, who took over in 1996 for a lifestyle change, have added five gas fireplaces to bring the total in bedrooms to seven.

Room 3, with a four-poster bed, comes with a jacuzzi for two in a marble bathroom that's larger than the bedroom. Room 18 is newly equipped with a gas fireplace, kingsize sleigh bed and a free-standing soaking tub in a corner near the bathroom.

Several common rooms are good for relaxing or watching television, and the pewter-topped bar in the tavern to the rear of the dining room is a popular gathering spot. Beyond is a cozy plant-filled sunroom with a TV/VCR atop an old iron stove.

The longtime breakfast cook prepares a healthy country breakfast buffet, which includes fresh fruits, homemade granola, yogurt, hot oatmeal in winter, apple brown betty, scones and corn muffins. The Baldwins added a choice of an egg dish and french toast in the winter.

The spacious and attractive grounds set back from the Newfane green include a landscaped swimming pool, rock gardens and a trout pond. Beyond are a trout stream and hiking trails up the inn's own little mountain.

(802) 365-7713 or (800) 787-6633. Fax (802) 365-0022. www.fourcolumnsinn.com. Fifteen rooms with private baths. Doubles, $110 to $130. Suites, $140 to $195. Foliage, $210 to $295 MAP. No smoking.

Windham Hill Inn, West Townshend 05359.

Up a steep hill so far off the main road that we had to stop to ask if we were on the right track is this gem of an inn, a speckled brick and white wood structure built in 1825 and distinguished by a suave oval sign and a commanding view of the West River Valley. Grigs and Pat Markham from Connecticut took over a going concern and, with skilled decorating touches and hospitable nuances like small decanters of Harvey's Bristol Cream in each room, have enhanced it as a destination unto itself. "There's not much to do but relax, admire our 160 acres of trees and hills, and enjoy two good meals a day," says Grigs.

Since their arrival, the Markhams have been remodeling bathrooms, adding fireplaces in rooms, and upgrading beds so that all but one room have king or queensize. All eighteen air-conditioned rooms have private baths, telephones and, Pat says, a "pet" on the bed from the Mary Meyer Stuffed Toys factory store in Townshend. But don't be misled. They're furnished with a panache that merited a six-page photo spread in Country Decorating magazine. Since our stay in the rear Tree House (so named because it gives the feeling of being up in the trees), it has gained a Vermont Castings stove and an idyllic deck from which to enjoy the view.

Among the most popular are the five rooms fashioned from nooks and alcoves in the White Barn annex, particularly the two sharing a large deck overlooking the mountains, and the renovated Taft Room with fireplace, bay window and floor-to-ceiling bookshelves. Even these have been upstaged by three deluxe rooms carved out of the former owners' quarters in the south wing. These come with kingsize beds, two armchairs in front of the fireplace, and jacuzzis or soaking tubs.

Not to mention the three extra-spacious rooms added in 1997 in the unfinished third-floor loft of the barn. Now the top-priced accommodations, each has a king

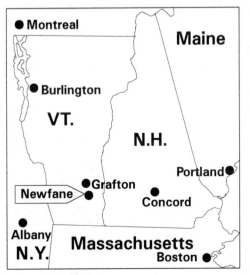

bed, fireplace and private deck facing the mountains. Two have double soaking tubs and the other a double jacuzzi. The one in the middle has a winding staircase up to the cupola with a window seat and a 360-degree view.

The Markhams offer pampering touches, from complimentary juices and Perrier in baskets in each room to candy dishes at bedside and Mother Myrick's chocolates on the pillows at nightly turndown, when small votive candles are lit.

Food is taken seriously at Windham Hill. The Markhams have enlarged their dining room to make more room for the public (see Dining Spots). Overnight guests enjoy a full breakfast served amid a background of taped chamber music, antique silver and crystal. Expect fresh orange juice in champagne flutes, breakfast breads and fresh fruits, and a main dish like waffles, eggs mornay or griddle cakes shaped like little doughnuts, made of winter wheat and cornmeal.

Other rooms at guests' disposal are a new bar room off the living room, another sitting room and a large and sunny game room with windows on three sides. Outside are a heated gunite swimming pool and clay tennis court.

(802) 874-4080 or (800) 944-4080. Fax (802) 874-4702. Eighteen rooms with private baths. Doubles, $245 to $370, MAP; $50 surcharge during foliage and Christmas week. Two-night minimum most weekends. Children over 12. No smoking. Closed first week in November, week before Christmas and month of April.

The Old Tavern, Grafton 05146.

Here is the epitome of an old Vermont inn in the epitome of an old Vermont hamlet. It's located at what passes for Grafton's main intersection, across from the small red brick town hall and down the hill from two white-spired churches. And it's been serving travelers since 1801, when it opened as a tavern on the old Boston to Montreal stage road.

This is no converted inn. It's the real thing – a living museum of the way things were, as preserved and restored starting in 1963 by the nonprofit Windham Foundation, which saved the inn and much of Grafton in a time warp. Staying in the inn's annexes or one its seven houses is "like staying in the beautiful old Vermont house you'd want to buy if you were moving here," in the words of the innkeeper. But the historically accurate ambiance comes with some of today's comforts, at least as far as private baths, Gilbert & Soames toiletries and afternoon tea are concerned.

The guest rooms, authentic to the period, range from cozy and a mite drab through a number of sizable, charming and quite comfortable quarters to the frankly elegant, luxurious hideaways demanded by today's boomers. None would qualify for a spread in a contemporary interiors magazine, let alone an AAA rating. Yet the special character of the place prompted travel connoisseur Andrew Harper to name it a hideaway of the year in the same breath as The Point in New York's Adirondacks and Carmel Valley Ranch in California in 1995.

For a family or group reunion from yesteryear, there may be no better place than the tree-shaded Barrett House, a snow-white, eighteenth-century beauty just across the Townshend Road from the main inn. Guests here enjoy the run of the house, a living room, dining room and kitchen down and four bedrooms with private baths up. Well-worn orientals on wide-plank floors, antiques, original prints, upholstered loveseats and chairs, and fishnet canopy queensize, double and twin beds are the norm as elsewhere. Somewhat more primitive accommodations are found nearby in the Woodard and Tuttle houses, some of which have private hall baths. Among the Woodard's rooms are two sharing a bath and rented as a family suite.

The most elegant quarters are in White Gates, around the corner from the landmark little White Church. It's light and elegant in the Federal style and appears much as it was originally furnished in 1908 by its former owner, Olga Dahlgren, whose name is on a plaque beside the entry. Guests in the four bedrooms here enjoy an enormous living room with fireplace, TV, game table and shelves of books, plus a formal dining room and big kitchen. Eight original Spy prints (part

Swimming pool behind annexes at The Old Tavern is a spring-fed pond.

of the inn's extensive collection by the Vanity Fair artist) line the curving staircase in the two-story-high hall. Upstairs is the bridal suite, the boomers' choice. Here is a handsome room with a queensize fabric canopy bed, a settee and two wing chairs, a writing desk in the window overlooking the stables, and a large and fancy new bathroom with double vanity, jacuzzi tub and separate shower.

Another hideaway is the Hillside Cottage, a half mile up the Middletown Road beside the inn's biggest (eight-room) Johnson House. Here, astride a hill with an endless view, is a two-room retreat with queen canopy bed and a living room with sofabed, TV and phone.

No two rooms are alike, and nearly every one is a favorite with someone among the inn's loyal following, many of whom return year after year to the same quarters. Our favorites would be among the 21 in the connected Homestead and Windham annexes across from the inn, perhaps the elegant rooms with plush chairs and twin canopy beds or twins and a sofabed in the rear overlooking the back lawn and a spring-fed swimming pond. We'd swim, amble about town, catch up on reading in a variety of comfy living rooms or the cozy den and do plenty of nothing, as Grafton addicts are prone to do.

Then we'd mosey across the street to one of the inn's three adjoining dining rooms – the Formal, the intimate and historic Pine Room or the casual skylit Garden Room – for a dinner of trendy Atlantic salmon steamed in an Asian bamboo basket or traditional cheddar and ale soup, New England lobster pie and apple pie with Grafton cheddar. The atmospheric Phelps Barn Pub, with live music on many weekends, would be just the place for a nightcap.

The complimentary continental breakfast the next morning would never do. We'd spring for something like pancakes with real maple syrup to complete this retreat to the good old days.

(802) 843-2231 or (800) 843-1801. Fax (802) 843-2245. Sixty-six rooms with private baths in main inn, two annexes and seven houses. Doubles, $125 to $165 weekends, $105 midweek. Jacuzzi suite and cottage, $250 weekends, $190 midweek. No smoking. Closed late March through April.

Entrées, $18.50 to $23. Lunch daily, noon to 2, Memorial Day through October, weekends rest of year. Dinner nightly, Sunday-Thursday 6:30 to 8:30, Friday-Saturday 6 to 9.

Three Mountain Inn, Route 30, Jamaica 05343.

The aromas of dinner emanating from the kitchen and a wood-paneled living room with a fireplace welcome guests to this charming inn, now encompassing three buildings and offering sixteen guest rooms, a two-room suite with woodburning stove, a honeymoon cottage beside the pool, a small conference center and good meals.

Charles and Elaine Murray took over the old Jamaica Inn with eight rooms in 1978, and have been adding rooms and private baths ever since. Accommodations in the main house vary from a corner room with private balcony and kingsize four-poster bed in shades of green and rose in the new "Wing Up" above a stable to a couple of simple rooms sharing a bath on the first floor. Architect Rodney Williams of the nearby Inn at Sawmill Farm designed the new wing with his trademark barnwood and beamed-ceiling touches, as well as the rear cottage with a queensize bed and a fireplace, perfect for honeymooners.

Next door in the Robinson House are six more guest rooms, one notable for a square bathtub and another that Elaine decorated around a lovely patterned rug. A small living room with a wood stove connects with a bedroom to make a suite. Guests enjoy a large deck out back. Across the street is the Sage House, a once-primitive place that the Murrays upgraded with a redecorated living room, two bedrooms, a kitchen and a whirlpool tub.

An inviting swimming pool is a favorite backyard gathering spot in the summer.

Pecan waffles, french toast, local sausage and eggs, homemade biscuits and blueberry muffins are typical fare at breakfast.

At night, Elaine offers straightforward meals for inn guests and the public in two fireplaced dining rooms dressed with pink and white linens, dainty curtains and ladderback or bow chairs. The handwritten menu changes nightly but retains signature dishes. Favorites among appetizers are tomato-dill soup, country pâté and smoked trout. Guests rave about the seafood or beef kabobs, trout amandine, chicken paprikash and pork tenderloin with red onion confit for main courses.

(802) 874-4140. Fax (802) 874-4745. Sixteen rooms, one suite and one cottage with private baths. Doubles, $130 to $190, MAP. Suite and cottage, $230 MAP. Closed November and April. Children over 6. No smoking.

Entrées, $12.50 to $18.50. Dinner nightly by reservation, 6 to 9.

The Inn at Woodchuck Hill Farm, Woodchuck Hill Road, Grafton 05146.

Without so much as a sign for identification purposes, this out-of-the-way farm complex astride a hill off unpaved Middletown Road has been housing guests since 1968. It was started by antique dealers who ran a shop on the property, but was taken over lately by their son and daughter-in-law, Mark and Marilyn Gabriel, both clinical social workers with an office in Grafton. Accommodations are varied and the feeling laid-back, reflecting the Grafton of old, without the meticulous refinements of the Windham Foundation.

The main floor of the rambling, unassuming white farmhouse holds an atmospheric country dining room with three tables set with woven mats, and a large beamed living room with a window seat, fireplace and well-worn oriental rugs. The living room opens onto a big square porch full of wicker furniture, including a glider swing, and hanging fuschia plants that frame a mountain view into New Hampshire. Beer and wine are available in a lounge or on the porch, where Grafton cheddar cheese and crackers are complimentary.

The largest of eight homey guest rooms here are in the west wing: a new suite with kingsize bed downstairs and, upstairs, a carpeted studio suite with quilt-covered queen bed, small kitchen and a private deck shaded by birch trees. Upstairs in the main house are six more bedrooms. They range from two with twins or a short antique double tester bed sharing a bath to a couple on the third floor with a double or king and an extra bed each and a hall sitting room with a TV.

The prime accommodations are across the road in a small barn. The Barn Residence on the lower floor sleeps up to four in a king-bedded loft with half bath and a large main-floor room with queen sofabed, full kitchen and dining area, TV and wood stove. There's a neat little sitting room in a silo with windows on three sides. Upstairs in another section of the barn is a beamed bedroom with private bath, double cannonball bed and corner fireplace. It can be rented alone or as part of the barn suite, which has two bedrooms, full bath, kitchenette and corner fireplace.

The Spruce Cottage in which Mark's late parents ran an antiques shop was converted in 1997 into a three-bedroom cottage sleeping seven.

The Gabriels serve a full breakfast of the cook's whim, he says. Those quarters with kitchenettes are stocked with the makings for breakfast.

Behind the barn is a small trout pond, complete with a canoe and a gazebo. Beyond in the woods is a wood-fired steam room and sauna.

The Gabriels sometimes close the main house in the winter for lack of use, but otherwise are open year-round.

(802) 843-2398. Five bedrooms and four suites with private baths; two rooms with shared bath; one three-bedroom cottage. Doubles, $110 to $140 with private bath, $89 with shared bath. Suites, $120 to $180. Cottage, $275. Children welcome.

The Inn at South Newfane, Dover Road, HCR 63, Box 57, South Newfane 05351.

What better way to approach a country inn than through a covered bridge? The one we have in mind is in Williamsville, the town next to South Newfane, where the handsome Inn at South Newfane, with its landmark porte cochere, opened in 1984.

The formerly private, turn-of-the century estate is situated at the front of 100 secluded acres. The porch in back is set with garden furniture and beyond are extensive grounds, embracing gardens and a pond for swimming in summer and skating in winter. Hiking and cross-country trails abound, some on the mountain that rises behind the inn. A slope has been cleared for a toboggan run. Croquet, bocce, badminton and horseshoes may be enjoyed on the back lawn.

British chef Neville Cullen and his wife Dawn took over as innkeepers in 1996. They have revived the dining operation (see Dining Spots) and made the overnight accommodations more comfortable. "There's no more 'look but don't touch' atmosphere," says Neville.

An expansive, well-furnished living room with fireplace and antique Estey pump organ and the "Great Room" that is just inside the front door, with shelves of books and an entire section of cookbooks, are available for guests' use. The rear morning room is where the Cullens serve an ample continental breakfast. They bake their scones and sticky buns, squeeze their orange juice and grind their coffee.

Upstairs are six guest rooms with private baths. Of varying sizes, three have queen beds, two have kings and one has twin cannonball beds. Colorful quilts made by "the ladies in the church across the street," floral wallpapers, frilly curtains and period furnishings convey a homey charm. The windowed back room has a bathtub in which, the innkeepers say, you can soak and look out at the birds and trees. French doors from the morning room open onto a wide back porch, furnished with rocking chairs and tables for breakfast, lunch and even dinner on warm evenings. Quiet and tranquil and off the beaten path, the Inn at South Newfane is a good place to relax and read that book you haven't had time for.

(802) 348-7191. Six rooms with private baths. Doubles, $80 to $115. No smoking.

The Old Newfane Inn, Route 30, Newfane 05345.
Built in 1787, this classic New England inn along the green proclaims itself "virtually unchanged for more than 200 years" and proud of it. Even the spectacular banks of vivid phlox outside the entrance have stood the test of time.

For more than twenty years, German chef Eric Weindl and his wife Gundy have run the place in the continental style, with an emphasis on their restaurant (see Dining Spots). Theirs is one of the few area inns we know of requiring a two-night minimum stay any time.

The ten old-fashioned (the Gundys call them quaint) guest rooms upstairs are meticulously clean. Most are furnished with twin beds, pretty floral wallpapers, samplers and wall hangings, wing chairs and rockers. Eight have private baths and one is a suite. Several rooms, which once were part of the ballroom, have gently curved ceilings and access to a side balcony looking onto the green.

Guests enter via a front porch with a lineup of rocking chairs into a lobby whose walls are hung with faded magazine articles touting the inn. Off the entry on one side is a parlor with fireplace, upholstered chairs and sofa. On the other side is a narrow and dark beamed dining room.

A continental breakfast is included in the rates.

(802) 365-4427. Eight rooms and one suite with private baths. Doubles, $115. Suite, $155. Two-night minimum. Closed November to mid-December and April to mid-May.

Green Valley Farm B&B, Auger Hole Road, Box 70, South Newfane 05351.
White Adirondack chairs facing the big side yard await guests at this 200-year-old working farm. Lois and Harold Kvitek share their white, dormered farmhouse with overnight guests in two bedrooms, both with private baths.

One room with twin beds, off an entrance/breezeway, is designed for privacy at one end of the structure. The other bedroom, upstairs in the main house, has a queen bed and a twin bed. The rooms are furnished in what Lois calls country style. "We're very casual," she says. "We try to make people feel at home."

She serves a continental breakfast of juice, fruit and homemade breads and coffee cake. Regular guests – of which this B&B seems to have many – may get treated to more substantial fare that would call for some of the maple syrup produced on the farm. Guests enjoy the animals and barns, walk the logging trails on the 56-acre property and wander down the street to Olallie Daylily Gardens.

(802) 348-7913. Two rooms with private baths. Doubles, $70. No credit cards. Smoking restricted.

Dining Spots

The Four Columns Inn, 250 West St., Newfane.
Beamed timbers from the original barn, a huge fireplace, antiques and folk art contribute to a country elegant look. Add white damask linens and an inventive

Adirondack chairs on side lawn await guests at Green Valley Farm B&B.

menu that changes seasonally and you have one of the premier dining experiences in southern Vermont.

The culinary tradition launched here by René Chardain has been enhanced by chef Gregory Parks, who was sous chef under Chardain.

The dinner menu is supplemented by daily specials. "Greg's an artist," says innkeeper Gorty Baldwin, "so the menu is constantly changing and getting more inventive all the time."

Starters are exotic: perhaps yellowfin tuna tartare with American sturgeon caviar, veal carpaccio, Thai-spiced quail with a watercress and vegetable salad, and a "martini" of hamachi sashimi with wakame and cellophane noodles. The night's soup, "composed daily," could be leek and onion with herbed biscuits or potato and spinach with shrimp and green-chile salsa.

A small green salad precedes the main course. Choices range from herb-stuffed poisson with chardonnay and cardamom sauce to breast of squab with foie gras. Others could be sauté of scallops and shrimp with a Thai lemongrass and coconut broth, pistachio-crusted swordfish fillet with a saffron-citrus sauce, and veal chop with sliced portobellos and truffle sauce.

The dessert repertoire here has long been famous. It might include pumpkin cheesecake, chocolate pâté, raspberry torte, hazelnut layer cake with mocha cream, and homemade sorbets and ice creams. You can stop in the lounge to enjoy one from the cart, even if you haven't dined at the inn.

(802) 365-7713 or (800) 787-6633. Entrées, $21 to $27. Dinner nightly except Tuesday, 6 to 9. No smoking.

Windham Hill Inn, West Townshend 05359.

Five-course dinners of distinction are served nightly to guests and, increasingly, the public, as innkeepers Grigs and Pat Markham expanded their dining operation with a new addition.

Guests gather for drinks and hors d'oeuvres in a new bar off the parlor. Then they adjourn to a dining room dressed in pale pink, with oriental scatter rugs, upholstered chairs at well-spaced tables, and views onto lawns and Frog Pond.

Talented chef Cameron Howard changes her menu seasonally. The meal is prix-fixe ($40), with up to four choices for most courses.

Dinner at our latest visit began with a choice of marinated shiitake mushrooms and parma ham en croustade or a beggar's purse filled with chèvre and grilled vegetables. A pear-leek soup and a salad of mesclun greens with French nut bread followed. An orange sorbet over raspberry sauce cleansed the palate for the main course, a choice of brioche and lemongrass-encrusted red snapper with warm rosemary or grilled medallions of beef tenderloin with horseradish-merlot sauce. Dessert choices included a raspberry-almond tart, a mocha chocolate terrine, a gingered-peach parfait and raspberry-cassis sorbet.

(802) 874-4080 or (800) 944-4080. Prix-fixe, $40. Dinner nightly, 6 to 8:30. Closed first week of November, week before Christmas and month of April.

The Inn at South Newfane, South Newfane.

British chef-innkeeper Neville Cullen mans the kitchen at this inn that has been known for fine dining since the 1980s. Trained under European chefs, he offers a short but wide-ranging menu.

Typical dinner entrées could be pan-seared mahi-mahi with gingered mango chutney, sauté of chicken breast with romano cheese and plum tomatoes, marinated beef tenderloin tips with portobello mushrooms and charbroiled filet mignon with sauce chausseur.

Expect starters like lobster bisque and a spinach and goat cheese tart with roasted red pepper coulis. Desserts at our latest visit included white chocolate mousse, chilled chocolate torte with raspberry and strawberry coulis and an apple-oatmeal crisp with french vanilla ice cream

A few dishes are offered under light fare. The lunch menu includes some of the dinner appetizers and salads, plus a turkey club sandwich and perhaps warm poached salmon with cucumber-yogurt-dill dressing.

Meals are served in a serene, 24-seat dining room with beige walls, sconces, comfortable bow or Queen Anne wing chairs and oil lamps. The napkins are different, each representing a color in the show plates.

(802) 348-7191. Entrées, $13.25 to $19.75. Lunch in season, 11:30 to 2. Dinner nightly, 5:30 to 9, Thursday-Sunday in off-season. No smoking.

The Old Newfane Inn, Route 30, Newfane.

Chef-owner Eric Weindl, who trained in a Swiss hotel, cooks in what he calls the classic French and continental style at this classic New England inn dating to 1787. The food is as predictable as when we first went out of our way to eat here more than two decades ago during a ski trip to Mount Snow – that is to say good, but not exciting.

A few daily specials spark up the enormous printed menu, which remains virtually unchanged over the years and lists most of the standards, ranging from a slice of melon through marinated herring and escargots bourguignonne to Nova Scotia salmon. Capon cordon bleu, duckling à l'orange or with peppercorns, veal goulash, brochette of beef bordelaise, frog's legs provençal, shrimp scampi and pepper steak flamed in brandy are a few of the entrées, accompanied by seasonal vegetables and salad. Châteaubriand "served the proper way" and rack of lamb bouquetière are available for two. Featured desserts include peach melba, Bavarian chocolate cream pie, cherries jubilee and pear hélène.

The decor matches the vision of what tourists think an old New England inn dining room should look like. Narrow and beamed with a wall of windows onto the green, it has white lace curtains, lamps on the window tables, pink and white linens, shiny dark wood floors, floral wallpaper and a massive fireplace.

(802) 365-4427. Entrées, $15.75 to $23.95. Dinner nightly, 6 to 9:30, Sunday 5 to 8:30. Closed November to mid-December and April to mid-May.

Casa del Sol, Main Street, Putney.

For a change of pace and one of the better Mexican meals of your life, try this pure place with refined food and prices from the past. It's run with great charm by Susana Ramsay, the cook from Mexico City, and her husband Richard, an anthropologist from Georgia, whom she met in Peru.

Working in a tiny kitchen, Susana turns out some great dishes, from her tortilla soup to her flan de leche. The tostada sampler, five small tostadas with toppings of tinga, mole, picadillo, cochinita pibil and refried beans, makes a superb lunch for $5.25. The suizas, a chicken casserole with green tomatillo sauce, sour cream and cheese, served with refried beans, would satisfy the heartiest of eaters, as it did one of us. At another visit, we ordered dinner plates of pork tenderloin in salsa verde and pollo en mole rojo and savored every bite. A third time, Susana outdid herself with a fantastic chile en nogada. End with one of Richard's plates of pecan balls, chocolate walnut squares and lemon curd.

The small dining room with a few tables beneath a cathedral ceiling is decorated with fine Mexican crafts (some are for sale in a little gift shop). More seats are at picnic tables in a garden outside. A lazy susan on the table holds five of Susana's homemade salsas, pickled jalapeños, serrano chiles and marinated onions. Bring your own beer or have a bottle of Penafiel, Mexican mineral water.

(802) 387-5318. Entrées, $7.65 to $11.50. Lunch, Tuesday-Sunday 11:30 to 2. Dinner, Tuesday-Sunday 5 to 8, Friday to 9. BYOB.

Diversions

There aren't many diversions – at least of the traditional tourist variety. For those, head for Brattleboro, Wilmington, Weston or Manchester, all within less than an hour's drive. In the West River Valley, you simply relax, hike or drive scenic back roads, and browse through flea markets, crafts shops and country stores.

One of the best selections of custom-made quilts in New England is carried at **Newfane Country Store,** a store chock full of "country things for country folks." Some of the quilts, which represent a local cottage industry, hang outside and beckon passersby in for herbs, jams and jellies, penny candy, maple syrup, sweaters, Christmas ornaments and such.

Other general stores are the **Newfane General Store,** a family-operated grocery store and deli, the **South Newfane General Store** ("experience nostalgia in a working general store and post office"), the **Townshend Corner Store** with a 1949 vintage soda fountain and the **West Townshend Country Store,** a fixture since 1848 with foods, gifts, cookware, old pickle and cracker barrels (would you believe pickled limes?), spruce gum and two-cent penny candy. There's an entire wall of beer steins with family crests in the $10 range.

Newfane's off-the-beaten-path West Street also is home to a couple of unusual, part-time enterprises. New and used books with a New England theme are represented seasonally at **Olde and New New England Books**, located in a barn behind the first frame house (1769) in Newfane. Just beyond, the British flag on the side door of a stark white house identifies **The British Clockmaker,** where antique clocks and music boxes are restored and sold.

Along Route 30 in Townshend, **Lawrence's Smoke Shop** carries maple products and corn-cob smoked bacon, ham and other meat products as well as jellies, honey and fudge, and they'll make up sandwiches. The factory outlet for **Mary Meyer** stuffed toys on Route 30 in Townshend is where doting grandmothers and the objects of their affections can go wild. The **Townshend Furniture Co.** factory has an outlet store with Colonial, country and contemporary pine furniture.

Flea markets seem to pop up all along Route 30. The original Newfane flea market, Vermont's largest now in its 28th year, operates every Saturday and Sunday from May through October one mile north of the Newfane common. The Old Newfane Barn advertises an auction every Saturday at 6:30. The Townshend flea market, beginning at the ungodly hour of 6 a.m. every Sunday, is considered a bit schlocky.

Swimming is extra-special in the Rock River, just off Route 30 up the road to South Newfane. Cars and pickup trucks in a parking area identify the path, a long descent to a series of swimming holes called locally "Indian Love Call," with sections for skinny-dippers, the half-clothed and the clothed. More conventional swimming is available in the West River reservoir behind the Townshend Dam off Route 30 in West Townshend.

Jamaica State Park, off Route 30, Jamaica. This 772-acre park with three hiking trails is considered a godsend for visitors to the area. From the parking area at the park entrance just north of town, an old railroad bed meanders along the bank of the West River for several miles and provides easy walking, jogging or biking. Near the start of the trail is Salmon Hole, with a beach for swimming. Near trail's end, an old switch road branches off along Cobb Brook for another mile. It leads to Hamilton Falls, a 125-foot-long stretch of three pools cascading into each other, so perfect that you'd think it was manmade. Park admission, $1.50.

Extra-Special

Grafton. For some, this postcard-perfect hamlet just north of Windham Hill and the West River Valley is a destination in itself. Off the beaten path, it was put on the map by the Windham Foundation, which was launched in 1963 after the town had gone downhill. More than twenty buildings in town have been restored, including the foundation-owned Old Tavern, and Grafton is recognized today as one of New England's finest 19th-century villages. There are other attractions in this tiny town of 600, where hilly dirt roads pass stately homes, both old and new. We enjoyed watching cheese being made as we bought some Covered Bridge cheddar at the Grafton Village Cheese Co., the foundation-backed cheese factory. Shoppers enjoy the excellent Gallery North Star, the crafts at Grafton Handmade and the seasonal Jud Hartmann Gallery. Also worth a look are the Grafton Village Store, a historical society museum showing area crafts and tools, a demonstration flock of sheep, and some of the marked nature trails at the year-round Grafton Ponds hiking and cross-country ski center. There are two covered bridges, a working blacksmith shop and two landmark churches. As Graftonites proclaim laconically, "there is always nothing to do, plenty of nothing."

West Dover Inn and West Dover Congregational Church are landmarks in center of town.

West Dover, Vt.

Fun Place in the Snow

If it weren't for the late ski pioneer Walter Schoenknecht and his vision for a showy ski resort called Mount Snow, West Dover might still be little more than a stagecoach stop on the back road from Wilmington to who-knows-where. It could have followed the path of Somerset, the sprawling township beyond Mount Snow's North Face, which has one of Vermont's largest lakes and nary a human resident – just the remnants of a ghost town vanished in the wilderness.

Flushed with success from his Mohawk Mountain ski area in northwest Connecticut, Walt Schoenknecht developed something of a skiing Disneyland on a 3,556-foot peak slumbering above West Dover. It had a glitzy gondola, enclosed bubble chairlifts, easy wide slopes and a heated outdoor swimming pool in which people frolicked all winter. Here was the closest major ski and fun resort to Eastern metropolitan areas, and the snow bunnies from the city turned out in droves.

Other ski areas, inns and lodges, restaurants and condos followed, and the boom was on all along the river that gives the Deerfield Valley its name, spilling into adjacent Wilmington. Mount Snow pioneered as a four-season resort with its own Snow Lake Lodge and an eighteen-hole golf course. It now bills itself as New England's mountain-biking capital, and began construction in 1997 of the 203-room Grand Summit Hotel and Conference Center.

Still, winter fun reigns around West Dover, and snowboarding and cross-country skiing are growing faster than the traditional downhill variety. High season is winter. Lodging rates generally are lower in summer, and vary widely depending on weekday or weekend, length of stay and holiday periods.

While Mount Snow has evolved under the ownership of Killington and the American Skiing Co., so has the Deerfield Valley. Inns and restaurants are proliferating as West Dover takes ever more advantage of its place in the sun and snow.

Inn Spots

The Inn at Sawmill Farm, Route 100, Box 367, West Dover 05356.

To hear Ione and Rod Williams tell it, they never planned to live in Vermont, much less run an inn. He was an architect and she an interior designer in New Jersey. On a ski trip to Mount Snow, a blizzardy day forced them off the slopes and into a real-estate office. The agent took them directly to the old Winston Farm they had been admiring for years. "We've never been sure who was more surprised that day when we bought the farm – we or the realtor," the Williamses recall.

That was in 1968. Their creative minds went to work and the idea for an inn evolved. They spent the next few years turning the 1799 columned farmhouse, a dilapidated barn, a wagon shed and other outbuildings on the site of an 18th-century sawmill into an inn that is a model of sophistication and distinction, one that recently was elevated to Relais & Chateaux status.

Not the usual country inn, this – even though it's in the country and is one of the world's most perfect hideaways, as Travel & Leisure magazine once described it. Rod Williams kept elements of the barn (hand-hewn beams. weathered posts, boards and doors) so guests would know they're not in the city. Dining rooms, the small bar, living room, loft room, entry, lobby and corridors to guest rooms all meld together rustic-fashionably and with unfolding fascination.

The twenty guest quarters in the inn, sawmill studios and fireplace cottages are large and comfortable. Our mid-price master bedroom typified the place. Extra-spacious, it had a kingsize bed, a desk-like table and chair, three upholstered chairs in a sitting area around a wood table with a good porcelain reading lamp, two sinks in a dressing area outside the bathroom, a dresser and a large plant in a wooden stand. Wallpaper, upholstery, bedspread and even the shower curtain were in the same country floral print, and the lush green towels matched the thick carpeting. Beyond was a small balcony overlooking the pool.

And then there are the extras: little gold packages of Lake Champlain chocolates in your room, afternoon tea with nut bread and ginger cookies in front of the large brick fireplace in the living room, superb dinners (see Dining Spots), hearty break-

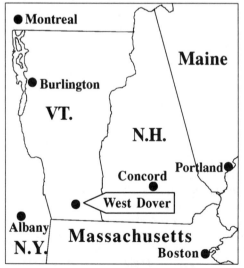

fasts, a sparkling swimming pool, a spring-fed trout pond, a tennis court and the historic part of West Dover just below.

Throughout, rooms are notable for a splashy, 1970s-style decor of color-coordinated fabric and chintz that nearly overwhelms in one room with busy pictures on the walls, but proves more restful in the outlying Spring House and Cider House. The ten cottage suites come with fireplaces and – sign of the times, as Sawmill Farm moves to keep up – five sport new jacuzzi tubs.

In the main inn, the hearth of the cathedral-ceilinged living

Lush plantings provide colorful welcome at entry to Deerhill Inn.

room, festooned with copper pots and utensils, is the focal point for guests who luxuriate on comfortable sofas or wing chairs covered in chintz and read the magazines displayed on a beautiful copper table. Other groupings are near the huge windows that give a perfect view of Mount Snow. The loft room upstairs has more sofas, an entire wall of books and the inn's only television set, which is rarely in use.

Breakfasts are a delight in the sunny greenhouse dining room facing the pool in summer and a flock of chickadees at the bird feeders in winter. You get a choice of all kinds of fruits, oatmeal and fancy egg dishes. We especially liked the baked eggs Portuguese and the eggs Buckingham, the latter an intriguing mix of eggs, sautéed red and green peppers, onion and bacon seasoned with dijon mustard and worcestershire sauce, served atop an English muffin, covered with Vermont cheddar cheese and then baked. What a way to start the day!

(802) 464-8131 or (800) 493-1133. Fax (802) 464-1130. Ten rooms and ten suites with private baths. Rates, MAP. Doubles, $340 to $370. Suites, $390 to $425. Closed April to mid-May.

Deerhill Inn, Valley View Road, Box 136, West Dover 05356.

High on a hill overlooking the valley and the Green Mountains, this rambling, multi-level inn is quiet and comfortable. And ever so eclectic, from the lavish garden décor in the restaurant (see Dining Spots) to the varied styles of the fifteen guest quarters, no two of which are at all alike.

The public rooms were originally decorated by Ione Williams of the Inn at Sawmill Farm, a former innkeeper's aunt, but they bear the unmistakable imprint of new owners Linda and Michael Anelli, well-known local restaurateurs who built the acclaimed Two Tannery Road nearby.

"Art and flowers are my passion," says Linda. The evidence is everywhere. A veritable gallery of local art hangs on the walls of the large first-floor living room, where dinner guests like to gather for cocktails on overstuffed sofas and wing chairs facing a gleaming copper-topped coffee table in front of a massive fieldstone fireplace. More art graces the second-floor living room, which is reserved for inn guests. It has another large brick fireplace, conversation groupings and enormous pillows to sit on. A library alcove with shelves of books and a TV set is at the head of the stairs.

The guest quarters, located in various sections and on different levels, are notable for bright and cheery decor. On a summer visit, we enjoyed one of the front rooms with a long, full-length balcony built by Michael and equipped with wicker rockers for watching the sun set over the mountains. The queen canopy bed was outfitted with fancy sheets and pillows – "one of my things," explained Linda, who switches to flannel sheets in winter. Two armchairs flanked the fireplace, a pastoral mural graced one wall, and bowls of fruit and candy were at hand. Behind was a 20-by-40-foot swimming pool, surrounded by cutting gardens that furnished the bouquets for guest rooms and restaurant tables.

Linda is partial to her cozy Waverly room, named for its decor and winner of Country Inns magazine's annual Room of the Year award in 1996. It has a king bed with a picket-fence headboard, sponge-painted walls and a deck facing the pool. Two rear rooms with vaulted ceilings and kingsize beds open onto private decks. A fan is displayed on the wall and the queen bed has a canopy of mosquito netting in a room with an oriental theme.

Breakfast, available from a full menu, is a culinary treat. Juice and strawberries with cantaloupe, garnished with a pansy, preceded our breakfast: a mushroom and cheese omelet with homefries in one case, a simple poached egg in the other.

(802) 464-3100 or (800) 993-3379. Fax (802) 464-5474. www.deerhill.com. Thirteen rooms and two suites with private baths. Weekends: doubles, $110 to $175, suites $220. Midweek: doubles $95 to $160, suites $205. Holiday periods: doubles, $150 to $215, suites, $260. Add $70 for MAP. Children over 8.

West Dover Inn, Route 100, Box 1208, West Dover 05356.

The area's original country inn began life as a stagecoach stop and tavern in 1846. Recently restored, the good-looking structure with columns outlining front porches on both the first and second floors is a cheerful presence in the heart of West Dover's historic district.

Energetic partners Greg Gramas and Monique Phelan moved here from California in 1996 and gave the establishment a breath of fresh air. Monique wanted to run an inn and Greg, who grew up in Westchester County, was familiar with the area because his family had a condo at Mount Snow.

The inn harbors guest rooms and four suites, all with private baths and TVs hidden in cupboards or armoires. Eight have queen beds, six have fireplaces and the four suites have whirlpool tubs. Expect period furnishings, antiques, light painted walls and floral wallpapers, and whimsical accents like a stuffed koala bear, made by a housekeeper and perched on the bed of the South Suite.

Most in demand are the four suites, which are located in rear sections away from the road. The Haystack and Mount Snow suites in a 1992 addition above the restaurant wing have thick carpeting, queensize brass or poster beds, and sitting rooms with gas fireplaces. They convey a feeling of contemporary luxury, as opposed to the North and South suites upstairs in the original structure, which retain their original wide-board floors and wood-burning fireplaces. Other rooms vary, from a small double with hooked rugs in the old house to an odd-looking family room that resembles a ski dorm, with a lineup of two twin beds and a double. Greg's favorite is the light and airy front room with double and twin bed opening onto the second-story porch.

He and Monique were about to refurbish the large main-floor common room at our visit. They already had redone the restaurant, "simplifying the former hodge-podge" (Greg's words) in the main dining room, the cozy tavern and the sunny rear breakfast room. The last is the site for an ample breakfast. Greg cooks eggs any style plus a choice of french toast or pancakes.

(802) 464-5207. Fax (802) 464-2173. Eight rooms and four suites with private baths. Summer: doubles $80 to $120, suites $125 to $135. Winter: doubles $90 to $150, suites $150 to $200. Children over 8. Closed most of May and first two weeks of November.

Trail's End, 5 Trail's End Lane, Wilmington 05363.

Tucked beneath towering pines off a quiet country road, Trail's End is an architecturally interesting blend of ski lodge and inn with thirteen guest rooms and two suites, all with private baths.

The centerpiece is the striking living room/dining room area, with soaring windows sloping up and outward, a cathedral ceiling, a gigantic stone fireplace, two stories of stone walls and an unusual wall of cistern wheels that must be seen to be believed. Against the windows is a lineup of built-in sofas, capable, no doubt, of seating half the house. Above is a ramp crossing to a corner loft television area overlooking the whole scene.

The low-ceilinged dining room has three large round tables, plus a smaller dining room for those who like privacy.

The heart of the house is the open kitchen, where new owners Debby and Kevin Stephens from Boston's North Shore, skiers both, prepare a full breakfast of the guest's choice. "We just finished serving 30 people homemade granola, eggs any style, belgian waffles and french toast," Kevin said one winter weekend. Since it was their first season, they had not yet found time to ski.

Scouring the East Coast to buy an inn in a year-round resort area, they took over what Kevin called "an incredibly solid business" from founding innkeepers Mary and Bill Kilburn, who moved to a smaller B&B in West Barnstable on Cape Cod. They planned few changes, other than perhaps adding a pub in a large, rustic fieldstone-floored room with books, games and bumper pool.

Over the years, the accommodations have been upgraded to the point where the innkeepers called them "picture-perfect in sophisticated country style," each done in a different color scheme and furnished with antiques. Each has a queen bed or a double and twin bed. Four with fireplaces also have TV.

Occupants of the two skylit fireplace suites seldom leave their quarters. Each has a queensize canopy bed, a bathroom with oversize whirlpool tub, a wet bar area with mini-refrigerator and microwave, a sitting area with small TV and a stone fireplace, and a sunken sitting room with a day bed. The one we liked added a second bathroom and a private outdoor deck.

The ten acres of grounds are most appealing with a heated swimming pool, a stocked trout pond, a hidden tennis court and beautiful English gardens.

(802) 464-2727 or (800) 859-2585. Thirteen rooms and two suites. Summer: doubles $95 to $115, suites $145. Winter: doubles, $115 to $145, suites $175. Two-night minimum weekends. Children welcome. No smoking.

Shield Inn, Route 100, Box 366, West Dover 05356.

They wanted to move from "the big city" (no, not New York – Boston and Washington) to run an inn. But Phyllis and Lou Isaacson had an unusual criterion.

Pianist Phyllis Isaacson and husband Lou host frequent concerts in living room at Shield Inn.

They needed a living room big enough to accommodate their seven-foot Steinway grand piano *and* an audience. They found it 1994 in the Shield Inn, a twelve-bedroom lodge screened from the road by evergreen trees.

Phyllis, a concert pianist and conductor who performed in college with the Boston Pops, found the inn's long living room – open to a smaller living room at one end and an area for dining at the other – an ideal setting for entertaining. She gathers visiting musicians around the piano and sets up folding chairs in rows for weekend jazz and chamber music concerts. Concerts are free to guests, $10 for the public, and are followed by a reception. "It's literally chamber music," Phyllis says. "The audience is right there, sometimes sitting as close as two feet from the performers.

Music, obviously, is the theme that sets this inn apart. Phyllis organized the Shield Inn Jazz Combo, lends her talents to a variety of musical endeavors in the area, is in demand for local functions and was invited to conduct the Vermont All-State high school chorus. But the music at the inn is scheduled and no background music is piped into the guest rooms. Phyllis, aghast at the thought, says people "come here for peace and quiet." They might hear her practicing in off hours, she concedes.

Phyllis and Lou, a retired engineer-chemist, are hardly one-track innkeepers, however. Both cook and like to entertain, and she has redecorated the inn with flair and an eye to guests' comfort.

Five guest rooms are in the original section of the house, built as a lodge in 1959. Six rooms and a suite are in a three-story wing added in 1991 by the previous owners. All have private baths and TVs, some hidden in cupboards. Seven have working fireplaces, and four have jacuzzis. Queen or king beds, comfortable chairs and floral fabrics abound. So do surprises, among them a jacuzzi tub in a 1959-style bathroom off a rear bedroom with a queensize bed and a sofabed, and a spacious end bedroom dramatic in black and pink, even in the bathroom. But none is more surprising than the two-room suite on the lower level with a queen bed, sofa and rocking chair in one room and a queen sofabed and rollaway cot in the other. Both rooms have TVs and there are not one but two bathrooms, one a raised affair with a paneled jacuzzi tub for two.

Lou does most of the cooking for breakfast, which could be omelets or seasonal pancakes – blueberry, of course, but also pumpkin or apple and even M&Ms. Phyllis pitches in at dinner, served in winter. A four-course meal, included in the rates, yields soup, salad, entrée and dessert on Monday, Tuesday, Thursday and Saturday nights.

The Isaacsons' passion for food also shows up in the loose-leaf notebook they put out in one of their several common areas. It's categorized by individual restaurants, and guests write their candid experiences at each. Some reports are quite at odds with their predecessors. "It makes for very interesting reading," Phyllis says slyly.

(802) 464-3984. Fax (802) 464-5322. Eleven rooms and one suite with private baths. April-November: doubles, $90 to $150 B&B. December-March: $140 to $200 MAP. Children over 10. No smoking.

Doveberry Inn, Route 100, West Dover 05356.
The former Tollhouse bed-and-breakfast establishment has been upgraded into this inn with a good restaurant and eight comfortable guest rooms.

Some of the guest rooms, all with private baths and TV/VCRs, convey a contemporary air. A few have skylights and one luxury suite adds a kingsize bed, a private deck and a sitting area with TV. The spacious East Room contains a queensize and a double bed, and, at our fall visit, had a basket of apples. A typical smaller double has two cat pillows on the chairs, floral curtains matching the wallpaper (which also covers the ceiling) and a bathroom with copper in the sink and shower. Young owners Michael and Christine Fayette are gradually redecorating the rooms. At our latest visit they had redone one in yellow and blue Laura Ashley decor.

Overstuffed dark blue sofas and armchairs are grouped around the open brick hearth that warms the large common room. Tea and cookies are served here in the afternoon.

Overnight guests order a complimentary breakfast from a full menu. Choices range from belgian waffles to eggs benedict with a crab cake.

(802) 464-5652 or (800) 722-3204. Fax (802) 464-6229. Eight rooms with private baths. Summer: doubles, $75 to $90 weekends, $68 to $85 midweek. Winter: doubles $110 to $145 weekends, $90 to $125 midweek.

The Nutmeg Inn, 153 Route 9, Box 818, Wilmington 05363.
Originally a 1770s farmhouse with a connecting carriage house and barn, this – like so many others in the area – was restored into a small ski lodge in 1957. Over the years it evolved into an authentic country inn of immense appeal: jacuzzis and woodburning fireplaces in guest quarters, gourmet breakfasts and afternoon treats, charming common rooms and a meandering layout that separates rooms into secluded retreats.

David and Pat Cerchio from Glastonbury, Conn., took over a going concern in 1996 and added embellishments. David, a former international consultant, likes to cook and went to the Cambridge School of Culinary Arts to specialize in baking. His loaves of peasant bread, fancy breakfast dishes and exotic tarts make eating here a pleasure.

Pat devotes her attention on the rooms, gradually lightening up and enhancing the décor. Early results showed in a side suite she redid in the French country look with queensize bed, oriental scatter rugs on a shiny southern white pine floor,

The Nutmeg Inn occupies 18th-century farmhouse with connecting carriage house and barn.

good reading lamps, an updated bathroom with tiled double jacuzzi, pedestal sink and solid brass fixtures. Waverly floral fabrics dress up a deluxe kingsize bedroom in front with a corner fireplace.

Altogether, ten rooms and four suites are clustered off four separate staircases in different parts of the house, providing unusual privacy. Although the front rooms are close to the highway, double-thick walls and insulation ensure quiet. All rooms have private baths, king or queen beds, air conditioning, telephones and TVs. Ten have working fireplaces or stoves. The most prized are the aforementioned queen suite and a deluxe rear suite with kingsize poster bed, skylit cathedral ceiling and spacious rear balcony overlooking the hillside.

David has his own starter for the breads he bakes every couple of days. Featured in 1997 at the Vermont Food and Wine Festival at Stratton, they turn up for breakfast. Samples of the day's French country sourdough and multi-grain loaves made us yearn for some of his other treats, among them tarts with apricots and almond cream or black mission figs and marsala wine. Breakfast could be a choice of eggs any way (with truffles on holidays) or wild blueberry-almond pancakes (strawberry romanoff pancakes on holidays). The meal is taken in any of three small dining rooms with round oak tables and ladderback chairs. A potbelly stove warms one and French impressionist paintings another.

Chocolate-chip cookies and tarts accompany beverages in the afternoon in a large beamed living room with fireplace and expansive BYOB wet bar. Given his cooking orientation, David was planning to offer prix-fixe dinners for house guests on Saturdays in winter.

(802) 464-3351 or (800) 277-5402. Fax (802) 464-7331. Ten rooms and four suites with private baths. Summer: doubles $78 to $120, suites $135 to $175. Winter: doubles $88 to $160, suites $150 to $215. Two-night minimum weekends. No smoking.

The Inn at Quail Run, 106 Smith Road, Wilmington 05363.
Young innkeepers Bob and Lorin Streim from Manhattan took over this inn in 1997 and refurbished it from top to bottom. That translates to new carpeting, paint and wallpaper, light floral print fabrics, furniture and accessories – even a green plant for every room. To prove the point, Bob left a bit of the "hideous green" wall paint on the light switch in the sitting room of his prized suite, now papered in red florals – "so people can see the changes we've made." They bill theirs as the "new" Inn at Quail Run, to distinguish it from its recent past.

The Streims offer ten rooms off a long corridor in the main house, four with king beds (the rest queensize) and four with gas fireplaces. One, a two-room suite, has a sitting room with small gas stove and TV/VCR and a bedroom with a queen bed. Three other bedrooms, two with king beds, are located in a house at the side.

Out in the country on fifteen acres, the large white house stands out with its purple shutters and silver roof. In back is a nicely landscaped, stone-lined free-form swimming pool, whose form took shape as Bob reconstructed it. The surrounding patio, framing a great view of Mount Snow and flanked by smart-looking lounge chairs, is a fine place to hang out on a summer day.

Inside, the large living room looking onto the pool is furnished with overstuffed chairs and sofas. Birds, chipmunks and squirrels at the feeders outside the long flagstone and glass-walled breakfast porch mesmerize guests, who also may watch the resident red fox trot by in search of breakfast. Also available for guests are a BYOB lounge with television and, downstairs, a larger television room with sofas, recent videos and a ping-pong table. Nearby is an eight-person sauna.

"We're child and pet friendly," stresses Lorin, a former lawyer who handles the business end of the inn and tends to their two infant children.

Bob, a chef who trained at Peter Kumps School of Culinary Arts in New York, is known for his gourmet breakfast. Banana-walnut pancakes and tomato-mozzarella-basil omelets are specialties. His special maple bacon or sausage, home fries and blueberry, cranberry-nut and corn muffins accompany.

The meal, cooked to order, is served from 8 to 10. Snacks and cocoa or lemonade are offered in the afternoon.

(802) 464-3362 or (800) 343-7227. Fourteen rooms and one suite with private baths. Summer: doubles, $105 weekends, $90 midweek. Winter: $125 weekends, $105 midweek. Fireplaces $10 additional; suite, $25 additional. Children and pets welcome. No smoking.

The Red Shutter Inn, West Main Street (Route 9), Box 636, Wilmington 05363.

Nestled on a hillside on the western side of Wilmington, this is best known for its restaurant, which is open to the public and attracts a loyal following. New owners Renée and Tad Lyon from Baltimore retained the chef and concentrated their resources on enhancing the accommodations, amenities and hospitality.

Upstairs in the main house, dating to 1894, are five guest rooms with queen or kingsize beds. The Lyons recently installed the inn's second jacuzzi tub in the newly tiled bath of the front Deerfield Room, the inn's smallest. That makes it nearly as popular as the wonderful Joseph Courtemanche Suite in back. The latter has a cathedral-ceilinged living room with a fireplace, TV and sofabed, full-length windows opening onto a private deck overlooking the hillside, and a bedroom with a queensize brass bed.

Also popular are the four rooms in the reborn carriage house, especially the fireplaced Molly Stark Suite with queensize bed, sitting room with loveseat and armchair, and a bathroom with two-person jacuzzi beneath a skylight. A vintage radio here is juxtaposed beside a new color TV.

Guests partake of a hearty breakfast cooked by Renée, perhaps western omelet with bacon or blueberry pancakes with sausage. They share a front common room and a cozy pub with dinner guests.

(802) 464-3768 or (800) 845-7548. Seven rooms and two suites with private baths. Summer: doubles $100 to $110, suites $135. Winter: doubles $105 to $125; suites $175. Children over 12. Closed April and early May.

The Hermitage, Coldbrook Road, Box 457, Wilmington 05363.

Nestled into a hill overlooking the Haystack Mountain ski area stands an 18th-century farmhouse that once was the home of the editor of the Social Register, the blue book for blue-blood society. Today it's the nucleus of an unusual inn, restaurant (see Dining Spots) and enough other enterprises to stagger the imagination.

"Please do not ask if you may bring your pets," the room confirmation card warns. Any doubts as to why are dispelled as you near the inn at the end of a dirt road. You hear the quacking of ducks and the squawking of geese. Off to the side is the liveliest group of gamebirds you ever saw. You can ogle the inn's peacocks and English setters, try your hand at fishing in the trout pond, cross-country ski at a large touring center, see the results of a vast maple-syrup operation, view the innkeeper's collections of decoys and paintings, and examine some of the bottles that comprise the largest wine list of any New England restaurant in the inn's wine and gift shop. A large banquet addition that also triples the size of the wine cellar provides space to show off a huge collection of wooden decoys and 200 lithographs from three artists, among them the largest hanging group of French artist Michel Delacroix. A 1997 addition doubled the size of the bar – always a focal point here – and made the main dining room roomier.

The Hermitage is the restaurant-turned-inn-turned-showcase of owner Jim McGovern, a man of many talents and interests. He pursues most of them 18 hours a day through the changing seasons on his 24-acre property. Part of the Hermitage experience is to wander the grounds, viewing the maple-sugar shed in which the innkeeper also produces more than 10,000 jars of preserves and the outdoor pens with as many as 60 different species of gamebirds, which are for sale and which also turn up on the lunch and dinner menus.

The scene is busy and the lodging almost seems an adjunct to all the other goings-on. The fifteen guest rooms in the main inn, the converted carriage house and the new Wine House have private baths, TVs, telephones and working fireplaces. Rooms are generally large and modern, individually decorated and furnished with antiques. The quality of housekeeping varies. In the Wine House, where pictures of ducks grace the small parlor, one room has a heavy carved bed with chenille spread, fringed curtains and a tiny sofa. Another has old wood and leather rockers in front of the fireplace. The carriage house with four guest rooms comes with its own living room and sauna.

A choice of eggs, omelets, pancakes and the like is offered at breakfast. All the maple syrup and preserves come, of course, from the Hermitage enterprises.

Brookbound Inn, the Hermitage's adjunct a mile down the road, conveys a ski-lodge atmosphere through and through. Ten of its fourteen paneled rooms have private baths and are pleasantly if spartanly furnished in a cross between country-inn and ski-lodge style. The attractive grounds astride a hill off Coldbrook Road contain a swimming pool and tennis court. Guests here have continental breakfast.

Jim McGovern considers the Hermitage an extension of his home and an expression of his hobbies. His eight-page inn brochure asks rhetorically: "Where else would one also find under one roof the breeding and training of English setter dogs...all with names like Cognac, Burgundy and Yquem. They're assistant inn-keepers and will be here to join in welcoming you and making you feel at home."

No cuddly inn cats or feminine frills here. It's eclectic, sporty and, yes, offbeat.

(802) 464-3511. Fax (802) 464-2688. Twenty-five rooms with private baths and four rooms with shared bath. Doubles, $225 to $250, MAP. Brookbound, $130 to $195 MAP.

Dining Spots

Deerhill Inn & Restaurant, Valley View Road, West Dover.
Fellow innkeepers and their guests generally consider this the best restaurant in the area, and some consider it among the best anywhere. It's well deserved praise for owners Michael and Linda Anelli, who earlier launched the Two Tannery Road Restaurant nearby.

Linda's passion for art and flowers shows up in two colorful dining rooms in the country garden style. There's a lot to look at, from a garden mural and floral paintings to ivy and tiny white lights twined all around.

Chef Michael's fare is contemporary continental-American. Our nicely paced dinner began with potato and leek soup and a portobello mushroom stuffed with lobster and crab. A good mixed salad followed. Entrées range from grilled chicken with white beans and peppers to black peppered sirloin steak. Wiener schnitzel and roast duckling are among the favorites. The sliced grilled leg of lamb with a wedge of saga blue cheese and the five-layer veal with roasted red pepper sauce were exceptional. A Forest Glen merlot accompanied from what Linda called "our NAFTA wine list." A marked departure from the famous wine cellars of two nearby establishments, it is totally North and South American – from Chile to Virginia to Oregon – and pleasantly priced in the teens and twenties.

Desserts were a refreshing lemon mousse parfait and peanut-butter/banana ice cream in a decorated pastry shell.

(802) 464-3100 or (800) 993-3379. Entrées, $18.50 to $24. Dinner nightly except Tuesday, 6 to 9:30.

The Inn at Sawmill Farm, Route 100, West Dover.
The food served up by engineer-turned-chef Brill Williams, son of founding innkeepers Rodney and Ione Williams, is worthy of the magnificent setting they created.

The three attractive, candlelit dining rooms display the owners' collection of folk art. The main room has white beams, theorem and oil paintings, rose and ivory wallpaper (even on the ceiling), a lovely china cabinet and tables set with white linens, heavy silver and pretty floral china. We like best the adjacent Greenhouse Room, a colorful plant-filled oasis.

The menu is larger and appears more dated – shrimp in beer batter, lobster savannah, breast of pheasant forestière, roast duck with bigarade sauce – than one might expect, with many favorites remaining year after year. But Brill Williams is not resting on reputation. For starters, we liked the thinly sliced raw prime sirloin with a shallot and mustard sauce, and the sauté of chicken livers with onion brioche and quail egg. Next came delicate green salads and a basket of good hot rolls and crisp, homemade melba toast. Entrées range from Indonesian curried chicken breasts to grilled venison au poivre served on a crouton with duxelle of wild mushroom. We found outstanding both the rabbit stew and the sweetbreads chasseur garnished with french-fried parsley.

Desserts are grand. Fresh coconut cake, apple tart with hard sauce, chocolate whiskey cake with grand marnier sauce and bananas Romanoff were among the choices at our visit. The espresso is strong, and better-than-usual decaffeinated coffee is served in a silver pot.

The inn's wine cellar, which Brill says he has developed "more as a hobby than a business," has been ranked one of the top 100 in America by Wine Spectator. Prices start in the twenties and rise sharply, but you can find any number of rare treats for a splurge.

(802) 464-8131 or (800) 493-1133. Entrées, $27 to $35. Dinner nightly by reservation, 6 to 9. Jackets requested. Closed April to mid-May.

Two Tannery Road, 2 Tannery Road, West Dover.

The first frame house in the town of Dover has quite a history. Built in the late 1700s, it became the summer home in the early 1900s of President Theodore Roosevelt's son and daughter-in-law. In the early 1940s it was moved to its present location, the site of a former sawmill and tannery. It became the first lodge for nearby Mount Snow and finally a restaurant in 1982.

Along the way it has been transformed into a place of great attractiveness, especially the main Garden Room with its vaulted ceiling, a many-windowed space so filled with plants and so open that you almost don't know where the inside ends and the outside begins. A pleasant lounge contains part of the original bar from the Waldorf-Astoria.

Longtime chef Brian Reynolds has spiced up the continental/American fare with starters like Acadian pepper shrimp, grilled cajun steak tips and Thai chicken satay. We enjoyed the garlicky frog's legs as well as the duck livers with onions in a terrific sauce.

Fourteen entrées plus nightly specials range from three chicken dishes to filet mignon with choice of sauces. Veal is a specialty, so we tried veal granonico in a basil sauce as well as grilled New Mexican chicken with chiles, herbs and special salsa, accompanied by a goodly array of vegetables – broccoli, carrots, parsley and boiled new potatoes in one case, rice pilaf in the other.

A four-layer grand marnier cake with strawberries – enough for two to share – testified to the kitchen's prowess with desserts.

(802) 464-2707. Entrées, $18.50 to $24.50. Dinner, Tuesday-Sunday 6 to 10.

Doveberry Inn, Route 100, West Dover.

Good northern Italian fare is offered here by young chef-owner Michael Fayette, who trained at Paul Smith's College in New York and 21 Federal in Nantucket, and his wife Christine, the baker. They have added a wine bar in the common room, and attract the public for dessert and cappuccino as well as dinner.

Thirty diners are seated in a two-part, beamed room at tables covered with handmade quilt overcloths that change with the seasons. The menu changes weekly. Typical starters include lobster ravioli, grilled shrimp with homemade gnocchi tossed with garlic and sage, and the evening's bruschetta. Main courses vary from grilled halibut over mascarpone polenta and rare grilled tuna over grilled vegetables to wood-grilled veal chop with wild mushrooms. Sautéed rabbit with apples, figs and dried cranberries is a seasonal treat.

Christine might prepare zuccota cake, mascarpone cheesecake, a plum napoleon and cannolis for dessert.

(802) 464-5652 or (800) 722-3204. Entrées, $18.50 to $28. Dinner nightly except Tuesday, 6 to 9.

Gregory's, Route 100, West Dover.

The restaurant at the West Dover Inn, bearing the name of co-owner Greg Gramas,

Northern Italian food is hallmark of chef-owned Doveberry Inn.

was earning accolades under new chef Dawn Hastings. It's a pleasant space with a cozy lounge and a paneled dining room with the requisite casual country look, white over blue cloths, flickering oil lamps and fresh flowers.

The short contemporary menu is supplemented by blackboard specials – the night we were there: cream of mushroom and roasted garlic soup, an appetizer of salmon quesadilla with boursin and jack cheeses, and grilled salmon fillet with lobster beurre blanc. Typical entrées are shrimp-stuffed phyllo triangles, honey-hoisin glazed duck, Jamaican jerk-spiced pork tenderloin and grilled black angus sirloin steak with a gorgonzola and caramelized onion cream sauce.

(802) 464-7264. Dinner, Thursday-Monday 6 to 9:30 in foliage and winter, Thursday-Saturday rest of year. Closed most of May and first two weeks of November.

Le Petit Chef, Route 100, Wilmington.

The outside of this low white 1850 farmhouse smack up against the road to Mount Snow looks deceptively small. The inside houses three intimate dining rooms, a spacious lobby abloom with spring flowers in midwinter and a veritable gallery of art work, plus an inviting lounge.

Chef-owner Betty Hillman, whose mother Libby is the cookbook author, studied in France and her formerly classic menu has become more contemporary of late. Appetizers include a tomato and goat cheese tart, roulade of smoked salmon with salmon caviar, and ragoût of escargots and shiitake mushrooms. Typical main dishes are fillet of salmon baked in a horseradish crust on a bed of mashed potatoes, a crab cake with confetti shrimp on a julienne of vegetables bordered by a Mexican corn sauce, free-range chicken roasted with garlic and lemon grass, filet of beef with a five-pepper sauce and noisettes of venison with sundried cherry sauce.

Homemade lemon sorbet and ice creams, fresh fruit tarts, apple cake, crunchy meringue and chocolate torte are among desserts.

(802) 464-8437. Entrées, $19.50 to $25. Dinner nightly except Tuesday, 6 to 9 or 10.

The Red Shutter Inn, West Main Street (Route 9), Wilmington.

Chef Graham Gill from London, who trained in Europe in the French style and whose good food we sampled earlier when he was at the Doveberry Inn, has made his mark in the dining room at the Red Shutter. So much so that despite Renée Lyon's background as a commercial chef, she and her husband Tad were not about to change chefs when they bought the inn. The pine-paneled main dining room is appropriately Vermonty. A canopied deck offers al fresco dining in front.

The blackboard menu lists about a dozen entrées, ranging from chicken chasseur to lamb tenderloin richelieu. Among the possibilities might be striped bass with ginger and sesame sauce, baked salmon with horseradish crust, pork tenderloin with sage and apples, veal orloff and Long Island duck with raspberry sauce.

Appetizers might be cream of broccoli and cheddar soup, escargots with wild mushrooms and smoked mozzarella ravioli. Homey desserts include apple crisp and maple-pecan pie, both with ice cream, and berry cobblers.

(802) 464-3768 or (800) 845-7548. Entrées, $16 to $22.50. Dinner, Tuesday-Sunday 6 to 9, mid-May to mid-October; Wednesday-Saturday rest of year. Closed Easter to mid-May.

The Hermitage, Coldbrook Road, Wilmington.

The dinner menu at the Hermitage rarely changes. It doesn't have to. Innkeeper Jim McGovern, one of whose talents is cooking, specializes in gamebirds that he raises on the inn's property. He also is a connoisseur of wines.

In season, lunch and brunch are served outside on a marble patio or inside in a recently expanded front dining room lightened up with cream-colored walls and gold-over-white tablecloths. Beyond the smoky, expanded bar is a large rear dining room generally used for functions. Upholstered and wing chairs flank widely spaced tables set with white linens and blue overcloths, fresh flowers, white china and heavy silver. Walls are covered with the "naif" prints of Michel Delacroix, and hand-carved decoys are everywhere.

The extensive dinner menu is basically variations on a shrimp, trout, veal and beef theme. You can get boneless trout, scampi, chicken amandine or wiener schnitzel. But who wouldn't opt for the nightly "homeraised gamebird" specials – perhaps pheasant, quail, duck, goose or, one time we visited, partridge?

As you dine, Jim McGovern may table-hop, chatting about his gamebirds or the Wine Spectator grand award-winning cellar, now containing more than 2,000 labels, remarkable for their quality and variety.

For Sunday brunch, we sampled the mushroom soup with a rich game pâté on toast triangles plus a house specialty, four mushroom caps stuffed with caviar and garnished with a pimento slice and chopped raw onion on a bed of ruby lettuce. The chicken salad was an ample plateful colorfully surrounded by sliced oranges, apples, green melon, strawberries, grapes and tomatoes on a bed of bibb lettuce. The portions were large enough that we could not be tempted by such desserts as a hot Indian pudding, a maple parfait made with Hermitage syrup or fresh strawberries on homemade shortcake.

(802) 464-3511. Entrées, $14 to $25. Dinner nightly, 5 to 11. Sunday brunch, 11 to 2.

Julie's Café, Route 100, West Dover.

Since Julie's is one of the few places where you can have lunch in the area, we're happy to report that it is worth the stop. It's small, but in summer you can eat on a deck in front by the road or on an enclosed deck in back beside a stream. Inside, skylights make the place bright and cheery, especially in the small, brick-floored front room.

The selection of salads and sandwiches is interesting (try the grilled chicken or the ground porterhouse burger, served on focaccia rolls).

At night, choices run from wood-fired pizzas to enchiladas, with an emphasis on pastas and vegetarian fare. Julie's signature dish blends chicken, olives, sundried tomatoes, artichoke hearts, garlic and white wine over chile pasta. Grilled salmon with salsa pesto and maple-glazed baby back ribs are the most expensive items. Each comes with a house salad.

(802) 464-2078. Entrées, $10.95 to $16.95. Lunch and dinner daily except Wednesday, 11 to 9 or 10. Sunday brunch, 10 to 2.

Diversions

Skiing. Mount Snow virtually put West Dover on the map and remains the stellar attraction today. Long known as a great beginners' area and a lively place for après-ski (with the stress on après more than ski), it nonetheless has always appealed to us for its wide-open, almost effortless intermediate skiing. Since founder-showman Walter Schoenknecht sold to the business types from Killington (now the American Skiing Co. behemoth), Mount Snow has been upgraded in terms of snowmaking and lift capacity. Gone is the heated swimming pool; more emphasis is on the North Face, a challenging area for advanced skiers, blessedly away from the crowds. Accessible from Mount Snow is the former **Carinthia** ski area, a low-key place that has been upgraded for beginners, intermediates and families. Now any skier can find his place – and space – at Mount Snow. **Haystack,** a smaller mountain (1,400-foot vertical, compared with Mount Snow's 1,900), is connected with Mount Snow by a free shuttle. In 1997, the new owners poured $24 million into Mount Snow/Haystack, the Grand Summit Hotel and Conference Center, but some went toward five new lifts, including the world's longest "magic carpet," a 400-foot-long surface lift moving people in the base and hotel area. Mount Snow now claims five mountain areas and the most lifts in the East.

Cross-Country Skiing. Where skiers gather, cross-country is usually available, too. So it is with the Deerfield Valley, which has three major touring centers. The **Hermitage Touring Center,** run by the Hermitage inn, has 50 kilometers of groomed trails next to Haystack. It is part of the rugged Ridge Trail, a five-mile-long mountaintop touring trail that winds up and down four peaks between Haystack and Mount Snow. **Timber Creek Cross Country Ski Center** offers a meandering, groomed trail system across from Mount Snow. The **White House Ski Touring Center,** run by the White House Inn in Wilmington, has fourteen miles of trails through woods and hills east of Wilmington.

Other Seasons. Two of Vermont's largest lakes are close at hand for boating, fishing and swimming: Somerset Reservoir in the wilderness northwest of Mount Snow and Harriman Reservoir/Lake Whitingham south of Wilmington. Golf is available at the eighteen-hole Mount Snow Country Club and the eighteen-hole Haystack championship course, plus the par-three, eighteen-hole Sitzmark Golf Course. Special events are scheduled throughout the summer and fall.

Transportation. For those who want to get around without wheels, ride **the MOOver,** the Deerfield Valley's community-sponsored shuttle system inaugurated in 1997. A free bus makes stops at more than 30 points along Route 100 between Mount Snow, West Dover and Wilmington. In the making is the five-mile **Valley Trail,** a state-funded pedestrian and bicycle pathway connecting the center of West Dover with Mount Snow. With an impressive **mountain biking center** and the country's first mountain bike school, Mount Snow claims to be the mountain bike capital of the East.

Southern Vermont Natural History Museum, Route 9, Marlboro.
This little-known attraction began as the collection of Luman Range Nelson, a noted taxidermist. More than 500 birds in 80 dioramas represent one of the largest collections of mounted birds in New England.
(802) 464-0048. Open daily 9 to 5, Memorial Day through October. Winter hours vary. Donation, $2.

Shopping. West Dover is little more than a hamlet with some landmark structures that make up what one innkeeper says is an emerging "Historic Mile." Most of the shopping opportunities are down the valley in Wilmington, where there are fascinating shops. The usual ski clothing boutiques abound, of course, and more trendy little shopping clusters open along Route 100 almost every year.

Hayloft Gallery claims the most eclectic display of fine art in Vermont, including an outdoor gallery of architectural artifacts around gardens and a pool. **Partridge Feathers** at Tollgate Village is where chef Brill Williams of The Inn at Saw Mill Farm hangs his hat by day. It's an exceptional pottery, glassware, furniture and woodenware shop carrying a few choice and expensive lines by Vermont artisans. **Swe Den Nor Ltd.** offers Scandinavian furniture, accessories and gifts. **The Cupola Ski & Bike Shop** and **Equipe Sport** are leading sports outfitters.

Taddingers is an expansive country store with seven unusual shops under one roof, including Orvis, a Christmas room and all kinds of antiques and accessories. We're partial to the Vermont specialty foods section, the Wilcox Ice Cream parlor and the Nature Room full of more kinds of birdhouses than we thought existed.

Wilmington is home to good gift shops, among them **For All Occasions, The Incurable Romantic** and **The Eclectic Eye.**

Extra-Special

The Marlboro Music Festival, Marlboro.
Popular with West Dover visitors is the summer tradition at Marlboro College in nearby Marlboro, where chamber music concerts are presented each weekend from mid-July to mid-August. The music school was founded in 1952 by pianist Rudolf Serkin. Considered to be the nation's best chamber music series, the concerts by 70 festival players are incidental to their studies. Tickets usually are sold out by spring, but seats may be available on the screened porch outside the 650-seat concert hall. For advance tickets, contact Marlboro Music Festival, 135 South 18th St., Philadelphia, Pa. 19103; after June 6, Marlboro Music Festival, Marlboro 05344, (802) 254-2394.

Lake Sunapee is quiet in early morning in this view from Scenic Three Mile Loop.

Sunapee Region, N.H.

The Lure of the Lakes

The fortuitous combination of lakes, mountains and meadows makes the Sunapee Region a choice year-round attraction, especially for the sportsman and those who are drawn to the water.

Lake Sunapee, New Hampshire's third largest, and its neighbors, Little Sunapee and Pleasant Lake, provide varied water pleasures within view of Mount Kearsarge, central New Hampshire's highest peak, and Mount Sunapee, a state park and ski area. In between on the rolling flatlands are four golf courses and two tennis clubs.

So it comes as no surprise that historic New London, the largest village in the region (year-round population, 3,200, but swelled by second-home residents, tourists and students at Colby-Sawyer College), is a mecca for the affluent. Its hilltop setting with posh contemporary homes, country clubs and trendy shops casts an unmistakable aura of prosperity. Legend has it that the song made famous by Kate Smith, "When the Moon Comes Over the Mountain," was written by a Colby-Sawyer student as she watched it rise above Mount Kearsarge.

Little Sunapee and Pleasant lakes, hidden from the tourists' path, are happily unspoiled. Some of the Lake Sunapee shoreline is surprisingly undeveloped as well, and old Sunapee Harbor – the heart of the lakes resort region – looks not unlike a cove transplanted from the coast of upper Maine.

The area's inns, many of which have been around a while, reflect the solitude and variety of the region.

Inn Spots

Dexter's Inn & Tennis Club, 150 Stagecoach Road, Sunapee 03782.

Its facilities and location a mile or so up a country lane, high above Lake Sunapee, make this self-contained small resort a retreat for sports enthusiasts as well as those seeking peace and quiet.

The main house, painted a pale yellow, was built in 1801, extensively remodeled in 1930 and converted into an inn in 1948. Longtime innkeeper Frank Simpson turned over the reins to his son-in-law and daughter, Michael and Holly Simpson Durfor, but still lives next door and retains the title of innkeeper emeritus. It was he who added "Tennis Club" to the name in 1973. Tennis buffs have use of three all-weather courts, with a tennis pro and tennis shop at hand, "and we've never heard of anyone who didn't get enough court time," Frank says proudly.

Tennis players – and others, for this is by no means exclusively a tennis resort – can cool off in the attractive swimming pool. The twenty-acre property offers shuffleboard, croquet and a horseshoe pit. The sports theme continues inside the large barn recreation room, with bumper pool and ping-pong tables.

The main inn has a living room full of chintz and walls of books, a pine-paneled lounge with games, fireplace and an alcove for TV, and a small gift shop. Particularly appealing is the screened porch with more chintz and wicker, a ceiling painted with red and white stripes, and tables covered with blue cloths.

All ten guest rooms in the main inn and seven in the annex have private baths. Each is decorated in vivid colors coordinated with the striking wallpapers. The front rooms afford glimpses of the lake in the distance. Rooms in the annex and barn have high ceilings; two have queensize canopy beds, another has sliding doors leading to a patio, and all are bright and cheery.

The newest lodging is in the Holly House Cottage, a two-bedroom, two-bath house that belonged to a grandmother in the family and contains a living room, kitchen and porch. Claiming the best views on the property and quickest access to the tennis courts, it's available for up to six people.

Coffee and juice are served in the bedrooms (and you could have your whole breakfast there), but most guests gather near the bay window in the dining room for a view of the lake and order, perhaps, eggs benedict or Michael's innovation, Dex-Mex omelets with salsa and cheese.

Dinners are table d'hôte, the price depending on the choice of entrée. A soup like chilled melon or a prize-winning clam chowder starts the meal, followed by a salad of tossed greens or kidney beans. Menu entrées like swordfish steak, chicken piccata, veal marsala, filet mignon and lamb chops are supplemented by such

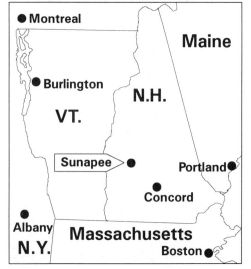

specials as poached salmon with hollandaise, scallops in cheese and white wine, rosemary haddock and brandied chicken with sauté of apples and walnuts. Dessert could be killer kahlua mousse or chilled butterscotch pecan pie.

(603) 763-5571 or (800) 232-5571. Seventeen rooms and one cottage with private baths. Doubles, $135 to $175, MAP. B&B $110 to $150, available only May-June and September-October. Cottage, $380; $1,200 weekly without meals. Children and pets welcome. Smoking restricted. Closed November-April.

Entrées, $15 to $18.50. Dinner by reservation, nightly except Tuesday 6:30 to 8.

Dexter's Inn & Tennis Club occupies house dating to 1801.

The Rosewood Country Inn, 67 Pleasant View Road, Bradford 03221.
    Electric candles are lighted in the windows of this expansive, rose-trimmed beige building that comes as a beacon for visitors arriving after a roundabout ride on back roads west of Bradford. The inviting facade is a sign of things to come. Inside this new B&B fashioned from an old summer resort is a stylish, comfortable place that's quite unexpected out here, seemingly in the middle of nowhere.
    Rhode Island transplants Lesley and Dick Marquis opened in 1992 after a year's worth of renovations to the abandoned Pleasant View Farm, once a summer resort accommodating 100 guests, including the likes of Jack London, Mary Pickford, Charlie Chaplin and the Gish sisters. "This was a nightmare," recalled Lesley, showing photos of the neglected interior.
    You'd never guess today. The Marquises and their contractor transformed the center section of the structure from head to toe, creating five spacious, handsomely appointed common rooms on the main floor and seven bedrooms with private baths upstairs. Lesley stenciled the intricate rose design that flows atop the walls from room to room, coordinating with changing fabrics and styles of window treatments along the way. The decor is handsome in rose colors in the formal living room and its arched annex. The side tavern room with TV and potbelly stove is bright and airy in the California style. In the center of the structure is an enormous dining room, big enough for a restaurant, with seven tables set for the inn's "candlelight and crystal" breakfast. Beyond the dining room is an open guest kitchen, family room and gift shop, all opening onto a broad deck overlooking the inn's twelve rolling acres of woods and fields.
    Upstairs, the comfortable bedrooms are nicely decorated in a range of styles with painted walls, stenciling and coordinated fabrics. Roses and grapevines twine around the canopy above the queensize bed in the bridal suite, where a wicker loveseat is cosseted in a corner turret. Ivy paisley fabrics are featured in an adjacent, more masculine room with queensize bed. An angled double bed is dressed in gold and black in a Victorian-style room in back. Sturbridge and Williamsburg are the respective themes of two third-floor Colonial rooms. Whimsical accents abound, from a little white dress hanging in the bridal suite to gloves resting on a table in the Victorian room to a bed warmer perched on the bed in the Williamsburg room.

Breakfast is served in the dining room, on the porches or the rear deck. A fruit course (at our visit, peaches with raspberries and vanilla yogurt) and pastries (perhaps cinnamon swirl muffins) come first. The main event could be a breakfast quiche or french toast with strawberry-maple syrup (made by a neighbor from maple trees on the inn's property). The signature dish is oven-baked cinnamon-apple pancakes with cider sauce.

Their first phase a success, the Marquises renovated one side of the building into a function room. In 1998, they added five suites with fireplaces above the function room. All have king or queensize beds. The bathrooms in two have double jacuzzis and the rest have five-foot-wide, double-headed showers for two.

(603) 938-5253 or (800) 938-5273. Seven rooms and five suites with private baths. Doubles, $69 to $85. Suites, $99 to $150. Two-night minimum weekends. Children over 10. No smoking.

Follansbee Inn on Kezar Lake, Route 114, Box 92, North Sutton 03260.

"Welcome to the Follansbee Inn – a great place to relax and enjoy a slower pace of living," greeted the sign at the porch entry to this rambling old inn fronting on Kezar Lake. And on a blackboard underneath: "Today's saying: Swallowing your pride occasionally will never give you indigestion."

Such are the distinctive touches that imbue the Follansbee with plenty of personality. A big place with a hotel-style main floor and 23 guest rooms, it seems smaller and is much more friendly than a hotel, thanks to innkeepers Sandy and Dick Reilein. Thus it is not unrealistic for Sandy to say that theirs is "like the country home you've always wanted to have – with none of the work." They do it, seemingly effortlessly, for you.

And with a church beside, a cemetery behind and a lake in front, the setting is classic rural New England.

Outgoing hosts who are apt to join arriving guests for a late-afternoon swim, they share the work in summer with their youngest son Matthew, a college student. He checks in guests, helps with luggage and tends to the waterfront with his lively English springer spaniel Samantha. Between food preparation and making small talk during cocktails in the living room, the Reileins can be counted on to bring out tray of munchies to those seeking solitude on the porch.

Off a second-floor hall full of antiques are eleven guest rooms with private baths, all spruced up with Eisenhart Vintage wallpapers, new mattresses, carpeting, large towels and bayberry soap made specially for the inn. Our corner room overlooking the lake had good cross-ventilation, a must on a sultry night. The third floor has twelve more bedrooms with shared baths.

Where the Follansbee once thrived on numbers, the Reileins stress intimacy and conviviality. They downsized the operation, closed the restaurant to the public and made the inn totally non-smoking. That last move has increased business, says Dick, a former IBM executive. "In our own small way, we feel we are helping people to live a healthier life style."

The homey main floor has a cozy sitting room paneled in barnwood and furnished with patchwork cushions, baskets and all kinds of games, and a large front parlor, more formal but most comfortable. It opens onto a dining room, where breakfast is with fresh fruit and Sandy's homemade granola and features an entrée such french toast, puffed apple pancake, egg soufflé or a choice of omelets.

night, Sandy occasionally cooks an optional, all-you-can eat dinner for groups.

Linda and Brian MacKenzie promote the dining experience at The Inn at Pleasant Lake.

Besides partaking of the Reileins' hospitality, guests enjoy peaceful Kezar Lake, where Matthew's armada now includes a sailboard, rowboat, canoe and paddle boat, and 500 wooded acres for hiking and cross-country skiing.

(603) 927-4221 or (800) 626-4221. www.follansbeeinn.com. Eleven rooms with private baths and twelve rooms with shared baths. Doubles, $75 to $105. Children over 10 welcome. No smoking. Closed part of April and November.

The Inn at Pleasant Lake, 125 Pleasant St., Box 1030, New London 03257.
Young Mississippi guy meets Connecticut gal at ski resort in Colorado. He trains at Culinary Institute of America. He cooks and she learns front office at top-rated inn in Virginia. Together they purchase old country inn in the state where she had summered with her parents.

Worldly beyond their years, Brian and Linda MacKenzie turned up in 1997 at the area's oldest operating inn, built in 1790 as a Cape farmhouse and converted in 1878 into a summer resort. They changed the name (from Pleasant Lake Inn), added a high-end guest room, offered a formal afternoon tea and a dining experience like that they'd understudied at Clifton, a top-rated inn in Charlottesville, Va., and lent youthful enthusiasm to an inn in need of a new lease on life.

The setting is super, down a long hill north out of New London at the end of Pleasant Lake. From the front windows and from the beach across the road, you look down the lake toward Mount Kearsarge at the far end.

The MacKenzies upsized some of the beds in eleven guest rooms on the second and third floors, all pleasantly furnished with country antiques and some with Laura Ashley accents. They saved the best for their new guest room, fashioned from the former innkeepers' quarters on the third floor. Here, with a fine lake view, are a queen bed and a day bed, plus a jacuzzi tub. Another good lake view is offered from a two-room suite with king bed, twin bed and sitting area.

The couple also instituted afternoon tea in the style of Clifton. Served on the

ardens mark entrance to New London Inn.

flagstone porch overlooking the lake, this is no ordinary tea. Besides the
'll get juices, fruit, a sampling of sweets and fancy imported cheeses and

inner time, chef Brian – who, except for a dishwasher, handles the kitchen
glehandedly – emerges toward the end of the cocktail reception to describe
g's dinner menu. Guests adjourn to the main dining room for a meal to
(see Dining Spots).
back in the kitchen in the morning to prepare a full country breakfast for
ter the preliminaries, guests can expect a hot entrée, perhaps poached
mushroom béchamel sauce and sausage or pecan and blueberry baked
st with bacon.
*-6271 or (800) 626-4907. Fax (603) 526-4111. Eleven rooms and one suite
baths. Doubles, $95 to $145. Suite, $145. Two-night minimum summer*
o smoking.

Farm Inn, Route 11, Box 1053, New London 03257.
Kathryn Joseph got their feet wet at a small B&B in Sutton Mills before
open a larger, full-service country inn east of New London. They took
some, 1836 center-chimney Colonial residence, of which they are only
wners, and spent five months renovating prior to opening. They now
e little restaurant (see Dining Spots), five bedrooms with private baths
ng antiques business.
it staircase and leading off rambling halls are the well-spaced bed-
lsomely decorated by Kathryn, who had been in the window design
erything in the guest rooms is carefully color-coordinated, from dust
lows to balloon shades on the windows. She used picture framing to
ead of the double bed in the Cabbage Patch Room. The rear Southport
ked out in white and blue Laura Ashley prints. The largest room is the

Wauwinet, with a queensize poster bed – it's named after an area in Nantucket, "where we were married," Kathryn advises. It comes with a handsome leather reading chair and a wicker rocker, and a pedestal sink in the modern bath.

Guests enjoy a spacious new common room with a vaulted ceiling on the second floor. Fashioned from an attic, it contains an antique pool table, games and a TV set. There's also a cozy front parlor shared with outside guests arriving for dinner.

A full breakfast includes fruit, muffins and a main dish, perhaps frittata, eggs or pancakes flavored with orange juice, blueberries or toasted walnuts.

In the carriage house beside the main house is Colonial Farm Antiques, where twelve dealers show their wares.

(603) 526-6121 or (800) 805-8504. Five rooms with private baths. Doubles, $95 to $110. Two-night minimum peak weekends. No smoking.

New London Inn, 140 Main St., Box 8, New London 03257.

This village inn next to the Colby-Sawyer College campus has been around since 1792, and was showing its age when Kim and Terence O'Mahoney from northern California arrived on the scene in mid-1996.

Taking over a going concern, the O'Mahoneys had no experience but considerable enthusiasm as they became resident owner/innkeepers. "I'd never run a bank before I started one in California," said British-born Terry, by way of dismissing his lack of background. He traded the bank president's role for one of hands-on innkeeping.

The first year the O'Mahoneys orchestrated the redecoration of eight of the inn's 27 guest rooms, with eight more scheduled to be done in 1998. Looking rather staid, even tired, the last time we'd seen them, the refurbished rooms appeared refreshed with queen or king beds, wicker furnishings, hooked rugs on freshly painted floors and tile-floored bathrooms with pedestal sinks. Choicest are the larger corner rooms (one of which accommodated Ronald Reagan when he campaigned in the New Hampshire primary). Mini-print and sprigged wallpapers, brass and spool beds, decoys and tin wall sconces characterize the remaining rooms, which come in various sizes and configurations. They retain a spare country look, many with double beds and only a single chair.

From a front porch stretching the width of the second floor, guests can view the passing scene and get a bird's-eye view of some of the award-winning gardens below.

Returning Colby-Sawyer and Dartmouth alums are surprised by the refurbished main floor, with a new entrance lobby, gracious parlors and a relocated tavern. The previous owners – for whom the restaurant took priority – redid the kitchen to allow for a bigger dining area near the fireplace, only to open up the fireplace and discover it was fake. Undaunted, they built one with 200-year-old bricks from the foundation.

Breakfast is expanded continental, with pastries and bagels obtained from a nearby bakery.

(603) 526-2791 or (800) 526-2791. Fax (603) 526-2749. Twenty-seven rooms with private baths. Doubles, $90 to $140. Two-night minimum in summer, fall and major college weekends. No smoking. Closed parts of April and November.

Hide-Away Inn, Twin Lake Villa Road, Box 1249, New London 03257.

This establishment gained a wide reputation as a restaurant under former owners Wolf and Lilli Heinberg. Subsequent owners tried to continue the restaurant and then closed it to focus on the accommodations. New owners Ginger and Roger Redifer revived the restaurant operation in 1996. Amazingly, they offer three meals a day, a schedule that keeps Ginger in the kitchen and Roger busy seating diners and tending bar.

The lodge-style structure, whose walls are paneled in Oregon fir, is outfitted with sturdy maple furniture and a few antiques. Upstairs are seven simple guest rooms with private baths, some in the hallways. Two have king/twin beds. One with a queen brass bed and windows on three sides is particularly popular. All the rooms are homey and retain their lodgey look and feeling.

Guests share the spacious entry parlor, which has a great stone fireplace, with waiting diners. A smaller common room is available on the side. The main gathering spot is the downstairs Pipedream Lounge, with a bar, game tables, a dart board and plenty of sofas and chairs for lounging around a TV/VCR. The wine cellar off the lounge is used for wine tastings.

Guests order breakfast from an extensive menu that draws the public.

The inn has an autographed copy of *Collected Poems* by Grace Litchfield, which turned up in nearby Potter Place. Signed "Hide-Away, New London," it is one of the prized works of the poet-author for whom the lodge was built as a hideaway in the 1930s.

(603) 526-4861 or (800) 457-0589. Seven rooms with private baths. Doubles, $85. Children welcome.

The Shaker Inn at the Great Stone Dwelling, Route 4A, Enfield 03748.

One of the most famous Shaker structures ever built, this six-story granite edifice was scheduled for reopening as an inn and restaurant in 1998. It had that use for a short period in the early 1990s, but the effort failed in the recession and lay dormant until 1997 when it went up for auction.

Threatened with the possible use as an orphanage, the small Museum at Lower Shaker Village on the property managed to raise enough money to buy the property. The building was leased to Don Leavitt and Rick Miller of Historic Inns of New England, owners of the Red Hill Inn in Holderness (see Squam Lakes chapter).

They were reopening the 1841 building as the centerpiece of the once-thriving, 330-member Shaker community in Enfield. The upper floors of what was then the largest building north of Boston have 24 spacious, high-ceilinged guest rooms, each with private bath. Most are in the original large sleeping rooms used by the Shakers and retain their original Shaker detailing, including built-in cabinets and shelves, peg boards on the walls and wood window shutters. The rooms were being furnished in new Shaker-style furniture, with many pieces based on original Enfield Shaker designs.

The original Shaker dining room was reopened as a restaurant – a status we experienced to good advantage earlier in the decade under the previous inn ownership. The plan was to serve "upscale American gourmet cuisine" based on Shaker cooking traditions. Inn guests are served a full breakfast in the restaurant.

The partners were working closely with the museum to develop programs, tours and exhibits about Shaker history. They planned special workshops on Shaker crafts, music and cooking on winter and spring weekends. The museum planned to conduct guided tours through the Great Stone Dwelling.

Inn guests have access to a beach along Lake Mascoma in back. A 2,000-acre nature preserve with paths for walking and cross-country skiing is across the road.

Rooms and meals are available at landmark Shaker Inn at the Great Stone Dwelling.

The inn also leased the beautiful Mary Keane Chapel, a remnant of the onetime La Sallette seminary that succeeded the Shakers on the property, for use as a wedding facility.

(603) 632-7810. Twenty-four rooms with private baths. Doubles, $85 to $145.

Dining Spots

The Inn at Pleasant Lake, 125 Pleasant St., New London.

Taking his cue from the Virginia country inn where he was sous chef, Brian MacKenzie is transplanting a successful upscale Southern formula up north.

"I like Craig's style," Brian says, referring to his mentor, chef-innkeeper Craig Hartman at Clifton, whose meals and inn experience have been among the highlights of our travels. The Clifton style is not unique, but it is delivered to perfection and with nuances rarely attempted, let along achieved, elsewhere.

Here, the style begins during the 6:15 cocktail reception. In chef's whites, Brian emerges from the kitchen to detail the evening's five-course, prix-fixe menu – which sounds simple but requires a bit of showmanship not to bore one's captives to tears. Dinner is served at 7 in a 40-seat dining room, where well spaced tables are set with white linens and crystal.

The night of our visit, the meal began with potage lyonnaise with chive oil and romano croustades, a salad of organic baby greens with roasted pinenuts and a sherried mango vinaigrette, and Italian bread with whipped butter. A raspberry sorbet with fresh kiwi prepared the palate for the main course, a choice of pan-seared swordfish with a marchand du vin sauce or roasted angus tenderloin with a chasseur sauce and basil pesto. Dessert was a dark chocolate terrine with two sauces and fresh raspberries.

The next night produced a choice of grilled wahoo with a citrus vinaigrette and roasted eggplant relish or baron of bison roulade with bordelaise sauce and an exotic mushroom duxelle. Dessert was cheesecake with a raspberry coulis, one of Brian's few departures from a chocolate theme.

(603) 526-6271 or (800) 626-4907. Prix-fixe, $40. Dinner nightly except Tuesday at 7.

La Meridiana, Route 11 at Old Winslow Road, Wilmot.
You can tell there's a culinary master in the kitchen of this old, rambling farmhouse, its dining room entered via a long corridor running the length of the building. A collection of Italian cookbooks is on display in the hall, and the wine list bears many interesting Italian vintages at prices mainly in the teens. You may hear chef-owner Piero Canuto singing arias in the kitchen. When he makes his rounds after dinner, he'll show you pictures of his hometown in northern Italy.

Peter makes most of his own pastas and encourages sharing of dishes at no extra cost. "Our menu is designed for you to choose as much or as little as your appetite allows." Prices are so low as not to be believed.

Start with crostini with chicken livers, squid salad, hot or cold antipasto or, the highest-priced appetizer, carpaccio ($4.95). Most entrées are in the $8 to $10 range, and veal chop baked with mushrooms and fontina cheese tops the price list at $15.95. When did you last see sautéed trout, calves liver, chicken cacciatore or pork cutlets for $8.95 or less in a top restaurant? Entrées come with fresh vegetable and potato of the day.

The menu is supplemented by many specials, among them osso buco and lamb casserole at our visit. People come especially for the rack of lamb, we were advised.

Desserts might be pumpkin pudding with mascarpone cheese, chocolate mousse cake, frozen chocolate soufflé and tirami su.

The candlelit dining room is country Italian with posts and hand-hewn beams, attractive hanging lights, handsome oak chairs with round backs at white linened tables, fresh flowers and a fieldstone fireplace.

(603) 526-2033. Entrées, $6.95 to $15.95. Lunch in season, Monday-Saturday 11:30 to 1:30. Dinner nightly, 5 to 9. Sunday, brunch 11:30 to 1:30, dinner 3 to 8.

Colonial Farm Inn, Route 11, New London.
Bob and Kathryn Joseph learned to cook at a small B&B in Sutton Mills before opening this small inn and restaurant. Their impressive center-chimney Colonial holds two fireplaced dining rooms seating a total of 30. The candlelit rooms have the requisite beamed ceilings and wide-plank floors, and are done in warm salmon and platinum colors, from the walls to the table linens to the china. Lately, Bob built a new screened dining porch in the rear. With five tables, it is quite elegant and graced with oriental rugs on the floors.

Bob, who does the lion's share of the cooking, offers four starters: on a typical night, a sampler of pâtés and terrines, wild mushroom soup, eggplant bruschetta and the signature house salad, a mix of red and green leaf lettuces tossed with dijon dressing and sprinkled with toasted walnuts and blue cheese. The house specialty is tenderloin of beef sautéed with burgundy-shallot sauce. Other main courses could be grilled swordfish with a compound butter of basil, ginger and lime; venison medallions served with a cranberry compote, and veal rib chop with a rosemary compound butter. Potatoes au gratin and carrots glazed with honey and brandy might accompany.

Desserts include apple-raspberry pie, homemade profiteroles with vanilla ice

Candlelight dinners as well as guest rooms are offered at Colonial Farm Inn.

cream and bittersweet chocolate sauce, and chocolate pâté with ground almonds and strawberry puree. Port and stilton are available after dinner.

(603) 526-6121 or (800) 805-8504. Entrées, $14.50 to $20. Dinner by reservation, Wednesday-Saturday 6 to 8:30 or 9.

New London Inn, Main Street, New London.
This inn's serene dining room, with its windows yielding full-length views of the colorful gardens outside, offered a couple of the best meals of our travels in years past. It's been downscaled in reach and price by new owners Kim and Terance O'Mahoney, but the ambiance remains and the food is considered quite good.

Their chef offers a short menu of contemporary New England fare. Typical main courses are baked Alaskan salmon with a brown sugar-lemon sauce, New England lobster cakes with horseradish-tomato cream, roast duckling with wild berry sauce and loin lamb chop with mint sauce. Starters include specialty soups "from simmering stockpots," smoked salmon mousse with melba toast, a wild mushroom, ham and oyster tart, and – a novel one, representative of the chef's occasional flair – escargots with garlic nutmeg butter on a hard roll.

The airy room is pretty in white and green. The pale green wallpaper is flecked with white peacocks and well-spaced tables are set with mint green-over-white cloths.

(603) 526-2791 or (800) 526-2791. Entrées, $10 to $16. Dinner, Monday-Saturday 5:30 to 9.

Hide-Away Inn, Twin Lake Villa Road, New London.
"An old friend is back in town," advertises this oldtimer. And so it is. After a lengthy hiatus, new owners Ginger and Roger Redifer revived the restaurant that founding owners Wolf and Lilli Heinberg made famous.

The fare is not the world-class caliber that prompted us once to drive two hours from Hartford for dinner. But locals applaud both the food and the prices, and were packing into three small dining rooms and a newly enclosed wraparound dining porch at our latest visit.

Ginger oversees the kitchen, which turns out wide-ranging fare. Dinner dishes range from swordfish en brochette, herb-roasted orange salmon and lobster fettuccine to apple-pecan chicken, pork chops and veal marsala.

There's an emphasis on soups (creamy cucumber, french onion, lobster bisque) and salads (citrus and avocado, spinach waldorf, mozzarella and tomato) on the dinner menu. Other starters include chicken satay, duck liver pâté and "oyster rockefeller prepared in the Hide-Away tradition." Desserts could be black forest cake, oreo ice cream pie, Bailey's chocolate parfait and lemon sorbet.

(603) 526-4861 or (800) 457-0589. Entrées, $8.95 to $14.95. Breakfast daily 8 to 11. Lunch, 11:30 to 3. Dinner, 5 to 9. Lounge with light fare until 1. Closed Tuesday for lunch and dinner, Labor Day to Memorial Day.

The Anchorage, Garnet Street, Sunapee Harbor.

Jaunty window treatments and artworks lit by track lighting give a fresh look to the old Anchorage. They are highlights of a total renovation undertaken by Jeffrey and Rose Follansbee, who helped make the New London Inn a mecca for fine dining.

Here they have a total of 140 seats in a couple of dining rooms, the rear bar and outside on an expansive deck right beside the water. Besides sprucing up the long and narrow main room with deep green booths and yellow walls, they've upscaled the menu from its traditional beer and sandwich days. Jeff oversees the cooking, featuring soups, salads, specialty sandwiches, fresh seafood and steaks – "pretty basic stuff and accessible to a broad clientele." Dinner entrées include seafood linguini diablo, grilled seafood brochette, broiled rainbow trout with sundried tomato pesto, barbecued chicken, sirloin steak and Yankee pot roast.

(603) 763-3334. Entrées, $7.99 to $11.99. Lunch daily, 11:30 to 4. Dinner, 4 to 9 or 10. Closed Monday and Tuesday in off-season. Open Memorial Day to Columbus Day.

Millstone Restaurant, Newport Road, New London.

A lofty cathedral ceiling with skylights lends an airy feel to this casually elegant place that is popular with the Colby-Sawyer College crowd. Owned by Tom Mills, it has a pleasant, canopied brick terrace for dining in the summer. Inside are well-spaced tables covered with linens.

Main courses on the large and varied dinner menu run the gamut from quite a variety of pasta dishes and Bavarian schnitzel to roast duckling, loin lamb chops, filet mignon with béarnaise sauce and New Zealand venison with juniper-coriander sauce.

Among appetizers are baked brie with almond herb crust, stuffed mushrooms gratinée and hummus served with Syrian bread points. Desserts include profiteroles au chocolat, marble cheesecake, chocolate mousse pie and maple crème caramel.

(603) 526-4201. Entrées, $11.95 to $18.95. Lunch daily, 11:30 to 2:30. Dinner nightly, from 5:30. Sunday brunch, 11 to 2:30. No smoking.

Gourmet Garden, 127 Main St., New London.

A specialty-foods shop par excellence ("give a gift of good taste with a local flavor"), this deli-bakery-cafe run by Sarah and Michael Cave also puts up great salads and sandwiches to eat in or take out. Curried chicken with water chestnuts and tortellini with artichoke hearts and turkey are two of the salad favorites. Smoked turkey or ham, tuna or chicken salad and pâté sandwiches are in the $4.75 range.

This is the place for a real continental breakfast: espresso, cappuccino or latte with a choice of pastries from the full bakery. The cafe has seats inside, plus more outside in season on a garden patio.

Gift boxes contain all kinds of New Hampshire goodies.

(603) 526-6656. Open Monday-Saturday, 7 to 5:30.

Diversions

Cultural Offerings. Since 1933, the **New London Barn Players,** New Hampshire's longest operating summer theater, have presented matinee and nightly performances of musicals and comedies from mid-June to Labor Day at the Barn Playhouse, 209 Main St., (603) 526-4631 or 526-6710. **Summer Music Associates,** (603) 526-8750, presents a series of concerts in the New London Town Hall or in the Sawyer Center Auditorium at Colby-Sawyer College. Band concerts are scheduled summer Wednesdays at 7 at the bandstand in Sunapee Harbor and Fridays at 7 at the Haddad Memorial Bandstand in New London.

Despite its generally low-key flavor, the area bustles during the League of New Hampshire Craftsmen's annual crafts fair, the nation's oldest, which attracts 1,500 craftsmen and 50,000 visitors for a week in August to Mount Sunapee State Park.

Mount Sunapee State Park, Route 103, Mt. Sunapee. A 700-foot-long beach is great for swimming in the crystal-clear waters of Lake Sunapee. Across the road is the 2,700-foot high Mount Sunapee, crisscrossed with hiking, mountain biking and ski trails and its summit lodge accessible in summer and winter by a 6,800-foot-long gondola lift. Summit barbecues are offered in summer. The park is also the site of such special events as a gem and mineral festival, the Great American Milk Bicycle Race and the New England championship Lake Sunapee Bike Race.

Sports. All the usual are available, plus some in abundance. Golfers have their choice of four semi-public country clubs and smaller courses: the venerable Lake Sunapee Country Club, the hilly and challenging Eastman Golf Links in Grantham, picturesque Twin Lake Village beside Little Sunapee, and the Country Club of New Hampshire, rated one of the nation's top 75 public courses by Golf Digest. Downhill skiers get their fill at Mount Sunapee, and cross-country skiers take over the fairways at the area's golf clubs in winter.

Lake Excursions. From Sunapee Harbor, the 150-passenger M.V. Mt. Sunapee II gives 90-minute narrated tours the length of Lake Sunapee at 10 a.m. and 2:30 p.m. daily from mid-June to Labor Day, and 2:30 on weekends in spring and fall. The steamer M.V. Kearsarge offers buffet-supper cruises at 5:30 and 7:45 nightly in summer. Another way to view the lake is to drive the **Scenic Three-Mile Loop** around Sunapee Harbor. You'll find striking new houses interspersed with older traditional cottages.

Shopping. For a town its size, New London has more than its share of good shopping – spread out along much of the length of Main Street and clustered in shopping centers and a mall along Route 11 on the southwest edge of town. Along Main Street are excellent crafts stores like **Artisan's Workshop** (which also has a branch in Sunapee Harbor), and the **Crafty Goose,** the **Spring Ledge Farm** flower and produce stand, and the kind of clothing stores one finds in college towns like **The Lemon Twist Shop, Lisann's** and **Church's. C.B. Coburn** has "unique gifts for home and palate." Its adjunct called **Not Just Balloons** offers children's items and gift baskets, and the related **Kearsarge Mountain Fudge & Candy Co.** speaks for itself. The new **Morgan Hill Bookstore** has a choice selection, plus cards and music. **Wildberry Bagel Co.** offers New York-style bagels, espresso, soups and sandwiches. **Baynham's,** an upscale country store and cafe, is a sprawling emporium of varied merchandise, some of it shown in room-style settings.

The **Woodbine Gift Shop** and the old-fashioned **Wild Goose Country Store** draw shoppers in Sunapee Harbor. The **Woodbine Gift Shop** and the old-fashioned **Wild Goose Country Store** draw shoppers in Sunapee Harbor.

Worth a side trip is **Nunsuch,** Route 114, South Sutton, the picturesque home and farm of Rita and Courtney Haase, producers of Udderly Delicious goat cheese. Not your ordinary cheesemakers, Courtney is a former cloistered nun and Rita, her proper New Orleans mother, has five offspring scattered around the world. Their 21 milking goats, all but one named for nuns Courtney has lived with (to the amusement and consternation of some), yield about 70 pounds of cheese a day, which the Haases sell herbed or plain from their kitchen. We bought some of the herbed variety to take home and it was delicious. At a recent visit, Courtney had acquired a smoker and was starting to smoke some of her cheese. She also was running day-long workshops on cheese-making "for the serious dairy person."

Muster Field Farm Museum, Harvey Road, North Sutton.

Atop a hill off a dirt road out in the middle of nowhere is this working farm museum, a 240-acre National Trust property where knowing locals buy their farm produce. Twenty farm buildings have been saved from destruction and moved to the militia muster field across from the 1784 Matthew Harvey Homestead. They include barns, an ice house, blacksmith shops, corn cribs and an 1810 schoolhouse, spread out plantation style in clusters. Visitors can obtain produce and enjoy the setting – a quite idyllic spot – during the week. A better time to visit and get a sense of the low-key evolving place is Sunday when the homestead is open for tours and guides help trace the evolution of early farming in New Hampshire. The best time is special weekends when coopers, quilters, a beekeeper, farrier and occasionally some of the militia demonstrate activities of days long gone.

(603) 927-4276 or 927-4616. Farm stand open seasonally, Wednesday-Sunday 10 to 6. House tours in July and August, Sunday 1 to 4. Grounds open daily, 10 to 5. Free.

Extra-Special _____

The Fells at the John Hay National Wildlife Refuge, Route 103-A, Newbury.

Three generations of diplomat John Hay's family have enjoyed the rugged landscape and cultivated gardens they developed along nearly 1,000 hillside acres above Lake Sunapee since 1891. Now the public also can enjoy a rare combination of nature preserve, botanical garden, library, historic house and landscape in a single location. The Fells Estate is maintained as a state historic site, and the gardens were replanted in 1994 by the national Garden Conservancy as a regional center for horticultural education. The property includes the 163-acre John Hay National Wildlife Refuge. Depending on season, masses of mountain laurel, rhododendrons, azaleas, blueberries, perennial borders, a rose terrace, a rock garden, an old walled garden and more can be seen.

(603) 763-4789. Garden tours Wednesday at 1 in July and August. House tours on weekends and holidays, Memorial Day through Columbus Day. Grounds open daily, dawn to dusk. Free.

Robert Frost worked at this desk in Franconia with a view of Cannon Mountain.

Franconia/Sugar Hill, N.H.
The Road Less Traveled

The lines are from Robert Frost: "Two roads diverged in a wood, and I – I took the one less traveled by, and that has made all the difference."

They were written when the poet lived in Franconia beneath Cannon Mountain, and the road less traveled has made a difference historically in maintaining the Franconia area as an island of serenity just beyond the crowds.

Even the opening of the beautiful Franconia Notch Parkway connecting completed portions of Interstate 93 on either side of the notch failed to bring in the hordes. Many people don't know about the area's history and beauty, said one innkeeper. "They think that beyond the Old Man of the Mountains, there are just woods and Canada."

Indeed, Franconia and its upcountry neighbor, Sugar Hill, are remote and relatively untouched by the usual trappings of tourism. They retain much of the look and the flavor of the late 19th century when they were noted mountain resort areas. In the 1930s, Austrian Sig Buchmayer established the country's first ski school at Peckett's-on-Sugar Hill (now designated by a primitive historic marker) and Cannon Mountain dedicated skiing's first aerial tramway.

But for the mystique of the name, one might not be aware of the area's storied past. Gone are the large hotels and, as ski areas go, Cannon keeps a low profile.

Today, the crowds and the condos halt below Franconia Notch to the south, leaving Cannon Mountain, Franconia, Sugar Hill, Bethlehem and even the "city" of Littleton for those who appreciate them as vestiges of the past.

For those who want action, the magnificent Franconia Notch State Park stretching eight miles through the notch offers outdoor activities and some of the Northeast's most spectacular sights.

But the road less traveled takes one beyond. There are few better places for fall foliage viewing than from Sunset Hill or the ridge leading up to Sugar Hill above Franconia. The heights afford sweeping vistas of the towering White Mountains on three sides and toward Vermont's Green Mountains on the fourth.

In winter, downhill skiers revel in the challenges of Cannon Mountain, the venerable World Cup area so full of skiing history that the New England Ski Museum is located at its base.

In spring and summer, the quiet pleasures of an area rich in history and character suffice. The Frost Place, the Sugar Hill Historical Museum and the Sugar Hill Sampler are classics of their genre.

Don't expect trendy inns, fancy restaurants or tony shops. Immerse yourself instead in the beauty and the tranquility of New England as it used to be.

It's little wonder that long after he left, poet Frost wrote, "I am sitting here thinking of the view from our house in Franconia." It's unforgettable.

Inn Spots

Rabbit Hill Inn, Off Route 18, Lower Waterford, Vt. 05848

If you have an iota of romance in your soul, you'll love this white-columned "inn for romantics" in a tiny hillside hamlet just across the Connecticut River from New Hampshire. Where else would you find, upon retiring to your room after a candlelight dinner, the bed turned down, the radio playing soft music, the lights turned off, a candle flickering in a hurricane chimney, and a small stuffed and decorated heart on the bed to use as a "do not disturb" sign and yours to take home?

That's just a sample of the care and concern that innkeepers Leslie and Brian

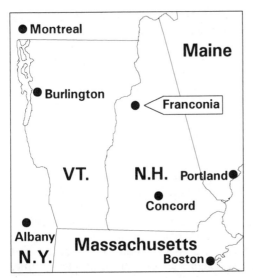

Mulcahy show for their guests. They served three years as assistants to innkeeper icons Maureen and John Magee before buying the highly revered establishment in 1997 when the Magees opted for a change of scenery. Taking their cues from their predecessors, who had a bent for the theatrical, the Mulcahys "set the stage, and our guests are the players."

Upon arrival, Brian is apt to greet you with a "welcome to our home." In your room is a personal note of welcome from Leslie, who already has sent a postcard to say they are "looking forward to your upcoming visit."

Aptly named Canopy Chamber awaits guests at Rabbit Hill Inn.

Depending on the season you'll find hot or iced tea, perhaps flavored with red clover, and delicious pastries in the afternoon in the cozy parlor. Next to it is a pub, the Snooty Fox, with comfortable sofas and upholstered chairs in one section and a newer section with game tables, an authentic 18th-century barn decor and handcrafted Vermont furniture. Across the road are a small gazebo near a pond for swimming and fishing, a bridge, a tree swing and nature trails.

The 21 guest rooms, all with private baths and most with air-conditioning, are in the 1825 main inn, a carriage wing and the 1795 tavern building next door. Part of the tavern's basement has been converted into a video den with a TV and VCR.

Rabbit Hill has been decorated with loving care. Each room has a theme and twelve have working fireplaces with andirons in the shape of rabbits. In Caroline's Chamber, the bed is draped with blue curtains. The Samuel Hodby suite (named after the original owner in the late 18th century) has a Georgian fireplace and a king bed covered with lacy pillows. Even in the carriage wing, where the rooms go off an interior corridor like that of many a motor hotel, they are done in a most unmotel-like way. Three rooms on the lower floor here were gutted and turned into two deluxe suites with corner fireplaces and sitting areas, and one has a soaking tub for two. Our room, Clara's Chamber, contained many mementos of its namesake as well as the standard room diary in which guests record their feelings and rave about the innkeepers.

Among the more prized accommodations is the Tavern's Secret, transformed from two existing rooms and a bath at the rear of the building next door. The

Mulcahys call it their "fantasy suite" and that it is. The secret? Pull forward what appears to be a floor-to-ceiling bookcase opposite the fireplace and you find a gleaming bathroom with brass fixtures and a double jacuzzi. Romantics can enjoy the fireplace from either the kingsize canopy bed or the jacuzzi.

No sooner was this completed than Rabbit Hill set about creating the Nest, converting an office and private quarters upstairs into a fireplaced bedroom with custom-made queen canopy bed, a European dressing room with a whirlpool tub for two and a private sun deck. The subsequent Loft and the Turnabout raise the total of "fantasy chambers" to four.

Two front porches, one on the second floor awash with wicker, are where guests like to sit and watch the distant mountains. Downstairs in the parlor, the innkeepers keep adding to a collection of books written by guests. Everywhere are rabbit items, many of them gifts sent by people who have stayed here.

Breakfast is an event at Rabbit Hill. It is served by candlelight in the dining room after 8:15 but you can find coffee in the pub earlier. To the accompaniment of the soundtrack from "The Sound of Music," we helped ourselves to a buffet spread of orange juice, a chilled fruit soup, a cup of melon pieces and tiny blueberries, homemade granola and assorted pastries. Two changing main dishes are prepared to order: at our visit, a poached egg on a croissant with cheese sauce, homefries and bacon as well as pancakes with bananas and strawberries. The granola is so good that guests buy packages to take home.

The inn's restaurant (see Dining Spots) is the finest in the area.

(802) 748-5168 or (800) 762-8669. Fax (802) 748-8142. www.rabbithillinn.com. Twenty-one rooms with private baths. Rates MAP. Doubles, $199 to $249. Fantasy chambers, $279 to $289. Two-night minimum weekends. Children over 12. No smoking.

Adair, 80 Guider Lane, Bethlehem 03574.

A "welcome slate," bearing the names of arriving guests and the fare for the next morning's breakfast, is posted in the wide entry hall of this country inn of uncommon charm. It's the first of many thoughtful touches guests will find at Adair. The hilltop mansion was built in 1929 as a wedding gift for Dorothy Adair Hogan from her father, nationally famous Washington trial lawyer Frank Hogan. The early guest list included presidents, governors, senators, judges, sports figures and actors. Helen Hayes visited each summer for many years.

Adair was restored to AAA four-diamond status in 1992 by Hardy Banfield, a Portland (Me.) contractor, who sold his construction business to return to college for a degree in hospitality management, and his wife Patricia, former owner of a knitting and needlework store in the Old Port Exchange section of Portland. They are joined here by their daughter Nancy, the fulltime inn manager.

The Banfields offer seven large bedrooms and two fireplaced suites. They lease their dining operation to Tim and Biruta Carr, owners of our favorite Tim-Bir Alley, who moved their restaurant lock, stock and barrel from an alley in Littleton to the main floor of Adair (see Dining Spots).

Adair's country-estate-style rooms on the second and third floors are named after nearby mountains, which is fitting given their scenic setting. Rooms are tastefully decorated and comfortable, and all have private baths and king or queen beds. We enjoyed the front Lafayette Suite, a commodious affair including a sitting room with a gas fireplace and a bedroom with feather pillows atop the kingsize bed. A stash of thick towels was wrapped and tied with green string. Also notable

Carriage on side lawn is trademark of Sugar Hill Inn.

were an assortment of the inn's own toiletries and a gift basket bearing an Adair bookmark and a crock of the inn's maple syrup.

Assorted hats that the Banfields found in the attic now rest atop a shelf on the landing of the main staircase, which is lined with a library's worth of books. Guests also enjoy a grand, fireplaced living room with several sitting areas and a remarkable, all-granite (from walls to ceiling) basement tap room with TV/VCR, an imposing old Oliver Briggs Boston pool table and a small bar with setups. Out back is a large flagstone patio, terraced gardens and a rear lawn sloping down to a tennis court and a water garden beside a gazebo. There's not a sign of civilization in sight.

The Banfields serve an elegant breakfast in the dining room, a potpourri of stunning black oriental fabric walls, pale yellow curtains, large Chinese figurines and mirrored sconces. It might start with juice, fresh berries, granola and popovers and end up with eggs florentine or blueberry pancakes. Cinnamon-raisin french toast with Vermont cob-smoked bacon was the delicious fare at our latest visit. Fruit and homemade cookies accompany afternoon tea.

(603) 444-2600 or (888) 444-2600. Fax (603) 444-4823. www.adairinn.com. Seven rooms and two suites with private baths. Doubles, $135 to $155. Suites, $185 and $220. Two-night minimum in foliage season and peak weekends. No children. No smoking.

Sugar Hill Inn, Route 117, Franconia 03580.
Nestled into the side of Sugar Hill is this old white inn, built as a farmhouse in 1789, its wraparound porch sporting colorfully padded white wicker furniture and a telescope for viewing Cannon Mountain.

When Barbara and Jim Quinn of Rhode Island took over as innkeepers, they knew they'd see deer but were quite unprepared for the bear that "pitched his camp at our dumpster for the summer," Barbara recalls. The bear since has departed, but the deer remain.

The Quinns have redecorated the ten inn rooms, all with private baths. They exude country charm with hand-stenciling, rocking chairs, quilts, eyelet curtains and even teeny pillows shaped like ducks on most beds. Among the neat touches are a lamp on an old sewing machine pedestal and a hooked rug in the shape of a heart. We found stenciling on the wood rim of the mirror in our bathroom. All rooms are different, with choice of twin, double, queen and king beds.

Lately, the Quinns have updated six cottage units in back with new windows and doors, free-standing gas fireplaces and king or queen beds. They come with front porches, plush carpeting, television sets and Barbara's trademark stenciling.

Two living rooms in the inn are available for guests. One next to the dining room has a wood stove and the other holds the reception desk and gift shop. A pub contains a small service bar and a TV set.

The Quinns have been joined by their daughter and son-in-law, Kelly and Stephen Ritarossi. He's a trained chef who teams with Jim in the kitchen, offering dinner to guests and the public.

Served by reservation in a country-pretty dining room, the four-course meal is available prix-fixe or à la carte. Choices vary from poached salmon with dill sauce and baked stuffed shrimp to beef wellington and, our choice, sautéed veal with champagne sauce, followed by chocolate kahlua mousse and bread pudding with warm whiskey sauce.

Their breakfasts are treats as well. We started with orange juice laced with strawberries, followed by blueberry muffins. Then came a choice of cinnamon french toast or swiss and cheddar cheese omelet, both excellent.

(603) 823-5621 or (800) 548-4748. Fax (603) 823-5630. www.sugarhillinn.com. Ten rooms and six cottages with private baths. Doubles, $95 to $135 B&B, $145 to $185 MAP. Two-night minimum in foliage season. No smoking.

Prix-fixe $25 or à la carte, $14.95 to $18.95. Dinner nightly, 5:30 to 8.

Sunset Hill House, Sunset Hill Road, Sugar Hill 03585

Michael Coyle, who had "a little house up the street," told friends that someday he would buy the landmark annex building that was all that was left of a famous hotel straddling the 1,700-foot-high ridge of Sugar Hill. The opportunity arose in a foreclosure auction in 1993 after it had been closed for fire-code violations.

Situated along a 1,700-foot-high ridge, the establishment has been nicely transformed into an urbane country inn by Michael, a gregarious ex-Boston entrepreneur who's into good food, golf and romance.

His spacious restaurant overlooking the mountain range provides the former. He took over and upgraded the derelict Sunset Hill nine-hole golf course across the road. And he married a Sugar Hill woman in what by all reports was the most festive wedding among many the Sunset Hill House has seen. At our 1997 visit, he had just become the proud father of a daughter.

The restored hotel holds eighteen guest rooms, all but two small singles containing king or queen beds and private baths, plus two jacuzzi suites, with four more suites in the works. All have new private baths (some with fiberglass showers or clawfoot tubs) with the inn's own toiletries. They also have a simple but stylish, uncluttered look with Waverly prints, coordinated colors and handmade draperies. We could see the sun both rise and set from our second-floor north corner bedroom with windows on three sides.

The adjacent Hill House is more like a typical B&B with five bigger, quieter rooms and a family suite. Because of Sunset Hill's size and variety, "we can be a

Enormous boulders at side identify The Inn at Forest Hills.

lot of things to a lot of people," says Michael, explaining how the inn can cater to both functions and the upscale couples market he seeks.

The public spaces are beauties. Along the front is a succession of three open, airy living rooms with fireplaces and splashy floral arrangements. One holds the inn's TV. Strung along the rear are four elegant dining rooms with windows onto the mountain panorama and one of the best fall foliage views in New England. On the other side of the reception desk is Rose McGee's tavern (named after Michael's 90-year-old great aunt), which is fun for drinks or light fare.

Outside in front are a pond on the golf course (for ice skating in winter) and a network of cross-country ski trails. Behind the inn is a most attractive rock-rimmed swimming pool – an all-new heated pool within a pool because the old one was deemed beyond repair. Beyond is a wedding arbor framing Mount Lafayette and an awesome mountain vista.

Rates include a full breakfast with juice, fresh fruit with yogurt and homemade granola, wonderful coffee cake and chocolate-chip scones and a choice of entrées, from a fabulous Cuban omelet to steak and eggs.

(603) 823-5522 or (800) 786-4455. Fax (603) 823-5738. Eighteen rooms and two suites with private baths. Doubles, $90 to $130. Suites, $150. Two-night minimum weekends. No smoking.

The Inn at Forest Hills, Route 142, Box 783, Franconia, N.H. 03580.

A basket full of thank-you cards from guests in the sun room indicates that new owner-innkeepers Joanne and Gordon Haym are on the right track. Taking over a deteriorating property from absentee investors, they reopened after a year's worth of renovations. The eighteen-room, English Tudor-style mansion, which had mildly piqued our interest in its earlier B&B days, has benefited from the Hayms' brand of TLC. "This is our home, our business, our future," acknowledges Joanne.

The inn is pleasantly situated off by itself on a knoll, hidden behind a clump of trees and enormous boulders with a grassy expanse on three sides. Off to the side is the Forest Hills residential association, successor to the old Forest Hills Hotel and later the short-lived Franconia College campus. The inn had been built as a private house to accommodate family groups and social functions for the hotel.

Now, inn guests are accommodated in seven guest accommodations, all with private baths, and lots of comfy common areas in which to spread out.

The spacious Franklin Pierce room with a stunning red birch floor holds a kingsize bed and a sitting area with two sofas. The other main bedrooms have queensize beds and new or updated bathrooms. They are colorfully decorated with quilts on the bed and walls of one, a floral cover and matching pillows in another. Reading lamps are placed over the beds. In their latest project, the Hayms transformed three small rooms sharing a bath on the third floor into a large bedroom and a two-room suite with bedroom and sitting room.

Most of the main floor is given over to common rooms. The focal point is an open, lodge-style living room with a wood stove in the corner fireplace. Beyond is a fireplaced dining room, where the day's breakfast menu is posted (at our visit, orange juice, homemade granola with wild blueberry yogurt and strawberries, poached bananas, coffee spice cake and sour-cream belgian waffles with raspberry sauce or warm New Hampshire maple syrup). At the rear of the inn is the timbered Alpine Room with vaulted ceiling, oversize fireplace and deep lounge chairs for reading or watching TV. A refrigerator is close by for guests' use. Along the side of the house is a cheery sun room, another inviting spot with a TV/VCR.

Hummingbirds are attracted to feeders beside the long, open front porch. They proved to be a pleasant distraction for one guest whom we observed spending the afternoon there with her laptop computer.

Her business approach was not the norm. The inn is so attractive for romance that Gordon has been commissioned a justice of the peace and calls himself "the marrying innkeeper. We can now perform weddings or renew vows on demand," he said. Joanne has been commissioned as well – for backup purposes. It seems she gets teary at weddings, so she's usually the photographer.

(603) 823-9550 or (800) 280-9550. (Fax) 603 823-8701. www.innatforesthills.com. Six rooms and one suite with private baths. Doubles, $85 to $105; suite, $105. Foliage: doubles $125 to $145, suite $145. Two-night minimum most weekends and foliage. Children over 12. No smoking.

Bungay Jar Bed & Breakfast, Easton Valley Road, Box 15, Franconia 03580.

Here is one exceptional B&B, tucked away in an 18th-century barn on eight acres without a neighbor in sight. The mountains of the Kinsman Range loom behind, providing an awesome backdrop for some rather awesome rooms and balconies on three floors.

The house – which looks like a small, two-story cottage in the woods in front – expands into a large, four-story structure overlooking gardens and mountains in back. The hayloft of the old barn became the two-story living room, where the fireplace is lit from fall to spring. Here are many sitting areas, a reading corner, an antique Steinway piano and Adirondack stick furniture. Some beams are draped with dried flowers and others bear a collection of birch-bark canoes. "It's a rustic setting, but the rooms are elegant," says Kate Kerivan, host with her lawyer-husband, Lee Strimbeck, and their young son, Kyle.

That's an understatement. You work your way upward through six rooms, two on each floor and varying in size. The higher you go, the more incredible the room and the more stunning the vista.

Start with the main floor, where two "modest" rooms full of antiques share a bath. They might be the ones of choice elsewhere, but here, move up to the second floor. The Rose Suite offers a kingsize pencil-post canopy bed, a full bath, a day bed and armchair in a sitting area, and a private reading balcony overlooking the common room and fireplace. Just outside the suite is a two-person sauna available to all. On the other side, the Cinnamon Suite has a quilted queen bed, french doors to a private balcony and a six-foot soaking tub that belonged to Benny Goodman. Kate acquired it at an auction, keeps a Benny Goodman record nearby and, at our visit, was looking for a clarinet to serve as a towel rack.

Banister rails made of lightning rods line the staircase to the third floor. Here is the Hobbitt Room, with a double bed beneath a skylight – "like being in a treehouse," says Kate. This has the best view, "Mount Kinsman staring you in the eyeball." The bed faces a tiled shower underneath another skylight.

The ultimate is the Stargazer Suite, where a telescope is aimed on the Kinsman Range or the tramway atop Cannon Mt. It has a kingsize bed beneath four skylights, an antique gas fireplace, a clawfoot tub under antique leaded-glass windows, a toilet behind a cloister table, and a twig loveseat and armchairs. Lovely in beige and brown, it's remarkable to the last detail.

New on the lower level are the Raspberry Garden Suite with kingsize bed, gas fireplace, free-standing double jacuzzi, TV/VCR and a small kitchen area. It opens through french doors onto a private patio overlooking the rear gardens.

Energetic Kate, a landscape architect, developed the showplace gardens around a lily pond, where she had a lotus flower blooming at our latest visit. She's also quite a cook, offering breakfasts with fresh fruit and edible flowers, popovers and perhaps zucchini quiche or french toast with crushed walnuts. She opened a small herb and perennial shop and runs garden symposiums on the property, and was planning to add a duplex cottage with two more fireplaced guest rooms.

Oh, the name? The Bungay Jar is a legendary wind that funnels from Mount Kinsman through the Easton Valley past this property. Kate has incorporated the name into a T-shirt, which she sells along with country antiques and other items. Check out the B&B's brochure: it's one of the most artistic we've seen.

(603) 823-7775 or (800) 421-0701. Fax (603) 444-0100. One room and three suites with private baths; two rooms with shared bath. Summer: doubles $100 to $120, suites $125 to $170. Foliage: doubles $115 to $135, suites $155 to $195. Rest of year: doubles $95 to $110, suites $120 to $150. Two-night minimum foliage season and holiday weekends. No smoking.

Foxglove, Route 117, Sugar Hill 03585.
A watercolor of foxgloves on the enclosed front porch welcomes guests to this inviting B&B, named for owner Janet Boyd's favorite flower. She "fell in love with the house" and all the prolific blueberry and raspberry bushes in back and decided to turn it into a small country inn.

A former recording studio manager and decorator for musicians in New York, Janet had a good eye for the both the potential and the execution of the rambling, three-section country house dating to the turn of the century. The original pantry is now a foyer and shop. The dining room opens onto a rear glassed-in porch and three acres of park-like gardens and woods, dotted with hideaway terraces, trickling fountains and quiet glades. The dainty living room, decorated to the max, is housed in a front turret.

Sloping lawn yields verdant setting for guests at Foxglove.

Each of five bedrooms with private baths has its own personality and comes with interesting decorative knickknacks. The Serengeti on the main floor has a black tiled bath and a deluxe queen bed dressed in black leopard sheets. Prints of old shoes along a wall adorn a lacy bedroom with English paisley wallpaper, an antique white cover on the Jenny Lind spool bed and hat boxes on the radiator. Upstairs in the turret is a queen bedroom, while a summery bedroom up and to the rear has lots of wicker and lace and a kingsize bed.

In 1998, Janet was adding a "very private" rear guest room with a Ralph Lauren Adirondack decor, screened porch, and a deck with outdoor shower and jacuzzi. A meeting room for corporate use was part of the addition.

Breakfast here turns out to be quite a feast. You might start with blueberry or orange juice and move on to a quiche of smoked salmon with asparagus and tomato slices, buttermilk banana-pecan pancakes garnished with blueberries and raspberries, and creamy scrambled eggs with fried apples. The fine linens, china and silver are coordinated to the day's fare.

Friendly and chatty, Janet serves afternoon tea, plus champagne or wine with smoked salmon and hors d'oeuvres before dinner. A silver tray bears chambord or cream sherry for after dinner. And occasionally she cooks romantic candlelight dinners by reservation for guests. Pampering service and attention to detail are her hallmarks.

(603) 823-8840. Fax (603) 823-5755. Six rooms with private baths. Doubles, $85 to $165. No smoking.

Lovett's Inn By Lafayette Brook, Profile Road (Route 18), Franconia 03580.
Although this inn, a fixture for two generations, added a swimming pool a few years ago for its summer clientele, it seems at its best in the winter – and we'll always remember it that way. We were lucky enough to stumble onto one of its fireplaced cottages during a snowstorm more than 25 years ago and liked it so well we stayed for two nights.

Innkeepers Tony and Sharon Avrutine are maintaining the reputation built over 70 years by the Lovett family as they upgrade the facilities and decor and seek to attract families.

The main house, dating to 1794 and listed in the National Register of Historic Places, holds candlelit dining rooms (see Dining Spots), a lounge with mooseheads perched over a curved marble bar and a sunken sunporch with TV. Upstairs are six renovated guest quarters, four with private baths, canopy beds and antiques. Sharon thinks the nicest is a two-room suite with kingsize bed and a sitting room.

Summer or winter, we'd choose one of the sixteen units in seven cottages scattered beside the pool and around the lawns. Each has a woodburning fireplace and a small patio with chairs for gazing upon Cannon Mountain. All come with sitting areas and small television sets. The elongated narrow bathrooms at the rear are ingenious as well as serviceable.

A full breakfast could include shirred eggs with mushrooms and herbed tomatoes or one of several renditions of pancakes.

In back, Sharon has opened the tiny Carriage House Gift Shoppe, and attracted a local following for her Lily Pulitzer fashions and upscale accessories.

(603) 823-7761 or (800) 356-3802. Three rooms, one suite and sixteen cottage units with private baths; two rooms with shared bath. Rates, MAP. Weekends: doubles, $145 to $150; suite, $165; cottages, $160. Midweek: doubles, $135 to $146; suite, $156; cottages, $146. Closed April to Memorial Day and mid-October to Christmas. No smoking.

The Franconia Inn, Easton Road, Franconia 03580.

Situated by a meadow with Cannon Mountain as a backdrop, this rambling white structure looks the way you think a country inn should look and is the area's largest and busiest. "We have a reputation for lots of activities," says Alec Morris, innkeeper with his brother Richard for their parents, who run a resort in the Ozarks.

Thirty-two rooms and suites on two floors have been gradually upgraded since the Morrises took over the vacant inn in 1980. Most of the changes were cosmetic, but every guest room now claims a private bath and carpeting.

Rooms vary in size and beds; some connect to become family suites. The Morrises have added matching window cornices and bedspreads and larger beds. We like pine-paneled Room 27 with a pencil-post, canopied queensize bed, a duck bedspread, matching curtains and a lamp base in the shape of a duck. A suite includes a bedroom with queen bed, a living room with fireplace and sofabed, a kitchenette, whirlpool tub and a balcony. The corner rooms are best in terms of size and view.

The main floor has a living room and oak-paneled library with fireplaces, a pool room, a game room with pinball machines, and a screened porch with wicker furniture overlooking a large swimming pool. Downstairs is the spacious **Rathskeller Lounge** with entertainment at night and, beyond, a hot tub in a large room paneled in redwood.

The attractive dining room, open to the public, features veal dishes on a broad-based menu with continental accents.

Outside there is swimming in a pool or in a secluded swimming hole in the Ham Branch River. Four clay tennis courts and a glider/biplane facility are across the street ("soaring lets you see the mountains from the ultimate vantage point – the sky," says Alec). The stables next door house horses for trail rides in what the inn touts as a western adventure. In the winter, the barn turns into a cross-country ski center; sleigh rides and snowshoeing are other activities. Movies are shown at night.

(603) 823-5542 or (800) 473-5299. Thirty-two rooms and three suites. B&B: doubles $93 to $113, suites $133 to $153. MAP: doubles $145 to $165, suites $185 to $205. Smoking restricted. Closed April to mid-May.

Entrées, $14.95 to $19.95. Dinner, 6 to 8:30 or 9. Closed Monday and Tuesday in off-season.

The Hilltop Inn, Main Street (Route 117), Sugar Hill 03585.

Prolific hanging baskets of fuschias on the front porch greet summertime visitors to the Hilltop Inn, whose flower beds have been featured in a floral magazine. Baskets of dried flowers or wreaths on the doors welcome them to their rooms.

Mike and Meri Hern have upgraded their 1895 Victorian home, adding private baths for every room and considerable stenciling and handpainted furniture. The homey guest rooms lack pretension. Handmade quilts, European cotton or English flannel sheets, a decorating motif of bunnies, and bedside mints are among special touches. One two-room suite includes a kingsize bed and a day bed, while two other rooms have either a king or a queen bed and a twin bed. A fully equipped cottage in back comes with two bedrooms, fireplaced living room, dining room and kitchen.

The fancy hand stenciling on the walls of the inn's Victorian living room matches the inn's china pattern of pink morning glories. Also striking is the Tiffany-era lamp against a backdrop of draped lace curtains.

A full country breakfast buffet is set out mornings from 8:30 to 9:30 in the large dining area, and may be taken in season to the side deck. Guests help themselves to baked goods, cob-smoked meats and perhaps cheese soufflé, quiche or golden raspberry and blueberry pancakes, made with berries picked by the innkeepers.

(603) 823-5695 or (800) 770-5695. Fax (603) 823-5518. Five rooms, one suite and one cottage with private baths. Doubles, $70 to $90. Suite, $100. Cottage, $200 for two to four. Two-night minimum summer weekends and foliage season. Pets welcome.

Dining Spots

Rabbit Hill Inn, Lower Waterford, Vt.

The doors to the Rabbit Hill dining room are kept closed until the dinner hour, so that first-time inn guests will appreciate the drama of a candlelit room, silver gleaming atop burgundy mats on polished wood tables and napkins folded into pewter rings shaped like rabbits. Even the electrified lanterns and chandeliers look like candles. Fresh flowers and porcelain bunnies on each table add to the charm, and a spinning wheel stands in the middle of the room. A second dining room has been added behind the original to accommodate a growing clientele attracted by the food and the magical atmosphere.

Chef Russell Stannard offers a changing, interesting prix-fixe menu with a choice of appetizer or soup, eight entrées, salad and dessert.

We feasted on cream of celery soup with pimento and chives and a great dish of scallops and three-pepper seviche with mint, papaya and toasted pinenuts, delicate salads with a creamy dressing, and a small loaf of piping-hot whole wheat bread served with the butter pat shaped like a bunny, with a sprig of parsley for its curly tail. Citrus sorbet drenched in champagne cleared the palate quite nicely. Main courses were a spicy red snapper dish and sautéed chicken with bananas, almonds

Tim-Bir Alley restaurant occupies dining room of Adair, an elegant country inn.

and plums, served with an asparagus-leek tart and garnished with baby greens. Sautéed potatoes shaped like mushrooms were a novel touch. With desserts of homemade peanut-brittle ice cream in an edible cookie cup and double chocolate-almond pâté with crème anglaise came brewed decaf coffee with chocolate shells filled with whipped cream to dunk in – a great idea.

Other choices might be steamed lobster tail and grilled shrimp presented with mango, ginger butter and pumpkin ravioli and garnished with marinated sesame seaweed and pineapple relish; sautéed duck breast with a maple-rhubarb sauce, and roasted beef tenderloin with a tamarillo barbecue sauce, garnished with corn relish.

A guitarist often plays gentle jazz and classical music during dinner. This is a serene dining room, in which no detail has been overlooked and solicitous service is well paced. Plan on at least two hours for a fulfilling meal and evening.

(802) 748-5168 or (800) (800) 762-8669. Prix-fixe, $37. Dinner nightly by reservation, 6 to 9. Closed early November and month of April. No smoking.

Tim-Bir Alley, 80 Guider Lane, Bethlehem.

For ten years, this little establishment named for its owners, Tim and Biruta Carr, was a culinary landmark in the basement of a building down an alley in downtown Littleton. It moved in 1994 from the alley to a 200-acre rural estate and the main floor of an inn called Adair. Inn owners Hardy and Patricia Banfield took advantage of the opportunity to provide a full-service inn without having to cook dinner themselves. The Carrs acquired a new commercial kitchen and twenty seats in Adair's main dining room plus fourteen more in a room converted from the inn's office. It's an elegant setting in which the Carrs continue to serve some of the most sophisticated and inventive food in the area.

After optional BYOB cocktails with snacks served in the inn's basement Granite Tavern or outside on the flagstone terrace, patrons adjourn to the dining room for a meal to remember. Our latest began with fabulous chicken-almond wontons with coconut-curry sauce and delicate salmon pancakes on a roasted red pepper coulis. From the selection of six main courses on a menu that changes weekly, we enjoyed the breast of chicken with maple-balsamic glaze and plum-ginger puree and the pork tenderloin sauced with red wine, grilled leeks and smoked bacon.

Follow this assertive fare with, perhaps, chocolate-hazelnut pâté with strawberry coulis, mango-coconut strudel with homemade banana-rum ice cream, or white chocolate-raspberry tart with sweet brandy sauce. The well-chosen wine list is affordably priced.

(603) 444-6142. Entrées, $13.75 to $16.95. Dinner by reservation, Wednesday-Sunday 5:30 to 9. Closed in November and April. No smoking.

Sunset Hill House, Sunset Hill Road, Sugar Hill.

Four elegant dining rooms seating a total of 100 are strung along the rear of this refurbished inn, their tall windows opening onto the Franconia, Kinsman and Presidential ranges. The rooms are handsome with yellow Schumacher bird-print wallpapers, oriental print carpets and well spaced tables set with white linens and china, candles in hurricane chimneys and vases of alstroemeria.

Owner/innkeeper Michael Coyle, who managed a restaurant after graduating from college, knows the food and service business and has succeeded handsomely here.

Chef Joe Peterson's contemporary fare and the staff's flawless service are the match for a mountain view unsurpassed in the area. We were impressed by starters of wild mushroom gratin and the unusual house salad tossed with a tequila-jalapeño dressing. Main courses included a superb roasted filet of beef with a lemon-spinach peanut sauce, served with shiitake mushrooms and roasted new potatoes, and a mixed grill of duck sausage, pork and lamb loin, slightly overcooked but redeemed by a cilantro pesto and served with wild rice. English trifle and bananas foster were sweet endings.

An appealing tavern menu offers most of the dining-room appetizers and light fare, from nachos to baked Cuban pork sandwich and a couple of entrées in the $6 to $11 range.

(603) 823-5522 or (800)786-4455. Entrées, $15.50 to $21.50. Dinner nightly, 5:30 to 9. Closed Monday and Tuesday in November and April.

The Grand Depot Cafe, Cottage Street, Littleton.

This handsome restaurant occupies the former railroad depot. The high-ceilinged dining room is dressed with white-clothed tables, tiny oil lamps and fine paintings, and the small lounge has an ornate gold mirror and quite a collection of hats around the bar.

Well-known local chef-owner Frederick Tilton has attracted a following for his contemporary continental fare, ranging from chicken forestière to tournedos of beef crusted with five peppers and filet mignon served with braised lettuce and mushroom caps and finished with a roasted garlic and cognac demi-glace. Appetizers could be terrine of smoked Scottish and fresh Atlantic salmon or blackened carpaccio of barbary duck marinated in armagnac and fennel. Desserts include lime cheesecake and cappuccino silk pie.

The blackboard menu appeals for lunch: perhaps grilled lamb sandwich, seafood crêpes or grilled chicken caesar salad.

(603) 444-5303. Entrées, $14.95 to $21.95. Lunch, Monday-Saturday 11:30 to 2. Dinner, Wednesday-Sunday 6 to 9.

Lovett's Inn By Lafayette Brook, Profile Road, Franconia.

A little concrete fisherman sits with his pole at the end of the diving board over a pond formed by Lafayette Brook across the road. Illuminated at night, he attracts the curious to this inn's well-known restaurant, a fixture in the area since the days of Charlie Lovett.

Before dinner, people usually gather around the curved marble bar (obtained from a Newport mansion) in the renovated lounge for socializing. Traditional, hearty New England fare is served in three beamed-ceilinged dining rooms.

A plate of pâté with crackers, marinated herring and the chilled White Mountain wild blueberry soup make good starters. Salad, warm biscuits and assorted relishes accompany. Main courses might be panfried trout, poached salmon with dill sauce, chicken stuffed with roasted red peppers and basil, curried lamb with Lovett's grape chutney and veal milanese.

Desserts are extravagant, from hot Indian pudding with ice cream to meringue glacé with strawberries. We remember fondly the chocolatey Aspen crud, a staple on the menu, from more than two decades ago. There's a choice but select wine list, and a new children's menu.

(603) 823-7761 or (800) 356-3802. Entrées, $12.95 to $16.95. Dinner nightly, 6 to 8.

Polly's Pancake Parlor, Hildex Maple Sugar Farm, Route 117, Sugar Hill.

Polly and Wilfred "Sugar Hill" Dexter opened their pancake parlor in 1938, when they charged 50 cents for all you could eat, mainly to have a way to use up their maple syrup. Their daughter, Nancy Dexter Aldrich, her husband Roger and their daughter and son-in-law operate the farm and restaurant now. They charge considerably more than 50 cents, but it's still a bargain and a fun place to go for breakfast, lunch or early dinner and a slice of local life.

Bare tables sport red mats shaped like maple leaves, topped with wooden plates handpainted with maple leaves by Nancy Aldrich, who, in her red skirt and red bow, greets and seats diners, many of whom seem to be on a first-name basis. Red kitchen chairs and sheet music pasted to the ceiling add color to this 1820 building, once a carriage shed. Big louvered windows afford a stunning view of the Mount Lafayette range beyond.

You can watch the pancakes being made in the open kitchen. The batter is poured from a contraption that ensures they measure exactly three inches.

Pancakes are served with maple syrup, granulated maple sugar and maple spread; an order of six costs $4.60 for pancakes made with white flour, buckwheat, whole wheat or cornmeal. All are available with blueberries, walnuts or coconut for $5.80. The Aldriches grind their own organically grown grains and make their own breads, sausage and baked beans (with maple syrup, of course). Waffles, seven inches wide, are available in all the pancake versions.

If, like us, you don't really crave pancakes in the middle of the day, try the homemade soups (lentil is especially good), quiche of the day (our ham and cheddar melted in the mouth) or a super-good BLT made with cob-smoked bacon. Cereals, eggs, muffins made with pancake batter, salad plates and sandwiches like grilled cheese and cob-smoked ham, croque monsieur and even peanut butter with a maple spread are available.

The homemade pies are outstanding. Hurricane sauce, made from apples, butter and maple syrup, is served over ice cream. The back of the menu lists, for extra-hearty eaters, all-you-can-eat prices.

The coffee, made with spring water, is great and a glass of the spring water really hits the spot (no liquor is served). The shop at the entry sells pancake packs, maple syrup and sugar, jams and jellies and even the maple-leaf painted plates.

(603) 823-5575. Open weekdays 7 to 3, weekends to 7, mid-May to mid-October; weekends only 7 to 2, April, early May and late October. No smoking.

Diversions

Franconia Notch State Park, south of Franconia. The wonders of one of the nation's most spectacular parks are well known. Thousands visit the Flume, a 700-foot-long gorge with cascades and pools (adults, $6), and the Basin and gaze at the rock outcroppings, most notably the Old Man of the Mountains. Echo Lake at the foot of Cannon Mountain is fine for swimming. Cannon Mountain has retired its original 1938 aerial tramway but a modern replacement carries tourists to the summit for the views that skiers cherish – and gets them back down without the challenges that hardy skiers take for granted. In the large visitor center at the southern entrance to the park, a good fifteen-minute movie chronicles years of change in the area and advises, "when you see Franconia Notch today, remember it will never be quite the same again."

Cannon Mountain. In an era of plasticized, free-wheeling skiing, the serious ski areas with character are few and far between. One of the last and best is Cannon, which considers itself the first major ski mountain in the Northeast (1937). Operated as a state park, it remains virginal and free of commercialism. The setting is reminiscent of the Alps, when you view the sheer cliffs and avalanche country across Franconia Notch on Lafayette Mountain and the majestic peaks of the Presidential Range beyond. From the summit, much of the skiing varies from tough to frightening, as befits the site of America's first racing trail and the first World Cup competition. But there is plenty of intermediate and novice skiing as well.

New England Ski Museum, next to the tram station at Cannon Mountain.

Skiers in particular enjoy this small museum that houses the most extensive collection of historic ski equipment, clothing and photography in the Northeast. The maroon parka belonging to the founder of the National Ski Patrol is shown, as is a photo of him taken at Peckett's-on-Sugar-Hill. One of the more fascinating exhibits traces the evolution of ski equipment. "Ski Tracks" is an informative and impressive thirteen-minute audio-visual show with 450 slides tracing the history of New England skiing.

(603) 823-7177. Open daily noon to 5, Memorial Day-Columbus Day; daily except Wednesday noon to 5, December-March. Free.

Sugar Hill Historical Museum, Sugar Hill.

Sugar Hill people say not to miss this choice small place, and they're right. It displays an excellent collection in a modern, uncluttered setting and gives a feel for the uncommon history of this small hilltop town, named for the sugar maples that still produce maple syrup ("everyone who can, taps the trees," reports the museum director). The life of the community is thoroughly chronicled in photographs and artifacts. The Cobleigh Room recreates a stagecoach tavern kitchen from nearby Lisbon. The Carriage Barn contains mountain wagons and horse-drawn sleighs, including one from the estate that used to belong to Bette Davis.

(603) 823-8142. Open July to mid-October, Thursday, Saturday and Sunday 2 to 4. Adults, $1.

Sugar Hill Sampler, Route 117, Sugar Hill.

A horse was grazing out front on our last visit to this store and museum behind the Homestead Inn, where commercialism gives way to personality and history. The large dairy barn, with nooks and crannies full of New England items for souvenir shoppers, is literally a working museum of Sugar Hill history. Owner Barbara Serafini is the sixth-generation descendant of one of Sugar Hill's founders and takes great pride in sharing her thoughts and possessions, even posting hand-written descriptions on the beams. In one rear section full of family memorabilia, she displays her grandmother's wedding gown, which she wore in a pageant written by her father and presented for President Eisenhower on the occasion of the Old Man of the Mountain's birthday in 1955. Amid all the memorabilia is an interesting selection of quaint and unusual merchandise, including maple syrup made by the Stewart family on Sugar Hill, and a special spiced tea mixture called Heavenly Tea. Many New Hampshire foods are featured, and you can taste samples of several. Toys, collectibles and Christmas decorations are displayed in nooks off the main barn.

(603) 823-8478. Open daily, 9:30 to 5, mid-June through October; weekends only in May, November and December.

Shopping. In Sugar Hill, **Harman's Cheese and Country Store,** a tiny place with a large mail-order business, proclaims "the world's greatest cheddar cheese." Many of its food and local items are one of a kind, according to owner Maxine Aldrich, who is carrying on the late Harman family tradition.

In Franconia, stop at the **Quality Bakery** (home of Grateful Bread) for a loaf of soy-sesame bread for $2.85. Two dozen varieties of breads and rolls are made; "we mill our own flour and our sourdough starter came from Germany 40 years ago," said the owner. A collection of frogs is featured amid the country gifts at the **Green Frog.** We liked the local handcrafts displayed by volunteers at **Noah's Ark,** a shop run by the Church of Christ.

Extra-Special

The Frost Place, Ridge Road off Route 116, Franconia.

The farmhouse in which the poet lived from 1915 to 1920 and in which he summered through 1938 is a low-key attraction not to be missed. It was here he wrote most of his best-known works, a spokesman said of the property opened by the town of Franconia as a Bicentennial project in 1976. The house remains essentially unchanged from the 1920s. Each summer a different visiting poet occupies most of it, but the front room and a rear barn are open with displays of Frost memorabilia, including his handwritten "Stopping by Woods on a Snowy Evening" and a rare, large photo of Frost at age 40 working at his desk in the room. Out back, a half-mile nature trail has plaques with Frost's poems appropriate to the site; in two cases, the poems are on the locations where he wrote them. As if the poetry and setting weren't enough, the stand of woods happens to contain every variety of wildflower indigenous to Northern New England.

(603) 823-5510. Open daily except Tuesday 1 to 5, July to Columbus Day; also weekends, Memorial Day through June. Adults, $3.

Squam Lake is visible through porte cochere at The Manor on Golden Pond.

Squam Lakes, N.H.

Midas Touches Golden Pond

The movie "On Golden Pond" cast the largest private lake in the country quietly into the public eye.

"Before the movie, not that many people knew the lake was here," said Pierre Havre, who with his wife Jan restored a rundown resort into The Manor, shortly after the movie debuted. Since retired, they started something of a boom in year-round innkeeping in an area that long has been a low-key haven for homeowner-members of the influential Squam Lakes Association, whose membership reads like a Yankee who's who.

Now, the Holderness area between Squam and Little Squam lakes has two inns and the surrounding area has at least half a dozen bed-and-breakfast establishments. Meredith, just east of the Squam Lakes at the closest section of better-known Lake Winnipesaukee, is the site of larger inns of more recent vintage.

"All of a sudden," notes Bill Webb of the Inn on Golden Pond, "the Squams have more than 50 beds and, with skiing close by, we're making this a destination area year-round."

Passersby see the striking sign in front of his inn and "stop just to ask if this is the place where the movie was filmed," he says. It isn't, but like most of the Squams' entrepreneurs, he takes full advantage of the association.

Visitors board pontoon craft for cruises along the 50-mile shoreline of Squam Lake to see the sights that Katharine Hepburn and Henry Fonda made famous (the Thayer house, Purgatory Cove) and sample the changing moods of a very special lake. Its water is so pure that the 1,000 or so homeowners drink straight from the lake and its setting is so quiet that it's a nesting place for loons, which are the lake's trademark.

Beyond the lake, quaint downtown Holderness is undergoing something of a rebirth. Nearby, the historic town of Center Sandwich – a picturesque crafts colony that is everybody's idea of what an old New England village should be – and the upscale pleasures of Meredith also beckon visitors.

Thanks to the continuing emergence of some good inns, they have a home base from which to enjoy the charms of Golden Pond.

Inn Spots

The Manor on Golden Pond, Route 3, Box T, Holderness 03245.

This is the largest and most luxurious of Squam Lake inns. It is also the only one with lake frontage and access, which is a major plus.

Built in 1903 by an Englishman who had made a fortune as a Florida land developer, the mansion with its leaded windows, gigantic fireplaces and oak and mahogany paneling is a gem. High on Shepard Hill, commanding a panoramic view of mountains and glimpses of Squam Lake, the honey-colored stucco structure has a porte cochere for an entrance and thirteen acres for a yard. A large swimming pool off to one side, a clay tennis court in the pines and a broad lawn set up for croquet enhance the picture. Down at the beach and boathouse, a raft, canoes and paddleboats are available.

Enthusiastic owners David and Bambi Arnold, transplanted Californians, grandly upgraded almost all aspects of the inn in their first few years. The new look begins in the expansive living room, where a custom-made area rug on the restored original floors, comfortable new furnishings and fine English antiques show taste and flair. Beyond is a cozy library opening through french doors onto a walled front patio with dark green molded chairs at marble tables – a delightful spot to which we repaired after helping ourselves to the sumptuous afternoon tea spread set out in the library. A cozy piano bar called the Three Cocks Pub, paneled in rich woods and ever so elegant with copper tables and a copper bar, is a convivial setting for cocktails or after-dinner drinks.

Upstairs is a small library/common room with a telephone for guests and a "squire's basket" stocked with necessities that a traveler might have forgotten. All seventeen guest rooms in the main house have private baths and ten have wood-burning fireplaces. Most have been redecorated by the Arnolds, who added double whirlpool tubs in three bathrooms. Handsome in coordinated Laura Ashley fabrics and fancy window treatments, they are outfitted with both antiques and remote-control TVs. We were happily ensconced in the front Windsor room, with a fireplace and big windows facing the lake. It was pretty in deep pink, white and hunter green, with the

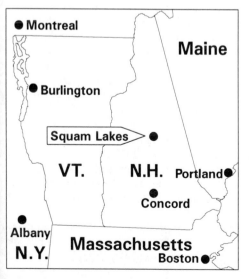

comforter on the queensize poster bed matching the balloon curtains and the cover on the night stand. A large antique armoire and a writing desk bearing an unusual desk lamp with a silver teapot as a base were other attributes. Another favorite is the Buckingham, a huge corner room with a marble fireplace and kingsize tester bed upon which the elegant blue and white checked canopy match the draperies. A small box of Godiva chocolates is presented on arrival, and gold-wrapped chocolate medallions are on your pillow in the evening.

Four bedrooms with private baths and a couple of two-room suites are available seasonally in the nearby Carriage House. Four more rustic efficiency cottages are rented by the week. Smack beside the lake is our favorite Dover Cottage, which has two bedrooms and a kitchen/living room with fireplace.

A full breakfast is served in the side Van Horne Room, which is also used for dinner on busy nights. An elegant room with french doors opening onto a side deck, it proved a cheerful spot for an ample breakfast of orange juice, lemon-poppyseed bread, unusually good coffee and a main dish, in our case shirred eggs and a quiche of tasso ham and shiitake mushrooms. Both came with potatoes sautéed with onions and peppers, and sausage or bacon.

The inn's restaurant (see Dining Spots) is known for special-occasion dining.

(603) 968-3348 or (800) 545-2141. Fax (603) 968-2116. Twenty-one rooms and six suites and cottages with private baths. Doubles, $210 to $325. Cottages by the week, $950 to $1,750 EP. Two-night minimum foliage and peak weekends. Children over 12. No smoking. Closed in April.

Red Hill Inn, Route 25B, RD 1, Box 99M, Center Harbor 03226.

The red brick summer estate that served as the administration building for the short-lived Belknap College is now a full-fledged country inn and restaurant atop a rural hillside with a view of Squam Lake.

"From your room you can see where they filmed 'On Golden Pond,'" the inn's publicity proclaims. All ten guest rooms on the second and third floors of the mansion have private baths. They vary from double rooms with twin beds to four suites with sitting rooms and working fireplaces, two with private balconies and pleasant views. A separate stone cottage contains another suite, and a second cottage has two guest rooms with franklin fireplaces and jacuzzis. Co-owners Rick Miller, a Meredith native who returned to the area after ten years of innkeeping in the Bahamas, and Don Leavitt added eight more guest rooms (three with jacuzzis, franklin fireplaces and queensize beds) in an 1850 farmhouse near a pond at the foot of the property. Surprisingly, given the fact there's plenty of space, only the five jacuzzi rooms have beds as large as queensize. Thirteen offer fireplaces, however, and the inn goes through some twenty cords of wood a year.

Room rates include a full country breakfast, with a choice of cereal, eggs, toast, muffins and such, served buffet style in a front dining room.

Dinner is served nightly in four dining rooms (see Dining Spots), two of them airy sunporches with large windows capitalizing on glimpses of Squam Lake. In the spacious Runabout Lounge in the rear woodshed, an old mahogany runabout was cut in half lengthwise to become a bar and the walls are lined with Don's old auto license plates.

Guests relax in the many lawn chairs and stroll along the labeled herb path, where hardy varieties are grown for the kitchen. In winter, the paths through the inn's 60 acres of fields and forests are used for cross-country skiing.

Snow blankets grounds of Red Hill Inn during holiday season.

Lately, Rick and Don acquired and started renovating the abandoned Kimball's Castle, built in 1895 by a railroad baron as a private home on Lake Winnipesaukee. Commanding a 360-degree view of the lake from its hilltop perch on a point, the new **Kimball's Castle Inn & Restaurant** was being anticipated as the jewel of the Lakes Region. Rick said it would have twenty deluxe bedrooms with jacuzzis and fireplaces, a 125-seat restaurant specializing in upscale regional New England cuisine, a cocktail lounge and a small pool. Left to the Nature Conservancy, the property ended up in the hands of the Town of Gilford, which sold the buildings to fund a 200-acre nature preserve around the castle. Rick said the property, listed on the National Register of Historic Places, would be restored to National Park Service standards, a process that was taking longer than anticipated. He and Don planned to divide oversight duties between their two establishments.

Meanwhile, they leased a six-story granite mill in 1998 and planned to reopen the Shaker Inn at the Great Stone Dwelling, a 24-room inn and restaurant in Enfield (see Sunapee chapter).

(603) 279-7001 or (800) 573-3445. Fax (603) 279-7003. www.redhillinn.com. Sixteen rooms and five suites with private baths. Doubles, $105 to $175. Suites, $135 to $175. Two-night minimum most weekends. Children accepted. Smoking restricted.

The Inn on Golden Pond, Route 3, Box 680, Holderness 03245.

Franconia native Bonnie Webb and her Massachusetts-born husband Bill opened this bed-and-breakfast inn in a 110-year-old residence with a rear section dating back 200 years.

No, the inn is not on Golden Pond (it's across the road from Little Squam, which is hidden by trees in summer) and "other than the fact that Jane Fonda once used the upstairs bathroom, we have no connection with the movie," the inn's fact sheet tells guests.

The Webbs have spruced up the place considerably. All eight guest quarters with private baths are handsomely appointed with queen or twin beds, pretty curtains with matching cushions, hooked rugs and needlepoint handwork done by Bonnie. A suite comes with a kingsize bed and a sitting room. Each room, named for an animal (Bear's Den, Raccoon's Retreat), has its needlepointed sign with the appropriate animal thereon. Bonnie also makes the mints that are put on the pillows when the beds are turned down at night.

The spacious, comfortably furnished living room, with a fireplace and numerous books and magazines, is particularly inviting for reading and quiet conversations. The large rear window looks onto a treed lawn with garden chairs and a hillside of 55 acres for cross-country skiing. A smaller room offers cable TV and, almost covering one wall, a fascinating map with colored pins locating "our guests' other homes." A 60-foot-long front porch is a relaxing spot in summer.

A full breakfast is served at individual tables in the attractive pine dining room, expanded when the Webbs added a second floor to the attached rear shed. Bacon and eggs as well as another hot dish like baked french toast or baked apple pancakes are among the daily choices. Bonnie sells a little cookbook of her breakfast specialties for $4. She also stocks New England foods and crafts in a small gift shop in the inn.

(603) 968-7269. Seven rooms and one suite with private baths. Mid-May through October: doubles $115, suite $140. Rest of year: doubles $90, suite $125. Two-night minimum weekends in season. Children over 12. No smoking.

The Glynn House Inn, 43 Highland St., Box 719, Ashland 03217.

The crown jewel on a residential side street in Ashland, this blends Victoriana and romance. Betsy Paterman and her Polish husband Karol, a chef of note, acquired the grand turn-of-the-century home and redid everything but the wallpaper in the dining room to achieve what she calls "a Victorian love affair." They offer four guest rooms and three suites with private baths, gourmet breakfasts and much TLC for guests.

The exterior of the house is lit all year with tiny Christmas lights, a disarming yet charming sight in summer. The parlor is decorated to the hilt in mauves and purples. Off it is the front veranda, a fine spot for relaxing with iced tea and cookies.

A basket in the upstairs hall contains every conceivable toilet article and necessity that you might have forgotten to bring along. Two of the four guest rooms on this floor have queensize beds and two have full baths. Our room in front, quiet as could be since this is a residential street with little traffic, contained a fishnet canopy queen bed with a Victorian loveseat at the end, a huge armoire, and a sink and a jacuzzi open to the room. A doll was ensconced on the mahogany bed in the corner facing the fireplace in the room next door, quite frilly with floral curtains and a little lace-covered table between two side chairs.

The third floor now contains a family suite with a sitting room and two bedrooms, each with a queensize and single bed.

At the side of the main floor is a honeymoon suite with a double jacuzzi beside the fireplace, a lacy canopy queen bed angled from the corner beneath a ceiling bearing gold embossed wallpaper, and a bathroom with a stall shower and pedestal sink. At the rear of the house is another honeymoon suite that was the owners' quarters until they moved out back. Reached by a separate entrance, it has a living room with TV, fireplace and queensize sofabed and a kingsize bedroom and whirlpool bath upstairs.

In 1998, the Patermans opened a fireplaced bedroom and two more honeymoon suites in their house in the rear.

Breakfast, prepared by Karol, is a treat. Early risers enjoy a pot of coffee before they sit down in a candlelit dining room at a lace-covered table expandable to seat sixteen. When we were there, a wooden goose with grapes wrapped around its neck was a striking centerpiece, and upwards of 50 dolls were looking on. Classical music played as Betsy served a fresh fruit cup, orange juice and a delicate cheese strudel with raspberry jam. The main course involved a choice of french toast or eggs benedict, the latter really special and served with hash browns. When he's not cooking breakfast, Karol collects and restores antiques for the inn.

(603) 968-3775 or (800) 637-9599. Fax (603) 968-9338. Five rooms and four suites with private baths. Doubles, $85 to $95. Suites, $125 and $145. Children accepted. Smoking restricted.

The Meredith Inn, 2 Waukewan St., Meredith 03253.
This Victorian "Painted Lady" on a Meredith hilltop was refurbished from top to bottom in 1997 by the former owners of the Rangeley Inn in Maine. Janet Carpenter wanted a smaller inn when her parents retired, so they helped get her started in the handsome Hawkins-Deneault House, once the home of a doctor and later a dentist but lately an apartment house that had stood empty for three years.

Starting from scratch with a new furnace, new electrical system and new bathrooms, Ed and Fay Carpenter undertook ten months of renovations before they and Janet launched an eight-room B&B.

Coming from an inn background in a resort area, they knew exactly what they wanted: jacuzzi tubs, large beds, a couple of fireplaces, TVs and telephones, lace curtains and a light Victorian feeling in a house full of 19th-century marvels. Rooms are spacious and handsomely furnished. The premier room comes with a king bed and an enormous bathroom, including a bidet. There are removable newel posts on several beds ("for hiding your jewels," Janet said as she pulled one open to show), etched brass doorknobs with matching plates, beautiful hardwood floors, shellacked Southern yellow pine woodwork and turrets with window seats (and one in which Ed hoped to install a circular bed). In a main-floor front room that was once the dentist's office, Janet found a dental pick when cleaning out the closet. She had it framed and planned to furnish the bedroom with other dental memorabilia.

Ed's father made the grandfather's clock and much of the furniture that graces the living room. Some of the furnishings were the family's and "some we picked up antiquing," Janet said with a wink.

Janet serves a full breakfast in a small breakfast room. Expect fresh fruit and yogurt, juice and perhaps french toast, omelets or an apple-filled crêpe with ricotta cheese, a recipe she borrowed from her sister Susan, who had been chef at the Rangeley Inn.

(603) 279-0000. Eight rooms with private baths. Doubles, $99 to $139.

The Pressed Petals Inn, Shepard Hill Road, Box 695, Holderness 03245.
Innkeeper Ellie Dewey presses flowers as a sideline, which accounts for the name she gave the inn she acquired in 1996. She thinks it has a better ring to it than the Curmudg-Inn, opened a few years earlier by a retired physician who billed himself as innkeeper and resident curmudgeon.

She retained the look and many of the furnishings, done in eclectic style, of her predecessor. The open living room and adjoining dining room, for instance, combine Victorian velvet sofas and oriental accents.

The eight guest rooms, all with private baths and six with queensize beds, are painted in different colors. A tour of the property is like walking through a rainbow. Bedrooms come in a variety of shapes and sizes, some with corner cupboards that you'd expect in a dining room. The beds, covered with white spreads and down pillows, bear damask linen sheets. Two rooms have sitting areas and all come with luxuriant towels, robes and Crabtree & Evelyn toiletries. Accents of Asian art stand out amid the decor that ranges from high Victorian and Eastlake to American country and oriental. Ellie has added a country flavor with her pressed flowers, including framed flowers on each doorway and in the large dining room. She gives complimentary pressed-flower bookmarks to guests.

Tea and pastries are served in the afternoon, and hors d'oeuvres on Saturday nights. Breakfast could be oven-baked french toast with apple cider, eggs Mexicali or vegetarian quiche, served by candlelight.

(603) 968-4417 or (800) 839-6205. Fax (603) 968-3661. Eight rooms with private baths. Doubles, $99 to $118. Children over 10. No smoking.

Strathaven, Route 113A, North Sandwich 03259.

There is artistry as well as hospitality here. Betsy Leiper, an embroidery teacher from suburban Philadelphia, and her husband Tony bought this rural manse as a summer home for their family of seven in 1978; upon his retirement from Bell Telephone in 1981, they decided to live here year-round. When the Corner House asked if the Leipers would take their overflow, Strathaven became a low-key B&B. "We found it an inexpensive way to entertain, which is what we like to do," says Tony.

And entertain they do, in a grand, beamed living room beneath a cathedral ceiling, amid bookshelves, an upright piano and sectional seating facing picture windows overlooking rear gardens and pond. Or in a front solarium facing more gardens – just the spot for soup and a sandwich between cross-country expeditions in the winter. Or in the fireplaced dining room with a twelve-foot-long table and a glass cabinet full of china. The sideboard here was carved by Betsy's father, who also fashioned the mantelpiece displayed over a bay window and painted the watercolors that grace the house. Betsy's maternal grandfather did the oil portraits throughout.

Betsy's embroidery shows up here and there, perhaps as crewel work on the valances in a pretty blue downstairs bedroom with private bath and two double beds. A second downstairs room in gold also has two double beds and a private bath. Upstairs in the older section of the house (1830 to 1840) are two more double rooms plus a single that share a bath with the host and hostess. The Quimby Room bears the maiden name and portrait of Betsy's mother, a musician who played with the Boston Conservatory. The Victorian Room contains a shelf of cottages and castles from England, acquired during her annual group tours for embroiderers. There's a canopied twin bed in the single room.

Guests enter the house through the kitchen, which says something about the hospitality of the place. Tony prepares a full breakfast: juice, cereal, homemade breads, omelets, three pancakes and sausages and coffee cake – "any or all of the above." Between meals, he serves as town treasurer and conducts cross-country ski expeditions on new trails he cut on the property, videotaping guests' exploits and recording their pratfalls. In summer he joins guests on the front or side porches where, he quips, it's so quiet that "we sit and count cars."

(603) 284-7785. Two rooms with private bath and three rooms with shared bath. Doubles, $70 to $75, including tax. Children and well-behaved pets welcome. No smoking.

Guest rooms and restaurant at The Inn at Bay Point face Lake Winnipesaukee.

The Mary Chase Inn, Route 3, Holderness 03245.

This 1895 Victorian landmark commands one of the area's best views from a granite ledge overlooking Little Squam Lake. John and Phyllis Chase from Michigan acquired it from his maiden aunt, who had occupied the place for nearly 60 years. When it became available, they saw the possibilities and read a book on how to run a B&B during their drive home. "We'd been staying in B&Bs for twenty years and felt this was something that could support the house," Mary said.

The Chases refinished the maple floors and papered the walls in Victoriana. They offer five rooms, one with private bath and the others sharing two hall baths. Each is named after one of the aunt's sisters. Four have antique double beds, some original to the house. The top accommodation is Mary's Suite, with a queensize poster bed, working fireplace, a clawfoot tub in the room, a lavatory in a closet, a private balcony with a glimpse of the lake through the trees, and a single rocking chair.

The floors of the rooms have been left uncovered and convey a spare look. That and the empty section of a double parlor contribute to what some guests consider an unfinished feeling. The Chases say they planned it that way, however.

A lace-covered table in the wainscoted dining room can seat up to fourteen for breakfast. Mary's specialties are breakfast lasagna, stuffed blueberry french toast and something she calls "eggs for brunch," a cross between a soufflé and an omelet.

(603) 968-9454. One room with private bath and four rooms with shared baths. Doubles, $125 with private bath, $85 to $95 with shared bath. No smoking.

The Inn at Bay Point, Route 3 at Route 25, Meredith 03253.

At last, here's a deluxe, full-service inn right on Lake Winnipesaukee. Rusty McLear, developer of the decade-old Inn at Mill Falls and Mill Falls Marketplace across the street, saw the need and obliged. He acquired the corner office structure that previously housed a bank and undertook a total rehab in 1995 to turn it into a 24-room inn with a ground-floor restaurant called **The Boathouse Grille** (see Dining Spots).

Guest rooms are on the three upper floors and all face the lake. Nineteen come with private balconies. Thirteen of the balconied rooms have queensize beds with a queen sofabed in the sitting area; three substitute leather wing chairs for the sofabeds and two premium rooms contain kingsize beds, jacuzzi tubs and fire-places. The spacious, front-corner penthouse on the fourth floor has a king bed, a queen sofabed in the sitting area, jacuzzi, fireplace, wet bar and balcony.

Rooms vary in size and shape, making use of nooks and crannies with a loveseat here, a shelf of books there. Those that look smaller compensate with large bathrooms.

Loveseats are in front of the fireplace in the lobby, which opens through french doors onto a waterside deck. The shoreline features a private dock, a beach and a whirlpool spa area.

Full breakfast is available in the restaurant. A complimentary continental breakfast is served in the lobby on weekdays in the off-season.

(603) 279-7006 or (800) 622-6455. Fax (603) 279-6797. Twenty-four rooms with private baths. Memorial Day to late October: doubles $149 to $225, penthouse $249. Rest of year: doubles $129 to $195, penthouse $235.

The Inn at Mill Falls, Mill Falls Marketplace, Route 3, Meredith 03253.

With two Bostonians as partners, local real estate broker Edward "Rusty" McLear developed this 54-room hotel as the last phase of an ambitious shopping and restaurant complex fashioned from an old mill site at the western end of Lake Winnipesaukee, about eight miles southeast of Holderness. "We couldn't understand why a beautiful resort area like this had nothing more than a couple of cottages in which to stay," Rusty explained.

A white frame structure on five levels, the inn has rooms of varying size and color schemes, decorated in contemporary French country style with matching draperies and bedspreads, plush chairs, television sets and spacious baths, each with a basket of amenities. Old samplers on the walls, framed pictures of 19th-century Meredith, plants in an old sleigh and antique headboards lend a bit of history.

The inn has a small indoor swimming pool, jacuzzi and sauna. A bridge over the waterfall that gives the project its name connects it to the busy marketplace, in which inn guests and the public can dine at the Millworks restaurant or pick up a gourmet pizza at Giuseppe's.

In 1997, Rusty acquired property southeast of the inn facing Route 3, razed a restaurant and started construction of a third inn, **The Chase House at Mill Falls.** Twenty rooms and three suites were scheduled to open in May 1998. Fireplaces were earmarked for most rooms and jacuzzis and lake-facing balconies for some. Rates range from $149 to $239 in summer, $129 to $205 rest of year.

(603) 279-7006 or (800) 622-6455. Fifty-four rooms with private baths. Doubles, $89 to $195 May-October, $69 to $175 rest of year.

Watch Hill Bed & Breakfast, Old Meredith Road, Box 1605, Center Harbor 03226.

The third oldest house in Center Harbor was built in 1772 by the brother of the village's founder. Barbara Lauterbach, who used to raise champion bullmastiffs from the Watch Hill kennel in Cincinnati, has imbued it with a dog motif and "dog sense." Also great food (she's a longtime cooking instructor). And personality-plus.

The personality reflects Barbara, whom we knew as a fellow ski club member when we all lived in Rochester, N.Y., more years ago than we care to remember. Since then she has lived around the world, ran a cooking school in the Lazarus department store in Cincinnati, does culinary programs and TV shows and teaches

Cooking instructor Barbara Lauterbach prepares breakfast in kitchen at Watch Hill B&B.

part time at the Culinary Institute of New England in Montpelier, Vt. So you'd expect her breakfasts to be good: perhaps maple-batter french toast with homemade sausage, belgian waffles or chunky apple and maple-syrup stuffed crêpes with maple butter. Local melons and blueberry buckle are other treats. It's taken on the front porch with a view of Lake Winnipesaukee or at a long table in the dining room, so full of depictions of dogs she calls it her "doggie room." Her champion bullmastiff certificates decorate the paneled walls.

Dogs play second fiddle to a huge leather hippo in the beamed living room, comfy with magazines, TV and VCR.

Four pleasant guest rooms upstairs share two baths. Each has a doggie touch, but you're more likely to notice that each has a little library and a basket of assorted toiletries collected by friends who travel. They are furnished with American and English antiques.

Barbara sells her own delicious jams, which vary from peach to tomato. She gives cooking lessons in her kitchen (where her Amazon parrot can do a pretty good imitation of a Cuisinart), and dreams about opening a restaurant in the area.

(603) 253-4334. Four rooms sharing two baths. Doubles, $65. Children over 10. No smoking. No credit cards.

Dining Spots

The Manor on Golden Pond, Route 3, Holderness.

The main dining room here is a picture of elegance, from its leaded windows and tiled double-sided fireplace to the crystal chandelier hanging from the beamed ceiling covered with rich floral wallpaper. New draperies and window treatments match the wallpaper. Exotic lilies and burgundy napkins fanned in crystal wine glasses accent the candlelit tables dressed in cream and burgundy linens.

Owners David and Bambi Arnold consider fine food and wine an integral part of the inn experience. The contemporary American menu changes nightly.

Dinner is prix-fixe, $38 for three courses and $50 for five courses. Ours began with a tasting of crab salad in a cheese puff, followed by a choice of three appetizers, among them scallop wontons with a wonderful tobiko beurre blanc sauce and bacon-wrapped veal sweetbreads in an Asian marinade. The third course was chilled cucumber-avocado soup or a calamari salad with balsamic vinaigrette.

Entrées were pistachio-crusted lamb loin with a dried cherry and juniper sauce with calvados and pan-seared filet mignon with black truffle and cognac sauce. These were nicely presented with julienned carrots and very thin asparagus, garbanzo and black beans. An $18 bottle of Conn Creek zinfandel accompanied from a choice but affordable wine list.

Dessert was an award-winning Remy-Martin chocolate torte and a hazelnut crème brûlée, two of the more decadent choices from a selection that also included plum crisp with buttermilk ice cream and fresh fruit parfait with grand marnier sauce.

New Age background music, flickering candlelight and exceptional food contributed to a memorable experience.

(603) 968-3348 or (800) 545-2141. Prix-fixe, $38 and $50. Dinner by reservation, nightly from 5:30 in summer and fall. Closed in April, also Monday and Tuesday November-May.

The Corner House Inn, Center Sandwich.

Over the years, innkeeper Jane Brown and her chef-husband Don have created one of the area's more popular restaurants in this delightful Victorian house in the center of town. They also teamed up with fellow restaurateur Alex Ray of the Common Man to open a restaurant and catering service at Glove Hollow, upcountry toward Plymouth a bit.

Dinner is by candlelight in a rustic, beamed dining room with blue and white tablecloths and red napkins, or in three smaller rooms off the other side of the entry. The striking quilted pieces on the walls are for sale by Anne Made; the same for the artworks from Surroundings gallery.

Lunches are bountiful and bargains; we saw some patrons sending half of theirs back for doggy bags. We, however, enjoyed every bite of the Downeaster, two halves of an English muffin laden with fresh lobster salad, sprouts and melted Swiss cheese. We also tried a refreshing cold fruit soup (peach, melon and yogurt, sparked with citrus rinds) and the crêpe of the day, a Corner House tradition and this time filled with ground beef and veggies. Desserts included cappuccino cheesecake, frozen chocolate kahlua pie or piña colada sherbet.

Except for specials, the menu rarely changes, nor do the prices. For dinner, you might start with a cup of the inn's famous lobster and mushroom bisque, mushroom caps stuffed with spinach and cheese, crab cake with cajun tartar sauce or sesame chicken with honey dip. Entrées range from chicken piccata or cordon bleu or a single lamb chop "for those who like to clean their plate" to a pair of two-inch-thick lamb chops. One diner said the last, a house specialty, were the best she'd ever had. Shellfish sauté, seafood mixed grill, brandied peach duckling, pork zurich, five pasta dishes and filet mignon bordelaise are among the choices. Grilled swordfish, venison au poivre and New Zealand rack of lamb were specials at a recent visit.

The wine list is affordably priced. "Sandwich was a dry town when we came

Windowed alcove offers view from small dining room at The Corner House Inn.

here and they finally granted us a beer and wine license," Jane said, "so they must think we're all right."

Upstairs, she has gradually redecorated three guest rooms – one up a separate steep staircase – each with private bath. A handstitched teddybear sits atop each queensize poster bed, surrounded by plants, antiques and handmade quilts. Doubles ($80) include a full breakfast.

(603) 284-6219. Entrées, $12.95 to $19.95. Lunch, Monday-Saturday 11:30 to 2, to 2:30 in season. Dinner nightly, 5:30 to 9, to 9:30 in season. Closed Monday and Tuesday November-May.

The Common Man, Ashland Common, Ashland.
Founded in 1971 by Alex Ray and hailed for food that is the some of the most consistent in the area, the Common Man attracts enormous crowds – we faced a half-hour wait at 8:30 one Wednesday evening. It also has spawned many other restaurateurs, Jane and Don Brown of the Corner House among them, as well as other restaurants around New Hampshire.

A jigsaw puzzle awaits on a table near the entrance. Inside, old records, sheet music and Saturday Evening Post covers are for sale. Upstairs is a vast bar and grill with buckets and lobster traps hanging from the ceiling, a long pine counter set for Chinese checkers and chess, plush sofas in intimate groupings and an outside porch overlooking the shops of Ashland Common. Pizzas, nachos, burgers and an uncommon number of snack foods are offered here nightly from 4 to 11.

The rustic, beamed main dining room, separated into sections by a divider topped with books, is crowded with tables sporting a variety of linens and mats, chairs and banquettes.

The dinner menu is straightforward and priced right, from four chicken dishes to rack of lamb. Planked "grate steak" serving "from one ridiculously hungry person to three very hungry people," complemented with a medley of vegetables, is one of the best bargains around for $26.95. We can vouch for the prime rib and the "uncommon steak," served with potatoes and excellent tossed romaine salads. A bottle of the house cabernet, specially blended by a California winery and something of a precedent among New Hampshire restaurants, was a fine accompaniment. Another innovation at our table was a box of menu recipes, marked "please don't steal" (they're meant to tempt the palate, rather than be specific).

Desserts vary from hot Indian pudding to a creamy cheesecake and white chocolate mousse. As you leave, a sign at the reception desk invites you to "take home a bar of our uncommon white chocolate."

(603) 968-7030. Entrées, $11.95 to $17.95. Lunch, Monday-Saturday 11:30 to 2. Dinner nightly, 5:30 to 9 or 9:30.

Red Hill Inn, Route 25B, Center Harbor.

Colorful china with a pattern of morning glories, fresh flowers and oil lamps accent the pink-linened tables in the two dining rooms and two airy sun porches of the Red Hill. The front dining room and the ends of the porches offer a view of Squam Lake. A warming fireplace compensates for the lack of view in the inner room.

Longtime chef Elmer Davis, who retired, was succeeded in 1997 by Stefan Ryll, a 27-year-old native of East Germany who trained in four-star Swiss kitchens. One of two chefs chosen from more than 100 applying for a program to cook in America, he offers an extensive menu of what he calls New England gourmet cuisine.

His signature appetizer, roasted garlic, is paired with Vermont goat cheese. The ravioli Golden Pond are stuffed with spinach, tomatoes, mushrooms, garlic and white wine. Other starters range from baked stuffed mushroom caps to mussels primavera.

Expect main courses like chicken Shaker style (topped with apples in a light cider cream sauce), roast duckling normandy with cranberry glaze, filet mignon wrapped in bacon, and rack of Vermont lamb with feta cheese and dijon mustard. The seafood medley combines scallops, mussels, shrimp and salmon in a light herb-wine sauce.

The traditionally popular Kentucky high pie retired from the dessert list with chef Elmer. Stefan has made up for it with his version of chocolate-peanut butter pie. He also does European pastries, tortes and cheesecakes. The wine list is extensive by New Hampshire standards.

(603) 279-7001 or (800) 573-3445. Entrées, $10.95 to $22.95. Lunch daily in summer and fall, noon to 2. Dinner nightly, 5 to 9:30. Sunday buffet brunch, 11 to 2.

Walter's Basin Restaurant & Bar, Route 3, Holderness.

Finally, a good restaurant right on the lake – at the channel where Little Squam joins Big Squam and named for the elusive fish in the movie "On Golden Pond."

Fashioned in 1997 from a bowling alley and a restaurant, it's a huge, unlikely sprawl of a place, from the plant-filled foyer with a fountain to the copper bar/lounge in which you feel as if you're on a boat. The two-level dining room in back has granite tables and a fish theme: quilted fabric fish on the walls, glass fish-shaped dishes, and salt and pepper shakers shaped like trout. With big windows onto the water, it's quite a stage for Andrew Cook, just out of college. He's a partner with friends of his parents, financial angels Charles and Dorothy Benson of Florida, all of whom were trying to handle the crowds at our early visit.

Their chef delivers an extensive menu of American fare, the kind that appeals particularly to the twentysomething crowd. Grilled portobello mushrooms, shrimp cocktail, baby back ribs and chicken wings are among the appetizers. Besides six standard pasta dishes, expect main dishes like pan-fried rainbow trout, baked scallops, lobster pie, grilled ribeye steak and combination rib platters.

Burgers, tortilla wrap sandwiches, boboli pizzas and fajitas are featured on the lunch menu.

(603) 968-4412. Entrées, $9.95 to $15.95. Lunch daily, 11:30 to 2. Dinner, 5 to 9. Closed Tuesday and Wednesday in winter, also all of November and December.

The Italian Farmhouse, Route 3, Plymouth.

Country Italian cuisine and atmosphere galore are offered by Jane and Don Brown of the Corner House in partnership with Alex Ray of the Common Man in this sprawling farmhouse and barn they dubbed a "cucina povera" (country kitchen).

Done with great style, as in their other restaurants, the tables in the barn dining room and four smaller rooms in the main 1849 structure are covered with red and white checkered cloths and topped with chianti bottles holding melting candles. There's lots to look at, yet the ambiance remains sedate.

The hearty Italian menu is country-priced. with portions divided into small and large portions. Cioppino, fettuccine alfredo with lobster and bifsteca portobello command top dollar, but the homemade pizzas, pastas and most dishes are under $11. The assertive farmhouse chicken and accompanying garlic bread were more than we could eat. Those with bigger appetites could start with mussels pomodoro, fried calamari or caesar salad and finish with tortoni, spumoni, citrus flan or pecan pie.

(603) 536-4536. Entrées, $8.95 to $14.95. Dinner, Monday-Saturday 5 to 9. Sunday, brunch 11 to 2, dinner 5 to 8:30. Closed Monday in off-season.

The Boathouse Grille, Routes 3 and 25, Meredith.

Local restaurateur Alex Ray, who started in 1971 with the Common Man up the road in Ashland, leased the main floor of the new Inn at Bay Point to develop this waterfront prize. The place is a beauty, with a cozy bar in front with Adirondack-style furniture and Indian print fabrics, a couple of rows of leather booths near or beside the windows, a partly open corner kitchen and a long and idyllic dining deck beside Lake Winnipesaukee. The deck holds an assortment of green picnic tables, some covered with white linens, and shiny wood tables flanked by green canvas boat chairs.

We gladly waited half an hour for one of the latter on a summer weekday. Ducks swam by looking for handouts as we sampled the veggie burger and the tuna salad plate, which turned out to be a mixed plate bearing tuna, pasta salad, coleslaw and fruit garnishes.

The menu expands and gets more interesting at night, when entrées range from New England shellfish stew to steaks and chops. Pan-fried soft-shell crab, grilled swordfish, shrimp scampi and rotisserie chicken are among the choices. Start with oysters or clams on the half shell, a pan-fried rock crab cake or grilled portobello mushrooms with baked polenta.

The wine list is affordable and interesting, as is typical of the Common Man group.

(603) 279-2253. Entrées, $11.50 to $18.50. Lunch daily, 11:30 to 3. Dinner nightly, 5 to 9. Sunday brunch, 10:30 to 4:30.

Diversions

Squam Lake. The lake made famous in the movie "On Golden Pond" is so screened from public view that passersby get to see it only from a distance or up close at precious few points. But you can – and should – experience it by tour boat. The newest is Capt. Joe Nassar's Squam Lakes Tour. He gives two-hour excursions on a 32-foot pontoon boat daily at 10, 2 and 4 from his residence off Route 3 half a mile south of Holderness; adults, $10.

We're partial to the original Golden Pond boat tour by Pierre Havre, who acquired a bigger boat in 1997. Former airline pilot Pierre is a knowledgeable and talkative guide as he conducts two-hour tours of the lake, leaving from the Route 3 bridge in Holderness three times daily at 10:30, 1:30 and 3:30 from Memorial Day through foliage season (adults, $10). He tells the history, relates vignettes, stops to watch nesting loons and visits the places made famous in the movie. "That's the Thayer cottage," he says from a distant vantage point before discreetly passing the house loaned for the summer's filming and so remote that many locals have yet to find it. Purgatory Cove with Norman's famous rock was as foreboding the stormy day we visited as it was during the dramatic scene in the film. "Even on a sunny day," he relates, "you'll generally see no more than a dozen boats on the second biggest lake in New Hampshire."

Chocorua Island, also called Church Island, is a favorite stop on both boat tours. The site of the first boys' camp in America, it has an inspiring outdoor chapel in which summer worship services, complete with crank organ, have been conducted continuously by area churches since 1903. On Sunday morning, the dock area is said to resemble the approach of the Spanish armada as upwards of 250 churchgoers arrive in a variety of boats.

Holderness. Huddled around the little Squam River channel that joins Big Squam and Little Squam lakes, the small downtown area of Holderness is on its way up. Town officials and merchants developed a meandering "reflection path" with benches upon which to sit and reflect along the waterfront. The **Loon's Nest Gift Shop,** situated in an 1812 farmhouse at Curry Place, purveys loon-related gifts, decorative accessories, jewelry, specialty foods and more. Authorized by the locally based Maxfield Parrish Family Trust, the first **Maxfield Parrish Museum Store** in a front section of the shop sells the New Hampshire native son's prints and derivative art products such as calendars, note cards and posters. The second-floor museum has a permanent exhibition of 60 Parrish pieces made from transparencies of the original works. Several are in frames made for the original works by Parrish himself.

Center Sandwich, an historic district, still looks much as it did two generations ago when Mary Hill Coolidge and the Sandwich Historical Society organized a display of hooked and braided rugs that led to the opening of a crafts shop. Known as **Sandwich Home Industries,** the shop became the first home for the League of New Hampshire Craftsmen. It is open daily from mid-May through mid-October with myriad craft and gift items, from carved birds to cribbage boards, handmade clothes to silver jewelry. We could spend hours (and a small fortune) here. Free crafts demonstrations are given several days a week in summer, and an outdoor art exhibit is staged during Sandwich Old Home Week in mid-August. The Sandwich Fair, one of New England's outstanding country fairs, has been held annually in mid-October since 1910. Summer residents might go home after Labor Day, but they often return for the Fair.

The main roads and byways of this picturesque village lead to any number of interesting crafts and antiques shops. Surroundings, long a favorite gallery in the center of town, occupies expanded quarters next to owner Jessie Barrett's home a mile south on Holderness Road. Now called **Surroundings at Red Gate,** its four rooms display fine and country art. We were intrigued by the handweaving (vests, pillows, jumpers and much more) at **The Designery,** a fascinating shop and studio in the former high school, open Tuesday-Saturday 10 to 5. We also admired the wonderful pillows, especially those with cat portraits, done by Anne Perkins of **Anne Made** at **Country Hill Antiques.** Her wall hangings, quilts and pillows decorate the walls of the nearby Corner House Inn and are snapped up by purchasers almost as fast as she puts them up.

Shopping. A new mecca for shoppers is **The Common Man Company Store** across from the landmark restaurant of that name in Ashland. It's chock full of gifts, accessories and specialty foods, including the restaurant's own-label wines.

The **Mills Falls Marketplace** in Meredith contains twenty enterprises from **The Country Carriage** with country gifts and accessories to the **Catalog Outlet Store** carrying women's apparel overstock from the Nicole Summers, The Very Thing and J.Jill Ltd. catalogs. We liked the birdhouses, garden benches and the cans labeled "Grow Your Own Forest" at **Upcountry Pastimes.** Absent are the souvenir shops indigenous to much of the Lakes Region. We overheard one customer ask if a shop had any T-shirts with "Meredith" printed on the front. No, was the reply – you have to go to Weirs Beach to find that kind of thing. Lamented the customer: "But then it won't say 'Meredith.'" Similarly, the loon items at the Science Center's Nature Store and Gift Shop in Holderness signify, but do not say, Squam Lakes.

Extra-Special _____

Science Center of New Hampshire, Junction of Routes 3 and 113, Holderness.

This 200-acre wildlife sanctuary has a nearly mile-long exhibit trail featuring more than 40 species of native New Hampshire animals – from white-tailed deer to bobcats and black bears – in natural enclosures. A new bird exhibit includes an outdoor songbird aviary. Trailside buildings are full of hands-on exhibits, games and puzzles of particular appeal to the young and young at heart, and daily programs are offered in summer. The Children's Activity Center is an entire barn full of fun and adventure; youngsters can climb a giant spider web or plunge into a groundhog hole. Two 28-foot pontoon boats offer a variety of nature cruises on Squam Lake. The visitor center contains an excellent **Nature Store and Gift Shop,** selling everything from stuffed animals to local jams and jellies. We admired a tile-top table bearing loons for $195. Displayed outside at one visit was a Maine woodsman's weather stick, a rustic weather predictor. "They really work," said a sign, noting that when the stick bends down, it portends bad weather. It was bending down, and a hurricane brushed by the next day. Upstairs in the **Favner Gallery** was a fascinating exhibit of stuffed birds and mammals, part of a collection on permanent loan.

(603) 968-7194. Trail and exhibits open daily 9:30 to 4:30, May-October. Adults, $8 in summer, $6 in spring and fall.

Sleigh rides and skating are featured on "Victorian Afternoon" at Nestlenook Farm.

Jackson, N.H.
A Rugged Mountain World

Drive through the old red covered bridge into Jackson and you enter another world.

It's a world isolated from the hubbub and congestion of the lower Mount Washington Valley. It's enveloped by mountains of the Presidential Range, tiptoeing toward the East's highest peak (6,288 feet). It's a highland valley of pristine air, scenic beauty, and peace and quiet. It's a European-style mountainside village of 600 residents and often a greater number of visitors.

Jackson is one of the nation's earliest year-round destination resorts, dating to pre-Civil War days (and not much changed since its heyday around the turn of the century when up to 40 trains a day delivered travelers to grand hotels in one of New England's most exclusive resort areas). It's a village of spirited tradition and pride, from the local book based on recipes used in Jackson's early lodges to the Jackson Resort Association's claim that "nowhere else in the world will you find a more concentrated area of diverse recreational opportunities."

Today, skiing is the big draw in Jackson and its sister hamlets of Glen and Intervale. There are two downhill ski areas, Wildcat and Black Mountain; a world-class cross-country center in the Jackson Ski Touring Foundation, and fabled Tuckerman Ravine, where the diehards climb to the headwall of Mount Washington for one last run in June.

The two worlds of skiing – alpine and nordic – co-exist in friendly tension. Explained the local leader who was staffing the village information center when we first stopped: "The foundation wanted to advertise 'Ski Tour Jackson' and Black Mountain wanted to stress alpine, so we ended up simply 'Ski Jackson.'"

There are modern-day amenities, two golf courses among them. But this is a rugged area, better epitomized by the Appalachian Mountain Club hiking camp at Pinkham Notch than the Mount Washington Auto Road (its bumper stickers boasting "This Car Climbed Mount Washington"), better experienced from a secluded mountain inn than from one of the chock-a-block motels down the valley in North Conway.

Inn Spots

The Inn at Thorn Hill, Thorn Hill Road, Box A, Jackson 03846.

Probably Jackson's best view of the Presidential Range is from the front porch of this handsome yellow structure, designed by architect Stanford White as a private residence in 1895 and converted into an inn in 1955. All the mountains are labeled for identification purposes on the painting at one end.

An even broader view, wide enough to encompass the weather station atop Mount Washington, opens through picture windows in the living room. Dressed in antiques, velvet upholstered furniture and fine oriental rugs, the room contains a soapstone wood stove and a baby grand piano. Between the living room and the entry hall is a Victorian parlor with the inn's only television and VCR.

Some of New Hampshire's best meals are served in an attractive dining room at the rear (see Dining Spots). Next to it is a cozy pub with a fireplace.

Innkeepers Jim and Ibby Cooper came here from Florida, where he was in food and beverage management for the Four Seasons hotel chain. They have added queensize or king beds in all the inn's rooms. They upgraded three cottages with gas fireplaces and double jacuzzis, and in 1997 redid the carriage house. For 1998 they were looking to add fireplaces and jacuzzis or soaking tubs in two suites in the main inn.

Until the cottage upgrades, the most choice rooms were the ten on the second and third floors of the main inn. They are richly furnished with Victorian antiques, colorful floral wallpapers and oriental rugs. Sachet pillows are scattered about the large antique beds, and there are many special touches. Katherine's Suite is stunning with a queensize canopy bed, ruffled curtains and a gorgeous patterned rug over wall-to-wall carpeting.

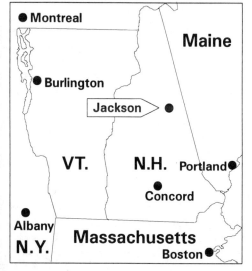

A deck and an outdoor hot tub were added to the carriage house, which lost its ski-chalet appearance. Five rooms and a suite were redone in a North Country look with Adirondack furnishings and new baths (four with jacuzzis).

We enjoyed our quarters in the Notch View cottage, a two-room affair equipped with a jacuzzi tub and gas fireplace, a queensize bed and a front porch that catches the evening breeze. Two other renovated cottages with decks are close by, and a pleasant swimming pool is screened from view by a hedge.

Breakfast, served formally on

white china, lives up to the inn's culinary reputation. It starts with five kinds of juices, homemade breads and muffins, and granola and cereals. The main course could be the inn's spicy chicken hash with poached eggs and peppered hollandaise sauce or grand marnier french toast with peach conserve, both excellent.

(603) 383-4242 or (800) 289-8990. Fax (603) 383-8062. Thirteen rooms, three suites and three cottages, all with private baths. Doubles, MAP, $160 to $260, $186 to $300 for foliage and Christmas week; B&B less $30. Two-night minimum weekends in season. Children over 10. No smoking.

Christmas Farm Inn, Route 16B, Box CC, Jackson 03846.

A basket of bright red buttons proclaiming "We Make Memories" is beside an arrangement of garden flowers inside the entrance to this ever-expanding property where Christmas is reflected all year long. The buttons are part of Sydna and Bill Zeliff's promotion effort for their lively inn (he was in marketing with du Pont and handles this venture accordingly, except for a period when he served in Congress and turned day-to-day operations over to his wife and son Will). The flowers are from the well-landscaped grounds, which are frequent winners in the valley's annual garden competition.

Few inns have such a fragmented history: part jail, part church, part inn, part farmhouse, part sugarhouse. The property was given by a Philadelphian as a Christmas present in the 1940s to his daughter, who tried and failed at farming on the rocky hillside before the place was revived as an inn. Hence the name, and whence all nicely detailed on the back of the dinner menu (see Dining Spots).

Located off by itself above Jackson Village, the inn posts a guest list beside the reception desk naming and welcoming the day's arrivals. The Zeliffs aim to bring people together for an inn-family experience, putting on everything from rum swizzle parties in summer to cross-country trail lunches in winter. They publish the North Pole Ledger, a fancy newsletter for guests, and keep a scrapbook for every year in the cozy Mistletoe Lounge "so that the guest experience becomes part of the memory," says Bill. Patrons reciprocate. Many of the wreaths, samplers and such on the walls are gifts from guests.

A brick fireplace is the focal point of the 200-year-old inn's living room, which is done appropriately in red and green with plaid loveseats, a big red velvet duck and holly on the pillows. Bingo, games and movies on the VCR are nightly features of the adjacent TV-game room. The rear barn has a huge game room with ping-pong, bumper pool, large-screen TV, an enormous fireplace and a sauna. Across the road are a swimming pool with a cabana where lunch is available, a putting green, shuffleboard and volleyball court. Everywhere you look are paths, brick walls and gardens with flowers identified by labels.

Oh yes, about the guest rooms, of which there are 35, all with private baths and telephones. Ten in the main inn have Christmasy names like Three Wise Men and those of Santa's reindeer, and are decorated in sprightly Laura Ashley style; the spacious Blitzen and Vixen have jacuzzis as well. The red and green 1777 Salt Box out back has nine deluxe rooms, and most luxurious of all are the four suites in the barn, each with a sitting area with sofa and velvet chair, television, high sloped ceilings, large baths and loft bedrooms. Five recently redecorated cottages, each with two kingsize bedrooms and private baths, large sun decks, TV and fireplace, are first to be rented in the winter. Other accommodations are in the Log Cabin and a honeymoon suite with living room and double jacuzzi in the Sugar House.

Lush flowers greet summer guests at Christmas Farm Inn.

The former Christmas theme has been toned down in the large, candlelit country dining room. The year-round decor now sports fanned napkins on mint green cloths with white overlays, delicate stemware, cushioned wood chairs, pretty floral window treatments and plants all around. Little white lights twinkle and classical music plays as diners enjoy a wide variety of pastas and entrées ranging from baked stuffed sole and turkey cutlets to Thai shrimp and veal dijon.

(603) 383-4313 or (800) 443-5837. Fax (603) 383-6495. Thirty-five rooms and cottages with private baths. Doubles, $156 to $220, MAP.
Entrées, $15.95 to $18.50. Dinner nightly by reservation, 5:30 to 9.

Dana Place Inn, Pinkham Notch, Route 16, Jackson 03846.
Harris and Mary Lou Levine never expected to own an inn, but they went to lunch with a broker and somehow got talked into buying Dana Place in 1985. They've been busy upgrading the inn ever since, except for a brief hiatus when they sold to an absentee owner who doubled the inn's size within a couple of years and nearly ran it into the ground. "We felt we had left the job unfinished," said the Levines, who reacquired the inn in 1989 and returned it to stability.

Following its expansion, the historic Dana Place is an unusual mix. It's at once a rural country inn with a few quaint rooms with shared baths rented as family suites, juxtaposed against luxury suites in three new additions. Its elegant, high-ceilinged Lodge Room with a fireplace, a huge sectional, oriental rugs and quite a library is New England traditional; the airy new addition with an indoor free-form swimming pool and a jacuzzi is anything but. The lobby and entry have been expanded and the side patio enclosed to make a bar and cocktail lounge with a dance floor. An addition nearly doubled the size of the dining room (see Dining Spots). Two clay tennis courts were installed.

The out-of-the-way location of the inn, which still carries the name of the original owners of the Colonial farmhouse/inn from which all these additions have sprung, is special. It's up in the mountains some 1,000 feet above North Conway, just before you reach Pinkham Notch in the midst of the White Mountain National Forest, and right beside the Ellis River at the base of Mount Washington.

The Ellis River cross-country ski trail, one of the most skied trails in the country, ends at the inn, and skiers often come inside for lunches of hearty soups and chili in the lounge. In summer, inn guests cool off in a scenic swimming hole in the rushing river.

The 35 guest quarters vary in size and decor from rustic to deluxe. All have been redone with pretty floral wallpapers, period furnishings and wreaths or straw flowers on the doors. The large room with sitting area in which we first stayed in the original inn has a view over the gardens toward Mount Washington, a kingsize platform bed and a large modern bathroom with tub and shower. At a recent visit, we enjoyed one of the ten large "porch rooms" in a rear addition, with decks or balconies overlooking the Ellis River and mountains. Our corner room had not one but two decks (on the rear and on the side), and the sound of the rippling river lulled us to sleep at night.

Six more rooms are available in two guest houses with contemporary cedar facades and more modern furnishings beside the river. One is called the Tree House for the tree growing through two of its porches. Its third floor contains a family suite for six, and the five bedrooms in the building can be private or inter-connected, making it good for groups.

A country breakfast is served (and available to the public from a menu). We liked the eggs benedict and the omelet of the day (onions, green peppers and cheese), the latter a huge plate bearing garlicky hash browns and whole wheat toast, more than one could finish. Afternoon tea produces a changing array of goodies, perhaps spice cake, peanut-butter squares and nut breads, served in the pleasant Pinkham Notch Pub. Aprés-ski nibbles are put out in winter.

(603) 383-6822 or (800) 537-9276. Fax (603)383-6022. www.danaplace.com. Thirty-five rooms and suites with private baths. Doubles, $135 to $155 MAP; peak, $175 to $225; B&B when available, $95 to $135.

Nestlenook Farm Resort, Dinsmore Road, Box Q, Jackson 03846.

The plaque out front understates: "A new romance, Nov. 1, 1989, Robert and Nancy Cyr." Local condominium developer Robert Cyr invested big bucks and grand ideas into the transformation of a rustic B&B specializing in horseback riding into a deluxe fantasyland built around the oldest house in Jackson.

The Cyrs sought romance and a gingerbread look and ended up with an abundance of both. Such is their appeal to passersby along Route 16 that tours of the property are given daily at 2 p.m. Behind the locked front doors of beveled glass lie a lovely living room with beamed ceiling and fireplace, a tin-ceilinged breakfast room, an intimate tap room and a bird cage full of finches in the lobby.

Upstairs are five bedrooms and two suites, each named for the Jackson artist whose paintings hang in the room. All have two-person therapy spa tubs and 19th-century parlor stoves or fireplaces and are decorated to the hilt. Everything is pink and mint green and ever-so-coordinated in the prized William Paskell Room, which has a handcarved four-poster kingsize bed with a crocheted canopy, cherry and mahogany furnishings and french doors opening onto a small balcony. The Horace Burdick Suite includes a queensize bed and a small sitting room with a ruffly day

Dana Place offers dining and lodging against a rural backdrop of river and mountains.

bed for a third guest. The penthouse master suite takes up the entire third floor and accommodates four guests in three rooms, including a jacuzzi room with wet bar.

A low-fat country breakfast is served in the dining room at seven tables set with high-back chairs and fine English china. It includes fresh oranges and grapefruit, cereals, homemade muffins and perhaps the house specialty, an omelet stuffed with fresh vegetables.

Gingerbread and romance continue outside onto landscaped grounds outfitted with statuary, gardens and even a big pond into which a waterfall trickles beneath a curving bridge. Music is piped into a huge gazebo, complete with a fireplace, park benches, a ceiling fan and a red sleigh in the middle. Horses, deer, sheep, llamas and donkeys from Nestlenook's petting farm graze in a nearby pasture.

A riverside chapel (for making or renewing marriage vows), a heated pool, sleigh or horse-drawn trolley rides and daily massages are among the offerings. Such amenities don't come cheap; Nestlenook charges the valley's highest prices in an effort to recoup some of its enormous investment. The expanding 65-acre "Victorian estate" resort lives up to its billing as "fantasyland."

(603) 383-9443 or (800) 659-9443. Five rooms and two suites with private baths. April to mid-September and mid-October to mid-December: doubles $125 to $210, suites $175 to $230. Foliage and mid-December through March: doubles, $175 to $280, suites $225 to $299. Two-night minimum stay. Children over 12. No smoking.

The Wentworth, Route 16A, Jackson 03846.

Built in 1869, the Wentworth was the grand hotel of Jackson at the turn of the century when Jackson had 24 lodging establishments. Abandoned for a time, it was restored in 1983 into a luxury resort with modern conveniences but retaining much of the style and charm from its golden era. It really came into its own after its acquisition in 1991 by Fritz and Diana Koeppel, he a Swiss-born hotelier who had been with the Ritz and Four Seasons chains and was general manager of the Banff Springs Hotel in the Canadian Rockies.

Their move East was a homecoming of sorts for Diana, a native of East Conway.

Restored Wentworth Resort Hotel retains style of its turn of-the-century beginnings.

A wide search for a three-season resort of their own near skiing, golf and the water led the couple to The Wentworth, where they have ambitious plans for upgrading and designs on five-diamond awards.

The eighteen-hole golf course behind the hotel is part of the Jackson Ski Touring Center layout in the winter. Other facilities include clay tennis courts, swimming pool, cocktail lounge and an elegant restaurant.

The turreted, yellow and green Victorian structure plus annexes and outbuildings (some with great views of the golf course) contain a total of 58 guest rooms with private baths and TV.

Plushly carpeted halls lead to twenty spacious guest rooms on the second and third floors of the main inn. All are beautifully restored in different shapes and sizes, with private baths (most have refinished, old-fashioned Victorian clawfoot tubs with showers), French Provincial furnishings, an upholstered chair under a reading lamp and color television. Beige patterned draperies and bedspreads are coordinated with restful cream walls and rust carpeting. Fritz warmed up the rooms with inn touches like dried flowers and stenciling.

Fireplaces were added in nine rooms, three with jacuzzi tubs. Top of the line is the ground-floor Thornycroft Suite with a king canopy bed, a Victorian settee in front of the fireplace, polished floors of white and flaming birch, an armoire holding a TV/VCR, and a three-room bath area with marble floors, a vanity with wet bar and a jacuzzi beside a fireplace.

The Koeppels also rebuilt the fireplace in the large, formal lobby and added Victorian antiques to cozy seating areas. A function room along a rear sun porch was converted into a pool room and library. Beyond is a dining deck with tables topped with Samuel Adams umbrellas. Antique couches and small tables were envisioned for the lounge. A health club with a pool was in the planning stage.

Regional American cuisine is featured in the candlelit dining room, its decor enhanced with sponge-painted walls, upholstered French Provincial chairs and skirted tables with floral prints. For dinner, expect main courses like steamed fillet of cod wrapped in savoy cabbage and roasted leg of lamb with black currant gravy. Five-onion soup with parmesan toasts and Thai curry barbecued quail are typical starters. Dessert could be peaches and cream pie, Maine raspberry-chocolate cake and blueberry napoleons served on vanilla anglaise.

(603) 383-9700 or (800) 637-0013. Fax (603) 383-4265. Fifty-eight rooms with private baths. Rates MAP. Mid-June to mid-September: doubles $159 to $249. Foliage and Christmas week: $169 to $259. Rest of year: $149 to $239.

Entrées, $17.50 to $21. Dinner nightly, 6 to 9 or 10 except closed in April and November.

Paisley and Parsley, Route 16B, Box 572, Jackson 03846.

The name reflects two of the many interests of energetic hosts Bea and Chuck Stone: paisley for the textiles, folk art and early antiques, and parsley for the gardening and cooking. Put them together and you have one fine B&B in a dramatic contemporary house on a hillside overlooking Mount Washington.

The house is oriented so "I can stand behind the kitchen sink and see Mount Washington," says Bea from her open kitchen, looking across the dining room and out tall windows onto an awesome view. The mountain also is on view through the "sky window" of the living room, where a brick wall encloses the fireplace.

The Stones offer three guest rooms with private baths. Most in demand is one on the main floor off the dining room. It contains a kingsize bed and two wicker chairs and a private porch with lounger and wrought-iron chairs. Its large, pale yellow bathroom is sensational: a cathedral ceiling, picture window, a two-person jacuzzi tub surrounded by a collection of small boats, a separate shower stall, a row of books on the back of the commode, and bottles of Poland Spring water.

Upstairs on what amounts to a balcony overlooking the downstairs are a teddy bear's tea party in the hall and a sitting area with TV, spinning wheel, books and games. One guest room here has two double beds, decorated in white, red and deep green. The other, all in blues, has a crocheted canopy four-poster bed, many botanical prints and a huge window with a view of the mountains. Antique clothing is hung in both rooms.

The dining room or the rear deck beside the herb gardens are the settings for elaborate breakfasts served on English bone china. Bea shunts blueberry pancakes in favor of the exotic: perhaps eggs benedict, belgian waffles, crêpes aux duxelles, eggs baked with shrimp, curried eggs, potato pancakes or frittatas. These treats look as good as they taste, accompanied by garnishes from Chuck's gardens – "we always serve the fruit on ferns," says Bea.

The Stones offer afternoon tea with cookies, have jacks for TV and telephones in the rooms, and take pictures of every guest to add to an album. Lately they added a grape arbor and a little covered bridge on the side yard for decorative purposes and for guests to sit in.

(603) 383-0859. Three rooms with private baths. Doubles, $75 to $115; peak, $95 to $135. No smoking. Closed May to mid-June.

Whitneys' Inn, Route 16B, Jackson 03846.

A somewhat Bavarian feeling pervades this self-contained resort – a rambling complex of inn, outbuilding, barn and cottages totaling 29 guest rooms – at the foot of Black Mountain. It has been granted new life after falling upon hard times and being closed for a spell. Bob and Barbara Bowman, who have a condo nearby for the winter, added it to their growing list of resort properties. They painted the Whitneys' facade blue in honor of their Nantucket connections, where they began with the old Wauwinet House.

Although primarily a winter place (with the family-oriented ski area out back, a lighted skating rink, sledding and tobogganing), summer fun is not overlooked. Tucked away in the trees across the street, the skating rink turns out to be a lovely spring-fed pond for swimming and lazing. The inn has a tennis court and volleyball, croquet and other lawn games. Once you're here, you're away from everything but nature. No wonder it's popular for an old-fashioned country vacation.

All with private baths, guest rooms vary from standard to deluxe with sitting areas and family suites with living rooms. Cottages come with two bedrooms, living room and fireplace.

Breakfast and dinner are served in a country-pretty dining room, open to the public. Dinner entrées range from a traditional roast turkey dinner to coconut grouper and roast duckling with a raspberry-almond sauce. A dining feature is the children's dinner table, since the inn's niche remains its family clientele.

(603) 383-8916 or (800) 677-5737. Nineteen rooms, eight family suites and two cottages with private baths. Doubles, $64 to $129 B&B; $76 to $140, foliage and winter. Entrées, $13.95 to $19.95. Dinner nightly, 6 to 9.

The Bernerhof, Route 302, Box 240, Glen 03838.

Long known for its European food, the Bernerhof has become a good place to stay. "Food had provided 85 percent of our revenues, but I want to get lodging up to 50-50," says Ted Wroblewski, owner with his wife Sharon. Their goal was to create the ambiance of a small, elegant European country hotel.

To do that, they expanded with a three-room addition featuring private baths, kingsize brass beds and, the crowning touches, jacuzzi tubs in window alcoves, where you can gaze at the stars as you soak. Since then, they have turned four rooms sharing baths into a couple of two-room suites with sofabeds in the sitting rooms and jacuzzis. All nine accommodations now have private baths, six with jacuzzis. One suite includes a sauna.

Guests have use of a second-floor sitting room with cable TV and VCR, and can walk to a secluded swimming hole in summer.

The main floor is devoted to things culinary, including the restaurant (see Dining Spots), a European-style lounge called the Zumstein Room (after the original owners), and the Taste of the Mountains Cooking School. A full breakfast is included in the rates, and a complimentary champagne breakfast with eggs benedict is served in bed on the fourth morning of one's stay.

Lately, the Wroblewskis have leased out the restaurant operation to their chef of recent years, Mark Prince, and his wife Ruth. "They didn't skip a beat," said Sharon. "The restaurant operation is as good as ever, and we can devote more time to the inn."

(603) 383-9132 or (800) 548-8007. Fax (603) 383-0809. Nine rooms and suites with private baths. Doubles, $95 to $130 weekends, $75 to $110 midweek. Suites, $150 weekends, $130 midweek. No smoking.

Carter Notch Inn, Carter Notch Road (Route 16B), Box 269, Jackson 03846.

During a varied career in retail and condominium management, Jim Dunwell always wanted to return to his roots as an innkeeper in Jackson. The opportunity arose in 1995 when the century-old owners' residence for the Eagle Mountain

Carter Notch Inn is former owner's residence for Eagle Mountain House (right).

House hotel became available. Located apart from but in the shadow of the six-story resort hotel, "it had the cute cottage-style façade and size we wanted," said Jim. "But it was a mess inside."

Renaissance man Jim, a former Navy helicopter pilot with a hotel degree from Michigan, undertook six months of renovations and alterations, doing most of the work himself and losing 50 pounds in the process. Wife Lynda did the decorating and pitched in during time off from her retail store. They created a sparkling main floor with an oversize living room, a dream of a kitchen, and a dining room with a built-in sideboard and a table for eight overlooking the side porch. Jim added central air conditioning and retained the original elevator in a closet to lift construction materials for a rear deck with a hot tub off the second floor.

They added private baths for each for seven guest rooms on the second and third floors. A light and airy look prevails in comfortable rooms of various sizes and bed configurations, ranging from queensize to double with twin. A front room with bow window has a queen bed and day bed done in Laura Ashley floral prints, the comforters matching the window shams. Quilts, straw hats, dried flowers, oak and wicker are the norm. With more improvements planned for the third floor, "those three rooms will become my best," Jim promised.

In the morning, he serves a full breakfast in the dining room or on the porch. Guests help themselves to the cold buffet set out on the built-in sideboard he made. Then he brings in "my choice" from a repertoire of twenty: grand marnier friend toast one day, scrambled eggs with brie and mushrooms in puff pastry the next. "I do everything myself," he says matter-of-factly. "Even the chambermaiding, except on days when we have a total turnover."

Having overseen start-ups at the Village House and the Inn at Thorn Hill locally and the Eastman House in North Conway, he and Lynda knew what they wanted for their own inn – "the best product at the lowest price in town." The location is quiet and the view from the wraparound front porch is of a golf course and mountains. "This is a perfect size for us to focus on our guests," says Jim.

(603) 383-9630 or (800) 794-9434. Seven rooms with private baths. Doubles, $79 to $89; foliage, $99 to $109; winter, $59 to $89. No smoking. Two-night minimum on winter weekends.

Eagle Mountain House, Carter Notch Road (Route 16B), Jackson 03846.

A picturesque row of high-backed rockers is lined up on the 380-foot-long veranda that's longer than a football field in front of this grand old hotel dating to 1879. The interior was restored in 1986 into a 92-room hotel and condominium center run by Colony Hotels & Resorts.

Although the establishment has an institutional-condo air, there's no denying the location – up in the mountains, facing a beautiful golf course and a colorful little pool and tennis court. Many rooms have sitting areas with sturdy mountain furniture, TVs hidden in the armoires and queensize beds.

Off a rambling front lobby are the Eagle Landing Tavern (lunch is served here or poolside in busy seasons), a health club, the Veranda Cafe and a huge dining room. The fare ranges from stuffed chicken to venison medallions and rack of lamb. Seniors and children eat for half price at the popular champagne jazz brunch and old-fashioned "suppah" buffet on Sundays.

(603) 383-9111 or (800) 966-5779. Fax (603) 383-0854. Ninety-two rooms with private baths. Rates EP. Summer: doubles $69 to $119, suites $109 to $149. Foliage and Christmas week: doubles $99 to $129, suites $129 to $149. Rest of year: doubles $49 to $109, suites $79 to $139.

Entrées, $12.95 to $20.95. Dinner nightly from 6, Sunday from 5.

Dining Spots

The Inn at Thorn Hill, Thorn Hill Road, Jackson.

The pretty dining room here is long and narrow with pressed-oak, high-back chairs at well-spaced tables set with pink damask linens and fanned napkins, white china, antique oil lamps and baskets of flowers from the gardens. New owner Jim Cooper, whose background was in food and beverage management for the Four Seasons chain, has built an award-winning wine cellar and former inn chef Hoke Wilson has returned to present inspired regional cuisine.

The formerly prix-fixe menu is now à la carte, with a number of choices. We started with a sensational cucumber soup with red bell peppers, diced tomato and mint and an appetizer of grilled shrimp on a bed of julienned cucumber and tomatoes with coriander. A basket of herbed sourdough bread accompanied. The optional salads were bursting with croutons, scallions, carrots, tomatoes, sprouts, mushrooms and impeccable greens, served with mini-carafes of poppyseed or honey dijon dressings. The sautéed pork medallions served with roasted red pepper puree and coated with a blend of cumin and other spices and sautéed hominy lived up to advance billing, as did the pistachio-crusted beef tenderloin with a bourbon and rosemary sauce. The sautéed scallops with a vodka and coconut sauce and the grilled chicken with chili-spiced peaches, feta cheese and couscous also sounded interesting. There was no letdown at dessert: frozen grand marnier soufflé, warm ginger-pear pie with cranberry swirl ice cream, profiteroles and Louisiana bread pudding with lemon sauce and chantilly cream.

Jim Cooper has expanded the wine list to more than 500 selections, starting around $20. He emphasizes French bordeaux and burgundies, with particular value on the high end. He also added single-malt scotches and grappas. In 1997, Wine Spectator upgraded the inn's ranking to "best of the award of excellence," the only restaurant in New Hampshire so honored.

(603) 383-4242 or (800) 289-8990. Entrées, $15.95 to $20.95. Dinner nightly, 5 or 6 to 9. No smoking.

Elegant country look prevails in dining room at The Inn at Thorn Hill.

Thompson House Eatery (T.H.E.), Route 16A at 16, Jackson.

An old red farmhouse dating from the early 1800s holds an expanded restaurant renowned for salads, sandwiches and original dishes plus a soda fountain.

In the twenty years since he opened, chef-owner Larry Baima has created many unusual dishes, some of them vegetarian. Sandwiches have flair: turkey with asparagus spears, red onions, melted Swiss and Russian dressing; knockwurst marinated in beer and grilled with tomatoes, bacon, cheese and mustard. Ditto for salads: a spicy vegetable salsa piled on greens with kidney and garbanzo beans, shredded cheddar, sweet peppers, sprouts and nacho chips, or cheese tortellini and rotini tossed with a sundried tomato and basil vinaigrette, served atop greens with artichoke hearts.

Dinner entrées often include "Baked Popeye," a notable spinach casserole with fresh mushrooms, bacon and cheese, with an option of adding scallops. At one visit, the pork tenderloin piccata and a special of scallops with spinach, plum tomato sauce and ziti made a fine dinner by candlelight on one of the flower-bedecked rear patios flanked by huge pots of tomatoes and basil.

Swiss chocolate truffle, Dutch mocha ice creams and wild berry crumble are great desserts. Kona coffee and black raspberry are among the flavors of ice cream available at the soda fountain. There's a full liquor license as well.

Patrons eat in several small, rustic rooms and alcoves at tables covered with pastel floral cloths, in a glamorous new skylit room (made by enclosing a former deck) with slate floors, chandeliers and hanging plants, or outside on canopied patios and a new front deck.

(603) 383-9341. Entrées, $12.95 to $16.95. Lunch, 11:30 to 3:30. Dinner, 5:30 to 10. Closed Tuesday and November to Memorial Day.

Prince Place at The Bernerhof, Route 302, Glen.

A turreted Victorian inn with sloping greenhouse addition is home for Swiss cuisine in an old-world setting, plus the noted cooking school, A Taste of the Mountains. Here is where visiting chefs Richard Spencer and Scott Montgomery teach weekend cooking courses in the spring and fall, and chef de cuisine Mark Prince adds Wednesday courses in winter.

"Our kitchen and cooking school set us apart," says innkeeper Ted Wroblewski, who created a culinary dynamic that pervades the establishment.

We can vouch for lunch, when we enjoyed the pâté platter and the day's raw plate of gravlax and vegetable salad, both appetizers but plenty for a meal after a hearty breakfast. The three pâtés of duck, trout and seafood-vegetable were memorable, and the smoked salmon was a generous serving around a salad in the middle, much enhanced by the melba toast that, upon request, the chef prepared from good French bread.

At dinner, the specialty is fresh Delft blue provimi veal, deboned by the chef and used in wiener schnitzel, emince de veau zurichoise and veal cordon bleu. Other main courses include a melt-in-your-mouth salmon and lobster sauté in a scallion-champagne cream sauce, pan-seared duck with wasabi and mango dressing, and sirloin of lamb roasted with garlic and rosemary. Cheese fondue with warm breads is available for two.

Traditional délices de gruyère and escargots compete with more contemporary appetizers like a tomato and artichoke pizza on chef Prince's changing menu. A delectable array of desserts includes a concoction of vanilla ice cream and kirsch in a meringue topped with bing cherries and whipped cream, profiteroles aux chocolat and chocolate fondue for two.

Meals are served in three dining rooms amidst pine paneling, beamed ceilings, crisp white linens, a piano and a Swiss stove. The more casual Black Bear Pub has an oak-paneled bar and an extensive pub menu, with more than 90 beers from micro-breweries. .

The wine list, large by New Hampshire standards, includes a few Austrian, German and Swiss vintages along with the predominantly French.

(603) 383-4414. Entrées, $16.95 to $22.95; pub, $5.95 to $9.95. Lunch daily in season, 11:30 to 3:30. Dinner nightly, 5:30 to 9:30.

Wildcat Inn and Tavern, Route 16A, Jackson.

Food is what the Wildcat Inn is known for. The old front porch had to be converted into dining space to handle the overflow from the original two dining rooms, as cozy and homey as can be. There's also patio dining at tables scattered around the prize-winning gardens.

Sitting beneath a portrait of Abraham Lincoln, we enjoyed an autumn lunch in a small, dark inner room with bare floors, windsor chairs, woven tablecloths and blue and white china. An exceptional cream of vegetable soup was chock full of fresh vegetables; that and half a reuben sandwich made a hearty meal. We also liked the delicate spinach and onion quiche, served with a garden salad dressed with creamy dill.

Dinner entrées range widely from lasagna to beef oscar. Wildcat chicken is served like cordon bleu but wrapped in puff pastry and topped with mustard sauce. Lobster lorenzo is the tavern's version of lobster fettuccine. You also can get mondo chicken with Italian sausage and apricot brandy, shrimp and scallop scampi and "the extravaganza" – shrimp, lobster and scallops sautéed with vegetables and served with linguini or rice pilaf.

The desserts slathered with whipped cream are memorable. Chocolate silk pie, mocha ice cream pie, frozen lemon pie and the Mount Washington brownie topped with vanilla ice cream, hot fudge sauce, whipped cream and crème de menthe are tempters.

Upstairs on the second and third floors, longtime tavern owners Marty and Pam Sweeney offer fourteen guest rooms, twelve with private baths. Most are billed as suites and contain sitting areas, sofabeds and reclining chairs.

(603) 383-4245 or (800) 228-4245. Entrées, $14.95 to $19.95. Breakfast daily, 7:30 to 9:30. Lunch in season,, 11:30 to 3. Dinner, 6 to 9 or 10.

Dana Place Inn, Route 16, Jackson.

The three dining rooms here are country elegant with an accent of Danish contemporary. There's a cozy room with Scandinavian teak chairs. The skylit and airy lower level has large windows for viewing the spotlit gardens, crabapple trees and bird feeders outside, and a large addition offers round tables at bay windows with views of the river. White cloths, pink napkins and oil lamps provide a romantic atmosphere.

The continental/American dinner menu is quite extensive and, we've found over the years, consistently good. Among signature dishes are brandied apple chicken (featured in Bon Appétit magazine), lobster alfredo, and chicken and portobello mushrooms in puff pastry. We've enjoyed appetizers of Dungeness crab cakes, moist and succulent, a chock-full fish chowder and blackened carpaccio served over an extra-spicy mustard sauce. The house mimosa salads were so abundant they nearly spilled off their plates. Main dishes of beef tenderloin wrapped in applewood-smoked bacon, veal oscar and tournedos choron came with sugar snap peas and choice of creamy cheese potatoes or broccoli and pesto pilaf. Among desserts were a good strawberry tart, a refreshing lemon mousse with chambord sauce, cappuccino cheesecake and original sin chocolate cake, the last described by our server as "just fudge."

Wintertime lunches are popular. Up to 300 people a day come in for sustenance off the Ellis River Cross-Country Trail that ends here.

(603) 383-6822 or (800) 537-9276. Entrées, $15.95 to $22. Lunch in winter, 11 to 3. Dinner nightly, 6 to 9.

Red Parka Pub, Route 302, Glen.

This is the perfect place for aprés-ski, from the "wild and crazy bar" with a wall of license plates from across the country (the more outrageous the better) to the "Skiboose," a 1914 flanger car that pushed snow off the railroad tracks and now is a cozy dining area for private parties. Somehow the rest of this vast place remains dark and intimate, done up in red and blue colors, red candles and ice-cream-parlor chairs. A canopied patio provides outdoor dining in summer.

The menu, which comes inside the Red Parka Pub Tonight newspaper, features hearty steaks, barbecued ribs, teriyakis and combinations thereof, and homemade desserts like mud pie and Indian pudding. Start with nachos, Buffalo wings, spudskins or spare ribs. Snack on soup and salad bar. Or go all out on prime rib or filet mignon. The full menu is available in the downstairs pub.

(603) 383-4344. Entrées, $9.95 to $17.95. Dinner nightly, 3:30 to 10.

Diversions

Downhill Skiing. Wildcat, looming across Pinkham Notch from Mount Washington, is a big mountain with plenty of challenge, a 2,100-foot vertical drop from its 4,100-foot summit, top-to-bottom snowmaking, five chairlifts and a gondola. **Black Mountain** is half its height and far smaller in scope, but its sunny southerly exposure and low-key, self-contained nature make it particularly good for families. Nearby are **Attitash** in Bartlett and **Mount Cranmore** in North Conway. **Tuckerman Ravine** on Mount Washington is where the hardy ski when the snows elsewhere have long since melted, if they're up to the climb (a 1,500-foot vertical rise for a half-mile run down).

Hikes and Drives. The Jackson Resort Association publishes a handy guide to nine walks and hikes, from the "Village Mile" stroll to Thorn Mountain trails. A good overview is offered by the Five-Mile Circuit Drive up Route 16B into the mountains east of Jackson, a loop worth driving both directions for different perspectives. Look for spectacular glimpses of Mount Washington, and stop for a picnic, a swim or a stroll through the picturesque cascades called Jackson Falls, part of the Wildcat River just above the village. The Appalachian Mountain Club has a guide for tougher hikes in the White Mountains.

Shopping. It's no surprise that Jackson's biggest store is the Jack Frost Shop, a distinctive landmark that's a serious ski shop as well as a fine apparel store with a few gift items. The **Jackson Trading Company,** located next to the Thompson House Eatery, offers sweatshirts, Christmas blankets, pottery, jewelry, collectibles and much more, artfully displayed in a rustic setting. Espresso, cappuccino and deli items are among the offerings at **As You Like It** and the **Jackson Bistro and Grocer.** Other than a couple of small galleries and antiques shops, "downtown" Jackson consists of a post office, a town hall, the Jackson Community Church and the tiny red 1901 Jackson Library, open Tuesdays from 10 to 4 and Thursdays from 10 to 4 and 7 to 9. For a more rigorous shopping foray, head down the valley to the stores of North Conway and its ever-expanding factory outlet centers and shopping complexes.

Other Attractions. Heritage-New Hampshire and **Storyland** are side-by-side destinations, of interest particularly to families. The former lets visitors walk through stage sets in which dioramas, costumed guides and talking figures depict 30 events in state history. Storyland is a fairytale village with buildings, themed rides and performances for children. Nearby is the **Grand Manor,** a museum of antique automobiles. Children and non-skiers also enjoy riding the **Wildcat Gondola,** a 25-minute round trip to the summit looking across to Mount Washington. You can look down on Wildcat and the rest of New England from the top of the Mount Washington Auto Road, a 90-minute round-trip drive.

Extra-Special ⎯⎯⎯⎯⎯⎯⎯⎯⎯⎯⎯⎯⎯⎯⎯⎯

Cross-Country Skiing.

Jackson was rated by Esquire magazine as one of the four best places in the world for ski touring. That's due in large part to the efforts of the non-profit Jackson Ski Touring Foundation, founded in 1972 and now with 91 miles of well-groomed and marked trails starting in the village of Jackson and heading across public and private lands into the White Mountain National Forest. They interlace the village and link restaurants and inns, as well as connecting with 40 miles of Appalachian Mountain Club trails in Pinkham Notch. It's possible for cross-country skiers to take the gondola to the summit of Wildcat and tour downhill via a twelve-mile trail to the village of Jackson 3,200 feet below.

Sherburne House (circa 1695) is one of the oldest structures at Strawbery Banke.

Portsmouth, N.H.

A Lively Past and Present

Settled in 1623, the Portsmouth area ranks as the third oldest in the country after Jamestown and Plymouth. In many ways it looks it. The early Colonial houses hugging the narrow streets and the busy riverfront concede little to modernity.

This is no Jamestown or Plymouth, nor is it a Newport, a similarly sized and situated community with which it occasionally is compared. The city has only one large hotel, its downtown blessedly few chain stores or trendy boutiques, its residents little sense of elitism. What it does have is a patina of living and working history, a pride in its past and present, and a noticeable joie de vivre.

The sense of history is everywhere, from the famed restoration called Strawbery Banke to the ancient structures dating back to the 17th century tucked here and there all across town. Named for the profusion of wild berries found on the shores by the English settlers, Strawbery Banke after 38 years of restoration efforts is a living museum of more than 40 historic buildings at the edge of downtown.

Portsmouth's pride in past and present evidences itself in the six museum homes of the Historic Portsmouth Trail and the creative reuse of old buildings around Market Square and on the Hill.

You can sense Portsmouth's joie de vivre in its flourishing restaurants (good new ones pop up every year). Their number and scope are far beyond the resources of most cities of 26,000 and give it claim to the title, "Restaurant Capital of New England." You can see it in its lively Seacoast Repertory Theater. You can feel it in its Prescott Park Arts Festival, the Ceres Street Crafts Fair, the Seacoast Jazz Festival. The people on the streets and in the shops exude friendliness.

Happily, Portsmouth retains its historic sense of scale. It is an enclave of antiquity along the tidal Piscataqua River, four miles inland from the Atlantic. The Portsmouth Navy Yard is across the river in Kittery, Me. The Pease Air Force Base is west toward Dover. The shopping centers and fast-food strips are out in Newington. The beach action is down in Rye and Hampton. Many tourists stay at motels near the Portsmouth Circle.

While travelers pass by on the New Hampshire Turnpike, Air Force jets stream overhead, and tugboats and ocean vessels ply the river to and from the sea, Portsmouth goes its merry, historic way.

Inn Spots

Martin Hill Inn, 404 Islington St., Portsmouth 03801.

The first B&B in Portsmouth (1978), the Martin Hill was acquired in 1983 by Jane and Paul Harnden, who with another couple were visiting their favorite town from Nashua, where they lived. "We had hardly heard of bed and breakfast," says Jane, "but during breakfast at the inn the owners said they would like to sell in about three years and, I thought, this is me."

It turned out that medical problems forced the owners to sell that summer, and since then the Harndens have been the friendly innkeepers who dispense gobs of information about the many restaurants in town, historic attractions and whatnot, as well as cooking delicious breakfasts and dispatching every innkeeping task themselves, without staff. "We still air-dry our sheets and iron the pillowcases while watching the TV news," says Jane. As innkeepers go, the Harndens are among the most dedicated we know.

Their handsome yellow house, built in 1820, is within a ten-minute walk of downtown. Although it is on a commercial street, it's quiet because of air conditioning and one can retreat in summer to a deep and nicely landscaped back yard where 400 plants thrive. The yard was featured one year in the Unitarian Church's annual pocket garden tour. The Harndens since have installed cedar fencing around the property and converted a courtyard into an illuminated water garden.

Although the inn lacks a common room inside, guests have plenty of room to spread out in the three spacious guest rooms in the main inn, plus a room and three suites in the Guest House. The downstairs front room, called the Library, is in shades of rose and holds a twin and a queensize pineapple poster bed. Upstairs, the Master Bedroom, in white and Wedgwood blue, has a canopy bed and oriental rugs on the wide-board floors. The Greenhouse Suite in the spiffy side annex contains a small solarium furnished in wicker looking onto the water garden, rattan furniture in an inside sitting room and a

Martin Hill Inn occupies handsome 1820 house.

bedroom with spindle bed and full bath. Balloon curtains frame the windows in the Green Room, which has a small sitting room, an antique tub with a hand-held shower, and an iron and brass bed that's so frilly it reminds Jane of a big crib. All rooms have modern baths, queen beds, loveseats or comfortable chairs, good reading lamps, writing desks, armoires, and nice touches like potpourri in china teacups and the inn's own wildflower glycerin soaps.

Breakfast is served on a gleaming mahogany table in the antiques-filled dining room, whose walls display three coordinated English wallpapers and paints. Orange juice might be followed by Jane's scrumptious baked apple, the core filled with brown sugar. Paul makes dynamite french toast with Italian sourdough bread, slathered with almonds and accompanied by Canadian bacon and homemade cranberry relish. Our scrambled eggs with cheese and chervil were served with cranberry bread, and the coffee pot was bottomless. It's a great time for guests to compare notes on the restaurants they visited the night before and to plan the day with the help of Paul, who can even plot you out a trip up to Canada and back. Clearly, the Harndens relish their role as innkeepers and go out of their way to be helpful and accommodating.

(603) 436-2287. Four rooms and three suites with private baths. July-October: doubles, $90 to $110, suites $95 to $115. Rest of year: all $80 to $90. Children over 12. No smoking.

Sise Inn, 40 Court St., Portsmouth 03801.

The first United States branch of a growing Canadian-based group called Someplace(s) Different Ltd., this is a fine operation. The company took the original Queen Anne home built in 1881 for the John E. Sise family, remodeled it with great taste and put on a rear addition that blends in very well. Walk in the front door past the stained-glass windows on either side, gaze at the rich and abundant butternut and oak throughout, marvel at the graceful staircase and three-story-high foyer, peek into the sumptuous living room and you're apt to say, as its marketing director did upon first seeing it, "this is the real Portsmouth."

The 34 rooms and suites on three floors and in a carriage house vary in bed configuration, size and decor. All are elegantly furnished in antiques and period reproductions with striking window treatments and vivid wallpapers. Geared to the business traveler, they have queen or twin beds, vanities outside the bathrooms (the larger of which contain whirlpool baths), writing desks, clock radios, telephones, and remote-control television and VCRs, often hidden in armoires. Some have sitting areas. Businessmen must like to watch TV in bed, for in many of the rooms we saw the TV wasn't visible from the chairs or, as is so often the case, the single chair. Windows that open, English herbal toiletries and mints on the pillow may compensate for the occasional lack of places to sit.

Or you can sit in the stylish main-floor living room, very much like an English library with several conversation areas and fresh flowers all around. Innkeeper Carl Jensen is the usually visible host.

A help-yourself breakfast of fruits, juices, yogurt, cheese, cereals, granola, bagels, toasting breads and all kinds of preserves and honey is available amidst much ornate wood in the dining room.

The lower floor, notable for an antique English phone booth in the hallway, contains three function rooms. A modern elevator shuttles guests between floors.

(603) 433-1200 or (800) 267-0525. Twenty-eight rooms and six suites with private baths. Mid-May through October: doubles $128 to $150, suites $175 to $225. Rest of year: doubles $109 to 125, suites, $140 to $165. Children accepted.

Gundalow Inn, 6 Water St., Kittery, Me. 03904.

The nicest of the B&Bs popping up across the Piscataqua River in Kittery is this appealing establishment facing the Portsmouth waterfront, which is within walking distance across the Memorial Bridge.

George and Cevia Rosol acquired the 1889 Italianate New England structure, formerly a two-family house, in an estate sale. They spent two years restoring the building, taking out the only two bathrooms and putting in seven new ones. They offer six guest rooms, each with private bath and several with views of the river. All are named after gundalows (a corruption of the word gondolas), the 250-year-old flat-bottom boats with sails that plied the Piscataqua and are believed to have transported the bricks for the house downriver from Dover.

Vivid Victorian wallpapers and ten-foot-high ceilings are the rule in the second-floor rooms, one of which has windows on three sides. The bathroom in the Minx room is big enough to include both a chair and a closet. A curved stairway beneath a skylight leads past a plant-filled shelf to a new third floor, where two guest rooms afford the best views of the river and of Portsmouth. We're partial to the Royal George, which has a wicker loveseat beneath a skylight, a queensize bed with a sturdy Colonial bedstead, an armoire, blue carpeting and walls with a yellow floral print. Thick white towels are in abundance in baskets and on towel racks. The Rosols added stained-glass interior windows to enhance those bathrooms without outside windows.

Guests gather in a large, comfortable parlor furnished in a mix of Colonial and Victorian styles. Focal points are a grand piano and an enormous table displaying half a dozen newspapers and some of the magazines and books that abound throughout the house. Tea, wine and sherry are offered here in the afternoons to

Facing Portsmouth waterfront is brick structure housing Gundalow Inn.

the accompaniment of classical music. A screened porch furnished with rockers catches a view of the river.

A full breakfast is served in a sunny garden room converted from a former passageway to the connecting barn, which the Rosols have transformed into their quarters. The room has a corner fireplace, three tables and windows on two sides onto colorful gardens. Breakfast starts with a fruit course, perhaps blueberry-lemon soup or baked apples with granola, and scones. Then come creamy scrambled eggs, pecan pancakes, zucchini fritters or bread pudding. Next is a meat or fish course – smoked salmon, fish cakes, homemade sausage or corned-beef hash. There might be a "dessert" of concord grape pie when the grapes are in season.

(207) 439-4040. Six rooms with private baths. Mid-May through October: doubles, $110 to $125. Rest of year: $80 to $90. Lower midweek rates in winter. Children over 16. No smoking.

The Inn at Strawbery Banke, 314 Court St., Portsmouth 03801.

You can't stay much closer to Strawbery Banke than this 1800 ship captain's house situated right up against the street, as so many in Portsmouth are. It also shows its age, but it's gradually getting improvements over the years.

All seven air-conditioned guest rooms come with private baths, although one is in the hall (and one in the attic suite is open to the room). Two rooms on the main floor share a common room. Strawberry stenciling, strawberry comforters and strawberry candies on the pillows accent the prevailing green and white color scheme here. More rooms go off an upstairs common room. One, done up in blues, has inside Indian shutters, two rattan chairs and pineapple stenciling. Another with windows on three sides contains a double and a single bed and three ice-cream-parlor chairs around a glass table. The aforementioned attic suite, with the open w.c. and shower added in the corner, must be for young, short people. It's up steep stairs and we had to duck to avoid the roof as we entered the sleeping alcove.

Innkeeper Sally Glover O'Donnell, who grew up in the family that formerly ran the Colby Hill Inn in Henniker, serves a full breakfast in a skylit breakfast room with an abundance of hanging plants. The main course at our visit was sourdough blueberry pancakes with sausages, supplemented by oatmeal, cold cereals and homemade pastries. The room looks onto a strawberry patch, bird feeders and the trellised rose garden of the historic Governor Langdon House just behind. Sally keeps cookie jars stocked for afternoon or evening snacks in the two small common rooms, both with television sets.

(603) 436-7242 or (800) 428-3933. Seven rooms with private baths. Doubles, $100 to $105 in season; $70 to $75 rest of year. Children over 10. No smoking.

The Inn at Christian Shore, 335 Maplewood Ave., Portsmouth 03801.

An abundance of antiques, an inviting dining room with a fireplace, and rather lavishly decorated, air-conditioned guest rooms with television are attractions in this 1800 Federal house, located in the historic Christian Shore area.

Across from the Jackson House, Portsmouth's oldest, this structure was renovated and redecorated in 1978 by three antiques dealers, who sold recently to Mariaelena Koopman.

In the main entry hall is a desk with baskets of candies and nuts, a grandfather clock and an etched-glass light.

The first and second floors contain five guest rooms, three with queensize beds, plus a tiny single available for $40 a night (rented only in conjunction with a queen-bedded room sharing its bath). The other two rooms have a double and a single bed. Two rooms have fireplaces. All contain handsome furnishings, antiques and crocheted afghans.

A harvest table dominates the beamed breakfast room, the heart of the house with its large brick fireplace. Three smaller dining tables with upholstered wing chairs are beside windows on the sides.

A full breakfast is served by the European-born innkeeper. "Excellent breakfast – gracious hostess" was the latest entry in the guest book at our visit.

(603) 431-6770. Fax (603) 431-6770. Five rooms with private baths. Doubles, $95, June-October; $75, rest of year. Pets accepted in winter.

The Bow Street Inn, 121 Bow St., Portsmouth 03801.

A succession of owners continues to improve this downtown riverfront establishment, which really is a cross between a motel and a small hotel. It occupies the second floor of a restored four-story brick brewery warehouse that also houses condominiums, a theater and a cafe.

Access to the inn is by buzzer and then up an elevator. Nine guest rooms with private baths go off either side of a center hallway. The views are of rooftops or the street, because the condominium blocks the view of the river except from Room 6. Unexpectedly small, the rooms are furnished simply but attractively in light pastel colors with queensize brass beds (except for one with a king/twins), thick carpeting, cable TV, telephones and a single chair. A mini-suite with a pullout couch and a town view accommodates four. A penthouse suite includes a kitchen and living room.

Juice, cereal, muffins, bagels and breads for toasting are put out in a pleasant brick dining room with three tables and a small refrigerator for guests' use. The owner "tries to make people feel at home," said one of the assistants on duty at our

Mural of farmers' market graces wall at Blue Mermaid World Grill.

visit. There's no specific parking area, but the inn supposedly pays if guests are ticketed for parking illegally.

(603) 431-7760. Ten rooms and one suite with private baths. Doubles, $114 to $149, July-October; $89 to $139 rest of year. Suite, $295. No smoking.

Dining Spots

Blue Mermaid World Grill, The Hill, Portsmouth.

Two restaurateurs from Boston took over the old Codfish restaurant here and found Portsmouth receptive to their idea of new world grill cuisine. They installed the town's first wood grill, gave the restaurant an arty and whimsical decor, and started dispensing spicy foods of the Caribbean, South America, California and the Southwest.

Partners Jim Smith and Scott Logan removed some walls for a more open feeling on two floors, added embellishments like a fascinating abstract mural of the Portsmouth Farmers' Market and iron animals atop some chandeliers, and identified the rest rooms with mermaids and mermen.

Our lunch testified to their success. As we sat down, tortilla strips with fire-roasted vegetables and salsa arrived in what otherwise might be a candle holder. These piqued the tastebuds for a cup of tasty black bean soup, a sandwich of grilled Jamaican jerk chicken with sunsplash salsa and a sandwich of grilled vegetables with jarlsberg cheese on walnut bread. These came with sweet-potato chips and the house sambal, and we also sampled a side order of thick grilled vidalia onion rings with mango ketchup. A generous portion of ginger cheesecake, garnished with the hard candy-like topping of crème brûlée, was a sensational ending.

The signature dinner dish is grilled lobster with mango butter, served with grilled vegetables and cornbread. Other treats include zuni vegetable stew with cilantro pesto, Southwestern skirt steak with roasted corn and red pepper salsa, pan-seared haddock with coconut cream sauce and a skewer of marinated lamb with couscous.

Bottles of incendiary sauces are on the tables to add fuel to the fire. Cool off with desserts like homemade caramel ice cream or tia maria flan.

(603) 427-2583. Entrées, $12.95 to $15.25. Lunch daily, 11:30 to 5. Dinner, 5 to 10 or 11.

Cafe Mirabelle, 64 Bridge St., Portsmouth.

French chef Stephan Mayeux and his wife Chris opened this casual gourmet restaurant in the former Fish Shanty. Now very un-shantyish, it's crisp and contemporary on two floors. There are a few tables for dining downstairs in a cafe near the bar called La Crêperie. Upstairs is a cathedral-ceilinged room with beams and pleasing angles, mission-style chairs at burgundy-linened tables up against tall windows, shelves of country artifacts along sand-colored walls and twinkling lights on ficus trees.

Stephan offers an interesting cafe-style menu as well as a four-course prix-fixe dinner. Bouillabaisse and frog's legs are menu fixtures. Also expect things like salmon épernay with scallops in a champagne and shallot-basil cream sauce, magret of duck with a tangy orange-ginger demi-glace, veal calvados, steak au poivre and roasted lamb loin with rosemary and horseradish sauce. Start with baked brie with walnuts and thyme in puff pastry, saffron mussels or grilled shrimp and scallops on a garlic-tomato coulis. Finish with lemon-bourbon cheesecake with a pecan crust, chocolate charlotte with raspberry coulis, homemade sorbet or tarte tatin.

Good-sounding crêpes and salads are offered at lunch, which is a available in season on a side courtyard.

(603) 430-9301. Prix-fixe, $32. Entrées, $11.50 to $19.95. Lunch, Wednesday-Saturday 11:30 to 2. Dinner nightly, 5:15 to 8:30 or 9. Sunday brunch, 10 to 2.

Anthony Alberto's, 59 Penhallow St., Portsmouth.

New owners took over the old Anthony's Al Dente, a local institution hidden in the Custom House Cellar. Tod Alberto and Massimo Morgia, who had been associated with the posh Ponte Vecchio in nearby Newcastle, renovated the space and named it after Tod's father.

It's elegant, dark and grotto-like with stone and brick walls, arches, exposed beams on the ceiling and oriental rugs on the slate floors. Aqua upholstered chairs, mauve fanned napkins and white tablecloths add a Mediterranean look. The service and attention to detail are said to be the best in town.

The menu is high Italian, as in grilled salmon with lentils, mushrooms and spinach served in a barbera wine sauce or grilled breast of duck in a port wine and ginger reduction with sautéed spinach and grilled peaches. Red snapper and vegetables might be baked in parchment paper and the veal sautéed with fontina cheese, sundried tomatoes and artichokes. Six pastas and risottos are available as appetizers or main dishes.

Expect such starters as carpaccio of yellowfin tuna, portobello mushrooms over arugula salad, grilled calamari stuffed with crabmeat and an antipasto plate meant for sharing. Desserts include tarts, bananas flambé, tirami su and crème caramel.

(603) 436-4000. Entrées, $13.95 to $21.95. Dinner, Monday-Saturday 5 to 9:30 or 10:30, Sunday 4 to 8:30.

The Metro, 20 High St., Portsmouth.

Very popular locally is Sam Jarvis's long-running art nouveau bar and bistro. It's decked out with brass rails, stained glass, old gas lights, mirrors and dark wood, leather banquettes, bentwood chairs and nifty Vanity Fair posters. Live background music is offered on weekends.

The Metro's award-winning clam chowder is a popular starter among the appetizers, which have been updated lately from their traditional continental bent to include grilled shrimp skewers with pesto vinaigrette, wild mushroom strudel with roasted garlic cream and pan-fried Maine crab cakes with lemon-herb aioli.

Main courses could be cedar plank-roasted salmon with honey-mustard glaze, herb-crusted red snapper with champagne citrus salsa, grilled free-range chicken with roasted shallot sauce, or roasted rack of lamb with mint-walnut pesto. Long Island duck might be grilled with a ginger and plum wine demi-glace and the pork chops glazed with cider.

Desserts, attractively displayed on a fancy old baker's rack, include cappuccino crème caramel, pecan fudge pie and walnut cake.

Salads, sandwiches, fettuccine alfredo and such entrées as baked haddock with brandied pecans are offered at lunch.

(603) 436-0521. Entrées, $14 to $23. Lunch, Monday-Saturday 11:30 to 2:30. Dinner, Monday-Thursday 5:30 to 9:30, Friday-Saturday 5 to 10.

Lindberg's Crossing, 29 Ceres St., Portsmouth.

The famed Blue Strawbery restaurant gave way in 1996 to this newcomer with obscure references to Charles Lindbergh. A propeller hangs on one wall of the brick and beamed downstairs bistro, site of widely acclaimed meals under its previous incarnation. A representation of Lindbergh's flight across the Atlantic flanks the stairway to the casual upstairs wine bar, where dinner also is available and no reservations are taken.

The contemporary Mediterranean fare has been downscaled since the heady days of former chef-owner Buddy Haller, but receives high marks from locals who found its predecessor a bit much. Expect such main courses as mixed seafood tossed with Israeli couscous, sautéed rainbow trout, pepper-crusted salmon roulade, pan-fried rabbit served over garlic mashed potatoes and organic beef tenderloin au poivre. The popular bistro steak sandwich is topped with caramelized onions and gruyère cheese.

Typical starters are two versions of mussels, escargots, seared rare tuna, and a pâté and cheese platter. Desserts are a signature "medium rare chocolate cake" (whose center is described as the consistency of chocolate pudding), almond-crusted cheesecake and crème brûlée. Espresso and cappuccino are finishing touches.

(603) 431-0887. Entrées, $11 to $21. Dinner nightly, 5:30 to 10:30. Wine bar from 4.

Porto Bello, 67 Bow St., Portsmouth.

Yolanda Desario, her brother Jerry and her mother run this intimate, L-shaped dining room overlooking the harbor. Yolanda, the founding chef, now assists Jerry when she's not tending to her young family. They prepare authentic and traditional northern Italian food from scratch, "cooked simply," says she, but sounding rather complex to anyone else.

Creative specials supplement the short dinner menu, which offers main dishes like grilled albacore tuna steak with a sauce of plum tomatoes and balsamic vinegar, chicken stuffed with prosciutto and porcini mushrooms, butcher-made grilled sausages with sweet peppers and roasted potatoes, and loin lamb chops roasted with garlic and rosemary. Friends who sampled the mozzarella appetizer with slices of parma prosciutto, plum tomatoes and basil said they never knew mozzarella could be so good. They also said the delicate homemade lasagna layered with five cheeses in ragu sauce is out of this world. Desserts include profiteroles, cannolis, poached pears and zuppa inglese. There's a short, pricey wine list.

Some of the white-clothed tables, set amid a beamed ceiling and brick walls, are flanked by windows onto the harbor.

(603) 431-2989. Entrées, $12.95 to $17.95. Lunch, Wednesday-Saturday 11 to 2:30. Dinner, Tuesday-Saturday 4:30 to 9:30.

Dunfey's Aboard the John Wanamaker, One Harbor Place, Portsmouth.

Walter Dunfey of the Hampton-based Dunfey chain purchased the old John Wanamaker tugboat that started life in Philadelphia and now is moored in the Piscataqua River beneath the State Street bridge. Come for lunch, perch on a stool at the mahogany bar around the outside railing and you can almost touch the water. Ships pass right in front of you. A bit more disconcerting for some is the below-deck dining room, where the portholes are at eye-level with the water, the engine is encased in glass and the bar is papered with nautical charts. An abundance of wood and brass make it all appear more like a yacht than a tugboat. The captain's dining room at the stern of the vessel is quite formal, with white-clothed tables against banquettes.

There's nothing subtle about the food, we hear. The chef comes right at you with appetizers like lobster and shrimp spring rolls with a spicy Thai sauce and main courses like pan-seared halibut with a smoky tomato vinaigrette, sesame-crusted salmon in a ginger sauce, Moroccan-spiced chicken with couscous and grilled black angus steak with a wild mushroom ragu. Dessert could be a chocolate-pear tart, peach torte or raspberry and blueberry shortcake.

The short lunch menu yields things like salad niçoise, grilled cajun shrimp tortilla, pesto ricotta pizza, a Texas steak sandwich with bananas and curried chutney, and a fried clam plate.

(603) 433-3111. Entrées, $16 to $23. Lunch daily in season, 11:30 to 2:30. Dinner nightly in summer, 5:30 to 10; closed Monday in off-season.

The Library Restaurant at the Rockingham House, 401 State St., Portsmouth.

The old Rockingham Hotel was converted to apartments, but part of the ground floor was restored into an extravagant restaurant. Its ornate carved-wood ceiling, rich mahogany paneling, fireplaces, huge mirrors and bright blue napkins set the stage for books on shelves in three rooms. A new owner removed some of the books and bookshelf-enclosed booths for a more open, elegant setting.

The fare is American/continental and highly regarded. For lunch, we tried a generous and tasty fennel and gruyère quiche, accompanied by a super spinach salad with a mustard dressing and homemade croutons. The mussels marinière arrived in a large glass bowl abrim with garlicky broth in which to dip chunks of the homemade rolls. The strawberry cheesecake for dessert was at least three inches high.

Dinner could be salmon béarnaise, baked stuffed shrimp, chicken marsala, grilled veal chop and prime rib. Start with chicken tenders, baked brie or smoked salmon. Finish with pecan pie, Indian pudding or a platter of biscotti.

(603) 431-5202. Entrées, $14.95 to $24.95. Lunch, Monday-Saturday 11:30 to 3. Dinner, 5 to 10 or 11. Sunday brunch, 11:30 to 4.

The Dolphin Striker, 15 Bow St., Portsmouth.

Considered the best of the touristy choices along the waterfront is this oldtimer rescued from foreclosure some years back. It was reopened by new owners and quickly garnered a number of culinary awards.

The atmosphere is strictly historic, with bare sloping floors, beamed ceilings, flickering oil lamps and a sense of Colonial times in three dining rooms and the cozy, stone-walled tavern beneath. The white napkins on each table are folded to look like schooners.

The recent seafood theme has given way to what the chef calls eclectic American fare. He shows a deft touch with things like broiled salmon with a lemon-onion vinaigrette, pepper-roasted haddock with corn relish, sautéed lobster, honey-grilled breast of duck with pineapple salsa, grilled veal porterhouse with a roasted plum tomato coulis and grilled beef tenderloin glazed with chèvre and served atop roasted red pepper-chipotle sauce. Typical appetizers are sautéed crab cakes with basil-mustard aioli and portobello mushroom stuffed with crabmeat and finished with roasted tomato coulis. Desserts could be chocolate mousse en croûte, key lime pie, grand marnier soufflé or Irish whiskey cake.

A light menu and live music are offered downstairs in the **Spring Hill Tavern.**

(603) 431-5222. Entrées, $14.95 to $23.95. Lunch daily, 11:30 to 2. Dinner, 5 to 9:30 or 10, Sunday 5 to 9:30.

The Portsmouth Brewery, 56 Market St., Portsmouth.

An award-winning restoration turned this downtown building into a brewery with a bar and restaurant that packs in a hip, young crowd day and night.

Sitting at booths or tables on one of several levels of a deep, high-ceilinged room full of brick, glass and mirrors, you can watch workmen pouring from 200-gallon tanks in the glass-walled brewery. You also can contemplate the incredible large wall collages designed by a friend of the owner. And you can sip some mighty good golden lager and pale ale from a choice of six brewed and sold on site by the pint or glass. With them we enjoyed a chicken salad Santa Fe, which came in a tortilla shell, and an oversize sourdough sandwich of feta cheese, vegetables and black olive garlic spread, served with corn chips and salsa.

The extensive menu pairs American with Mexican, anything from a cajun swordfish sandwich to chicken fajitas. Dinner entrées at our latest visit ranged from fish and chips to hickory-smoked sirloin steak.

(603) 431-1115. Entrées, $10.95 to $16.95. Lunch daily, 11:30 to 5. Dinner, 5 to 11.

BG's Boat House Restaurant, 191 Wentworth Road, Portsmouth.

If you're hankering for lobster and down-home surroundings, head for this popular restaurant with waterside decks and a marina out past the old Wentworth resort in Newcastle.

The walls are pine paneled, the floors bare and tables have captain's chairs and paper mats, the better for gorging oneself on a lobster dinner, a lobster roll with french fries, fried oysters or a seafood platter. The lobsters are delivered to the back door by boat by BG's own lobstermen. The Graveses accommodate other tastes with BLT sandwiches, hamburgers, potato skins and mozzarella sticks, but most people come here for lobster and seafood, plain and simple.

(603) 431-1074. Entrées, $8.95 to $13.95. Lunch, daily in summer, 11 to 4. Dinner nightly, 5 to 9. Closed Monday-Tuesday in spring and fall and October to mid-March.

Cafe Brioche, 14 Market Square, Portsmouth.
Lately expanded into an old stationery store to twice its original size, this large sidewalk café and meeting spot is a good place to stop anytime for a light breakfast like a ham and cheese croissant with cappuccino. It's also popular for lunch, with several kinds of quiche, salads and great soups (caldo verde and curried crab bisque at one visit). Sandwiches range from hummus to country pâté.
(603) 430-9225. Open daily 6:30 to 6, weekends to 11.

Diversions

Portsmouth offers much for anyone with an interest in history. The Greater Portsmouth Chamber of Commerce publishes a "Walking Tour of Downtown Portsmouth's Waterfront," which also can be driven (although directions get confusing because of one-way streets). The 2.3-mile tour takes in most of the city's attractions, including some we had passed for years unknowingly. Such is the charm of an area crammed with discoveries at every turn. A new way to tour is by horse and carriage with **Portsmouth Livery.** Talkative Ray Parker, in beard and top hat, adds dimension to the city's history as he gives sightseeing tours for $15 to $25, leaving from the Market Square carriage stand from noon into the evening, daily May-October.

Strawbery Banke, Marcy Street, Portsmouth.
Billed as "an American original," this walk-through museum is the careful restoration of one of the nation's oldest neighborhoods. Its more than 40 structures across ten acres date from 1695 to 1945 and depict four centuries of cultural and architectural change. Some have simply been preserved. Some are used by working artisans (independent of the museum, they are earning their living as well as re-enacting history). Others are used for educational exhibits including archaeology, architectural styles and construction techniques and, on the outside, historic gardens. Strawbery Banke's collection of local arts and furniture is shown in ten historic houses. Significantly, these are not all homes of the rich or famous, but rather of ordinary people. As the museum's 35th anniversary program noted, "This is the real story of history – the dreams and aspirations, the disappointments and frustrations of common people." That is the glory of Strawbery Banke, and of much of Portsmouth.
(603) 433-1100. Open daily 10 to 5, mid-April through October; also evening candle-light stroll, first two weekends in December. Adults, $12 (good for two consecutive days).

The Portsmouth Trail. Six of Portsmouth's finest house museums are open individually and linked by a walking tour. Considered the one not to miss is the 1763 **Moffatt-Ladd House,** a replica of an English manor house located just above Ceres Street restaurants and shops. The yellow 1758 **John Paul Jones House,** the imposing **Governor John Langdon House** (1784) and the Georgian-style **Wentworth-Gardner House** (1760) are others. Most are open six or seven days a week from June to mid-October and charge $4 each.

The Isles of Shoals. This group of nine rocky islands located about ten miles off shore are reached by the Isles of Shoals Steamship Co. cruises from Barker Wharf at 315 Market St. Charted by Capt. John Smith when he sailed past in 1614, the islands originally drew European fishermen for their "shoals" or schools of fish. The two largest islands, Appledore and Star, became summer resorts in the

1800s. Since early in the 1900s, Star Island has been operated as a religious conference center by the Congregational and Unitarian churches. Visitors hear the legends of these barren islands during cruises. The one at 11 a.m. includes a Star Island stopover that allows passengers to spend an hour exploring the island.

(603) 431-5500 or (800) 441-4620. Variety of cruises daily, mid-June to Labor Day. Adults, $9 to $41.95.

Shopping. Most of the traditional tourist shopping attractions have passed Portsmouth by, heading for the outlet strip along Route 1 north of Kittery or the shopping malls of Newington. But downtown Portsmouth has plenty of interesting local shops concentrated around Market Square.

In one of its four stores, **Macro Polo Inc.** has inventive children's toys; we were transported back to our childhood while gazing at the assortment of marbles in the window. **Wholly Macro!** stocks handmade Texas boots among its wares. **Macroscopic** struck us as rather New Agey. **Not Just Mud! Craft Gallery** stocks great hand-blown art glass, kaleidoscopes, pottery, jewelry and titanium clocks among its contemporary crafts. The **Paper Patch** is the shop for funny cards. **Bow Street Candle and Mug** is room after room of – you guessed it – but also has a section called **Southwest Passage** where you'll find things with the Santa Fe look. **Worldly Goods** purveys birdhouses, oil lamps, interesting baskets and adorable cat pins.

Among its treasures, **Les Cadeaux** stocks exotic bath salts, fancy stationery, boxes of decorated sugar cubes from Kentucky, chocolate spoons to dip in hot chocolate, lovely china casseroles with different fruits on top for handles, and preserves and mustards from Le Cordon Bleu in France. You'd have to see them to believe the high-heeled shoes made of papier-mâché and trimmed with jewelry at **Gallery 33;** we also liked the hand-carved whimsical animals here. Wearing a T-shirt urging "squeeze me, crush me, make me wine," jovial proprietor David Campbell brings a sense of fun along with expertise to his wines, specialty foods and gift baskets at the **Ceres Street Wine Merchants.** We did some Christmas shopping at **Salamander Glass** and the **N.W. Barrett Gallery,** which has some of Sabra Field's woodcuts and fantastic jewelry. Strawbery **Banke's Museum Shop** at the Dunaway Store on Marcy Street is a classy gift shop. **Strawbery Banke's** working crafts shops offer the wares of potters, a cabinetmaker, a weaver, and dories made in the boat shed.

Extra-Special

Newcastle. Drive or bicycle out Newcastle Avenue (Route 1B) through the quaint islands of Newcastle, the original settlement in 1623, dotted with prosperous homes. The meandering roads and treed residential properties, many with water views, mix contemporary-style houses with those of days gone by. You can view Fort Constitution with one of several towers built during the War of 1812 and visit the seacoast park at **Great Island Common,** where there are a playground, waterfront picnic tables and views of the Isles of Shoals. The old Wentworth-by-the-Sea, a majestic resort hotel if ever there was one, was in transition. Its golf course was sold to make way for expensive houses, but in 1998 Ocean Properties Inc. was restoring the hotel with its original shell into an upscale, 180-room hotel and conference center. Another rewarding drive is out Maine Route 103 past the Naval Yards in Kittery to Kittery Point, where attractive houses large and small seem to be surrounded by water on all sides.

The ocean lies just beyond guest rooms at Stage Neck Inn in York Harbor.

The Yorks
Great Gateway to Maine

The visitor quickly agrees with what the Chamber of Commerce directory proudly proclaims: "The Yorks are a perfect introduction to Maine. They have everything for which the Great State is famous: rocky coast, sandy beaches, a lighthouse, a mountain, rivers,...lobsters, folks who really do say 'ayuh.'"

The focal point of the Yorks is, of course, the water – specifically, the harbor where the river confronts the sea. From fashionable York Harbor, whose waters are as protected as its seaside homes, it's barely a mile inland along the York River to historic York Village, the oldest surviving English settlement in Maine. From the harbor, it's also barely a mile along the shore to York Beach. Abruptly, the rocky coast yields to sand; the trailer parks symbolize the transition from tree-shaded affluence to honky-tonk strand.

Beyond are Nubble Light, one of America's most photographed lighthouses, and Cape Neddick Harbor, a quieter and quainter fishing site. Sand gives way again to rocks as Bald Head Cliff rises off the forested Shore Road near the Ogunquit town line.

Yes, the Yorks provide a good introduction to Maine, from the Cape Neddick fishermen to the amusement areas at crowded York Beach.

But much of the appeal of the Yorks lies elsewhere. It's in York Village, where a national historic district embraces both private structures and eight house museums and inspires the slogan, "Where Maine's History Begins." It's in York Harbor, a verdant enclave of Colonial homesteads and gracious estates whose occupants in 1892 formed the York Harbor Reading Room men's club, an offshoot of which was the York Harbor Village Corporation. It established the first zoning laws in Maine and prevented the hordes and development of York Beach from spilling into York Harbor.

Growing numbers of inns are concentrated in York Village and York Harbor, allowing visitors to partake of quiet places in which past melds into present.

Inn Spots

Stage Neck Inn, Off Route 1A, Box 97, York Harbor 03911.

Once an island and now a promontory where the York River becomes a harbor, Stage Neck was the site of the Marshall House, the first of the area's resort hotels. It was razed and rebuilt in 1973 as the Stage Neck Inn, a low-profile contemporary resort whose understated luxury fits the setting.

Disproportionate numbers of Cadillacs are in the parking lot, indicating the clientele for whom Stage Neck is designed. There are tennis courts, a swimming pool and private beach, an indoor pool and jacuzzi, golf privileges, posh public rooms with water views, and a handsome dining room in which the traditional jacket requirement has given way to "proper dress" for dinner.

There also are water views from the private patios or balconies of 60 guest rooms on three floors. The sprawling building was designed into the landscape and opens on three sides to ocean, river and beach. Guest rooms are comfortably furnished in restful shades of deep rose and moss green, with two doubles or queen or kingsize beds, two comfortable chairs and a table, color TV and phone. Rates vary with the view. The most choice are corner rooms with wraparound porches and views of the water in two directions.

Three meals a day are served in the Sandpiper Bar & Grille or the main Harbor Porches dining room. Baked stuffed shrimp, veal with mushrooms and steak au poivre are menu standbys. Locals are partial to the **Sandpiper Bar & Grille,** where the extensive all-day menu offers pizzas, sandwiches and light entrées.

(207) 363-3850 or (800) 222-3238. Fax (207) 363-2221. Sixty rooms with private baths. Rates EP. Doubles, $165 to $230, Memorial Day to Labor Day; $135 to $200, spring and early fall; $110 to $145, November-March. Three-night minimum in summer; two-night minimum in off-season. No smoking. Closed first two weeks of January.
Entrées, $15.95 to $23.95. Lunch daily, noon to 2. Dinner nightly, 6 to 9 or 10.

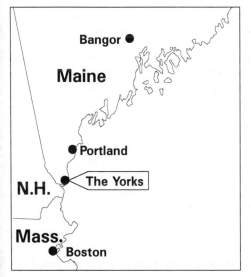

Bangor ●

Maine

● Portland

N.H. ● The Yorks

Mass.
● Boston

Wooden Goose Inn, Route 1, Cape Neddick 03902.

Tantalizing aromas and spirited classical music greet visitors to the Wooden Goose Inn. The aromas come from the kitchen, where innkeepers Jerry Rippletoe and Tony Sienicki take turns baking their specialties, perhaps a flourless chocolate torte for afternoon tea or date bread for breakfast. The music comes from myriad speakers, which send Mozart and Vivaldi across the house.

This is one decorated inn, from its Terrace Room breakfast area and two comfy parlors to the seven guest rooms. All would do

Elegant furnishings enhance guest bedroom and parlor at Wooden Goose Inn.

any house and garden magazine proud. Jerry was a decorator in New York and New Jersey before he and Tony acquired the derelict house in 1984; he still commutes to the metropolitan area for consulting jobs. Lately they bought 750 yards of fabric to redo three bedrooms and learned to use a sewing machine when they found it would cost $11,000 to have done what they wanted. Their do-it-yourself window treatments, billowing canopies and coordinated pillows are remarkable. So are the decorative birdhouses that Tony builds and displays around the house. They're for sale at up to $350 each. Guests had purchased three the weekend before our recent revisit.

As befits the inn's name, geese and ducks are everywhere – even on the white-lit Christmas tree during the holiday season. Many are gifts from guests.

The rooms have been sumptuously outfitted with Victorian country furnishings in a masculine style and the walls are hung with many paintings. Each air-conditioned room has a queensize bed, private bath and a sitting area. Blinds are down and curtains drawn to screen out distractions from the road outside. There are bedside lights for reading, and the setting epitomizes escape and romance. "The room is the important part of the stay," contends Jerry. "We try to provide a tranquil, peaceful house."

He and Tony keep their charges well fed. Afternoon tea is taken in the rear Terrace Room or outside in lush gardens around a trickling pond bordered by rocks. Eleven varieties of tea are offered, and come with pâtés on toast rounds and a choice of desserts, perhaps a tart of Granny Smith apples and lemons, a butter pecan cheesecake or other fancy desserts prepared by Tony.

They now offer weekday BYOB dinner packages in the off-season and on July weekends. They even close their inn to the public in July, opening only by invitation for weekend guests who book three nights, two dinners, two continental breakfasts and a full breakfast, $375 for two. The same package also has proven successful

Monday-Wednesday in the off-season. A typical dinner might be five-onion soup, salad with dijon vinaigrette, chicken breast with shiitake mushroom sauce, oven-roasted rosemary and thyme potatoes, pan-fried asparagus, and a choice among several tempting desserts.

Breakfasts are sumptuous as well. The day begins with coffee on a silver tray outside your room at 8 o'clock. The main event opens with fresh juice, homemade baked goods and such fruit courses as strawberries romanoff or peach and cherry soup. Then comes the pièce de résistance: eggs oscar, hard-boiled eggs with shrimp and creamy dill sauce, or baked egg in puff pastry on smoked Canadian bacon with hollandaise sauce, garnished with pimento and black olives. Recent dishes have included shepherds pie made with chicken instead of lamb, topped with cheddar cheese and mashed potatoes; country French chicken with a poached egg encased in puff pastry, and haddock sautéed in brandy with honey and apples, served with thyme-roasted potatoes and garlic-fried broccoli. "People sometimes remark how nice it is to have dinner for breakfast," says Tony. After all this, he concedes, you might need to go back to your room for a snooze.

In 1998, the partners opened an adjacent retail adjunct, a shop specializing in antiques and accessories.

(207) 363-5673. Seven rooms with private baths. Doubles, $150. Closed to public in July.

Dockside Guest Quarters, Harris Island, Box 205, York 03909.
Just across the river from Stage Neck on a peninsula unto itself is the Dockside, which in 1954 began taking in boaters in the handsome late 19th-century white homestead. Owners David and Harriette Lusty enjoyed innkeeping so much they added the Crow's Nest with an apartment and two studios on the water, then built the Quarterdeck cottages, and finally added the contemporary Lookout on the hill. They retain the name "guest quarters," such is the tradition of the place.

The lovely grounds lead to water's edge and are dotted with lawn chairs, flower gardens and picket fences.

The day's tides are posted on the blackboard in the Maine House, where the dining room and parlor are furnished with antiques, marine paintings and models of ships, and the rambling wraparound porch opens to sea views. Scrapbooks full of pictures of inn guests are displayed on a coffee table. There's a TV set in the parlor, and a table holds tea bags and apples for afternoon snacks.

The house has five guest rooms, ranging from two twin rooms sharing a bath to a studio sleeping two to four. The front corner room is the choice of many, with its full-length porch from which to view the buoys bobbing in the harbor.

The three multi-unit cottage buildings scattered around the property hold twin or double bedrooms, studios, an efficiency and apartment suites for two to four. Each has a porch or deck with a view out the harbor entrance to the ocean. You can't get much closer to the water than the balconies in the Crow's Nest, but some prefer the wider decks of the Lookout, higher up on the lawn. We reveled in the waterside setting of a Crow's Nest studio, complete with kingsize bed with floral spread and matching pillows and shams, two chairs, good reading lights, a small color TV, light colors and french doors onto a balcony beside the water. Very private and comfortable, it was the kind of "guest quarters" we wish we could buy for our very own in coastal Maine.

Son Eric Lusty and his wife Carol have infused new enthusiasm and creature comforts into Dockside. They keep the Maine House and Crow's Nest open weekends in winter. They hoped to add another building with four more rooms, two with fireplaces.

A continental-plus breakfast buffet featuring fresh fruit and just-baked muffins is offered in the dining room for $3. Lunch and dinner are available next door at The Restaurant at Dockside Guest Quarters (see Dining Spots).

(207) 363-2868 or (800) 270-1977. Fax (207) 363-1977. Thirteen rooms and six suites with private baths; two rooms with shared bath. Late June to late September: doubles $66 (shared bath) to $108 (private bath), studios $112 to $124, suites, $155 to $159. November to early May (weekends only): doubles $45 to $60, suites $100 to $150. Rest of year: doubles, $60 to $93, studios $83 to $104, suites $104 to $128. Two-night minimum in summer and weekends. Children welcome.

York Harbor Inn, Route 1A, Box 573, York Harbor 03911.

A history dating back to 1637 and a family's labor of love. That's the story of this busy turn-of-the-century inn restored by twin brothers Joe and George Dominguez, their younger brother Garry and Joe's wife Jean.

Listed in the National Register of Historic Places and built around a 1637 post-and-beam sail loft that was moved to the site and now serves as a common room, the 33-room inn once was headquarters for the York Harbor Reading Club, which continues to this day. The Dominguez brothers, all graduates of Colgate University, spent a year and a half restoring the inn, and are still adding and upgrading. Recently, they redid three larger rooms with solid cherry furniture, queensize four-poster beds, color TVs and jacuzzi tubs, and created a three-room suite with fireplaced living room and a whirlpool tub. In 1997, they opened The Harbor View Inn, a B&B next door (see below).

But for the fifteen newer rooms, this is an old-fashioned, full-service inn with a character you sense immediately when you enter the main Cabin Lounge, its pitched ceiling (the former sail loft) now covered with tiny white Christmas bulbs lit all year. The dark, English-style Wine Cellar Pub Grill with a long solid cherry bar and lots of sofas clustered around the corner fireplace offers frequent entertainment, and the dining rooms serve three meals a day (see Dining Spots).

All rooms now have private baths and poster beds (many of them king or queensize) and four have working fireplaces. Eaves and dormers contribute to interesting shapes, nooks and crannies in many rooms. They are nicely furnished with such touches as white wicker headboards and rocking chairs, pink puffy quilts, good-looking prints and perhaps a writing desk. A deluxe suite includes a kingsize bed and a whirlpool tub.

Eleven guest rooms are located next door in the newer Yorkshire House, which has an outdoor hot tub. A large front room here has an oak bed, a working fireplace and a case full of books. From most rooms you can hear the ocean rolling up against the inn's beach beneath the Marginal Way across the street. With the town removing structures across the street to prepare a public harborside park in 1997, water views were opened up for some rooms.

Guests get a continental breakfast of fruit, cereals, yogurt and homemade pastries and muffins. Mineral water and soft drinks are complimentary in the afternoon.

(207) 363-5119 or (800) 343-3869. Fax (207) 363-3545. Thirty-two rooms and one three-room suite with private baths. Doubles, $109 to $189. Suite $199. Some rooms $10 less November-March. Two-night minimum weekends.

Edwards' Harborside Inn has own wharf where harbor meets ocean.

The Harbor View Inn, Route 1A, York Harbor 03911.

The Dominguez brothers from the York Harbor Inn acquired the handsome white mansion next door in 1997. They converted the private home dating to the late 1800s into an elegant seven-room B&B. The accommodations, Garry assured, surpass the top-of-the-line rooms of their existing inn.

All rooms here have TVs and phones, three have working fireplaces and two have whirlpool spas. Two are two-bedroom suites, each with an antique single bed in the extra bedroom. Bathrooms in several are tiled in marble.

A spiral staircase leads to the premium third-floor room, an elegant attic space with beadboard ceilings and wide hardwood floors. The oceanfront wall is lined with windows and a door opens onto a spectacular balcony with ocean view. The room has both a gas fireplace and a marble bathroom with whirlpool spa.

Other rooms are no slouches. Done in floral fabrics and colors, the garden room at the rear of the main floor has a fireplace and spa, queensize four-poster bed, and a view of the back patio and gardens. The master bedroom on the second floor has a kingsize poster bed and a sitting area in front of the fireplace.

The main floor also has a large common room with a fireplace and a picture window with ocean view. Continental breakfast is taken on the porch overlooking the water, on the rear garden patio or in an inside dining area.

(207) 363-7187. Five rooms and two suites with private baths. Doubles, $149 to $219.

Edwards' Harborside Inn, Stage Neck Road, Box 866, York Harbor 03911.

An inn with a grand location at the entrance to Stage Neck, "where harbor and ocean meet," this three-story, turn-of-the-century residence has been renovated by owner Jay Edwards. A recently retired Portsmouth auto dealer and third-generation innkeeper, he says he jumped at the chance of acquiring what he thinks is "the prettiest place in the world."

The property faces water on three sides, has its own long wharf (from which Jay has been known to take guests on his boat for whale-watching or moonlight cruises) and a crescent beach beyond the lawn.

All ten bedrooms have air-conditioning and television and most have queensize beds plus a view of harbor or ocean – or both. Friends who stayed in the second-floor York Suite with water views on three sides felt as if they were on a yacht. The suite is a beauty: a queensize bed, a sofabed against one picture window, two Queen Anne chairs, blue carpeting, colorful floral wallpaper and an enormous blue bathroom with a tub, shower, double sink and what Jay says is "the only potted bidet on the East Coast" (a plant sprouts from inside). A tiled spa in the suite's entry overlooks the harbor. Other rooms are of different sizes and shapes. Two have two double beds and one has a kingsize. Eight have private baths.

The Bay View Room on the main floor is a guest living room in the off-season. It's richly furnished with a plush white sofa, chairs and a red oriental rug that Jay brought home from Hong Kong. In the summer it's rented as part of a suite connecting with the adjacent bedroom.

A lobby area contains books and games, and a complimentary decanter of sherry is available for guests to help themselves. A continental breakfast buffet is put out on the sunporch with those all-encompassing water views. Expect several kinds of juice, fruits, cereals and homemade muffins, breads and bagels.

Jay and his staff work hard "to project a homey touch." He also is so adamant against smoking that he stipulates a $150 room cleaning charge for any violation. Several guests reluctantly paid the fee. One woman who said ahead of time she'd gladly pay to smoke was told "Oh no you won't" and was directed elsewhere.

(207) 363-3037 or (800) 273-2686. Fax (207) 363-1544. Six rooms and two suites with private baths; two rooms with shared bath. July and August: doubles $110 to $170, suites $240. May-June and September-October: doubles $100 to $150, suites $220. Rest of year: doubles $90 to $120, suites $200. All rates $30 to $40 lower midweek. No smoking.

Inn at Harmon Park, 415 York St., York Harbor 03911.

Maine artists and books are well represented in this homey B&B run with TLC by Sue Antal, a font of local lore. Her 1899 Victorian home at the corner of Harmon Park Road comes with a wide front porch, a side sunporch, a fireplaced parlor, an open kitchen that seems to be the heart of the house and five guest accommodations, all with private baths. The B&B is known for food, value and personality.

The second floor holds four rooms with wicker furniture. Largest are the front-corner Georgeanne suite with a queen bed and a plush sofa facing the fireplace and the Blue Heron with a king bed and a clawfoot tub with shower. Two smaller rooms with double beds, one with a glimpse of the harbor down the street, recently gained private baths as Sue managed make good use of every nook and cranny. The main floor also has a bedroom with a double bed and a new private bath. All rooms are appointed with lovely quilts and comforters.

Sue compensates at breakfast for "not being on the water," and fellow innkeepers report the fare worthy of Gourmet magazine.

Apple-blueberry crisp was the main course the morning of our visit. Belgian waffles with blueberry sauce were on tap the next day.

Other treats include apple torte, baked french toast, crustless spinach pie, apple-cinnamon quiche and several potato dishes, since Sue doesn't serve breakfast meats. The meal is taken on the pleasant side sunporch or, in good weather, on the front porch.

She sends guests on their way with a packet of her favorite recipes. She also has become a notary and now numbers among her services "wedding celebrations," as listed on her business card.

Sue, who has been innkeeping since 1983, obviously subscribes to the slogan we spotted in her kitchen: "Enjoy life – this is not a dress rehearsal."

(207) 363-2031. Fax (207) 351-2948. www.yorkme.org/inns/harmonpark.html Four rooms and one suite with private baths. Doubles, $79 to $89. Suite $109. Off-season, $59 to $89. Children over 12. No credit cards.

Tanglewood Hall, 611 York St., Box 12, York Harbor 03911.

The substantial Shingle-style house in which Tommy and Jimmy Dorsey supposedly summered with a relative is now an elegant, low-key B&B. Michael and Jean Stotts from Wellesley, Mass., bought the fifteen-room Victorian cottage as a retirement home, with the idea of running a B&B.

It served first as the site for the York Historical Society's annual Decorator Show House in 1994. After the decorators and crowds left, the Stottses spent months readying the B&B for opening a year later. Only the wallpapers, some landscaping and a few artistic touches remained from the show house, but the owners' own furniture and acquisitions filled in well.

The main floor holds a formal parlor, a chandeliered dining room and an octagonal sun room with oriental wallpaper and a red ceiling that the couple turned into a game room.

Upstairs are three guest quarters, all with private baths and queensize beds. Located on the mezzanine level of a "good morning" staircase is the front Winslow Homer Room, formerly a library. Named for the artist who stayed here, it is spacious and cheery with a wicker loveseat and chair appointed in peach. The side Tommy Dorsey Room overlooks gardens and woods. The York Harbor Suite in the rear comes with an enclosed sunporch, a large sitting room and a spacious bedroom with poster bed. Country Curtains did this room and pulled out all the stops, Mike related. Still evident to guests are the fancy handpainted floral designs gracing the floors and walls.

A custom-made pine table, fashioned from wide boards obtained from a Pennsylvania silo, is the focal point of the dining room. Here is where the Stottses serve a full hot breakfast: perhaps french toast or pancakes, accompanied by fruit cup and croissants. Guests also enjoy a wraparound porch and a broad lawn.

(207) 363-7577. Two rooms and one suite with private baths. Doubles, $90. Suite, $120. Children over 12. No smoking. Closed November-May.

Riverbank On the Harbor, 11 Harmon Park Road, Box 1102, York Harbor 03911.

Ice damage from the hard winter of 1994 was a blow to owner Marie Feuer after part of the second floor of her family's home of eight years collapsed onto the first floor. But she and her husband rebuilt and redecorated their century-old house, and guests in the six upstairs bedrooms are the beneficiaries of all new furnishings.

They are also the beneficiaries of some great water views, best enjoyed from the broad rear porch perched on the York River bank above the harbor. Along with an abundance of chairs and loungers, the porch contains an ice chest that guests find handy during happy hour. The porch is reached from a wonderful, long living room/dining room with large windows onto the harbor scene. The latter is pleasantly furnished in contemporary style with oriental rugs, oriental prints and screens, and maritime paintings done by Marie's uncle. The dining end of the room is the setting for a full breakfast buffet, which includes fruit, cereal, muffins, danish pastries

Water is on view from back porch at Riverbank On the Harbor.

and perhaps omelets or quiche, accompanied by a signature maple syrup sausage. Sherry and chocolates are put out at 4.

Upstairs are six guest rooms with kingsize beds. The only shortcoming is the bath configuration. The front Garden Room enjoys a private bath, and the Sunset Room with a water bed has its own marble bath in the hall. The other bedrooms, including the prime waterfront Harbor and Balcony rooms, share a large bath and a half bath. Rooms are bright and cheery with thick carpeting and designer bedspreads or duvets.

You probably will not spend much time in your room here, given the common areas inside and out. All you need to do is to step off the back porch and descend the stairs to the shore to hook up with the Captain's Walk, a scenic path that runs along the harbor from Edwards' Harborside Inn to the Hutchins House. Those more laid-back can hang out on the sunken afternoon sun terrace hidden down the river bank.

(207) 363-8333. Fax (207) 363-3684. Two rooms with private baths and four rooms with shared baths. Doubles, $120 to $165. Off-season, $80 to $125. No smoking.

RiverMere, 45 Varrell Lane, Box 141, York Harbor 03911.

Gourmet breakfasts, harbor views, wondrous gardens and artistic floral arrangements are the hallmarks of this small new B&B, opened by Brian and Paulette Chernack after their second floor became vacant when their daughter left for college.

The breakfasts are something else, prepared in a kitchen open to the living room and served on the side deck or in the sun room. The latter, a plant-filled aerie outfitted with a comfy sofa and lots of wicker, affords a head-on view of the harbor. Here you might enjoy fresh raspberries from the garden, baked eggs and homemade scones, as we did at a mid-October visit. Brian proved himself to be quite the breakfast cook, and we particularly liked his elder-plum jelly, one of the preserves he and Paulette make from six kinds of berries they grow in their exotic gardens. Other breakfast treats could be a clafouti filled with fruit, belgian waffles, omelets or french toast.

Upstairs on the second floor is a double-bedded room with private hall bath, a settee that folds into a single bed and a corner fireplace.

The premier lodging takes up the entire third floor. On one side of the staircase is a library and sitting room with a single wing chair. The bedroom holds a queensize brass bed, wicker chairs, a settee and, as is the case throughout the house, a lot to look at (actress Jane Seymour wore the white dress displayed in the corner in a movie). You get a distant view of the ocean from the window above the bed, although most guests are content with the wide-angle view of the harbor through the side windows. A spice rack in the bathroom holds all manner of soaps and perfumes that the Chernacks have picked up on their travels.

Artistic touches abound, reflecting the talents of Paulette, who is cultural coordinator for the local school district. Splashy dried plants, wreaths and collections make the entry foyer look like a gift shop. Brian's talents are evident in the front and side vegetable and flower gardens. We could spend hours here marveling at their varied output and getting ideas to try at home.

(207) 363-5470. Fax (207) 363-3268. One room and one suite with private baths. Double, $80. Suite, $90 to $125. No smoking.

Dining Spots

Cape Neddick Inn Restaurant, 1233 Route 1, Cape Neddick.

This interesting combination of restaurant and art gallery has been going strong since 1979. In 1997, owner Glenn Gobeille and his original chef, Michele Duval, teamed up again to redesign the two-level dining room and expand the menu. New place settings and a pianist playing five nights a week were part of what Glenn called the "upscale casual" theme.

Michele designed her menu to reflect the way people want to eat: "a little of a lot." The list of starters is as extensive as the entrées, and diners may make an entire meal of appetizers. These include a fabulous fish chowder, the house pâté (a Duval original of chicken livers, Italian sausage and cognac, served with the proper accompaniments and wheat crackers), a sampler of applewood-smoked salmon, mussels and scallops, and risotto with gorgonzola, swiss chard and prosciutto.

Main courses run the gamut from wasabi and sesame-crusted halibut to Maine lobster fra diavolo over cappellini and braised lamb osso buco over spinach fettuccine. A typical presentation is grilled mustard-coated pork tenderloin in pinenut cream, served with baked prosciutto-wrapped mission figs stuffed with stilton cheese and smashed yams.

Desserts range from a mudcake pyramid built around mango buttercream and resting on raspberry coulis to a frozen French fantasy of vanilla-amaretto and chocolate-cognac ice creams and frozen grand marnier mousse, layered like a parfait and topped with fudge sauce.

Seventy-five wines, categorized by grape or region, comprise the wine selection. Twenty are available by the glass. The new partners' plans included adding an on-site microbrewery.

(207) 363-2899. Entrées, $12 to $20. Dinner nightly, 5:30 to 9.

The Restaurant at Dockside Guest Quarters, Harris Island, York.

Overlooking the harbor next to the Lusty family's Dockside Guest Quarters, this gray-shingled structure houses an airy dining room on two levels, several round tables on the porch screened from floor to ceiling and an outdoor dining deck from which you're apt to spot cormorants, blue herons and seals. The restaurant is run by Philip Lusty, who had been a catering director at the Crowne Plaza Hotel in White Plains, N.Y., and his wife Anne.

The Lusty family and staff made the striking tables inlaid with nautical charts and topped by blue mats. Nautical pieces on shelves and colored glassware in the windows provide accents for the decor, which is secondary to the water view.

It's an especially fine setting for lunch. You can get broiled scrod, fried scallops, English-style fish and chips, grilled chicken caesar salad, smoked turkey BLT or seafood tostada. Most are accompanied by crudités and dip, mini-loaves of fresh bread and the "salad deck" – items from a salad bar set in half of an old boat.

The same appetizers are offered at lunch and dinner, among them onion soup gratinée, bruschetta, gravlax, lobster raviolis and crab-stuffed mushrooms.

Dinner entrées run from broiled scrod to bouillabaisse seasoned with garlic and saffron. Perennial favorites are the roast stuffed duckling with orange-sherry glaze, baked haddock with a crab soufflé, a sauté of lobster and scallops splashed with Irish whiskey in a cream sauce, grilled swordfish served on a bed of fried spinach and finished with a strawberry salsa, pesto chicken, braised lamb shanks and beef tenderloin au poivre. Anne Lusty is responsible for such desserts as bread pudding, apple crisp, key lime pie and a terrine of chocolate and pistachio ice cream with raspberry crème anglaise.

(207) 363-2722. Entrées, $10.95 to $19.95. Lunch, Tuesday-Sunday 11:30 to 2. Dinner, Tuesday-Sunday from 5:30. No smoking. Closed Columbus Day to Memorial Day.

York Harbor Inn, Route 1A, York Harbor.

From their hilltop perch, three of the four charming dining rooms here look onto (and catch the salty breeze from) the ocean across the street. One room, the main Cabin Loft lobby with fireplace, is used in winter. Another is an enclosed porch, and a third beamed room looks like a pub.

Mismatched chairs, small paned windows, blue and white plates displayed below the beamed ceiling, rose-colored napkins shaped like swans, small oil lamps and sloping floors convey an old-fashioned feeling.

Highly regarded fare is served up by veteran chef Gerry Bonsey, who was inducted in 1997 into the American Culinary Federation's prestigious Academy of Chefs. Signature dishes on the continental/New England menu are Yorkshire lobster supreme, stuffed with scallops and shrimp, baked with parmesan cheese and laced with thermidor sauce; chicken breast stuffed with lobster, and veal Swiss, the recipe for which was requested by Gourmet magazine. Other entrées range from Moroccan seared salmon to pecan-crusted rack of lamb.

Brie cheese soup, mussels provençal and Maine crab cakes are favorite starters. Special desserts include a chilled lemon-caramel soufflé, homemade maple-bread pudding and strawberry shortcake. The well-chosen wine list is fairly priced.

Soups, salads, sandwiches and a few entrées are listed on an extensive luncheon menu. A bar menu is offered in the cozy cellar pub.

(207) 363-5119 or (800) 343-3869. Entrées, $16.95 to $24.95. Lunch, Monday-Friday 11:30 to 2:30. Dinner nightly, 5:30 to 9:30. Sunday brunch, 8:30 to 2:30.

Dining tables are right beside the water at The Restaurant at Dockside Guest Quarters.

Fazio's, 38 Woodbridge Road, York.

Started as a neighborhood storefront restaurant in a shopping plaza, Annette Fazio's expanding enterprise moved into a former lumber shed and it's quite a place. The main entrance is in the rear past an awninged courtyard that's popular for summer dining. Inside are a bar/lounge with Italian murals and an attractive dining room with booths and banquettes around the perimeter and tables covered with pinkish oilcloths. Not to mention the casual La Stalla Pizzeria at the side, or the function rooms upstairs.

The main dining room, although rather brightly illuminated, is immensely popular with the locals. Many items are available in smaller portions, and nobody goes away hungry. The pastas are homemade, and the kitchen knows what it's doing. We were well satisfied with the chicken française and the seafood tecchia, accompanied by good house salads with blue cheese or raspberry vinaigrette dressings and a $14 bottle of Murphy-Goode fumé blanc.

Besides the predictable Italian fare, there are interesting specials – at our visit, grilled swordfish with red pepper vinaigrette and roasted garlic aioli, served with garlic-herb risotto and tomatoes provençal; grilled lamb medallions with a sweet red pepper sauce, teamed with mashed potatoes and broccoli with garlic, and grilled beef tenderloin with a horseradish-dijon demi-glace, served with oven-roasted herb potatoes and a mushroom-onion compote. Such treats hint of the special wine-tasting dinners that Fazio's stages periodically in the off-season.

La Stalla Pizzeria offers pizzas, subs and salads daily from 11 a.m.

(207) 363-7019. Entrées, $10.50 to $15.95. Dinner nightly, 4 to 9 or 10.

Frankie & Johnny's, 1594 Route 1 North, Cape Neddick.

"Food that loves you back" is the hallmark of this gourmet natural-foods restaurant. It isn't much to look at – a manufactured home beside the highway, painted with colorful triangles and sporting a Haagen-Dazs sign in front. But stop and venture in for a healthful meal, either inside in a whimsical dining room, outside at a couple of picnic tables or to go.

Personable Frank Rostad handles the front of the house while partner John Shaw cooks in a state-of-the-art kitchen. Everything here is made from scratch and almost all of it on site, say these purists (it took them fourteen months to find an all-natural cone to serve with their Haagen-Dazs ice cream). They even squeeze juices at their juice bar.

The soups could be vegetarian or vegan (dairy-free). Eight entrée salads range from smoked lobster to blackened chicken on assorted greens. Favorites among entrées are grilled tofu with ginger-soy sauce, grilled portobello mushroom, a variety of spaetzles, poached or blackened Atlantic salmon and baked chicken stuffed with spinach and house-smoked mozzarella. New at our latest visit was farm-raised ostrich, grilled and fanned on an orange liqueur glaze or blackened and topped with goat cheese. Sweet endings could be fresh peach pie with a crunchy streusel topping or whole wheat honey cake.

The place is best known for its trademarked crustolis ($10.75), ten-inch-round French bread crusts made from unbleached flour and not unlike pizzas. For dinner, we ordered one with shrimp, pesto and goat cheese and another with capers, olives, red onions and feta cheese, split a house salad and had more than enough left over for lunch the next day.

Dinner is by candlelight and the food is fairly serious, but it's dispensed in a relaxed and playful environment. Decor in the pine-paneled room is nil except for a few abstract oils by Frank's sister at one end and a handful of rocks and perhaps a miniature dinosaur on each table. "It's hard to take yourself seriously with rocks and a little dinosaur in front of you," says Frank, whose aim is to help customers enjoy healthful food and have a good time.

(207) 363-1909. Entrées, $12.75 to $18.75. Dinner from 5, nightly in summer, Thursday-Sunday in spring and fall. Closed Dec. 21 through March. BYOB. No smoking.

Chef Mimmo's Restaurant, Route 1A, York Beach.

A brick arch frames the open kitchen and garlands of tiny white lights outline the enclosed porch windows onto the beach at this ever-so-Italian-looking restaurant in a white house in the thick of the York Beach action. Chef Mimmo is an Italian of the old school, a big man who flings pots around and when he leaves the kitchen for the noisy and intimate dining room, the fun begins.

The food is Tuscan. We hear great things about the vermicelli godfather with mussels, shrimp and clams. The extensive menu lists seven veal dishes, seven chicken and four seafood dishes, all served with vermicelli, salad and garlic bread.

Appetizers, all for two, include a cold antipasto platter, pimento and artichokes, calamari salad, stuffed mushrooms and mussels marinara or fra diavolo.

(207) 363-3807. Entrées, $15.95 to $17.95. Breakfast in summer, 7 to noon. Dinner nightly, 5 to 10 or 11. BYOB.

Cape Neddick Lobster Pound, Shore Road (Route 1A), Cape Neddick.

A gray shingled building practically over the water, this sprawling place offers glorious views (especially at sunset) from every window inside the two-level bar and dining area, which has shiny wooden tables, deck chairs and paper mats decorated with lobsters. There's a large deck outside. Loud rock music plays in the background – live on weekends – and it's all very picturesque and casual.

Offering more than just lobster, the menu lists things like vegetable stir-fry, teriyaki steak and filet mignon. Boiled or baked stuffed lobster, a shore dinner, broiled scallops, shrimp scampi and bouillabaisse are among seafood items. Fried clam baskets, fried haddock sandwich, fish and chips, lobster roll, lobster salad, chicken fingers and a multitude of appetizers round out the selection.

(207) 363-5471. Entrées, $12.95 to $19.95. Dinner nightly from 5, Thursday-Monday in off-season. Closed in winter.

Diversions

Beaches. Inn guests probably will be grateful for the peace and quiet of the inn grounds and sheltered beaches. Or you may be as lucky as we were and find a parking spot and place at Harbor Beach, next to a private club. But if you want surf, join the throngs on Long Sands Beach, one of Maine's sandiest and deservedly crowded. It was a refreshing oasis on one unforgettable 100-degree day when we and everyone else placed our sand chairs in the ocean and lounged in the water to keep cool. If there's not enough action on the beach, surely there is in the amusement area of downtown York Beach. On past Short Sands Beach at Cape Neddick Harbor is a sheltered beach good for children.

Nubble Light. Don't miss the landmark Cape Neddick Lighthouse on the nubble separating Long Sands and Short Sands beaches. From the bluffs you can see up and down the coast and out to Boon Island and the Isles of Shoals off Portsmouth. Along Nubble Road you'll pass tiny cottages and institutions like Fox's Lobster House and Brown's Old-Fashioned Ice Cream ("We make our own"). Another spectacular view is from Bald Head Cliff off Shore Road.

Not far inland is 673-foot-high **Mount Agamenticus,** a landmark for sailors and the highest spot on the southern Maine coast. You can drive up a paved road or hike a steep but pleasant, .8-mile trail to the top for a panoramic view of the area. The York recreation department operates a saddle horse livery stable offering scenic trail rides at the summit. You also can rent mountain bikes there.

Marginal Way. A three-mile walk along the ocean between shore and homes begins at Harbor Beach and extends to Nubble Light. It's more rugged than nearby Ogunquit's better known Marginal Way, but well worth the effort for the views and the natural landscaping (wild roses, bayberry, blueberries and ground juniper).

York Historic District, 207 York St., York Village.

The history of the first chartered English city in North America (a refuge for early Puritan settlers from Massachusetts) is on display in York Village. The **Old York Historical Society** in the historic **George Marshall Store** at 140 Lindsay Road offers guided tours of its six properties. Costumed guides begin tours in the 1750 **Jefferd's Tavern,** a Colonial hostelry facing the Old Burying Yard and the village green in the center of town. An introductory video tour of Old York is shown here. One of New England's best collections of regional decorative arts is displayed in more than 30 period rooms and galleries spanning the period from 1719 to 1954. The **Old Gaol,** once the King's Prison, is the oldest surviving public building of the British Colonies in this country; on view are the dungeon, cells, jailer's quarters and household effects. Also open are the **Emerson-Wilcox House** (1742) and the enormous **Elizabeth Perkins House** (1730) beside the river, the 1745 **Old School House** and the **John Hancock Warehouse & Wharf,** with old tools and antique ship models in a warehouse owned by a signer of the Declaration of Independence.

(207) 363-4974. Open Tuesday-Saturday 10 to 5, Sunday 1 to 5, mid-June through September. Adults, $2 each building. Combination ticket, $6.

The Chamber of Commerce has an excellent brochure detailing walking and driving tours. Most of the historical society buildings are concentrated along Lindsay Road, which leads to **Sewall's Bridge,** a replica of the first pile drawbridge in America dating to 1761. Nearby, Route 103 passes an intriguing looking mini-suspension bridge for pedestrians (called the "wiggly bridge," for good reason), which leads to a neat pathway along the river from York Harbor to Sewall's Bridge. The rambling **Sayward Wheeler House** (1718) at 79 Barrell Lane is opened weekends noon to 4, June through mid-October, $4, by the Society for the Preservation of New England Antiquities. Out Route 91 is a small stone memorial next to the trickling **Maud Muller Spring,** which inspired John Greenleaf Whittier's poem.

Shopping. A landmark church built in 1834 in the center of York Village now houses **York Village Crafts & Antiques,** a cooperative featuring more than 100 area craftsmen and dealers. Also in the village is the **Williams Country Store,** which has evolved from a general store into an antiques shop. Along York Street, **River Place** is a gallery of fine arts, crafts, garden ornaments and more. Artist JoAnne Campbell shows her works in **The Powder House Gallery.**

Stonewall Kitchen Company Store, 469 Route 1, is the upscale retail outlet in front of Stonewall Kitchen, the fast-growing producer of jams and condiments housed in an old grocery store at York Corner.

The Goldenrod, which has been operated every summer since 1896 by the same family in York Beach, is where everyone stops for saltwater taffy kisses – choosing from dozens of flavors. It's also a restaurant with a nice old-fashioned menu, listing sandwiches like fried egg and bacon or cream cheese and olives, club sandwiches, toasted "frankfort" and lots of soda-fountain goodies. Also in York Beach is **Shelton's Gift Shop,** which offers attractive clothing, cards and jewelry.

Extra-Special

Factory Outlet Shopping. Anyone who rejoiced as we did when **Dansk** opened its first large factory outlet at Kittery is probably ecstatic about the several miles of outlets along Route 1 from Kittery to York. Although some are the same kinds of clothing outlets that you find in Freeport, the specialty here seems to be china, glass and kitchenware. We have found tremendous bargains at **Villeroy & Boch** (place settings and oversize dinner plates at up to 75 percent off), **Mikasa, Royal Doulton** and **Waterford/Wedgwood.** You can admire the river view from benches outside the **Corning Revere** store at the Maine Gate Outlets. There are **Lenox** and **Oneida, Le Creuset, Reed & Barton** as well as all the usual suspects in various malls and small plazas on both sides of the highway. New ones pop up all the time (a **Bose** factory store was there at our latest visit), and it takes policemen to untangle the bumper-to-bumper shopper traffic on summer weekends.

Harbor at Cape Porpoise is on view through rose trellis at The Inn at Harbor Head.

Kennebunkport, Me.
The Most and Best of Everything

For many, the small coastal area known as the Kennebunk Region has the most and best of everything in Maine: the best beaches, the most inns, the best shops, the most eating places, the best scenery, the most tourist attractions, the best galleries, the most diverse appeal.

It also plays a starring role as the summer home of George Bush, a visible figure around town.

All combine to create a Kennebunk mystique that has strong appeal for tourists. Actually, there are at least three Kennebunks. One is the town of Kennebunk and its inland commercial center, historic Kennebunk. The second is Kennebunkport, the coastal resort community that was one of Maine's earliest summer havens for the wealthy, and adjacent Kennebunk Beach. A third represents Cape Arundel, Cape Porpoise and Goose Rocks Beach, whose rugged coastal aspects remain largely unchanged by development in recent years.

Even before George Bush's election as president, Kennebunkport and its Dock Square and Lower Village shopping areas had become so congested that tourists were shuttled by bus from parking areas on the edge of town. Although some of the luster faded after its favorite son left the White House, visitors still are drawn much as they are by the Kennedy name to Hyannis Port.

While the downtown area can get congested, you can escape. Walk along the ocean on Parson's Way. Drive out Ocean Avenue past Spouting Rock and the Bush estate at Walker Point and around Cape Arundel to Cape Porpoise, a working fishing village. Bicycle out Beach Avenue to Lord's Point or Strawberry Island. Visit the Rachel Carson Wildlife Preserve. Savor times gone by among the historic homes of Summer Street in Kennebunk or along the beach at Goose Rocks.

One of the charms of the Kennebunks is that the crowded restaurants and galleries co-exist with events like the annual Unitarian Church blueberry festival and the Rotary chicken barbecue, and the solitude of Parson's Way.

Watercolorist Edgar Whitney proclaimed the Kennebunks "the best ten square miles of painting areas in the nation." Explore a bit and you'll see why.

Inn Spots

The White Barn Inn, Beach Street, Box 560 C, Kennebunkport 04046.

Long known as one of the area's premier restaurants (see Dining Spots), the White Barn has become a top-rate inn under Australian owner Laurie Bongiorno. Indeed, shortly after he took over, refurbished the facility and added deluxe suites, the inn became only the second in New England to be accepted into Relais & Châteaux, the international group of prestige hotels.

The inn's 25 rooms and suites vary, as their prices indicate. A renovated cottage beside the elegant new pool area is the ultimate in plush privacy with a living room, porch, kingsize bedroom, double-sided fireplace and two-person jacuzzi. Equally sumptuous are six in the refurbished Carriage House, the height of luxury with library-style sitting areas, dressing rooms, spacious marble bathrooms with jacuzzis and separate showers, Queen Anne kingsize four-poster beds and secretary desks, chintz-covered furniture and plush carpeting. The desk in the Blue Suite here contains a detailed book on everything about the inn and the area except how to fill the ice bucket (just phone, we were told after walking across the way to the bar area). The only other drawback was that the armoire containing the TV was positioned so that it was not comfortably visible from the sitting area in front of the fireplace. The fireplace was laid with real wood and we were wrapped in total luxury with a personal note of welcome from the innkeeper, a bowl of fresh fruit, Poland Spring water, no fewer than four three-way reading lights, much closet and drawer space in the bathroom, terry robes, Gilchrist & Soames toiletries and a couple of cookies when the bed was turned down.

Four large rooms in the Poolhouse, considered intermediate, have cathedral ceilings, whirlpool tubs, sitting areas with wing chairs, queensize sleigh beds, chintz spreads and fine art on the walls.

Less regal are the smaller rooms upstairs in the inn, all refurbished with modernized bathrooms and whimsical artistic touches to enhance what the owner calls their "basically quaint, country-style" nature. A local artist did the delightful trompe-l'oeil accents in each room – robin's eggs on a desk, car keys on a night stand, a shell book on a side table, a crane on an armoire, even a beach scene at the end of one bed and a lighthouse on the bureau. The inn's trademark straw bonnet is placed atop each bed, which come in double, queen or twin sizes.

Fireplace warms Oriental guest room at The Captain Lord Mansion.

The inn's handsome main floor contains a reception area, three sitting rooms with comfortable furniture and an inviting sunporch. An elaborate tea spread is set out in one room. Flowers, mints, decanters of brandy and port, newspapers and magazines are all around, and oriental rugs are scattered over the polished wood floors. Lush flowers and prolific herbs add color to the grounds.

Guests enjoy a substantial continental buffet breakfast in the quietly elegant Colonial dining room. Fresh orange juice and slices of cut-up fruits are brought to your table by a tuxedoed waiter, and you help yourself to assorted cereals, yogurts, and an array of muffins and pastries like we've seldom seen before – including a wonderful strawberry-bran muffin with a top the size of a grapefruit and a cool crème d'amandes with a sliced peach inside.

(207) 967-2321. Fax (207) 967-1100. Eighteen rooms and seven suites with private baths. May-December: doubles $160 to $250, suites $350, cottage $395. January-April: doubles $130 to $160, suites $295, cottage $320. Two-night minimum most weekends. No smoking.

The Captain Lord Mansion, Pleasant Street, Box 800, Kennebunkport 04046. For starters, consider the architectural features of this beautifully restored 1812 mansion: an octagonal cupola, a suspended elliptical staircase, blown-glass windows, trompe-l'oeil handpainted doors, an eighteen-foot bay window, a hand-pulled working elevator.

The inn is so full of historic interest that public tours are given in summer for a nominal fee. You'd never guess that it was converted in 1978 from a boarding house for senior citizens.

Guests can savor all the heritage that makes this a National Historic Register listing by staying overnight in any of the sixteen sumptuous guest quarters and enjoying hot cider or iced tea in the parlor or games beside the fire in the Gathering Room. Rooms on three floors have been carefully decorated by Bev Davis and her husband Rick Litchfield, whose innkeeping energy and flair are considered models by their peers. Fourteen rooms have gas fireplaces, much in demand in the autumn and winter. All have private baths (though some created from closets are rather small), and the corner rooms are especially spacious. Nice touches like sewing kits, Poland Spring water, and trays with wine glasses and corkscrews abound.

Bev makes pin cushions and needlecraft "Do Not Disturb" signs for the rooms and oversees the gift shop on the main floor. Breakfast is served family-style at large tables in the kitchen. It includes fruit, yogurt, whole-grain muesli, a changing entrée (perhaps cheese strata, quiche or apple-cinnamon pancakes), freshly-ground coffee with a flavor of the day, hot muffins and sticky buns. Bev's zucchini bread is renowned, as are some of the hors d'oeuvres she prepares for holiday gatherings.

Always on the move, Rick and Bev opened an annex called Phoebe's Fantasy with four more guest rooms, all with king or queen beds and fireplaces. Guests here take breakfast at a seven-foot harvest table in a gathering room with a chintz sofa, fireplace and television.

The mansion's basement summer kitchen with large fireplace has become a second common room that doubles as a conference area.

In 1997, the inn's main-floor Merchant Room was expanded into a deluxe suite with king canopy bed, fireplace, double jacuzzi and a hydro-massage shower. Another double jacuzzi was added to the third-floor Union Room.

(207) 967-3141 or (800) 522-3141. Fax (207) 967-3172. www.captainlord.com. Nineteen rooms and one suite with private baths. June-October and weekends through December: doubles, $149 to $249; suite, $349. Rest of year: weekends, doubles $112 to $199, suite $289; midweek, doubles $75 to $159, doubles $249. Two-night minimum on weekends. Children over 6. No smoking.

Old Fort Inn, Old Fort Avenue, Box M, Kennebunkport 04046

The main lodge in a converted barn is the heart of the Old Fort Inn. You enter through the reception area and Sheila Aldrich's antiques shop. Beyond is a large rustic room with enormous beams, weathered pine walls and a massive brick fireplace, the perfect setting for some of Sheila's antiques.

That's where she and husband David, transplanted Californians, set out a buffet breakfast each morning. Guests pick up wicker trays with calico linings, help themselves to bowls of gorgeous fresh fruits and platters of pastries, and sit around the lodge or outside on the sun-dappled deck beside the large swimming pool. Sheila bakes the sweet breads (blueberry, zucchini, banana, oatmeal and pumpkin are some); the croissants are David's forte and there are sticky buns on Sundays. They added granola and yogurt to the spread, and quickly found they were going through twenty pounds of granola a week.

The stone and brick carriage house out back contains fourteen large and luxurious guest rooms and two suites, all newly air-conditioned. All are decorated in different colors, all have private bathrooms, wet bars with microwaves, plush carpeting and color television, plus such nice touches as velvet wing chairs, stenciling on the walls and handmade wreaths over the beds. "My wife agonizes over every intricate detail," says David. "I call her Ms. Mix and Match." Her decorating flair shows; even the towels are color-coordinated. In the hall, her framed shadow boxes containing Victorian outfits are conversation pieces.

In the most deluxe rooms, of which there seem to be more at every visit, the TV may be hidden in a handsome chest of drawers, the kingsize four-poster beds are topped with fishnet canopies, and the baths are outfitted with jacuzzis and Neutrogena amenities. The sitting room in the carriage house has two settees and a pine hutch; a small adjoining room has wicker furniture.

The inn is a quiet retreat away from the tourist hubbub but within walking distance of the ocean; at night, David says, the silence is deafening. The inn offers a tennis court as well as the pool. Many guests are repeat, long-term customers, and it's easy to see why.

(207) 967-5353 or (800) 828-3678. Fax (207) 967-4547. www.oldfortinn.com. Sixteen rooms and two suites with private baths. Doubles, $135 to $285, mid-June to late October; $95 to $225 rest of year. Two-night minimum stay in summer and all weekends. Children over 12. No smoking. Closed mid-December to mid-April.

The Inn at Harbor Head, 41 Pier Road, Cape Porpoise, RR 2, Box 1180, Kennebunkport 04046.

The location of this rambling shingled home on a rocky knoll right above the picturesque Cape Porpoise harbor is one of the attractions at this small B&B. Out front are gorgeous gardens with a sundial. A rear terrace and lawns lead down to the shore for swimming from the floats or just relaxing in one of the oversize rope hammocks, watching the lobster boats go by.

Breakfast is another attraction. From the country kitchen come such dishes as pineapple boats decorated with edible flowers, pears poached with lemon and vanilla and topped with a cointreau-laced custard sauce, and broiled grapefruit with nutmeg. The "Maine" course could be vegetable frittata, blueberry strata, mushroom omelet topped with salsa or "the bakery lady's special from Montana" – grated potatoes, scallions and sausages with monterey jack cheese and salsa – so named because her daughter got the recipe from a bakery lady in Montana. No one ever leaves a bite of the roast beef hash made from scratch with red and green peppers and a touch of garlic. Pecan sticky buns and fruit croissants might accompany this feast. The meal is served at 9 in the dining room at a long table where there is much camaraderie. Coffee for early risers is put out at 7 in the sitting room or the library, where a telescope is at the ready.

The four guest quarters, three up and one two down, have private baths and king or queensize canopy beds. They were decorated to the nth degree by the former owner, a sculptor and artist. The murals are exquisite. In the newly expanded, three-room Harbor Suite, they show Cape Porpoise on the walls, with clouds and sky on the ceiling, mirroring the view from the window. The gas fireplace is tiled with ivy and birds crafted by local artist Lou Lipkin of Goose Rocks Pottery. A new sitting room, a kingsize bedroom and a bathroom with a soaking tub and a chaise lounge all have windows onto the water. The entrance to the Garden Room is paved with stones and a little fountain, and original drawings of peach and plum blossoms float on the wall. French doors open onto a private, trellised deck overlooking the harbor. The downstairs Greenery, where we stayed, with its mural of fir trees by the shore, has become the quarters of new innkeepers Eve Sagris a nd Dick Roesler from Massachusetts. Next time we'd opt for the upstairs Summer Suite, with the best view of the harbor from its balcony. It's painted with clouds drifting across the ceiling and comes with a kingsize bed, gas fireplace and a cathedral-ceilinged bathroom with skylight, bidet and jacuzzi.

Tables are set for breakfast beside water at Bufflehead Cove Inn.

The recently renovated Ocean Room is different from the rest – bold and masculine with a library of books about sailing, the sea and shipwrecks, plus a trompe-l'oeil window scene she painted in its skylit bathroom to simulate a window.

Rooms are outfitted with thick towels, terrycloth robes, hair dryers, irons and boards, books and magazines, good reading lights, clock radios, a decanter of sherry and fresh flowers from the backyard cutting garden.

The innkeepers put out wine and cheese in late afternoon and, after guests leave for dinner, turn down their beds, light soft lights and leave silver dishes of Godiva chocolates on the pillows. It's little wonder that some guests stay for a week or more, and that many are honeymooners.

(207) 967-5564. Fax (207) 967-1294. Two rooms and two suites with private baths. Doubles, $180 and $190, off-season $125 and $135. Suites, $295, off-season $195. Two-night minimum weekends. Children over 12. No smoking. Closed in winter.

Bufflehead Cove Inn, Gornitz Lane, Box 499, Kennebunkport 04046.

Down a long dirt road and past a lily pond is this hidden treasure: a gray shingled, Dutch Colonial manse right beside a scenic bend of the Kennebunk River, the kind of summer home you've always dreamed of. Owners Harriet and Jim Gott hardly advertise and don't need to. Their five-room B&B is filled by word of mouth.

The public rooms and the setting are special here. A wide porch faces the tidal river and downtown Kennbunkport in the distance; there are porches along the side and a huge wraparound deck in back. A large and comfy living room contains window seats with views of the water, and the dining room, which is shaped like the back of a ship, has a dark beamed ceiling, paneling, stenciling and a carpet painted on the floor. There are a dock with boats and five acres of tranquility with which to surround oneself.

All bedrooms are bright and cheerful. The Balcony Room is perhaps the most appealing of those in the main house. It has a fabulous, wicker-filled balcony overlooking the river, a sitting area with window seats, a queensize brass bed, a gas fireplace and dramatic decor with splashes of black, including the striking glossy stenciling – green leaves on a black band. Reflections of sun on the river shimmer on the ceiling of the River Room, which has a queen bed and a balcony. The walls and ceilings are handpainted with vines in the Cove Suite, two rooms with lots of wicker, a gas fireplace and a private bath. The Garden Studio in back has its own entrance and patio, a wicker sitting area, gas fireplace, a handcrafted queensize bed and grapevine stenciling that echoes the real vines outside the entry.

The crowning glory is the secluded Hideaway, fashioned from the Gotts' former quarters in the adjacent cottage. Mostly windows, it holds a kingsize bed, a tiled fireplace open to both the bedroom and the living room, rattan chairs, and an enormous bathroom with a double jacuzzi surrounded by a tiled border of fish. Pears seem to be a decorative theme, showing up on the fireplace tiles and at the base of a huge twig wreath over the mantel. Outside is a private deck where early-morning coffee was provided and we would gladly have spent the day, had we not been working.

Breakfast on the inn's front porch brought fresh orange juice and an elaborate dish of melon bearing mixed fruit and homemade pineapple sorbet. The main event was a delicious zucchini crescent pie, teamed with an English muffin topped with cheddar, tomato and bacon, and roasted potatoes with onions and salsa. Soufflés, asparagus strata, green-apple stuffed french toast, waffles and popovers are other specialties.

Wine and cheese are served in the afternoon, and there are decanters of sherry plus bottles of sparkling water in each room.

Jim is a lobster fisherman. Guests may not see much of him unless they get up to join his fishing expedition at 4:30 a.m., but they know he's around by the lobster in the quiche and omelets.

(207) 967-3879 or 967-5151. www.buffleheadcove.com. Three rooms and two suites with private baths. June-October: doubles $135 to $250, suites $155 to $250. Rest of year: doubles $95 to $165, suites $125 to $165. Two-night minimum weekends. Smoking restricted.

The Captain Jefferds Inn, 5 Pearl St., Box 691, Kennebunkport 04046.

This handsome 1804 sea captain's mansion – once pictured on the cover of House Beautiful – has been nicely revitalized by new owners. Dick and Pat Bartholomew from the Brandywine Valley renovated and refurbished for four months before reopening in 1997 with a fresh new look.

The changes are evident from the outset. The original main entry, which had not been used for years, was reopened as the front entrance. The dining room was returned to its original place in the middle of the house, freeing up space for a quiet parlor away from the sunny garden TV room. All common rooms and most of the sixteen bedrooms were redecorated. Seven bathrooms were renovated and tiled, with fir ceilings overhead in the showers.

Assisted by their daughter Jane, the Bartholomews named and furnished each room in the spirit of their favorite places. Six have fireplaces, and beds are queensize except for two king suites and three small rooms with double beds. Hat boxes are a decorating trademark. Most coveted are two third-floor suites. The Assisi has a kingsize verdigris iron bed, a corner fireplace and an indoor water garden complete with plants, statue and a fountain. The Adare has a double-sided fireplace, one side facing the sitting area and kingsize sleigh bed and the other facing the bathroom with clawfoot soaking tub and a walk-in shower with two shower heads. The Florida Room has a more contemporary look, while the Charleston Room enjoys a newly tiled bath with sliding Indian shutters in the windows. Four guest rooms in the rear Carriage House are done in a country motif. We liked No. 4 with a wicker sitting room and a screened porch. Dick is partial to Bilbo's Hideaway, a cozy, skylit retreat with a double bed and private entrance – a good value for $105.

Breakfast is served outside on the side terrace or at a candlelit table for ten beside the fireplace in the expansive dining room. The backs of the chairs have been handpainted with different floral designs. The fare at our visit was fresh fruit, fresh orange juice and a fluffy lemon pancake with strawberry glaze. Eggs benedict was on the next day's menu. Other treats include stuffed french toast and creamy hash brown potatoes with fennel sausage and broiled tomatoes. Tea or hot mulled cider with homemade sweets are offered in the garden room in the afternoon.

(207) 967-2311 or (800) 839-6844. Fax (207) 967-0721. Eleven bedrooms and five suites with private baths. Doubles, $105 to $195. Suites, $155 to $220. Two-night minimum weekends. Children over 8. Dogs accepted. No smoking.

The Kennebunkport Inn, Dock Square, Box 111, Kennebunkport 04046.

In a nicely landscaped setting just off busy Dock Square, with a view of the river, is the graceful, clapboard turn-of-the-century mansion housing the Kennebunkport Inn, plus a 1930 motel-style River House annex in the rear. A small octagonal swimming pool with a large wooden deck fits snugly in between.

Innkeepers Rick and Martha Griffin, both schooled in hotel management, knew what they wanted after apprenticing at inns elsewhere. They sought an appealing location, spacious rooms, a large dining room, a bar and a swimming pool in a town with character. "We found everything we were looking for here," says Rick. They have decorated the twenty guest rooms in the annex with period pieces, chintz, Laura Ashley wallpapers and different stenciling everywhere. One of the larger rooms has a four-poster bed, sofa and velvet chair. All rooms have private baths and color TV.

Five more bedrooms are upstairs in the main inn. Nine deluxe rooms with four-poster beds have been added behind the restaurant in a wing that also provided the handsome piano bar and lounge, the last of the Griffins' requisites. A pianist entertains nightly in summer through foliage season.

The Griffins, who live with their daughters in an apartment attached to the inn, are hands-on innkeepers, assisted by a professional staff.

Excellent meals can be sampled in the inn's lovely dining rooms (see Dining Spots). Breakfast is extra, but includes such interesting dishes as custard french toast with pear-honey sauce and potato skins stuffed with scrambled eggs and mushrooms in a mornay sauce.

(207) 967-2621 or (800) 248-2621. Fax (207) 967-3705. Thirty-four rooms with private baths. Doubles, $99.50 to $249, EP, late June through October, $79.50 to $229 rest of year. Three-night minimum on summer and holiday weekends. Children welcome.

Cape Arundel Inn, Ocean Avenue, Box 530A, Kennebunkport 04046.

A choice location facing the open ocean and an excellent dining room commend

Graceful, turn-of-the-century mansion houses Kennebunkport Inn.

this Maine-style inn containing seven oceanview rooms with private baths and seven motel units at the side.

Jack Nahil of the Salt Marsh Tavern, who formerly owned the White Barn Inn, acquired the Cape Arundel in 1997 and started a modest upgrading. He added queensize beds and in-room telephones, created more windows for ocean views and completely refurnished the motel units. He also refurbished the living room and added oriental rugs. Throughout, his emphasis was on enhancing this "great Shingle-style structure. It's a wonderful property. It just needed some attention."

Rooms upstairs in the inn are spacious and pleasantly traditional. Master Bedrooms 2 and 3 are most coveted, the former with queen bed, a loveseat and chair by the picture window, and a private balcony. We liked Room 4 on the far-front corner, where white organdy curtains fluttered in the breeze and a white chenille spread covered the kingsize bed. The walls were wood and the carpeting attractive, but the view was all: two chairs in the corner from which to take in the bird's-eye panorama of the ocean and the George Bush compound at Walker Point.

Also in demand are the motel rooms, each with a full bath and TV, and a little balcony with striped chairs and a front-on view of the ocean beyond the wild roses. Some have kitchenettes.

The spacious front porch of the inn is a super place to curl up with a good book, enjoy a cocktail or a nightcap, or the morning newspaper before breakfast. Breakfast is hearty continental, featuring homemade pastries. The inn traditionally served lavish breakfasts for the public, but the new owner found them to be intrusive for the inn guests. He downscaled the breakfast service and planned to offer lunch instead (see Dining Spots). He also extended the inn's season.

(207) 967-2125. Seven inn rooms with private baths and seven motel units. Late June to mid-October, doubles $140 to $175, motel $165. Rest of year: doubles $100 to $130, motel $110 to $140. Two-night minimum weekends. No smoking. Closed January to mid-April.

The Captain Fairfield Inn, Pleasant and Green Streets, Box 1308, Kennebunkport 04046.

A new lease on life has been given this Federal sea captain's mansion, listed on the National Register and overlooking the River Green. Bonnie and Dennis Tallagnon, formerly of the Red Clover Inn in Mendon, Vt., bought the inn after it was closed and in bankruptcy. "We failed at a normal life," Dennis quipped as to why they re-entered the hospitality business.

After serious upgrading, they now offer nine guest rooms, all with new full baths, queensize beds dressed with pretty linens and lots of pillows, and comfortable sitting areas. Three have fireplaces. The one downstairs on the corner opposite the living room is a beauty. Called the grand library suite, it has a fishnet canopy queen bed, two armchairs, a desk, a fireplace and its own porch with two rocking chairs. Its bathroom recently has been enlarged and contains a jacuzzi tub. Three rooms lined up off a hall in the rear wing each offer four-poster beds draped with sheers and chintz, a day bed, and a wicker loveseat and chair. Bonnie has

Breakfast room at Captain Fairfield Inn.

outfitted each room with fluffy towels, Gilchrist & Soames toiletries and night lights, and hung grapevine wreaths on the doors.

Beautiful woodwork and molding and fresh flowers are evident throughout. The formal living room is elegant and pretty, yet comfortable. French doors open from the library/TV room onto the garden and a large side lawn.

Breakfast, a highlight here, is served in a fireplaced dining room and a sun room. It's prepared by Dennis, the son of a Swiss chef, who was off demonstrating how to make blueberry crêpes at Filene's in Boston at our first visit. That morning, he'd served fruit compote and juice, homemade muffins and croissants, and then a choice among three entrées: Spanish frittata topped with Vermont cheddar cheese and homemade toasted bread, apple pancakes, and granola with fruit, nuts and yogurt. Tea and treats are offered in the afternoon.

(207) 967-4454 or (800) 322-1928. Fax (207) 967-8537. Nine rooms with private baths. Doubles, $139 to $225, mid-June through October; $89 to $225 rest of year. Two-night minimum on weekends. Children over 6. No smoking.

The Maine Stay Inn & Cottages, 34 Maine St., Box 500A, Kennebunkport 04046.

A wraparound veranda and a cupola identify this 1860 house, listed on the National Register. It's been nicely upgraded by innkeepers Lindsay and Carol Copeland, who live nearby with their children and welcome families in their suites and cottages out back.

The main house offers a stylish living room, dining room and six guest quarters with private baths. The largest is a suite on the main floor, with a pullout sofa and woodburning fireplace in the sitting room and a queensize bed tucked into a corner of the bedroom, which also has a sitting area. Another main-floor room with a gas fireplace has a private deck onto the back yard. Up a graceful, suspended spiral staircase are four more rooms, one a fireplaced suite with a kingsize mahogany plantation bed, a sink in the sitting room and the bathroom in a closet. All rooms here have TVs hidden away in armoires or credenzas. Bathrooms contain the inn's own brand of toiletries.

In back are eleven cottages. Six have fireplaces, most have queensize or two double beds, and all but three have kitchenettes. Three of the ones with fireplaces have new whirlpool tubs.

A spacious, shady back lawn between inn and cottages contains a multitude of lawn chairs and a play area with an elaborate climber-swing apparatus that was "supposed to take eight hours and took two of us sixteen hours to assemble," Lindsay recalls. Carol cooks breakfast and he serves: juice, fresh fruit, homemade granola, fresh breads and muffins, and such entrées as featherbed eggs, egg strata with sausage and cheese, baked french toast, apple bread pudding, fruit-filled blintzes and apricot or currant scones. Cottage guests may have a breakfast basket delivered or share breakfast in the inn. Afternoon tea and desserts are served to all.

(207) 967-2117 or (800) 950-2117. Fax (207) 967-8757. Four rooms, two suites and eleven cottages with private baths. July-August and foliage: doubles $145 to $205, suites and two-bedroom cottage $185 to $225. November to Memorial Day: doubles $85 to $165; suites $115 to $175. Rest of year: doubles $95 to $195, suites $115 to $215. Two-night minimum most weekends. No smoking.

The Tides Inn By-the-Sea, 252 Goose Rocks Beach, Kennebunkport 04046.

Innkeeper Marie Henriksen used to call hers "a casual, crazy place with a true Maine air." After years of investment and hard work, she and her daughter Kristin have upgraded the turn-of-the-century inn into a comfortable, eclectic Victorian charmer, barely a stone's throw from Goose Rocks Beach. It's still casual, but nicely so, and not so crazy nor primitive as we first found it. All but three of the 22 refurbished guest rooms on the second and third floors now have modern baths (some of them admittedly small), and all but the shared-bath rooms contain king or queensize beds replete with an abundance of pillows.

Eleven yield ocean views. Plush carpeting and floral fabrics co-exist with antiques. The spaces are ingenious: one L-shaped family suite contains a queen bed, two twins and a day bed. There are whimsical and arty touches, from the flowers painted on the doorways to the faux designs atop bureaus. A mural of Teddy Roosevelt, who signed an early guest book, graces the third-floor stairwell, and Marie likes to show off a surprise visitor lurking behind one doorway.

The inn has a large Victorian living room with a TV set, a well-regarded restaurant (see Dining Spots), a rough-paneled pub in the rear and a decidedly Victorian/beachy feeling.

(207) 967-3757. Nineteen rooms with private baths and three with shared bath. Mid-June through Labor Day and all weekends: doubles, $135 to $185 with private bath, $89 to $99 with shared bath. Rest of year: doubles, $95 to $185 private, $65 to $99 shared. Three-night minimum in season. Children welcome. Smoking restricted. Closed mid-October to mid-May.

Dining Spots

The White Barn Inn, Beach Street, Kennebunkport.

Soaring up to three stories, with a breathtaking backdrop of flowers rising on tiers outside its twenty-foot-high rear picture window and illuminated at night, the elegant White Barn is almost too atmospheric for words. A local florist designs the dramatic backdrops that change with the seasons (lush impatiens in summer, assorted mums in fall, and a Christmas scene that begins with potted red cabbage and escalates to full spruce trees dressed with velvet bows, golden bells and tiny white lights). Talented executive chef Jonathan Cartwright oversees the kitchen, which seems to get better every year. And owner Laurie Bongiorno, a personable but perfectionist Australian of Italian descent, is the host who ensures that the dining room runs flawlessly.

Seasonal floral backdrop at White Barn Inn.

Little wonder that the White Barn became the AAA's first five-diamond dining establishment in all New England. It's *that* good.

The food is in the vanguard of contemporary American regional cuisine. Dinner is prix-fixe in four courses, with eight to ten choices for most courses. It's prepared by a kitchen staff of sixteen and served with precision by a young wait staff who meet with the chef beforehand for 45 minutes each night. Guests at each table are served simultaneously, one waiter per plate.

Up to 120 diners can be seated at tables spaced well apart in the main barn and in an adjoining barn. They're filled with understated antiques and oil paintings dating to the 18th century, and the loft holds quite a collection of wildlife wood carvings. The tables are set with silver, Schottsweizel crystal and Villeroy & Boch china, white linens and white tapers in crystal candlesticks. At one visit, a Russian pianist, here on a scholarship, played seemingly by ear in the entry near the gleaming copper-topped bar.

Our latest dinner, the highlight of several over the years, began with a glass of Perrier-Jouët extra brut (complimentary for house guests) and the chef's "welcome amenity," an herbed goat cheese rosette, an onion tart and a tapenade of eggplant and kalamata olives. Really interesting olive bread and plain white and poppyseed rolls followed. We'd gladly have tried any of the appetizers, but settled on a lobster spring roll with daikon radish, savoy cabbage and hot and sweet glaze, and the seared Hudson Valley foie gras on an apple and celeriac tart with a calvados sauce. Both were sensational.

Champagne sorbet in a pool of Piper Heidsieck extra-dry cleared the palate with a flourish for the main courses. One was a duo of Maine rabbit: a grilled loin with roasted rosemary and pommery mustard and a braised leg in cabernet sauvignon, accompanied by wild mushrooms and pesto-accented risotto. The other was pan-seared tenderloin of beef topped with a horseradish gratin and port-glazed shallots on a pool of potato and Vermont cheddar cheese, with a fancy little side of asparagus. A $29 bottle of Firestone cabernet accompanied from an excellent wine list especially strong on American chardonnays and cabernets.

Dessert was anything but anti-climactic: a classic coeur à la crème with tropical fruits and sugared shortbread and a trio of pear, raspberry and mango sorbets, served artistically on a black plate with colored swirls matching the sorbets and decorated with squiggles of white and powdered sugar. A tray of petits-fours gilded the lily. After an after-dinner brandy in the inn's living room, the little raisin cookies we found on the bed back in our room sent us happily into dreamland.

(207) 967-2321. Prix-fixe, $56. Dinner nightly, 6 to 9:30. Closed first two weeks of January. Jackets recommended. No smoking.

Seascapes, On the Pier, Cape Porpoise, Kennebunkport.

When President and Mrs. Bush first dined here, the First Lady exclaimed as they were seated, "my, what a pretty table." Owner Angela LeBlanc could not have been more pleased. The table settings, her pride and joy, won Restaurant Hospitality magazine's national table-top competition shortly after she and husband Arthur opened the restaurant. The table – pictured on the cover of our book, *The Restaurants of New England* – bears a teal cloth, a napkin ringed with fishes, handpainted Italian pottery in heavenly colors and fluted wine glasses. The setting is the match for the view of lobster boats in Cape Porpoise Harbor through large windows on three sides.

The chef handled the unexpected Bush visit with aplomb, as he does the lunch and dinner chores throughout the season. Waiters in Hawaiian shirts serve lunch from an interesting, extensive menu. You can order anything from a grilled pizza to a Maine lobster tortilla with mixed greens and daikon sprouts, from a caesar salad with lobster to a risotto of wild mushrooms, peas and artichokes.,

Excellent dark wheat rolls get dinner here off to a good start. For appetizers, we've enjoyed a stellar bisque of lobster and crab with crème fraîche, crispy phyllo shrimp with a Thai mint melon salad and sweet chili sauce, and the fabulous Maine lobster and crab egg roll with a seasoned seaweed pickled ginger salad. We thought the Maine crab cakes with crispy outsides and a tomato-rosemary sauce even better than the Chesapeake Bay variety. Almost a meal in itself is the unusual Caesar salad – chiffoned lettuce wrapped in a grilled flour tortilla and served sliced with prosciutto, reggiano-parmigiano and chives.

A sorbet precedes the entrées. At one dinner they were a classic Mediterranean bouillabaisse with rouille and a roulade of chicken stuffed with ginger, shiitake mushrooms and baby bok choy; at another, a rich lobster tequila over linguini, a garlicky shrimp Christina with feta and saffron rice, and grilled salmon with a sesame-soy-sherry marinade and a trio of julienned vegetables.

We're usually too full after the main courses to order dessert, but you might succumb to an ethereal strawberry torte, blueberry cheesecake, chocolate decadence or polenta pound cake with berry sauce. The reasonably priced, primarily American wine list has been honored by the Wine Spectator.

Keeping a family tradition launched when the LeBlancs owned the nearby Kennebunk Inn, half a dozen entrées bear the first names of their grandchildren.

The sale of the inn has allowed them to concentrate on Seascapes and to launch the **Lively Lobster,** a seafood shanty on the wharf next door. In the walkout basement beneath Seascapes they run the casual **Cape Porpoise Pub.** And in a corner off the entry to Seascapes is a piano bar, where a pianist entertains on weekends. The latest addition is a hidden side terrace with a little pond and fountain for lunchtime dining beside the harbor.

(207) 967-8500. Entrées, $17.25 to $27.50. Lunch daily, noon to 3, late June to late October. Dinner nightly, 5:30 to 9 or 10, Wednesday-Sunday in May and June. Closed late October to April. Lively Lobster open seasonally, daily 11 to sunset.

Grissini Trattoria & Panificio, 27 Western Ave., Kennebunkport.

This new Italian bistro is run by Laurie Bongiorno of the White Barn Inn, who took over the old Cafe Topher property in 1996. He opened it up into a perfectly stunning space, with vaulted beamed ceilings three stories high and a tall fieldstone fireplace. Sponged pale yellow walls, large tables spaced well apart, comfortable lacquered wicker armchairs, white tablecloths covered with paper, pinpoint lighting, and fancy bottles and sculptures backlit in the windows add up to a thoroughly sophisticated feeling. The talented chef and much of the staff are direct from Italy.

Opera was playing in the background as a plate of tasty little crostini, some with pesto and black olives and some with gorgonzola cheese and tomato, arrived to start our dinner. The bread, prepared in the in-house bakery, is served in slabs smack onto the table, with the server pouring an exorbitant amount of olive oil into a bowl for dipping. Everything else came on enormous white plates, except for the wine (in beautiful stemmed glasses) and the ice water (in pilsener glasses).

The exciting, oversize menu is made for grazing. Among antipasti, we loved the wood-grilled local venison sausage on a warm caramelized onion salad and the house-cured Maine salmon carpaccio with olive oil, herbs and lemon juice and topped with pasta salad. Pastas come in small and large sizes, as do pizzas.

Secondi are dishes like osso buco, wood-oven roasted half duck on a bed of baked tomato and eggplant, and pan-seared lobster tail with olive oil, smashed potato and herbs. We split the wood-grilled leg of lamb steak with Tuscan white beans, pancetta, garlic and rosemary. The "insalata mista della casa" was a nice mixture of field greens, kalamata olives, tomato, gorgonzola and pinenuts. Accompanying the meal was a fine reserve chianti for $18 from an affordable, all-Italian wine list.

A sampler plate of tirami su, a chocolate delicacy and strawberries in balsamic vinegar with mascarpone cheese ended a memorable dinner.

The turnaway crowds spill on warm nights onto a tiered outdoor courtyard that looks rather like a grotto.

(207) 967-2211. Entrées, $10.95 to $13.95. Lunch daily, 11:30 to 2. Dinner, from 5:30. Closed mid-February to mid-March.

Salt Marsh Tavern, 46 Western Ave. (Route 9), Lower Village, Kennebunkport.

If this reminds people of the old White Barn, that's the way its owner planned it. Jack Nahil recreated the White Barn restaurant he used to own after a brief hiatus in Florida. "There's a lot of déjà-vu here," he said. "Barns speak to me, I guess."

This barn speaks with a piano bar in the center beneath a soaring barn ceiling, oriental scatter rugs on the wide plank floors, the owner's oil paintings on the barnwood walls, farm implements and wood carvings on the lofts, and large rear

Loft floor and far dining room are on view from bar area at Salt Marsh Tavern.

windows onto a salt marsh stretching toward Kennebunk Beach. Tables dressed with white-over-forest green cloths and brass candlesticks are spaced throughout the open main floor and the upstairs loft. Up to 130 diners can be seated in "four different atmospheres under the same roof," Jack says.

The food speaks with the authority of the old White Barn, blending the classic and the creative with equal flair. Among main courses the grilled salmon fillet might be served with a julienne of basil and sundried tomatoes with cumin-scented spaetzle, the roast duckling with a raspberry-rhubarb demi-glaze and gingered whipped potatoes, and the sliced medallions of lamb leg with a roasted garlic bread pudding and lemon-mint sauce. Steamed or stuffed lobster and pepper-coated sirloin of beef with a brandy dijon sauce revive memories of the former surf and turf years.

Among starters, roasted chicken and green chile soup with cilantro cream is a counterpoint to the traditional lobster, scallop and shrimp bisque, lately enlivened with Thai spices. Baked oysters come with wild mushroom duxelles and double smoked bacon, the grape leaves are stuffed with lobster and basmati rice, and the salmon pot stickers marry fried scallions with a hot and sour lobster sauce. Dessert could be profiteroles, bittersweet chocolate torte or fruit tartlets.

(207) 967-4500. Entrées, $17.95 to $25.95. Dinner, Tuesday-Sunday 6 to 9 or 10. Closed in March.

Cape Arundel Inn, Ocean Avenue, Kennebunkport.

What could be more romantic than dining at a window table at the Cape Arundel, watching wispy clouds turn to mauve and violet as the sun sets, followed by a full golden moon rising over the darkened ocean? That the food is so good is a bonus.

The ocean and sky outside provide more than enough backdrop for an attractive dining room with lots of windows and plants, dark wood and white linens. An excellent warm pheasant salad on radicchio with Thai dressing and a lobster cheesecake garnished with nori salad preceded our main courses, sweetbreads with a tart grapefruit sauce and roast rack of lamb, accompanied by rice pilaf, ratatouille, and julienned carrots and turnips. Other entrées include roasted halibut crusted with a lemon and lime gratin and paired with a mango-leek couscous, seared roulade of salmon with mussels on lemon linguini and pan-seared filet mignon napped with roasted red pepper coulis and chive oil.

The dessert tray harbors some interesting indulgences, a fruit shortcake and brandy pound cake among them.

New owner Jack Nahil of the Salt Marsh Tavern extended the inn's season and planned to offer lunch service starting in 1998.

(207) 967-2125. Entrées, $19.95 to $26.95. Dinner, Monday-Saturday 5:30 to 8:30 or 9. Closed January to mid-April. No smoking.

Kennebunkport Inn, Dock Square, Kennebunkport.

The pristine dining rooms on either side of the inn's entry are extra pretty, with fringed valances, lace curtains, Laura Ashley wallpaper and stenciling, hurricane lamps, jars of fresh flowers on the fireplace mantels and tables with white-over-beige linens.

Innkeeper Martha Griffin, a graduate of La Varenne in Paris and the Elizabeth Pomeroy Cooking School in London, oversees the kitchen. She and husband Rick go to France frequently to learn new dishes with which to dazzle regular customers.

Seared carpaccio, grilled bruschetta with garlic bulb and caesar salad with shrimp are favorite starters.. Entrées range from sautéed breast of chicken on a bed of ratatouille to dijon-crusted rack of lamb, roasted lobster with a creamy risotto cake and the inn's signature bouillabaisse, served with a hot pepper sauce on the side. We remember an artfully presented grilled duck breast with raspberry sauce and an extraordinary mustard-ginger rack of lamb from past visits.

An ethereal key lime pie and a white chocolate mousse with strawberries in kirsch are good desserts. The wine list has been honored by Wine Spectator.

There's piano entertainment in the Victorian pub.

(207) 967-2621 or (800) 248-2621. Entrées, $17.50 to $24.95. Lunch, noon to 2:20. Dinner nightly, 6 to 9. Closed Sunday in off-season and November-April.

Arundel Wharf Restaurant, 43 Ocean Ave., Kennebunkport.

This riverfront landmark had been plodding along for years until co-owner Bob Williamson got married. His wife Michelle gave the place a facelift, a new chef, a new menu and an extended season. The locals responded in droves, joining tourists to pack the place at all hours.

The location has much to do with it. The blue-awninged deck (heated in fall) affords 125 patrons some of the best harbor views in town. Another 75 can be seated inside, at shiny nautical chart tables amidst wooden ship models, mahogany accents and a yacht club feel. Two half-circle tables extend out over the wharf for the most in-your-face waterfront dining we've encountered anywhere.

The food earns accolades for its quality as well as its breadth. For dinner, you can order a lobster roll, a hamburger, lobster stew or an avocado stuffed with lobster or crab at the low end; coastal paella or bouillabaisse at the high end. Sea-food reigns, from seven lobster dishes to charbroiled swordfish with corn-pepper relish, shrimp scampi and "bag of fish" (scallops and haddock steamed in parchment with orange, ginger and sesame). Other possibilities include pork gorgonzola, mango chicken, venison and prime rib.

Start with a smoked seafood sampler. But save room. Some people come here for the desserts alone. Consider the chocolate cake, the bread pudding with whiskey sauce, the mixed four-berry pie or the blueberry-apple crisp.

(207) 967-3444. Entrées, $7.25 to $18.95. Open daily, 11:30 to 9. Closed November to mid-April.

The Tides Inn By-the-Sea, 252 Goose Rocks Beach, Kennebunkport.

Some of the area's more intriguing fare comes from this beachy Victorian inn of the old school beside Goose Rocks Beach. "Real food for real people" is how chef Pam White describes her fare.

That translates to such dinner specialties as a lobster burrito, shellfish ragoût, pan-seared sea scallops on a bed of wilted greens, seared buffalo medallions, and flambéed veal medallions with cognac and portobello mushrooms. Still etched in our memories is a sensational dinner here of grilled lamb with a side of salsa containing the proper amount of cilantro and a delectable grilled shrimp and fettuccine with green onions, sundried tomatoes, basil and garlic cream.

The food is assertive and the setting, colorful. Pink Lalique-style oil lamps and cobalt blue wine glasses accent the floral-clothed tables in the enclosed front porch and the interior dining room. Appetizers, light fare and four entrées are available in the rear **Sandy Bottom Yacht Pub.**

(207) 967-3757. Entrées, $16.25 to $27.95. Dinner nightly except Tuesday, 6 to 9. Closed mid-October to mid-May.

Diversions

Beaches. Gooch's, a curving half-mile crescent, and **Kennebunk** are two beaches with surf west of town (parking by permit, often provided by innkeepers). The fine silvery sand at Goose Rocks Beach looks almost tropical and the waters are protected. Beachcombers find starfish and sand-dollar shells here in early morning. More secluded is **Parson's Beach,** a natural sandy strand set among the tall grasses and undeveloped area next to the Rachel Carson Wildlife Refuge. The beaches are at their uncrowded best at non-peak periods and early or late in the day.

Parson's Way. A marker opposite the landmark Colony Hotel notes the land given to the people of Kennebunkport so that "everyone may enjoy its natural beauty." Sit on the benches, spread a blanket on a rock beside the ocean, or walk out to the serene little chapel of St. Ann's Episcopal Church by the sea.

Ocean Avenue. Continue past Parson's Way to Spouting Rock, where the incoming tide creates a spurting fountain as waves crash between two ragged cliffs, and Blowing Cave, another roaring phenomenon within view of Walker Point and the George Bush summer compound. Go on to Cape Porpoise, the closest thing to a fishing village hereabouts, with a working lobster pier and a picturesque harbor full of islands.

History. The Kennebunkport Historical Society has its attractions: the 1853 Greek Revival Nott House called **White Columns** and the 1899 **Town House School** with exhibits of local and maritime heritage. But inland Kennebunk is more obviously historic: There's a treasure behind every door on the block at the 1825 **Brick Store Museum,** which has an excellent collection of decorative and fine arts, Federal period furniture, artifacts and textiles. It mounts a couple of major exhibits each year (photos of the great fire of 1947 were on at one visit) and offers walking tours of Kennebunk's historic district. Summer Street (Route 35) running south of downtown toward Kennebunkport is considered one of the architecturally outstanding residential streets in the nation; the 1803 **Taylor-Barry House** is open for tours, and the aptly named yellow-with-white-frosting Wedding Cake House (1826) is a sight to behold (though not open to the public).

Arts and Crafts. Its scenery has turned Kennebunkport into a mecca for artisans. The Art Guild of the Kennebunks numbers more than 50 resident professionals as members and claims the Kennebunks are the largest collective community of fine art on the East Coast. Art and galleries are everywhere, but are concentrated around Kennebunkport's Dock Square and the wharves to the southeast. Out over the water in the Wharf Lane Shops is Lou and Bob Lipkin's distinctive **Goose Rocks Pottery.** More than 95 artists show at **Mast Cove Galleries,** a lovely Greek Revival home and barn next to the library on Route 9. For a change of pace, visit the grounds of the **Franciscan Monastery** (where, as some savvy travelers know, spare and inexpensive bedrooms are available) and St. Anthony's Shrine. The shrines and sculpture include the towering piece that adorned the facade of the Vatican pavilion at the 1964 New York World's Fair.

Shopping. Dock Square and, increasingly, the Lower Village across the river are full of interesting stores, everything from **Dunne Roman** for gifts and home accessories inspired by the garden to the **Port Canvas Co.,** with all kinds of handsome canvas products. Crowning the main corner of Dock Square is the decidedly upscale **Compliments,** "the gallery for your special lifestyle." It features lots of glass, including lamps and egg cups, trickling fountains and cute ceramic gulls, each with its own personality. Another extraordinary shop is **Punctilio,** stocking one-of-a-kind items from innovative designers. You might pick up a feather quill pen set or a beaded scarf that looks like a piece of jewelry. **Alano Ltd.** has super clothes, and we liked the contemporary crafts at **Kennebunkport Arts** and **Plum Dandy.** The splendid **Kennebunk Book Port, Paper Plus,** the **Good Earth Pottery, Port Folio** ("paper with panache"), **The Whimsey Shop** and the shops at Union Square and Village Marketplace are other favorites.

Extra-Special _____

Rachel Carson National Wildlife Refuge, Route 9, Kennebunkport.

A mile-long interpretive trail through saltwater marshes and adjacent grasslands leads one through an area rich in migratory and resident wildlife. The 5,000-acre reserve is named for the environmental pioneer who summered in Maine and conducted research in the area for several of her books. The trail, "paved" with small gravel, and boardwalks lead through tranquil woods until – just when you begin to wonder what all the fuss is about – the vista opens up at the sixth marker and a boardwalk takes you out over wetlands and marsh. Cormorants, herons and more are sighted here regularly, and benches allow you to relax as you take in the scene. An even better view of the ocean in the distance is at Marker 7, the Little River overlook. The widest, best view of all is near the end of the loop at Marker 11. If you don't have time for the entire trail, ignore the directional signs and go counter-clockwise. You'll get the best view first, though you may not see much wildlife.

(207) 646-9226. Open daily, dawn to dusk. Donation.

Fine view of Camden Harbor is offered from porch at Smiling Cow gift shop.

Camden, Me.
Where Mountains Meet Sea

From where she stood in 1910, all that native poet Edna St. Vincent Millay could see were "three long mountains and a wood" in one direction and "three islands in a bay" the other way. Her poem, written at age 18 and first recited publicly at Camden's Whitehall Inn, captures the physical beauty of this coastal area known as the place where the mountains meet the sea.

Today, the late poet might not recognize her beloved Camden, so changed is the town that now teems with tourists in summer. The scenery remains as gorgeous as ever, and perhaps no street in Maine is more majestic than High Street, its forested properties lined with the sparkling white homes that one associates with the Maine coast of a generation ago. Back then, when you finally reached Camden after the slow, tortuous drive up Route 1, you unofficially had arrived Down East.

Those were the days, and visitors in ever-increasing numbers still try to recapture them in a town undergoing a bed-and-breakfast inn boom and a proliferation of smart, distinctive shops. A sign in the window of Mariner's Restaurant, proclaiming itself "the last local luncheonette," caught our eye: "Down Home, Down East; no ferns, no quiche."

A small-scale cultural life attract some; others like the

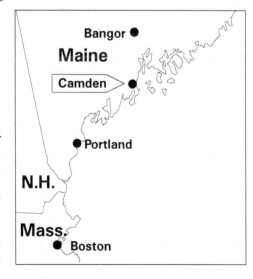

outdoors activities of Camden Hills State Park. But the focus for most is Camden Harbor, with its famed fleet of windjammers setting forth under full sail each Monday morning and returning to port each Saturday morning.

Camden has an almost mystical appeal that draws people back time and again. Sometimes, amid all those people, you just wish that appeal weren't quite so universal.

Inn Spots

Norumbega, 61 High St., Camden 04843.

Imagine having the run of a grand Victorian castle overlooking Penobscot Bay – a "castle to call home," in the words of businessman-turned-innkeeper Murray Keatinge.

It's possible, thanks to Murray, a Californian who summers in Camden and acquired Norumbega in 1987. "We're trying to build the best inn in the U.S.A.," he said on one of his not-infrequent trips back and forth from Pasadena, "and we're close to it."

One of the great late-19th-century villas along the Maine coast, the 1886 cobblestone and slate-roofed mansion was built for Joseph B. Stearns, inventor of the duplex system of telegraphy, and for a few years was the summer home of journalist Hodding Carter. It has eight sumptuous guest quarters on the second and third floors, four more in the walk-out basement, a penthouse suite to end all suites and a main floor with public rooms like those in the finest estates.

Indeed, this is a mini-Newport-style mansion, from its graceful entry with oriental carpets and ornate staircase (complete with a cozy retreat for two beside a fireplace on the landing) to the smallest of guest rooms on the garden level, which has a queen bed, TV and an ocean view from its own little deck. The room that was once the smallest has now become a sitting room for the Library Suite, a two-story affair with windows on three sides and a wraparound mezzanine to get at the books.

The other rooms, all high-ceilinged and airy, are decorated in a fresh California style with lots of pastels and plush rugs. Each includes a kingsize bed, sitting area and private bath. The Sandringham has one of Norumbega's five in-room fireplaces in the corner and a sofa and two chairs beneath balloon curtains in the turret window. The Canaervon, full of wicker, has its own little rear porch with deck chairs. A bay window with a window seat and a private deck afford full bay views for guests in the Warwick Room, also with fireplace. Even the basement rooms, with windows and private decks onto the garden, are cheery, and the Arundel comes with a jacuzzi tub. The ultimate is the penthouse suite, up a spiral staircase from the third floor. It harbors a kingsize bedroom beneath a skylight, a regal bath with pillows around a circular whirlpool tub for two, a wet bar, a sitting room in pink and green, and a see-through, three-sided fireplace, plus a porch with two deck chairs and a fabulous ocean view.

The parlors, the conservatory, the downstairs lounge with pool table and TV, the flower-laden rear porches on all three floors and the expansive lawns are all available for guests' relaxation.

Murray or his staff greet guests and pour tea or wine in the afternoon. You also can help yourself to goodies from the cookie jar and a refrigerator stocked with mineral water and soft drinks. In the morning, guests gather at the large table in the formal dining room, in the sunny conservatory or outside on the deck for a

Norumbega is a grand Victorian mansion overlooking Penobscot Bay.

breakfast feast: platters of fresh fruits, homemade muffins and breads, breakfast meats and, the pièce de résistance, the main course – perhaps featherbed eggs with shrimp and hash-browns, lemon pancakes with blueberry sauce, raspberry crêpes or, in our case, french toast topped with a dollop of pink sherbet and sliced peaches, which all eight at our table agreed was about the best we'd ever had.

Being thrown together with strangers somehow works here – there's enough room for togetherness and also for escape, if you want. The price is steep, but most guests find it worth it.

(207) 236-4646. Fax (207) 236-0824. Nine rooms and three suites with private baths. July to mid-October: doubles, $155 to $325; suites, $345 to $450. Late spring and late October: doubles, $125 to $275; suites, $295 to $375. November to mid-May: doubles, $95 to $225; suites, $245 to $295. Two-night minimum weekends in season. Children over 7.

The Inn at Sunrise Point, Route 1, Box 1344, Camden 04843.
Here's a switch: Travel writer visits more than 2,000 inns and decides to open his own on the coast of Maine. Finds old house within 100 feet of the ocean on four forested acres and 150 feet of waterfront near Lincolnville Beach. Doubles size of house, adds conservatory, builds new cottage and doubles size of another. Opens B&B and awaits travel writers' reactions "with trepidation."

Jerry Levitin, a Californian who took over the late Norman Simpson's *Country Inns & Back Roads* guidebook for a time and ruffled the feathers of some longtime innkeepers along the way, found out again what it's like to be on the receiving end of the pen (he opened the White Swan residential hotel on San Francisco's Nob Hill in 1979 before turning to travel writing).

"I built what I'd like to stay at," says Jerry with characteristic candor. Incorporating "the best of what I've seen," he and resident innkeepers have run what he calls a combination "English manor/country casual/seaside cottage." His goal was to join the ranks of Norumbega – which, he opines, is the only inn for the high-end market on the Camden coast, "and it isn't on the water."

The main house offers a living/dining room that's mostly windows onto Penobscot Bay, an English hunting-style library with cherrywood shelves and a stone fireplace, and a small conservatory with a breakfast table for two, a wicker couch and the sky visible above. Upstairs are three rather small guest rooms with fireplaces, tiled showers, queensize beds with swing reading lamps, two swivel upholstered or wicker chairs in front of the window, built-in desks, telephones and honey-pine armoires holding TVs, VCRs, music systems and guests' clothing. They are decorated variously in yellow, raspberry and light blue.

Four fireplaced guest cottages are bigger and offer the same amenities plus microwaves, wet bars and double jacuzzis with separate showers. The Winslow Homer Cottage that we occupied right beside the bay features a kingsize bed and an enormous bathroom almost as big as the bedroom. We were surprised there was no space to stash luggage other than in the bathroom, and the waterfront deck was so narrow as to be useless (the front porch of the main house compensated). New at bay's edge is the prized Fitz Hugh Lane Cottage, light and airy with a vaulted ceiling. Lie in one of its two queensize beds "and your feet are in the water," Jerry points out, with an understandable bit of hyperbole. There's a kitchenette in the Edward Hopper Cottage in the old barn and carriage house. All four cottages have been enhanced with paintings, accessories and deck chairs to make them more warm and homey.

Jerry or his innkeepers greet guests with tea, coffee, wine and hot and cold appetizers, served from 4 to 6 "and substantial enough so you won't need to eat dinner until 8 or 9." At breakfast, we feasted on fruit, pecan coffeecake, a terrific frittata with basil, bay shrimp and jack cheese, potatoes dusted with cayenne, crisp bacon and hazelnut coffee. Corn muffins, potatoes and crabmeat strata were on tap at a later visit, and lobster hash was the main dish last time we stopped by.

Upon departure, we found a card under our windshield: "Our porter has cleaned your windscreen to allow you to get a clear picture of our Penobscot Bay."

(207) 236-7716 or (800) 435-6278. Fax (207) 236-0820. Three rooms and four cottages with private baths. Doubles, $150 to $205. Cottages, $250 to $325. Open May-October. Children by special arrangement. No smoking.

Windward House, 6 High St., Camden 04843.

Guests enter this handsome 1854 Greek Revival through the dining room, which is appropriate, for its gourmet breakfasts are well-known. A gleaming silver service, lace curtains, blue patterned rug and lots of plants immediately catch the eye. Owners Tim and Sandy La Plante from Ontario may greet you here and lead you to the nicely furnished parlor, where the fireplace seems to be ablaze morning and night, for orientation purposes before showing you to your room.

Upstairs are five guest rooms, each with queensize bed and private bath, and a suite with sitting area, gas stove and a new clawfoot soaking tub in the enlarged bathroom. The most choice accommodations are more recent, and reflect the La Plantes' determination to attract the winter trade. In the rear Garden Room, a favorite of honeymooners, light pours through a skylit cathedral ceiling to reveal a pink and green space with a Maine maple cannonball bed and a Vermont Castings stove. The La Plantes consider the newest Carriage Room their signature: a ground-floor space in the front carriage section of an old barn with pine-board floors, two wing chairs in front of the gas stove and a queen canopy bed with Ralph Lauren sheets and a fluffy duvet. The oversize bathroom has a clawfoot soaking tub and a corner shower.

Guests gather in the parlor, a library where tea and coffee are available all day, a cozy game room stocked with puzzles and board games, and on the rear deck. The deck looks onto a long back yard and an English garden, a showplace of annuals, perennials and herbs, carefully planned and tended for color all season long.

The culinary background of the couple, who owned food stores in Ottawa, ensures exotic breakfasts. They also serve afternoon tea with cookies and dessert squares, offer complimentary port and sherry, and put chocolate mint truffles in every room.

Breakfast is taken at individual tables in the elegant dining room or outside on a rear deck. Sandy does the baking and Tim prepares the entrées. We were mighty impressed with a bowl of fresh strawberries and blueberries in cream, the raspberry-cream cheese coffee cake and the peaches-and-cream french toast with bacon. Orange-yogurt pancakes, ham and cheese strata, frittatas and eggs olé with homemade salsa are other treats.

After breakfast, you may be temporarily immobilized. Linger over coffee on the deck overlooking the gardens and revel in the good life.

(207) 236-9656. Fax (207) 230-0433. www.windwardhouse.com. Seven rooms and one suite with private baths. Mid-May through December: doubles, $100 to $170. Rest of year: $85 to $115. Children over 12. No smoking. Closed two weeks in March.

Edgecombe-Coles House, 64 High St., Camden 04843.

On a hilltop almost across the street from Norumbega, this is another substantial summer home run by former Californians and listed on the National Register. Innkeepers Terry and Louise Price named it for their fathers and furnished it rather spectacularly with antiques, oriental rugs, original art, stenciling that Louise did herself (she also loves to wallpaper), and interesting touches like draperies around the showers and English soaps and herb shampoos for guests.

All six guest rooms come with TV/VCRs and telephones. Each is different, but most have lacy canopies and quilts and bedspreads made by Louise's mother. The most elegant is the huge front room with kingsize bed, fireplace and picture windows framing a grand ocean view for the occupant of the chaise lounge. A large end room with kingsize bed, loveseat and water view comes with a collection of antique toys and teddybears.

Somewhat hidden in every room is what Terry calls "a snooper's box" in which guests leave messages for each other and the housekeeping staff has fun moving around.

In the luxurious living room are a leather chesterfield, plush sofas and antique chairs angled around the fireplace, a baby grand piano, and many books and magazines. There's a book-filled den, which also has a fireplace.

A full breakfast is served in the pretty rear dining room or on the wraparound front porch, restored to its original look and furnished in wicker. Omelets, scrambled eggs with lox, strawberry waffles, blueberry pancakes and dutch babies (giant sweet popovers) are among the specialties. The innkeepers will bring continental breakfast to your bedroom, if you wish. They also provide free bicycles, including a tandem bike, for guests to use.

(207) 236-2336 or (800) 528-2336. Fax (207) 236-6227. Six rooms with private baths. Doubles, $100 to $185; winter, $85 to $145. Children over 8. No smoking.

The Hawthorn, 9 High St., Camden 04843.

Elegance and comfort are the hallmarks of this 1894 Queen Anne-style beauty, nicely upgraded by Nicholas and Patricia Wharton from Texas. Moving to Maine in 1995 because of their love of the ocean and sailing, they enhanced a landmark B&B that had suffered under previous ownership. The Whartons redecorated most of the ten guest rooms and suites, adding their own furnishings and antiques plus warmth and a personal touch. They also did extensive landscaping in the back yard, which slopes down toward Camden Harbor and a gate opening onto the town amphitheater.

Six guest rooms are in the main inn and four in the rear carriage house, newly repainted in barn red with a pale yellow trim that matches the house. All have private baths, telephones and queensize beds (except one with twins). The rear Regency Room comes with an extra-large bathroom and the best water view from the washstand – if you turn sideways. Oriental art and a pine English maid's closet add interest. Framed botanical prints enhance the Jillian Suite, formed by dividing a large room into a front sitting room with french doors into the bedroom. The Turret Suite has a wicker chaise and a rocker in the turret, while the Victorian Room on the lower garden level has a free-standing clawfoot tub right in the room with a European water closet nearby.

The four prime accommodations, three with double jacuzzis and three with gas fireplaces, are in the carriage house. All have private decks or patio and TV/VCRs. A "wow" view – "the one that people come to Maine for," says Nick, with his native British accent – greets guests in the Norfolk. It's a huge room with white iron queen bed, extra day bed, gas stove and private deck overlooking shady lawn and harbor. Downstairs is the Watney with a mahogany sleigh bed and an unusual canopy headboard. A collection of birdhouses is hung as art on the walls of the Cabriolet, prized for its garden patio. Nick's favorite is the upstairs Broughman Room, with a mahogany poster bed, two upholstered rocker chairs, stenciling around the jacuzzi and another great water view.

Back in the main house are a double parlor with not one but two turrets. Breakfast is served in a formal dining room or on a delightful rear deck. The fare the day we visited included a fresh fruit plate, coffee cake, homemade granola and a turkey sausage frittata. Other main courses range from crème caramel french toast to crab strata with roasted red bell pepper sauce.

(207) 236-8842. Fax (207) 236-6181. Ten rooms with private baths. Doubles, $100 to $195 in season, $80 to $150 rest of year. Children over 12. No smoking. Closed mid-January through February.

Maine Stay Inn, 22 High St., Camden 04843.

Three of the most doting innkeepers we know pamper guests in this rambling house that never seems to end. Retired Navy Capt. Peter Smith, his wife Donny and her twin sister, Diana Robson, go the extra mile. That means anything from keeping the cast-iron wood and coal stove in their kitchen gathering place aglow from November to April, to sending guests on their way with a map and a computer print-out of directions and sights to see for almost any destination – more than 80 at last count.

"We try hard to make people feel they're staying in a home, not just renting a room," says Peter. Starting simply in 1988 with nine bedrooms and three shared baths in their handsome 1802 farmhouse, they have conscientiously upgraded to

Upgraded Maine Stay Inn houses guests in comfort and style.

the point where they have eight bedrooms and suites, all with private baths. The effort pays. While their colleagues were posting vacancy signs in July and August 1997, the Maine Stay had been filled every night since May. Service and value are the reasons cited by these engaging innkeepers.

As guests arrive, Peter tells them they're welcome to light the fireplaces in two parlors and a library/TV room, or come into the expansive kitchen for company and cheer. They're also invited to use the rear deck, which was about to be enclosed for a solarium in the next phase of renovations, or to enjoy the seats and paths in the two-acre back yard, which backs up to Camden Hills State Park. Peter pointed to the spot where they planned to install a gazebo and a bridge over a creek.

Room 3, upstairs front, is typical of the future rooms as envisioned by these visionary innkeepers. Formerly two small rooms with a shared bath, it is now the Clark Suite with a sofabed and gas fireplace in the front sitting room, a queen brass bed in back and a private deck. The rest of the bedrooms vary in size and décor, but all live up to the term charming. They also have private baths (some with Corian tiled showers), except for two on the third floor that are rented as a family suite. In the ongoing renovations, that was to become a suite with bedroom and sitting room.

The attached carriage house harbors a delightful downstairs guest room, cheery in white with blue trim and yellow accents, with gas stove and private stone patio. You'd never guess it had been transformed from a root cellar with no windows and a dirt floor. The Smiths were vacating their upstairs suite in the carriage house to move into a spacious new apartment in the attached four-story barn. That yielded the largest guest suite yet, this one with cathedral ceiling, tall windows and a fire-place. The pricetag, as with the other suites: a mere $125.

Breakfast is a convivial gathering, served on fine china at three tables in the dining room or, eventually, in the solarium. The buffet table might hold fresh fruit, homemade granola, bundt cake and an egg casserole, french toast or pancakes.

(207) 236-9636. Fax (207) 236-0621. Five rooms and three suites with private baths. Doubles, $95. Suites, $125. November-May: 20 percent less. Children over 8. No smoking.

A Little Dream, 66 High St., Camden 04843.

This is a lacy valentine of a B&B, decorated with great flair by Joanne Fontana. She and her sculptor husband Billy (most of his time is spent in remodeling these days) bought the white Victorian turreted house in 1988. Former owners of toy stores in New York City and Boston, they seem to have brought their entire inventory with them. The collection of dolls and teddybears in their little dream world is not to be believed.

From the pretty wicker and chintz furnished parlor to the elaborately decorated dining room to the conservatory they added off the dining room, everything is accessorized to perfection. Lace pillows on a chaise, tea sets, old playing cards, tiny sentimental books tucked here and there – you know that Joanne, who says "I have the nicest guests in the whole world," loves to pamper them.

The choicest lodging in the main house is the master bedroom on the second floor. Done in greens and roses, it has its own porch, a four-poster bed entwined with pussy willows, a TV with a VCR and video library and a chaise lounge in a reading nook. When the leaves are off the trees, this room has a great view of Norumbega across the street and Penobscot Bay beyond. The newly expanded Yellow Room adds a bidet and an expansive deck and balcony. A large turret room is popular because it adjoins a sitting area in the turret. Every room has a private bath, a basket of hand towels and Crabtree & Evelyn amenities, everything is tied with ribbons, there are about eight pillows on each bed and Victorian clothing is displayed everywhere.

Always perfecting, Joanne was redoing the side carriage house in 1998 as a replica in miniature of the main house. A basement addition for Billy's new studio freed up space for the prime accommodation on the middle floor. It's a large room with fireplace and kingsize bed, a sitting area with TV and bay window facing the bay, a porch and a bathroom with large oval soaking tub and separate shower. Upstairs is a second unit with a separate sitting room, wet bar, a balcony and a queensize brass bed.

Breakfasts are gala happenings at A Little Dream. On lace cloths topped with flowered mats and heavy silver, you might find fresh orange juice in champagne flutes, Kentucky butter cake with crème fraîche and local blueberries, a fruit platter with honeydew melon, black raspberries, kiwis, strawberries and grapefruit, and heart-shaped banana-pecan waffles with country sausage. Smoked salmon or apple-brie omelets, fruit crêpes, lemon-ricotta soufflé pancakes or baked featherbed eggs with pears, smoked ham and a raspberry puree sauce are other specialties. At check-in, the Fontanas will serve strawberry or peach herbal iced tea, with fresh mint from the garden, and at cocktail time, perhaps a tray of pâtés, including smoked trout, and olives.

(207) 236-8742. www.camdeninns.com. Four rooms and three suites with private baths. Mid-May through October: doubles, $95 to $159; suites $169 to $195. Rest of year: doubles $95 to $110, suite $115 to $135. Two-night minimum weekends from July to mid-October. No children. No smoking.

Victorian B&B features turrets and wraparound veranda.

The Victorian By the Sea, The Other Road, Box 1385, Camden 04843.

New Yorkers Marie and Ray Donner moved with their almost-teenagers in 1993 to a Victorian house built in 1889, added 5,000 square feet and created a comfortable B&B. They offer six spacious bedrooms and suites with private baths and a superior location – 800 feet down a wooded hillside off Route 1, with views and a nature trail reaching to Penobscot Bay.

You can tell this place is special when you first see the substantial house – painted beige with lots of striking apricot-colored trim – and the broad, wrap-around veranda that was part of the addition built by Ray, who was involved in heavy construction work in New York. The wicker-filled veranda is perfect for taking in the tranquil setting and the watery scene through a break in the trees. So is a shady gazebo overlooking gardens. Also comfortable is the guest living room, a fireplaced dining room that opens onto an appealing eight-sided sun porch in a corner turret, and a large butler's pantry in which guests are free to use the microwave, refrigerator and such.

Little cloth dolls from their daughter's collection reside amid the pillows on the queensize beds in each room. Family heirlooms, quilts, window treatments and beds reflect the Victorian period, but without the clutter often associated with the era. Each room has a fireplace, two upholstered chairs, antique writing desks and complimentary Poland Spring water. A second-floor suite comes with a sitting room with original wainscoting in the turret. A skylit suite encompasses the entire third floor. It has a loft with two twin beds above the bedroom, a sitting room with sliding glass doors onto the ocean-view balcony, enough sitting areas to seat a small army and an enormous bathroom in which Ray built wash basins into a library table and installed a clawfoot soaking tub with separate shower.

Breakfast is served buffet style in the octagonal sun porch, recently expanded and winterized with six individual tables placed beside tall windows around the perimeter. At our visit the fare was juice, muffins, granola and blueberry pancakes. Other main dishes include stuffed french toast with cream cheese, chocolate belgian waffles with raspberries picked on the grounds, and crêpes filled with homemade jams.

The Donners serve afternoon tea and cookies or hot apple cider, depending on the season, to arriving guests. Marie also runs a small Victorian gift shop in a section of the carriage house beside the inn.

(207) 236-3785 or (800) 382-9817. Four rooms and two suites with private baths. Mid June to mid-October: doubles $135 to $150, suites $205. Rest of year: doubles $95 to $115, suites $145. Children over 12. Smoking restricted.

Blue Harbor House, 67 Elm St., Camden 04843.

Still more ex-Californians in Camden, Dennis Hayden and Jody Schmoll own this old-timer, which they have upgraded and expanded. They offer ten guest accommodations, ranging in size from tiny front Room 4, formerly occupied by a lady who lived in the house for 96 years, to two large suites converted from a rear apartment. All have telephones and most have TVs.

The rooms are notable for attractive and varied stenciling, done by the former innkeeper who returns as Jody adds more rooms. It turns up in the most interesting motifs and places. Seagulls, tulips, pineapples – you name it, you may find it stenciled somewhere. Colorful quilts, period furnishings and treasured pieces from the couple's past abound. Traffic noise in rooms near the street has been reduced with the installation of thermopane windows and air-conditioning.

For privacy and comfort, we'd spring for one of the two rear suites, each with kingsize bed, circular whirlpool tub, TV and comfy sitting area. An antique posting board once used for stock prices adorns a wall in one.

Guests share a side porch, a small parlor, a sun porch/common room with TV where breakfast is served, and a second dining room for overflow. Dennis does the cooking. His favorite is blueberry pancakes, light and fluffy. He also does soufflés, rum-raisin french toast with rum-raisin ice cream, dutch babies filled with fruit, shirred eggs and lobster quiche – "I try to make every day a Sunday brunch," he says. Iced tea, cookies and sometimes homemade ice cream are served in the afternoon.

Candlelight dinners at 7 o'clock are available for house guests by reservation. The $30 tab might bring lobster stew, a green salad with basil vinaigrette, rack of lamb stuffed with spinach and hazelnuts, and chocolate brownie soufflé or blueberry pie. Steamed lobster was on the docket at our latest visit. Dennis says he enjoys cooking better than his former executive job with the Korbel champagne company.

(207) 236-3196 or (800) 248-3196. Fax (207) 236-6523. Eight rooms and two suites with private baths. Doubles, $85 to $125. Suites, $145. No smoking.

Swan House, 49 Mountain St., Camden 04843.

"Birds and gulls – not traffic – wake you up here in the morning," says Ken Kohl, formerly of Chicago, who with wife Lynn took over the Swan House from a consortium of local innkeepers and began imbuing it with the renovations and TLC that energetic, on-site owners provide. Their location on a wooded double lot on a residential street away from busy Route 1 is an asset. So are the six comfortable, quiet guest rooms in the main 1874 Victorian house built by the Swan family, on which the Kohls built an addition for their living quarters, and in the rear carriage house nestled in the trees.

Two guest parlors are full of interesting touches. Among them are a sleigh transformed into a coffee table, covered with old Life magazines, and a game table made by Amish woodworkers. The latter has an astonishingly realistic Monopoly board made of needlepoint inlaid inside. Breakfast is served on butcher-block and glass tables in a front sun porch with a view of a hillside gazebo. Juice, strawberries in a pineapple half, homemade granola and pastries like almond coffeecake and apple crisp started the repast when we visited. Main dishes vary from pancakes to baked french toast to egg casserole.

Two bedrooms on the first floor of the main house and four more in the carriage house called the Cygnet Annex are named for swans. All have private baths and all but one come with canopied queensize beds. Especially popular are the upstairs Swan Lake loft with skylights, two queen beds and a day bed, a wicker loveseat and knotty pine walls hung with baskets, wreaths and artifacts. Also in demand are the quiet and cool Lohengren Suite with queensize sofabed in the sitting area, and, our choice, the Trumpeter Room in back with a vaulted ceiling and a private deck in the trees. From it, you can see the start of the Mount Battie hiking trail.

(207) 236-8275 or (800) 207-8275. Fax (207) 236-0906. Five rooms and one suite with private baths. June-October: doubles $85 to $120, suite $100. Rest of year: doubles $70 to $105, suite $85. Children over 12. No smoking.

The Belmont, 6 Belmont Ave., Camden 04843.

Camden's oldest inn, this cottage-style Victorian on a residential side street has sheltered guests first as the Green Gables and, later, as Aubergine. Gerald Clare and John Mancarella changed the name, enlarged a reception room/parlor, added a side porch and switched the cuisine from French nouvelle to regional American (see Dining Spots).

All six upstairs guest quarters come with private baths. They are nicely decorated with a mix of new and traditional furnishings, floral wallpapers and a light, sunny quality in keeping with the yellow exterior. The two third-floor rooms we once occupied with our sons have been converted into one extra-large room. A suite offers a separate sitting room.

Wicker rockers on the side porch invite dalliance with a pre-dinner drink from the small bar off the parlor. The parlor, done up in rose and celadon with an oriental rug over the bleached wood floor, has a nifty window seat made from mattress ticking and small built-in benches beside the fireplace.

A full breakfast, perhaps with shirred eggs or dutch babies, is served in the country-pretty dining room or on the enclosed sun porch sparkling with white summer furniture.

(207) 236-8053 or (800) 238-8053. Two-night minimum stay, including two breakfasts and one dinner: doubles, $260 to $320. Suite, $360. Single-night stay with dinner, space permitting, $165 to $195, suite $215. Closed December-April. No children. Smoking restricted.

Dining Spots

The Belmont, 6 Belmont Ave., Camden.

The first fine restaurant in the Camden area (indeed, a pioneer in nouvelle cuisine on the Maine coast), Aubergine gave way to The Belmont and chef-owner Gerry Clare, who had a restaurant in Fort Lauderdale and a guest house in Nantucket. He changed the emphasis from French to modern American cuisine (lately with oriental accents).

The serene dining room is lovely with its white linens and aubergine carpet. The

Fine dining is an attraction for guests and public at The Belmont.

adjacent sunporch has pristine white tables and chairs, accented by new curtains. Floral china and flowers from the cutting garden provide color.

The menu changes every few days. Some of the fare is inspired, as in an appetizer of grilled oysters in pancetta with two sauces and a white gazpacho with delicious homemade croutons. Peeky toe crab summer roll with Asian dipping sauce, hazelnut dredged sweetbreads with roasted portobello and grilled seafood sausage are typical of other starters.

The seven entrées, one of them always vegetarian, might range from calves liver with pancetta and onions to an exotic lobster pad thai. We enjoyed grilled chicken with toasted polenta and a tri-pepper compote – accompanied by julienned carrots, creamed spinach and new potatoes – and a special of poached salmon with a citrus sauce.

The wine list is distinguished and priced accordingly, though there are plenty of affordable choices.

Among desserts, always a strong point here, the sour-cream blueberry cheese-cake is sensational. Other tempters are chocolate mascarpone dacquoise, warm plum tart, raspberry gratin and the trio of sorbets, perhaps piña colada, passion fruit and watermelon. "It could be anything," says Gerry; "when we run out of one kind, we make another."

(207) 236-8053 or (800) 238-8053. Entrées, $15 to $26. Dinner nightly except Monday, 6 to 9:30. Closed December-April.

The Youngtown Inn & Restaurant, Route 52 and Youngtown Road, Lincolnville 04849.

The dining rooms here are exceptionally pretty, the setting is rural and the food is French-inspired. It's run by Manuel Mercier, a chef who trained in Cannes, and his wife Mary Ann, a former Wall Street bond trader whom he met on a cruise ship. They live on the premises in the French style with their young family.

Manuel's cooking is "strictly traditional French, using American products." The short menu lists ten entrées, of which the salmon fillet with potato crust and the rack of lamb with fresh thyme are house favorites. Contemporary accents show up in the grilled Atlantic swordfish with pineapple salsa and the chicken breast stuffed with sundried tomato and goat cheese. Starters include a stellar lobster ravioli with fennel sauce, duck sausage with white beans, and rabbit and veal pâté with currant chutney. Dessert brings a sensational crème brûlée, classic soufflés, cappuccino mousse cake and homemade sorbets in a meringue shell.

Four upstairs guest rooms and a family suite with private baths are appointed simply but attractively in country French style. Doubles, with full breakfast, are $80 to $99.

(207) 763-4290. Entrées, $15 to $23. Dinner nightly, 5:30 to 9. Closed Monday in off-season.

Frogwater Cafe, 31 Elm St., Camden.
Innovative, healthful cuisine at modest prices is offered by Erin and Joseph Zdanowicz, young New England Culinary Institute graduates who moved across the country from Tacoma, Wash., to open this homey little storefront cafe in 1995 in the former Galloway's, a family diner. They named it for Frogwater Lane on their favorite Bainbridge Island and stress Oregon and Washington wines on a select wine list.

Joseph's menu ranges widely, from a grilled pork foccacia sandwich or a vegetarian spaghetti cake with sweet bell pepper salsa to cioppino and beef medallions served with homemade pierogies and roasted shallot-mustard sauce. Start with some of the signature onion rings, sweet potato cakes or grilled flatbread. Finish with Erin's caramel shortcake with peaches and strawberries, peach bread pudding with butterscotch sauce, chocolate-hazelnut layer cake or a creamy summer breeze tart of lemon-lime splashed with gin.

We sampled this talented pair's fare at lunch (since discontinued, when they decided after two years to concentrate on dinner). Quite tasty were a hearty bacon-leek-potato soup, an open-faced grilled baguette with feta cheese, tomato, cucumber, black olives and sundried tomato pesto, and a "BLT and Then Some Club" sandwich adding onions, cucumber and cheddar cheese on Texas toast. Sides of nippy macaroni and vegetable salads came with each, and the meal indicated the style that this couple added to the Camden dining scene. The locals return the favor by packing the place at night.

(207) 236-8998. Entrées, $9 to $16. Dinner, Tuesday-Sunday 5 to 9.

The Waterfront Restaurant, Harborside Square off Bay View Street, Camden.
Rebuilt following a damaging 1995 fire, this popular restaurant is notable for its large outdoor deck shaded by a striking white canopy resembling a boat's sails, right beside the windjammers on picturesque Camden Harbor, and for its affordable, international menu. Some say the location surpasses the food, though we've been satisfied each time we've eaten here.

It's a great spot for lunch, when seven delectable salads in glass bowls are dressed with outstanding dressings, among them sweet-and-sour bacon, lemon-parmesan, dijon vinaigrette and blue cheese.

The dinner offerings turn more eclectic, although the luncheon salads are still available. Among appetizers are calamari and shrimp, mussels marinière, clam fritters and soups, perhaps chilled raspberry accented with grand marnier. The superlative smoked seafood sampler was our choice for sharing. We've enjoyed the Maine crab cakes with creamy mustard sauce, an assertive linguini with salmon and sundried tomatoes, shrimp with oriental black beans over angel-hair pasta and a special of swordfish grilled over applewood with rosemary, which was juicy and succulent. Grilled chicken with quinoa polenta and sirloin steak are the only meat offerings. Mint chocolate-chip pie with hot fudge sauce and whipped cream proved to be the ultimate dessert.

All sorts of shellfish and light fare from hamburgers to lobster rolls are available at the oyster bar and outdoor grill, open from 2:30 until closing.

(207) 236-3747. Entrées, $11.95 to $21.95. Lunch daily, 11:30 to 2:30. Dinner, 5 to 10.

Chez Michel, Route 1, Lincolnville Beach.

Michel and Joan Hetuin, he a former chef at the Helm restaurant in Rockport, run this country French restaurant that's many people's casual favorite.

The main floor is crowded with formica tables and pink-painted wood chairs with green upholstered seats. The seats of choice are upstairs in a cheery dining room that offers a head-on view of the water, or at the four tables on a screened balcony off the side.

For a quick lunch, we enjoyed an avocado-tomato-cheddar melt and a fried clam roll, plus Joan's fantastic raspberry pie with a cream-cheese base and an extra-good shortbread crust, so good that regulars call to reserve a slice before it runs out. A subsequent dinner began with great french bread, two slabs of rabbit pâté with cornichons on lettuce, and house salads dressed with creamy Italian and pepper-parmesan. A special of salmon béarnaise arrived on a bed of spinach. The only disappointment was the bouillabaisse, with haddock substituting for most of the usual shellfish. Other dinner dishes include vegetarian couscous, scallops provençal, mussels marinière, grilled chicken béarnaise, beef bourguignonne, lamb kabob and steak au poivre. We know folks who think there's no better place for lobster or even a crab roll with homemade potato chips and a bowl of Maine chowder.

Save room for the superlative desserts, including strawberry torte, caramel custard, chocolate mousse and especially that raspberry pie. The short, mainly French wine list is priced in the teens.

(207) 789-5600. Entrées, $10.95 to $14.95. Lunch and dinner daily except Monday, 11:30 to 9. Closed December-March.

Cappy's Chowder House, 1 Main St., Camden.

"The Maine you hope to meet" is one of the catchy slogans surrounding Cappy's, and local color is said to be its strong point. The scene is barroom nautical: lobster traps hang above the bar, and green billiards-room lamps light the bare wood tables. The upstairs Crow's Nest offers a view of the harbor. The something-for-everyone menu is Down East cutesy: Maine pigskins, burgers on the bounty, Camden curly fries, mussel beach pasta and desserted islands.

The place packs in the crowds for clam chowder, a lobster salad croissant, crab cakes topped with salsa on a bed of spinach, seafood stir-fry, chicken cappenesca "and all the latest gossip." Main courses come with French bread from Cappy's Bakery & Coffee House below, rice pilaf and salad with a good house dressing. Burgers, sandwiches, salads and lighter fare are available day and night.

Locals gather here for breakfast. The placemat is the menu, offering things like "pure eggstasy" and blueberry pancakes. For a snack, try a spinach and feta croissant or a Miss Plum's cookie sandwich from the bakery.

(207) 236-2254. Entrées, $9.95 to $15.95. Open daily, 7:30 a.m. to midnight. Winter hours vary.

Mama & Leenie's, 27 Elm St., Camden.

Stop at this little cafe and bakery for a cup of that good Green Mountain coffee and a breakfast of blintzes, french toast or the ever-so-good eggs in a frame – grilled in thick toast.

At lunch you could order Mama's special beef stew, or a baconburger with blue cheese. Melted cheese and tomato on a bagel might hit the spot, or how about a pasta salad primavera?

Mama does a lot of the cooking. Daughter Leenie, an artist, is a master baker as evidenced by the apricot strudel with coconut and walnuts, the double chocolate fudge brownies with orange zest, and the pure butter shortbread. The fresh berry pies with real whipped cream are masterpieces. The decor is simple, with ladderback chairs and wild flowers in little jars. Leenie has painted flowers and ivy leaves all over the place, and "Vaya con Dios" is painted above the door. There's a pleasant outdoor patio on one side.

Bring your own wine for dinner, when you might find Indonesian marinated chicken on a skewer or a bowl of chili with homemade bread.

(207) 236-6300. Entrées, $5 to $8. Open daily, 7 a.m. to 11 p.m., Sunday to 8; fewer hours in off-season. BYOB.

Sea Dog Brewing Co., 43 Mechanic St., Camden.

The Maine beers and ales are all the rage at this no-expense-spared microbrewery cum restaurant run by the Camplin family in one of the former Knox Mill buildings. Most visitors gravitate to the fancy tavern – a mix of booths, beams, oriental runners and stone walls that's too atmospheric for words. The splashy waterfall outside the soaring windows adds to the effect. The large outside patio beside the Megunticook River is the icing on the mix.

The brewery's Penobscot Maine lager, Windjammer Maine ale, Owl's Head light and Old Gollywobbler Brown Ale are featured, along with a variety of snacks and sandwiches. The food is surprisingly good, considering – anything from peel and eat shrimp to seafood-stuffed mushrooms, beef or chicken fajitas to a lobster club sandwich. Sample the haddock chowder, caesar salad and a burger and you've made yourself a meal.

(207) 236-6863. Entrées, $6 to $15. Open daily, 11 a.m. to 1 a.m.

Diversions

Water pursuits. Any number of boat cruises on Penobscot Bay leave from the Camden landing, where there are benches for viewing the passing boat parade. The famed windjammers are a class apart, but lately the Appledore has been giving morning and afternoon cruises, there's a Sunday buffet lunch sail on the Timberwind and the Wendameen offers an overnight with dinner and breakfast. For more cruises or ferry rides to the islands, go to Rockland or Lincolnville Beach (a favorite excursion is the ferry trip to Islesboro). The Lincolnville Beach is popular for swimming. A more secluded, picturesque setting is the little-known Laite Memorial

Beach with treed lawns sloping down to the water, a small beach, picnic tables and old-fashioned fireplaces off Bay View Street.

Camden Windjammers. Long known as the windjammer capital of the world, Camden Harbor is quite a sight when the windjammers are in. On Sunday evenings from June through September, people sit at the wharf to watch as passengers board the old-time sailing vessels for their week's cruise through Penobscot Bay. After breakfast on Monday, the sixteen or more windjammers set sail for who knows where; their routes depend on whim, wind and tides. Mates sleep and eat on board, helping the crew if they like but most relaxing and savoring a sail from yesteryear. Many beds are bunks, but at least one of the newer windjammers has double beds, and some have running water for showers. Generally, the captain handles the sea-going chores while his wife does the cooking – everything from chowders to roasts – on a wood stove. The evening lobster bake on a deserted island is usually the week's highlight. On Saturday afternoon, the watching resumes in earnest as the windjammers return to Camden. Passengers can count on paying $400 to $800 each for the experience. Landlubbers can watch the comings and goings free.

Inland pursuits. Some of the East Coast's most scenic hiking is available on trails in Camden Hills State Park. Mount Megunticook is the highest of the three mountains that make up the park and the second highest point on the Eastern Seaboard. If you're not up to hiking, be sure to drive the toll road up Mount Battie, an easy one-mile ride. The view is worth the $1-per-person toll. More rugged hiking is available on the trails of Camden Snow Bowl overlooking Hosmer Pond. A scenic drive is out Route 52 to Megunticook Lake, an island-studded lake that emerged eerily from the clouds the first foggy afternoon we saw it. A walking tour of Camden and a bicycle or car tour of Camden and adjacent Rockport are available through the Camden-Rockport Historical Society.

Cultural pursuits. Summer entertainment, from band concerts to vaudeville, is provided periodically in the outdoor Bok Amphitheater next to the town library, just a few hundred feet from the harbor. The **Camden Civic Theatre** produces plays at the restored brick Camden Opera House. Classical and chamber music concerts are offered year-round at the Rockport Opera House by **Bay Chamber Concerts.** The **Conway Homestead and Cramer Museum,** a mile south of town along Route 1, includes a restored 18th-century farmhouse, a barn displaying antique carriages and sleighs, a blacksmith shop and an 1820 maple sugar house. The **Camden-Rockport Historical Society** complex is open Tuesday-Friday 10 to 4 in July and August. The **Farnsworth Museum** in nearby Rockland ranks among the finer regional art museums in the nation. The collection focuses on American art from the 18th century to the present, with prized paintings by the Wyeth family, who have selected it as the permanent repository for their works. Included in the $5 museum admission is the adjacent **Farnsworth Homestead,** considered one of the most beautiful Victorian houses in the country.

Vesper Hill Chapel, Calderwood Lane, Rockport. (207) 236-4594. Built of pine and resembling a Swiss chalet, this non-denominational outdoor chapel atop a rock ledge affords a great view of Penobscot Bay. It's the legacy of Helene Bok, who fulfilled a dream of building a chapel that would open out onto the world on the site of a summer estate-turned-hotel that was destroyed by fire in 1954. Mrs. Bok, friends and children created a garden showplace and a chapel sanctuary for the ages. Up to 50 people can be seated for informal meditation on Sunday mornings.

Not wishing to intrude on the Quaker Meeting we came upon, we bided our time in the wonderful formal perennial and Biblical herb gardens below. More than 60 wedding ceremonies take place here annually, but the casual visitor can stop by to enjoy peace, quiet and beauty any other time from mid-April through October.

Shopping pursuits. Camden is a mecca for sophisticated shopping, and all kinds of interesting specialty stores and boutiques pop up every year, particularly along Bay View Street. A major presence on Main Street is **Planet,** a world marketplace that started small in 1993 and expanded into an old department store across the street. It quickly became a department store in itself with a trendy selection of gifts, hip clothing, housewares, accessories, medicinal herbals, toys, children's things and much more, many with a nature or planetary theme. **The Smiling Cow,** a large and venerable gift shop with a myriad of Maine items, has a great view from its rear porch over the Megunticook River, which ripples down the rocks toward the harbor; you can take in the picturesque scene while sipping complimentary coffee or tea between shopping forays. Along Bay View Street, **The Owl and the Turtle** is an excellent, many-roomed bookstore on two floors. **Wild Birds Unlimited** has an amazing collection of bird feeders, carved birds, birdsong tapes and the like. In relocated quarters, **Lily, Lupine & Fern** pairs a thriving floral business with the sale of cheeses, gourmet foods and a huge selection of wines and microbrewery beers. In 1997 it added a wine bar and espresso cafe upstairs. A large carved gull wearing a windjammer tie drew us into the **Ducktrap Bay Trading Co.,** a gallery of wildlife from decoys to paintings. **The Admiral's Buttons** has preppy clothing and sailing attire. We bought a handcrafted Maine wooden bucket for use as a planter from **Once a Tree,** which also has great clocks, toys, bracelets and everything else made from wood. **Unique One** stocks a great selection of sweaters done by local knitters. **The Oracle** offers interesting gifts from around the world. Traditional favorites are the **House of Logan** and **Margo Moore,** for distinctive clothing and gifts.

Extra-Special

Kelmscott Farm, Vancycle Road off Route 252, Lincolnville.

Eighteen rare livestock breeds are raised on this unique working farm dedicated to the preservation of endangered species. Cotswold and Shetland sheep, Gloucestershire Old Spots pigs, Kerry cattle, Toulouse geese, Aylesbury ducks, Ancona chickens and Nigerian dwarf goats are housed in barns, arks and even a piggery. Most of the animals that visitors see there or in pastures lost their commercial value years ago because they are not as productive as modern farm animals. Executive director Robyn Shotwell Metcalfe, whose family moved from California to launch the farm in 1996, says they are trying both to preserve rare breeds and to re-establish their commercial value by making products from sheep's wool and, through conservation efforts, helping farmers solve genetic problems with their animals. The old Wool Shed in the center courtyard is the farm's compass rose, a visitor center with museum exhibits and a farm shop. Special events every weekend draw those in the know for wool festivals, border collie trials, cooking demonstrations and even a pig's birthday celebration.

(207) 763-4088. Open Memorial Day to Labor Day, Thursday-Sunday 11 to 4. Adults, $5. Family, $8.

Rowantree Pottery inspired others and put Blue Hill on the map.

Blue Hill/Deer Isle, Me.

Treasure of Tranquility

Between the chic of Camden and the bustle of Bar Harbor lies a largely unspoiled peninsula jutting into East Penobscot Bay. The area stretches across Eggemoggin Reach onto Deer Isle and Stonington. Its focal point is the tranquil treasure known as Blue Hill.

So small that the unknowing tourist almost could miss it, the village lies between the 940-foot-high hill from which it takes its name and an inlet of Blue Hill Bay. A few roads and streets converge from different directions and, suddenly, here it is: Blue Hill, Maine, population 1,941.

This is the center of an area long known for fine handicrafts, especially pottery. Indeed, Rowantrees Pottery owner Sheila Varnum says it is the pottery that "put Blue Hill on the map." Founded more than 50 years ago, Rowantrees has inspired a number of smaller ventures by craftspeople who cherish the simplicity of the area. Another draw in summer is the Kneisel Hall Chamber Music Festival. Blue Hill also supports a volunteer radio station, WERU (We Are You), with a down-home cultural programming mix.

Not for water nor resort pursuits do most visitors come to Blue Hill or Deer Isle. It's the kind of place where the sign at the outdoor phone booth warned, "This phone doesn't work the way you're used to. Dial your number, wait for the loud tone and after your party answers, deposit twenty cents." We managed to get through the second time around.

Blue Hill has no town beaches or marinas, no shopping emporiums to speak of, and only one motel. What there are, instead, are world-famous potteries and crafts cooperatives, a handful of exceptional inns and restaurants, rural byways that remain much the way they were a generation ago and invite aimless exploration, and a sense of serenity that draws the knowing few back time after time for the utter peace and quiet of it all.

Go, but don't tell too many others about your find.

Inn Spots

Blue Hill Inn, Union Street, Box 403, Blue Hill 04614.

Its flag flying out front, this trim white Colonial inn with Wedgwood blue shutters – a landmark in the heart of Blue Hill for nearly 150 years – has been considerably spiffed up by Mary and Don Hartley.

The energetic Hartleys have enhanced the thirteen guest accommodations with plush carpeting, new wallpaper and modernized bathrooms. All come with private baths and three with fireplaces. Some have sitting areas converted from small bedrooms. Our rear bedroom – occupied the previous night by Peter of Peter, Paul and Mary fame following a concert for Paul's hometown fans at the Blue Hill Fair Grounds – was comfortable with a kingsize bed, two blue velvet wing chairs, colorful bed linens, plump towels and windows on three sides to circulate cool air, which was welcome after a heat wave. The other rooms we saw also were nicely furnished with 19th-century antiques and traditional pieces reflecting what Mary calls "a homey Down East style." Homemade chocolates come with nightly turndown service.

In 1997, the Hartleys added a luxurious efficiency suite next door in the inn-keeper quarters. Now the Cape House, the cathedral-ceilinged space offers a kingsize canopy bed plus an antique bed in a box, a fireplace, living room with telephone and TV, kitchen and a rear deck for enjoying the back yard.

Back in the main inn, a small library-game room, where old Life magazines are prominent, is furnished in antiques. The larger main parlor with a fireplace and a ten-candle Persian chandelier is where the Hartleys serve hors d'oeuvres (perhaps smoked bluefish or local goat cheese) during a nightly innkeepers' reception for guests and outside diners.

The prix-fixe meal is served by candlelight at 7 p.m. at white-clothed tables in a sunporch and dining room where classical music plays in the background.

Chef André Strong, an American whose mother came from France, changes the handwritten menu nightly. Braised shiitake mushrooms with saffron risotto was the appetizer at our latest dinner, which was artistically presented and exceptionally

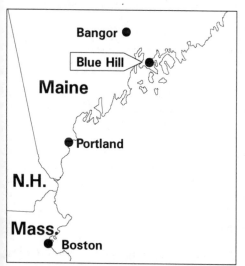

tasty throughout. A blueberry-campari ice cleansed the palate for the main course, a choice of ethe-real paupiettes of trout with salmon mousseline and mint or tender noisettes of lamb with cob-smoked bacon, garlic and chèvre. A mesclun salad preceded the dessert, a remarkable frozen nougat with spiced orange rum.

Breakfast is a culinary event as well. Ours started with the usual juices, a plate of cut-up fresh fruit and a wedge of apple-custard pie that one of us thought was dessert. The main course involved a choice of eggs scrambled with garden chives in puff pastry, an omelet with chèvre or brie and Canadian bacon, waffles with strawberry topping or blueberry pancakes. Excellent french-roast coffee accompanied.

Outside, guests enjoy the Hartleys' perennial garden with lawn furniture, a gazebo and a profusion of huge yellow lilies. The innkeepers occasionally charter a schooner to take guests out on East Penobscot Bay for day trips. They also sponsor seasonal concert weekends, schooner day trips on Penobscot Bay and themed wine-tasting dinners in the off-season.

(207) 374-2844 or (800) 826-7415. Fax (207) 374-2829. Eleven rooms and two suites with private baths. Mid-June through early October: doubles $120 to $150; suites $220. Off-season: doubles $110 to $140, suites $160. Add $40 for MAP. Two-night minimum weekends. Children over 10. No smoking. Closed December to mid-May.

Prix-fixe, $30. Dinner by reservation, nightly at 7, June-October; weekends in off-season.

John Peters House, Peters Point, Box 916, Blue Hill 04614.

Looking somewhat like a Southern plantation, this white pillared and red brick structure commands an idyllic hilltop location on 25 acres just outside Blue Hill, with water on two sides. Built in 1815, it's listed on the National Register of Historic Places.

Personable owners Barbara and Rick Seeger offer eight comfortable bedrooms with private baths in the main house. Five have fireplaces. Rick recently added a rooftop deck for the Brooklin Suite, which has a queen bed in one room and twin beds in the other. Everybody's favorite remains the expansive Blue Hill Room, which has a kingsize bed, lovely carpets, a wet bar with refrigerator and a large private deck where we lazed away the early evening while gazing up at Blue Hill. The deck is so pleasant that many guests bring dinner in and eat right there.

Six newer rooms are located in a rear carriage house. There you can stay in one of two first-floor rooms with a queensize brass bed and a loveseat looking onto a private deck. Four larger rooms on the first and second floors are almost studio apartments, each with queen bed, fireplace, kitchenette and private deck.

Now with fourteen guest quarters, the Seegers were eyeing the rear barn at our latest visit – possibly as the site for an antiques co-op. "No more rooms," stressed Barbara.

Nice touches include fresh fruit and flowers in the bedrooms, the morning newspaper, a living room with a grand piano (many musicians stay here) and cozy sofas and chairs for reading or socializing, an old-fashioned swimming pool, a canoe and a couple of sailboats.

The Seegers put out quite a spread for breakfast, served on the enclosed side porch amid fine china, silver and classical music. Our three-course repast began with cantaloupe with ice cream or fresh berries with champagne (extra champagne is poured in glasses for those who wish it – one couple finished off a bottle and retired to their room for an early nap, Barbara reported). Then came fresh orange juice with sliced and grilled blueberry and corn muffins. The main event was a lavish choice including eggs benedict, blueberry or banana waffles, cheese and eggs or, the pièce de résistance, a lobster and artichoke omelet – so colorful that it cried out to be photographed. Garnished with lobster claws, it was accompanied by bacon or ham and hash browns and was so good that one of us ordered it two mornings in a row.

(207) 374-2116. Thirteen rooms and one suite with private baths. Doubles, $105 to $165. Suite, $130 for two, $175 for four.

John Peters House has the look of a Southern plantation.

Blue Hill Farm, Route 15, Box 437, Blue Hill 04614.

Located out in the country north of Blue Hill, this B&B really has a farm feeling – from the rambling farmhouse and the barn exterior of a newer addition to the goats grazing outside to the garden, stone wall, trout pond and 48 acres of woods and brooks out back.

The barn, full of fanciful touches and furnishings, includes a spacious and lofty main floor where meals are served and where there are all kinds of sitting areas – perfect for the occasional summer jazz concerts to which the inn plays host. Upstairs are seven modern, smallish guest rooms with private baths and double beds. Seven more guest rooms with double or twin beds and shared baths are in the original farmhouse to which the barn is attached. It offers a cozy, old-fashioned parlor for those who prefer more seclusion.

From an ample kitchen, innkeepers Marcia and Jim Schatz serve what they call a Maine continental breakfast: fresh orange juice, a plate of fruit and cheese, homemade granola, cereals and, every third or fourth day, a treat of lox and bagels.

The table settings are charming: woven cloths and napkins, white china and dried flowers in baskets. Dinners are served by advance request. A typical meal might be poussin with Sicilian barbecue sauce or peasant bouillabaisse plus salad and a dessert of homemade ice cream for $25, BYOB.

Jim, who serves as a town selectman, ran for the state legislature in 1996. "I came in second," he recalls, "and did pretty well for a Democrat around here."

Blue Hill Farm gives off good vibes. It's the kind of simple, homey place that many inn-goers look for.

(207) 374-5126. Seven rooms with private baths and seven rooms with shared baths. Doubles, $75 to $90, June-October; $60 to $70 rest of year. Children over 12. No smoking.

Eggemoggin Reach Bed & Breakfast, The Herrick Road, RR 1, Box 33A, Brooksville 04617.

At the end of a long driveway lies this prize of a waterside B&B. It's the transformation of a summer/retirement home for an energetic couple who decided they weren't ready for retirement.

Susie and Mike Canon built their summer home along a particularly picturesque section of Eggemoggin Reach, looking out past the Pumpkin Island lighthouse toward Penobscot Bay, with a view of the Camden Hills beyond. They liked it so much that he sold his business in Jacksonville, Fla., they had the house winterized and moved here in 1989 "without a plan." Mike started a brokerage business in the garage and, in 1993, Susie opened their home as a B&B.

The house lends itself perfectly for the purpose. The open main floor of post and beam construction has pine paneling and high ceilings. A large brick fireplace warms the living room, and a wood stove enhances the den. Comfortable period furnishings and oriental rugs make the place more than a summer home. Across the rear of the house is a full-length porch, partly screened and partly open. As Susie served iced tea, we watched the resident osprey and cormorants and looked for the seals that cavort daily in Deadman's Cove.

The Wheelhouse Suite spreads across the entire third floor with bath, king bedroom and a large living room with a sofabed, chairs, a desk and two twin beds tucked beneath the eaves.

Our idea of a night in paradise is a stay in one of the rustic-looking but ever-so-plush duplex cottage units facing Deadman's Cove. Paneled in pickled pine, it has a cathedral ceiling, king bed, an efficiency kitchen and a sitting area with sofabed and franklin stove. The screened porch overlooking the water was perfect for enjoying a takeout lobster dinner by candlelight (the Canons sometimes put on lobster bakes by the shore for groups of eight guests or more).

In 1997, they built the nearby Bay Lodge, a Maine-style farmhouse with six efficiency suites on three levels. Patterned after the cottage units but larger, each offers a king bed, sitting area with queen sofabed, kitchenette and a substantial screened porch or deck facing Deadman's Cove head-on. The views from the porches here are fabulous. Stylish draperies, arty touches, shell mirrors and cedar showers are the rule in accommodations like the huge, lower-level Vinalhaven in which we spent a night and would gladly stay the summer.

The Canons also rent out a neighbor's carriage house as Tuckaway, with a huge great room, rear bedroom, Stickley mission-style furnishings, fully equipped kitchen and water-view decks up and down.

Guests gather for breakfast on the large porch or in the open dining area of the main house. Susie, whose background is in catering, provides quite a spread: juice, fruit, cereal, and a broccoli-cheese casserole with sausage and almond-poppyseed bread at one visit, a zesty frittata and coffeecake another. Eggs benedict, Mexican eggs, chiles rellenos, and Yankee hash and egg casserole are other favorites.

(207) 359-5073. Fax (207) 359-5074. Seven suites, two cottages and one apartment with private baths. Suites, $160. Cottages, $150. Tuckaway, $175. Two-night minimum weekends. Children over 12. Closed mid-October to mid-May.

Pilgrim's Inn, Deer Isle 04627.

A welcoming, tasteful Colonial inn run with flair by Dud and Jean Hendrick beckons visitors south from Blue Hill to Deer Isle. The striking, dark red 1793 house is on a spit of land with a harbor in front and a mill pond in back.

Listed on the National Register of Historic Places, the inn exudes an aura of history. The main-floor library contains an exceptional collection of books, while another parlor is a showroom for local artists.

Jean has added appropriate art in the inn's thirteen guest rooms, each with a

Rocking chairs take in water view from front porch of Eggemoggin Reach B&B.

wood stove and ten with private baths. Most in demand are the larger rooms at the back. Two bedrooms on the newly renovated third floor have private baths featuring vanities topped with Deer Isle granite. The rooms have been decorated in sprightly Laura Ashley style, mixing and matching artworks and plants. Oriental rugs and quilts lend elegance to the prevailing simplicity. Duvets and down pillows are typical of the Hendricks' caring touches.

In 1997, they bought the adjacent property to double the size of their grounds and converted its vintage house called Ginny's into two efficiency suites. Each has a living room with sofabed and cable TV, cast-iron gas stove, queen bedroom with full bath, an efficiency kitchen and dining area, plus a large deck overlooking the water.

Dud Hendrick, a former Dartmouth College lacrosse coach, tends an extensive herb and vegetable garden on the grounds behind the inn during the day. At night he tends bar in the paneled tap room, serving drinks to guests (he even made a fresh raspberry daiquiri for one when we were there) who gather at 6 o'clock in the comfortable downstairs common room with its eight-foot-wide fireplace and beehive oven for abundant and delicious hors d'oeuvres.

The inn's longtime chef, Terry Foster, prepares a prix-fixe, single-entrée dinner at 7 in the charming dining room (in a former goat barn). Decorated simply with farm utensils and quilts on the walls, mismatched chairs, and fresh flowers and dark green overcloths on the tables, it has ten outside doors that open to let in the breeze.

We'll never forget a Sunday night dinner: salad with goat cheese, homemade peasant bread, a heavenly paella topped with nasturtiums (such a pretty dish it should have been photographed for Gourmet magazine) and sensational raspberry chocolate pie on a shortbread crust. Depending on the night, you might be served rainbow trout stuffed with lobster and crab or rack of lamb. A large outdoor barbecue, which occupies a prominent spot on a rear deck, is used for grilling. A mixed grill marrying tenderloin of pork, marinated scallops and free-range chicken is a weekly special. Arugula and radicchio from the garden turn up in the dinner salads, and a dynamite six-herb risotto is a frequent accompaniment. Many are the repeat guests who return for a succession of interesting meals. Their wishes were answered in 1997 when Terry revealed 130 original recipes in the long-awaited Pilgrim's Inn Cookbook ($14.95).

Homemade granola, ginger scones, fresh melon and omelets are featured at breakfast.

The Hendricks recently transformed a rear shed into The Rugosa Rose, a stylish craft and gift shop.

(207) 348-6615. Fax (207) 348-7769. Dinner by reservation, nightly at 7. Ten rooms and two efficiency suites with private baths; three rooms with shared bath. Doubles, $150 to $175, MAP. Suites, $205. Two-night minimum requested. Children over 10. No smoking. Closed mid-October to mid-May.

Prix-fixe, $29.50. Dinner by reservation, nightly at 7.

Inn on the Harbor, Main Street, Box 69, Stonington 04681.

Four 19th-century buildings joined by a flower-covered common deck over-looking the harbor have been transformed into comfortable guest quarters on their way to becoming a full-service inn.

Christina Shipps, an international jeweler based in New York, bought the old Captain's Quarters Inn & Motel in 1995 and spent two winters renovating and refurbishing. "This place had so much potential it was just screaming for this," she said as she showed the results.

The original seventeen rooms and efficiency apartments in the complex became thirteen. The result is larger rooms with sitting areas, many queen or kingsize beds, updated bathrooms and new overstuffed furnishings good for "putting up your feet and vegetating" as you study the harbor scene through binoculars thought-fully provided in every ocean-view room. That is, if you can tear yourself away from the lounge chairs on the enormous flower-bedecked deck open to all guests.

All different, rooms vary from small and cozy to suites that are rather substantial. They're named for schooners that sail into Stonington harbor and all but three yield harbor views. Those on the village side compensate with extra space. In those facing the water, you're lulled to sleep by the sounds of gulls and foghorns. We especially liked the second-floor Heritage room with kingsize bed, a fireplace of Deer Isle granite and a chaise and plump club chair for taking in the scene. The other view room with granite fireplace is the main-floor Victory Chimes, also with king bed and two loveseats placed together as a sectional facing the deck garden and harbor. A former barber shop became the adjacent Stephen Tabor cottage with high cream-colored tin ceiling and walls, queen bed, full bath, a sectional and a private deck. A two-bedroom seaview suite with sitting room is available in the Shipps House, the owner's residence out West Main Street.

Christina, who's here in summer, and innkeeper Janet Blanchette put out a breakfast buffet in the reception room, which operates as an espresso bar open to the public from 11 to 4:30. Fresh fruit, homemade granola, yogurt, cereals and muffins are augmented by one main dish, perhaps strata or frittata.

In the off-season, Christina planned dinner weekends in preparation to becoming a full-service inn, eventually open year-round.

(207) 367-2420 or (800) 942-2420. Fax (207) 367-5165. Ten rooms, three suites and one cottage with private baths. Doubles, $100 to $120. Suites and cottage, $100 to $125. Children over 12. Closed January to early April.

Waterside decks for picnicking and lounging are featured at The Inn on the Harbor.

Island House, Weedfield Road, RD 1, Box 3227, Stonington 04681.

Stylish accommodations arrived in old-fashioned Stonington in a big way with the opening of this contemporary showplace commanding a private hilltop over-looking the ocean in the distance.

The interior of the large redwood house is light and summery, with walls painted in sunny pastels, modern furnishings, lots of wicker and splashy rugs. Computer whiz John Metcalf built the house in 1988 to hold his treasures from across the world. When his business took him in 1995 to Colorado, he called upon old friend Rebecca Cennamo, a Nantucket innkeeper, to run his house as a B&B. Her instructions were to go first-class.

"This is an innkeeper's dream," she said as she led a tour. Full-length windows in the great room look out across a deck to end all decks, a full-length affair running across the back of the house, and looking across the treetops onto the island-studded harbor. A modern white seating area faces a fieldstone fireplace. A linen-covered dining table adjoins the open kitchen. There's a small TV room as well.

Upstairs are five breezy guest rooms, all with private baths, queen beds and ocean views. Poland Spring water and bedside chocolates are in each. We like the Merchants Room, with a cut-lace comforter atop the poster bed, a wicker-furnished sitting area, organdy curtains fluttering in the breeze, a private balcony and a large bath with bidet and soaking tub and a floor tiled in aqua. Others prefer the third-floor Lookout, an enclosed widow's walk with a bed surrounded by windows on all sides. A nearby cabin is billed as a private guest house with two bedrooms, a kitchen and a sitting room with wood stove.

Rebecca serves guests an ample breakfast, including juices, fresh fruit, granola, cereal and an egg dish, quiche or berry pancakes. She likens the evening refreshments to a Viennese coffee shop with coffee, tea and perhaps sacher torte. A spa and laundry facilities are available for guests.

A bullfrog croaking in the lilypond might punctuate your reveries as you loll in the rope hammock on the front lawn.

(207) 367-5900. Fax (207) 367-2270. Doubles, $100 to $150. Closed mid-October to Memorial Day.

Goose Cove Lodge, Goose Cove Road, Box 40, Sunset 04683.

"Simple, rustic and comfortable lodging," distinguished meals and a distinct sense of place are offered at this oldtimer, lately upgraded by innkeepers Joanne and Dom Parisi.

Their 1.5-mile-long dirt access road leads to the End of Beyond – the loveliest sight in the world, according to the lodge brochure. The 70-acre preserve marked by trails, wide sandy beaches and tree-lined shores is a paradise for nature lovers. At low tide, you can walk across a sand bar to Barred Island, a nature conservancy full of birds and wildlife. At night, Dom, an astronomy buff, lets guests peer through his telescope.

Geared to families, accommodations are MAP and booked by the week in summer, B&B in the off-season. Most in demand are nine secluded cottages and four attached cottages, each sleeping four to six and each with ocean view, sundeck, kitchenette or refrigerator and fireplace. Two new cottages, each with a beamed living room with a queen bed in an alcove, two bedrooms with twin beds and country French doors onto front decks, were added in 1997.

Ten less expensive bedrooms and suites, most with woodland views, are available in two annexes off the main lodge. The deluxe new two-bedroom Lookout Suite on the lodge's second floor provides an expansive ocean view.

The lodge is the epitome of a Maine lodge: an enormous stone fireplace and a mishmash of lodge chairs, benches, sofas and bookcases. The shiny pine tables in the paneled, wraparound dining room – with windows onto a new deck and the water below – are graced with stoneware by local potter William Mor and bud vases holding field flowers. Guests gather for BYOB drinks and hors d'oeuvres in the lodge before dinner at 6:30. Counselors entertain children, who have their own dinner beforehand.

The innovative, prix-fixe menu changes with every meal, and a special vegetarian appetizer and entrée are offered nightly. A typical dinner might start with black bean soup with cornbread croutons and cilantro-lime cream. The main course could be grilled butterflied leg of lamb with roasted shallot juice, garlic mashed potatoes and butternut squash puree, followed by a salad of mixed field greens wrapped with prosciutto in a sunflower seed vinaigrette. Cardamom crème brûlée with a tuile might be the finale.

Breakfast ($9 for the public) is quite a feast, too. One Sunday's fare included fresh pineapple, bananas and nutmeg flamed in spiced rum, homemade granola with yogurt, an assortment of breads, buttermilk pancakes with spiced plum topping and a choice of eggs or omelets prepared any style, served with pan-seared red bliss potatoes and grilled ham.

(207) 348-2508 or (800) 728-1963. Fax (207) 348-2624. Six rooms, six suites and thirteen cottages with private baths. Accommodations MAP by the week (Saturday to Saturday) in summer. June 21 to Sept. 6: doubles, $170 to $260 MAP. Off-season: $90 to $170 B&B, two-night minimum. Closed mid-October to mid-May.

Prix-fixe, $30. Breakfast daily, 8 to 9:30. Lunch, 11:30 to 2. Dinner by reservation, nightly at 6:30 in summer, 7 in spring and fall.

The Inn at Ferry Landing, 108 Old Ferry Road, RR 1, Box 163, Deer Isle 04627.

An 1850s farmhouse at a point along Eggemoggin Reach where the ferry from Sargentville once landed has been converted into a charming waterside B&B.

Jean and Gerald Wheeler bought the property in 1996 when he left after 31 years as music director for Christ Church Cathedral in Montreal to take a similar position at St. Francis By the Sea Episcopal Church in Blue Hill. They have furnished the place with family antiques and Jean gets to exercise her passion for cooking, serving up exotic breakfasts at a mahogany table for six in the dining room. French toast with oatmeal bread and orange slices, omelets or pain au chocolat might be the fare, leavened with organic fruit and a healthful, vegetarian orientation.

The huge living room, white with mauve trim, is airy and open with large windows on three sides. It harbors lots of seating and – given its owner's music propensity – not one but two grand pianos covered with framed family photos

Four guest quarters, two up and two down, have water views. One at the rear of the main floor has twin beds, a clawfoot tub and french doors that make a private entrance from the yard. We're partial to the second-floor suite with a brass queensize bed, a huge tub and walk-in shower, a pullout sofa and chair, a wood stove and skylights in the pitched ceiling.

Families go for the apartment in the rear annex. It's rented by the week and offers a living room with a queen sofabed, a full kitchen, a sunroom, two upstairs bedrooms and a new waterfront deck.

(207) 348-7760. Fax (207) 348-5276. Three rooms, one suite and a two-bedroom apartment with private baths. Doubles, $95. Suite, $130. Annex, $1,000 per week, EP. Two-night minimum encouraged. Children under 10 in annex. No smoking.

Dining Spots

Firepond, Main Street, Blue Hill.

It's hard to imagine a more enchanting setting than the dining porch beside the stream at Firepond, on the lower level of a mill complex. The screened porch, which wraps around the small bar/waiting area and an interior dining room, is the place to be on a summer evening, with its garden-type glass tables lit by candles and topped by linens or woven mats, fresh flowers and Blue Hill pottery, the sounds of water rippling below and spotlights illuminating the gleaming rocks. It's almost magical, and usually must be booked well in advance.

The food is often magical as well, thanks to chef-owner Craig Rodenheiser, who recently expanded the kitchen and dining space. We like to start with the selection of terrines or pâtés – country pork, salmon mousse and vegetable at one visit – with croutons, cornichons, and interesting mustards and chutneys, or the smoked salmon ravioli with gruyère. Other recent choices included baked brie en croûte, escargots in puff pastry, smoked duck breast, wild mushroom sauté on a roasted garlic crostini, grilled polenta with chèvre and house-cured tuna pastrami served with smoked mussels and two sauces.

Entrées range from fish of the day to a sensational pork tenderloin with pancetta and chargrilled black angus sirloin steak. We've enjoyed sea scallops paired with leeks and mushrooms in a vermouth cream sauce, a fabulous fettuccine with crabmeat and pine nuts, a zesty halibut espagnole topped with mussels and saffron beurre blanc, and roast duckling with raspberry-chambord sauce.

Porch dining beside the brook is magical experience at Fire Pond.

Desserts are few but select, among them a superior lemon-raspberry cheese-cake, chocolate-truffle dacquoise, chocolate ravioli, fresh fruit terrine and pavlova.

Two dining rooms have been added on the main floor. One looks like a library, with shelves full of old books lining the walls and oriental carpets dotting the original wood floors. French doors look onto a flower-bedecked outdoor dining terrace facing Main Street. Craig also renovated the kitchen to handle the extra seats and the debut of patio service, an assortment of light fare from hummus and tziki with pita chips to assorted cheeses and a smoked seafood platter.

Celebrating Fire Pond's twentieth anniversary in 1997, Craig added a small rear deck for cocktails and cigars near his herb gardens. He also helped open Firebird, a grand Czarist Russian restaurant, in New York City.

(207) 374-9970. Entrées, $16.95 to $22.95. Patio daily, noon to 5:30, weather permitting. Dinner nightly, 5:30 to 9:30, mid-May through October.

Jonathan's, Main Street, Blue Hill.
How can one small town support two such good, full-service restaurants? Who knows, but Blue Hill does, and both get better and better.

Innovative Mediterranean-inspired cuisine and an award-winning wine list are the hallmarks of this cheery, informal spot run by Jonathan Chase. He started here with somewhat close and intimate quarters in front, and expanded into an open and airy rear section with rough wood walls, pitched ceiling, bow windows and a bar.

The newer area is a welcoming and comfortable place for an assertive summer meal. Our latest dinner started with a crostini with roasted elephant garlic and chèvre, served with ripe tomatoes, and a remarkable smoked mussel salad with goat cheese and pinenuts. Other choice starters are an Algerian salad of grilled shrimp and roasted corn, baja fish taco with fresh tomato salsa and minted yogurt, and some good soups, which come with all entrées.

The specials here are really special. We've enjoyed scallops sautéed with mint and tomatoes, and grilled swordfish with tequila-lime mayonnaise, as well as Jonathan's signature dish, shrimp flamed in ouzo and served with feta on linguini. Pan-seared rainbow trout with scotch whiskey and scallions, rabbit braised with smoked bacon and sundried tomatoes, and braised lamb shank with Bass ale, bourbon and maple barbecue sauce were other recent choices.

Kahlua-mocha mousse, frangelico cheesecake, peach crisp and cantaloupe sorbet with macaroons are among the worthy endings. The exceptional and extensive wine list, honored by Wine Spectator, is reasonably priced.

(207) 374-5226. Entrées, $17 to $22. Dinner nightly, 5 to 9. Closed Monday and Tuesday in winter.

The Landing, Steamboat Wharf Road, South Brooksville.

The schooners and windjammers sailing into the harbor provide a colorful backdrop for the food of personable new Swiss owners and their talented chef. Kurt and Verena Stoll took over the second-story waterfront restaurant, raised the ceiling, installed more windows and placed mirrors on the back wall and added pine paneling in two serene, candlelit dining rooms. Forrest Lyman, a New England Culinary Institute grad, changes the exotic dinner menu every week or so.

The best value is the four-course prix-fixe dinner, which changes nightly. Or you can order à la carte. Our party was impressed with such starters as the pheasant and chèvre beggars purse, chilled peach and cantaloupe soup, cold smoked salmon ravioli and a salad of watercress and frisée with duck confit and toasted pecans. Also good were the main dishes: tempura fried Maine lobster with saffron aioli, plank-roasted filet of salmon, roasted poussin and a grilled wild boar chop.

Worthy endings included a mango-rhubarb tart, raspberry crème brûlée, and a bing cherry and dark chocolate napoleon.

(207) 326-8483. Prix-fixe, $29. Entrées, $17.50 to $23.50. Dinner, Tuesday-Sunday from 5. Open Memorial Day to Oct. 20. No smoking.

Jean-Paul's Bistro, Main Street, Blue Hill.

Gaelic charm and a great view of Blue Hill Bay emanate from this compelling bistro opened by Jean-Paul Lecomte, a former waiter at prestigious New York City restaurants, including the 21 Club. He moved into a classic white Maine house with green shutters and started serving lunch and tea with the best water view in town. Jean-Paul takes care of the front of the house and several members of his family help out.

You can come in anytime after 8 a.m. for a cup of cappuccino and one of the delectable pastries from the patisserie. You may decide to stay for lunch. The French menu yields things like salade niçoise, croque monsieur, pasta salad, a smoked seafood platter, a New Orleans muffuletta sandwich or grilled chicken with roasted red pepper on focaccia. One of us thoroughly enjoyed a spicy gazpacho and the sausage tart de provence, while the other liked the grilled chicken caesar salad, layered rather than tossed and served with a baguette. The side terrace with its custom-made square wooden tables topped with canvas umbrellas proved such a salubrious setting that we lingered over a strawberry tart and a slice of midnight chocolate cake that Jean-Paul insisted we taste, calling it a French-Japanese cake (why, we don't know).

You might even decide to stay on for tea and a snack, served from 3 to 5, amid prolific flowers and some Jud Hartmann sculptures on that great terrace or at side-by-side Adirondack chairs for two on the lawn sloping toward the water.

All the atmosphere is not outside. Jean-Paul seats 80 inside in a couple of stylish dining rooms. The photogenic main room comes with cathedral ceilings, local art, white tablecloths, and blue and white spattered Bennington pottery for a simple and fresh yet sophisticated look. Wines and beers are available.

(207) 374-5852. Entrées, $5.95 to $9.95. Breakfast from 8. Lunch, 11 to 4. Tea, 4 to 5. Open July to mid-September.

The Mill Stream, Mill Street, Blue Hill.

The old Pie in the Sky pizza emporium on an out-of-the-way-street gave way in 1997 to this establishment of broader appeal. New owners Ann and Bill Rioux renovated three dining rooms and a bar area in what they call "country contemporary pink and green." A chef from Jonathan's took over the kitchen at dinner time, offering a variety of dinner salads and such main dishes (each accompanied by soup) as baked haddock with calamata olives and lemongrass, scampi over linguini, grilled swordfish with pesto mayonnaise, chicken marsala and black angus sirloin cooked on the outdoor grill.

The new owners still serve pizzas day and night. They also offer an extensive array of sandwiches and pitas for lunch. Microbeers are the beverages of choice.

(207) 374-2233. Entrées, $9.95 to $14.95. Open daily except Monday, 11:30 to 9:30, weekends to 11.

Diversions

Culture and crafts vie with picturesque coastal scenery for the visitor's attention. Pottery and handcrafts abound in Blue Hill and, indeed, all across the East Penobscot Bay peninsula and onto Deer Isle and Stonington.

The world-famous **Haystack Mountain School of Crafts** at Sunshine on Deer Isle, which sometimes has shows, is worth the drive simply for the breathtaking view from its unsurpassed setting on a steep, forested slope with stairs down to East Penobscot Bay. Public tours are offered daily at 1 p.m. in summer..

Rowantrees Pottery, the institution inspired in 1934 by Adelaide Pearson through her friend Mahatma Gandhi, is still going strong in a rambling house and barn reached by a pretty brick path through gardens at the edge of Blue Hill. Inside, you may be able to see potters at work; veteran employees like Grace Lymburner in the upstairs shop might recall for you the days when as children they joined the story hours and pottery classes run by Miss Pearson and her protégé, Laura Paddock. Sheila Varnum, who was associated with the founders since she was 3, has owned the pottery since 1976 and has continued its tradition. Named for the mountain ash trees above its green gate along Union Street, Rowantrees is especially known for its jam jar with a flat white lid covered with blueberries, as well as for unique glazes. Items are attractively displayed for sale.

Rackliffe Pottery at the other end of town is an offshoot of Rowantrees, Phil Rackliffe having worked there for twenty years. He and his family make all kinds

Owner Jean-Paul Lecomte greets customers at entrance to Jean-Paul's Bistro.

of handsome and useful kitchenware in a work area next to their small shop on Route 172. The soup tureens with blueberry, strawberry or cranberry covers are especially nice.

Kneisel Hall Chamber Music Festival, Pleasant Street, Blue Hill. (207) 374-2811. Concerts by well-known faculty members are given Friday evenings and Sunday afternoons from late June to early August in a rustic concert hall off upper Pleasant Street. The series is part of the summer session of the Kneisel Hall School of Music, founded by Dr. Franz Kneisel and called "the cradle of chamber music teaching in America." Innkeepers say a summer tradition for many of their guests is to arrive on Thursday and stay through Sunday, taking in two concerts, visiting the potteries and dining at Jonathan's and Firepond. Concert tickets, $19; unreserved veranda seats, $10.

Blue Hill Farmer's Market, Route 172 at the Blue Hill Fairgrounds. Each Saturday in July and August from 9 to 11:30 a.m., local farmers and artisans gather here for a real down-home event. Horse-drawn wagons give the youngsters hayrides, while residents and visitors browse through a small but interesting display of everything from local produce to goat cheese, jellies, handmade gifts, lamb's wool and patterned ski sweaters. The well-known Blue Hill Fair, incidentally, has been going strong since 1891.

Shopping. Along Blue Hill's Main Street, big spenders are drawn to the famed **Jud Hartmann Gallery.** Here, sculptor Jud Hartmann shows quite spectacular paintings by artist-friends along with the exceptional bronze sculptures he crafts at his studio in nearby Brooklin (he also has a gallery in foliage season in Grafton, Vt.). Everything is artfully arranged at **The Handworks Gallery,** which shows super contemporary crafts. Artist Judith Leighton's **Leighton Gallery** off Parker Point Road is considered one of the best galleries in Maine. Other favorites include **Liros Gallery** and **Mark Bell Pottery.** Birdhouses, carved birds, hooked fish hangings, tables with driftwood bases and Victorian twig furniture appeal at **Belcher's Country Store,** an offshoot of the main store in Deer Isle. **North Country Textiles** has moved its main store here from South Penobscot, offering wonderful throws, rugs, table linens, wicker and wooden furniture, pottery and more. Even non-smokers are enticed by the aromas at **Blue Hill Tea & Tobacco Shop,** something of an anachronism modernized by a selection of fine wines. The community supports not one but two bookstores. After **North Light Books** opened on Main Street, oldtimer **Blue Hill Books** doubled its space by expanding into the basement of its historic building on Pleasant Street.

Beside the causeway on Little Deer Isle is **Harbor Farm,** a store and showroom in an 1850 schoolhouse and a wreath-production building moved there by barge. Starting by making wreaths of wicker, Dick McWilliams and company have expanded into an impressive mail-order and retail operation of fine crafts, down-home knickknacks, practical gadgets and Christmas items. Something of a cross between, say, Tiffany's and Brookstone, it features unique, made-to-order items from birch twig swan baskets, woven coverlets, and gold and silver jewelry to wooden hooks, folding stools, English bathracks and garden shears. Behind the country store is a Christmas shop with ornaments from around the world.

In Deer Isle, the **Maine Crafts Association** shows contemporary works by members. The **Blue Heron Gallery** exhibits contemporary American crafts, featuring works by the Haystack faculty. **The Turtle Gallery** has changing exhibits of watercolors, oils, drawings, photographs and wood carvings by area artists. **The Periwinkle** stocks books, cards, knit goods, stuffed animals and local crafts. **Dockside Quilt Gallery** is known for colorful quilts.

Stonington's long slumbering downtown is awakening. The **Deer Isle Granite Museum** opened in 1997 along Main Street. Three galleries caught our eye, **West Main Street Gallery, Good Prospect Gallery** and the **Hoy Gallery,** displaying Jill Hoy's vibrant paintings of coastal Maine. **The Clown** is a remarkable venture, combining English antiques, contemporary art and Italian ceramics with Italian specialty foods and wines. The wonderful olive oil is produced on the owners' farm in Tuscany. The charming **Dockside Bookstore,** right beside the water with chairs for reading on a little deck, specializes in Maine and marine books and nautical gifts. **Penobscot Bay Provisions** features fresh breads made from natural ingredients, soups and sandwiches, smoked fish and prepared foods.

Extra-Special

Community Steel Bands. Spend any time in Blue Hill in the summer and you're sure to hear of the local steel-drum bands. The area now claims the largest steel band ensemble in the country, with hundreds of players in a variety of bands. The phenomenon started as a cooperative effort of Mary Cheyney Gould, director of the 80-member Bagaduce Chorale and the Bagaduce Music Lending Library, and Carl Chase, maker of steel drums and founder of the Atlantic Clarion Steel Band. An adult-education course was offered, one thing led to another and soon many folks hereabouts were playing steel drums. The Clarion band, which Carl started in Brooksville in 1974, is the most well known (it has played across the Northeast, including a concert at Lincoln Center). Another of the ensemble's sub groups, called Flash in the Pans, gave a wildly popular series of Monday night concerts across the peninsula one summer, culminating in an appearance at Kneisel Hall. "I did it for therapy," advised local innkeeper Barbara Seeger, one of the Flash in the Pans at the time. "We had people dancing in the streets."

Lobsters and harbor view draw visitors to Thurston's Lobster Pound in Bernard.

Mount Desert Island, Me.

The Other Harbors

Mount Desert Island has long held a special appeal, first as a summer resort for society and later as the site of a national park beloved by campers and naturalists.

Its focus for us, as well as for increasing numbers of others, has always been Bar Harbor and the eastern part of Acadia National Park. Since our first vacation there more than 30 years ago, we've witnessed the changes – for better and worse – as tourism impacted relentlessly. And still Bar Harbor remains dear to our hearts.

Be advised, however, that there are other harbors and another side to Mount Desert Island. The other side is the quieter side, one that its devotees call "the right side" of this fabulously varied island. This side celebrates its own identity in its annual Quietside Festival, three days of activities the last weekend in June.

Even the quiet side is wonderfully diverse. Northeast Harbor and Southwest Harbor are barely two miles across Somes Sound from each other, but far apart in spirit and character.

Northeast Harbor is the yachting harbor, a haven for Rockefellers and some of the world's great boats, a moneyed place where sailing is the seasonal preoccupation. Southwest Harbor is the working harbor, where fishing and boat-building are the year-round occupation. Here and in Bass Harbor, the oldtime flavor of coastal Maine remains.

Some of the choice portions of Acadia National Park are close at hand: Seawall, Wonderland, Beech Mountain, Echo Lake and Eagle Cliff. Thuya and Asticou gardens are special treats, and we know of few better views than those up and down Somes Sound, the only natural fjord in North America.

For a different perspective than most visitors get of Mount Desert, try the other harbors on the "right side" of the island.

Turn-of-the-century sea captain's house has been stylishly refurbished as Lindenwood Inn.

Inn Spots

Lindenwood Inn, 118 Clark Point Road, Box 1328, Southwest Harbor 04679

Towering linden trees shade this turn-of-the-century sea captain's home, now grandly refurbished by Jim King. Jim, who had opened the Kingsleigh Inn here, returned from traveling around the world in 1993 to purchase the Lindenwood, which had fallen on lean times.

With a decorator's eye, international tastes and an assortment of cosmopolitan possessions, Jim redid the entire place. You'll find palm trees on the front veranda, Italian chairs and glass tables in a dining area he dubs "tropical primitive – I got tired of the country look," a collection of shells and stones in each bedroom, sleek black modern lights, potted cactus plants on the tables, pottery from Mexico and Indonesia here, a contemporary mission bed there. He splashed around lots of color, from walls to down comforters to carpets. Call it different, call it eclectic, call it international. Jim calls it "a blend of old and new" and wants the Lindenwood to be "in the vanguard of the new look."

The two parlors are contemporary, accented with green and white striped upholstered chairs. Potted plants throughout the main floor bring the outdoors inside. Upstairs are nine guest quarters of varying sizes, all with private baths and several with fireplaces. Check out Room 6 with its six-foot-long clawfoot tub. It's one of six rooms with private decks or balconies affording views of the harbor. The ultimate is the penthouse suite with a curved sofa and gas fireplace, opening onto an enormous rooftop deck holding an oversize spa.

Next Jim redid two waterfront cottages and converted an adjacent apartment house into six efficiency suites he called the Lindenwood Annex. He converted another house across the street into yet another annex with six rooms with private baths. The breakfast room evolved into a small, full-fledged restaurant (see Dining Spots). Outside at the side, screened by a trellis from the street, is a heated gunite pool and a separate spa topped by a sculptured mask spraying a stream of water.

We stayed in the pool-side cottage with cable TV in the cathedral-ceilinged living room, an efficiency kitchen and a queensize bedroom.

In the morning, seated in one of the three small dining rooms, we helped ourselves to fresh fruit and raspberry-banana muffins from the buffet and were served a main dish of fruit crêpes. We vowed to return the next year to see what whirlwind Jim and his staff were up to.

(207) 244-5335 or (800) 307-5335. Fax (207) 244-3643. www.acadia.net/lindenwood. Twelve rooms, two suites, six efficiency suites and three cottages with private baths. July and August: doubles $95 to $155, efficiencies $115 EP, suites, $185 to $225, cottages $1,085 to $1,295 weekly. Rest of year: doubles $75 to $135, efficiencies $95 to $105, suites, $145 to $195, cottages $95. Smoking restricted.

Asticou Inn, Route 3, Northeast Harbor 04662.

Majestically situated at the head of Northeast Harbor on a hillside where the mountains slope to the sea, the Asticou has been a bastion of elegance since 1883.

The fireplace in the lobby is always ablaze – "to take the chill off foggy mornings or late afternoons," our friendly guide informed. The lobby with its huge oriental rug and wing chairs gives way to a comfortable parlor. Beyond is a bright and breezy cocktail lounge with sliding doors onto the outdoor deck. Amid white furniture, yellow umbrellas and petunias in planters, it's a great place from which to view the goings-on in the harbor. The enclosed east porch is used for games and television viewing. The spacious dining room (see Dining Spots) serves three meals a day and a Thursday evening buffet that draws people from all over the island.

A carpeted staircase and a turn-of-the-century elevator lead to 35 simple guest rooms on the second and third floors. Rooms vary from those with twin beds, rose carpeting and frilly white curtains framing views onto the harbor to a suite with a sofa, two peach chintz chairs and a desk in a sitting room plus two twins in the bedroom. Four have private balconies viewing the water. Seven more rooms and suites are available in the popular Bird Bank and Blue Spruce guest houses, two in Cranberry Lodge, and six in the Topsider cottages. Most striking are the contemporary, circular Topsiders, each with two identical suites. Their interiors painted

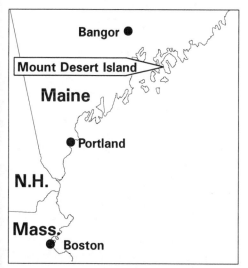

yellow with mauve accents, they come with decks, full-length windows, king beds, sitting areas with floral chintz fabric and wicker, wet bars and microwaves.

Joseph Joy, innkeeper for the inn owned by a group of summer residents and businessmen, has overseen $500,000 worth of infrastructure improvements since 1995. All the common areas and the Topsider rooms have been redone, and rooms in the inn were scheduled for enhancement in 1998.

The perfectly landscaped grounds offer a swimming pool, tennis, gardens and, all the while, changing vistas of the harbor. Guests have privileges at the Northeast Harbor Golf Club. The inn also has a new massage therapy center.

The MAP meal plan is no longer required – nor are jackets and ties in the dining room – as the inn continues to evolve with the times.

(207) 276-3344 or (800) 258-3373. Forty-six rooms and suites, most with private baths. Rates, MAP. July and August: doubles $264 to $299, suites $299 to $349. Late spring and early fall: doubles $184 to $249, suites $224 to $279. Deduct $67 for B&B. Two-night minimum in season. Children over 6. Smoking restricted. Closed mid-October to mid-May.

The Claremont, Clark Point Road, Box 137, Southwest Harbor 04679.

The other grand dowager of Mount Desert, the Claremont was founded in 1884, a year later than the Asticou. It's the island's oldest continuously operating inn, with only three owners in its first century.

Entered in the National Register of Historic Places in 1978 as a reminder of the "prosperous, relaxed and seasonal way of life" of Maine's early summer-resort era, the original light yellow wood structure has been considerably spiffed up of late and the name has been shortened from the Claremont Hotel and Cottages. But the inn's wraparound veranda and the heavy white Adirondack chairs lined up side by side on the rear lawn still provide a relaxing view of Somes Sound, and croquet remains the sport of choice. The annual Claremont Croquet Classic is known as the home of nine-wicket croquet.

The main building contains a lobby and living rooms full of wicker chairs and sofas, a handsome dining room and 24 guest rooms with queen or twin beds (a few singles) on the second and third floors, all with private baths. Twenty were renovated for 1994 to include heat, telephones and full bath, and furnishings remain comfortable yet simple. Also available for longer stays are twelve housekeeping cottages with living rooms, franklin or stone fireplaces and decks, and two guest houses. The Phillips House with five large rooms, a suite and a massive fieldstone fireplace in the parlor is particularly inviting. The Clark House provides an additional suite.

Besides croquet, boating and tennis are offered, and the hardy can swim from the dock in chilly Somes Sound. The Boat House and its decks are a favorite spot for a light lunch or cocktails in summer.

Dinner is available for guests and the public in a candlelit dining room with windows onto the water. The American/continental menu includes such dishes as grilled salmon on a bed of spinach with citrus salsa, grilled lamb tenderloin with sauce robert and veal steak au poivre.

(207) 244-5036 or (800) 244-5036. Twenty-nine rooms, two suites and twelve cottages with private baths. Hotel and guest houses: doubles, $195 MAP, $120 B&B, July and August; $175 MAP, $120 B&B, late June and September to mid-October. Guest houses: $65 to $75 B&B, Memorial Day to mid-June. Cottages, EP, $153 to $183, mid-June to mid-September; $95 to $135 rest of season; three-night minimum. Smoking restricted. Inn open mid-June to mid-October, cottages and guest houses Memorial Day to late October.

Entrées, $16 to $19. Lunch at Boat House daily in July and August, noon to 2. Dinner nightly, 6 to 9, mid-June to mid-October; jackets required.

Harbourside Inn, Harbourside Road (Route 198), Northeast Harbor 04662.

Built in 1888 in the style of the Seal Harbor Club, this shingled hilltop inn is

Lawn chairs are lined up for visitors to take in view at The Claremont.

fresh and pleasant and unusually comfortable. "We're old-fashioned and intend to keep it that way," Geraldine Sweet explains. She and her husband, who formerly managed the Jordan Pond House, acquired the mansion in 1977 from a woman who would sell only to Maine residents who would maintain the heritage.

The heritage indeed remains, from the nasturtiums nurtured from the original seeds still brightening the entry circle and the blueberry plants along the entry path to the original carpets from China, repaired when they became worn because they were too prized to be discarded. Guests gather in a pleasant parlor with wing chairs in shades of blue or on the front sun porch, all done up with bright cushions and curtains in appropriate Northeast Harbor colors, preppy pink and green.

All but one of the ten guest accommodations on the first and second floors have working fireplaces, and three have their own sunporches. Four more bedrooms on the third floor raise the total to fourteen. All have private baths and are furnished in 19th-century style. "We had great fun with the wallpapers," Geraldine said. One bathroom's paper has small red bears with big hearts on the borders, and one bedroom is papered with irises and another with fuschias. Room 1 with a wallpapered ceiling has a Wallace Nutting bed, a collector's item. The floral-papered honeymoon suite includes a kingsize bed and an enclosed porch with cathedral ceiling, wicker rockers, a glider and a teak deck chair from the liner Queen Elizabeth. A first-floor suite offers a sitting room with comfortable chairs grouped in front of the fireplace and a kitchenette in an alcove, a bedroom with a kingsize four-poster and a chaise lounge, and an old-fashioned tub in the bathroom. White organdy curtains in the windows frame the dark fir trees outside.

Outside are perennial gardens and a path for hiking up Norumbega Mountain and around Haddock Pond.

A continental breakfast with blueberry muffins is served on the sunporch.

Lest the inn's name mislead, the Sweets stress that the once-sweeping view of the harbor from their hilltop is now obstructed by a century's growth of trees. "We're only the third owners of this wonderful property," said Geraldine. "Hopefully, our children will take it over."

(207) 276-3272. Eleven rooms and three suites with private baths. Doubles, $90 to $125. Suites, $150 to $175. Open mid-June to mid-September. No smoking.

The Maison Suisse Inn, Main Street, Box 1090, Northeast Harbor 04662.

Pick a couple of blueberries along the entry path as you arrive at this inn, surrounded by gardens designed by a previous owner who trained as a landscape architect in Switzerland. Beth and David White took over in 1987, did a total renovation and ended up with six bedrooms and four suites.

Canopy beds, silkscreened wallpaper, feather pillows, down comforters, dust ruffles, antiques and Bar Harbor wicker comprise the decor. In-room telephones have been added lately. Rooms come in a variety of configurations, with suites ranging from one to two and one-half bedrooms. We're partial to an upstairs suite, which has a small balcony with a wicker loveseat, and the Garden Room with a separate entrance and a charming little garden ringed by cedars to make it private. Two main-floor rooms open onto outdoor porches. The suites with two bedrooms, one with eight sides, have fireplaces.

Three downstairs common rooms with fireplaces are handsomely furnished. Beach stones form an unusual inset in the mantel of the brick fireplace in the main hall of the circa-1890 summer mansion, designed in the shingle style. There are more seating areas in the gardens outside, and in 1998 the Whites purchased an abutting acre for more outside seating and to clear some trees to provide "more water glimpses from our rooms," in Beth's words.

Room rates include a full breakfast with the inn's compliments at Colonel's Restaurant across the street.

(207) 276-5223 or (800) 624-7668. Fax (207) 276-9814. www.acadia.net/maison. Six rooms and four suites with private baths. Mid-July through August: doubles $125 to $175, suites $195 to $245. Early July and September to mid-October: doubles $105 to $155, suites $185 to $225. May-June: doubles $75 to $135, suites $145 to $195. No smoking. Closed mid-October to mid-May.

Grey Rock Inn, Harbourside Road, Northeast Harbor 04662.

Remarkable gardens and a prolific hanging begonia on the porch at the front door greet visitors to this little-publicized inn, said to have been a gathering place for Northeast Harbor socialites after it was built in 1910 as a private residence.

Inside the inviting large fieldstone and shingled mansion with yellow trim is a veritable showcase for British owner Janet Millet's decorating tastes: an array of wicker like you've never seen, fans and paintings from the Orient, fringed lamps, masses of exotic flowers – rather overwhelming, some find.

People who stay at Grey Rock must like eclectic elegance, for that's what they get. The two fireplaces in the living room and parlor are kept aglow, even in mid-summer, because the innkeeper finds her guests want it that way. Wicker serves as furniture and art, from table lamps to loveseats, from desk to plant stand.

The nine guest rooms are equally exotic. The huge main-floor corner room with canopied four-poster bed, oriental screen and private balcony could not be more romantic. The upstairs rooms are lacy, frilly and flowery, with much pale pink and green, all kinds of embroidered towels, and porches all around. Some have fireplaces, and all have views of the trees or gardens atop this wooded hilltop.

Assisted by her sons Adam and Karl, Janet serves an exemplary continental-plus breakfast, including a fruit compote with eight to ten kinds of fresh fruit, assorted baked goods and bacon, occasionally eggs, and what she states is "a good cup of coffee for a British lady."

(207) 276-9360 or 276-5526. Doubles, $110 to $190 July-October, $85 to $145 in June. Closed November-May.

Lush plantings and hanging begonia grace entry to Grey Rock Inn.

The Kingsleigh Inn 1904, 373 Main St., Box 1426, Southwest Harbor 04679.
A wraparound veranda full of wicker, colorful pillows and flowers distinguishes this B&B with an unusual pebbledash stucco-stone exterior. Guests enter through the country kitchen, which seems to be the heart of the house, where refreshments are available throughout the day.

Ken and Cyd Champagne Collins from Newburyport, Mass., who took over in 1996, added their own antiques and artworks to the eight bedrooms, some with harbor views and all with private baths. One has a new balcony with chairs over-looking the water. The Turret Suite on the third floor offers television and a great view from a telescope placed between two cozy wicker chairs; the bedroom comes with a kingsize bed and fireplace. The other rooms are lavishly furnished with queensize beds, Waverly wall coverings and fabrics, plush carpeting, lace window treatments, country accents and woven baskets filled with thick towels.

Afternoon tea and homemade cookies or lemon bars are served on the porch or in cool weather by the fireplace.

Breakfasts are bountiful, taken by candlelight at tables for two in a dining room with gleaming hardwood floors, dark green tablecloths, and pink and green china. Juices, fresh fruit, homemade granola and muffins preceded baked German eggs at our latest visit. Other treats include crab soufflé, lemon french toast with warm Maine blueberry sauce, eggs florentine and belgian waffles with fruit topping.

(207) 244-5302. Fax (207) 244-0349. Seven rooms and one suite with private baths. July through mid-October: doubles $90 to $125, suite $175. Mid-May through June: doubles $75 to $85, suite $135. Rest of year: doubles $55 to $65, suite $105.

The Inn at Southwest, Main Street, Box 593, Southwest Harbor 04679.
This inn has been taking in guests since 1884, first as a rooming house and lately as an attractive Victorian B&B, acquired in 1995 by Jill Lewis, a computer programmer from Michigan. She took over a going concern and started upgrading bathrooms, redecorating and adding plush carpeting.

Southwest Harbor and islands are on view from on high at Island Watch.

All nine guest rooms on the second and third floors have private baths, two down the hall. Jill named them after historic Maine lighthouses and decorated them accordingly. All are furnished with designer linens, down comforters, antique wicker or rattan tables and desks, ceiling fans, potpourri, plants and the like. The Cape Elizabeth, second-floor front, is the most spacious, with a kingsize bed, a sitting area with a sofabed and an antique writing desk, and a bay window. All the rest of the rooms but one have queensize beds, and two on the third floor have large window seats beneath unusual chapel windows.

Guests gather in a comfortable living room with a big sofa, TV and stereo, a game table and an ornate fireplace mantel. Waverly and Schumacher wallpapers, stenciling and old pictures are included in the main-floor decor.

Jill, who did most of the redecorating herself, appointed the dining room in white with blue accents. She serves a fancy, two-course breakfast here or on the wraparound porch lined with geraniums and overlooking Victorian gardens. Strawberry shortcake and eggs benedict were the fare the day we visited. A cranberry-apple compote and belgian waffles with raspberry sauce were to be on tap the next day. Other possibilities include her specialty crab-potato bake, summer fruit soups and Irish cream french toast.

In the afternoon, she offers homemade cookies and brownies in the living room.

(207) 244-3835. Nine rooms with private baths. Mid-June to mid-September: doubles $90 to $135. Off-season: $50 to $95. Closed November-April. Children over 8. No smoking.

The Moorings, Shore Road, Southwest Harbor 04679.

Genial Downeasters Leslie and Betty King have run this delightfully informal, old-fashioned place since 1960 in a location they call the "Little Norway of America," and one we find the most scenic on the island, smack on the shore at the start of Somes Sound in Manset.

The rambling white house with dark shutters in the Maine style contains ten guest rooms, two of them small singles and all with private baths. There also are three motel-style units (one with two exposures billed as having "probably the finest view on the coast") and five units in three trim white cottages with wicker porches and a garden apartment. The Kings have upgraded their rooms with cheery new wallpapers and furnishings, and the five on the inn's second floor now sport decks and balconies to take advantage of the view. Most rooms have double or twin beds.

We dubbed our front-corner bedroom the Agatha Christie Room because several of her paperbacks were on the bureau (Betty makes the rounds of all the lawn sales to pick up the books, son Storey volunteered). It's the only one without a water view but, as with the other rooms, the towels were large and fluffy, the double bed had colorfully patterned sheets, and a candle was in a ceramic holder beside the bed. The Pilot House cottage with living room, fireplace, screened porch and television provided more expansive accommodations at a later visit.

The fireplace glows on cool mornings in the living room, which has a television set in a windowed alcove and enough books and magazines to start a library. The coffee pot is kept filled all day in the adjacent office, where complimentary orange juice and donuts are put out every morning.

Outside, two rowboats filled with geraniums brighten the path to the front door. In back are canoes, bicycles, a pier and a stony shoreline for swimming (if you can stand the icy water), beachcombing, clamming and musseling. The Kings provide charcoal for the grills beside the shore, a memorable spot to barbecue a steak for dinner as you watch the sunset.

We're obviously fond of the Moorings. It's unpretentious and the prices are, too.

(207) 244-5523 or 244-3210. (800) 596-5523. Thirteen rooms and six cottage units with private baths. July to mid-September: doubles $65 to $80 (two small singles, $55), cottage units $80 to $100. Rest of year: doubles $60 to $70, cottages $75 to $85.

Island Watch, Freeman Ridge Road, Box 1359, Southwest Harbor 04679.

Little known but aptly named, this B&B in a contemporary ranch house occupies the top of a high ridge west of town. Floor-to-ceiling windows in the living room/dining room stretching across the rear of the house and an expansive deck take full advantage of the panoramic view of islands and water.

Maxine Clark, who says she's the only native-born hostess in the B&B business locally, grew up in the Bass Harbor Lighthouse as the daughter of the lighthouse keeper. Here, in a rather spectacular house, she offers six homey guest rooms (one a single) and an efficiency suite in a separate building. All have private baths, and three afford water views. One room with a private entrance on the ground floor has a double and single bed and built-in pine counters. An adjacent room offers a similar bed configuration plus a wood stove and a large bathroom with a clawfoot tub. Everything except the red carpet is white in Room 1 upstairs, a simple room with a kingsize bed and a glorious view. The efficiency in the outbuilding contains a queensize bed in back and a small living room with a TV and half a kitchen in front, plus a small private deck.

The living room in the main house has a huge stone fireplace and TV, VCR and stereo for guests' use. We settled down on the rear deck in the early evening and found it hard to leave for dinner (there's also a front deck that catches the late afternoon sun).

The next morning we were back on that great rear deck, but managed to arise long enough to enjoy Maxine's festive breakfast at a big round table in a dining room open to the country kitchen. Her french toast with ricotta stuffing and strawberry-raspberry sauce was the main event. Fresh fruit and cereal preceded. Belgian waffles and a ham and spinach quiche are other favorites.

Maxine since has added a greenhouse at the end of the dining room so folks can now enjoy breakfast amid the plants and with an island view.

(207) 244-7229. Five rooms and one efficiency suite with private baths. Doubles, $75. Efficiency, $85. No smoking.

Dining Spots

Redfield's, Main Street, Northeast Harbor.

The sign on the door is apt to say "Thank You – Full" at this, the hottest dining ticket on Mount Desert Island. Scott and Maureen Redfield, who got their start serving dinners in the off-season at the Cranberry Lodge of Asticou Inn, decided it was "time for us to open our own place."

Northeast Harbor proved highly receptive to their casually elegant, contemporary 30-seat establishment, which would be quite at home on Nantucket but for the prices and the refreshing lack of pretensions.

The decor in two small dining rooms is simple yet sophisticated. Tiny lamps hanging from long cords over most tables illuminate some large, summery, impressionist-style paintings and make the rooms rather too bright for our tastes. But they do highlight the food, which is worth the spotlight here.

We staved off hunger with a basket of Maureen's fabulous foccacia topped with tomatoes and goat cheese, exquisite house salads and a shared appetizer of venison carpaccio as we nursed the house La Veille Ferme wine. Lemon sorbet in a lotus dish

Art is backdrop for dining at Redfield's.

prepared the palate for the main dishes: sliced breast of duck with fresh chutney and marinated loin of lamb with goat cheese and black olives, both superb. Strawberry sorbet and a chocolate-almond mint tart ended a memorable meal.

Scott changes his menus frequently. Recent choices included silken red snapper with smoked cilantro and chile mayonnaise, arctic char with chive and parsley compound butter, veal scaloppine with caper wine sauce and rack of lamb with green peppercorn demi-glace. Starters ranged from chilled five-berry soup finished with grand marnier to seared ostrich with grilled portobello mushrooms and sautéed duck foie gras and apples flamed with chartreuse. Among desserts were chocolate and dried cranberry chiffon tart, ginger ice cream and a chocolate genoise and almond mousse torte.

(207) 276-5283. Entrées, $17 to $22. Dinner, Monday-Saturday 6:30 to 8:30; weekends only in off-season.

The Bistro at Seal Harbor, Route 3, Seal Harbor.

Their kitchen isn't much bigger than that in a studio apartment, they grow their own herbs in wine casks on the back porch and they have only eight tables for dining. But Donna Fulton and Terri Clements earn plaudits for their homespun bistro in the heart of old-money Seal Harbor.

The storefront room is pristine with tables topped with white napkins, votive candles, fresh flowers and white china. Behind is a small service bar and aforementioned kitchen, snug with ten-burner stove. Donna handles the cooking chores, preparing half a dozen main courses like Maine crab cakes with Creole sauce, sautéed pork tenderloin with mangos and shallots, and grilled loin lamb chops with rosemary jus. The Bistro salad comes with feta, apples and spiced pecans. Other starters range from scallops with heirloom beans, preserved lemon and parmigiano-reggiano to smoked salmon with ginger-scallion pancake. Soup might be salmon chowder or lobster with jalapeño peppers and corn.

Desserts could be crème brûlée, lemon tart and intense ice creams (coffee-almond-praline or ginger) and orange-buttermilk sorbet served with biscotti. The choice, all-domestic wine list is priced mostly in the twenties.

This is obviously a pure place, where the owners make everything from scratch. They even pick their own berries for the blueberry pie and grate their own vanilla beans for the extract.

(207) 276-3299. Entrées, $16 to $21. Dinner, Tuesday-Sunday from 6. Open Memorial Day to October. No smoking.

The Burning Tree, Route 3, Otter Creek.
It's a bit of a trek, but folks from Northeast Harbor are particularly fond of this simple restaurant in a rural setting along the road to Bar Harbor. There are tables on the long front porch, one section of which is a waiting area. Beyond are two small dining rooms, cheerfully outfitted in pinks and blues, their linened tables topped with tall, blue-edged water glasses. Colorful paintings by local artists adorn the walls, and the dining room manager designed the arty menu covers.

The summer-cottage setting is the backdrop for inspired "gourmet seafood" offered by chef-owners Allison Martin and Elmer Beal Jr. A couple of chicken dishes are the only meats listed among entrées ranging from baked codfish with black bean sauce to curried pecan flounder served over a dried apricot, currant and pistachio couscous. Vegetarians hail offerings like a the cashew, brown rice and gruyère terrine and spring risotto with artichokes, peas, spinach and hazelnuts.

Our party was quite delighted with such appetizers as mussels with mustard sauce, grilled scallops and an excellent vegetarian sushi. The cioppino came so highly touted that two of us ordered it, and the choice measured up. The others enjoyed grilled monkfish with a spicy tomato coulis, served with creamy potatoes with cheese and sautéed zucchini and peppers, and baked sole with crab and leek mousse. A couple of bottles of Chilean sauvignon blanc accompanied. Fresh strawberry pie, nectarine mousse cake and a rich chocolate kahlua cheesecake finished off an entirely satisfying meal.

(207) 288-9331. Entrées, $16.50 to $21.50. Dinner nightly except Tuesday, 5 to 10. Open June to mid-October.

Asticou Inn, Northeast Harbor.
The $28.95 buffet every Thursday night draws up to 300 people in peak season to the posh dining room of the Asticou Inn. Thursday happens to be maid's night off hereabouts, so summer residents join inn guests for the extravagant spread and an evening of socializing. A band plays for dancing on the deck twice a month.

The pillared dining room is restful with handpainted murals of trees and flowers on the deep yellow walls, oriental rugs, lovely flowered china and tiny plants in clay pots. Most coveted seating is in the adjacent enclosed porch, with great views through picture windows onto the harbor beyond.

The continental/American dinner menu ranges widely, from salmon en croûte, coq au vin and pistachio-crusted pork chop with port wine sauce to lobster grand marnier, filet mignon forestière and grilled elk medallions with cabernet demi-glace. Starters could be shrimp cocktail, escargots and brie in garlic butter, mozzarella salad or smoked seafood sampler. Dessert possibilities are raspberry meringue glacé, chocolate-truffle torte and key lime pie.

On a sunny day, we lunched on the outdoor terrace high above the sparkling harbor. The menu produced a crabmeat club sandwich with potato salad, garnished with colorful specks of bell peppers and nasturtiums, and a superior seafood salad of lobster, shrimp and crabmeat tossed with vegetables and field greens.

(207) 276-3344 or (800) 258-3313. Entrées, $21.95 to $25.95. Lunch, Monday-Saturday in July and August, 11:30 to 5. Dinner nightly, 6 to 10:30 to 9, mid-June to mid-September. Sunday jazz brunch, 11:30 to 2:30.

Lindenwood Inn, 118 Clark Point Road, Southwest Harbor.

The former breakfast room at this expanding inn has become part of a superior restaurant, thanks to owner Jim King and his chef, Bill Morrison. They seat 30 in three stylish dining rooms and offer a short, changing menu that is every bit as eclectic as the rest of the inn. Organic foods and vegetarian dishes are among the wholesome fare

For dinner in the small bar room, a basket of breads with pesto sauce and butter in mini-crocks arrived at a table flanked by sleek European-style chairs and dressed with exotic flowers, a silver elephant and an oil lamp bearing a shade atop a wrought-iron twig. A South African chardonnay accompanied what proved to be a superb meal: for one, a pair of appetizers – crab, avocado and cilantro Japanese mako sushi rolls and Thai mussels steamed in sake with basil, cilantro, ginger and hot pepper; for the other, a spinach salad with roasted portobello mushrooms and parmesan cheese and a main course of crab and cod cakes with saffron rémoulade. Choice ranged from pan-seared salmon with saffron beurre blanc to grilled ginger duck breast with crème de cassis sauce.

Homemade bourbon ice cream with chocolate biscotti and a strawberry tart with mascarpone were refreshing counterpoints to such assertive tastes.

(207) 244-5335 or (800) 307-5335. Entrées, $16 to $28. Dinner by reservation, Tuesday-Saturday 6 to 9:30 in season, weekends through Christmas.

XYZ Restaurant & Gallery, Shore Road, Manset.

The letters stand for Xalapa, Yucatan and Zacatecas, and the food represents the Mexican interior and coastal Maine. Owner Janet Strong had the West Side Gallery here for a year before opening this enterprise with cook Robert Hoyt, who's traveled in Mexico for years and describes himself as "a nut for the food there for a long, long time."

We could easily become nuts for his food, too, after a couple of dinners here. Everything is, as Robert says, "real," from the smoked jalapeño and tomatillo sauces served with the opening tortillas to the fine tequila he offered with dessert as a chaser. Busy hostess Janet recommended we try her partner's sampler plate ($11 each): two chiles rellenos and a chicken dish with mashed potato and pickled cucumber. Thoroughly smitten, we returned the next year to enjoy the pollo deshebrada (shredded chicken in a rustic sauce of chiles with cilantro and onions) and tatemado (pork loin baked in a sauce of guajillo and ancho chiles). Dessert was the sensational XYZ pie, layered ice cream and chocolate covered in warm kahlua chocolate sauce.

Part of the main floor of the Dockside Motel, the L-shaped dining room is colorful in white, red and green, the colors of the Mexican flag. The front windows look out onto Somes Sound across the road.

(207) 244-5221. Entrées, $12 to $14. Dinner nightly in summer, from 5:30. Seasonal.

Keenan's, Route 102A, Bass Harbor.

This little place where Route 102A meets Flat Iron Road at "the Triangle" looks like a seafood shack, what with lobster traps perched on the roof and steaming pots of water out front. Inside it's bigger than it looks and pleasantly rustic with driftwood paneling and a roll of paper towels on each table.

From the galley-size kitchen come remarkable treats that draw locals-in-the-know: lobsters, of course, but also barbecued back ribs marinated in a mysterious red sauce known only to contain tomatoes and vinegar, crab cakes, seafood gumbo, shrimp étouffée and blackened swordfish. Chef Frank Keenan, of French-Canadian descent, and his wife Liz call their blend of Cajun and Down East cooking "Acadian cuisine," much like that you find around the bayous of southwestern Louisiana.

(207) 244-3403. Entrées, $6.95 to $12.95. Dinner nightly in summer, from 4:30; fewer days in off-season.

The Deck House Restaurant & Cabaret Theater, 11 Apple Lane, Southwest Harbor.

An island tradition since 1970 at Bass Harbor, this moved in 1997 to grand new quarters upstairs in the loft of an old canning factory in the Hinckley Great Harbor Marina complex. It's a much larger and more substantial venue for cabaret theater presented, as always, by the singing wait staff.

The new Deck House serves lunch and Sunday brunch, but the main event is at night. The dining room opens at 6:30 for dinner. The ten dinner entrées include grilled swordfish, cornish game hen, prime rib and tournedos rossini. At 8:15, the servers become players, singing solos, duets, quartets and ensemble numbers in the round. No customer is more than four tables from the action. The emphasis is on Broadway show tunes, but barbershop quartet, mime numbers and dance also have been featured. Some attendees consider the event the highlight of their visit to Down East Maine.

(207) 244-5044. Entrées, $17.95. Lunch, Monday-Saturday 11 to 2. Dinner nightly, from 6:30; show at 8:15. Sunday brunch, 10:30 to 1.

Thurston's Lobster Pound, Steamboat Wharf Road, Bernard.

From the jaunty upstairs deck at this newish lobster pound, you can look below and see where the lobstermen keep their traps. Thurston's is a real working lobster wharf. And if you couldn't tell from all the pickup trucks parked along the road, one taste of the lobster will convince you.

We enjoyed our lobster dinner ($7 to $8 a pound, plus $3 for the extras, from corn to blueberry cake). Together we also sampled the lobster stew (bearing tons of lobster), a really good potato salad, steamers and two pounds of mussels (about one pound too much). Oh well, this *was* our first lobster feast of the summer. You wait in line for one of the square tables for four on the covered deck, place your order at the counter and select from a choice wine and beer list. They provide the candles, and a little wash basin outside the kitchen so customers can wash the lobster debris off their hands.

This is a true place, run by Michael Radcliffe, great-grandson of the lobster wharf's founder, and his wife Libby. A local couple, whose license plate said "Pies," was delivering the apple and rhubarb pies for the day when we stopped by. *(207) 244-7600. Open daily 11 to 8:30, Memorial Day through September.*

A sampling of other, more casual eating spots, particularly good for seafood or local atmosphere:

Head of the Harbor, Route 102, Southwest Harbor. A lobster dinner was $9.95 when we ate at Alan Hartling's rustic indoor-outdoor restaurant on a hill above Somes Sound. You see the lobsters steaming and place your order at the outdoor steamer and grill. Then a waitress delivers your order to the citronella-lit picnic tables on the expansive outdoor deck overlooking the water or on a screened porch adjacent. A fried clam platter with coleslaw and potato salad or french fries and chowder with a clam roll made a good lunch, washed down with a wine cooler and a Bud Lite. At a recent visit, we enjoyed a sunset dinner of stuffed shrimp with potato salad and sautéed scallops with french fries and three-bean salad (each $12.95), followed by fresh raspberry pie. Open daily, noon to 10, Memorial Day to mid-October.

Northeast Harbor Cafe and Ice Cream Parlor, Main Street, Northeast Harbor. Green checked cafe curtains and green marble-top tables identify this newcomer inspired by an heiress to the Godiva chocolate fortune who felt the town needed a good ice cream parlor. There's far more than ice cream, however: sandwiches, pizzas, stir-fries, quiches and entrées from $5.95 to $11.95 (for baked stuffed haddock or shrimp scampi). The cafe has a beer and wine license. Open daily in season, 11 to 8.

Maine-ly Delights, Ferry Road, Bass Harbor. From a van that dispensed hot dogs and crabmeat rolls opposite the Swans Island Ferry terminal, Karen Holmes Godbout has expanded over the years to the point where she now has a roof over her head, a room with an open kitchen and an outdoor deck. A hot dog costs $1.50 and a lobster roll $6.95; last we knew, you could get a complete lobster dinner with french fries and coleslaw for $7.95. Karen's fryolator is famous for her original O'Boy Doughboys, and she still picks the blueberries that go into her muffins and pies. Even with a beer and wine license, she stresses, "I am quaint, not fancy, Down East all the way." Open daily, 7 a.m. to 9 p.m., June-September.

Jumpin' Java Espresso Cafe, Garden Street, Southwest Harbor. Relocated to a larger location in 1997, this is a happening espresso bar and bakery. The latte is perfectly made, and there are all the usual yummy and caloric baked goods to go with. A few tables in the shady garden out front are where to partake.

Little Notch Bakery, based in The Shops at Hinckley Great Harbor Marina in Southwest Harbor, is a great bakery producing more than 4,500 loaves of bread weekly for a knowing clientele, some of Down East Maine's finest inns and restaurants. Specialties include Italian breads, focaccia, olive rolls and onion rolls. In 1996, young owners Art and Kate Jacobs opened the year-round **Little Notch Cafe** and retail outlet at 340 Main St. in the center of town. Art said the bittersweet belgian chocolate brownie he urged us to sample tasted like fudge, and it sure did. Had it been lunch time, we'd have gone for the grilled flank steak sandwich with roasted peppers and onions on a French baguette for $5.95.

Diversions

Acadia National Park. The most famous sites are along Ocean Drive and the Park Loop Road out of Bar Harbor, but don't miss the park's other attractions on this side of the island. The Beech Mountain area offers Echo Lake with a fine beach, changing rooms and fresh water far warmer than the ocean. Hike up Beech Cliff for a great view of Echo Lake below (yes, you may hear your echo). Past Southwest Harbor and Manset are Seawall, created naturally by the sea, and the Wonderland and Ship's Harbor nature trails, both well worth taking.

Somes Sound and Somesville. Follow Sargent Drive out of Northeast Harbor along the fjord-like Somes Sound for some of the island's most spectacular views (it's the closest thing we know of to the more remote areas around California's Lake Tahoe). At the head of the sound is Somesville, a classic New England village and a joy to behold: the whites of the houses brightened patriotically by red geraniums, white petunias and morning glories in flower boxes that line the street. Converted from a general store, the excellent **Port in the Storm Bookstore** stocks two floors with books and recordings. On the mezzanine, books are displayed the way they ought to be on slanted shelves around the atrium. Two resident cats and a pair of binoculars occupy a reading area in back beside Somes Sound, and you could not wish for a more beautiful spot for a bookstore. Also check out the old library with its new-fangled, wired-for-sound lounge chairs, and maybe an arts and crafts show outside. The entire town is listed on the National Register of Historic Places, and the **Mount Desert Historical Society** buildings chronicle the history of the island's earliest settlement. The Somesville Village Improvement Society conducts a biennial historical walking tour. The Masonic Hall in Somesville is home of the **Acadia Repertory Theater,** which has been staging five plays in two-week cycles each summer since 1973.

Museums. Southwest Harbor is widely known for its variety of birds (many consider it the warbler capital of the country), so fittingly this is the home of the **Wendell Gilley Museum,** a monument to the memory of one of the nation's outstanding bird carvers. Occupying a solar-heated building, it shows more than 200 of the late local wood carver's birds and decoys, ranging in size from a two-inch woodcock to a life-size bald eagle. The museum also has special exhibitions, and films and programs on woodcarving and natural history (admission, $3).

Also in Southwest Harbor is the main **Mount Desert Oceanarium,** a building full of sea life and lobster lore, with a touch tank, whale exhibit, fishing boats and more (adults, $5.95). Lately, the institution has branched out with a second oceanarium and a lobster hatchery, both in Bar Harbor.

New in Northeast Harbor is the **Great Harbor Collection Museum** in the old Town Hall/Fire Station. Artifacts from fire trucks to forks, toys to tools and sewing machines to sleighs reflect the heritage of Northeast, Southwest and Seal harbors. Adults, $1.

Boat cruises. Untold numbers of cruises – public, private and park-sponsored – leave from Northeast Harbor, Southwest Harbor and Bass Harbor. You can take a naturalist tour to Baker Island, a lobster boat or a ferry ride to Swans Island or the Cranberry Islands, and the park's cruises are particularly informative. If you'd rather observe than ride, poke around one of the ten or more boat-building yards in Southwest Harbor.

Shopping. The area's best shopping is in Northeast Harbor, although Southwest Harbor is catching up. In Northeast Harbor, **The Kimball Shop and Boutique** are two of the snazziest shops we've seen. The shop is a pageant of bright colors and room after room of pretty china, furniture, kitchenware and almost anything else that's in. A couple of doors away is the newer Boutique, filled with zippy clothes. **Beals Classics,** with an emphasis on fine dishware and wines, is a branch of one of our favorite gift and clothing stores in Ellsworth. **Mrs. Pervear's Shop** is a nice hodgepodge of painted furniture (we loved the table with lupines painted on), handknit sweaters, yarn and more. Behind a wild awning, **Local Color** purveys marvelous handpainted clothing. **The Romantic Room** stocks a range from wicker and straw hats to brass beds. Try **Animal Crackers** for adorable clothes for children, **Sherman's** and **McGrath's** for books, **Shaw** for contemporary jewelry and glass, and **Provisions** for suave groceries. There are several fine art galleries in which to browse, including **Smart Studio and Art Gallery,** with Wini Smart's wonderfully evocative paintings of Maine, and her new **Wini Smart's Garden Gallery** around the corner..

In Southwest Harbor, things are happening around the Hinckley Great Harbor Marina, a new state-of-the-art marina (it was the site of the international Wooden Boat Show when it opened) with a burgeoning complex of retail businesses. Check out the plants growing in all kinds of shoes, boots and sneakers outside **Hot Flash Anny's,** the hip showroom for Ann Seavey's stained-glass pieces. Almost everything is made of glass and is one of a kind; you could spend from $4 to $4,000 here. In the downtown area, **Home Port** has super clothes and gifts. Great sweaters and skirts are for sale at **Common Threads,** where we fell for the lupine earrings and pins. **Mrs. McVety's Ice Cream Shop** is where school teacher Judy McVety offers heath bar and cappuccino frozen yogurt, many flavors of ice cream and good sandwiches in summer. Little Notch Bakery products and Seal Cove goat cheese are hot numbers at **Sawyer's Market,** the local grocery with all the right stuff. Across the street is **Sawyer's Specialties,** an excellent gourmet food and wine shop.

Extra-Special

Asticou Terrace and Thuya Gardens, Route 3, Northeast Harbor.

You can drive up, but we recommend the ten-minute hike nearly straight up a scenic, well-maintained switchback path and stairs to the prized gardens above Northeast Harbor. A plaque relates that landscape architect Joseph H. Curtis left this "for the quiet recreation of the people of this town and their summer guests." It is easy to enjoy the showy hilltop spread combining English flower beds with informal natural Japanese effects, some common and uncommon annuals plus hardy rhododendron and laurel that appear as a surprise so far north. As you might find on a private estate, which this once was, there are a gazebo, a free-form freshwater pond, and a shelter with pillowed seats and deck chairs for relaxing in the shade. Thuya Lodge, the former Curtis summer cottage, houses a rare botanical book library. Nearby are the **Asticou Azalea Gardens,** where twenty varieties of azaleas compete for attention with a Japanese sand garden and amazed us with their Southern-style lushness in late June.

(207) 276-3344. Open daily in July and August, 7 to 7. Free.

Campobello Island is on view across Passamaquoddy Bay from Eastport Lobster & Fish Co. wharf.

Eastport, Me./St. Andrews, N.B.

Quoddy Loop: An International Wonderland

Franklin Delano Roosevelt chose to build his summer home on Campobello, his beloved island. The titans of Canadian industry turned St. Andrews By-the-Sea into one of Canada's poshest summer resorts. And sea captains, fishermen and sardine packers fished for a living around Lubec and Eastport, the smallest "city" in the United States.

The two-nation wonderland where easternmost Maine meets southwestern New Brunswick is undeniably remote – a mixed blessing – and incredibly picturesque. Naturalists call it the last coastal frontier on America's East Coast.

Although linked geographically and by water, each section of the Quoddy Region has its own distinctive aura.

Eastport, on a hilly peninsula called Moose Island overlooking Passamaquoddy Bay, is America's easternmost city (population, 2,000). It was considered a sister port to Boston by seagoing travelers during the 19th century and, along with Lubec across the bay, boomed as a fishing and sardine-packing town in its heyday. After decades of decline, both now are making a comeback with port and marina facilities and a growing aquaculture industry.

Lubec (accent second syllable, as in Quebec), is the closest American point to Campobello Island, famed for the Roosevelt summer home and 2,600 acres of nature preserves in the unique Roosevelt Campobello International Park. Although Canadian, its proximity and American ties ally Campobello more with Lubec, just a short bridge's length across the Lubec Narrows, than either Eastport – to which FDR and Eleanor used to go by boat to shop – or St. Andrews.

Ah, St. Andrews. One of us will forever cherish the summer days (and nights)she spent as a teenager with a friend whose family owned a house in St. Andrews, a low-key watering hole for old-money Canadians and knowing Americans. The town, settled in 1783 by British Loyalists after the American Revolution, still looks and feels much as it did in her youth. But change is under way with the opening of deluxe new inns and the world-class Kingsbrae Horticultural Garden, along with a much-heralded upgrading of the championship Algonquin golf course.

Granted, this area is way down east. But the trip is worth it and, once here, you'll want to stay. So allow time to complete the Quoddy Loop. Tour the Roosevelt home at Campobello. Eat lobster on the Eastport wharf. Luxuriate in a sumptuous inn in St. Andrews. Explore the craggy coastline. Savor an area of earthy (and watery) pleasures. Watch the monumental tides rising and falling up to 26 feet a day, ebbing and flowing with life in a quieter time and place.

Inn Spots

Accommodations are grouped here according to location. Prices quoted are in local currency. American dollars stretch about 40 percent farther in Canada, where a $250 suite might translate to $175 U.S., with a refund available on the new harmonized sales tax. This part of Canada is in the Atlantic Time zone, one hour ahead of Eastern Time.

St. Andrews, N.B.

Kingsbrae Arms, 219 King St., St. Andrews E0G 2X0.

It was sheer serendipity, according to the owners of Canada's first five-star inn. Long Island innkeepers Harry Chancey Jr. and David Oxford were returning from a Maritimes vacation in 1995 when they detoured on a whim to St. Andrews.

"We thought we'd arrived in the magic kingdom," recalled Harry. They extended their vacation, started house hunting and within a week took possession of an abandoned mansion in which to run a second inn.

The rambling 1897 cedar-shingled house and its neighbors on a ridge at the top of King Street were among the finest in one of Canada's ritziest summer colonies. Time had taken its toll, however. Abandoned for eight years, it was "a real mess," in Harry's words. "We see something like this and it becomes a challenge." The partners were up to the challenge, having restored seven houses before buying a Victorian farmhouse in East Hampton and turning it into the Centennial House, a deluxe B&B.

With the blessing of town officials and neighbors Lucinda and John Flemer, who funded the adjacent Kingsbrae Horticultural Garden, the partners began 24 months of renovations that temporarily made them the second biggest employer in St. Andrews. When finished, they welcomed

Kingsbrae Arms is the second inn for owners David Oxford (left) and Harry Chancey Jr.

guests to a full-service inn with five luxurious rooms, three suites and all the amenities required for a designation by Canada Select as Canada's first five-star inn, membership in Relais & Châteaux and selection as a hideaway of the year in the Harper Report. Wide publicity flowed their way when they were invited to host the annual Canadian premier's conference in August 1997, filling up their guest rooms, serving two working lunches for the premiers and staging the farewell reception and garden party dinner, complete with fireworks over Passamaquoddy Bay.

"This is the realization of a vision," Harry said as he led a tour before settling us like old friends into the King Suite, offering the run of the house and preparing an intimate dinner for three. Kingsbrae Arms is five stars with a difference – the warmth and hospitality of its owners.

A crystal Austrian-style chandelier hangs in the entry foyer, a gift of Mrs. Flemer, with whom the owners worked closely so the world-class inn and the world-class gardens would complement each other. The entry foyer leads into a plush, paneled and beamed library. Off the side of the foyer is a drawing room elegant in cream and peach colors, with a grand piano on a platform for recitals at one end, fireplaces on either side and two comfortable seating areas in between. Across the foyer is the dining room, where the owners commissioned a handsome table for twelve in time for the premiers' conference. Beyond is a professional kitchen in the staff wing. A conference facility in the side carriage house includes a dining porch beneath a veranda.

The luxurious guest quarters ramble across the second and third floors and are just the right size and scale – room enough to spread out, but not so big as to rattle around in. They're comfortable, cozy and anything but sterile. Harry designed the Canadian birdseye and maple four-poster beds and the patterned mahogany armoires that were built by local craftsmen. Except for antiques from their own collection (and a set of Indian shutters imported from a friend's inn in East Hampton), all the furnishings, fabrics and accessories were obtained locally, with Harry orchestrating the way. Along with instant gas fireplaces, each room has TV, a writing desk, telephone with data port, three-way reading lamps, sumptuous seating, porcelain doorknobs and original art on the walls. There are double whirlpool tubs, glass-enclosed showers and five-foot marble vanities in the six bathrooms that could accommodate them. The finest Neutrogena toiletries, thick towels and embroidered waffle-weave sauna robes come with. Chocolate truffles are at bedside, complimentary beverages and snacks are in a little guest kitchen down the hall, and room service offers mini-meals. Rates include breakfast, and guests may order lunch and dinner in the dining room or on the terrace.

Whimsy and surprises abound. The Queen Room has not one but two queensize rice-carved poster beds, a sitting area beside the fireplace and a deep window seat with a chandelier – a great place for reading poetry, advises Harry, who has slept in every room in the house, as good innkeepers do. An antique matrimonial bed from Shanghai, original to the house that was built by a merchant involved in the China trade, plays a decorative role beneath an elliptical window in a third-floor hallway. On the third floor, the masculine Duke and its mirror-image companion, the feminine Duchess room, offer panoramic views of the horticultural gardens and Passamaquoddy Bay. Their fireplaces are ornamented with English garden tiles, each different. The Earl is a triple-gabled suite with a sitting area in one gable, a queen sleigh bed in another (with the window enveloped in a crown canopy), and the bathroom in a third gable. The King Suite has a kingsize four-poster with a draped canopy to keep out the morning light, fireplaces in bedroom and sitting room, and a wide balcony overlooking showy gardens in the rolling back yard that ends at a swimming pool. The marble in the bathroom extends to the vanity, shower, whirlpool tub and floor. These are the designs of which decorator magazines dream.

The food here is up to the rest of the experience. A "casual supper" with the innkeeper produced a salad topped with lobster meat, tiny marinated green and yellow beans, bowtie pasta primavera and a frozen lemon mousse with apricot coulis, topped off by chocolate-covered cherries in the library. Breakfast the next day included dainty cut-up fruit with yogurt sauce, a first-rate eggs benedict and hazelnut coffee. An optional five-course dinner with table wine costs $65. A four-course lunch with wine is available for $35.

The partners' vision has been masterfully realized. Kingsbrae Arms offers all the five-star extras the owners wanted. Happily, they're leavened with an easygoing personality that makes guests feel as if they're staying with friends at a magnificent country estate.

(506) 529-1897. Fax (506) 529-1197. Five rooms and three suites with private baths. Doubles, $225. Suites, $250 to $350. Off-season, $150. Two-night minimum weekends. Children over 10. No smoking.

A Hiram Walker Estate Heritage Inn, 109 Reed Ave., St. Andrews E0G 2X0.
The former summer home of the Hiram Walker Distillery family occupies eleven sylvan acres bordering the renowned Algonquin golf course at the edge town. Deer browse in the back meadow morning and evening, and there's a distinct sense of tranquility and privacy.

Elizabeth Cooney, who was born in St. Andrews and lately summered at the Algonquin with her family, returned from Toronto when her husband Roger planned to retire. Starting small in 1994 with five double rooms and private baths, she soon

Rear of A Hiram Walker Estate Heritage Inn opens onto new deck and pool.

converted most into suites and added five more for what she considers to be the grandest accommodations in New Brunswick. The Hiram Walker became the second five-star inn in St. Andrews in 1997 after the Cooneys started offering three meals a day to guests and installed the requisite swimming pool, an octagonal affair surrounded by decking, along with a hot tub topped by a pagoda.

Restored to its 1912 grandeur, the house has a somewhat forbidding English Norman facade in front and a more inviting French château facade in back. The elegant interior speaks of romance. "Love" is embroidered on throw pillows, a "honeymoon table" occupies a prime position beside the window in the dining room, and a crib holds lacy pillows in the upstairs hall. Fine Canadian art collected over the years enhances the walls, and decorative magnums of Canadian Club convey the Hiram Walker heritage.

Silk damask-covered sofas, an 1851 square grand piano, oriental carpets, crystal chandeliers, antique mahogany furniture and wood-burning fireplaces accent the inn's drawing room, library and music room, a dining room and a dream of a kitchen. An enclosed rear porch with windows onto the pool area allows dining al fresco. At the side is a handicapped-accessible room with two double canopy beds and a jacuzzi in one end of the room and a private porch at the other end.

Upstairs on the second and third floors are nine more rooms and suites with four-poster beds, gas fireplaces, marble baths and TV/VCRs. The seven with kingsize beds have double whirlpool tubs. Each comes with monogrammed towels, fine linens and duvets, Gilchrist & Soames toiletries, chocolate truffles, the inn's own bottled water and coffeemakers. Attractive in mauve florals, the premier Edward Chandler Suite has a step-up canopied four-poster king bed, a sitting area overlooking the pool and a marbleized tile bath with jacuzzi beneath the skylight. The opulent Hiram Walker Suite is notable for a Waterford crystal chandelier, armoire, wood-burning fireplace, two wing chairs in celadon green, a walk-in cedar closet and a double vanity and jacuzzi in the bathroom. The Albert Kahn Suite has a jacuzzi in one corner of the bedroom and a fireplace in another corner. The newest Meadow Suite, third floor rear, offers big dormer windows with a water view.

For the future, the inn has a carriage house with two kingsize suites downstairs and a three-bedroom suite upstairs. It also started phased construction in 1998 of eleven one-bedroom cottages with queen beds, whirlpool tubs and sitting rooms with fireplaces. Situated along the side of the property facing the golf course, each cottage is designed as a replica in miniature of the main house.

Amid much silver and crystal, Elizabeth serves breakfast by candlelight at a long table beside the dining-room fireplace. Fresh fruit with lemon yogurt in a brandy snifter precedes the main dish, perhaps gourmet french toast that her husband describes as "a picture on a plate" or scrambled eggs made with whipping cream, ham glazed in maple syrup and whole wheat toast spread "with my mummy's jams and jellies."

English tea is served in mid-afternoon. Candlelight dinners for house guests are available at 7 o'clock by reservation. The menu lists four entrées for $17.95 to $24.95, or a prix-fixe five-course meal for $49.95. Atlantic salmon poached with white wine and beef tenderloin with peppercorn sauce are house favorites. Elizabeth does all the cooking, and is proud that one reviewer said she had raised dining locally to an art form.

"We quickly found a thriving niche market," says Elizabeth, who caters to "people seeking romantic getaways." She bills her estate as "the jewel in the crown of historic St. Andrews."

(506) 529-4210 or (800) 470-4088. Fax (506) 529-4311. www.townsearch.com/ walkerestate. Two rooms and eight suites with private baths. May-October: doubles $155 to $165, suites $235 to $335. Rest of year: doubles $105 to $115, suites $125 to $175. No children. No smoking.

The Windsor House of St. Andrews, 132 Water St., Box 1209, St. Andrews E0G 2X0.

A third potential five-star establishment emerged in 1998 with the opening of this six-room inn and restaurant along the town's main street. The 1810 Georgian house, which once served as a Victorian inn and later a rooming house, was undergoing massive renovations at our 1997 visit. The owners are two Americans who summered in St. Andrews: Jay Remer of Delaware and Greg Cohane of New York. They planned to make St. Andrews their primary residence and start an antiques business, when friends badgered them into considering the downtown property. "We looked at it and put a down payment on it an hour later," Jay recalled in the midst of eighteen months of renovations.

Jay had restored about twenty properties in Wilmington and worked at Sothebys for five years, while Greg had a background in the restaurant industry, so they decided to combine talents on an inn.

Architectural sketches for the main floor showed a restored veranda, a 24-seat front dining room, a Victorian mahogany bar/parlor across the hall with leather banquettes along two walls, what Jay called "a really cool" rear billiards room with a nine-foot antique pool table from a Newport mansion and a 1939 Rockola jukebox, and an enclosed rear courtyard with a lap pool, hot tub and gardens. Four large bedrooms, each with a different mantle over the original fireplace, were being readied on the second floor, with verandas to be restored front and rear. Two suites with cathedral ceilings, sitting areas and gas fireplaces were planned for the third floor.

Designs called for four rooms with queen beds and two with a pair of double

The Pansy Patch offers lodging and dining in fairy-tale white stucco cottage.

sleigh beds each. All have sitting areas, telephones and TV/VCRs concealed in armoires. Jay said the furnishings, crafted by well-known New Brunswick cabinet makers, would be Georgian with a bit of Victorian. Décor was to be "relatively simple but quite decorative." The hallways were to be adorned by 19th-century English prints and paintings, part of the owners' extensive art collection.

The partners were looking to hire a top chef for the restaurant, which was to be open to the public for dinner and possibly lunch. Jay promised the food would be "as good as it gets up here." Dinners will include lobster, char-grilled steaks and continental cuisine. Food also will be served on both the front and back verandas and through room service.

A full breakfast features such specialties as eggs benedict with locally smoked salmon. They partners planned to offer single-malt scotches, quality wines and perhaps Cuban cigars in the bar.

(506) 529-3330 or (888) 890-9463. Fax (506) 529-4498. Six rooms with private baths. Doubles, $150 to $200. No children. No smoking. Open May to mid-January.

The Pansy Patch, 59 Carleton St., St. Andrews E0G 2X0.

Said to be the most photographed house in New Brunswick, this fairy-tale white stucco cottage, with small-paned windows, towers and turrets and a roof that looks as if it should be thatched, stands across the street from The Algonquin.

Built in 1912 by the superintendent of Canadian Pacific Hotels, it was fashioned after a Cotswold cottage. Michael and Marilyn O'Connor from Massachusetts bought it in 1994 from a Connecticut antiques dealer who ran the largest rare book store in Atlantic Canada on the main floor and offered four B&B bedrooms with shared baths upstairs.

The O'Connors have upgraded and expanded considerably. They converted the living room, with its beamed ceiling and huge fireplace, into the stunning **Gallery**

New Brunswick specializing in fine art and crafts. They opened up a stylish rear sunporch and veranda full of wicker for guests to enjoy the water views, and converted a small room nearby into a library and game room. In 1997 they added lunch and dinner service for guests and the public in a gallery dining room formal in burgundy and white and outside on the landscaped terraces, where the restored gardens put on quite a show.

They first renovated the upstairs into five guest rooms with private baths (most with showers only). One with a queen bed has a fireplace and another with a king bed has a window seat with a bay view. An attic suite with queen bed and sofabed includes a kitchenette. In 1996 the O'Connors acquired the adjacent Cory Cottage. It offers four more bedrooms with private baths. One upstairs room here has a double bed and a clawfoot tub beneath a window in the gable. Another with a queen bed adjoins a common room opening onto a balcony with a great water view; the sofabed in the common room can turn this into a two-bedroom suite, but the private bath is in the hall (robes provided). A downstairs room with a hunt theme offers a queen bed and oriental rugs.

The staff serves breakfast for guests in the main inn's sunroom on pansy-rimmed china at individual tables set with white linens and pansy napkin rings. The fare might be eggs benedict, mushroom quiche or egg bake, accompanied by homemade granola, muffins and croissants. Tea is served in the afternoon, and chocolates appear at nightly turndown. Rates include use of the pool and spa at The Algonquin.

The dining operation offers a short menu of starters and light meals, from crab bruschetta and caesar salad to lobster stew and seafood paella ($6.95 to $14.95). The dinner menu is even shorter: three appetizers, stuffed chicken breast and baked salmon for entrées and two desserts.

(506) 529-3834 or (888) 726-7972. Eight rooms and one suite with private baths. Doubles, $120 to $175. Suite, $190. Children accepted. Closed mid-October to mid-May. Entrées, $13.95 to $17.95. Lunch daily, 11:30 to 3. Dinner nightly, 4 to 9.

Treadwell Inn, 129 Water St., St. Andrews E0G 2X0.
The license plate on the MG sports convertible parked beside this waterfront B&B says simply "The Inn." Erected in 1820 by ship's chandler John Treadwell, the house once served as the town's customs house, as noted in a stained-glass window over an entrance. Annette Lacey and Jerry Mercer restored it into a B&B, winning a preservation award from the St. Andrews Civic Trust for their effort.

They opened in 1994 with four bedrooms with queen or two double beds covered with duvet comforters, private baths and sitting areas with period furnishings and TVs on the second floor. Two in the rear open onto a common second-floor deck overlooking the harbor. Two in front are up close to the busy street.

An efficiency suite was added later on the third floor with beamed and vaulted ceiling, a tiled whirlpool bath in the main room, a queen bed, a sitting area with a sofabed and two wicker chairs. French doors open onto a private balcony high above the water.

A nutritious continental breakfast of homemade muffins and breads is served in an eat-in country kitchen with panoramic view of the bay. The kitchen opens onto yet another deck overlooking the water. Guests relax in an attractive common room when they're not out on the decks or enjoying the waterside garden.

(506) 529-1011 or (888) 529-1011. Fax (506) 529-4826. Four rooms and an efficiency suite with private baths. Doubles, $85 to $125. Suite, $145. No children. No smoking.

Tara Manor Inn, 559 Mowat Drive (Highway 127), Box 30, St. Andrews E0G 2X0.

Locally alone in touting the AAA four-diamond rating in an area where everyone else claims Canada Select stars, this old-timer goes its own pleasant way. Once a private estate, Tara occupies twenty secluded acres crisscrossed by sculptured, century-old hedgerows on a hill overlooking Passamaquoddy Bay.

Innkeepers Norman and Sharon Rymmall started with two rooms in their residence in 1971, opened a dining room in 1980, and in the early 1990s added what Norman called six "ultra suites, the best in the Maritimes." Three more ultra suites were planned in 1998. The ones we saw had kingsize brass beds partitioned off from sitting areas containing a sofa, two chairs and a remote-control TV. The three secluded "ultra" suites with spacious patios overlooking the gardens command top-dollar, but we like better the panoramic view of the bay from the six "deluxe suites" off the third-floor balcony.

We booked one of the other sixteen rooms located in the old carriage house, boat house and servant's quarters, all with full baths and cable TV and comfortable indeed. Decor varies from French provincial to early American. All rooms are different but have striking draperies and Tara's signature collections of plates displayed in bays on the walls. Some have adjoining sunrooms or private balconies. The park-like grounds include a pleasant pool, a whirlpool spa and a tennis court.

(506) 529-3304. Fax (506) 529-4755. Sixteen rooms and nine suites with private baths. Doubles, $100 to $120. Deluxe rooms and suites, $125 to $158. Closed November-April.

The Algonquin, 184 Aldolphus St., St. Andrews E0G 2X0.

No report on St. Andrews lodging facilities is complete without mention of this landmark, one of the grand old Canadian Pacific hotels that span the country. The 240-room Algonquin preserves a tradition of gracious resort life that has nearly vanished.

One look at the turreted, Tudoresque hotel surrounded by lavish flower beds atop a knoll overlooking St. Andrews and Passamaquoddy Bay indicates that this is a special place. Add bellhops in kilts of the New Brunswick tartan (with incongruous-looking intercom beepers on their belts), the long lobby with comfortable peach chairs on which people actually are sitting, the enormous 375-seat Passamaquoddy Dining Room with windows onto the grounds, the book-lined Library Bar with nightly piano music, a large pool, tennis courts, a health club, a championship golf course and good conference facilities. The result is a resort of world renown.

The historic hotel, started by Boston businessmen in 1889 as a private club, fell on hard times in the post-war period. Rescued by the provincial government in 1974 and managed since by CP Hotels, the Algonquin is undergoing slow upgrading. Recently, it has completed a five-year refurbishing program for all rooms and added 50 efficiency mini-suites designed for families in a new wing. Those we saw had two queensize beds, two pillowed wicker chairs, a dining ell with refrigerator and microwave, a large bathroom loaded with amenities and a closet that lights automatically when the door is opened.

The new wing repeats some of the architectural traits of the older section, which is wonderfully quirky in decor and layout. As one guest volunteered, "I like to walk through the old part and stay in the new." Because the hotel was rebuilt with concrete walls, ceilings and floors after a 1914 fire, the rooms are unusually quiet.

The Algonquin is a landmark for visitors in St. Andrews.

Water views enhance rooms on the third and fourth floors. The best view of all is claimed by the roof garden, which frames Passamaquoddy Bay through flower-bedecked trellises and a turreted gazebo. It provides a sylvan retreat for reading and sunbathing.

Upwards of 500 people turn out for the Sunday brunch. The daily lunch buffet for $8.95 also is a treat. We enjoyed selecting from a lavish display of salads, cold salmon, peel-your-own shrimp, hot curried pork, halibut and pasta with shrimp, among others. The dinner menu features salmon from Passamaquoddy Bay.

With accommodations in the new wing, the hotel is now open year-round.

(506) 529-8823 or (800) 441-1414. Fax (506) 529-4194. A total of 240 rooms and suites with private baths. Rates EP. Mid-May to mid-October: doubles, $119 to $219. Efficiency mini-suites, $169 to $249. Suites, $189 to $349. Rest of year: efficiency suites, $79. Closed Christmas week.

Entrées, $22.95 to $25.95. Lunch and dinner daily in season, from 11:30.

Eastport/Lubec, Me.

Peacock House, 27 Summer St., Lubec 04652.

Once the sardine packing capital of the world, Lubec is home to the R.J. Peacock Canning Co., which now packs farmed salmon from pens in Passamaquoddy Bay and is still run by the Peacock family. Hence the name for this early Victorian beauty built in 1860 by a sea captain from England for his bride. Located on a residential side street, it passed by marriage into the Peacock family twenty years later. Four generations of Peacocks have lived here, including Carroll B. Peacock, a state senator, who entertained prominent guests – from Dwight Eisenhower to Edmund Muskie to Margaret Chase Smith – here over the years.

Today, owners Chet and Veda Childs and daughter, Debra Norris, entertain overnight guests in a nicely eclectic B&B.

The main floor is handsomely furnished with pieces "collected from 30 years of living around the world," says Chet. That helps explain the large gathering room, which is unexpectedly appointed in Southwest style, with TV and a bar found in an antiques shop near Fort Leavenworth, Kansas. Beyond are a library/living room with an organ and a fireplace, oriental rugs and, hidden in the foyer, an antique telephone booth.

The Peacock offers five bedrooms, all with private baths and a couple with glimpses of the water. The Margaret Chase Smith Suite, in which the Maine senator frequently stayed, has a sitting room with TV, a queensize brass bed and a spacious bath. Also pleasant is the Summer Room, furnished in wicker with a queen bed and white sheer curtains framing a water view.

Breakfast is served family style in the dining room at two seatings. From a repertoire of eighteen choices you might have an egg dish called cactus flowers, chocolate belgian waffles with raspberries and cream or strawberry-banana french toast. English tea is served in the afternoon on the side deck.

The innkeepers have restored the house to its latest 1937 renovation period and added a wing in back as family quarters. Chet calls that section "The Looney Bin" – you have to be to be in this business," he quips. Very much in business they are, however, with all the prerequisites and energy necessary for an AAA three-diamond rating.

(207) 733-2403. Five rooms with private baths. Doubles, $70. Suite, $80. Open mid-May to mid-October. Children over 7. Smoking restricted.

Weston House, 26 Boynton St., Eastport 04631.

You don't expect to find fig trees and cactus plants in the bedrooms of a B&B in Eastport. Nor do you expect to find transplanted Californians as the innkeepers.

Jett and John Peterson made the transition with ease after their arrival from the West Coast in 1985. "We love this area," says energetic Jett, now president of the Eastport Chamber of Commerce. "It's a very special world and we're very content in it."

She has furnished the majestic yellow, Federal-style house with flair and exotic plants, among them a potted fig tree in a corner of the Audubon Room, much greenery and the odd cactus plant here and there. The house, built in 1910 by Eastport lawyer-politician Jonathan Weston, commands a broad lawn atop a hill with a view of Cobscook Bay in the distance.

The five upstairs rooms share two-and-one-half baths. The bayview Audubon Room, in which John James Audubon stayed as the guest of the owner while awaiting passage to Labrador in 1833, has a queensize four-poster bed with eyelet-edged sheets, a couple of Audubon prints on the walls and lovely scatter rugs on polished floors. The front Weston Room offers a bay view, a kingsize poster bed, fireplace, TV and telephone. "You can sit up in bed and watch the freighters in the bay," Jett advises. Terrycloth robes are provided for guests to reach the full bath in the hall.

The rear of the house harbors three smaller guest rooms, sharing a bathroom with shower and a lavatory. The side Rose Room, named for its wallpaper, has a queen bed. The rear Abbot Room contains a double bed, and the adjacent Corner Room, a brass twin bed.

The public rooms are impressive. There's a library with books and TV. In a formal front parlor with a pressed-tin ceiling, afternoon tea and sherry or port are poured in front of the fireplace beside a century-old melodeon. Meals are served beneath baskets hung from the ceiling in a more casual kitchen-dining area. The front porch yields a view of the gardens with a glimpse of the distant water.

Jett Peterson wants guests to "enjoy all of our house." They certainly enjoy her breakfasts of fresh orange juice, melon balls with mint and silver-dollar pancakes doused with lingonberry or hot apricot syrup one day, peach-yogurt muffins and smoked salmon-scrambled eggs the next. "I believe eating is half visual," says Jett, explaining the garnishes she adds to the presentation.

Jett will dish up five-course gourmet dinners by reservation, the price determined by the menu. A $35 meal includes hot broccoli or chilled cucumber soup, an appetizer of smoked salmon, poached salmon with cumin mayonnaise and fresh salsa, a red lettuce salad with goat cheese and red grapes, and tirami su or a rhubarb tart based on an original recipe from her grandmother. Complimentary wine accompanies, and coffee and mints follow.

(207) 853-2907 or (800) 853-2907. Five bedrooms with shared baths. Doubles, $60 to $75. Single, $50.

The Inn at Eastport, 13 Washington St., Eastport 04631.

Bob and Brenda Booker have nicely upgraded this early 1800s Federal house, built by a sea captain who owned a large fleet of schooners anchored in Eastport, into a five-room B&B. She's on hand in the summer, while he commutes weekends from Massachusetts, where he has a computer service business.

The front foyer leads to an elegant double parlor with black marble hearths and wide-plank hardwood floors. There's a TV in one section and compact disc player in another.

Upstairs are two bedrooms above the double parlor and three smaller bedrooms in back. All have private baths, three in the hall. One in front has a queen canopy bed. Antique oak beds and country touches are the rule.

Brenda is known for elaborate breakfasts, starting with fresh fruit, orange juice and coffee cake or muffins. The main event could be scrambled eggs with salmon, lobster oscar, pecan waffles or wild blueberry pancakes. Nightly turndown brings liqueurs at bedside and mints on the pillows.

An outdoor hot tub on the rear deck is available for guests.

(207) 853-4307. Five rooms with private baths. Doubles, $55 to $65. Closed in winter except weekends.

Kilby House Inn, 122 Water St., Eastport 04631.

Built in 1887, this Victorian house overlooks Passamaquoddy Bay and Campobello Island. Gregory Noyes, a high school teacher who has an unbelievable commute to school at Steuben at the western end of Washington County, opened his house as a B&B "to survive," he concedes.

His ancestors lived here and family heirlooms abound. He has decorated the property as "an English house of the period" and resisted an oppressive look in favor of an open and airy feeling with light painted walls and lace curtains on the windows.

The main floor holds a double parlor with pocket doors between, a dining room with a formal table and cane-seat chairs, and a welcoming kitchen with a wood-burning stove.

Upstairs are five bedrooms with double or twin beds. Three have private baths. One in front with a canopy poster bed enjoys a bay view, as does a side room. A rear room with private bath is considered the nicest.

Gregory prepares a full breakfast in summer, perhaps strata with coffee cake or

Weston House occupies handsome Federal-style structure overlooking Eastport.

blueberry pancakes. Weekday guests in winter are on their own, since Greg leaves early for his long commute.

(207) 853-0989 or (800) 435-0989. Three rooms with private baths and two rooms with shared bath. Doubles, $55 to $75. No children. No smoking.

Dining Spots

St. Andrews

L'Europe, 48 King St., St. Andrews.

Showy flowers and hanging baskets grace the alpine-looking façade of this rustic low brown structure we remember as a dance hall in our teen years. Copper pots and pottery bedeck the white stucco walls of the charming little dining rooms. Beamed ceilings, hanging lamps covered with fabric, crisp linens, fresh flowers and candles in antique candle holders make you feel you could be in the heart of Europe. Since 1984, Alex Ludwig and his wife Anita, the chef, have been serving up some of the best food in town from an extensive menu.

Our dinner started with a good, hearty, complimentary pâté and farmer's bread, followed by an interminable wait for the salad plate bearing carrot and potato salads. Fresh seafood is the specialty, including arctic char, Atlantic perch and fried oysters at our latest visit. We liked the whole pork tenderloin flambéed in brandy, an enormous affair served with small potato balls and cauliflower, and the rack of lamb with a superb garlic sauce. Options range from wiener schnitzel to filet mignon with morels.

The desserts of choice were a chocolate truffle torte (a huge slab of cake topped by a truffle), peach cream cheesecake, and butter cream mocha cake.

(506) 529-3818. Entrées, $16.50 to $34.50. Dinner nightly except Monday, 6 to 11. Closed in winter except for Christmas week.

The Evening Star at Tara Manor Inn, 559 Mowat Drive, St. Andrews.

Crystal chandeliers, burgundy draperies, pink linens and live piano music create an elegant, big-city setting in this country-inn dining room with a fancy name. And yet, from a window table as we watched the shadows lengthening on the lawns outside, we were entertained by all the rabbits hopping around.

The extensive and steadfast continental dinner menu includes a stellar New Brunswick fiddlehead soup and entrées like turkey stir-fry, chicken à l'orange, coquilles St. Jacques, poached salmon, roast leg of lamb and delmonico steak. Our latest dinner here began with a complimentary cheese spread with crackers and crab bisque, followed by good, small caesar salads. Main courses were an excellent stuffed trout with crisp carrots and snow peas, and a curried shrimp and chicken dish ringed by rice with little mounds of coconut, chutney and almonds. Curries are a house specialty, and on another occasion, we tried the curried lamb and rice (much more rice than lamb), served with a tray of sliced almonds, chutney and bananas in sour cream, and a braised citrus pork with rice, green beans and almonds. A light blueberry cheesecake and Spanish coffee were worthy endings.

(506) 529-3304. Entrées, $13.95 to $22.75. Dinner nightly, 6 to 9:30. Closed mid-October to late May.

The Gables, 143 Water St., St. Andrews.

A pleasant, three-level rear deck shaded by a chestnut tree beside the water is the most appealing part of this restaurant, lately under the ownership of Ted Michener, an artist and cartoonist whose works grace the walls and the menu. In nice weather, it's far preferable to the interior with a small dining room and bar, a large licensed dart room with pool tables in front, and a pub upstairs.

The all-day menu offers casual, contemporary fare, with a few specials for lunch or dinner. Among the possibilities are caesar salad with smoked salmon, a haddock burger, spanakopita and a Mideastern plate. On a recent afternoon, one of us liked the zesty gazpacho and an appetizer of smoked salmon, served with a baguette. The other splurged for the lobster club sandwich with choice of tossed salad or french fries. At an earlier visit, we quite enjoyed a casual waterside supper of bruschetta, a Greek salad that unfortunately lacked the advertised calamata olives, a good caesar salad and a large bowl of steamed mussels. Praline ripple cheesecake, kiwi-lemon meringue pie and bumbleberry cobbler are among the desserts.

(506) 529-3440. Entrées, $9.50 to $17.95. Open daily, 11:30 to 11.

Eastport

Eastport Lobster & Fish Co., 167 Water St., Eastport.

Fish and sardine canning started in this country in the 1870s in Eastport on the wharf upon which the Eastport Lobster & Fish Co. stands today. For twenty years the site of the Cannery restaurant, it stood idle in the 1990s until Frank Crohn reopened the property in 1997 after extensive renovations.

It's quite an establishment. The main restaurant is in two pine-paneled rooms on the upper floor. The lower level, former home to the Cannery, is now a bar with more casual pub and dining available. It opens onto a wharf with picnic tables, a lobster pound, the Trap and Buoy Shop (where those so inclined can have a lobster buoy personalized for $18.95), and the Whistling Pig Gift Shop. Whale watching and charter boat excursions leave daily from the wharf.

The upstairs dining area, with big windows onto the water, has the trappings of fine dining: captain's chairs at well-spaced tables set with cream-colored cloths, fresh flowers and cut-glass oil lamps. The fare is a cut above the area's norm and quite good, according to locals. The all-day menu runs from haddock and chicken sandwiches through lobster salad (on a bed of mesclun greens), a smoked salmon

Outdoor diners at The Gables eat beside water amid maritime memorabilia.

platter, steamed mussels and lobster stew. The specialty local seafood is poached, pan-seared or baked, as in crab cakes with lemon butter, scallops with white wine and herbs, and salmon with dill sauce. Bouillabaisse is a signature item. You also can get a chicken brochette, grilled porterhouse steak or a kabob of organic vegetables on a bed of couscous. Desserts include blueberry pie, seasonal fruit tarts and assorted Maine-made ice creams. A good wine list is priced in the teens.

(207) 853-6006 or (888) 327-8767. Entrées, $11.95 to $17.95. Lunch and dinner daily in season, 11:30 to 9.

La Sardina Loca, 28 Water St., Eastport.

Housed in the former A&P store where Eleanor Roosevelt shopped for groceries while summering on Campobello, this is billed as the easternmost Mexican restaurant in the United States. "The crazy sardine" name was chosen to give the sardine back to the community after many packing plants had closed, according to owner Chuck Maggiani. His son Lenny, the chef, married a woman from Mexico, which accounts for the theme.

Wait until you see the place – a double storefront with big round tables, plastic patio chairs, a Christmas tree hanging upside down from the ceiling, posters, sign boards and a dark cantina bar in back. It's crazy and colorful, to say the least.

Blackboard specials at the entry proclaimed lobster and steak dinners for $11.95 at a recent visit. The regular menu might offer rancho grande bifstek with salad, baked potato and corn on the cob and a Rosarita beach lobster dinner, Mexican style, with salad, rice, beans and tortillas. Of course, you can order chicken fajitas, burritos, enchiladas, tostadas, nachos and even pizzas. Start, if you dare, with La Sardina Loca, billed as herring steaks with hot chiles on a bed of lettuce with crackers, onions and sour cream. Dessert could be strawberry delight, kahlua parfait or caffe loca with tequila and kahlua.

(207) 853-2739. Entrées, $4.95 to $12.95. Dinner nightly except Tuesday, 4 to 10.

Diversions

Life is simple and oriented to the water in these parts, although St. Andrews adds a touch of sophistication for those who wish. Because of the enormous range of the tides, a wide variety of marine life can be found along the shore between high and low tides. Walk the beaches or explore the coastline to find shells, mussels, sea urchins, starfish, sand dollars and such. Traditionally the area's biggest tourist attraction has been the Roosevelt summer home on Campobello. The new Kingsbrae Horticultural Garden in St. Andrews and the upgraded Algonquin golf course promise to be other major draws.

Roosevelt Campobello International Park, Campobello Island.

From 1883 when he was a newborn until 1921 when he was stricken by polio here, Franklin D. Roosevelt spent most of his summers on Campobello. Here are the cottage and the grounds where the Roosevelts vacationed, the waters where they sailed, and the beaches, bogs and woods where they hiked and relaxed. The park reception center provides a touching introduction both to the Roosevelts' tenure here and to the island. Movies like "Beloved Island" are shown on the hour; "Campobello, the Outer Island" was particularly helpful in understanding the unusual nature of this area.

The Roosevelt Cottage, a 34-room red house high above Passamaquoddy Bay, is one of the most pleasant we've seen. The house still looks lived in, almost as if the Roosevelts had simply left for a quick boat ride to Eastport to pick up groceries. You can walk right into most rooms, which are human-size rather than grand. Unobtrusive hostesses answer questions or leave you on your own. Most of the furnishings were used by the family. You'll see the megaphone used for hailing latecomers to meals, a collection of canes, the large chair used to carry the handicapped President, the family telescope, and eighteen simple but inviting bedrooms. Outside are lovely gardens and paths to the shore. Next door, the main floor of the Victorian **Hubbard Cottage** is open periodically for tours.

(506) 752-2922. Roosevelt Cottage open daily 9 to 5, Memorial Day to mid-October. Park open year-round. Free.

Lubec. The one-time sardine capital of the world is down to one remaining sardine packing plant. Other canneries now process and pack salmon harvested from pens in Cobscook Bay. Lubec Landmarks Inc. publishes a brochure for a walking tour of twelve historic landmarks. The **Sardine Village Museum,** billed as the only one of its kind, is located in an old barn on Route 189 near the turnoff to West Quoddy Head. The owner-curator guides visitors through the process of transforming herring into sardines. Open in summer, Wednesday-Friday 2 to 5, Saturday 2 to 3:45; adults, $3.

Curiously, the easternmost point of land in the United States is at West Quoddy Head in South Lubec. The **West Quoddy Light,** an 1809 landmark with red and white candy stripes, stands atop a cliff pounded by the open ocean. The 483-acre **Quoddy Head State Park** offers trails to the lighthouse, an island and a bog. A raised boardwalk goes through the rare coastal plateau peat bog.

Eastport. America's smallest city is evolving from an isolated Down East fishing village into something of a tourist destination. After the great fire of 1886 destroyed the downtown and much of the surrounding area, Eastporters rebuilt within one year with impressive – and fire-resistant – brick and granite structures. Many are listed on the National Historic Register, and sixteen landmarks are outlined in an Eastport walking tour guide.

The waterfront is the scene of port and aquaculture development. Whale watch expeditions are offered. The annual Old Home Week over the Fourth of July draws thousands of returnees from across the country for five days of activity, culminating in a parade featuring the governor and congressmen and an evening fireworks display. **Stage East**, corner of Dana and Water streets, presents five productions a season from April through November. More than 100 plant species and nearly 30 bird species have been observed at **Shackford Head,** a new park with three miles of craggy shoreline jutting into Cobscook Bay.

Shopping. On the outskirts of Eastport at 85 Washington St., **Raye's Mustard Mill** is a must stop. The country's last remaining stone-ground mustard mill produces the mustards in which the area's sardines used to be packed. Various mustards, other Maine-made foods and crafts are on sale in the Pantry Store, which has a new Coffee Express bar in front. Jim Blankman processes farm-raised salmon, along with smoked mussels and rainbow trout at **Jim's Smoked Salmon,** 37 Washington St. Cappuccino and espresso, teas and sandwiches are offered along with antiques and artworks at **Timeless Reflections** frame shop. Works of an artist who painted in Belize are shown at **Le Petite Gallery.** Don Sutherland produces monumental pots and vases, some with amazing blue glaze, at **Earth Forms,** a most unusual pottery at 5 Dana St. In Lubec, **Cottage Garden** out North Lubec Road is a fascinating enterprise. Gretchen and Alan Mead share their many talents with visitors to their showy perennial and herb gardens. Their Herb Shop is full of dried flower wreaths, birdhouses, framed bird and botanical prints, hanging potpourri and even painted garden benches, all made by the owners.

St. Andrews. Settled in 1783 by United Empire Loyalists who floated their dismantled homes here from Castine, Me. (they were rebuilt and three are still standing), St. Andrews is said to have more examples of fine New England Colonial architecture than any other Canadian town. Everything from Cape Cod cottages to saltboxes to large Georgian houses with Federal detailing can be seen scattered across a grid of neatly squared lots laid out by town planners two centuries ago. More than 250 structures, many of them legacies of the prosperous era when St. Andrews was a port of call on the West Indies trade route, are over a century old. The 1824 **Greenock Presbyterian Church** looks like any white Colonial New England church, except for the unique bright green oak tree carved on the exterior beneath its spire. Other St. Andrews churches, particularly those along King Street, are architecturally interesting.

Other attractions are as diverse as the famed **Algonquin Golf Course** (contrary to belief, not patterned or named after the Old Course in St. Andrews, Scotland, but currently undergoing a $7 million upgrading for "serious golf"), **Huntsman Marine Science Center and Aquarium,** the new **Atlantic Salmon Center,** and the landmark **St. Andrews Blockhouse,** a two-story National Historic Site built of hand-hewn timbers in 1813 to protect St. Andrews from American privateers. Costumed guides provide tours of the **Sheriff Andrews House,** an 1820 Neoclassic historic site.

The bar to **Minister's Island**, which we drove nervously across a decade ago, is under seventeen feet of water at high tide, so you don't want to get stranded out there. Spearheaded by Canadian Pacific Hotels & Resorts (The Algonquin), a local advisory committee is working with the provincial government on long-range plans to develop the 500-acre island as a destination site for the public. Visitors on guided tours get to peek at **Covenhoven,** the shuttered nineteen-bedroom estate of CP railroad magnate Sir William Van Horne, which is under restoration as a museum, and at the bathhouse for a tidal swimming pool. The architect-designed barn is envisioned as an equestrian center and a petting zoo. Hiking and riding trails are in the works. Two-hour tours are timed twice daily in summer according to the tides.

Ross Memorial Museum, an imposing red brick Neo-Classic house built in 1824 at 188 Montague St., is a true house museum. It was acquired and given to the town by Henry Phipps Ross and his wife Sarah as a means to display their extensive collections of decorative arts and furniture. Ross, a onetime Episcopal minister in Providence, R.I., and his wife, the daughter of the Bradstreet of Dun & Bradstreet in New York, summered here from 1902 to 1945. Guided tours, Monday-Saturday 10 to 4:30, mid-June to early October; closed Monday after Labor Day.

Shopping. Stores here come and go, but some endure and more good ones pop up every year. FDR sometimes rode the mail boat into St. Andrews to discuss politics with town notables at our favorite **Cockburn's Corner Drug Store,** still a fixture at Front and King streets. **Stickneys Wedgwood Store,** founded in 1842, is the oldest Wedgwood store in North America and the oldest store in St. Andrews. **Cottage Craft,** on the waterfront at Town Square, with brightly colored skeins of wool draped around its cork fence in front, shows knit goods in lovely colors, knitting bags (one shaped like a house in which the door opens), and the neatest collection of mittens for kids you ever saw. **Boutique La Baleine** stocks cute things like stuffed animals, cards, apparel and a large toy section. We were struck by the $195 sweaters bearing images of a whale and a covered bridge at **Serendipin' Art,** which shows local handicrafts and has a jewelry and metal smithing studio on site. We coveted some of Richard Gill's unique sculpted clay wall plaques and murals, from a traditional lobster scene to an intricate rendering of the Algonquin hotel, at the **Tom Smith Pottery** on Water Street. Tom's wife Ellen, who manages the studio, makes the drawstring bags for Tom's handsome raku teabowls. **Beacon House Casuals,** on the ground floor of the Treadwell Inn, carries Tilly Endurables among its wares.

Extra-Special ⸻

Kingsbrae Horticultural Gardens, 220 King St., St. Andrews.

Lucina and John Flemer, who sold the house that became the new Kingsbrae Arms inn, also donated an adjacent 27-acre property and funds to operate this world-class horticultural garden, expected to be in full bloom in the spring of 1998. Work started in 1995 to re-create formal gardens, naturalized areas, butterfly sections, an aviary, a knot garden, therapy garden, orchards, a seaside theme area and a labyrinth on a magnificent hilltop site sloping toward Passamaquoddy Bay. Andreas Haun, executive director, said 900 varieties of perennials and 800 of trees would complement existing mature trees and wildflower fields. One of four manor houses originally on the property, the Edward Maxwell-designed Les Goelands, once owned by Lucinda Flemer's parents, is the site of a tea room serving sandwiches, salads and desserts, a gift shop and an art gallery, with an artist in residence. The gardens are a joint venture between town, province and the Flemers.

(506) 529-3335. Open daily in season, 9 to dusk. Adults, $6.

Peter Thibodeau Photo

Moose-watching is a major pastime in Moosehead Lake region.

Greenville/Moosehead Lake, Me.
The Maine You Remember

The drive through interior Maine on Route 6 and 15, the only road into the Moosehead Lake region, seems endless. But the intrepid traveler need not despair. Suddenly, the road crests atop a hill and now, before you in all its glory, unfolds the majesty of Moosehead, the Northeast's largest lake.

At the near end lies Greenville (population 2,200), the region's only town of note. On all sides are mountains – small ones, to be sure, but enough to alter the landscape of what to the south had been essentially rolling flatlands. The sky-blue glacier lake spreads its tentacles like the antlers of a moose head around islands and into coves. Think of an inland sea stretching into a forest of green, rather like a freshwater version of Penobscot Bay.

The pristine lake, shaped vaguely like a moose head, is 40 miles long and 20 miles across at its widest. It's up to 300 feet deep at the base of the landmark Mount Kineo cliffs. Most of the 400 miles of shoreline, owned by paper companies more interested in raw lumber than in vacation condominiums, is undeveloped. Forestry and recreation are the area's industries.

Moosehead's mystique has always been that of a sportsman's paradise in the North Woods wilderness. The area has long been a mecca for hunters and fishermen. Increasingly, its lure is broadening to embrace nature and wildlife lovers, hikers, rafters and canoeists in summer, and cross-country skiers, downhill skiers and snowmobilers in winter.

The area is poised for what one proponent calls "eco-travel, the tourism of the future," for those who like to pursue sports year-round in the great outdoors. Already the rough co-exists with the refined. National publicity has been accorded the original Road Kill Cafe, a restaurant poking fun at the pretensions of some of its peers, and the Lodge at Moosehead Lake, an inn revising the standards for creature comforts and style in the Maine woods. New owners are improving the Squaw Mountain ski area. True, much of the area remains raw and primeval. But its virgin veneer is leavened by a gentleness that the great lake gives to the mountains, by a subtle sophistication that escapes other north woods destinations.

Moose-watching is a mania, and few visitors leave without spotting at least a few, front and center during a moose cruise or safari or unexpectedly, simply feeding beside the road. The region stages the annual Moosemania, a month of moose-related activities in late spring. At least three shops convey a moose theme.

This is the natural state of "the Maine you remember," as the Moosehead Lake Region Chamber of Commerce touts it. Just you and the moose, and a few others who like to get away from the crowds.

Inn Spots

The Lodge at Moosehead Lake, Lily Bay Road, Greenville 04441.

High up Blair Hill overlooking Squaw Mountain and Moosehead Lake, this small hostelry sets a standard for low-key luxury in the wilds. Jennifer and Roger Cauchi, former resort and hotel managers in the Poconos, converted a Shingle-style summer home into a light and airy refuge. From the ultra-comfortable common rooms and guest quarters to some fairly exotic meals, guests are in for a treat.

As you enter the foyer with its artful arrangement of fishing creels and other piscatory accessories, you know this is no ordinary inn. The foyer leads to a broad living room, its windows opening onto a full-length deck where you can look down on the lake activity in the distance and watch a sunset that's apt to be spec-

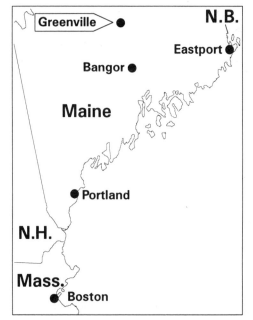

tacular. Here and elsewhere, the high-style lodge decor is striking for flair employed with restraint. Adjoining the comfortable living room, filled with books and magazines, is a smaller parlor/library called the Toby Room. Its lineup of toby jugs reflects Roger's British heritage. Beyond is a summery dining room where breakfast and, at certain times, dinner are served to house guests. Opening onto a patio on the lower level is the Moosehead Room, a large game room with English darts and a billiards table.

A neat little "Gone Fishing" sign, complete with a miniature rod and two tiny wooden fish, hangs gracefully on the door of each of the five bedrooms and three suites. The lodge's version

Elegant woodsy decor enhances living room at The Lodge at Moosehead Lake.

of a "Do Not Disturb" sign, it flips over to say "In Camp." Utter comfort with a wildlife theme prevails within. Each room has a TV/VCR in a cabinet above a gas-lit fireplace outlined in stone, a private bath with jacuzzi for two, hand-carved four-poster queensize beds with fine linens, plush sitting areas and such amenities as toiletries, hair dryers, ironing boards, terrycloth robes and little Coleman ice chests.

Our quarters in the Bear Room came with plush carpeting, an assortment of loveseats and wing chairs richly upholstered in woodsy fabrics, and a private deck. Small black climbing bears were carved upon each bed post. The mirror in the bathroom, with a bear head on top, was carved to match. Whimsical bear accents (such as small needlepoint rugs depicting black bears, one on either side of the bed) enhanced the room at every turn.

Jennifer repeated the sophisticated decorative scheme with other wildlife motifs in other rooms. There are loon books and a loon-patterned table in the Loon Room, pillows in the shape of fish in the Trout Room, and antlers holding the valances in the Moose Room. Expect to find such decorative accents as a twig birdhouse in a corner, twig branches and pine cones outlining the hall windows, and full-length curtains draped smartly like an upside-down L in the bedrooms. The latest handiwork is twig stenciling – twigs running around the tops of walls in intricate patterns. These are the designs of which decorator magazines are made.

The ultimate accommodations are three fireplaced "retreat suites" in the adjacent structure, a converted boathouse. On two levels, they have sunken living rooms with lake views through sliding glass doors that open onto a deck and, below, a landscaped patio set into rocks and gardens along the hillside. Our recent stay in the Katahdin included a step-up bed with a moose antler canopy and a large, mirrored bathroom with double vanity, double jacuzzi, fireplace and crystal chandelier. Birch branches formed decorative molding around the vaulted ceiling. The other two suites are notable for unique queensize beds hung on boom chains from the ceiling and swaying lengthwise to rock occupants to sleep. "It rocks like a cradle and you sleep like a baby," one guest told Roger.

A deer bounded across the back lawn as we prepared for breakfast the next morning. Roger served a "wake-up cocktail," which turned out to be a small mixed berry milkshake in a wine glass, and soufléed eggs garnished with cantaloupe, pineapple and wild blueberries. A choice of juices and toasting breads awaited on a side table. Other entrées include Finnish pancakes, breakfast pizza and stuffed french toast with cream cheese and fruits.

Dinner here is a paced experience that can best be described as romantic. Prepared by Roger and Jennifer, it is served to house guests at 7:30 two nights a week in season and five nights a week in winter and spring. The night's menu is recited, and the four-course meal is prix-fixe ($40).

Rush-seat chairs are at well-spaced, green-linened tables beneath a pitched ceiling in the airy dining room. The candles are in wrought-iron holders shaped like moose. The "flowers" on the tables may be pussy willows or more colorful exotica from Jennifer's extensive gardens. Jazz, New Age and classical music plays in the background, interspersed occasionally with loon calls and sounds of the wild.

We started with a cup of the dynamite apple cider and onion soup, a house specialty, and the house salad, on this night described simply as broccoli. Presented nouvelle style, the small pieces of broccoli were tossed with onions, walnuts and raisins and carried a distinct bite. Main courses were sautéed chicken breast poached in white wine and oregano and sherried seafood over moose-shaped puff pastry. Side plates produced samplings of the day's three vegetables: braised celery, sautéed carrots with cumin and sesame seeds, and green beans with walnuts.

Desserts from the "moose cart" included raspberry pudding, rum cake and a novel chocolate mousse maximus with a surprise in the middle. The food was assertive, the service friendly and, as the sun set across Moosehead Lake, the setting spectacular.

The innkeepers have kept the lodge small so guests can be pampered in style. And style their lodge has in spades.

(207) 695-4400. Fax (207) 695-2281. www/lodgeatmooseheadlake.com. Five rooms and three suites with private baths. Doubles, $165 to $250. Suites, $275 to $350. Two-night minimum stay. Rates are B&B in summer and fall; dinner included in winter and spring. No children. No smoking. Dinner at 7:30, Wednesday and Saturday in season, five nights in off-season.

Greenville Inn, Norris Street, Box 1194, Greenville 04441.

Old money and solid furnishings prevail in this established inn, built as a summer home in 1895 by a wealthy lumber baron. Embossed Lincrusta walls and gas lights convey an air of antiquity in the halls, as does the old telephone fixture on the wall. A large spruce tree painted on a leaded glass window adorns the stairway landing. Carved mantels, mosaic and English tiles surround the fireplaces.

Foremost a restaurant of distinction run by Elfie Schnetzer and her two grown offspring (see Dining Spots), the inn recently added to its lodging business with six deluxe new cottages clustered off to the side on a slope above the inn. Each has a sitting area, TV and front porch. Four have queensize beds and two have a full and a twin bed. Four more bedrooms with king or queen beds and private baths and two suites are available in the main inn. Here, the best glimpses of the water are obtained from the Master Suite in front. It has a sitting room with fireplace and TV, a queen bedroom, and a spacious tiled bath with a deep tub and a separate needle-spray marble shower. Another prime accommodation is a two-bedroom

Greenville Inn occupies restored 1895 lumber baron's mansion.

suite in the attached Carriage House, which offers a queen bed and a sitting area with a wood stove and TV, a second bedroom with double bed, and a private deck with mountain views.

The rooms are nicely furnished in uncluttered Victorian style and beds are covered with colorful quilts. Ours had one of the inn's two kingsize beds and one of its two fireplaces, but had only one chair and a clawfoot tub without a shower. Our stay in the inn proved somewhat confining, what with the only common room doubling as a pre-dinner gathering place and bar for restaurant-goers and the few chairs on the side porch being in full view and earshot of people eating in the dining rooms. We don't know who was more disconcerted – we, blocking their views, or they, spoiling our quiet reading time. (Next time we'll avoid the problem by staying in one of the new cottages.)

At breakfast the next morning, classical music muffled conversations in the three small dining rooms. The innkeepers, nowhere in evidence, had put out a European buffet spread of fresh fruit, cereals, bagels, croissants, breads, ham and cheese. It was perfectly filling, but seemed rather impersonal.

The Schnetzers offer dinners by reservation for house guests in the off-season.

(207) 695-2206 or (888) 695-6000. Four rooms, two suites and six cottages with private baths. Late June to mid-October, doubles $115 to $195. Late spring and early fall: $95 to $165. November to mid-May $85 to $155. Children over 7.

Evergreen Lodge, Route 15, HCR 76, Box 58, Greenville 04441.

Five miles south of town is this attractive, all-cedar structure, built as a physician's home and set back from the road amid evergreens and birches and showy flower gardens on 30 acres.

New owners Bruce and Sonda Hamilton from Maryland have added their personal touch to this comfortable B&B with six bedrooms, each with private bath. The rooms, paneled in varieties of cedar, are outfitted with king, queen, two double or twin beds to suit a clientele that varies from couples to families with older children. Colorful quilts and lots of pillows enhance the contemporary lodge-style décor. Bedtime mints are on the pillows.

Gas log stoves have been added to the two first-floor bedrooms, each with kingsize bed. Sonda redid the Moose Room with a moose theme, incorporating a green quilt with a moose design on the queen bed and twin bed.

Guests gather in two cheery sitting rooms with TVs and fireplaces. Breakfast is served at a pair of glass-topped tables for six in a sunroom with a greenhouse section overlooking the perennial gardens. The fare includes fresh fruit, pastries, breakfast meats, pancakes, eggs or puff french toast, "and people can come back for seconds," Sonda advises. Moose and deer are sighted occasionally on the property.

The Hamiltons keep their lodge open year-round, and offer dinner by reservation from December to May.

(207) 695-3241 or (888) 624-3993. Fax (207) 695-3084. Six rooms with private baths. Doubles, $65 to $90. Children over 12. No smoking.

The Sawyer House, Lakeview Street, Box 521, Greenville 04441.

A view of East Cove Harbor, a residential in-town location and comfortable accommodations commend this small B&B in an 1849 farmhouse long occupied by the Sawyer family, who were boat captains on Moosehead Lake and whose matriarch weathered 100 Maine winters. Pat Zieten, a former local newspaper reporter who seems to know everyone and everything going on in town, and her husband Hans, a plumber, offer three bedrooms and enthusiastic hospitality.

Our quarters in the main-floor Captain Fred Sawyer Suite could not have been more commodious. The large room contained a kingsize bed at one end, a sofabed in a sitting area at the other, light patterned wallpaper and fresh flowers. The bathroom held a collection of amenities, from shampoo to toothpaste to disposable razors. Two smaller rooms upstairs have private baths, queen beds, mini-print wallpapers, thick carpeting and beribboned bonnets hung on the walls here and there. "Hans wanted to panel but I'm partial to wallpaper," says Pat, who prevailed. Her

Breakfast for two at The Sawyer House.

light and airy decorating scheme complements the wallpaper, and vice-versa.

Guests spread out in a common room with dining area, a stylish side deck beside the woods and a front porch overlooking the harbor. The Zietens and their sons occupy a separate section of the house.

Popovers are Pat's trademark at breakfast, a treat that begins with orange juice and fresh fruit and ends with a choice of eggs, pancakes or french toast. We liked the scrambled eggs with chain-link sausages and thick homemade toast, accompanied by frequent insights and suggestions from the ebullient hostess.

(207) 695-2369. Fax (207) 695-3086. Doubles, $65. Suite, $75. Children over 12. No smoking.

The Lakeview House, Lakeview Street, Box 524, Greenville 04441.

They got their feet wet for five years operating a small B&B here with shared baths. But Concetta and Dick Edwards realized they would be better off with private baths and a lakefront location. So they sold the Whitman House and resurfaced in 1997 in a modified Victorian farmhouse. Here they offer three bedrooms with private baths, queensize four-poster beds and lake views in two directions.

Said rooms are simple but tasteful. The premier front room has a queen poster bed, a bathroom with pedestal sink and shower, a bureau, one chair and a TV. The bedside tables in a side room are handpainted with loons and a view of the islands in the lake visible through the windows. A third room on the other side of the house has an iron bed and a ceramic tile shower in a cubbyhole open to the room, with separate lavatory in a former closet.

The main floor holds a guest living room with a desk and three chairs, and a richly wainscoted dining room open to a country kitchen with a corner fireplace. Breakfast includes french toast, pancakes or a popover with scrambled eggs and cheese along with juice, a fresh fruit plate, yogurt and sausage.

Adirondack chairs occupy a corner of the side lawn, a prime vantage point for observing the lake. "The view up the lake is quite a surprise," Concetta says. The house is on a corner lot and only those who round the corner know there's such a view beyond East Cove Harbor in front. The flower and vegetable gardens are a visual treat as well.

(207) 695-3543. Three rooms with private baths. Doubles, $95 to $125. Closed Columbus Day through June. Children over 12. No smoking.

Pleasant Street Inn, Pleasant Street, Box 1261, Greenville 04441.

A rather unusual spired turret on the fourth floor tops this rambling 1890 Victorian house on a residential side street. Sue Bushey, an attorney, converted a private home into a B&B that became so time-consuming she was planning to give up her law practice.

Victoriana reigns throughout, especially on the main floor where lace curtains cover the windows in the dining room and five Victorian sofas and loveseats provide seating in the living room. There's more seating on wraparound porches outside.

Upstairs are a television room with a collection of videos and eight bedrooms, four with private baths and four others sharing two baths. Rooms vary widely in size and style, but the rates for each are the same. All have queen beds except for one with twins. The front second-floor bedroom is done up in white wicker and retains its original bathroom fixtures. Another that Sue calls "my sort of African room" has a renovated bath and is outfitted with a floral bedspread and two wing chairs. Two wing chairs and pink walls that turned out more vivid than she expected highlight a front room on the third floor, while its neighbor has a large bathroom with a curved wall and marble shower. The most unusual room is a sitting room with a futon sofa and distant view of the lake in the fourth-floor turret.

Local artworks are displayed and for sale throughout the house. Sue, a gourmet cook, offers elaborate breakfasts. Fresh fruit cup and blueberry-banana-walnut pancakes with ham were the fare the morning of our visit. French toast made with homemade cinnamon-raisin bread was on tap the next day. Sue offers weekend lunches and dinners to house guests by reservation in the off-season.

(207) 695-3400. Four rooms with private baths and four rooms with shared baths. Doubles, $75, mid-May through October; $65 rest of year. Children over 12. No smoking.

The Devlin House, Lily Bay Road, Box 1102, Greenville 04441.

Ruth Devlin and her late husband, Jim, built this large contemporary ranch on Blair Hill specifically to run as a B&B. They'd become enamored with the setting during their tenure running the acclaimed Lakeview Manor restaurant next door in the building that is now the Lodge at Moosehead Lake.

"Isn't this peaceful, quiet and gentle?" Ruth asked rhetorically as we took in the stunning lake vista through the sliding doors and windows of her living room, while a hummingbird hovered outside at a feeder. The main floor is devoted to the owner's quarters (Ruth also runs a computerized bookkeeping business from a front room).

Upstairs are two large guest rooms with kingsize beds, full baths, thick carpeting, color TVs and comfortable sitting areas for reading or taking in the view. Downstairs in the walkout lower level is a suite with a double bed and two twins, a huge bath and a family room with two sturdy couches, three lounge rockers and a big TV.

Ruth serves a hearty breakfast between 6 and 9. "I'll feed people at 6 if they're going rafting," she says cheerily. Her repertoire includes cereal, muffins, bacon and eggs, raspberry pancakes and french toast.

(207) 695-2229. Two rooms and a suite with private baths. Doubles, $75. Suite, $125. No smoking.

Kineo House Inn, Kineo Island, Box 397, Rockwood 04478.

With the fabled old hotel of the same name long gone, this is the only public lodging and dining facility on idyllic Kineo Island. It occupies one of eight privately owned cottages left on the island, a sylvan retreat in the shadow of the famed Mount Kineo cliffs, and is a must visit – if not for overnight, at least for lunch or dinner.

Lynn and Marshall Peterson, mainlanders who used to camp nearby at Casey's at Spencer Bay, purchased the property in 1993 and set about its upgrading into what they call a casual island inn. Besides a popular restaurant (see Dining Spots), they offer six upstairs guest rooms, four with private baths. There's a water view from every room, this being located at the tip of a peninsula opposite Rockwood at the midpoint of Moosehead Lake, with water on three sides and Mount Kineo looming behind. The rooms are simple and rather cottagey, but sport good-looking floral prints on the walls. Some rooms connect to offer both double and bunk beds. Four-poster beds were in the works for others. A continental breakfast of cereal and bagels is included in the room rates.

On the main floor are a pub, a restaurant and a nifty little common room with windows right beside the water. Outside are lawn chairs and tables facing a nine-hole golf course, the abandoned Kineo House annex and a wildlife sanctuary. There's itinerant activity during the day, thanks to visiting boaters, golfers and sightseers. But the last scheduled shuttle leaves at 6, and overnighters have the island to themselves.

The Petersons are hands-on innkeepers, to put it mildly. "We wear nine hats each," says Lynn, who does the cooking and housekeeping. Her husband tends bar, greets guests and shuttles people back and forth to Rockwood on his pontoon boat. In winter, he picks up house guests by snowmobile or dog sled. Life here is simple, the Petersons say, but has its rewards.

(207) 534-8812. Four rooms with private baths, two with shared bath. Doubles, $70 in summer, $60 in winter. Closed in April.

Northern Pride Lodge, HX 76, Box 588, Greenville 04441.

Out in the semi-boondocks in Kokadjo, eighteen miles northeast of Greenville, this occupies prime waterfront property at the end of First Roach Pond at the headwaters of the famed Roach River, a fisherman's mecca for salmon and trout. Jeff and Barb Lucas left careers as respiratory therapists in Ohio for a new life in the Maine wilds in 1993. They quickly gained avid following for some of the area's more creative meals (see Dining Spots) and they redid their guest quarters with considerable style. Only the basic necessities are lacking, since guests occupying the five bedrooms share two intimate bathrooms on the ground floor, one for men and the other for women but each seemingly big enough for only one at a time.

The Lucases make the best of the situation, however, as do their guests. The two most appealing rooms are on one side of the main floor, one with a queensize four-poster and the other with two double beds. Both have good-looking comforters and suave decorative touches. Upstairs are three rooms, two holding four twin beds each and the other a queen bed and a twin. Greenville wood carver Joe Bolf carved the striking wildlife scenes on the doors of each bedroom, as well as the lodge's sign.

The common rooms in this lodge, built in 1896 by a logging baron as his summer home, are uncommonly attractive. A moose head in stained glass adorns the top of the french doors in the living room opposite a huge fieldstone fireplace. Meals are served in a summery dining area on an enclosed porch, part of a long screened porch that wraps around the front and sides. Guests also like to chat with Barb as she works in her large commercial kitchen. Her breakfast the day of our visit included a choice of scrambled eggs or blueberry pancakes, fresh fruit (cantaloupe with kiwi), sausage and bacon. The optional American meal plan adds an interesting box lunch and full dinner for $35 per person.

The Lucases rent canoes, paddle boats and motor boats as well as mountain bikes. They also offer 24 primitive campsites, which account for all the picnic tables scattered across the shady grounds beside the water. The five-acre property is nestled in the woods with 550 feet of shoreline.

(207) 695-2890. Five bedrooms sharing two baths. Doubles, $80 B&B, $150 AP. Children over 12.

Dining Spots

Greenville Inn, Norris Street, Greenville.

Among Greenville folk, this restaurant is "the toast of the town," in one fellow innkeeper's words. Since 1988, the Schnetzer family has been serving some of northern Maine's fanciest fare in elegant surroundings. Three small dining rooms are clad in white linens amid rich wood paneling, ornate fireplaces, embossed Lincrusta walls and distant views of Moosehead Lake's East Cove Harbor. Austrian-born chef-innkeeper Elfie Schnetzer and daughter Susie are in the kitchen. Son Michael oversees the front of the house and the wine list, which is the best around.

Dining is taken seriously here, as is the solicitous service. Our leisurely mid-summer meal began with a shared appetizer, a silken pâté of duck liver, truffles and port wine, served with the appropriate garnishes and a homemade roll rather than the traditional melba toast. Next came green salads on glass shell-shaped dishes and huge, piping-hot popovers, with butter presented in a silver shell.

Among main courses, we liked the breast of chicken in a very spicy peanut sauce and a trio of lamb chops with rosemary butter. Both were fairly unadorned and served with rice and a mix of yellow and green beans. Chocolate-coffee ice cream cake and plum strudel were refreshing endings among such exotic treats as profiteroles, chocolate truffle tart and citrus cheesecake with mango coulis.

Other favorites include Maine crab cakes with tarragon tartar sauce and smoked rainbow trout for appetizers; grilled swordfish steak provençal, pork tenderloin with paprika sauce and spaetzle, and beef tenderloin with green peppercorn sauce. Elfi says she has guests who come especially for her Atlantic salmon, which she marinates, broils and serves with sauce verte. She keeps the favorites from year to year, but rewrites her dinner menu seasonally.

A wood stove warms the inn's lounge/living room in which many diners choose to have cocktails or after-dinner drinks. The impressive wine list features Maine Bartlett wines as well as numerous California cabernets and a mix of French, Australian, Spanish, German and Chilean labels.

(207) 695-2206 or (888) 695-6000. Entrées, $15 to $19.50. Dinner nightly, 6 to 9, May-October.

Northern Pride Lodge, Kokadjo.

A small and pleasant dining porch and an inspired-for-the-area menu draw people for dinner to this small lodge in out-of-the-way Kokadjo (whose sign says Population; Not Many), just before the paved road ends on the back way to Baxter State Park and Mount Katahdin.

Ohio transplant Barb Lucas does the cooking. The short, à la carte menu starts with things like smoked trout pâté, pheasant or duck sausage and, Barb's favorite, a baked brie cheese wheel with warm caramel sauce, seasonal fruit and french bread. Seasonal greens enhance the Mediterranean and smoked shrimp salads that come with the meal.

Main courses always include filet mignon topped with sautéed mushrooms. Two other choices are offered, depending on the night: perhaps southwestern chicken, smoked buffalo ravioli, bacon-wrapped shrimp or roast quail. Dessert could be amaretto cheesecake, apple crêpes and hot caramel sundae. The full bar offers a number of choice brands.

"We'd never been in the food business before," says Barb, "so we're just winging it." Winging it rather well, their fans say.

(207) 695-2890. Entrées, $12.95 to $16.95. Dinner by reservation (before 1 p.m.), Thursday-Sunday 5 to 9.

The Road Kill Cafe, Pritham Avenue, Greenville Junction.

Only in Greenville, you think, could they get away with a place like this. Wrong. The concept debuted here, but national publicity made it such a success that the owners branched out with more locations across northern and eastern New England – a total of nine at last count.

"Greenville is not your normal town," explained Leigh Turner, who launched the cafe in 1992 to lampoon what he called "the pretensions of fine dining."

Here you'll find an irreverent menu ("Oh deer! The buck stopped here"), assorted roadside memorabilia, sassy servers and staff theatrics that defy description. Locals and tourists alike pack the tables in the brightly lit dining room and bar, in the screened rear porch or on the umbrellaed side deck overlooking Moosehead Lake.

Heaping portions, affordable prices and fun, fun, fun are the Road Kill's hallmarks. Although there are a few nightly dinner specials, this is basically sandwich

Northern Pride Lodge offers lodging and dining in former logging baron's summer home.

and snack fare. "Never assume it's a raisin," warns the menu as "the most important advice for dining in the Moosehead area." The food is categorized as skidbits (starters like chicken knuckles, potato pelts and Canadian nachaux), mower clippings (salads), pot holes (soups, chili and chowder), bye-bye Bambi burgers, brake and scrape sandwiches, and ribs, fips, bucks and balls, served with nightcrawlers (french fries) and house mower clippings.

The cafe's theme is "where the food used to speak for itself," doled out with an audacious sense of humor (as in kitchen staff throwing handfuls of feathers through the kitchen door, the bartender yelling "you're overdressed" and the waitress plopping herself down at your table as she takes your order). If you're in the mood, it's lots of fun.

(207) 695-2230. Entrées, $9.95 to $14.95. Open daily, 11:30 to 11:30.

Flatlander's, Pritham Avenue, Greenville.
Billed as "a country place for food and drink," this small downtown emporium is a cut above, thanks to its specialty of broasted chicken. You can order a three-piece chicken dinner ($6.50), including french fries and coleslaw, to eat here or take out to a picnic table in the pocket-size park facing the harbor across the street.

If broasted chicken is not your bag, owners Jim and Millie Young offer other options, from appetizers to burgers, soups to salads. Among main courses, expect a few things like beans and a long dog, spaghetti with meat sauce, shrimp with linguini, fish and chips, country ribs and ribeye steak.

Decor in the long, narrow room with a bar at the back is minimal. The handsome bare wood tables are made of Maine pine – "you can hardly find trees like this any more," says Millie.

(207) 695-3373. Entrées, $4.25 to $12.95. Lunch and dinner daily in summer, 11 to 9; sharply reduced hours in off-season.

Kineo House Inn, Kineo Island.

A pleasant summer outing involves a six-minute trip by shuttle boat from Rockwood out to storied Kineo Island for a bit of sightseeing and lunch at the Kineo House. Lynn Peterson, who handles the cooking, has attracted quite a following, serving up to 50 people a day in her summery, Victorian-style dining room and outside on the front lawn facing a golf course.

Because of her location and the numbers of patrons, her lunch menu is rather basic. We ordered the chicken salad in a pita pocket, which turned out to be a half sandwich, good but a niggardly portion, and a burger with jalapeño cheese. Both were served on paper plates with potato chips and a bit of pasta salad. The iced tea came in plastic glasses.

Dinner gets a tad fancier in the old-fashioned dining room outfitted with floral-print tablecloths, captain's chairs and Victorian fluted lights. You might start with mushrooms stuffed with crabmeat, Mexican shrimp cocktail or the house pâté. Main courses include chicken stir-fry with vegetables, shrimp scampi on pasta, ribeye steak and catch of the day. Cheesecake with strawberries is a favorite dessert.

Marshall Peterson offers drinks in his convivial pub across the hall from the dining room. He also shuttles diners back to the mainland after dinner.

(207) 534-8812. Entrées, $8.95 to $12.95. Lunch daily, 11 to 3. Dinner by reservation (before 4 p.m.), 5:30 to 8. Reduced hours off-season. Closed in April.

Pittston Farm, West Branch Area, Moosehead Lake (Box 525, Rockwood).

People fly in or drive 40 miles from Greenville to have one of the all-you-can-eat logger's dinners at this remote fishing camp at the point where the north and south branches of the Penobscot River meet twenty miles above Rockwood. There's no phone (reservations are taken through Folsom's Air Service, with which it maintains radio contact) and the farm is primitive, as you might expect from its heritage as the main hub of Great Northern's lumber operations in the West Branch area and later as a Boy Scout camp.

Ken Twitchell offers meals to house guests and the public. The dining room seats 60, but this is the kind of place where folks help themselves and are likely to take their plates outside to eat on the porch or on the front lawn. The farm features "lumber camp cooking," which means hearty, homemade fare and lots of it. Expect two main courses, vegetables, real mashed potatoes, homemade breads and rolls, half a dozen items from the salad bar, pies, cakes and desserts.

Ken remodeled nine upstairs guest rooms, which share four bathroom facilities on the main floor. They rent for a modest $40 a day, which includes three meals.

(207) 695-2821. Full meal, $7.95. Dinner by reservation, seatings at 5 and 6:30. BYOB.

Diversions

Outdoor Sports. Fishing and hunting have traditionally been the leading activities here, although neither is quite as good in terms of take as in days gone by. "Overkill," explained a Maine Guide of our acquaintance. To compensate, some of the old sporting camps have altered their focus to appeal to nature lovers, wildlife watchers and photographers. White-water rafting is popular on the Kennebec and Penobscot rivers. Hikers like the 75-minute hike up the 700-foot-high landmark Mount Kineo to a renovated fire tower, which yields a panoramic view of Moosehead Lake. One of the prime waterfront spots is occupied by Lily Bay State Park, an uncrowded favorite of swimmers, picnickers and campers.

In winter, skiing at **Squaw Mountain Resort** is improving under new owners (from Florida, of all places), who took over in 1995. Just outside Greenville, Squaw has two chairlifts and a 1,700-foot vertical rise, facing Moosehead Lake. It offers plenty of skiing for $15 on weekdays and $20 on weekends – especially with an increase in snowmaking coverage to the top of the mountain. Cross-country skiing also is popular, but tends to get overshadowed by the snowmobilers who make this their noisy base.

Moose Watching. Everyone looks for moose, and local promoters say more moose reside in the Moosehead area than anywhere in the East. You'll likely spot them feeding in ponds and rivers after dawn and before dusk. They're said to be at their most numerous around the roads and waterways near Rockwood and Kokadjo. A brochure outlines "moose safari" packages by land, sea and air.

One of the best ways to see moose and understand their habitat is to take the two-hour moose cruise offered by the Birches Resort in Rockwood. Unexpectedly plush seats accommodate up to sixteen passengers on a 24-foot-long pontoon boat. Moose were spotted on 96 of 100 excursions in the previous summer, resort co-owner Bill Willard advised. We thought we were going to be among the four percent failure rate until, at the end of our two-hour cruise up and down a jungle-like river, a lone moose suddenly obliged up close. "Every trip is different," our laconic boat pilot-guide said. Two more moose were spotted from a distance on the return trip to the resort. We also encountered two moose along Route 15 on the drive back to Greenville after dinner. Next morning, the pilot pointed out one feeding in an inlet during a half-hour sightseeing flight. That was it for moose of the live variety on our four-day visit.

Airplane Adventures. Almost as much as moose, seaplanes define the Moosehead area, and their sheer numbers convey a different look and feel to this lake. Indeed, the lake is so favored by backwoods pilots that they converge every September on Greenville for the International Seaplane Fly-In, the largest of its kind in the Northeast. Since much of the Moosehead Lake shoreline and many sporting camps are not accessible by road, seaplanes get quickly where motor vehicles and boats cannot.

Three commercial air services offer sightseeing excursions. We found a half-hour flight around the lower half of the lake with **Folsom's Air Service** ($30) the best way to appreciate the vastness of both lake and wilderness. Folsom's provides a canoe-and-fly service ($85) in which customers are flown to Penobscot Farm. There they board canoes for a leisurely three-hour paddle upstream to Lobster Lake, where they are met for the return flight to Greenville.

Other airplane sights may be of interest. Folsom's bases the last operating DC-3 seaplane, an ark of an Army Air Force plane fitted with pontoons, at Greenville's tiny municipal airport. The curious also may view remnants of the wreckage of a B-52, which crashed due to air turbulence against Elephant Mountain during the Cuban missile crisis in January 1963, killing seven crewmen. Access is via a logging road maintained by Scott Paper Co.

Boat Excursions. Another good way to see this area is by boat, and a variety of craft seems to be everywhere for rent or hire around Moosehead and its tributaries. Experience a bygone era with a cruise on the **Katahdin,** the last of 50 steamboats that plied the lake, ferrying cargo and people to resorts and sporting camps before cars and trucks reached the area. Now the star floating exhibit of the tiny **Moosehead**

Marine Museum beside the lake at the municipal parking lot, the diesel-powered Katahdin gives three-hour cruises of the lower third of the lake daily except Monday and Friday at 12:30; adults, $16. A small galley offers hot dogs, candy and the like. We didn't know this, so had picked up good sandwiches at Auntie M's Family Restaurant (open for breakfast and lunch) across the street.

Shopping. Greenville's little downtown is of interest to browsers. Wonderful birdhouses (some made in the Smokies), fishing scenes painted on saws, twig furniture, moose mobiles and T-shirts are among the offerings at **Maine Street Station.** A moose theme also prevails, from banners to tea towels, at **Moosin' Around Maine.** In addition to its namesake items, **Maine Mountain Soap and Candle Co.** carries baskets, pottery and home accessories. A fine selection of gourmet foods is interspersed among the antiques at **The Village Outpost.** We were impressed with Nancy Ward's lines of salsas, mustards, pastas and such, along with her own Ward Farm products. Look for jams and jellies, cards, baskets, books, Hummel figurines, Christmas villages and more at **The Corner Shop.** Souvenirs of a more basic nature, as well as items from a rock shop, are offered at the **Indian Shop,** which appears to be the biggest store in Greenville. Young Mike Boutin stocks everything the sportsman needs at **North Woods Outfitters,** where his partner serves up fancy coffees, baked goods and Internet services in the new **Hard Drive Café.** Rustic lamps with carved bears for the base, carved birds, prints and moose, of course, are available at **The Woodcarver's Shop.**

The original wood carver, **Joe Bolf,** has since moved on to his own quirky studio and shop across from the Municipal Building. Widely known for his wildlife carvings and signs, he spearheaded the National Institute for Hospital Art, launched in Greenville to provide artworks in hospitals. He provided its first gift, a large statue carved not by chisel but by chain saw. "After twenty years' making a living by carving wood," he volunteered, "I just discovered I can do it three times as quickly and just as well with a chain saw." We're believers.

Extra-Special

Kineo Island. You want to get away from the "crowd?" A nostalgic place to visit on a sunny day is this island, actually a peninsula and site of the late Kineo House resort. For $10, you can play golf on a scenic nine-hole course (the midway point is almost at the foot of the sheer Kineo cliffs). Rent a golf cart ($10 an hour) to poke along three miles of bumpy roads on this island attached to the mainland by a 500-foot stone causeway on the far side of the lake. Swim at the secluded and picturesque Pebble Beach beside the causeway, where knowing boaters often tie up for the afternoon. Observe moose, deer, loons and eagles in the wildlife sanctuary. Hike up Mount Kineo or scale the rocky cliffs. Take a peak at the abandoned yacht club building known as the Breakers on the point, and dream of turning it into a restaurant or a B&B. Enjoy lunch or dinner or a drink at the Kineo House Inn, the endearing little successor to the large resort of the same name. The island is reached by or pontoon boat (Kineo Shuttle, every two hours from 8 a.m. to 6 p.m. from the state boat ramp in Rockwood, 534-8812, $4 round trip). Another Kineo shuttle leaves by reservation or on demand from Rockwood Cottages, 584-7725. Jolly Roger's Moosehead Cruises, 534-8827, operates daily cruises with lunch at the Kineo House.

White Mountains provide backdrop for boating on Kezar Lake.

Oxford Hills and Lakes, Me.
Not Where It's At – Yet

The famous – some locals call it infamous – milepost sign out in the middle of nowhere giving distances to nearby places like Norway, Denmark, Mexico, Poland, Paris, Naples, China and Peru would deceive no one.

This is anything but the center of the universe. It's more like the name on the school bus we passed, "State of Maine, Unorganized Territory."

The Oxford Hills region is an unspoiled land of sparkling lakes, hills that back up to the mighty White Mountains and tiny hamlets with English-sounding names like Center Lovell and Lower Waterford. It's an area of great beauty – we hear that the National Geographic called Kezar Lake one of the nation's ten most beautiful (its other claim to fame is that Bridgton native Stephen King has a summer home along its forested shore). There's a fortuitous concentration of small country inns that epitomize the genre.

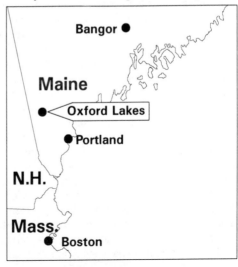

Unusual as a time capsule from the past, the area offers little in the way of formal activity or tourist trappings. "You are on your own," one inn brochure advises.

More and more people seek the serenity of western Maine. "We're

Former home of Arctic explorer is now Admiral Peary House, a deluxe B&B.

really out in the country," concedes Barbara Vanderzanden of the Waterford Inne. "But we have a central location not far from North Conway or the Maine coast."

The charms of this rural retreat have yet to be discovered by the crowds. But that may be only a matter of time. Says restaurateur Michael Myers of the Lake House: "Western Maine is where it's going to be at."

Happily, it's not there yet. That remains its special joy.

Inn Spots

Admiral Peary House, 9 Elm St., Fryeburg 04037.

Splendid gardens, a clay tennis court, an outdoor hot tub and five deluxe guest rooms commend this B&B run by Nancy and Ed Greenberg in a white clapboard house that once was the home of Arctic explorer Robert Edwin Peary. Not to mention a great rear porch, screened on three sides and full of wicker rockers and loungers, from which to view the back yard. Plus a side patio with an outdoor spa.

Avid tennis players, the Greenbergs formerly ran the tennis shop at Mount Cranmore Recreation Center in nearby North Conway, N.H., so their tennis court is a natural. So is the house they bought to convert into a B&B.

Each of their air-conditioned guest rooms contains a queen or kingsize bed, its own sitting area and a spacious bath with dressing table. All are spiffily decorated with an eye to flair and detail. Paintings by a local artist in some rooms are for sale. Slanted roof lines and odd nooks and crannies lend an air of coziness to the Jo, a kingbedded room named for Peary's wife. A spacious attic room called the North Pole has been transformed into everyone's favorite, with a great pink and teal quilt atop a kingsize brass bed and another quilt displayed on a rod. "I tried to decorate with a lack of clutter," says Nancy.

The public rooms are equally comfortable. Just inside the rear entrance is a billiards table on a raised floor, separated by a railing from a large rear living room. The latter has a barnwood wall behind the fireplace, a TV in an armoire, four wing chairs and two couches. Ten people can sit around the table in the open kitchen, all brick and barnwood and notable for stained glass and a chevron floor. Several smaller, more formal sitting rooms, one with an unusual Korg piano, are available in the front of the house for guests who seek privacy. The library contains a portrait of Nancy's great-great-great-grandparents from Newport.

Breakfasts could include the Admiral Peary breakfast pie (like a crustless quiche, says Nancy, with lots of cheese and meats but few eggs), belgian waffles, stuffed french toast and wild Maine blueberry pancakes. Fresh fruits and homemade breads and muffins accompany. The rhubarb and berries are obtained on the property.

The Greenbergs recently cut snowshoe trails for guests on eight acres behind their house.

(207) 935-3365 or (800) 237-8080. Doubles, $108 to $128, foliage $118 to $138, winter $70 to $80. No children. No smoking.

Acres of Austria, Route 5, RR 1, Box 177, Fryeburg 04037.

These 65 tranquil, utterly secluded acres with a half mile of river frontage are full of surprises. Not the least of which is the name. The property reminded new owner Franz Redl of his native Austria. He thought the German way of saying Acres of Austria sounded better and was more catchy than Austrian Acres.

With his New Jersey-born wife Candice, Franz transformed an empty dark wood and stone residence into an unusual B&B of style and comfort in 1997. They offer four spacious guest rooms with private baths and telephones plus five common areas, if you include the nicely furnished, 50-foot-long screened porch.

The great hall with its two-story ceiling is centered by a fieldstone fireplace. Big enough to seat a small army, the hall contains five tables for dining, a small bar, spacious window seats, a corner spiral staircase to the mezzanine library (the book collection is half German language and half English) and a cuckoo clock that plays Edelweiss.

Off the great hall are a living room with three dark green suede couches and TV, a game room with a carombal billiards table from Vienna and a rear reading room with rattan furniture.

The guest rooms were transformed from what had been a four-bay garage. The main-floor Innsbruck Room has a kingsize bed covered, as are the others, with floral duvet covers from Austria. The bed is made up in the Austrian style with two single-size down duvets placed horizontally. The couple moved the entire contents of the bathroom, including a nearly round tub in the corner and a double marble vanity, from their newly renovated house in Vienna. Across the way, the Salzburg Room offers two twin beds and a corner sectional that converts into a queen sofabed. Its fancy new bathroom sports gold fixtures and built-in shelves.

Upstairs is the Graz Suite, with a queen bed and a sitting room with a queen sofa bed. The Vienna Room also has a queen bed with an intricate wood slat headboard and footboard, an armoire and a wood stove.

Candice has quite an eye for décor and comfort. She stenciled most of the walls and achieved a remarkable spray-painted effect in the Salzburg Room with a paint scraper pad. Beamed ceilings and the occasional barnwood wall create a lodge effect.

Franz, a Vienna business owner who aspired to become a chef, got his opportunity here. He offers dinner to guests by reservation. The menu can be arranged, but his two standby meals are wiener schnitzel and spinatknockn (homemade spinach dumplings with onions and cream sauce). He planned cooking seminars and fondue weekends.

For breakfast, guests may have eggs cooked to order or a choice of sweet apricot crêpes, belgian waffles or blueberry pockets. It's taken in summer on a great side porch that extends beyond the building, letting air in on three sides at the end.

The young owners offer canoes for exploring the old course of the Saco River

The Waterford Inne occupies hilltop setting way out in the country.

that flanks their property, and were marking cross-country ski trails for their first winter. They planned to offer two more guest rooms above the horse stables in their carriage barn.

(207) 925-6547 or (800) 988-4391. Three rooms and one suite with private baths. Doubles, $85 to $120 in summer, $75 to $90 in off-season. No smoking.

The Waterford Inne, Chadbourne Road, Box 149, Waterford 04088.

This handsome inn and antiques shop really is out in the country – half a mile up a rural lane in East Waterford. The pale yellow and mustard structure commands a hilltop view and contains nine well-furnished guest rooms, a comfortable and charming living room full of folk art, a more formal parlor and a semi-public dining room of note.

Former New Jersey school teachers Rosalie and Barbara Vanderzanden, a mother and daughter team, carefully restored and furnished the 1825 farmhouse in 1978, eventually augmenting the original five bedrooms with more in the old woodshed leading to the red barn out back.

The common rooms and porch are unusually nice and ever so tasteful. Special touches abound in each bedroom, seven of which have private baths. Duck pillows, duck wallpaper and a duck lamp grace the deluxe Chesapeake Room, which has a kingsize bed, a working fireplace and a super second-story porch overlooking the farm pond and mountains. A quilted whale hangs behind the bed in the Nantucket Room, complete with a map of the island and a bathroom almost as large as the bedroom itself. The Strawberry Room in the woodshed has strawberries on the lamp, rug, quilts, pillow and sheets, and even strawberry-scented potpourri in a strawberry-shaped dish.

Fresh flowers decorate each room in summer. Electric blankets are provided in winter. And "you should see this place at Christmas," says Barbara. "Every nook and cranny is decorated and red bows are put on even the smallest folk-art lambs." In summer, the principal activity is watching the bullfrogs and birds, including a great blue heron, around the farm pond.

Full breakfasts, included in the rates, are served in the beamed dining room or in good weather on the porch. "We'll cook whatever you want," says Barbara.

Dinners for $29 are served to guests and, by reservation, to the public in the dining room filled with her pewter collection. Up to twenty can be served when the front parlor and porch are used as well. Although there is no choice, Barbara will work around special diets and asks large parties for their preference.

A typical dinner might start with cream of broccoli soup, go on to dilled scallops over angel-hair pasta with vegetables and salad not long out of the garden, and end with a fresh berry pie. Chilled cucumber soup and veal marsala might make up another dinner. Leg of lamb often appears, as do shrimp with pernod, game hens, duckling, sole, and pork or beef tenderloin. Grand marnier soufflé and pumpkin ice cream cake are frequent desserts. Guests may bring their own wine.

(207) 583-4037. Seven rooms with private baths, two with shared bath. Doubles, $75 to $100, B&B. Smoking discouraged. Closed in April.

The Noble House, Highland Road, Box 180, Bridgton 04009.

Once a senator's home on four acres in a residential section overlooking Highland Lake, the Noble House is now a comfortable B&B with six bedrooms and three suites, run with much warmth and personality by Jane and Dick Starets with summertime assistance from their college-student offspring. Although they share a Victorian-antique theme, five rooms in the rear carriage house seem more modern – some with jacuzzi baths, large windows overlooking the grounds, a window seat and perhaps a private porch. They're decorated primarily in whites and mauves, furnished in wicker and have wall-to-wall carpeting, period antiques, floral quilts with matching draperies, and frilly touches like eyelet curtains and pillows, one in the shape of a heart.

Guests gather in the fireplaced parlor, which harbors lots of books and a grand piano outfitted with sheet music, or in the pine-paneled family room in back, with its huge mushroom-colored sectional and a grand fireplace.

Breakfast is served on one of the porches or at a table for six in a Victorian dining room clad in blue and green. Tropical fruit salad, whole-grain cereal, raisin bran muffins and vegetable frittata were served the morning we were there.

Guests can swim, canoe or use the paddle boat from the inn's lakefront property across the road, where a hammock, barbecue grill and picnic table are available. Jane Starets has printed up several handy guides to area restaurants and attractions.

(207) 647-3733. Six rooms and three suites with private baths. Doubles, $78 to $88. Suites, $95 to $125. Two-night minimum weekends in season. Children welcome. No smoking. Closed November to mid-June except by reservation.

Center Lovell Inn, Route 5, Center Lovell 04016.

The former owners who first saw this 1805 homestead bought it because of the view of Kezar Lake with the White Mountains beyond. They sat on the front porch, surveyed the scene "and that was it," Susie Mosca recalled.

The new owners acquired the inn in a novel way. Susie and Bill Mosca had conceived the idea of a contest to sell the inn to the winning essayist. Some 5,000 entrants paid $100 each for the chance. The winners were Maryland restaurateurs Richard and Janice Cox, who had always wanted to own and operate an inn of their own. "Our dream came true when we won the contest," said Janice.

The Coxes arrived in 1993 and had three days in which to get ready for the summer season. They gradually renovated most of the ten guest rooms, five in the inn and five in an annex (all except two in each section with private baths). "There were a few problems," Richard conceded. "But what do you expect for $100?"

Janice's parents moved with the couple to make the inn a family operation (they ask guests to call them Mom and Pop.) The foursome had two houses full of antiques, which proved helpful in furnishing the place. Richard proudly showed "our room," the front corner bedroom in which they had stayed upon winning the contest. It now has a queen bed, an oriental rug and two chairs from which to absorb the lake view out the front window.

The three-story structure has something of a Mississippi steamboat appearance, thanks to the Floridian who added a mansard roof topped by a cupola in the 1860s. The 1835 Norton House, a former barber shop, was moved to the site from Lovell to become a side annex. The Coxes have stripped the floors, put in some new baths and added queensize beds. Their main-floor common room has patterned rugs, a fireplace and an upright piano.

Breakfast the day of our visit included fresh fruit, hot baked grapefruit and eggs benedict. Other of Richard's specialties are eggs Chesapeake with Maryland crab, smoked salmon omelet and raspberry french toast. He's also the chef at dinner (see Dining Spots). Janice does the baking for the evening meal.

(207) 925-1575. Doubles, $68 to $98 EP, $109 to $144 MAP.

Bear Mountain Inn, Routes 35 and 37, South Waterford 04081.

Lorraine Blais likes to consider her new B&B a mini-resort. The 52 acres at the foot of Bear Mountain come with a private beach on Bear Pond, canoes and kayaks, hiking and nature trails, cross-country skiing and snowmobiling. Not to mention eighteen acres of mowed fields – "I know, because I mow them and it takes two days."

An interior designer, she returned in 1996 to her native Maine from Boca Raton, Fla. "I promised my mother I'd come home someday and I'm glad to be back," she said. She's in her element, catering to guests like the Disney Channel crew who stayed here in 1997 while filming "Bug Juice" at nearby Camp Waziyatah.

The 1820 farmhouse rambles hither and yon, through a paneled living room and into a large dining room with a paneled ceiling and a fieldstone fireplace in the center. Beyond are a crafts shop that doubles as a snowmobile headquarters in the winter, featuring custom-designed sweatshirts, and a 170-year-old barn "that's my favorite part of the house." Here she came across the old wood that she had made into one of the beds in a guest room.

The front of the main floor houses said bed in one of two guest rooms that share a bath. Décor is country style, but comfortable, she notes. Upstairs, the Grizzly Bear Room with shared bath and one of the inn's five queen beds is done in Ralph Lauren style. The queen-bedded Black Bear Room has a private hall bath. Two bedrooms in a family suite share a master bath. The rear Fuzzy Bear Room with queen bed, jacuzzi tub and view of the pond is considered the honeymoon suite. A guest refrigerator and "convenience center" are stocked with complimentary wines, beverages and snacks.

The hearty breakfast typically includes a fresh fruit cup, banana bread or muffins, and a main dish ranging from eggs benedict to an herbed cheese soufflé casserole. Everything served is organic and without preservatives. In season you may enjoy it on a rear deck overlooking the wildflower field.

(207) 583-4404. Two rooms and a family suite with private baths and four rooms with shared baths. Doubles, $85 to $125. Children over 8.

Pleasant Point Inn, Pleasant Point Road, Box 218, Center Lovell 04016.

Working reproduction antique radios in every room are a feature at this lakeside inn, vastly upgraded from a lodging establishment of the old school by Sue and Alan Perry from Plympton, Mass.

Taking over in 1992, they redid the entire main building, reducing the number of guest rooms from 22 to 8. They also operated a highly regarded restaurant, although they closed it suddenly in 1997 because of the press of wedding functions. "A lot of people were disappointed it closed," said Sue, the chef. She hoped to reopen the restaurant in the future.

The renovated guest rooms on the second and third floors have queensize or two double beds, sprightly decor, swivel recliners or wing chairs and updated bathrooms. Most look out onto the lakeshore, where guests enjoy a great beach and dark green wooden lounge chairs beneath the pines.

The fourteen-acre property along Kezar Lake also includes rustic lakefront cottages, most with fireplaces and porches.

A continental breakfast is put out for guests in a pine paneled dining room. We can vouch for Sue's biscotti and a delectable raspberry coffee cake, fresh from the oven. There are a lodge-style living room with a fieldstone fireplace and a wrap-around porch, but no television. Says Sue: "I tell people if you're coming to Maine to watch TV, stay home."

(207) 925-3008. Eight rooms with private baths. Summer: doubles, $115 to $125 weekends in summer, $79 midweek. Winter: $58 to $68.

Kedarburn Inn, Route 35, Box 61, Waterford 04088.

Built in 1858, this handsome white Colonial house with dark green shutters and broad lawns brightened with flower beds has been upgraded since its acquisition by Margaret and Derek Gibson, who had run a B&B in their native England.

They added three guest rooms for a total of seven, plus a third-floor suite with a sitting room, and installed private baths in each. Beds come in a variety of configurations from kingsize to twins, but most are doubles. The Balcony Room is a double-deck affair with stairs up to twins in a loft, with a double bed and a new private bath below. The bedrooms are enhanced by pleasant country touches, including antiques, quilts, arrangements of dried flowers and handsewn linens. Margaret sewed the curtains bearing ducks and learned upholstering "to redo the furniture myself." Mints, thick colorful towels and stuffed Paddington bears are extra touches.

The front guest parlor invites with a television set, comfortable sofas and books. An outdoor patio is within earshot of Kedar Brook.

Margaret's prime interest has turned to making quilts, wreaths, baskets and dolls, which she sells in the Kedar Craft Shop that has taken over the walkout basement. "The quilts in gold frames sell as fast as I make them," Margaret advises.

Her daughter and son-in-law operate Peter's Restaurant, serving dinner to guests and the public on the main floor (see Dining Spots). The full breakfast offers a choice of eggs, omelets, pancakes or french toast in a sunny front breakfast room.

Four versions of English tea are served by reservation most afternoons from 3 to 4.

(207) 583-6182. Seven rooms and a two-room suite with private baths. Doubles, $71 to $125. Children welcome.

Lake House, Routes 35 & 37, Box 82, Waterford 04088.

A landmark structure that had been Waterford's first inn (operating until the 1940s) was reopened in 1984 as the Lake House. A well-regarded restaurant (see

Dining Spots) and a small parlor with a fireplace take top billing on the main floor. Two rooms and two suites with private baths are available on the second floor.

The Waterford Flat Suite had more than enough space in which we could spread out during a record hot spell, in spacious sleeping quarters with a ruffly queen bed and an adjoining reading room with a sofa, shelves lined with books and a coffeemaker. Two rooms are smaller, but like ours had a homey, lived-in feeling. Not at all home-like is the air-conditioned grand ballroom suite, which lives up to its name with a huge curved ceiling, a queensize bed, seven windows, a sitting area and an open, carpeted platform for a bathroom. Lately, owner Michael Myers has added the Dudley House, a bungalow with queensize bed, TV and screened porch.

Breakfast, taken at 9 o'clock in the rear dining room or on the front porch, could be scrambled eggs, pancakes or waffles, accompanied by juice and a fresh fruit salad – in our case, bananas and blueberries with cream.

(207) 583-4182 or (800) 223-4182. Fax (207) 583-6078. Two rooms and two suites with private baths. Doubles, $84. Suites, $110 and $130. Bungalow, $130. Closed April and November. No smoking.

The Oxford House Inn, 105 Main St., Fryeburg 04037.

Known primarily for its food (see Dining Spots), this inn run by John and Phyllis Morris also offers five guest rooms with private baths. They're located upstairs in an attractive, pale yellow and green house fronted with a wraparound piazza.

One front corner room has a bow window and two double beds. Velvet is draped behind the queensize bed in another room. All rooms are furnished with period furniture and antiques.

Guests share a parlor with waiting dinner patrons, but can retire as well to the large Granite Room Lounge downstairs pub with four small tables and a sitting area with a wood stove and a large TV favored by the innkeepers' young sons. The wicker-filled wraparound porch is great for relaxing, and the back yard opens onto a super view of the Presidential Range.

The Morrises serve a complete breakfast. Eggs benedict, grand marnier french toast, berry pancakes and french toast with cream cheese and marmalade or raspberry jam are among the possibilities.

(207) 935-3442 or (800) 261-7206. Five rooms with private baths. Doubles, $75 to $125.

Dining Spots

The Oxford House Inn, 105 Main St., Fryeburg.

Opened in 1985, this 1913 country house is run quite personally by John and Phyllis Morris, formerly of North Conway, whose dinner fare commands a wide reputation.

Seventy-five people can be seated on white chairs (their tops hand-stenciled by Phyllis) on the rear porch with a stunning view of Mount Kearsarge North, in the former living room called the Parlor, and along the screened front piazza. Tables are set with delicate pink crystal, heavy silver and Sango Mystique peach china, with candles in clay pots and napkins tied like neckties. Floral wallpaper, Phyllis's handmade curtains and draperies, and handsome paneling enhance the parlor.

The menu, which changes seasonally, comes inside sheet music from the 1920s. Dinner begins with complimentary homemade crackers and a cream cheese spread, a salad of fresh greens and fruits (blueberries and watermelon), perhaps with a

The Oxford House Inn is known for good food and lodging.

tomato-tarragon dressing or a cranberry vinaigrette, and fresh nut and fruit breads. Starters might be salmon fricassee, hot buttered brie, a house pâté and Maine crab crêpes.

The ten entrées include poached salmon pommery, scallops à l'orange in puff pastry, grilled pork tenderloin with plum-cinnamon port sauce, veal madeira, rack of lamb with mint-apple chutney, and pan-fried venison flamed with sherry and port and finished with currant and guava jelly, dried cherries, cloves and cinnamon. John does most of the cooking, but the desserts are Phyllis's: fruit trifles, cheese-cake terrine, praline truffle, chocolate mousse, spumoni and frozen peach yogurt at one visit. Her bread pudding with peaches and blueberries is acclaimed.

We can vouch for a masterful summer lunch that yielded a creamy corn chowder made with native corn and chunks of potato, half an avocado filled with a curried salad of shrimp, crabmeat, scallops and fish, and the Oxford salad, a cucumber stuffed with ham, chicken and waldorf salads on a plate of greens. The very generous salad plates were garnished with cornichons, black olives, cucumbers, cherry tomatoes, watermelon and blueberries. Date nut and french breads with raspberry and herb butters accompanied.

(207) 935-3442 or (800) 261-7206. Entrées, $19 to $23. Lunch daily in summer and fall, 11:30 to 2. Dinner by reservation, 6 to 9, nightly in summer and fall, Thursday-Saturday rest of year.

Center Lovell Inn, Route 5, Center Lovell.
Maryland restaurateurs Richard and Janice Cox won this venerable farmhouse-turned-inn in a much-publicized essay contest.

The chef is Richard, who started cooking with his Italian mother as a youngster and had been with the Loew's hotel chain, most recently as chef in Annapolis. His wife was a restaurant manager at the well-known Busch's Chesapeake Inn there. Their experience stood them in good stead for taking over the small inn overlooking

Kezar Lake and the Presidential Range. They redecorated the 40-seat Victorian dining rooms in muted peach and pink colors, and added colorful quilts and print cloths to the wraparound screened dining porch overlooking Kezar Lake and the Presidential Range. And they quickly earned wide acclaim for their food.

The ambitious menu features three veal dishes, grilled salmon with cucumber sauce, smoked pheasant ravioli, muscovy duck breast with lingonberry sauce, and filet mignon forestière. In season, Richard adds Maryland items, perhaps crab cakes or soft-shell crab with ginger, and game specials like rabbit and venison. He's known for his soups, especially the four-onion variety; the night's offering was scallop and artichoke soup at our visit. Other starters could be mussels provençal, grilled venison sausage, and brie baked with honey, toasted almonds and sliced apples.

Janice does the baking. House favorites proved to be strawberry-rhubarb and blueberry cream pies, strawberry shortcake and her mother's key lime pie. The short, select wine list is priced from the teens.

(207) 925-1575. Entrées, $17.95 to $21.95. Dinner nightly, 5:30 to 10:30, May-October. Ski season, Friday and Saturday for public, nightly for house guests. Closed November and April.

Lake House, Routes 35 & 37, Waterford.

Almost since it reopened in 1984, the restaurant at Waterford's first inn has been making culinary waves in western Maine. A changing menu of creative regional cuisine, flaming desserts and an award-winning wine list are offered by chef-owner Michael Myers.

Each dining room is pretty as a picture. The small front room has burgundy wallpaper above pale green woodwork, burgundy carpeting, shelves of glass and china, a collection of bird paintings and a picture of puffins over the fireplace. The larger rear, pine-paneled dining room has a remarkable corkscrew collection, linen-clad tables set with two large wine glasses at each setting and oriental rugs on the floor. Patrons enjoy the antics of birds at window feeders.

On a mild summer night, we chose to eat outside on the screened front porch. The menu is prix-fixe for three courses, with about half a dozen choices for each, the price depending on the entrée. The Rhode Island squid sautéed with spinach ravioli and garlic sauce and the signature duck pâté seasoned with apples and grand marnier were excellent starters.

A dollop of kiwi sorbet preceded the entrées, a generous portion of sliced lamb sauced with curry and vodka and roast duckling in a sauce of peppered blackberries and red wine. Sliced potatoes, cucumbers, tomatoes and pickled corn accompanied. Veal stuffed with prosciutto and mozzarella, filet mignon and fresh salmon filleted on site and served with tequila-lime butter were other choices.

For dessert, we succumbed to a parfait pie and a light chocolate-espresso mousse served on a grand marnier sauce. Bananas foster are flamed tableside for two.

(207) 583-4182 or (800) 223-4182. Dinner nightly, 5:30 to 9, fewer days in off-season. Closed April and November. No smoking.

Peter's Restaurant, Route 35, Waterford.

Their daughter married the then-executive chef at Sunday River ski area, so the new restaurant at Margaret and Derek Gibson's Kedarburn Inn was a natural. Forty diners can be seated at white-linened tables in two rooms on the inn's main floor.

Peter Bodwell does the cooking and his wife Emma, the Gibsons' daughter, oversees the dining room. The menu mixes continental flair with American standbys.

Expect main courses like stuffed sole, poached salmon with a citrus-hollandaise sauce, chicken oscar, veal marsala and steak au poivre. A garden salad comes with, but those who are hungry can indulge first in baked brie, crab cakes or escargots. Desserts like ice cream puff and banana kahlua surprise and international coffees are worthy endings.

The wine list is exceptional, given Peter's daytime work as owner of the Wine Market at 74 Main St. in Bridgton. There's a small bar at the entry to the restaurant.

(207) 583-6265. Entrées, $10.95 to $17.50. Dinner nightly except Tuesday, 5 to 9.

Ebenezer Kezar's Pub, 405B Old Narrows Road, Lovell.

Good food is offered at this casual establishment beside the second hole of the Kezar Lake Golf Course. The short blackboard menu at our visit listed gazpacho, crab cakes, tandoori chicken, mussels marinière, a fried haddock dinner, black angus sirloin steak and lobster pie. The Hungarian mushroom soup here is extraordinary, according to our informant. Desserts run to profiteroles and hot fudge sundaes. Dining is on an enclosed porch or a covered, trellised outdoor patio.

(207) 925-3200. Entrées, $7.95 to $13.95. Lunch and dinner from 11:30 in season.

Diversions

The area has many attributes, but they tend to be quiet and personal. As one inn brochure states: "Whether you prefer browsing through local antique shops, visiting the country fairs, watching the sun rise over the misty lake as you fish from your canoe at dawn or spending a quiet evening around the fieldstone fireplace, you are on your own." Some ideas:

The Villages. General stores and the odd antiques or crafts shop are about the only merchandising in places like Waterford, North Waterford, Center Lovell and Lovell. But do not underestimate the villages' charms. As humorist Artemus Ward wrote of Waterford: "The village from which I write to you is small. It does not contain over forty houses, all told; but they are milk white, with the greenest of blinds, and for the most part are shaded with beautiful elms and willows. To the right of us is a mountain – to the left a lake. The village nestles between. Of course it does. I never read a novel in my life in which the villages didn't nestle. It is a kind of way they have." Waterford hasn't changed much since, nor have its surrounding towns. For action, you have to go north to Bethel, east to Bridgton or southwest to Fryeberg and North Conway.

The Lakes. Kezar, peaceful and quiet and somewhat inaccessible, lies beneath the mighty Presidential Range, its waters reflecting the changing seasons and spectacular sunsets. The lake is relatively undeveloped and private, with access only from the marina at the Narrows, the beach at the end of Pleasant Point Road and a point in North Lovell. The rest of the time you can rarely even see it (much to our dismay, for we got lost trying). Keoka Lake, at Waterford, has a small, pleasant and secluded beach just east of the village and an unexpectedly crowded village beach just to the south. Hidden lakes and ponds abound, and not far distant are more accessible Long Lake and Sebago Lake.

Antiques. The Bridgton area, in particular, is a center for antiquers; a special brochure described 23 antiques shops at last count. The **Oxford Common Antique Center** on Route 26 south of Oxford is a collection of dealers and shops. Cynthia Hamilton's antiques and folk art in the **1836 Brick Schoolhouse** in Lovell and the **Kayserhof Alpine Village** with a country store and Christmas shop in North Waterford are shopping destinations.

Other Shopping. The handpainted gifts, crafts and furnishings of the talented Quisisana resort staff are featured at the interesting **QuisiWorks** shop along the main highway at Center Lovell. We also liked all the pottery, jewelry, carved birds and the kitchen corner with themed cookbooks at the nearby **Kezar Lake Handcrafts**. More crafts are shown in **The Loft** at the Center Lovell Market. The handthrown porcelain feeders for hummingbirds caught our eye at **Wiltjer Pottery**, Route 37, South Waterford. At **Craftworks,** ensconced in a refurbished church in Bridgton, we browsed through the baskets, rugs, candles, clothing and Maine foods and wines. We also liked the gifts and handicrafts at **The Maine Theme** in Bridgton. Exceptional glazed pottery reflecting the colors of the mountains makes the studio and showroom of **Bonnema Potters** in Bethel worth a special trip.

Extra-Special

Quisisana, Point Pleasant Road, Center Lovell.

The chef prepares four-star dinners and then repairs to the music hall and sings his heart out at this music-oriented resort beside Kezar Lake. When Randy Braunberger received standing ovations after playing the leading roles in "Fiddler on the Roof" and "My Fair Lady," resort owner Jane Orans said, the audience was cheering both for his stage performances and his gastronomic prowess. The latter is not inconsiderable, prompting one well-traveled New Yorker to tip us off to what he called one of the finest restaurants in the land.

Magazine writers have long sung the praises of the venerable 75-room family resort that attracts a devoted following for music, Mozart and tranquil lakeside pleasures during mostly week-long stays. Two lodges totaling eleven rooms and 37 guest cottages with names like Sonata, Symphony and Pianissimo are strung along the beach or nestled deep in the woods. Most of the 80 staffers are students at the nation's leading music schools, which gives the place a decided musical air – when the dining room staff sing as they dry the silver, Jane says, "it's an incredible sound." The sleeper in the publicity department has been chef Randy, something of a Renaissance man who studied cooking at the Ritz Hotel in Paris, has a master's degree in acting and paints incredible floral tapestries.

When space is available in the 150-seat, lodge-style dining room with screened windows on three sides, the public may join resort guests for an evening to remember. The prix-fixe menu changes daily. A typical dinner begins with a choice of steamed vegetable spring rolls or curried zucchini soup. After a house salad, the main course could be salmon-leek roulade with roasted yellow pepper sauce or saddle of lamb provençal with a black olive tapenade and confit of red peppers. Dessert could be a blueberry pie or frozen cappuccino mousse cake. Beer or wines from a good selection of reasonably priced Californias accompany.

After dinner, adjourn to the music hall and enjoy the chef's grand finale.

(207) 925-3500. Prix-fixe, $25 to $30. Dinner nightly by reservation, 6:30 to 7:30. Open mid-June through August.

Motif No. 1 is on view from rear dining room at The Greenery Restaurant.

Rockport, Mass.
Bargains by the Sea

They certainly don't need more crowds, these habitués of Bearskin Neck, Pigeon Cove and Marmion Way. Nor do those who cater to them.

But bargain-conscious travelers can seldom do better than in Rockport, the seaside Cape Ann resort town where the costs of food and lodging consistently remain five years behind the times. Last we knew, lobster dinners were going for $7.95 at Ellen's Harborside. Rooms in some of the better inns and motels cost $70 to $100, about one-third less than they'd command in equivalent locations elsewhere.

Why such bargains? Because Rockport was developed earlier, when costs were lower, than many such coastal resorts. "We were bed and breakfast long before the craze started," notes Leighton Saville of Seacrest Manor. Adds William Balzarini of the Old Farm Inn: "The inns here keep their prices down because they don't have new

mortgages with high rates." Rockport's century-old ban on the sale of liquor has influenced prices, if only in lowering restaurant tabs when patrons BYOB.

The bargains help swell Rockport's year-round population of 7,500 to 35,000 in summer. Most folks, it seems, are on the streets near Dock Square and Bearskin Neck, the rocky fishing and commercial promontory that juts into the harbor. Parking is usually a problem. Arrive early or expect to park on distant side streets and walk. Or better yet, take the Cape Ann Trolley.

Visitors are drawn by the rocky coast more typical of Maine, the atmosphere of an old fishing village crammed with shops, the quaintness of a "dry" town in which Sunday evening band concerts are the major entertainment, and the lively arts colony inspired by a harbor listed by Walt Disney Productions as one of the nation's most scenic. In fact, Motif No. 1, a fishing shack on the wharf, is outranked as an artist's image only by the Mona Lisa. When it collapsed in the Blizzard of 1978, villagers quickly rebuilt it – such is the place of art (and tourism) in Rockport.

All around Rockport are the varied assets of the rest of Cape Ann. They range from the English look of quiet Annisquam, which is New England at its quaintest, to the commercial fishing flavor of busy Gloucester.

The allure of Rockport is so strong that its devotées return time and again. Crowded it may be, but it's hard to beat the prices.

Inn Spots

Eden Pines Inn, 48 Eden Road, Rockport 01966.

You can't get much closer to the ocean than on the rear patio that hovers over the rocks – or, for that matter, in most of the upstairs guest rooms – at this delightfully secluded B&B by the sea.

The setting in what was formerly a summer home could not be more attractive. The lodge-like front parlor with stone fireplace, the California-style side breakfast porch with white wicker furniture and picture windows, the rear porch full of wicker lounge chairs with a neat brick patio below, even a couple of bathroom windows take full advantage of the water view across to Thatchers Island and its twin lighthouses. Although the shore here is rocky, the inn is within walking distance of two beaches.

The seven guest rooms, all with private baths, are unusually spacious. Six come with idyllic private balconies overlooking the ocean. Three have king beds and three have two double beds. Although each appeals, we'd choose premier Room 4, all beige and blue in decorator fabrics with two double beds linked by a crown canopy. It has thick carpeting, a comfortable sitting area with Queen Anne chairs and an enormous bathroom done in Italian marble with a bathtub, a separate shower and a large window onto the ocean next to the marble vanity.

Innkeeper Inge Sullivan, who is partial to marble baths and Laura Ashley and Bill Blass fabrics, has redecorated all the rooms in California style. Although her favorite colors are blues and yellows, Room 6 with a full canopy queen bed is romantic in pink and green florals. Her new third-floor penthouse room is a beauty with a crown canopy above the kingsize bed, a wicker sitting area facing the window as well as a balcony, and a large bathroom.

She and her husband John serve a continental breakfast that includes fruit salad, Scandinavian pastries, and muffins, as well as mid-afternoon tea, lemonade and setups for drinks. We know of few more picturesque places for the last than the wicker lounge chairs on the rear patio smack beside the ocean.

Atlantic Ocean lies just behind Eden Pines Inn.

The Sullivans also rent four bedrooms in their smashing, California-style **Eden Point House** down the street at 34 Eden Road, a corner lot with a sweeping ocean view. You can rent the entire house for $380 a night or it can be divided into two two-bedroom sections for $280 a night each.

(978) 546-2505 or (508) 443-2604 (November-May). Seven rooms with private baths. Doubles, $100 to $165. Two-night minimum. No young children. Smoking restricted. Open mid-May to mid-November.

Seacrest Manor, 99 Marmion Way, Rockport 01966.

Lawns and gardens and a breakfast to remember – these are the hallmarks of Seacrest Manor. So is the sweeping view of the ocean beyond the trees from the second-story deck above the spacious living room of the inn, situated in a prosperous residential area. Leighton T. Saville and Dwight B. MacCormack Jr. have run their inn since 1972, so personally that many repeat guests have left gifts – their own watercolors of the inn, crocheted pillows and countless knickknacks, including a collection of rabbits "which just keep multiplying, as rabbits are prone to do," according to Leighton.

The main-floor library displays so many British magazines that "our English guests tell us it feels like home," he adds. The elegant living room, where afternoon tea is served, has a masculine feel with leather chairs, dark colors and fine paintings, as well as exquisite stained glass and tiny bottles in the bow windows.

The formal dining room is decked out in fancy linens, Wedgwood china and crystal glasses at five tables for a breakfast that Town & Country magazine called one of the 50 best in America. It begins with fresh fruit cup and fresh orange juice, continues with spiced Irish oatmeal and bacon and eggs, and ends with a specialty like blueberry or apple pancakes, french toast or corn fritters.

Guests have the run of the two-acre property, which includes a remarkable, century-old red oak shading the entire front yard, prolific gardens, a couple of statues and a rope hammock strung between trees in a rear corner. The flower beds supply the small bouquets scattered through the inn. Flowers even turn up in stand-up frames, unusual English vases that the partners discovered in Bermuda. They purchased one for every room and now stock them for guests to purchase.

Six guest rooms and a two-bedroom suite have private baths. Three have full ocean views and three partial ocean views. Rooms are comfortable and have been redecorated lately. Each has twin/king or queen beds, color television, a clock radio, a couple of chairs and a desk. The suite has a double bed in each room, which may be reserved individually if available. Amenities include mints on the bedside table at nightly turndown service, fine soaps and shampoos, overnight shoe shines and a complimentary Boston Globe at the door in the morning.

Seacrest Manor is a special place that measures up to its motto, "decidedly small, intentionally quiet."

(978) 546-2211. www.rockportusa.com/seacrestmanor. Six rooms and a two-bedroom suite with private baths. May-October: doubles $124 to $138, suite $196. April and November: doubles $108 to $118, suite $176. Two-night minimum weekends. Children over 16. No smoking. No credit cards. Closed December-March.

Yankee Clipper Inn, 96 Granite St., Box 2399, Rockport 01966.

One of Rockport's larger and older inns, the Yankee Clipper continues to be upgraded by Barbara and Bob Ellis, daughter and son-in-law of its founders. It takes full advantage of a remarkable setting on a bluff, with beautifully landscaped lawns on a bit of a point jutting into the ocean.

Now with 26 rooms and suites, all with private baths and telephones and fifteen with ocean views, the inn began in 1946 with nine rooms in a 1929 art deco Georgian mansion beside the ocean. More were added in the 1840 Bulfinch-designed neo-classic mansion across the road, and premium, somewhat contemporary rooms are in the Quarterdeck built in 1960 beside the water. The last has a knockout penthouse on the third floor with ruffled pillows on two double beds, a sofabed, and two velvet chairs facing floor-to-ceiling windows onto the ocean. Two ground-floor oceanfront lodgings that Barbara calls her "wow rooms" have been transformed lately with colorful chintz and wicker and look across gardens to the open sea.

Another drawing card is the new Intrepid guest room in the Bulfinch House, created from two small rooms. It boasts a canopied, Queen Anne-style king bed beside a mirrored, in-room jacuzzi, an audio-visual center and, for those who cannot be without their electronic gadgetry, a modem outlet.

The main inn's rooms, all named after clipper ships, have been upgraded. Some offer spectacular close-up ocean views from sunporches or decks. We like the Sea Witch, with a queen canopy bed and an enclosed porch in rose and wicker, with a queen hideabed and a deck facing the ocean. The Red Jacket, favored by actress June Allyson during a filming stay here, offers a double and a twin bed plus a long porch with green wicker furniture that has been in the family for a century. We'd sink into the curved wicker sofa, the chaise or the rockers and never want to get up. Everyone shares a beauty of a deck off the third floor. Also in the inn is a grandly furnished living room on the main floor. Downstairs is a function room, in which chairs are lined up in front of a huge VCR, with a bunch of videos at the ready.

The dining porch is leased to a chef who runs it as **The Veranda,** a restaurant open to the public (see Dining Spots). The inn's longtime cook continues to prepare breakfast for guests and the public, offering treats like poached eggs with spinach-basil sauce on a puff pastry nest for $6 to $8.

Century-old red oak shades front of Seacrest Manor.

The heated saltwater pool is hidden from the public eye on the landscaped, terraced grounds beneath the road.

(978) 546-3407 or (800) 545-3699. Fax (978) 546-3407. www.yankeeclipperinn.com Twenty-one rooms and five suites with private baths. Memorial Day to mid-October: doubles, $109 to $209 B&B, $179 to $319 MAP. Off-season: $115 to $157 B&B weekends, $82 to $115 B&B midweek. Open March-November. No smoking.

Addison Choate Inn, 49 Broadway, Rockport 01966.

An in-town location and a rear swimming pool draw guests to this attractive, flower-bedecked house built in 1851 and boasting Rockport's first bathtub – in the kitchen, no less.

That bathtub has been replaced, of course, but all five air-conditioned guest rooms and a two-room suite come with large and modern hand-tiled bathrooms with reproduction fixtures. Innkeepers Knox and Shirley Johnson have renovated and redecorated the inn from top to bottom. Shirley's touch as an interior designer shows in the main-floor Captain's Room, dressed in nautical navy and white with a fishnet-canopied, queensize mahogany poster bed, and the second-floor Chimney Room done in wedgwood blue with rose accents and a lace queen canopy bed. The third-floor Celebrations Suite, furnished in white wicker with a queen canopy bed draped in lace, has a skylight in the bathroom, television, refrigerator and a view of the ocean across the rooftops. All rooms come with wicker chairs, wide-board floors and hair dryers.

The comfortable living room with its restored antique mantel over the fireplace, a small rear library with TV and a dining room with a beehive oven are cheery. Each contains antiques and original art. A continental-plus breakfast buffet includes fresh fruit, cereal, granola, homemade coffeecake and house-ground coffee. It's taken in the dining room or at intimate tables for two on the narrow side porch facing showy perennial gardens across the driveway. Shirley and Knox, a landscape architect, transplanted more than 60 potted plants from the couple's previous home in nearby Lanesville.

The rear Stable House contains two housekeeping suites with TV and loft bedrooms available by the day, week or month. The Choate with a spiral staircase and skylights in the bathroom and bedroom has particular flair.

Beyond is the tree-shaded pool area, a delightful refuge with chaise lounges and umbrella-topped tables away from the hustle and bustle of Rockport.

(978) 546-7543 or (800) 245-7543. Fax (978) 546-7638. Five rooms and a suite with private baths, plus two housekeeping suites. Doubles, $98. Suite, $125. Housekeeping suites, $695 weekly. Two-night minimum summer weekends. Children over 12. No smoking.

Old Farm Inn, 291 Granite St. (Route 127), Rockport 01966.

For years, this was tops on everyone's list of favorite eating spots on Cape Ann. Susan and Bill Balzarini, whose family ran the restaurant with tender loving care since 1964, closed it to concentrate with equal TLC on their growing B&B operation.

The inn is housed in a red farmhouse with white trim and creaky floors, built in 1799 and once part of a dairy farm (the Balzarini grandchildren's ponies still graze in the meadow). One of the original dining rooms has been converted into a parlor; here, in something that resembles grandma's sitting room, sherry and cookies are available in the afternoon. Another of the former dining rooms is now part of the Garden Suite, which has a bedroom with queen bed, a sitting room with two twins and TV, and a private deck.

The main garden dining room with 80-year-old cast-iron stove and full-length windows looking out onto birch trees is where guests take breakfast in the morning. Colorful as can be, it's a tropical paradise of hanging plants and tables covered with floral cloths in vivid yellows, greens and reds. The fare includes fresh fruit and juice, cereals (and sometimes oatmeal in winter), yogurt, muffins and coffeecake.

Upstairs are three guest rooms with fireplaces, each with private bath, queen bed, television and wide-plank floors and furnished in antiques. The barn out back has four guest rooms, all with private bath and TV and small refrigerators. Three have a queen and a twin bed and the other a king bed. They're recently upgraded, comfortable with country decor and rather motel-like. The Fieldside Cottage offers one to three bedrooms in various configurations.

Secluded woodland paths lead through the inn's five acres to the rocky coastline and a scenic quarry at Halibut Point, Rockport's only oceanfront state park.

(978) 546-3237 or (800) 233-6828. Fax (978) 546-9308. Seven rooms, one suite and one cottage with private baths. Doubles, $95 to $135, July-October; off-season, $83 to $115. Cottage, $1,025 weekly in July and August. Smoking restricted. Closed December to mid-April.

The Inn on Cove Hill, 37 Mount Pleasant St., Rockport 01966.

Close to the heart of town and with a fine view of Motif No. 1 and the harbor from its rear third-floor deck is this Federal-style mansion built in 1791. It's surrounded by a white picket fence and lovingly tended gardens.

Innkeepers Marjorie and John Pratt completed a lengthy restoration and redecoration of the former guest house. Nine of the eleven bedrooms have private baths; two on the third floor share. Each is nicely decorated in Laura Ashley fabrics and wallpapers, and each has a small color television set. Most rooms sport handmade quilts and afghans and crocheted coverlets as well as oriental-style rugs.

The Pratts like to point out the structure's architectural features – such as the spiral staircase with thirteen steps in the entry hall – and the antique furnishings in the small common room. On the coffee table is a book called "Taster's Tattles and Titillations," written by guests who share their local dining experiences. It makes for lively reading.

A continental breakfast with muffins is served on English bone china at outdoor tables topped by umbrellas in the side garden or on trays in the bedrooms.

Recipes for some of the Pratts' popular muffins (oatmeal, orange-buttermilk and pumpkin, among them) have been printed for guests. A note is appended to the end: "If you find that your muffins are failing, we have conspired to leave out one essential ingredient from each of the recipes; that is umbrella tables in the summer and breakfast in bed in the winter. For access to both, come see us."

(978) 546-2701 or (888) 546-2701. Nine rooms with private baths and two rooms with shared baths. Doubles, $47 shared bath, $65 to $101 private bath, mid-June to late October, $61 to $93 in spring. Two-night minimum in summer and most weekends. No smoking. Closed late October to mid-April.

Linden Tree Inn, 26 King St., Rockport 01966.

Flowery and fragrant and about two centuries old, an enormous linden tree spreads its limbs beside this Victorian-style house dating to about 1850. Dawn and Jon Cunningham offer stylish common rooms and eighteen bedrooms with private baths.

Guests enter through a pleasant side sun porch into a dining room and a formal living room with elegant Victorian furnishings and oriental rugs. Twelve bedrooms in the main inn are nicely appointed with period furniture, carpeting, fresh flowers and a mix of twin, double and king beds. The third-floor Room 34 with a double bed and a sitting area with a loveseat and chair has windows on two sides onto the distant ocean and the nearby Mill Pond, where the locals ice skate in the winter. For an even better view, Jon leads guests up to the cupola, lit by Christmas lights in the windows and visible from all around town. An annex to the main house holds two connecting bedrooms rented as a suite.

The premium rooms are in a carriage house behind the inn. Here you'll find four modern, year-round rooms, each with a double and twin bed, TV, kitchenette and private rear deck.

Dawn, a town native, is known for her baking. Some of her treats are served with afternoon tea and lemonade, and the aroma of her blueberry cake emanating from the kitchen nearly did us in upon arrival (it tasted delectable, too). The main event is breakfast around the large table or at smaller individual tables in the dining room. Expect all kinds of fresh fruits, juice and homemade coffeecakes and breads, from mango to apple-walnut. Rhubarb cake, fig-pineapple coffeecake and banana/chocolate-chip bread are other favorites.

(978) 546-2494 or (800) 865-2122. Twelve rooms, one suite and four efficiency units with private baths. Mid-June to mid-September: doubles $97, efficiencies $107, suite $137. Off-season: doubles $75, efficiencies $79, suite $107. Two-night minimum in summer. Closed in February.

Sally Webster Inn, 34 Mount Pleasant St., Rockport 01966.

A good-looking gray house with red shutters and a lovely fan door, this 1832 structure contains eight guest rooms, each named for one of its former occupants and each with private bath. The house has six fireplaces, original wide-plank pine floors, period door moldings, brick terraces and herb gardens.

The front parlor is known as "Sally's Share," because that is the part of the house that Sally Choate Webster inherited from her father, the local "housewright" who built it. Bearing a rather grim-faced portrait of her, the room contains family artifacts given to the inn by Sally's great-great-granddaughter, who has stayed here. Across the hall is Sally's Room, a bedroom with twin beds joined as a kingsize.

Double canopy, pencil-post four-poster and Jenny Lind beds are in the guest rooms. Each is attractively furnished to the period and outfitted with the inn's own toiletries.

Young owners Tiffany and David Muhlenberg, who arrived as newlyweds from New York's Westchester County, prepare a continental-plus breakfast, including cereal, yogurt and muffins. It's served with silver coffee pots and antique china in the dining room or, beyond through french doors, on a new brick patio they added.

(978) 546-9251. Eight rooms with private baths. Doubles, $69 to $96; off-season $55 to $85. No smoking. Closed in January.

The Captain's House, 69 Marmion Way, Rockport 01966.

A fabulous location at water's edge commends this white stucco mansion, billed as "a comfortable and casual guest house" by owners Carole and George Dangerfield. Although they've owned it for 30 years, both the exterior and interior have been upgraded lately.

There's a wraparound porch, part of it open to the ocean and the rest enclosed for a library and TV. Inside are a huge parlor with beamed ceiling and fireplace, and a handsome dining room that catches a glimpse of the ocean.

Upstairs are five guest rooms with private baths. Two rooms are particularly large, and those in front yield the best views. Each is done in turn-of-the-century wallpaper and has hand-creweled embroidery on the valances and reproduction Williamsburg furnishings.

Sour cream blueberry coffeecake, muffins and fruit breads are served for continental breakfast in the dining room or on the porches, where guests "feel closer to the water," Carole says. They really feel close to the water in the lounge chairs spread out on neat little cement patios nestled here and there among the rocks along the craggy shore.

(978) 546-3825. Five rooms with private baths. Doubles, $90 to $115. Closed in January and early February. Two-night minimum weekends.

Seaward Inn, 62 Marmion Way, Rockport 01966.

Facing the ocean on attractive grounds full of gardens, lawn chairs, boulders and stone fences is this complex of inn, cottages and guest lodge, totaling 38 rooms with private baths.

Jane and Fred Fiumara took over the old-fashioned establishment in 1995 from founders Anne and Roger Cameron, who had operated it for 51 years. They kept it much as it had been, a low-key and rustic place to which guests return year after year. They extended the season and also upgraded the dining operation, opening the Sea Garden Restaurant to the public as well as to house guests. Following Fred's untimely death, Jane was running the establishment herself in 1997, with help from staff and family.

The main inn offers ten old-fashioned rooms furnished with period pieces and vintage maple bureaus and desks. Adjacent is the Carriage House with nine rooms and several two-room suites with ocean vistas. Some guests prefer the oceanfront Breakers Lodge, a shingled house atop granite ledges with a common room and nine homey guest rooms. Others like the accommodations in nine single or multi-unit, pine-paneled cottages, eight of which have kitchenettes and fireplaces.

Guests may swim in a small spring-fed pond with a sandy beach, surrounded by beach chairs, situated on the property. Or they can enjoy the view of Sandy Bay from the lawns in front of the main inn or beside the Breakers.

Dining is in three beamed and paneled dining rooms and a small oceanfront bistro. The walls are hung with paintings by local artists, and diners are surrounded by windows on three sides on the side sun porch. Live piano music may accompany.

The extensive dinner menu changes every few days. The four-course meals are prix-fixe. You might start with Asian poached salmon with Asian coleslaw or duck pâté with grilled onion relish. The salad could be caesar or Greek with baked eggplant, goat cheese and vegetable brochette. Typical main courses are grilled swordfish with corn relish and mango salsa, free-range chicken with pinenuts and almonds over linguini, and pan-seared black angus ribeye steak topped with lobster.

(978) 546-3471 or (800) 648-7733. Twenty-nine rooms and suites and nine cottages, all with private baths. Mid-May through October: doubles $115 to $175 B&B, cottages $850 to $1,700 weekly. Off-season: doubles $100 to $140, cottages $125 to $155.

Prix-fixe, $35. Dinner in summer, Tuesday-Sunday 5:30 to 9:30, Thursday-Saturday in off-season. BYOB.

Dining Spots

Rockport is dry, but most restaurants invite patrons to BYOB. Some of the more prominent restaurants and biggest advertisers are considered tourist traps.

My Place By the Sea, 68 South Road, Rockport.

You can't get much closer to the ocean than at this restaurant at the very end of Bearskin Neck. In fact, it's so close to the ocean that twice in recent years it has been damaged in storms. After the latest event, owners Charles Kreis and Annie Russell rebuilt the structure and reopened with a crisp summery look. A two-level outdoor porch wraps around the tiny interior, with an open lower level resting right above the rocky shore and a smaller side level covered by an awning and enclosed in roll-down plastic "windows" for use in inclement weather. Floral cloths cover the white molded tables and the atmosphere is romantic in rose and aqua.

Called "My Place" because a former owner couldn't think of anything else, Charles added "By-the-Sea" to its name when he took over. To complement the magical setting, he's built a reputation for the best food in town. Indeed, a recent entry in one innkeeper's restaurant diary was by Californians who proclaimed My Place "the best over-all restaurant on our thirteen-state foliage tour. Excellent service, food and ambiance."

New chef Kathy Milbury has upgraded the menu with such starters as asparagus and morel mushroom soup with a parmesan crouton, and lobster quesadilla with sundried tomato cream cheese and spicy salsa. The kitchen shines on such seafood items as baked swordfish with a tangy béarnaise sauce, pan-seared szechuan salmon on an Asian noodle pancake and seared ocean catfish over wilted spinach. Meat-eaters hail the grilled lamb loin with saffron couscous and grilled plum tomato salad.

Georgian mansion beside ocean houses Yankee Clipper Inn and The Veranda restaurant.

The restaurant's creative desserts are displayed in a glass case that diners pass on their way to their table. Favorites include warm chocolate cake with homemade maple walnut ice cream, chocolate hazelnut mousse and raspberry crème brûlée.

(978) 546-9667. Entrées, $14 to $18. Lunch daily, 11:30 to 4. Dinner, 4 to 9:30 or 10. Fewer days in the off-season and closed in winter. BYOB.

The Veranda, Yankee Clipper Inn, 96 Granite St., Rockport.

The restaurant at this seaside inn is aptly named. It's a long and narrow enclosed porch running alongside the inn, with great views of the water off to the side. Curved arches are overhead, pink and white linens dress up the wrought-iron furniture, and fresh flowers are at each candlelit table. It's a simple but effective setting for chef Carl Kosko's regional American fare with an Italian accent.

Expect such main courses as shrimp and artichoke hearts in a champagne chèvre sauce over polenta, poached sole layered with jarlsberg cheese and crabmeat, and garlic-roasted duck stuffed with a homemade port and wild rice stuffing. Bruschetta, baked stuffed artichoke hearts and Swedish onion soup with cognac and cambozola cheese are featured starters. Homemade pies are among the desserts.

(978) 546-7795. Entrées, $14 to $22. Dinner nightly, 5:30 to 9, Memorial Day through mid-October. No smoking. BYOB.

The Greenery, 15 Dock Square, Rockport.

The name bespeaks the theme of this casual and creative place, but hardly prepares one for the view of Motif No. 1 across the harbor from the butcherblock tables at the rear of the L-shaped dining room.

Seafood and salads are featured, as is a salad bar and an ice cream and pastry bar out front. Otherwise the fare runs from what owners Deborah Lyons and Midge Zarling call gourmet sandwiches to dinner entrées like grilled swordfish, poached salmon, seafood casserole, bouillabaisse linguini and chicken milano. Dinners include the extensive salad bar, as do such lighter fare as pesto pizza and crab salad quiche.

At lunch time, we savored the crab salad quiche with a side caesar salad and the homemade chicken soup with a sproutwich. The last was muenster and cheddar cheeses, mushrooms and sunflower seeds, crammed with sprouts and served with choice of dressing. We liked the sound of the crab and avocado sandwich, now a menu fixture, and overheard diners at other tables raving about the lobster and crab rolls.

Apple pie with streusel topping, key lime pie, tirami su and cheesecake with fresh strawberries are popular desserts. The chocolate chambord and amaretto cheesecakes are available to go.

(978) 546-9593. Entrées, $11.95 to $15.95. Open daily, 10 to 9 weekdays, 9 to 10 weekends. No smoking. BYOB. Closed November to mid-April.

Brackett's Ocean View, 29 Main St., Rockport.

The old Oleana-By-the-Sea gave way to this family restaurant that receives good reviews from residents. It's simple as can be, except for the sweeping view of the water on two sides of the main dining room tucked around to the rear and not visible from the entry. Windsor chairs are at bare tables topped by paper mats.

The all-day menu is priced right and contains some interesting fare, including grilled portobello salad and a cajun chicken rollup. More substantial fare includes broiled sea scallops, fried seafood platters, baked scrod au gratin, codfish cakes, chicken parmigiana and grilled liver and onions.

Start with the crispy thin fried onion rings – the best anywhere, according to a local innkeeper. Desserts of the day could be grapenut custard pudding, strawberry-rhubarb pie and french silk pie.

(978) 546-2797. Entrées, $7.95 to $14.95. Lunch daily from 11:30. Dinner from 4:30. BYOB.

Ocean Cafe, 8 Old Harbor Road, Rockport.

The restaurant at the Old Harbor Yacht Club has been leased to Eric and Kim Lorden, caterers and owners of Passports restaurant in Gloucester. Here, most of the dining is outside on the deck and on picnic tables perched on the seawall.

The menu has been ugraded lately. For lunch, you can get a burger or a haddock sandwich, but also spring rolls and a grilled chicken club. The dinner menu starts with Jamaican fish cakes, Mayan vegetable soup and Vermont smoked duck salad. Main dishes include lobster as well as grilled salmon, seafood Mediterranean over linguini, shrimp and pork shangri-la, southwestern chicken and grilled sirloin steak.

(978) 546-7172. Entrées, $10.50 to $18.50. Open daily in summer, from 11:30.

Diversions

The Seashore. Rockport is aptly named – it has the rocky look of the Maine coast, in contrast with the sand dunes associated with most of the Massachusetts shore. Country lanes lined with wild flowers interspersed between interesting homes hug the rockbound coast and crisscross the headlands in the area south of town known as Land's End. We like the California look of Cape Hedge Beach from the heights at the end of South Street, the twin lighthouses on Thatchers Island as viewed from Marmion Way, and the glimpses of yachts from the narrow streets along the water in quaint Annisquam (stop for a lobster roll on the deck right over the water at the Lobster Cove).

Swimming is fine at Front and Back beaches in the center of town, the expansive

Good Harbor Beach near the Gloucester line, the relatively unknown Cape Hedge and Pebble beaches at Land's End, and the Lanesville beach north of town. Parking can be a problem, but we've always lucked out.

Halibut Point State Park, Pigeon Cove. On a clear day, you can see Crane's Beach in Ipswich, the Isles of Shoals in New Hampshire and Mount Agamenticus in Maine from this 54-acre park along the rocky coast. In the middle of the park is an abandoned, water-filled quarry from which tons of granite made their way to some of the more notable buildings across the Northeast. Guided tours and demonstrations about the quarry are given Saturdays at 9:30. The park is popular with hikers and sunbathers. Parking, $5.

Bearskin Neck. The rocky peninsula that juts into the harbor was the original fishing and commercial center of the town. Today, most of the weather-beaten shacks have been converted into shops and eateries of every description. Glimpses of Sandy Bay and the Inner Harbor pop up like a changing slide show between buildings and through shop doors and windows; arty photo opportunities abound. The rocky point at the end of the neck provides a panoramic view, or you can rest on a bench off T-Wharf and admire Motif No. 1 – the Rockport Rotary Club sign beckons, "This little park is just for you, come sit a while and enjoy the view."

Shopping. Most of Bearskin Neck's enterprises cater more to tourists than residents, and T-shirt and souvenir shops abound. We found some nice sweaters at **Bearskin Neck Sweaters** and some interesting crafts at **The Waxing Moon**. Main Street and the Dock Square area generally have better stores. Colorful fused glass plates in the window drew us into **Square Circle,** where we marveled at incredible porcelain depictions of antipasto platters, fruit salad and the like, done by a woman from Virginia. **Gatherings** stocks a unique collection of English greeting cards, gifts, jewelry and garden accessories. **Hannah Wingate House**, two shops across the street from each other, and **Woodbine Antiques** are two of the better antiques shops. The **Granite Shore Gallery** specializes in maritime art, decoys and fishing collectibles. **The Sandpiper** is an excellent kitchen shop. **London Ventures** displays exceptional pottery and jewelry. Proceeds from the well-stocked **Toad Hall Bookstore** in the old Granite Savings Bank building further environmental causes; it carries a great selection of children's books. Interesting casual clothing and jewelry are offered at **Willoughby's**

The Art Galleries. For many, art is Rockport's compelling attraction, and by 1900 the town had become *the* place for artists to spend the summer painting. More than 200 artists make the town their home, and 29 galleries are listed in the Rockport Fine Arts Gallery Guide. The 76-year-old **Rockport Art Association,** with exhibitions and demonstrations in its large headquarters at 12 Main St., is a leader in its field. You could wander for hours through places like Paul Strisik's slick gallery next to the art association or Geraci Galleries in a 1725 complex of buildings at 6 South St.

Concerts. The summer Sunday evening concerts presented at 7:30 by the Rockport Legion Band at the outdoor bandstand near Back Beach have been a Cape Ann summer tradition since 1932. A few of the original members remain active today, providing stirring concert marches, overtures and selections from Broadway musicals under the stars. The annual Rockport Chamber Music Festival presents performances Thursday-Sunday from mid-June to early July in the Rockport Art Association's main gallery. Other than these, the best entertainment in town may well be, as a couple of guests at Eden Pines Inn put it, "sitting on Dock Square and watching the world go by."

Museums. The Sandy Bay Historical Society and Museum shows early furnishings and exhibits on shipping, fishing, the local granite industry and Rockport history in the 1832 Sewall-Scripture House built of granite at 40 King St., a new wing and in the Old Castle, a 1715 saltbox on Granite Street (both open daily 2 to 5 in summer, $3). The **James Babson Cooperage Shop** (1658) on Route 127 just across the Gloucester line, a small one-story brick structure with early tools and furniture, may be the oldest building on Cape Ann (Tuesday-Sunday 2 to 5, free). In Pigeon Cove at 52 Pigeon Hill St. is the **Paper House,** built nearly 50 years ago of 215 thicknesses of specially treated newspapers; chairs, desks, tables, lamps and other furnishings also are made of paper (daily in summer 10 to 5, $1.50).

Extra-Special ————————————————

Like the rest of Rockport, its museums are low-key. But you only have to go next door to Gloucester to see two of New England's stellar showplaces.

Beauport, 75 Eastern Point Blvd., Gloucester.
Interior designer Henry David Sleeper started building his summer home in 1907 to house his collection of decorative arts and furnishings. Most of the 40 rooms are small, but each is decorated in a different style or period with a priceless collection of objects. Twenty-six are open to the public. Sleeper designed several rooms to house specific treasures: the round, two-story Tower Library was built to accommodate a set of carved wooden draperies from a hearse; the Octagon Room was built to match an eight-sided table. One of the breakfast tables in the Golden Step Room is right against a window that overlooks Gloucester Harbor; many visitors wish the place served lunch or tea.
(978) 283-0800. Guided tours Monday-Friday 10 to 4, mid-May to mid-September, daily mid-September to mid-October. Adults, $6.

Hammond Castle Museum, Hesperus Avenue, Gloucester.
Cross the drawbridge and stop for lunch or tea and castle-baked pastries at the Roof Top Cafe in this replica of a medieval castle, built in the late 1920s by inventor John Hays Hammond Jr. to house his collection of Roman, medieval and Renaissance art and objects. Concerts are given on the organ with 8,600 pipes rising eight stories above the cathedral-like Great Hall. Marbled columns and lush plantings watered by the castle's own rain system are on view in the Courtyard.
(978) 283-7673 or (800) 649-1930. June-August: daily 10 to 6. May, September and October: Wednesday-Sunday 10 to 5. Rest of year: weekends 10 to 4. Adults, $6.

Marblehead, Mass.

Jewel of the North Shore

It's not difficult to understand why some call this beautiful town with so much cachet the jewel of the North Shore.

Poised on a rocky headland jutting into the Atlantic, Marblehead has a lot going for it. It is seventeen roundabout miles northeast of Boston, whose skyline can be seen on clear days across the water, much as San Francisco's can be seen from suburban Tiburon. Yet it's a world removed – from big-city Boston, and even from tourist-jammed Salem, its better-known neighbor on the mainland.

Founded in 1629 and apparently named for all the rocky (not marble) ledges upon which it grew without regard for 20th-century traffic needs, Marblehead was one of the earliest and richest settlements in America. Sea captains, merchant traders and cod fishermen erected houses and public buildings grand and small. Their edifices remain in use today, posted with discreet markers saying "Built for Ambrose Gale, Fisherman, 1663" and "Joseph Morse, Baker, 1715." The more than 300 pre-Revolutionary structures in the half-mile-square historic district have changed little since. A walking tour takes one past (and occasionally inside) the one-of-a-kind Jeremiah Lee Mansion, the art galleries in the King Hooper Mansion, the 1727 Old Town House that predates Boston's Faneuil Hall, the brick-towered Abbot Hall landmark (permanent home of the famous painting "The Spirit of '76"), the Lafayette House (whose corner was removed, legend has it, to let General Lafayette's carriage pass), the Fort Sewall harbor fortification and the second oldest Episcopal church still standing in this country.

As opposed to restored Colonial Williamsburg or relentlessly perfect Nantucket, Marblehead is a "real" historic town, lived in year-round and bearing well any foibles or blemishes. Its original character endures – and townspeople fight fiercely to keep it that way. Small treasures abound: glimpses of the harbor through vest-pocket side yards, lush impatiens in window boxes and cosmos blooms waving beside doorways, oversize benches in the many small parks, antique signs, friendly townspeople, winding and impossibly narrow streets whose one-way directional signs thwart unknowing motorists at every turn.

The fact that Marblehead is rather isolated and so difficult for visitors to navigate is both its bane and its charm. There are none of the tourist trappings that coax visitors to Salem, Gloucester or Portsmouth. It's at the end of the road, so you do not pass through town on your

Winding residential street is typical of old Marblehead.

way to somewhere else. You may come here for a quick visit and leave perplexed as to what the fuss is about. Or you may be smitten and stay awhile.

Until recently, Marblehead – a bedroom suburb that seems far smaller than its official population of 20,000 – offered few overnight accommodations. The first inn of note emerged in 1986, and there has been a proliferation of small B&Bs only in the 1990s. The '90s have brought a changing succession of trendy restaurants and tony shops catering as much to the resident gentry on Marblehead Neck as to visitors in Old Town.

Sailors have long been lured to Marblehead, which claims to be the birthplace of the American Navy and now the yachting capital of the nation. Some 2,500 pleasure craft bob at their moorings in Marblehead's harbor. Members and guests assemble at six yacht clubs, where cannons are fired in a sonic ritual at sunrise and sundown. Thousands turned out in 1997 when the USS Constitution ("Old Ironsides") visited the harbor and fired a salute to the fort that was its salvation during a life-or-death chase with two British frigates in the War of 1812. Ordinarily, the town is at its busiest in late July during its century-old Race Week.

Otherwise, as the world becomes homogenized, Marblehead retains a singular sense of place. As a local newspaper put it, "There is plenty of room for hollyhocks in 18th-century dooryards, but only grudging space made for automobiles. The arts flourish, public debate is often spirited, and Santa arrives by lobster boat."

Inn Spots

Spray Cliff on the Ocean, 25 Spray Ave., Marblehead 01945.

One of the best oceanfront locations in town is enjoyed by guests at this substantial English Tudor home perched on a sea wall above the open Atlantic. After 35 years as corporate gypsies, Roger and Sally Plauché returned in 1994 to the town in which they'd once resided to purchase Spray Cliff, a residence turned B&B. They

Rear patio is perched above water at Spray Cliff on the Ocean.

totally redecorated, undertook many enhancements and became hands-on innkeepers. "We want to capitalize on a captivating place," said Sally.

And capitalize they did – with great style and hospitality. The Plauchés offer seven large bedrooms with private baths. The spacious main-floor guest hospitality room is dressed in colorful painted wicker furniture, with breakfast tables near the oceanfront windows and a sitting area with club chairs and an overstuffed sofa in front of the fireplace.

We'd gladly settle in the adjacent rear Winnetka bedroom, summery and cheery with a queen bed, two club chairs dressed in chintz and doors onto a private patio facing the Atlantic. The larger front bedroom, originally dark and masculine with fireplace and kingsize bed, has been lightened up with denim and plaids and some of the handpainted furniture that artistic Sally painted herself.

A professional decorator, she also left her mark on the upstairs bedrooms, all named for places in which they'd lived. "This house shouldn't be New England quaint," she advised. "It can be whimsical, fresher and freer, with a California feeling. The house lends itself to accessorizing."

She upgraded the linens and towels, incorporated splashy Ralph Lauren-style fabrics and added fresh flowers, bottled waters, and current magazines and novels in the bedrooms and amenities in the bathrooms. The result is seven truly eclectic bedrooms, five with ocean views and one on the side with a glimpse. The third-floor Athens room is a rainbow of colors, from the fabrics to the sun hat perched on a doodad atop the bureau. Fraternity pictures from Roger's days at Ohio University add interest on the pale yellow walls. A wooden lighthouse is on a shelf in the corner here as in every room. The premier accommodation is the second-floor Manhasset room with king bed, fireplace, reading nook, dramatic wall coverings and bay windows affording head-on ocean views.

The Plauchés also enhanced the continental breakfast with the help of their daughter-in-law, a nearby resident and gourmet cook "who likes to experiment." Juice, exotic fresh fruit, cereals and yogurt are supplemented by strawberry muffins, pumpkin biscuits, lemon-apple breads and homemade croissants. In the afternoon, they serve complimentary cocktails, tea and light hors d'oeuvres.

Guests have access to a smashing rear brick terrace, nestled amid flower gardens overlooking the ocean. Just below, Adirondack chairs and loungers invite relaxation atop the sea wall. Outgoing hosts, the Plauchés may offer guests a look at their handsome family quarters, including an expansive living room in California white. and their outdoor pool. "Of all our homes," Roger says, "this is our best yet." Guests feel fortunate to share it.

(781) 631-6789 or (800) 626-1530. Fax (781) 639-4563. www.marbleheadchamber.org/ spraycliff. Seven guest rooms with private baths. May-October: doubles $175 to $200. November-April, $140 to $180. Two-night minimum stay July-October and all weekends. No children. No smoking.

Harbor Light Inn, 58 Washington St., Marblehead 01945.

Born and raised in Marblehead, Peter Conway had long wanted to operate an inn here but, like others, was stymied by the town's strict zoning regulations. Instead, he opened the Carlisle House in Nantucket, became immersed in the innkeeping business and bided his time. That time arrived in 1986, when he purchased a grand Federal mansion along the town's principal through street. He was able to win approvals from neighbors and four regulatory agencies, and opened a twelve-room B&B – "without a sign and without advertising."

Success was immediate, thanks to receptive townspeople (old-line residents were happy finally to have a quality place in town in which to put up relatives and friends) and a ready market (all the daytrippers who heretofore had had no place in which to stay overnight). The fact that Peter was catering to the upscale market – "I wanted to have the best rooms on the North Shore" – didn't hurt. His rooms, constantly being upgraded, are handsomely furnished to the period, generally spacious and outfitted with private baths, TVs and telephones, fine antiques, oriental rugs, Crabtree & Evelyn toiletries, private-label sparkling water and local chocolates from Stowaway or Harbor Sweets – many of the modern-day comforts and amenities generally missing in Nantucket and other historic-house accommodations are found here.

Never content, Peter bought the Federal mansion next door in 1993, connected it to his existing building and added eight more elegant guest rooms with modern baths. Five bedrooms have whirlpool tubs, eleven have working fireplaces, most have sitting areas and several have private balconies and decks. A big (for Marblehead) back yard contains lounge chairs and a heated swimming pool. Here, on a sloping lawn with a screen of thick trees, we almost thought we were in the woods, except for the sounds of the harbor in the distance (a sight now visible only from the rooftop deck when the leaves are off the trees).

Peter and wife Suzanne, who has an eye for creative decor, continue to improve their inn. At our visit, they'd just installed a gas fireplace to warm the new formal dining room and were adding 300-count sheets in the deluxe bedrooms. Especially in demand are the front-corner Room 22, with hand-carved mahogany queensize bed, two wing chairs, a double vanity and a double jacuzzi beneath a skylight, with a mirrored wall beside, and Room 5, with deep-red walls above the wainscoting, built-in settees beside the fireplace, two wing chairs, a hand-carved four-poster queen bed and a double jacuzzi with glass brick wall. Smaller rooms have charms as well: the third-floor Room 34 has its own sun deck, Room 36 a beamed and vaulted ceiling, and Room 4, a summery-looking ground-floor room with a pine-poster bed, has a double jacuzzi and a private screened deck near the pool. There are no curtains in the inn, Peter points out – "just inside window shutters that are easily opened and closed." Elegant touches include fancy wallpapers, fine paintings and prints, brass or porcelain doorknobs, silver ice buckets and candy dishes, and votive candles beside the jacuzzis. The inn maintains a video library for the VCRs in the deluxe rooms.

An elaborate continental breakfast spread is put out in the dining room, which holds a table for eight and a tea table for two. Or the meal can be taken on trays to four tables beside the pool, or to one of the two elegant but cozy front parlors, where the day's newspapers await. The fare when we were there included orange juice, cut-up melon, lemon bread and especially good blueberry and cranberry-walnut muffins. Choices range from blueberry scones to Suzanne's no-fat bundt cake incorporating applesauce and yogurt. Tea is offered in the afternoon. On Saturdays in the off-season, the Conways serve hot hors d'oeuvres by candlelight for BYOB social gatherings.

(781) 631-2186. Fax (781) 631-2216. Nineteen rooms and two suites with private baths. Doubles, $95 to $175. Suites, $160 to $275. Two-night minimum weekends. Children over 8. Smoking restricted.

The Seagull Inn B&B, 106 Harbor Ave., Marblehead 01945.

When Skip Sigler suddenly found himself "redundant in corporate America" at age 58, he opened his family home of 25 years as a B&B. It's about the only one on posh Marblehead Neck – and thus viewed skeptically by some of his neighbors, says Skip, although the property had been the site of a hotel, which burned down in 1940. He and his wife Ruth offer a bedroom and two suites, each with private bath and cable television. Bright and airy, their home up a hill from Marblehead Harbor is distinctly lived-in and laid-back.

Skip is a hands-on innkeeper (his wife works for an insurance company), from preparing breakfast to socializing with guests to housecleaning ("six years of college for this, but I love it"). His sideline is woodworking, and he made most of the furniture in the house.

The gathering spot is the spacious living room, with its cherry floor and door, homemade furniture and valances, and a remarkable carved wooden chess set on a table in the corner.

All guest quarters come with refrigerators and TV/VCRs. The smallest is the book-lined Library, paneled in barnwood, with a queensize bed, bathtub and separate shower. Skip painted the sea scenes on a bedroom wall in the two-room Seabreeze Suite with queensize bed and a sitting room with a sofa and daybed. The biggest accommodations are in the two-story Lighthouse Suite with its own side deck. It offers a living area with sofabed, daybed and kitchen and, upstairs, a bedroom with queensize bed. Climb one more flight of stairs to the rooftop deck, from which the Boston skyline can be seen when the leaves are off the trees.

In his newfound profession, Skip is a convivial host, chatting away the morning and pouring wine in the evening. His continental breakfast includes fresh fruit and lemon or banana-walnut breads.

(781) 631-1893. Fax (781) 631-3535. One room and two suites with private bath. Doubles, $100. Suites, $150 and $200. Children welcome. No smoking.

Oceanwatch, 8 Fort Sewall Lane, Marblehead 01945.

A more watery location could not be imagined, even in Marblehead where water seems to be on all sides. From this point at the entrance to Marblehead Harbor,

The Seagull Inn B&B occupies choice hilltop property on Marblehead Neck.

there's water on three sides. You get a view of it from three guest rooms and a cottage, from the second-floor common room and breakfast deck and, especially, from the widow's walk above the nautical fourth-floor watch and sitting room.

Diane and Paul Jolicoeur, who had renovated twenty properties in Boston, had the vision and resources to transform an abandoned residence that had been in the same family since 1880. "It was a wreck that no one else wanted," bubbly Diane acknowledged. They bought it for a song in 1996, began restoring it for resale and decided to make it their home. They set up a separate section with its own entrance as a B&B. The last was an after-thought – "we'd never stayed in a B&B before," Diane said.

The bedrooms on the second and third floors are cheery in what Diane calls a "happy country, elegant beachy" look. Each has kingsize bed with floral sheets and covers, an updated bathroom with an oversize shower, a closet, TV and telephone. The Little Harbor Room has a velvet loveseat in front of a fireplace, but the other quarters are rather tight. No matter. Guests spread out in a snug common room with a fireplace and a deck, enjoy sherry in the Jolicoeurs' fourth-floor sitting room with all its nautical accoutrements and classical music playing, or climb to the widow's walk for a bird's-eye view of town and water.

Diane serves fresh fruit and local baked goods for continental breakfast at three wrought-iron tables on the harbor-view deck.

For 1998, the Jolicoeurs were readying an outlying kitchen house as a duplex cottage for guests. The main floor holds a living room with sofabed, kitchen and bathroom. The upstairs has a king master suite with a second bathroom and a deck for enjoying the harbor view.

(781) 639-8660. Three rooms and one cottage with private baths. Doubles, $165. Cottage, $250. No smoking.

Stillpoint, 27 Gregory St., Marblehead 01945.
Blessed with a choice location that catches a glimpse of Marblehead's harbor, this fine old house also is blessed with an innkeeper who cares. Sarah Lincoln-Harrison, who founded the local bed-and-breakfast association, is devoted to wholesome living, environmental innkeeping, healthful food, sustainable resources and eco-tourism. She's an innkeeper with a mission, you might say.

"This B&B is a good teaching tool to show by experience how people can live more wholesome lives," says Sarah as she warms to her subject. If asked, she'll tell about the energy-saving compact fluorescent lights in the front parlor and the four varieties of plants that line a shelf above the bed in the front guest room, "which eat up bad toxins from the air." The tap water is all right, she advises, but you may be happier with the pitcher of purified water in the bathroom.

This serene lady is particularly proud of an "edible landscape" – her former side lawn now transformed into a medley of herbs, vegetables, flowers and medicinals. We weren't the only guests to be fooled in mid-October by the still lush ripening "tomatoes," which turned out to be a rare variety of Turkish orange eggplant. She and her husband have since started an organic gardening organization and were spearheading establishment of a farmer's market locally in 1998.

The accommodations are comfortable as well as comforting, simple yet refined. There are two bedrooms (one with a double bed and one with twins and windows on three sides). They share a full hall bath, and the first taker gets a private bath if desired. There are lots of local magazines and environmental literature, but no television "because that's not what we're about," says Sarah. She prefers restful atmosphere – which includes a side deck beneath a flowering crabapple tree, with a good view of the harbor below.

Breakfast is an assortment of juices and organic cereals, homemade applesauce, muffins (perhaps morning glory) and no-fat bread for toasting, along with local preserves.

Proceeds from the small selection of environmental and crafts items for sale in the hallway go to local programs for the homeless and environmental causes. Stillpoint "welcomes guests from all cultures, races and lifestyles," says its brochure, which is printed on recycled paper. Guest-room diaries are full of praise and uplifting messages written by sensitive or sensitized guests. Wrote one Atlanta couple who stayed three weeks: "Sarah's serenity and sense of connectedness to the earth and people is a calming force in this retreat from the mainstream hubbub. Her edible landscape is both beautiful and delicious."

(781) 631-1667. Two rooms with shared bath. Doubles, $75 shared or $85 private. Children over 10. No smoking.

The Herreshoff Castle Carriage House, 2 Crocker Park, Marblehead 01945.

You can stay in a replica of a Viking castle – or at least in the carriage house of one. Chris and Michael Rubino, who occupy the three-story stone castle formerly owned by yacht designer Francis Herreshoff, offer the adjacent carriage house overlooking a shared garden courtyard.

The hideaway is a beauty. A sofa/daybed, bathroom with shower and a galley kitchen bearing framed photographs of the designer of America's Cup yachts are on the first floor. Upstairs is a wow of a bedroom with a 25-foot high ceiling, its four wood-planked sides tapering inward and upward as in a boat. The stone walls, gothic doors, stained-glass windows, antique double bed and massive armoire impart a look of antiquity. The telephone and TV set give access to the outside world. A stairway leads down to the walled courtyard/dining area surrounded by perennial gardens, gargoyles and griffins. Guests think they're in Europe next to a castle with parapets, turrets and gothic windows. And just outside are Crocker Park and the waterfront, where Michael swims every day when he gets home from work.

Guests in carriage house (right) of Herreshoff Castle may think they're in Europe.

Chris puts out pastries and the makings for an expanded continental breakfast in the galley kitchen.

(781) 631-3083. Double, $150. Two-night minimum. No smoking.

The Guest House at Lavender Gate, One Summer St., Marblehead 01945.
Two lavender doors brighten the facade of what the owners call their raspberry-mocha colored house, built in 1714 in the heart of Old Marblehead. It faces a strip of lawn leading to historic St. Michael's Church, also built in 1714, the second oldest Episcopal church still standing in the country. Except for the Shakespearean garden nestled between the house and the ancient gravestones alongside the church, you'd never guess that this is actually a very English, very literary B&B.

Any doubts vanish the moment owners Cate Olson and Nash Robbins open the main lavender door. Inside is their home, a repository chock full of antiques and accessories collected by these much-traveled anglophiles and bibliophiles, who own the nearby Much Ado Bookstore, which holds more than 35,000 volumes of old and out-of-print books. Their house is also full of books and literary accoutrements, of course.

Prepare to be overwhelmed in the living room, painted a lavender-blue color and draped with garlands of dried flowers from their gardens. Here a proper British tea is served in the afternoon amidst a clutter of books and bric-a-brac, unopened boxes of gifts from the couple's latest English buying trip and even a grand piano. That may pale beside the dining room, where a continental breakfast is set out buffet style on a table beside a framed pair of Eugene O'Neill's monogrammed boxer shorts, shelves of literary cookbooks and autographed pictures of authors, both famous and obscure.

Upstairs are two spacious suites with private baths. The second floor holds the airy Hogarth Suite, where a pastel patchwork quilt covers the queensize poster bed. There's space for a dinette table as well as a sitting room with a loveseat in a book-filled alcove in which we could get lost for hours. That is, if we weren't out on the suite's patio overlooking the garden, enjoying the flowers and a great birdhouse replicating the Globe Theater.

On the third floor is the smaller Kelmscott Suite, furnished with William Morris wallpaper, a brass double bed and a clawfoot tub. A cushioned doorway (so that tall folks don't hit their heads) leads to a small alcove with a day bed, but the principal reading area is in the main room.

Breakfast is a festive affair, overseen by the chatty owner-occupants. Expect fresh orange juice, fruits, homemade coffeecake, fresh breads or croissants and cheeses.

"We're only the fifth family that has owned the house," says Cate, "so it's been well-loved."

Now its guests can be well-read and well-fed.

(781) 631-3243 or (800) 800-6824. Two suites with private baths. Doubles, $100. Two-night minimum stay. No smoking.

Brimblecomb Hill B&B, 33 Mechanic St., Marblehead 01945.

Built in 1721 by one of the first summer visitors to Marblehead, this house in the heart of Old Marblehead is run as a B&B by Gene Arnould, art gallery owner, organizer of jazz concerts and ex-Congregational minister who's considered one of the more interesting people in town. He lives on the second floor, and turns over the first floor to guests.

Everything here is properly historic. "Ben Franklin stopped by to visit," the B&B advertises. "You can spend the night."

The Isaac Mansfield Room (named for the original owner) is the largest, an end room with private bath, queensize maple poster bed, cottage pine chest, shelves of books and wide pumpkin pine flooring. Two small rooms in the rear, reached by a separate entrance, share a full bath. Each has a double bed, basic furnishings, carpeting and a rocking chair.

Guests enjoy a small common room with fireplace, games table and a grand piano. A buffet breakfast of fruit, cereal, muffins and croissants is put out here in the morning.

(781) 631-3172 or 631-6366. One room with private bath and two rooms with shared bath. Doubles, $65 to $80. No smoking.

The Golden Cod, 26 Pond St., Marblehead 01945.

A bulletin board full of thank-you notes is a focal point in the small third-floor sitting room of this B&B, named for the town's early, lucrative codfish industry. The notes testify to the hospitality of gregarious hosts Jean and Rufus Titus, community leaders. Their late 19th-century house is located in a residential section a bit removed from Old Town. Besides the sitting room that's occasionally pressed into service as a third bedroom for a single, the third floor holds two skylit guest rooms with private baths. One has a queen bed and the other has two twins that can be joined as a king. Both come with small black and white TVs.

Jean stenciled the borders that enhance the main-floor dining area opening into a large country kitchen. It's full of notable displays of gleaming silver and china. Here is where Jean serves a full breakfast, from juice and a bowl of cut-up fruit to blueberry pancakes or eggs benedict.

The Tituses sometimes share their comfortable living room with TV, if only to show their fine collection of framed, handpainted paintings of original Wallace Nutting photos. They also share their rear deck for lounging beside the gardens.

(781) 631-1846. Two rooms with private baths. Doubles, $80. Children over 14. No smoking.

Dining Spots

Pellino's, 261 Washington St., Marblehead.

This diminutive downtown hideaway is almost universally first on locals' lists of favorite restaurants. Naples-born chef-owner Francesco (Frank) Pellino's white-clothed tables as well as five booths ensconced behind arches and fitted out with old church pews are much in demand. Twinkling white lights outline the front windows above a colorful vest-pocket garden.

Whole roasted garlic cloves are served with olive oil for spreading on the crusty Italian bread that begins each meal. The signature veal pellino is sauced with port wine, shiitake mushrooms, sundried tomatoes and herbs. Other main-course treats vary from jumbo scallops pan-seared with ginger and orange soy sauce to roasted veal rib chop stuffed with prosciutto, spinach and gorgonzola, fanned and served on mushroom risotto.

Pasta dishes here are the best in town, from to shrimp diavolo tossed with linguini to lobster ravioli. Favorite starters are grilled calamari with bruschetta crostini and wild greens salad, summer vegetable terrine and grilled portobello mushrooms with whole roasted garlic, grilled asparagus and warm polenta.

Tirami su, chocolate mousse cake on strawberry coulis, cappuccino gelato and sorbets are among the homemade desserts. The wine list has been honored by Wine Spectator. Wine-tasting dinners and cooking classes are offered here in the winter.

(781) 631-3344. Entrées, $15.95 to $20.95. Dinner nightly, 5 to 10.

The King's Rook, 12 State St., Marblehead.

Every town should have a cafe and wine bar like this. Occupying the lower floor of a restored 1747 house in the historic section of Marblehead, it was established as a coffee house in 1959 – when a coffeehouse was radical and radical was a bad word, according to owner Frank Regan. "We've stayed with the concept for all these years, but we express it in today's terms."

As the clientele has matured, so has the Rook. "We still have the same basic menu and the same cheesecake," says Frank, "but we keep looking for new items." Among the newest are gourmet pizzas, cafe latte and liqueurs. The wide-ranging, all-day menu is perfect for lunch, an afternoon drink, a casual supper or late-evening snack. House favorites are a frittata with salad of the day, a Middle Eastern plate, a pesto turkey sandwich on baguette or croissant, shrimp scampi pizza and a classic pâté platter or sandwich. Desserts here are special, particularly the creamy and rich cheesecake, the carrot cake and the Neopolitan mousse torte.

There are many coffees, teas, frappes and exotic beverages, and a fantastic selection of beers and wines by the glass. Frank often circulates through the

Owner Frank Regan at The King's Rook.

beamed, low-ceilinged rooms, and a casual, coffeehouse ambiance prevails. We know local folks who love to sip coffee or wine, listen to the classical music or jazz, read the newspapers or the Tatler from the magazine rack, and while away an afternoon.

(781) 631-9838. Light entrées, $4 to $7. Open Monday-Friday noon to 2:30; Tuesday-Friday 5:30 to 11:30; Saturday and Sunday, noon to 11:30.

Maddie's Sail Loft, 15 State St., Marblehead.

This kind of local hangout (a fixture since 1946) is not our cup of tea, but we're obviously in the minority because it's generally packed at all hours and the bar is a favorite watering hole, known for wickedly potent drinks. Except for the mural of Marblehead and the harbor at the foot of the stairs, the scene and the setting could be anywhere, which is probably why we don't find it particularly alluring.

Nevertheless, for lunch you won't go wrong with the prize-winning clam chowder, a basic burger, grilled cheese or roast beef sandwich in the $2 to $5 range. You might be stunned to find a clam roll for $10.50 or Boston scrod for $13.95. The latter are also available at dinner, when the fare ranges from fish and chips to a combination seafood platter, baked stuffed jumbo shrimp or Marblehead seafood pie. Hearty portions and a convivial seafarer's atmosphere draw the throngs.

(781) 631-9824. Entrées, $8.95 to $15.95. Lunch, Monday-Saturday 11:45 to 2, Sunday 11:45 to 4. Dinner, 5 to 10. Pub serves continuously from 11:45 to 11:30. No credit cards.

The Barnacle, 141 Front St., Marblehead.

Considered on a par with Maddie's Sail Loft, this crowded, no-nonsense restaurant at least has a water view – one of the best in town. In fact, you can sit at a narrow counter running the width of the restaurant smack dab against the windows at the rear and feast on the panorama as you eat, or on a small outdoor deck during the summer.

The short menu lists New England seafood basics at fairly steep prices; for instance, a clam roll for $8.95 and a lobster roll for $10.50 – a bit stiff, we thought, for a weekday lunch. Featured at dinner are such standards as haddock au gratin, broiled scallops, baked stuffed shrimp, "jumbo shrimp scampi" and broiled sirloin. All entrées are served with salad, potatoes, rolls and butter – "no substitutions." The tables are almost on top of each other, the nondescript decor is vaguely nautical and the small, crowded bar in front also has a good view.

(781) 631-4236. Entrées, $10.95 to $15.95. Lunch, daily 11:30 to 4; dinner, 5 to 10. Closed Tuesday in winter. No credit cards.

The Rockmore, Salem Harbor, Marblehead.

Here is a restaurant with a difference. It's located on a floating pontoon barge, and reachable only by boat. A free launch service from the Village Street Landing takes people to the barge moored in the harbor, where the dining experience is likened to that of eating on someone's yacht – a favorite Marblehead pastime. Youngsters like to flip their french fries into the water to attract a school of fish.

The menu is surprisingly extensive, and lately rollups have been added. Expect salads and sandwiches as well, and grilled or fried seafood, chicken and steak dishes. Frozen drinks, regional beers and wines by the glass go with or on their own.

(781) 639-0600. Entrées, $10.95 to $16.50 Open daily in summer, 11:30 to 9, weather permitting. No smoking.

Diversions

On a presidential visit more than 150 years after it was founded, George Washington remarked that Marblehead had the look of antiquity. It still does (even more so, no doubt), particularly in the Old Town historic district near the harbor. It has so many ledges and glacial outcroppings that early settlers simply built where they could. Streets are winding and narrow, many seem to be one-way the wrong way, parking is limited and directional signs are few. A map of town from the seasonal Chamber of Commerce information booth at Pleasant and Essex streets is a must. Even then, it takes most visitors several days to get their bearings.

Driving Tour. With said map and a willingness for trial and error, orient yourself by driving along Pleasant Street (Route 114), the main drag from Salem through the uptown commercial center. It eventually intersects with **Washington Street,** the historic main street winding from uptown through Old Town, where the most notable landmarks are located. Get to the start of one-way **Front Street** to drive along the harbor and out to the views from **Fort Sewall,** the 1742 fortification at the mouth of the harbor, where during the War of 1812 the frigate Constitution found shelter from the pursuing British. Another good view is from **Old Burial Hill** off Orne Street, one of the oldest graveyards (1638) in New England; a plaque notes that 600 Revolutionary heroes and several early pastors are interred at the top of the hill, the highest point in town. Return to Pleasant Street and head west to **Ocean Avenue,** the access route to Marblehead Neck. At the causeway is **Devereux Beach,** a sandy strand for sunning and swimming. The other side of the causeway overlooks Marblehead Harbor with all its moored pleasure craft and affords vistas of Old Town and **Marblehead Neck.** Turn left on Harbor Avenue and then Foster Avenue and pass the posh Eastern and Corinthian yacht clubs and lovely homes beside the harbor. At the tip of the neck is **Chandler Hovey Park,** where protected benches on the rocks are good vantage points for Marblehead Light and the passing boats. Continue around to Ocean Avenue with a stop at the alley leading to **Castle Rock** (one of the many public access points to the water throughout Marblehead). The rock may be of less interest than the multi-million-dollar castle residence beside. More palatial homes face the ocean on the way to the **Audubon Bird Sanctuary,** unmarked but reached off Risley Road. Head back to the causeway and where Ocean Avenue intersects with Harbor Avenue you'll be surprised by a stunning view of the Boston skyline across the water.

Walking Tour. Thus oriented, get out and walk – the best way to see and sense Marblehead. A Chamber of Commerce map outlines rewarding walking tours of one or two miles. We did ours just after daybreak, when all was still and many Marbleheaders were out walking their dogs and taking their morning constitutional. Go slowly, so as to savor (and not miss) all the little treasures and to make your own discoveries. Here are some highlights, in addition to those itemized below. Colorful houses and gardens enliven winding **Lee Street,** including a residence marked by one of Marblehead's ubiquitous plaques, this one saying "Built in 1735 for Thomas Roads, innholder." (Others to be encountered were built for merchants, bakers, boat builders, blacksmiths, shoremen, fishermen and countless others, giving a fascinating who's who of early Marblehead.) Off Gregory Street, climb the steps of **Prospect Alley** to reach Boden's Lookout, a hilltop aerie above the harbor, next to a gray house built in 1710 for John Boden, shoreman. Pass the

Lafayette House, with its cutout corner beside Union Street, and head down Water Street to the imposing **Boston Yacht Club,** one of the nation's first, where rockers are lined up on the long waterfront porch. Beyond is **Crocker Park,** a stony outcrop harbor blessed with long benches for viewing the harbor goings-on. A plaque, dedicated to George Washington's Navy, tells of "the first American vessels to engage in naval operations against an enemy...the forerunners of the U.S. Navy." They were manned by Marblehead sailors. Stop at the **Town Landing** at the foot of State Street to see working fishing boats. From the 1727 **Old Town House** area in the center of Old Town, take brief side trips to see Old North Church, the Unitarian-Universalist Church and St. Michael's Episcopal Church. None is quite as imposing as **Abbot Hall,** the 1877 town hall whose red brick tower is Marblehead's most visible landmark. The creaky main floor displays much Marblehead memorabilia; foremost is Archibald Willard's famed "Spirit of '76" painting, a larger-than-life piece made famous during the nation's centenary celebration and now framed permanently against a red velvet backdrop in the selectmen's meeting room here. The walking tour goes near or past many restaurants, B&Bs and shops detailed herein.

Jeremiah Lee Mansion, 161 Washington St., Marblehead.

Step through the door of this impressive house and you're back in 1768. Almost every feature of this house, built by one of the richest traders in the local "codfish aristocracy," is original. Lee's residence was described by a Boston newspaper at the time as "the most elegant and costly home in the Bay State Colony." You're told that Lee emulated the houses of the British aristocracy, from the simulated cut-stone blocks of the Georgian wooden facade to the original rococo carving and architectural features inside. Guides point out the intricate carved spindles and newel posts (bearing spirals within spirals) of the unsupported Santo Domingan mahogany staircase with its free-standing landing, a focal point of the massive entry foyer. On either side of the landing are copies of portraits of Jeremiah and Martha Lee, among the few full-length portraits by John Singleton Copley. Most unusual is the exotic, handpainted wallpaper created in England to exact specifications for the hallway and several grand chambers; the Lee is the only public house this old where you can see the original wallpaper on the same walls. The house is full of unique attributes and furnishings, from original fire backs and fireplace tiles to Colonial Revival gold draperies and "important" North Shore furniture – all gifts to the sponsoring Marblehead Historical Society from local families and Louise du Pont Crowninshield, an honorary director who summered in Marblehead and contributed much toward saving the house. The bedchambers and servants' quarters on the third floor have been turned into museum rooms to display local artifacts, including dolls, children's furniture, shoes, a wonderful sea captain's crib and a room full of paintings by local folk artist J.O.J. Frost. This mansion, billed as the most beautiful Colonial mansion in the country, is not to be missed.

(781) 631-1069. Open mid-May through Columbus Day, Monday-Saturday 10 to 4, Sunday 1 to 4. Adults, $4.

Shopping. Especially good specialty stores are concentrated around Washington Street in Old Town. They're also scattered along School Street, Atlantic Avenue and Pleasant Street in the newer uptown area.

In the heart of Old Town is **Tyme,** featuring one-of-a-kind works of leading artisans from across the country. We coveted a floral-painted corner table, not to mention all the Christmas ornaments of Charles Dickens characters that owner Julia Bantly chose because of their connection with the local Jacob Marley's restaurant, or the fabulous pins that call out to women to purchase a few. Across the street is **Uncommon Stock,** with an uncommonly choice selection of kitchenware, cookbooks, pottery and accessories that lure us inside at every visit.

Most unusual is Joan Wheeler's **Russian Gallery,** a trove of things Russian, including dozens of matrioshka nesting dolls, lacquered boxes, shawls, small colorful pens and eggs, even T-shirts. Downstairs are Russian watercolors and prints. **The Marblehead Kite Co.** carries everything that says Marblehead – T-shirts, coffee mugs, sweatshirts of sailboats on the harbor titled Marblehead Rush Hour and, yes, kites. Some of the cards here made us laugh out loud. Also specializing in Marblehead items is **Arnould Gallery,** with many local prints and some carved swans clad in straw hats. Nearby, **Much Ado** has two floors crammed with rare books and **O'Rama's,** which started selling antique lingerie and linens, expanded into a line of jewelry, frames, soaps, teapots and boxes, all very dainty and feminine. **Atlantic Rancher** is the only retail store of the local company that manufactures functional apparel and accessories. **Hector's Pup** is a great toy store, and **Shay's Rebellion** a better-than-average souvenir shop.

Uptown are **C'est la Vie** with imaginative gifts of the kind found in decorator showhouses, as well as unusual picture frames, china and glass, and exquisite baby things; **Accessories by Blass,** with unusual pins, pocketbooks and umbrellas, and the excellent **Spirit of '76 Bookstore.** At 189 Pleasant St. is the **Garden Collection,** where proprietor Rebecca Ellis stocks all kinds of flowery gifts, botanical notecards, floral aprons and pottery with a floral or garden theme. We liked her T-shirts with cats or bird feeders.

For a break from shopping, stop at **Delphin's Gourmandise** at 258 Washington St., where you'll likely be overpowered by the most heavenly aromas of any bakery anywhere. Master pastry chef Delphin Gomes creates delectables for eating in the cafe, on the side patio or to go. We can vouch for the plum tart, one of the best pastries we've ever eaten.

Extra Special

Hestia Handcrafts, 13 Hawkes St., Marblehead.

Generally unknown by residents as well as visitors, the little showroom here displays fine miniatures produced in the rear "factory" and sold to collectors across the country. Linda Macdonald, a Marblehead mother of four, turned her hobby of designing unique products in clays and porcelains into a lucrative business. Her original designs, which range from Christmas ornaments and miniature buildings ($8 to $15) to figurines and garden statues ($35 to $45), are first sculpted in clay. Latex molds are made for mass-producing air-dried plaster units, which then are individually handpainted and sealed by fifteen employees, many of whom work at home. We were struck by the AmeriScape ornaments devoted to different places, from Charleston to Cape May to Breckenridge to Natchez – not to mention Marblehead, for which a different design is produced each year. There are garden statues of cats, rabbits and dogs, as well as nativity scenes (to which collectors add characters over the years). We picked up a few finely sculpted and detailed woodland animals for Christmas gifts.

(781) 639-2727. Open Monday-Saturday, 9 to 5.

Renovated 1846 octagonal rotunda is a focal point of Williams College Museum of Art.

Williamstown, Mass.

Arts Town of the East

Blessed with an uncommonly scenic setting and the riches that prestigious Williams College attracts and returns, this small college town in the northern Berkshires is an arts center of national significance.

Newsweek called the annual Williamstown Theatre Festival "the best of all American summer theaters." Connoisseur magazine said its three leading museums make it "an unlikely but powerful little art capital." U.S. News and World Report revealed that educators consider Williams College tops among academic institutions in the country.

Local promotion pieces note that Williamstown has been cited as "the most culture-saturated rural spot in the nation."

Williams, its associates and benefactors have inspired these superlatives. But they have geography and nature to thank for what some call "The Village Beautiful." Somewhat isolated in a verdant bowl, Williamstown dwells at the foot of Mount Greylock, the highest peak in Massachusetts, surrounded by Vermont's Green and New York's Taconic mountains. Not only do these provide great outdoor activities (in particular, golf, hiking and skiing). They also help Williamstown retain a charmed rural flavor that seems far more village-like than its population of 8,200 might suggest.

Williamstown is a sophisticated little town of great appeal, one that unfolds as you delve. The youthful dynamic of 2,000 college students is not always apparent in the broader community – at least in summer, during tourist season. Besides natural and cultural attractions, there are good restaurants, selective shops and a handful of inns and B&Bs.

This is one place that has long been special. If you simply drive around town, you may not sense the subtle blend of sophistication and small town that is the real Williamstown. Here you must stop, stay awhile and explore.

Inn Spots

The Orchards, 222 Adams Road (Route 2), Williamstown 01267.

Opened to the tune of many millions of dollars in 1985, the Orchards was designed to fill a conspicuous gap in terms of inn accommodations. It succeeds "along the lines of an English country hotel" (its words). But its billing as the Berkshires' "most gracious country inn" and "the finest inn in the Northeast," as its early publicity hoopla claimed, was a stretch. (Indeed, passersby along Route 2 sometimes mistake its odd-looking, salmon-colored stucco facade for a condominium project). Its early status always rather tenuous, The Orchards was rescued from foreclosure in 1993 by Sayed M. Saleh, a hotel executive from Boston, who acquired the inn from the FDIC.

Despite its initial "newness," The Orchards has aged surprisingly well. The 49-bedroom, three-story structure meanders around a small, open courtyard containing a free-form, rock-bordered pond with a fountain. Recently enlarged, the pond is surrounded by an outdoor dining area, lawns and flowers.

The interior layout separates the restaurant and lounge from the guest rooms. Winding corridors expand into a gracious drawing room, where intricate chandeliers hang from the cathedral ceiling and polished antique furniture of the Queen Anne style warms the space. Complimentary scones and English tea are served on fine china in the afternoon and, perhaps, dessert and coffee or liqueurs after dinner. Coffee and breakfast pastries are served there (gratis) before the dining room opens in the morning. Check out the inn's collection of antique silver teapots and the Victorian-era tin soldiers and guardsmen on display.

The guest rooms are large, comfortable and colorful in the Orchards' pink and green theme (the area was long an orchard, but lately has been developed).

Amenities include telephones in bathrooms as well as bedrooms and TVs secreted in armoires, their remote controls at bedside. Each room is different within the prevailing theme: marble bathrooms with terrycloth robes and Lord & Mayfair bath oils and soaps, separate dressing area and small refrigerator. Twelve have working fire-places, and some have four-poster beds and bay windows. Cookies are served when the beds are turned down at night.

The inn has a sauna and jacuzzi, four function rooms, an

antiques shop, a cocktail lounge with fireplace and small outdoor pool flanked by a sundeck. Three meals a day are available in the elegant dining room, where the short dinner menu at our latest visit ranged from $23 for grilled swordfish with citrus-ginger sauce to $28 for crepinette of lamb loin on a bed of spicy spinach. A pub menu is available from 2 to 9 p.m.

Although the dining room is considered lately to have slipped under a succession of chefs, the inn merits its ranking as the only Mobil four-star, AAA four-diamond hotel in Massachusetts west of Boston.

(413) 458-9611 or (800) 225-1517. Fax (413) 458-3273. Forty-nine rooms with private baths. Memorial Day to mid-November: doubles, $160 to $225. Rest of year: $125 to $175.

Field Farm Guest House, 554 Sloan Road, Williamstown 01267.

When the 1948 American Modern-style home of arts patron Lawrence H. Boedel became available following the death of his widow in 1984, The Trustees of Reservations didn't quite know what to do with it. Restorationists David and Judy Loomis of River Bend Farm B&B (see below) proposed running it as a B&B and ended up doing just that. They got it up and running, turning over operations in 1996 to the Trustees and resident innkeepers Sean and Jean Cowhig.

A stay in one of the five guest rooms in this rural hilltop home surrounded by 296 acres of conservation land is intriguing, given the home's history. The word "home" is used advisedly, for that's exactly what it is – looking much as the Bloedels left it, with the exception of some of the fabulous collection of paintings they donated to the Williams College Museum of Art and the Whitney Museum of Art in New York City. At a recent visit, eight of the original pieces were back on indefinite loan from the Williams Museum.

Guests have the run of a spacious living room, dining room, galley kitchen and grounds, which are striking for their sculptures, views and trails. Throughout the 5,000 square-foot house, most of the furniture was made by Mr. Bloedel, a 1923 Williams graduate and onetime college librarian. All five bedrooms retain their original private baths and vary in size.

The huge main-floor Gallery Room, which the original owner used as a studio, has a queen bed as well as two twins, a black walnut floor and a separate entrance.

Upstairs in this house that might be described as a mixture of art nouveau and Danish modern are four more guest rooms. Two have queen beds, one has twins and the other has a queen and two twins.

In the North Room, tiles of butterflies flank the fireplace (fascinating tiles surround all the fireplaces). It has its own balcony, a dressing table with mirrored surface and a walk-in closet with sliding drawers. The master bedroom contains a built-in corner dressing unit, a fireplace with tiles of trees and birds, and an enormous private deck. The other rooms also are comfortable but considerably smaller.

The Cowhigs serve a full breakfast in the dining room, which opens onto a small porch. Fresh fruit, yogurt, homemade granola and banana bread precede the main course, perhaps a cheese omelet, blueberry pancakes or tomato-basil frittata (the ingredients for the last picked from the garden).

The architecturally interesting house, built of Western cedar and fronted by a mass of yellow creeping hydrangeas, was designed by architect Edward Goodell.

Outside are the original swimming pool fed by an underground spring, a tennis court, picnic tables, woodlands, pastures, a pond, and four miles of trails for wildlife

Field Farm Guest House backs up toward pond.

watching or cross-country skiing. The property has been a working farm since Williamstown was incorporated in 1765. It's now leased to a farmer who raises corn and cows.

Don't be misled by the name. Field Farm Guest House is not a farm in the usual sense, but rather it is a home lived in by a wealthy and interesting man. You'll be charmed staying here among the furnishings of the period and enjoying the tranquil grounds.

But book early. Field Farm charges the same price for each room and enjoys one of the highest occupancy rates of any New England B&B – so much so that the rates were raised substantially for 1998 in an effort to reduce occupancy and subsequent wear and tear. "The B&B is here to preserve the house," explains Jean. "Not to hurt it."

(413) 458-3135. Five rooms with private baths. Doubles, $125.

The Williamstown Bed and Breakfast, 30 Cold Spring Road, Williamstown 01267.

An attractive white Victorian house built in 1880 with room to spare, this was turned into a sparkling B&B in 1989 by partners Kim Rozell and Lucinda Edmonds. "I cook and Lucinda cleans," quipped Kim at our first visit. Both perform their functions to perfection, although now they share the duties and sometimes switch roles.

Kim's breakfasts are feasts, taken at a table for eight in the dining room. Start with fruit, cereals and homemade baked goods, but save room for the main course – perhaps blueberry pancakes, waffles, baked eggs or cheese blintzes. Spinach pie and oatmeal scones were treats when we last were here.

Lucinda's "cleaning" is evident throughout the house. Besides the comfy living room outfitted in a crisp, almost contemporary style, there are four spiffy guest rooms with private bathrooms and comfortable wing chairs on the second floor. Two rooms have queensize poster beds, a third has a double bed and one has two twins. White cotton comforters top each bed.

Appointments are a blend of antiques and modern, with an emphasis on oak furniture, mini-print wallpapers with vivid borders and a refreshing absence of clutter often associated with Victoriana. Typical of the caring touches are the bottles of Poland Spring water in each room.

The personable hosts, who do all the work themselves, seem to know everything there is to know about the area and share their enthusiasm with guests.

(413) 458-9202. Four rooms with private baths. Doubles, $70 to $80. Children over 10. No smoking. No credit cards.

River Bend Farm, 643 Simonds Road (Route 7 North), Williamstown 01267.
This handsome Georgian Colonial was built in 1770 by Col. Benjamin Simonds, one of Williamstown's thirteen founders, and the house exudes 18th-century authenticity.

Preservationists David and Judy Loomis acquired the house in 1977, spent years restoring it with great care and attention to detail, and started sharing its treasures with B&B guests.

Guests enter the rear keeping room, where black kettles hang from the huge hearth, one of five fireplaces off the central stone chimney. The room is full of hooked rugs, antiques, dried flowers and grapevine wreaths. Here's where the hosts serve what they call a healthful continental breakfast of fresh fruit, homemade granola, honey from their own beehives, muffins and breads.

All the lighting here and in the adjacent parlor comes from small bulbs in tin chandeliers and period lighting fixtures. The Loomises removed layers of flooring atop the original 1770 boards in the parlor. "Just to think that Ethan Allen stood here on the same floor is exciting," says Dave. The house contains what authorities consider to be the best examples of period woodwork in town, as well as notable corner cupboards, paneling and iron work.

Four bedrooms share two baths, one upstairs with a tub and the other downstairs in the old pantry and harboring an ingenious corner shower with tiles that Dave fashioned from roof slate. Three rooms are upstairs off a hall containing a giant spinning wheel. The front corner room has a crocheted coverlet over the four-poster double bed and plenty of room for two wing chairs in a sitting area. Two other upstairs rooms, each containing a double and a twin bed, are good for families. A downstairs bedroom in a former parlor is lovely, decorated in blues and whites with well-worn oriental rugs.

Dave says the B&B proceeds help finance the ongoing restoration of this old home and tavern, which is listed on the National Register of Historic Places. Spending a night or two here is to immerse oneself in history. Or, as Judy tells it, "guests say it's like staying in a museum but you can touch the stuff."

(413) 458-3121. Four rooms with two shared baths. Doubles, $90. Closed November to mid-April.

Le Jardin, 777 Cold Spring Road (Route 7), Williamstown 01267.
A wooded hillside lush with pachysandra, a pond, a waterfall from the passing brook and, of course, colorful gardens welcome guests to this French-style restaurant and country inn converted from a 19th-century mansion two miles south of town.

The Williamstown Bed and Breakfast occupies Victorian-era house set on broad lawn.

A narrow stairway beside the entrance to the main dining room leads from the entry foyer through a rustic hallway to the six guest rooms, all with full baths and four with fireplaces. Most choice is the front corner room with a four-poster bed ensconced in a niche, stenciling, hooked rugs and TV, and a tub with a jacuzzi in the large bathroom. Particularly popular in summer is a small room in the rear with a queensize bed and a private balcony facing the woods. The other rooms, outfitted in country style, are rather more plain.

Foremost a restaurant, the inn's only public sitting area is in the front bar. Continental breakfast is served in the formal dining room, where friendly German chef-innkeeper Walter Hayn has achieved a good reputation in his 25 years (see Dining Spots).

(413) 458-8032. Six rooms with private baths. Doubles, $75 to $95.

The Williams Inn, Junction of Routes 7 and 2, Williamstown 01267.

After the old Williams Inn was taken over by Williams College, the Treadway built a replacement (supposedly "on-the-green at Williams College," though not by our definition). Not a typical country inn, this is a Colonial-modern hotel/motel. A pianist was playing in the almost-empty cocktail lounge and a gaggle of giggling girls was being shepherded through the lobby for a swimming/birthday party the first Friday afternoon we stopped in.

The 103 air-conditioned rooms and "junior suites" on three floors come with full baths, color TVs, oversize beds and early American furnishings. Facilities include a spacious and comfortable lobby, indoor pool, a whirlpool and sauna, elevators, lounge and a restaurant serving three meals a day.

The large and formal dining room with ten big brass chandeliers and high-back, leather-seat chairs is in vivid shades of raspberry with black trim and beige table-cloths. The extensive dinner menu includes such continental choices as chicken dijonnaise, pork tenderloin madagascar, roast duck bigarade and veal oscar.

The buffet tables for the popular Sunday brunch ($16.95) take up the entire lobby. With choices from baked eggs in ham, belgian waffles and cheese blintzes to scallop and langoustine pie, swordfish Louisianne, roast pork, sweet and sour duck, sauerbraten, roast sirloin and carved leg of lamb, no one leaves hungry.

The inn's gift shop features quilted bags, baskets, beveled glass ornaments, porcelain Christmas tree angels, appliquéd denim jumpers, animal sculptures and such.

(413) 458-9371 or (800) 828-0133. Fax (413) 458-2767. Ninety-eight rooms and five junior suites with private baths. Memorial Day to late October: doubles $120 to $175, suites $175 to $190. Rest of year: doubles $100 to $135, suites $150 to $175.

Entrées, $13.95 to $19.95. Lunch, Monday-Saturday 11:30 to 2:30. Dinner nightly, 5:30 to 9:30 or 10. Sunday, brunch 11:30 to 2:30, dinner 5 to 9.

Dining Spots

The Mill on the Floss, Route 7, New Ashford.

Genial Maurice Champagne, originally from Montreal, is the chef-owner at this established and well-regarded restaurant, tops on everyone's list for special-occasion dining.. He loves to socialize, and one reason he designed the open, blue and white tiled kitchen was so that patrons could come up and talk with him as he cooked.

The dark brown wood building, pleasantly landscaped, was once a mill. Inside it is cozy, with beamed ceilings, paneled walls, a hutch filled with Quimper pottery, white linens and many hanging copper pots.

Assisted by his daughter Suzanne, Maurice presents classic French fare. Among starters are duck pâté with plum wine, escargots, prosciutto and melon, crab cakes and soups like cold cucumber or black bean. Entrées range from steak and kidney pie to rack of lamb. Sweetbreads in black butter, chicken amandine and sliced

Chef Maurice Champagne in his kitchen.

tenderloin with garlic sauce are some. The fish of the day could be halibut meunière, poached salmon or grilled swordfish.

For dessert, you might find crème caramel, deep-dish pie and grand marnier soufflé, or try café diablo for two. Wines are quite reasonably priced.

(413) 458-9123. Entrées, $18.50 to $26.50. Dinner, Tuesday-Sunday from 5.

Wild Amber Grill, 101 North St. (Route 7), Williamstown.

The old Le Country restaurant, a bastion of French cuisine, became contemporary American with its reincarnation by identical twin brothers Ned and Sandy Smith, well-known local chefs.

Ned, who used to cook at The Orchards, is the chef at this sprawling establishment with a couple of white-clothed dining rooms and a large screened porch, where meals are served in season. The signature sesame-seared tuna with soy-ginger vinaigrette got its start at the brothers' Cobble Café, where Sandy continues to hold forth as chef. Other main courses on the with-it menu include shrimp sautéed in a red curry coconut sauce, marinated chicken with pineapple-papaya salsa, sautéed duck breast with plum sauce and green tea noodles, and osso buco. The shrimp and scallops lotus, served in a pastry shell with coconut lime and cilantro, and the arugula and endive salad with goat cheese are favorite starters. All the cooking for outdoor dining is done on a grill on the porch.

Live entertainment is scheduled Friday and Saturday nights in the lounge.

(413) 458-5000. Entrées, $14.50 to $21. Dinner nightly except Tuesday, 5:30 to 9:30 or 10.

Mezze, 84 Water St., Williamstown.
What one innkeeper called the "Smithification of Williamstown restaurants" reached a high point with the opening of this wildly popular bistro and bar in the former Potter's Wheel craft gallery. Owner Nancy Thomas, who is married to Sandy Smith, gave the food a Mediterranean and Moroccan theme initially, thanks to her mother from Morocco. But a new chef, trained at the Culinary Institute of America, added a contemporary American accent.

The curving interior, white with shiny birch walls and banquette seating, is the place to see and be seen. There's usually a wait for a table, a wait made agreeable in season with drinks served on the small deck above the Green River in back.

The short menu ranges from light fare like a Turkish white bean salad and a smoked trout plate to entrées such as Mezze chicken (a changing presentation) and grilled flank steak. You can stop in for an appetizer, dessert, drinks or dinner.

(413) 458-0123. Entrées, $11 to $14. Dinner nightly, 5:30 to midnight or later.

The Cobble Cafe, 27 Spring St., Williamstown.
Three meals a day are offered in this colorful and casual storefront operation by chef Sandy Smith, who used to cook in New York and on private yachts. He and his twin brother Ned started here as partners with local liquor-store owner Gerard Smith, no relation. Walls hung with contemporary art and a rear wall checkered in black and white are the backdrop for tables dressed in white and teal green.

The prices are modest and the fare interesting. For dinner, how about blackened tuna steak on greens tossed in a tomato vinaigrette, roasted pork tenderloin with tomatillo sauce, or New Zealand venison medallions with morel mushrooms and a cranberry gastrique? Those are "large plates." Among "small plates" are oyster stew, Thai duck salad and Asian mussels steamed in ginger, garlic, chile peppers, lime leaves and more. Homemade desserts include apple crisp, linzer torte and cheesecake.

The lunch menu yields interesting salads, sandwiches (the Cobblewich teams grilled eggplant with tomato, goat cheese and basil) and main dishes like chicken quesadilla, chicken gumbo filé in puff pastry and vegetable burrito. French almond toast, pecan pancakes and breakfast burrito are among the morning offerings, but we'd splurge for eggs Edward (with smoked trout, chives and crème fraîche in puff pastry).

Gerard oversees the wine list, offering boutique wines at affordable prices.

(413) 458-5930. Entrées, $12 to $16. Breakfast, Monday-Saturday 7 to 11:30, Sunday 7 to 1. Lunch, Monday-Saturday 11:30 to 3. Dinner, Tuesday-Saturday 5 to 9.

Robin's, Spring and Lathrop Streets, Williamstown.
A California chef who moved east when her husband joined the Williams College faculty, Robin MacDonald started a catering business before opening her dream restaurant in a house at the foot of Spring Street. She is known for innovative Mediterranean-style fare and expanded into the adjacent shop for more space.

Although it receives generally good reviews, the place did not meet expectations when we stopped for a Columbus Day lunch. After an interminable wait in the coffee/tableware area that doubled as a holding tank, we finally were seated in one of the two small dining rooms. There was a slice of lemon in the carafe of ice water, a good sign, but the cutlery was so small and wimpy we felt as if we were eating with plastic. We ordered the carrot-ginger soup (which had sold out) and settled for focaccia topped with sausage, tomato and cheese (a pizza-like spread so ample that half went home for lunch the next day) and the smoked Asian chicken salad with sesame soy noodles (a small portion that was niggardly in terms of chicken).

Nonetheless, we would return at a slower time – perhaps for dinner, when the changing menu emphasizes locally raised food and organic produce. Main courses range from grilled tuna with thyme butter to grilled ribeye steak with green peppercorn sauce. The rainbow trout roasted with oranges, lemons and herbs and the lobster ravioli with pesto, cream and tomatoes come highly rated.

Desserts include a dynamite lemon tart, chocolate torte, blueberry shortcake, banana cheesecake and apple-raspberry-almond crumb cake.

Interesting local art adorns the walls, white butcher paper covers the tablecloths and an energetic staff scurries back and forth through the holding tank from kitchen to table. A side deck allows outdoor dining in season beneath three stately white pine trees growing through the floor.

(413) 458-4489. Entrées, $14 to $22.50. Open daily 11 to 11, Sunday 9 to 9. Shorter hours in winter.

Le Jardin, 777 Cold Spring Road, Williamstown.

The two partitioned dining rooms here are country French and quite elegant, with velvet striped seats, white linens and dark napkins placed sideways, hanging lamps with pierced tin panels, white draperies and plants in the windows.

German chef-owner Walter Hayn has the distinction of the longest tenure in town (26 years), now that colleague Raymond Canales of Le Country restaurant has retired. Walter shows no signs of retiring, but has turned the kitchen duties over to his chef. They produce an extensive American-continental menu of the updated Long Island duckling school.

Starters range widely from onion soup and herring in sour cream to escargots bourguignonne and shrimp cocktail. Main courses pair classics like sole florentine, frog's legs and filet mignon with bordelaise sauce with such contemporary offerings as grilled swordfish and chicken kabobs. The specialty rack of lamb is $48 for two, and four vegetarian dishes are listed under "on the light side."

Desserts tend to be rich, among them death by chocolate, New York cheesecake and pecan pie. The wine list is stunningly short but serviceable and affordably priced.

Traditionalists dote on the low-key place, which has remained comfortably the same over a quarter century of culinary change.

(413) 458-8032. Entrées, $15 to $24. Dinner nightly, 5 to 9 or 10. Closed Tuesday, November-May.

Hobson's Choice, 159 Water St., Williamstown.

This country-rustic place with paneled walls and beamed ceilings is a favorite of locals. Old tools hang on the walls, Tiffany-type lamps top tables and booths, and there are a few stools at the bar in back of the room. Around the front door are wonderful panes of stained glass with flowers and birds therein.

Chef-owner Dan Campbell moved from Montana to lend a Western accent to the extensive steak and seafood menu. Hand-cut steaks, prime rib, chicken Santa Fe, cajun shrimp and grilled or blackened Norwegian salmon and tuna are featured for dinner. Or you can make a meal out of chopped sirloin and the salad bar, which is known for its organic produce.

Start with shrimp wontons, sautéed mushrooms or fried calamari. Finish with mud pie, grand marnier fudge parfait or apple strudel.

(413) 458-9101. Entrées, $10 to $18. Lunch, Tuesday-Friday 11:30 to 2. Dinner nightly, 5 to 9:30.

Diversions

Williamstown's scenic beauty is apparent on all sides, but less known is the composite of its art and history collections. You get a hint of both on arrival simply by traversing Main Street east from the green at Route 7. The hilly street with broad lawns leading to wide-apart historic homes, imposing college buildings and churches – totally lacking in commercialism – is more scenic and tranquil than the main street of any college town we know.

Art and history are best appreciated when viewed close up, away from the crowded settings of the huge museums. As Connoisseur magazine reported, this intimacy is "the great gift" of Williamstown.

Williams College Museum of Art, Main Street.

A $4.5 million extension to its original octagonal building in Lawrence Hall makes this museum a sleeper in art circles. Itself a work of art, it contains an 1846 neoclassical rotunda with "ironic" columns that are decorative rather than functional. The eight sides of the rotunda are repeated in soaring newer galleries with skylights, some of their walls hung with spectacular wall art. Once headed by Guggenheim director Thomas Krens, the museum houses fourteen galleries and a staggering 10,000 works, from 3,000-year-old Assyrian stone reliefs to the last self-portrait by Andy Warhol. In an effort to complement the better-known Sterling and Francine Clark Art Institute's strengths in the 19th century, this museum stresses contemporary, 17th- and 18th-century American art and rare Asian art. It features traveling and special exhibitions rivaling those of many a metropolitan museum.

(413) 597-2429. Open Tuesday-Saturday 10 to 5, Sunday 1 to 5. Free.

Nearby is the **Hopkins Observatory,** the oldest working observatory in the United States (1836), offering exhibits on the history of astronomy plus planetarium shows and viewings through college telescopes.

Chapin Library, Stetson Hall, Williams College.

Nowhere else are the founding documents of the country – original printings of the Declaration of Independence, the Articles of Confederation, the Bill of Rights and drafts of the Constitution – displayed together in a simple glass case on the second floor of a college hall. This remarkable library contains more than 30,000 rare books, first editions and manuscripts. You might ask to see James Madison's copy of Thomas Paine's *Common Sense.* One floor below is the Williamsiana Collection of town and gown, while the lowest level of Stetson contains the archives of band leader Paul Whiteman, with 3,500 original scores and a complete library of music of the 1920s.

(413) 597-2462. Open Monday-Friday, 9 to noon and 1 to 5. Free.

Williamstown Theatre Festival, Adams Memorial Theater, Williams College. Founded in 1955, the professional summer festival presents "some of the most ambitious theatre the U.S. has to offer," in the words of the Christian Science Monitor. Such luminaries as Christopher Reeve, Dick Cavett, Edward Herrmann and Marsha Mason return summer after summer to the festival they call home for productions of everything from Chekhov and Ibsen to Tennessee Williams and Broadway tryouts, all the while mingling with the townspeople. The festival uses the theater's main stage, but also includes the smaller Other Stage, emphasizing newer works in the 96-seat Extension added in 1982 to the same building.

(413) 597-3400. Festival performances Tuesday-Saturday, late June through August.

Williams College. Besides the aforementioned highlights, the campus as a whole is worth exploring. Its 50 buildings, predominantly in red brick and gray granite, range through almost every period of American architecture. The lawns and plantings and sense of nature all around contribute to a pleasant walking tour.

Nature. The prime spot – as well as the area's dominant feature – is the **Mount Greylock State Reservation,** a series of seven peaks with a 3,491-foot summit that is the highest in Massachusetts. You can drive, hike or bike to the summit for a spectacular five-state view. Other memorable views are obtained by driving the Taconic Trail through Petersburg Pass and the Mohawk Trail above North Adams. The 2,430-acre **Hopkins Memorial Forest** northwest of the campus is an experimental forest operated by the Williams College Center for Environmental Studies, with nature and cross-country trails, plus the Barn Museum showing old photographs, farm machinery, implements and tools, and the Buxton Gardens, a farm garden designed to have certain flowers in bloom at all times. Williams College also recently acquired **Mount Hope Park,** a former estate with extensive gardens and grounds.

Recreation. Golf is the seasonal pastime at the Taconic Golf Club, on the south edge of town and ranked as one of the tops in New England, and at Waubeeka Golf Links in the valley at South Williamstown. In summer, you can swim in the 74-degree waters of Sand Springs Pool and Spa, founded in 1813 and the oldest springs resort still in operation in the country. In winter, there's skiing nearby at Jiminy Peak and Brodie Mountain ski resorts.

Shopping. The college-community stores are generally along Spring Street, which runs south off Main Street opposite the main campus between such campus appendages as museum, science center and sports complex. The **House of Walsh** is an institution for traditional clothing, and **Zanna** is a newcomer for women's apparel. Try the **Clarksburg Bread Co.** for chunky cheddar cheese bread or an oatmeal-cranberry scone. More than 40 varieties of coffees and 25 of loose teas are available at **Cold Spring Coffee Roasters. Library Antiques** shows dhurrie rugs, English country pine furniture, linens, china and more.

Water Street, a parallel street that blossomed later, has distinctive shops including the **Cottage** gift shop and outdoors equipment at the **Mountain Goat.**

For foodies, the most interesting shopping of all may be at **The Store at Five Corners,** an 18th-century general store gone decidedly upscale, just south of

Neoclassical white marble temple houses Sterling and Francine Clark Art Institute.

Williamstown at the junction of Routes 7 and 43. Ex-New Yorkers Stuart Shatken and his wife Andy seek out the unusual as they stock their store with one-of-a-kind items. Expect to find things like Epicurean spices, Mendocino pastas, interesting wines, gifts, Italian biscotti and homemade fudge along with an espresso bar, baked goods from the store's bakery, "real NYC bagels," and an assortment of breakfast and lunch items from the deli. There are tables upon which to enjoy, inside or out.

Extra-Special _____

Sterling and Francine Clark Art Institute, 225 South St., Williamstown.
The most widely known of the town's museums chanced upon its Williamstown location through an old family connection with Williams College and the fact that eccentric collector Sterling Clark, heir to the Singer sewing machine fortune, wanted his treasures housed far from a potential site of nuclear attack. Clark's neoclassical white marble temple opened in 1955 (he and his wife are buried under its front steps) and was expanded in 1973 by a red granite addition housing more galleries and one of the nation's outstanding art research libraries. Lately mounting major exhibitions that draw more than 100,000 visitors a summer, the Clark has particularly strong holdings of French 19th-century paintings (more than 30 Renoirs), English silver, prints and drawings (the Clark was the single largest source for the Renoir exhibition at Boston's Museum of Fine Arts). Shown mostly in small galleries the size of the rooms in which they once hung, the highly personalized collection of Monets, Turners and Winslow Homers quietly vies for attention with sculptures, porcelain and three centuries worth of silver (Sterling Clark liked good food and the silverware to go with it). All this is amid an austere yet intimate setting of potted plants and vases of dried flowers, furniture and benches for relaxation. Amazingly, it's all free.
(413) 458-9545. Open Tuesday-Sunday and Monday holidays, 10 to 5.

Blantyre is a Tudor-style replica of a castle in Scotland.

Lenox, Mass.
The Good (and Cultured) Life

The gentle beauty of the Berkshires has attracted generations of artists, authors and musicians – as well as their patrons who appreciate the good life. At the center of the Berkshires in both location and spirit is Lenox, a small village whose cultural influence far exceeds its size.

In the 19th century, Lenox was home for Nathaniel Hawthorne, Edith Wharton, Henry Ward Beecher and Fannie Kemble. Herman Melville, Henry Adams, Oliver Wendell Holmes, Henry Wadsworth Longfellow, William Cullen Bryant, Daniel Chester French and (later) Norman Rockwell lived and worked nearby.

Such was the allure of this tranquil mountain and lake country that many prominent Americans built palatial homes here. Lenox became "the inland Newport" for such families as Westinghouse, Carnegie, Procter, Morgan and Vanderbilt. Indeed, some of America's 400 summered in Newport and spent the early autumn in the Berkshires.

The artists and the affluent helped make Lenox in the 20th century a center for the arts. Tanglewood, across from Hawthorne's home, is the summer home of the Boston Symphony Orchestra. Edith Wharton's Mount is the stage for Shakespeare & Company. Nearby are the Lenox Arts Center, the Berkshire Theater Festival, Jacob's Pillow Dance Festival and the Aston Magna Festival concerts. Lenox is now the home of the National Music Foundation, whose mission is to build a National Music Center there.

The Lenox area's cultural attractions are well known. Less so are some of its hidden treats: the picturesque Stockbridge Bowl (a lake), the Walker sculpture garden, the Pleasant Valley wildlife sanctuary, the Church on the Hill, and the mansions along Kemble and Cliffwood streets.

Attractions of a more specialized nature are offered at the Kripalu Center for Yoga and Health and at Canyon Ranch in the Berkshires.

Staying in some of Lenox's inns is like being a house guest in a mansion. Besides lodging in style, visitors may dine at some of New England's fanciest restaurants and enjoy $72 orchestra seats in the Shed at Tanglewood. The budget-conscious can find more reasonable places in which to stay and eat, and, while picnicking on the Tanglewood lawn, can hear the BSO almost as well as those in the Shed.

Except perhaps for the prices, the charms of Lenox appeal to almost everyone.

Inn Spots

Most Lenox inns require a minimum stay of three nights on summer weekends, and weekend prices usually extend from Thursday through Sunday.

Blantyre, 16 Blantyre Road, Box 995, Lenox 01240.

This rambling, Tudor-style brick manor off by itself on 85 private acres was built in 1902 as a summer retreat for a millionaire in the turpentine business. A replica of the Hall of Blantyre in Scotland, it used to be called Blantyre Castle, and was a memorable place for dining in the baronial style. Today, "castle" has been dropped from the name, but the regal feeling remains in lodging as well as in dining (see Dining Spots).

In 1981, the structure was carefully restored even to the insides of the huge closets by owner Jane Fitzpatrick, whose Red Lion Inn in adjacent Stockbridge has welcomed guests in the New England tradition for so many years. The result is worthy of a castle, or at the very least an English country-house hotel, says general manager Roderick Anderson with his trace of Scottish accent: a majestic foyer with staircase of black oak, public rooms with high beamed ceilings, rich and intricate carved paneling, crystal chandeliers and fireplaces with hand-carved mantels, and eight elegant suites and guest rooms, five with fireplaces.

The ultra-deluxe Paterson Suite ($675 a night) contains a fireplaced living room with a crystal chandelier, a large bedroom with kingsize bed and two full bathrooms. Victorian-style sofas and chairs make comfortable sitting areas at the foot of the ornate queensize four-poster beds in the Laurel and Cranwell suites. Even the smallest Bouquet and Ribbon rooms are fit for would-be barons and baronesses, if only for a night or two. And the two-room Ashley suite is considered a steal at $350 a night.

A typical bathroom has terrycloth robes and piles of towels, a scale, a wooden valet, heated towel racks, embroidered curtains and at least ten kinds of soaps and assorted toiletries.

Twelve rooms in more contemporary style, several of them split-level loft suites, are available in the carriage house. They were totally renovated in 1994, down to the handpainted tiles and marble floors of their sparkling bathrooms. All have decks or balconies and wet bars. There also are three cottages, two with kitchenettes. The other, formerly a simple little affair with a queen bed and shower, was tripled in size for 1998 with a kingsize bedroom, a sitting room with fireplace, a full bath and a veranda.

Fees include the use of four tennis courts (whites required), a swimming pool, jacuzzi, sauna and competition bent-grass croquet lawns on the property.

Fruit, cheese and mineral water await guests on arrival. Cocktails and after-dinner coffee and cordials are served in the main foyer and the crystal-chandeliered music room. "Proper evening dress" is required in the house after 6 p.m.

A complimentary continental breakfast is served in the breakfast room or on the terrace.

Guests are pampered within an inch of their lives. Blantyre was the first American hotel to win the coveted International Welcome Award from the prestigious Relais & Châteaux association. It also is the top-rated inn and resort in New England in the Zagat hotel survey. Guests don't mince words in the oversize guest book in the entry hall. Many write simply: "Perfection."

(413) 637-3556. Fax (413) 637-4282. Twelve rooms, eight suites and three cottages, all with private baths. Late June to early September and foliage: doubles $285 to $475, suites $350 to $675, cottages $415 to $550. Off-season: doubles $265 to $440, suites $325 to $650, cottages $375 to $510. Two-night minimum weekends and foliage. Children over 12. Smoking restricted. Closed early November to early May.

Wheatleigh, Hawthorne Road, Lenox 01240.

People who demand opulence and luxury are partial to this Italian palazzo built in 1893 as a wedding gift for the Countess de Heredia. It's romantic, extravagant, dramatic and ornate.

The imposing entrance of the honey-colored brick building framed in wrought iron leads into a soaring Great Room with a couple of sitting areas, a majestic staircase rising to the second floor, parquet floors and fine art all around. For its centennial year in 1993, owners Susan and Linwood Simon redecorated most of the establishment, "bringing in antiques we've been collecting for years," in Susan's words. Window treatments now match the fancy partial canopies draped above the beds, and bathrooms sport new tiles and fixtures.

All seventeen air-conditioned guest rooms are different. Seven are huge, two merely large, two medium and the rest, frankly, small. Nine have fireplaces, half have kingsize beds and some have terraces or balconies. One two-story affair has two queensize beds.

Susan's aim was to be "true to the period of the house and its architectural style" (it took her five years to find the right pattern of English axminster, for the carpeting in the halls). The period can be austere; some guests think the rooms could use more furnishings and more of a cozy feeling. Having seen all the rooms, we'd urge would-be guests to splurge for the best to avoid disappointment; the small rooms seem claustrophobic in comparison. The exception would be what

Cliffwood Inn is classic Colonial built about 1890 by an ambassador to France.

Wheatleigh considers a last-choice designation called 2NO: a small bedroom with queen bed and a separate sitting room, both quite serviceable for $255 a night. To us it appealed far more than the premium room 2I with, surprise, a crib in one corner and an antique writing desk in another, renting for almost twice the price. Even the best appear dressed for show. We saw no good lights for reading, nor few places one would wish to curl up.

Things have been looking up under general manager François Thomas, a suave Parisian who had managed a four-star hotel in Bordeaux. Each room now has a TV/VCR and – a first in our experience – a portable phone for those who want to be in touch wherever they are. François redid seven rooms, added $50,00 worth of artworks and turned a portion of the basement into a state-of-the-art fitness room with computerized equipment that tallies how you're doing as you watch the overhead TV. Adjacent is a massage room with a masseur on call.

Outside are the joys of a 22-acre property within walking distance of Tanglewood, a tennis court and a swimming pool hidden in a sylvan glade.

(413) 637-0610. Fax (413) 637-4507. Seventeen rooms with private baths. Doubles, $225 to $565, Tanglewood and foliage weekends; $175 to $425, rest of year. Three-night weekend minimum in season. Smoking restricted.

Cliffwood Inn, 25 Cliffwood St., Lenox 01240.
A magnificent classic Colonial built in Stanford White style about 1890 by the then-ambassador to France, this is almost a stage set for the furnishings of inn-keepers Joy and Scottie Farrelly, acquired during their periods of residence in Paris, Brussels, Italy and Montreal when he was with Ralston Purina Co. Among them are 24 pieces of fine Eldred Wheeler antique reproduction furniture, which are scattered through the house and available for purchase.

The three-story mansion has ten working fireplaces, one of them in the bathroom off a third-floor guest room.

A large foyer gives access to all three main-floor public rooms, each of which has French doors opening to the full-length back porch overlooking a swimming pool and a gazebo. At one end of the house is a living room with twelve-foot-high mirrors and a white marble fireplace. The music room in the center leads to the formal dining room, which has a dark green marble fireplace.

Upstairs are seven air-conditioned guest rooms, all with private baths and six with working fireplaces. Each is named for one of the Farrellys' ancestors (a scrapbook describing the particular one is at the foot of each bed, and it turns out they were an illustrious lot). The Walker-Linton Suite, with a sitting room fashioned from a former bedroom, has a step-up four-poster bed. A Victorian loveseat faces the fireplace in the Helen Walker Room, pretty in pink, white and rose. The Nathaniel Foote Room on the third floor comes with a canopied queensize Sheraton field bed and side tables, two wing chairs in front of the fireplace, a plush armchair in the window corner and no fewer than four oriental rugs, one from Saudi Arabia. A gaily painted lunch pail is a decorative accent in one room, and Joy has crafted folk-art boxes for Kleenex in the others. You'll be intrigued by her many ingenious decorating touches.

In the early evening, the Farrellys put out wine and hors d'oeuvres, perhaps salmon mousse, marinated olives and hot artichoke dip. Joy occasionally offers "dinners in a party atmosphere" in the spring.

For what they call a "copious continental breakfast," the Farrellys serve a re-nowned fruit compote and baked apples with nuts and crème fraîche, homemade yogurt, granola, muffins and cornbread. Wonderful popovers emanate from their prized AGA cooker. The meal is served in the paneled dining room with tapestried, high-back chairs or on the back porch.

Underneath the porch is a new, cedar-walled enclosure housing a counter-current pool and spa for folks to work off the calories year-round.

(413) 637-3330 or (800) 789-3331. Fax (413) 637-0221. www.cliffwood.com. Seven rooms with private baths. Mid-May through October: doubles $123 to $213. Rest of year: $83 to $142. Three- or four-night minimum stay Tanglewood weekends. Three-night minimum some other weekends. Two-night minimum foliage weekends. Children over 11. No smoking. No credit cards.

The Gables Inn, 103 Walker St., Lenox 01240.

Edith Wharton made this her home at the turn of the century while she was building her permanent edifice, the Mount. Her upstairs room is one of the most attractive in the original Berkshire "cottage" built in the Queen Anne style. Ask innkeeper Frank Newton to show you the famous eight-sided library where she once wrote some of her short stories.

The seventeen guest rooms and suites, all with private baths, are full of verve and Victorian warmth. The Jockey Club Suite offers a brass bed in a niche, an ample sitting area with two sofas facing a big-screen TV, and a private entrance from the back-yard pool area. Also in demand are two large second-floor suites built out over a former roof. Both have cathedral ceilings, high windows, swagged draperies, working fireplaces and TVs. One, the Teddy Wharton, is masculine in hunter green and mauve. It contains a leather sofa, two wing chairs and a carved bas relief of Shakespeare in the bedstead. More feminine in pink and teal floral prints is the Edith Wharton Suite with a four-poster bed and Gibson Girl prints on the walls.

The new Tanglewood Suite, downstairs in back, is the only one with a private garden patio. Fashioned from two former guest rooms, the bedroom with a queen canopy bed opens onto the secluded patio and the walls of the sitting room are hung with framed Boston Symphony Orchestra programs from 1899 and 1900.

We like the Show Business Room, full of signed photos of old stars and a library of showbiz volumes, with which to curl up on the chintz loveseat in front of the fireplace. The Presidents' Room is aptly named, with lots of memorabilia and

Lenox inns are known for sumptuous dining facilities, like this breakfast room at The Gables.

memoirs, including a long handwritten letter from Michael Dukakis thanking the Newtons for their hospitality after he was stranded here when his car broke down following a Tanglewood concert in 1989.

Frank, a former banker and sometime pianist, writes and produces summertime shows featuring name entertainers at the Lenox Town Hall Theater. His wife Mary conducts quilting seminars and takes in guests down the street in the home they restored in 1992, built by a cousin of Edith Wharton and called **The Summer White House.** Here (at 17 Main St., 637-4489), Mary "really fusses" as she pampers overnight guests in six spacious bedrooms with private baths and prepares fancy continental breakfasts. "This is our home," she says, "and we treat everyone here as our house guests."

The Newtons first operated the Gables as a restaurant before converting their banquet hall into lodging and making theirs "a special inn." That explains the spectacular breakfast room, with one long table in the center and, along the sides, six round tables for two skirted in pink, green and white. Full breakfasts are served. French toast, pancakes, waffles or eggs are typical fare, supplemented by sour-cream cake, bran muffins and pumpkin, lemon-almond and banana breads.

In the back yard are a tennis court and an enclosed, solar-heated swimming pool with a jacuzzi.

"We like to be hosts and to enjoy our guests," says Frank. That they do very well.

(413) 637-3416 or (800) 382-9401. Fax (413) 637-3416. www.gableslenox.com. Thirteen rooms and four suites with private baths. Mid-May through October: doubles $90 to $160, suites $210. Rest of year: doubles $80 to $120, suites $160. Three-night minimum stay during Tanglewood and some holidays. Two-night minimum in October and holiday weekends. Children over 12.

Six rooms with private baths at Summer White House, doubles $160, July and August only.

Garden Gables Inn, 135 Main St., Box 52, Lenox 01240.

What a difference a change of ownership and a few years can make! The woman who had run this triple-gabled house as a homey little inn since 1951 retired in 1988 and sold to Mario and Lynn Mekinda, an energetic couple with two then-teenagers from Toronto. Mario, an engineer who says he loves to tinker and fix things, has done wonders in renovating the main structure and undertaking major expansion projects, including an attached house behind for their family quarters. The returning visitor from a decade ago scarcely would recognize the place.

First, Mario added private baths for each of the eleven original guest rooms. Some rooms remain rather small, but are cozy and clean. All have been pleasantly redecorated by Lynn with attractive comforters and floral wallpapers. All but three now have queensize beds, and a corner room has the first of eight new fireplaces. All rooms are equipped with telephones and small clock-radios.

The most dramatic changes result from new construction. Two new suites have been added above the inn's expanded dining room. They offer hexagonal cathedral ceilings, corner fireplaces, whirlpool baths, kingsize canopy beds, sitting areas and sliding doors onto private balconies. "Everything people ask for we've got in these suites," says Mario. Also popular is a bedroom in back on the main floor containing a kingsize bed with a solid Germanic-looking headboard, a private deck and a large bathroom with jacuzzi.

The latest additions are four deluxe, light and airy units in a new detached front cottage, which continues the gabled-dormer theme of the other buildings. Here you'll find more cathedral ceilings, fireplaces, air-conditioning, cable TV/VCR, sitting areas and queensize Eldred Wheeler canopy beds.

The eighteen accommodations offer quite a range in size and price. Everyone enjoys sherry from the decanter in the cozy entry parlor. The Mekindas have totally redone it and the larger living room, which has a TV/VCR and a Steinway baby grand.

The former innkeeper's gift shop has been transformed into a charming dining room, which has been expanded by opening onto a new wraparound screened porch. A substantial buffet breakfast of juice, fruit, cereal, yogurt, homemade pastries and things like hard-boiled eggs, sausages, smoked salmon and quiches is served.

A 72-foot-long swimming pool and prolific gardens also are attractions at this verdant, five-acre oasis set well back from the road in the heart of Lenox.

(413) 637-0193. Fax (413) 637-4554. Twelve rooms and six suites with private baths. Summer: doubles $120 to $175 weekends, $90 to $145 midweek; suites, $225 weekends, $180 midweek. Off-season: doubles $70 to $125, suites $140 to $160. Three-night minimum summer weekends; two-night minimum weekends in June, September and October. Children over 12. Smoking restricted.

Walker House, 74 Walker St., Lenox 01240.

It's clear that ex-Californians Peggy and Richard Houdek, who opened this B&B eighteen years ago in the heart of Lenox, like music. A pecan Kimball grand piano in the living room is used for recitals and singalongs, a pump organ is in the front hall and the guest rooms are named for composers, with appropriate memorabilia of the person and the period in each. Dick Houdek was a music critic and Peggy in administration at the San Francisco Opera, which is where they met.

It's clear also that the Houdeks like flowers, which are in profusion everywhere,

Dramatic renovations and expansion have upgraded Garden Gables Inn.

inside and out, and cats (they have seven live ones and uncounted inanimate replicas in the form of pictures, pillows and the like). We coveted the poster in the dining room picturing three earnest-looking cats with the message, "we don't want you to smoke."

The result is an engaging clutter that shows the public rooms are clearly meant to be used. Ditto for the screened side porch and the wide rear veranda looking onto a landscaped yard and three acres of woods in back.

All eight guest rooms in the house, built in 1804 as the Walker Rockwell House, come with private baths and five with working fireplaces. Some have clawfoot tubs, most have hooked rugs and comforters, and several have canopied beds with high oak headboards. The Verdi room with its wild green and white wallpaper, white iron bedsteads and wicker furniture is in airy contrast to the dark colors and period wallpapers in most of the rooms. The Puccini room downstairs has rose walls, queen iron canopy bed, modern bathroom, fireplace and its own little porch.

Guests watch foreign films, operas, concerts and special events like the Olympics in the inn's Library Video Theater with a stereophonic sound system and a giant 100-inch screen. They also keep a running commentary on local dining experiences in an informative guest book. Tea is offered in the afternoon, and a half liter of wine awaits in each guest room.

Continental breakfast of fresh fruit or baked apples, assorted cereals, muffins and croissants is served in the dining room, where a stuffed tiger, lion, bear and cat are seated at one table, and on warm mornings on the back porch. The welcoming aroma of spices fills the room day and night. More than 100 mugs with all kinds of logos on them are hung on a wall. If you're late for breakfast, Peggy advises guests, your cup may be from Cleveland or Fargo, N.D.

(413) 637-1271 or (800) 235-3098. Fax (413) 637-2387. www.regionnet.com/colberk/ walkerhouse.html. Eight rooms with private baths. Late June through October: doubles, $110 to $190 weekends, $80 to $120 midweek,. Rest of year: $80 to $120 weekends, $70 to $90 midweek. Three-night minimum stay summer and holiday weekends. Children over 12. No smoking.

The Birchwood Inn, 7 Hubbard St., Lenox 01240.
The sophisticated tastes, food and travel magazines, accessories and collections of owners Joan and Dick Toner have upgraded this lovely inn, listed on the National Register and dating to 1767 when it was the site of Lenox's first town meeting.

Their purchase was inspired by son Dan, a Cornell hotel graduate who had worked for the Marriott and Sheraton chains. "He got us interested," said Joan, as her husband, an Air Force brigadier general, was looking for something to do in retirement. "We love to travel and to entertain." With Dan helping run the inn, they have time for both.

The Toners have repainted the exterior and restored the gardens of their hilltop property across from Lenox's landmark Church on the Hill. Inside, they have spruced up the ten comfortable guest rooms with designer towels, linens and pillows, joined twin beds to make them kingsize and added oriental decorative accents here and there. All but two rooms have private baths, most quite large since they were fashioned from former maid's quarters. Most bedrooms also are large, one in the front corner containing a canopy queen four-poster bed, two plush chairs and a settee for reading. Some have oriental rugs and fireplaces, three have TV and all contain telephones. Old hat pins stuck into an oversize pin cushion make a striking decorative accent in a rear room. There's a teddy bear's picnic in the window of a third-floor hallway, part of an assortment Joan started collecting for her grandchildren "and then I couldn't bear parting with all of them." Two suites with kitchen facilities are available in a rear carriage house.

Food and travel magazines are displayed in every room from the Toners' complete sets that are stocked in the enormous sunken living room, where walls of books are available for the borrowing. There are two separate seating arrangements here, one in front of the fireplace, as well as window seats along an outside wall. The Toners have hung in the living room a remarkable rendering of Strasbourg, which looks like a painting but turns out to have been done totally in different kinds of wood by Europe's foremost practitioner of wood marquetry. Another cozy parlor with a TV set leads into the large dining room, where Hitchcock chairs are at five tables set with woven cloths and coffee mugs bearing the inn's logo.

Breakfast starts with a buffet of fruit, juice, cereals, homemade breads and muffins. The main course, posted by the week on a blackboard, might be tarte d'alsace, ham and cheese omelet, eggs benedict or cranberry pancakes. Tea, wine and cheese are served in the afternoon, taken seasonally on a wide front porch outfitted in wicker.

(413) 637-2600 or (800) 524-1646. Fax (413) 637-2600. Eight rooms and two efficiency suites with private baths; two rooms with shared bath. July-October: doubles, $100 to $210 weekends, $90 to $180 midweek. Rest of year: $75 to $150 weekends, $60 to $125 midweek. Three-night minimum during Tanglewood season and holidays. Children over 12. No smoking.

Applegate Bed & Breakfast, 279 West Park St., RR 1, Box 576, Lee 01238.
Just across the Lenox town line is this sparkling white Georgian Colonial with a pillared porte cochere. It was built by a New York surgeon in the 1920s as a weekend retreat and now is one of the area's more inviting B&Bs. Applegate is set nicely back from the road on six tranquil acres bearing venerable apple trees, towering pines, flower gardens and a beckoning swimming pool. Inside are elegant common rooms, six guest rooms with private baths and an effervescent welcome by Nancy and Rick Cannata, she a retired flight attendant and he a retired pilot, who decided to alight here in 1990 and convert their large home into a B&B.

Off a lovely entry foyer are a fireplaced dining room, where three tables are each set for breakfast for four, and a large living room equipped with a grand piano. To the side of the living room is a sunporch, newly enclosed for use as a reading and TV room. Off the dining room is a screened back porch facing the pool and gardens.

Porte cochere dignifies Applegate entry.

A carved staircase leads to the four main guest rooms, one the master suite with a kingsize poster bed, family photos on the mantel above the working fireplace, a sitting area with a sofabed and two chairs, and a great steam shower. The other rooms are slightly less grand in scale, holding queensize beds. One has Shaker-style pine furniture, another a walnut sleigh bed and a third an antique white iron bed and white and blue wicker furnishings. Two newer rooms are situated in a far wing of the house. One is a sunny corner space swathed in pale lavenders and greens with a tiger-maple four-poster, a sitting area and the best view of the grounds. The other is a smaller room done up in Victorian style with an antique bed and matching marble-topped dresser and a hat rack holding an opera cape and granny hats. A rear carriage house has been renovated into a two-bedroom, condo-style apartment, available for $330 a night, three-night minimum.

Godiva chocolates and decanters of brandy are in each room. The Cannatas offer wine and cheese around 5 p.m. The continental-plus breakfast, including cereal and yogurt, is served amid stemware and antique cups and saucers.

(413) 243-4451 or (800) 691-9012. Fax (413) 243-4451. www.applegateinn.com. Six rooms with private baths. June-October: doubles, $135 to $225 weekends, $100 to $190 midweek. Rest of year: $100 to $190 weekends, $85 to $165 midweek. Three-night minimum summer and holiday weekends, two-night weekend minimum in June, September and October. Children over 12. Smoking restricted.

Brook Farm Inn, 15 Hawthorne St., Lenox 01240.

This would be just another charming inn, were it not for the owners' bent for literature and music. "There is poetry here," says the stylish cover of their brochure, and indeed there is.

You'll find it in each of the twelve guest rooms as well as in the front parlor, where there are shelves full of poetry volumes, tape recorders and a collection of poetry tapes. The poetry tradition launched by the former owners has continued under Joe and Anne Miller, New Jersey transplants who had never heard of Lenox – "we must have been living under a rock," quips Anne – until they arrived on an inn-buying trip, walked in the door of Brook Farm Inn and decided this was the one.

Fortunately, the Millers have taken to poetry, and Anne says her contractor-husband has turned into "quite a reader." As did his predecessor, he displays a poem of the day on the lectern. He does a poetry reading every Saturday at tea time, when guests enjoy his wife's scones, and sponsors a writing seminar every spring. Such is to be expected from an inn that takes its name from the mid-19th-century Brook Farm literary commune in West Roxbury, Mass.

The Millers also have upgraded seven of the inn's twelve air-conditioned guest rooms. The results show throughout, from the pretty sand-colored facade with green shutters and cream trim to the new bridal suite, where white sheer fabric is draped around the canopied queen bed and guests enjoy two wing chairs beside the fireplace. That is one of two front rooms that the Millers gutted to redo into their premium lodgings, right down to the enlarged bathrooms and "new everything," in Anne's words. All guest rooms have private baths, handsome furnishings and, of course, good reading lights on the bed headboards. Some include fireplaces, colorful stained-glass windows and skylights.

There is more than intellectual nourishment at Brook Farm. A hearty breakfast could include cheese strata or french toast casserole topped with fruit after preliminaries of sliced fruit, homemade granola and assorted pastries. Each bedroom contains a decanter of sherry. And Joe has put in an upstairs pantry where guests can help themselves to ice and prepare hot beverages any time they want.

Guests also enjoy a heated swimming pool and pretty gardens in back.

(413) 637-3013 or (800) 285-7638. Twelve rooms with private baths. Mid-June through October: doubles, $125 to $200 weekends, $115 to $145 midweek. Rest of year: $90 to $130 weekends, $80 to $120 midweek. Three-night minimum weekends in summer and some holidays; two-night minimum other weekends. Children over 15. No smoking.

Amadeus House, 15 Cliffwood St., Lenox 01240.

Music is the theme and in the air at this newish B&B, nicely restored by classical music buffs John Felton, an ex-Midwestern newspaper reporter and former deputy foreign editor of National Public Radio, and his wife Marty Gottron, a freelance editor. With a renovation crew of fifteen, they breezed through the former seasonal tourist home in ten weeks, repainting every inch inside and out.

The result is eight varied accommodations, from the deluxe ground-floor Mozart Room to two small bedrooms that share a bath to a two-bedroom apartment rented by the week. Plus a location on quiet Cliffwood Street, known to Lenox residents as *the* street but one often missed by tourists.

Some would say the heart of the house is the cozy parlor/music room. It harbors a collection of 500 classical CDs that are played throughout the day, and the walls are hung with musical posters. Others gravitate to the larger dining room with brick wall and cast-iron stove, which opens into a country kitchen. Here is where three tables are set for breakfast – perhaps mushroom quiche, frittata with seasonal vegetables, orange waffles, omelets or honey-baked french toast with honey syrup. The tables are used for games or puzzles at night.

Guests are housed in style in the prized main-floor Mozart Room, with an Eldred Wheeler queensize tiger maple bed, a wicker sitting area facing the wood stove in the fireplace and a private porch. Also popular are the spacious rooms with queensize beds and private baths on the second floor: the Brahms Room in back with a wicker sofa and two rockers, and the Bach in front with an extra double bed and two rockers. Two mid-size rooms with private baths comprise the "Tanglewood wing." Here, John points out a couple of prized acquisitions: a Japanese Sony record catalog signed by Leonard Bernstein, and a framed album cover signed by Aaron Copland. John bills two small bedrooms sharing a bath in the rear as the best B&B

values in Lenox. The third-floor Beethoven Suite offers a full kitchen, two bedrooms with king/twin beds and a small, window-less library/living room in the middle.

Marty has taken to identifying each room with an appropriate T-shirt bearing the composer's name. "Finding Sibelius ain't easy," John quipped. But knowing their journalistic instincts, we're sure his will turn up.

Afternoon tea is served on the wraparound porch. Guests also enjoy the flower gardens and a wooded, undeveloped greenbelt in back.

(413) 637-4770 or (800) 205-4770. Five rooms with private baths, two with shared bath, one two-bedroom suite. May-October: doubles, $85 to $145 weekends, $60 to $105 midweek; suite, $900 weekly for two, $1,100 for four. Rest of year: $75 to $110 weekends, $60 to $85 midweek; suite $130 to $135 nightly. Three- or four-night minimum weekends during Tanglewood; two-night minimum some midweek stays during Tanglewood and most weekends and holidays. Children over 10 in suite. No smoking.

Gateways Inn and Restaurant, 71 Walker St., Lenox 01240.

The landmark white, dark-shuttered mansion, built in 1912 by Harley Procter of Procter & Gamble and said to resemble a cake of Ivory soap, has long been a fixture in Lenox. After several years of ups and downs, it was upgraded in 1996 by new owners Fabrizio Chiariello from Naples and his American wife Rosemary, who moved here to escape the New York corporate world. They redid the bathrooms, were installing working fireplaces in all the bedrooms, did extensive refurbishing and were making their presence felt in an inn that needed hands-on oversight.

Architect Stanford White inspired the two leaded windows by the main side entrance and the sweeping central staircase, which upon descending makes you feel as if you're floating into a ballroom. The nine accommodations with private baths on the second floor are richly furnished with antiques, oriental rugs and four-poster, canopy or sleigh beds, all but one king or queensize.

A huge front corner suite lined with books and containing a couch and two fireplaces was home for Arthur Fiedler during the years of his Boston Pops concerts at Tanglewood. The living room is enormous; the kingsize canopy bed takes up most of the bedroom, and occupants enjoy a new jacuzzi tub in the suite's modernized bathroom. Elsewhere, a semi-suite has a pillar in the middle with the bed at an angle, while the west corner room harbors an eight-piece bird's-eye maple and black walnut Victorian bedroom set. One room with a queensize bed, called Cozy on the rate sheet, is priced far lower than the others with a peak weekend price of $120. Three rooms at the rear of the main floor have king beds and plush carpeting and convey an air of luxury in keeping with the rest of the place.

A complimentary continental breakfast is served in the dining room, which also houses a restaurant that has been redecorated with orange terra cotta walls and oriental rugs. Chef Janice Wheeler's contemporary American/continental dinner menu offers a good selection from escargots and bruschetta to pan-seared duck breast and twin tournedos.

(413) 637-2532 or (888) 492-9466. Fax (413) 637-1432. Eleven rooms and one suite with private baths. June-October: doubles, $215 to $240 weekends, $125 to $160 midweek; suite, $380 weekends, $265 midweek. Rest of year, doubles, $140 to $175 weekends, $110 to $112 midweek; suite, $305 weekends, $225 midweek. Three-night minimum weekends during Tanglewood. No children. No smoking.

Dining Spots

Church Street Cafe, 69 Church St., Lenox.

This is the casual, creative kind of place of which we never tire, the one we keep returning to for a quick but interesting meal whenever we're in Lenox. We're not alone, for it's generally No. 1 on the list of everyone's favorite eating establishments in town.

Owners Linda Forman and Clayton Hambrick have furnished their small dining rooms and outdoor deck simply but tastefully. On one visit we admired all the amusing paintings of zebras on the walls, part of the changing art exhibits and all for sale. We also like the bar stools painted like black and white cows, udders hanging below, as well as the ficus trees lit with tiny white lights, the white pottery with colorful pink and blue flowers, the artworks lit by track lights in the adjacent gallery, the flute music playing in the background, and the jaunty outside dining deck.

Once Ethel Kennedy's chef, Clayton also worked in a creole restaurant in Washington and that background shows. Blackened redfish might be a dinner special. Louisiana shrimp and andouille filé gumbo is apt to be a dinner appetizer and a luncheon entrée. Lately, the fare has acquired Southwest and oriental accents, as in an appetizer of smoky black bean ravioli in a red chile broth or a main dish of grilled mirin- and soy-glazed salmon with ginger sauce, wilted greens and scallion rice. These join such traditional favorites as sautéed Maine crab cakes, roasted free-range chicken and crispy sautéed duck breast with roasted fig sauce.

Our latest lunch included a super black bean tostada with three salsas and the Church Street salad, a colorful array of goat cheese, chick peas, sprouts, eggs and red pepper, with a zippy dijon vinaigrette dressing on the side and whole wheat sunflower seed rolls, so good that we accepted seconds.

Among desserts, the chilled cranberry soufflé topped with whipped cream, the apple walnut crisp and the chocolate macadamia nut torte are superior.

(413) 637-2745. Entrées, $16.50 to $18.95. Lunch, Monday-Saturday 11 to 2. Dinner nightly, 5:30 to 9. Sunday brunch in summer and fall. Closed Sunday and Monday in off-season.

Blantyre, Route 20 and East St., Lenox.

An English country-house hotel setting is the backdrop for the contemporary cuisine offered by chef Michael Roller, who returned to Blantyre after a stint at Restaurant Million in Charleston, S.C. Prix-fixe dinners of three to five courses are offered to house guests and the public in the formal dining room and two smaller rooms. The tables are set with different themes, the china and crystal changing frequently as owner Jane Fitzpatrick adds to the collection.

A typical dinner here starts with a "surprise," perhaps foie gras or veal sweetbreads with sauternes and carrot juice. The appetizer could be Maine crabmeat and ossetra caviar with avocado and ginger or seared foie gras with caramelized mango, frisée and mixed herb salad. Main courses include sautéed lobster with chanterelles, pan-roasted saddle of rabbit with foie gras and grilled loin of antelope with pink peppercorns. Desserts could be bitter Swiss chocolate cake with sour orange compote and blackberry sorbet or lemon meringue tart with blueberry compote and passionfruit coulis.

The wine list is exceptionally strong on California chardonnays and cabernets

Wheatleigh and its noted restaurant occupy this Italian palazzo built in 1893.

and French regionals, priced up to $220. Most guests take coffee and armagnac in the Music Room, where a harpist and pianist play on weekends.

The entire experience evokes superlatives in the Blantyre guest book. "The best dinner we ever had" was one of the latest.

(413) 637-3556. Prix-fixe, $70. Lunch, daily except Monday in summer, 12:30 to 1:45; dinner nightly in summer and foliage season, 6 to 9, otherwise Tuesday-Sunday. Reservations and jackets required. Closed early November to early May.

Wheatleigh, Hawthorne Road, Lenox.

When he arrived here, general manager François Thomas from Paris was so impressed with resident chef Peter Platt that he took him to Paris the next spring to demonstrate American cooking – "the first time that's ever happened back there," he said. It's a mark of the expertise of Peter, a Williams College history graduate who's been at Wheatleigh since 1986. He oversees a cooking staff of fourteen, some of whose foreign backgrounds lend an international flavor to what Peter describes as "new French classic cuisine."

Chippendale armchairs imported from England are at white-clothed tables in the high-ceilinged main dining room. Three tile murals from England, each weighing 500 pounds, give the walls a luminescent glow in the candlelight.

Dinner here and on the adjacent sunporch is serious business. Three four-course tasting menus are prepared each evening – regular, low-fat and vegetarian, each prix-fixe for $68. You can pick and choose between them. Or the entire table can try the grand tasting menu to sample seven dishes from the three menus for $90. A smaller, à la carte menu ($16.50 to $24.50) is available seasonally in the Grill Room.

Wheatleigh's kitchen uses exotic ingredients and is said to be labor-intensive. You know why when you see one night's regular offerings: warm squab salad with foie gras flan, chanterelles and black truffle sauce; fillet of Maine salmon with lobster roe-mashed potatoes and port wine sauce; pan-roasted Texas antelope with roasted vegetable couscous and Italian porcini sauce, and warm apple tarte tatin with iced sour quenelles.

Owners Susan and Linwood Simon have doubled the size of their wine list, with a number available in half-bottles. "At the high end," says Linwood, "our wines become very reasonable. If you're of a mind to drink Château Lafite, this is the place to do it." François also had in mind adding some wines in the $30 range, a price point conspicuously missing at previous visits.

(413) 637-0610. Prix-fixe, $68. Lunch in summer, Tuesday-Saturday noon to 1:30. Dinner nightly by reservation, 6 to 9; closed Tuesday in winter. Grill Room, 5 to 9, July and August only.

Cafe Lucia, 90 Church St., Lenox.

Jim Lucie transformed an art gallery cum cafe into an expanded cafe with art as a sideline. "We're a restaurant that shows and sells art," explains Jim, who opened up the kitchen so patrons can glimpse the goings-on.

Jim's Italian cuisine is favored by locals, who praise his pasta creations, baked polenta with homemade sausage and Italian codfish stew. The osso buco with diced vegetables and risotto is so good that it draws New Yorkers back annually, and Jim reports he almost had a riot on his hands when he took the linguini and shrimp alla medici off the menu (it was promptly restored, even though he had offered it on specials). Lamb stew served over white Tuscan beans with celery, carrots, shallots and escarole appealed at one visit. Another time we were tempted by the mixed grill of pan-seared duck leg and hot Italian sausage, finished with a fig sauce on a bed of braised escarole.

Start with carpaccio with arugula and shaved reggiano or a ragu of rabbit and wild mushrooms over soft polenta. End with a fruit tart, flourless chocolate torte or one of the gelatos. Those desserts, a fine port or brandy and cappuccino can be taken on a spacious awning-covered deck or at tables spilling onto a gravel patio and lawn on summer evenings.

(413) 637-2640. Entrées, $13.95 to $25.95. Dinner, Tuesday-Sunday from 5.

Semolina, 80 Main St., Lenox.

Fresh out of the Culinary Institute of America, Lina Aliberti got a job as garde manger at Wheatleigh and awaited the day when she could open her own restaurant in the house her father had bought in the center of Lenox and leased out for commercial purposes. That day came in 1997 when the main floor was transformed into a Mediterranean-style bistro and bar focusing on a large center fireplace with a Count Rumford oven. Forty-two diners can be seated at well spaced tables inside, with an equal number on the front porch that quickly became a popular gathering spot to sit and watch the passing parade.

The restaurant's name is a natural because of the chef's name and because she uses semolina flour in her focaccia and a semolina pudding.

The menu is Mediterranean in spirit: pan-seared scallops with artichokes over penne, salmon en papillote with salsa verde, breast of chicken stuffed with prosciutto and fontina cheese, veal forestière and filet mignon au poivre with caramelized shallot sauce. Expect starters like roasted garlic soup with polenta croutons, kataifi-wrapped goat cheese on a bed of field greens, pernod house-cured salmon with fennel relish and a Mediterranean antipasto that spans many countries. Desserts vary from the predictable tirami su to the surprise Greek spiced honey almond-walnut nest with orange-raisin compote.

(413) 637-4455. Entrées, $14.50 to $20. Lunch daily except Tuesday, 11 to 2. Dinner, 5 to 9. Closed Tuesday, also Wednesday in off-season.

Diversions

Tanglewood, West Street, Lenox.

The name is synonymous with music and Lenox. The summer home of the Boston Symphony Orchestra since 1936, the 210-acre estate above the waters of Stockbridge Bowl in the distance is an idyllic spot for concerts and socializing at picnics. The 6,000 seats in the open-air Shed are reserved far in advance for Friday and Saturday evening and Sunday afternoon concerts. Up to 10,000 fans can be accommodated at $12.50 each on the lawn (bring your own chairs, blankets, picnics and wine, or pick something up from the cafeteria). Free open rehearsals for the Sunday concert are scheduled Saturday mornings at 10:30. The acoustically spectacular Seiji Ozawa Hall seats 1,200 inside and another 200 on sloping lawns so situated that you can see right onto the stage. It's used for chamber music concerts and student recitals most weeknights in summer and for community events in spring and fall.

(413) 637-1940 or (800) 274-8499. Concerts, Friday and Saturday at 8:30, Sunday at 2:30, last weekend of June through August. Tickets, $14 to $72.

Shakespeare & Company, Plunkett Street, Lenox.

The evening sky and the gardens of **The Mount,** novelist Edith Wharton's former estate above Laurel Lake, yield a natural amphitheater for one of America's largest Shakespeare festivals. Fourteen productions are staged each summer and fall in four theaters, including the recently renovated Stables Theatre and the outdoor Oxford Court Theatre, tucked in a quiet glen that was once a grass tennis court. Some are presented in the intimate Wharton Theater in the drawing room of the Mount. The novelist and her niece, landscape architect Beatrice Farrand, designed the 50-acre estate. The neo-Georgian home, an ongoing restoration project, has several areas open for guided tours.

(413) 637-3353. Mount open daily 9 to 3, June-October, weekends 9 to 3 in May. Adults, $6.

Lenox Town Hall Theater, Walker Street, Lenox. Local innkeeper Richard Houdek headed the committee that refurbished the auditorium of the town hall into a community theater in 1992. Another local innkeeper, Frank Newton, writes and produces a number of shows with name entertainers here.

The National Music Center, 70 Kemble St., Lenox, 637-1800 or (800) 872-6874. Ending a long nationwide search, the National Music Foundation settled on the 63-acre campus of the former Lenox School for Boys as the home for its planned $30 million Music Center. The 1,200-seat Berkshire Performing Arts Center, once a gymnasium and hockey rink, presents an occasional concert by name entertainers. But in its first five years, the center has never really gotten off the ground for lack of funding. If it does, up to 200 musicians are expected to live, teach and perform here, adding a year-round dynamic to an already vibrant musical community.

Pleasant Valley Wildlife Sanctuary, West Road off Route 7 north, Lenox. The Massachusetts Audubon Society maintains a 1,500-acre nature preserve high up

Lenox Mountain next to Yokum Brook. A museum of live and stuffed animals and seven miles of nature trails through forests, meadows and marshes are a pleasant refuge for a few hours. Open daily except Monday year-round.

Shopping. Lenox offers some of the most exclusive shops in the Berkshires. Along Church Street, **Mary Stuart Collections** has wonderful needlework, potpourris and fragrances, children's clothes fit for royalty, heavenly lingerie and fine glass, china and antiques. Neat casual, natural-fiber clothes are at **Glad Rags,** children's clothing and accessories at **Gifted Child,** and fine American pottery and jewelry at the **Hoadley Gallery. Tanglewool** sells English cashmeres and other handknits, Italian bags, Arche shoes from France, creative jewelry, and imported yarns and knitting patterns; everything here has flair. **Weaver's Fancy** displays lovely weavings, from placemats to pillows to coats.

On Walker Street you'll find **Talbots** for classic clothes and **Evviva!** for contemporary by designers with a background in the arts. **Hand of Man** shows works of more than 300 artisans in its craft gallery at the Curtis Shops.

Stop at **Crosby's** for gourmet foods and the makings for wonderful picnics, or enjoy an old-fashioned turkey sandwich at **Blue Heaven Rotisserie & Sandwich Shop.** Some of the area's best breads and pastries come from **Suchèle Bakers. Savori** is a Manhattan-style food and dessert bar.

For an ice cream fix, head to **Bev's Homemade Ice Cream,** 26 Housatonic St., where Beverly Mazursky and sons Dan and Jeff make all the wonderful flavors in two machines behind the counter. They're known for their raspberry-chocolate chip, served in a sugar cone. You can order gelatos, frappes, smoothies, sherbet coolers and even a banana split ($5.50). Soups and sandwiches are available except in summer, when their popular Jamaican patties (different kinds of Caribbean breads with such fillings as beef, mixed veggies and broccoli-cheese, $2.50) are the only things that get in the way of their ice cream.

Extra-Special

Chesterwood, 4 Williamsville Road, Stockbridge.

Lenox's next-door neighbor, Stockbridge, has so many attractions – from the relocated Norman Rockwell Museum to Naumkeag to the Berkshire Garden Center (even the Red Lion, the epitome of old New England inns) – that it should not be missed. Our favorite is Chesterwood, the secluded estate of sculptor Daniel Chester French, who fashioned the Seated Lincoln here for the Lincoln Memorial in Washington. Visitors start at a gallery in the old cow barn, where many of French's sculptures are shown, and tour the 30-foot-high studio in which the sculptor worked. Here you see plaster-cast models of the Seated Lincoln and a graceful Andromeda, which he was working on at his death. It's placed on a flatcar on a 40-foot-long train track and wheeled outdoors so students can see, as French did, how a sculpture looks in natural light. Gracious rooms flank the wonderfully wide, full-length hall of the grand Colonial Revival home in which he spent six months a year until he died there in 1931. The period garden, nature trail and museum shop appeal as well.

A two-bedroom apartment called Meadowlark, part of the sculptor's studio, is available for overnight guests through the nearby Red Lion Inn, (413) 298-5545. It's a special experience for $350 a night.

(413) 298-3579. Open daily 10 to 5, May-October. Adults, $7.

Two churches and Dunbar House B&B lie beyond Shawme Pond in center of Sandwich.

Sandwich, Mass.

Cape Cod's First Town

If you've never detoured off the highway on your way out Cape Cod, it's time you did.

Hidden off main Route 6 and even out of reach of meandering Route 6A is a little enclave – very different from the prevailing norm – representing Cape Cod's oldest town and a different way of life.

Established in 1638 by settlers from the Plymouth colony, the center of Sandwich is a quiet village untouched by creeping commercialism. "People bypass us on the way out to Hyannis or Provincetown," said the docent at the Sandwich Glass Museum. "They don't realize the treasures they are missing."

The Old Boston & Sandwich Glass Co., founded in 1825, grew to be the largest industry on the Cape for half of the 19th century. It transformed a rural farm town into a thriving mill center known worldwide for blown and pressed glass. But the glass company's fortunes faded in the late 1800s, and with it ended the growth of Sandwich. It's now a museum center and, actually, a museum of living history.

Sandwich's museums and its aura of history attract knowing visitors who like to combine their beach expeditions with a dose of culture. As the first town on the Cape – in terms of geography as well as history – Sandwich also attracts daytrippers, weekenders and people who prefer intimate B&Bs to the anonymity of chain motels.

The renowned Dan'l Webster Inn dates to 1692, but only lately has really come of age. Also relative latecomers are a cluster of eight smaller inns and B&Bs in historic structures in the heart of the village. The structures were there, but the B&Bs didn't exist a decade ago.

"Sandwich is quietly becoming a destination," notes Harry Dickson of the Capt. Ezra Nye House, dean of the village's innkeepers.

From any inn it's a leisurely stroll through the village center around Town Hall Square along Water Street and Main Street and onto Jarves Street. You'll pass the Town Hall (now undergoing restoration), the library, the Christopher Wren-inspired spire of the First Church of Christ, three museums, an English tea room, a working grist mill and an artesian well. You'll likely see swans and ducks paddling on Shawme Pond, which glistens beside the Thornton Burgess museum and, beyond, one of Cape Cod's oldest houses. Dozens more houses, part of a National Register historic district, catch your eye.

Spend a few hours at Heritage Plantation, famed for showy rhododendrons among its 76 acres of gardens. It also houses a military museum, an art museum and a renowned collection of antique and classic cars.

Cross the picturesque salt marshes on the citizen-built Sandwich boardwalk to view Cape Cod Bay from the sand dunes. Bicycle along the Cape Cod Canal and the scenic Old King's Highway (Route 6A).

You may decide to save Hyannis and Provincetown for another time.

Inn Spots

The Dan'l Webster Inn, 149 Main St., Sandwich 02563.

This village inn likens itself to a boutique hotel and looks and feels far newer than its heritage dating to 1692. That's because the old parsonage-turned-Fessenden Tavern, a Patriot headquarters during the Revolution, and subsequent inn was destroyed by fire in 1971. It was quickly rebuilt in modern style to look old, but was little more than a fancy motor inn with a dining room when we first stayed here in 1977. The Daniel Webster connection results from the lengthy stays of the famous orator here and the personal legacies found in some of its rooms.

The Catania family – restaurateur Vincent of the regional Hearth 'n Kettle chain and his five sons and a daughter – purchased the establishment in 1980 and began turning it into a full-fledged inn and small hotel. They retained the old Jarves Wing, where traditional rooms come with poster beds, TVs enclosed in armoires, pleasant sitting areas, fresh flowers and all the inn's considerable amenities, from

hair dryers to nightly turndown service. They built the Fessenden Wing, with deluxe rooms including a corner room with side balcony, queen canopy bed, a sofa and a wing chair. They purchased and gutted the Fessenden House in front, turning its apartments into four deluxe suites with fireplaces and jacuzzi tubs. They created a luxury penthouse suite in the main inn with a canopy king bed, skylit jacuzzi encased in Italian marble and a handsome living room. Lately, they turned the 1832 Quince Tree House

Quince Tree suite is ready for guests at The Dan'l Webster Inn.

down the street into five more suites with jacuzzis and fireplaces. One even has a grand piano in the living room.

Our quarters in the Fessenden House's Ezra Nye suite, named for the Sandwich sea captain who built the house in 1826 for his bride, were most comfortable. The sizable living room with a marble fireplace has a plush sofa, coffee table, two wing chairs, a writing desk and a low reproduction chest that opens to reveal a TV. The bedroom contains a step-up queen canopy bed. The bathroom has a jacuzzi tub and another sink in the dressing area, which has a substantial vanity containing aloe shampoos and toiletries, a Saks Fifth Avenue soap, a handy little sewing kit and a leather ice bucket filled with ice.

The inn operates a well regarded restaurant and tavern (see Dining Spots) at the rear of the main building, plus a gift shop where some of the stock appeals to doting grandmothers. There's a "gathering room" for reading or card-playing off the lobby. In season, a pool, almost hidden by flowers and shrubs, beckons in the rear gardens beside a gazebo and the salt marsh. The flowers and seasonal displays in front of the inn's porte-cochere attest to the caring touches offered by the Catania family and their friendly staff.

(508) 888-3622 or (800) 444-3566. Fax (508) 833-3220. Thirty-seven rooms and nine suites with private baths. Memorial Day through October: doubles, $139 to $179, suites $209 to $335. Rest of year: doubles, $99 to $149; suites $159 to $285. Two-night minimum weekends.

The Belfry Inne & Bistro, 8 Jarves St., Sandwich. 02563.

Stylish accommodations and a small and well-regarded restaurant and bar (see Dining Spots) are the hallmarks of this new, expanding inn occupying a former rectory. The Eastlake newel post, double door with Sandwich glass, shuttered windows and other original features have been salvaged from the 1879 residence of a clothing merchant. The house was in considerable disrepair when Christopher Wilson, a local banker, took possession in 1995 and "restored it to the way it was."

The nine guest rooms come with private baths, ceiling fans and telephones. Each is spiffily decorated and enhanced by good art, some of it done by Christopher's mother, an artist in Jaffrey, N.H., and the handpainted creations of local artist Kathleen Hill. A discreet sign warns of a $125 "fine" if evidence of smoking is found in the room. Cut-lace duvet covers are atop down comforters on the antique beds, most of them queen or kingsize. There's a clawfoot soaking tub near the bed in the front Martha Southworth Room with a shower in the bathroom for those who prefer. An English griffin-footed brass soaking tub occupies a raised platform by a window in the front George Drew Room, which also has a separate shower as well as a gas fireplace. French doors open onto a side balcony overlooking the gardens in the Seth Drew Room which has dramatic sponged green walls with multi-colored accent streaks. The premier John Drew Room and its mirror image, the new Cottage Room, have double jacuzzi tubs in the bathrooms as well as gas fireplaces in the sitting areas.

Ingenious decorative touches such as an arch above a jacuzzi, Laura Ashley accents and whimsical colors are employed throughout. On the third floor, the Sara Drew Room with kingsize bed and corner fireplace is delightful in mint green and white, while the companion Ida Drew Room with twin cottage spool beds and double skylights is stunning in black and white with an English rose trellis theme. Handpainted murals of Alice in Wonderland characters brighten the hallway and stairs leading to the belfry tower. Here three pillowed seats face more wonderland scenes, a view across the treetops (the ocean is on view after the leaves fall) and a handwritten poem from the book on the ceiling, "...up above the world you fly, like a tea tray in the sky."

Besides the tower, guests relax on the main floor in a comfortable common room with TV or the appealing bistro bar.

Before heading off to his banking duties, hands-on innkeeper Chris prepares a full breakfast for inn guests. Fruit, cereal and pastries on the buffet in the dining room pave the way for such treats as individual omelets, tarragon eggs with diced ham and béarnaise sauce, asparagus-mushroom quiche and peach french toast. His chef handles kitchen duties at night, and his two school-age sons may lend a hand during the week.

Chris was negotiating to buy the former Catholic church next door to increase his wedding business and add seven large guest rooms, each with jacuzzi and TV.

(508) 888-8550. Fax (508) 888-3922. Nine rooms with private baths. June to mid-October: doubles, $95 to $165. Rest of year: $85 to $145. Smoking restricted.

The Inn at Sandwich Center, 118 Tupper Road, Sandwich 02563.
Facing the village square, this beautifully restored 18th-century saltbox commands an expansive hillside across from the Sandwich Glass Museum. Paris-born Eliane Thomas lived around the world before she and her Boston-born husband moved to the Cape in 1995 from California to run a B&B. They refurnished and redecorated five guest rooms with great style.

Eliane, whose family ran hotels in France and elsewhere, does things right. From the turndown service with chocolates to the coordinated sheets and fabric patterns to the matching terrycloth robes in each room, you see the assured hand of an experienced traveler at work.

The downstairs Green Room sets the stage: a queensize poster bed is awash in floral sheets and pillows that match the poof curtains and even the shower curtain

The Inn at Sandwich Center commands prime hillside location in center of town.

in the bathroom. It is one of three guest rooms with working fireplaces. Upstairs are four more rooms with private baths. The Yellow Room is a delightful pale yellow, with a handsome comforter atop the bed, lace curtains beneath the swag fabric, and a bathtub beside a window overlooking Town Hall Square. Handsome oriental rugs and a Claire Murray rug bearing a picture of the inn grace the Beige Room. The rear Blue Room has a queensize bed, a private terrace onto the hillside and the smallest bath – "like a ship's," Eliane admits, "but better than none." Beyond is the White Room, "small and charming," with twin beds, wicker chairs and a hooked rug.

The heart of the house – literally – is the elegant dining room with its original 1750 beehive oven and fireplace. The rest of the structure was built around it in 1829. The furnishings are Jacobean. Two tables, one with a window seat at the end, are set with fine silver and Farberware china of the English Garden pattern. Here, Eliane offers an extensive continental breakfast of fruits, yogurt, cranberry and banana breads and sometimes pancakes.

The handsome front parlor contains a multitude of coffee-table books on Sandwich and Cape Cod. Antiques and artworks acquired from around the world are shown here and throughout the house to good advantage.

(508) 888-6958 or (800) 249-6949. Five rooms with private baths. June-October: doubles, $85 to $110. Rest of year: $75 to $99. Two-night minimum certain weekends. Children over 12. No smoking.

Bay Beach, 1-3 Bay Beach Lane, Box 151, Sandwich 02563.

If you love the luminous light of the Cape as we do, you'll love Bay Beach, which has an abundance of it. Facing Cape Cod Bay, almost beside the wide-open marshes over which the Sandwich boardwalk is built and with colorful gardens in front, this is a perfect place for those who crave an oceanfront location with all the comforts of home – and then some.

Real and Emily Lemieux sold their nearby motel in 1988, built a glamorous home on the beach, bought the land next door, erected a four-room B&B and added two suites in their home as their children vacated.

The result is six of the most amenity-laden accommodations and one of the top locations on Cape Cod. Yet for some reason this showy but low-profile B&B remains relatively unknown among its peers in Sandwich.

"We're a well-kept secret," Real said as he led a tour of the complex. Even so, they have been happily filled ever since they won an AAA four-diamond rating.

Arrangements of flowers from the gardens abound. On the ground level of the B&B house is a mirrored exercise-recreation room. On the first floor, huge windows frame a view of the ocean and marshes in the large California contemporary style living-dining area, off which is a spacious deck. From here you can see the entrance to the Cape Cod Canal and, on a clear day, Provincetown. The raised hearth fireplace is welcome on stormy days. From the modern open kitchen come lemonade or cider and cookies in the afternoon (gourmet teas on cooler days). Breakfast is put out buffet style from 8 to 10:30, and guests may take it on trays to their rooms, private decks or common decks or socialize in the dining area. There's always a hot dish like belgian waffles, fruit crêpes or egg casserole. Real has plans to build a boardwalk between the two houses to a private beach.

Wine, cheese and crackers in their own mini-refrigerators are ready for guests upon arrival. Each bedroom comes with thick carpeting, TV/VCR, private phone lines and mostly rattan-type furnishings. Chocolates are at bedside. Three guest quarters have king beds, double jacuzzis and private decks. A large main-floor suite has a huge bath with a jacuzzi under a skylight, a separate shower and a double vanity. In the garden-level room that has two double beds, the couple was putting in a jacuzzi with a view of the gardens

In their own house, the Lemieuxs offer a first-floor suite with two double beds dressed in florals and an enormous jacuzzi in the center of the room, plus a double shower in the skylit bathroom. Upstairs is a suite with king bed, a better view and a merely ordinary-size double jacuzzi.

(508) 888-8813 or (800) 475-6398. Three rooms and three suites with private baths. Doubles, $160 to $225. Three-night minimum weekends, two-night minimum midweek. Children over 16. No smoking. Closed November-April.

Capt. Ezra Nye House, 152 Main St., Sandwich 02563.

The most celebrated shipmaster Sandwich ever produced built this house because he felt his earlier residence – now the Fessenden House at the Dan'l Webster Inn – too confining after days at sea with the sky as his ceiling. A painting of his packet ship, The Independence, hangs over the fireplace in the parlor today.

Harry and Elaine Dickson moved here from New Mexico in 1985 to become only the sixth owners of the Federal-style house built in 1829. The deans of Sandwich innkeepers, they offer pleasant common rooms and six accommodations with private baths.

Beyond the parlor, which has a sofa and not one but two Victorian-style settees, are a stenciled dining room and a small den with a TV. Harry's collection of export china is displayed on shelves in both.

The Dicksons consider their grandest accommodation to be the Blue Room, upstairs in the front corner of the rambling house. It has a queensize carved mahogany four-poster bed and a loveseat beside the working fireplace. Decor in

Capt. Ezra Nye House was built in Federal Style by famous shipmaster in 1829.

three other rooms with queensize canopy beds varies from mahogany to wicker to country pine. The Calico Room is named for the calico cat on the pillow and the calico spread on the bed. At the rear of the second floor are the Peach Room with twin century-old Jenny Lind spool beds. It has a private hall bath that is shared if rented as a family suite with the adjacent Yellow Room.

Out back on the ground level is the Rose Suite, with a private entrance, a queen bed and a small sitting room with TV.

The couple's Blue Willow china is the backdrop for a gourmet breakfast. At our visit, Elaine had prepared Dutch baby pancakes with apples as the main course following starters of orange juice, fresh fruit and blueberry-cranberry muffins. Ham quiche, praline french toast and red pepper or goat cheese and walnut soufflés are other morning treats.

(508) 888-6142 or (800) 388-2278. Fax (508) 833-2897. Five rooms and one suite with private baths. June-October: doubles $100 to $110, suite $110. Rest of year: doubles $90 to $95, suite $95. Two-night minimum weekends. Children over 6. No smoking.

Isaiah Jones Homestead, 165 Main St., Sandwich 02563.

This 1849 Italianate B&B is elegantly furnished with prized antiques and oriental carpets in high Victorian style. It's been that way since it was launched by Cathy Catania of the Dan'l Webster Inn family and maintained thus by subsequent owners.

Doug and Jan Klapper, corporate dropouts from Connecticut, took possession of a turnkey operation in 1997. Caring little about antiques, they recognized a going concern and have maintained the status quo, although Jan was about to replace the corona canopy, wicker and chintz in the side Lombard Jones Room with a stately Victorian cherry queen bed with matching chairs and end tables.

The Deming Jarves Room in the front of the house is the largest of the five guest rooms, all with private baths. Its Victorian half canopy queen bed facing out from the corner is part of an antique set with an armoire and matching cheval mirror. The floral draperies match the bedspread and pillows. There's a sofa, and a large bath with jacuzzi and separate shower.

Downstairs beneath the Jarves in what once was the parlor is the Dr. Jonathan Leonard Room, with fishnet canopy queen poster bed, two wing chairs and a massive

History pervades Seth Pope House, erected in 1699 and full of charm.

armoire. Two side closets have been converted into a two-part bathroom. A jacuzzi tub is a feature of the Lombard Jones Room, while the Samuel Beale Room offers a working fireplace, step-up mahogany queen bed and an alcove sitting area. The rear Thomas Dexter Room comes with an Eastlake double and a twin poster bed, an Eastlake dresser and two Victorian parlor chairs. Hat boxes and old christening dresses are among the decorative accents.

Beyond a small reception room is a long side parlor with a dining area at one end and a Victorian sitting area at the other. An enormous Victorian breakfront of carved mahogany is a focal point and showcases prized dining pieces. The Klappers serve a full breakfast by candlelight at 8:30. Eggs florentine and lattice yeast coffee cake were featured the day of our visit. Broccoli quiche, sausage and sticky buns were the fare the day before. Afternoon tea is available upon request.

(508) 888-9115 or (800) 526-1625. Five rooms with private baths. Late May through October: doubles, $95 to $155. Rest of year: $75 to $135. Children over 12. No smoking.

Seth Pope House, 110 Tupper Road, Sandwich 02563.

Few B&Bs convey a feeling of history better than this gray Cape/Colonial saltbox, a 1699 beauty of size and substance on a hillside acre of trees north of the village square. John and Beverly Dobel, who retired here from Michigan, converted the private residence listed on the National Register into a comfortable B&B in 1991.

"This house works its charms on people," says Beverly. And so it does. Just inside the front entry are a handsome Colonial parlor and a small den with TV. Beyond, running across the back of the house, is a beamed keeping room to end all keeping rooms. The dining area is set for a candlelit breakfast, and there's a sitting area in front of a wood stove in a large fireplace with a beehive oven. Here is where Beverly offers a full breakfast, featuring a baked omelet, three-grain pancakes or french toast scones. Her signature starter is a breakfast parfait layering fruit, yogurt and granola.

Up steep stairs are a small sitting room and three comfortable guest rooms with private baths. Antique four-poster twin beds are in the Pineapple Room with a hooked rug on the wide-plank floor, a dressing room closet and a large bathroom with a lineup of old school desks for decoration. A floral comforter tops the Lincoln-era walnut queen bed in the carpeted Victorian Room, dressed in rose and cream shades and holding an armoire, dresser and a marble-topped vanity and washstand. The rear Colonial Room with exposed beams offers a queen canopy bed, a sloping floor, an unusual twelve-over-twelve window and a large sit-down shower.

In the shady back yard, guests enjoy a slate patio surrounded by old stone walls and an herb garden.

(508) 888-5916 or (888) 996-7384. Three rooms with private baths. Memorial Day to Labor Day: doubles, $95. Off-season: $85. Two-night minimum weekends in season. Children over 10. Closed November to mid-April.

The Village Inn, 4 Jarves St., Sandwich 02563.

Painting workshops by area artists whose works grace its walls are the hall-marks of this Federal-style inn under new ownership. Susan Fehlinger gave up a career as a TV producer in New York to move here in 1997 with her teen-aged son. She took over an inn opened in 1989 by a man who did much of the renovation to the 1830s structure himself and left the furnishings, most of which he made.

Professional artists conduct workshops for all levels of painters in the new Sand-wich Artworks studio behind the inn. The area's colorful marshes, cranberry bogs, beaches and historic buildings offer subjects aplenty, and give participants an opportunity to improve their skills in the company of others of similar persuasion.

Susan has concentrated on refurbishing the common rooms. She took a rather spare Victorian décor and made the double parlor more comfortable yet sophisticated. A wooden cat is curled around the leg of the antique coffee table in the front parlor. "I'm allergic to cats," she explains, "so this is the only kind I can have." Off the rear parlor is a wet bar, where complimentary wine is stored and guests make their own tea.

Susan painted the checkered floor in the breakfast room – "it took a lot of tape" – and added color with her Fiestaware stored in open shelves. Here is where she puts out a buffet for continental breakfast on weekdays and adds hot entrées on weekends. Frittata with zucchini and peppers might be the main course one day, and egg strata the next.

White cotton duvets, down comforters and antique pillow shams dress the hand-some beds made by the previous owner. Six rooms – two on the first floor and four on the second – have queensize beds and private baths. Two have working fire-places. One at the rear of the main floor has a handpainted armoire, a polished floor and crisp décor. What Susan calls two "cute and cozy" rooms with twin beds on the third floor share a hall bath and are good for families.

(508) 833-0363 or (800) 922-9989. Fax (508) 833-2063. Six rooms with private baths and two rooms with shared baths. June-October: doubles, $85 to $105. Rest of year: $70 to $95. Children over 8. No smoking. Closed most of January-March.

The Summer House, 158 Main St., Sandwich 02563.

This 1835 Cape Cod Greek Revival house was occupied by the family and descendants of a Sandwich Glass mold-maker until 1981, when it became one of Sandwich's earliest B&Bs with four rooms sharing two baths. As their first order of business in 1996, new owners Kevin and Marjorie Huelsman added two bathrooms so all would be private. They also gave birth to their first child, "who was born here to a full house," Marjorie recalls. They moved here from Nantucket to advance Kevin's career as a middle school principal.

The bedrooms, three with working fireplaces, have queen or twin/king beds. The largest front corner room has a king mahogany poster bed and a faux rug painted on the floor. A rear bedroom that lacks a fireplace compensates with its view of the gardens. Antique roses wrap around the rear of the house and envelop a downstairs bedroom, where their sweet smell intoxicates in June.

Guests spread out in the double parlor along the front of the house. The Victorian sitting room opens into a colorful, rather exotic dining room with white window trim accenting the Chinese-red walls, a black and white checkerboard floor, a black marble fireplace, three floral-clothed tables and an abundance of green plants. A rear sunporch that's warm enough to enjoy on sunny winter days is outfitted with wicker furniture and a TV. Afternoon tea is served here overlooking a large side and rear yard with a linden tree and showy phlox in an English perennial garden.

In the morning, Marjorie serves a full breakfast starting with fruit cup, juices and cinnamon rolls or muffins. Spinach and cream cheese omelets, a breakfast puff with eggs and bacon, or banana-raspberry pancakes could be the main event.

(508) 888-4991 or (800) 241-3609. Four rooms with private baths. May-October: doubles, $75 to $95. Rest of year: $65 to $85. Children over 6. Smoking restricted.

The Dunbar House, 1 Water St., Sandwich 02563.

"Home-style lodging" is offered at this B&B overlooking Shawme Pond in the heart of village. Make that home-style of the 18th century, for the interior of the yellow Colonial with green shutters remains true to its 1741 heritage. Add an English accent, for David Bell, son of the founding innkeepers who retired, is from Great Britain. He and his wife, Nancy Iribarren, operate a thriving tea room.

The Bells are only the fourth family to occupy the house, which was being used for town offices when they took over in 1989. They named the three guest rooms, all with views over the pond, after favorite lakes in England's Lakes District. The main-floor Buttermere has twin beds and simple décor. Upstairs are the Loweswater with queensize bed, three chairs, a hooked rug and an antique mirror, and the Ennerdale with a canopy queen bed and a sofa. The furniture is English pine.

In the dining room, overnight guests are served a full breakfast. David cooked baked strawberry french toast the day of our visit, but ordinarily Nancy does the cooking. Eggs on crumpets with cheese is a favorite. A red and white, authentic Colonial parlor at the rear of the house faces a large fireplace. Out back are a patio and, nearby, the tea room (see Dining Spots).

(508) 833-2485. Fax (508) 833-4713. Three rooms with private baths. May-October: doubles, $85 to $95. Rest of yea: $65 to $75. No smoking.

Dining Spots

The Dan'l Webster Inn, 149 Main St., Sandwich.

Upwards of 350 dinners a night are served in the three dining rooms and tavern at this popular inn. The wonder is that they do it so successfully, offering excellent food, deftly served, with piano entertainment and an impressive wine list.

The Catania family's ownership of the Cape Cod-based Hearth 'n Kettle restaurant chain stood them in good stead for this adventure in fine dining. Rob Catania, the Culinary Institute-trained executive chef here, oversees the kitchen,

Stylish dining and lodging are offered in former church rectory known as The Belfry.

markets his lobster chowder and founded the family's pioneering aquafarm in nearby Barnstable to raise striped bass and hydroponic produce. Brother Richard Catania put together the award-winning wine list that's notable for only nominal markup on select French vintages. The entire family was behind the $500,000 worth of 1997 renovations that enlarged the atmospheric tavern into a tavern dining room, and opened up the Music Room and adjacent Heritage Room.

The inn now can offer all things to all people, supplementing its traditional fine-dining fare with an extensive tavern menu featuring thin-crust gourmet pizzas and offering a selection of main courses in half portions at lower prices.

Many of the dining areas were fairly crowded starting at 4:30 the weeknight we stopped in to make a reservation. Returning at 8:15, we found a glamorous crowd of inn guests and locals enjoying sophisticated fare in the stunning, high-ceilinged Conservatory that brings the outdoors in. The extensive menu is made for grazing, which is what we did. The daily sampler of the signature lobster chowder and two soups served with crostini (chicken-vegetable and an assertive roasted garlic with shrimp that was a standout) was more than enough for two to share. One of us noshed on the scallops casino appetizer and a huge salad of aquafarm greens with gorgonzola cheese, white raisins and pistachios. The other sampled a half entrée of lobster, shrimp and scallops with julienned vegetables over cappelletti from a choice of five, representing about one-third of the menu that ranged from baked scrod to prime rib, grilled veal chop and lobster with filet mignon. Kiwi sorbet was a refreshing ending to a satisfying meal.

(508) 888-3623 or (800) 444-3566. Entrées, $16.50 to $26; light entrées, $10.95 to $13.95. Lunch and dinner daily, 11:30 to 9 or 10.

The Belfry Inne & Bistro, 8 Jarves St., Sandwich. 02563.
The hot spot in town for fine dining is the stylish bistro on the main floor of this

new inn. Thirty-two lucky diners can be seated at white-clothed tables in two small rooms with pale yellow rag-rolled walls and oriental rugs. The front common room is pressed into service for overflow, and a few more can eat in the bar.

Culinary Institute-trained chef Peter Martin prepares what he calls a French neo-classical menu. You might start with a marinated shrimp antipasto salad, smoked salmon terrine, a mushroom and polenta tart or a lobster, scallop and leek strudel. Or try butternut squash soup topped with blue cheese and toasted pepitas.

Expect main dishes like pan-seared salmon fillet on a bed of wild rice with carrots, asparagus and a shallot-pernod beurre blanc; sautéed duck breast with a cassis and currant demi-glaze; fricassee of cornish game hen, or rack of New Zealand lamb with an herbed red wine sauce.

White chocolate cheesecake, crème brûlée and mixed berry tart typify the selection of desserts. They are so highly regarded that many people stop in late in the evening for a sweet and a drink.

(508) 888-8550. Entrées, $16 to $23. Dinner, Wednesday-Sunday 5 to 9.

The Bee Hive Tavern, 406 Route 6A, East Sandwich.

Townspeople are partial to this replica of a Colonial tavern with an extensive menu catering to family tastes. Inside a newish looking roadhouse built in 1950 is a dark and beamed interior with booths, hanging lamps and 19th-century accessories. It is billed as "exactly the kind of spot that locals and weary travelers alike hope to find on historic Olde King's Highway."

Everyone faced at least a fifteen-minute wait for a table the sunny and warm autumn Tuesday we stopped for lunch (alas, the umbrellaed outdoor tables and benches were for waiting only, not eating, we were advised). At a booth in the dark and intimate interior, customers and staff streamed by as we lunched on french onion soup, a mediocre spinach salad and a good fried oyster plate with french fries and coleslaw. The blackboard specials were numerous but as standard (baked scrod, liver and onions) as the rest of the menu. Desserts were less predictable: homemade gingerbread with cranberries, grapenut custard and a specialty Schneeball, a German snowball of homemade ice cream wrapped in nuts and more.

The dinner menu touches all the traditional bases from baked cod and lobster pie to back ribs and lamb chops. The onion-dill rolls are famous, we're told.

(508) 833-1184. Entrées, $9.95 to $14.95. Lunch daily, 11:30 to 3. Dinner, 5 to 9. Pub, 11 to 9. Sunday breakfast (also Saturday in season), 8:30 to 11:30.

Horizons on Cape Cod Bay, 98 Town Neck Road, Sandwich.

Scores of college pennants hang from the beams in the vaulted-ceilinged upstairs at this informal tavern and restaurant with a sports bar atmosphere. But it was the outdoor deck overlooking a curved beach along Cape Cod Bay that attracted us for lunch.

Watching barges come and go from the entrance to the Cape Cod Canal added interest to a meal in which the food played second fiddle. The trademarked imitation crab and seafood sandwich was passable and the grilled chicken tortilla okay. The chowders and pizzas at the next table were said to be great.

Fried seafood, lobster and prime rib are specialties at night, upstairs in the tavern or downstairs in a large dining room. But the waterfront location takes priority.

(508) 888-6166. Entrées, $9.95 to $14.95. Lunch daily, 11:30 to 4. Dinner, 4 to 9. Closed November-March.

The Dunbar Tea Shop, 1 Water St., Sandwich.
This charming shop – a haven for anglophiles – offers Cape Cod's only British tea room. The Bell family from England started in 1991 with a gift and book shop and added a tea shop in the former garage beside their soon-to-open B&B.

Now, with David Bell and wife Nancy Iribarren at the helm, the enterprise has added a tea room with a charming tea garden outside. British treats are featured for lunch, afternoon tea and, in cooler months, the more substantial high tea. Spicy pumpkin soup, crab tart, cheshire lamb crumble and blueberry sour cream cheesecake were blackboard specials at our visit. They supplement such standbys as scones, mushroom and walnut soup, Welsh tarts, shepherd's pie, ploughman's lunch and rich Trafalgar squares.

The tea shop in front is a trove of loose and bagged teas and tea-related accessories, from kettles to cozies. A book shop annex advertises British topics and first editions.
(508) 833-2485. Entrées, $6.75 to $9.95. Shop open daily, 10 to 5. Tea room, 11 to 4:30.

Sandwich's Sandwiches, 132 Route 6A, Sandwich.
The neat name of this storefront establishment tells the story. The menu lists ten specialty sandwiches – perhaps chicken cordon bleu or curried chicken salad bombay – in the $3 to $5.50 range. Most are served in pita pockets or on jumbo onion rolls. Also available are ten salads in the same price range.
Open daily from 10 a.m.

Diversions

Sandwich Glass Museum, 129 Main St., Sandwich.
The transformation of Cape Cod's oldest town from small farming community into one of the world's leading manufacturers of glass objects is traced chronologically in this colorful museum operated by the Sandwich Historical Society. The Boston & Sandwich Glass Co. thrived here starting in 1825, its more than 500 employees refining the art of pressing glass in molds and creating exquisite blown pieces. Competition and lower prices took their toll, however, and a prolonged strike closed the factory permanently in 1888. More than 5,000 pieces of Sandwich glass are on permanent display in fourteen galleries, with occasional video areas for explanation. The pieces, from 800 cup plates to rare banquet lanterns and iridescent Trevaise art glass, are of particular interest to collectors. The Historical Society adds some idiosyncratic finds, including an old rocking cradle on wheels and a Quaker marriage certificate above a display of glass remnants. The remarkable map-like rendition of Cape Cod, made of Sandwich glass fragments, fascinates on the way out from the gift shop.
(508) 888-0251. Open daily 9:30 to 4:30, April-October; Wednesday-Sunday, 9:30 to 4 rest of year. Closed in January. Adults, $3.50.

Heritage Plantation of Sandwich, Grove and Pine Streets, Sandwich.
The incredible display of rhododendrons are the primary attraction for most at the former estate of Charles O. Dexter, but there's much more at this museum of Americana founded by the Lilly pharmaceutical family. Dexter's renowned rhodies – more than 125 varieties – are at their best in late May and early June. We were surprised to find some late-bloomers still a brilliant red in mid-October. The remains of the day lily, heather, herb and hosta gardens and the holly dell appealed around the 76 tranquil acres as well. Also impressive were the Lilly collections of firearms

and hand-painted miniature soldiers, a working 1912 carousel (well visited by school groups) and wonderful folk art exhibits at the Art Museum. The collections of duck decoys and shore birds, the scrimshaw and Nantucket lightship baskets, the children's chocolate mug collection are stunning. So is the American flag fashioned from plastic objects found on local beaches. Some people spend hours ogling the 37 shiny antique and classic cars in the Shaker Round Barn, a perfect display space with two circular floors showing Gary Cooper's 1930 Duesenberg and William Howard Taft's White Steamer, the first official White House auto. A free shuttle bus makes stops every twenty minutes around the far-flung property. The Carousel Café offers light breakfast, lunch and afternoon snacks. The Old Barn Garden Shop sells plants and garden supplies, and there are all kinds of neat things in the main gift shop by the parking area.

(508) 888-3300. Open daily 10 to 5, Mother's Day to Oct. 19. Adults, $8.

Thornton W. Burgess Museum, 4 Water St., Sandwich.

The works and spirit of the renowned children's author and naturalist, the best-known Sandwich native in this century, are preserved in this restored 1776 Cape Cod house beside Shawme Pond. His animal characters like Peter Rabbit, Reddy Fox and Grandfather Frog are in evidence in the pint-size museum with nature exhibits on one side and a shop on the other. A couple of herb gardens are out back.

Two miles east off Route 6A in East Sandwich are the **Green Briar Nature Center and Jam Kitchen,** operated by the Thornton W. Burgess Society and featuring the 57-acre Briar Patch conservation area, nature trails and a fascinating, turn-of-the-century jam kitchen producing and selling jams, chutneys and relishes in the style of a century ago.

(508) 888-6870. Open Monday-Saturday 10 to 4, Sunday 1 to 4. Winter hours vary. Donation.

Yesteryears Doll and Miniature Museum, River and Main Streets, Sandwich.

Dolls of every age, description and size as well as rare early dolls from Germany, France and Japan are on display in this quirky museum showing the collections of founders Eloise and Ronald Thomas on two floors of an old church, the 1833 First Parish Meetinghouse. The 50 dollhouses (including a four-story Victorian) are a highlight for some, while others are charmed by the miniature grocery stores, toy shops and candy stores. All the ingredients for one grocery store were made of real candy, including marzipan sausages strung above the meat counter. The family-run museum is considered one of the best of its type in the country.

(508) 888-1711. Open Monday-Saturday 10 to 4, mid-May to mid-October. Adults, $3.

Hoxie House, 18 Water St., Sandwich.

One of the oldest houses in Cape Cod's oldest town, a restored 1675 saltbox overlooking Shawme Pond, looks its age. One hardly knows what to make of its fortress-like front façade or its curving room in back. Inside is a two-story wonder of primitive antiquity – all the more so when you learn that people lived here until 1953 without the benefit of running water, plumbing or electricity. Our guide called it "the best, most inexpensive tour on the Cape." A combination ticket gives admission to **Dexter's Gristmill,** built in 1640 and still in operation at the foot of Shawme Pond in Sandwich Center. Corn is ground daily here, and you can usually see ducks and swans on the adjacent pond.

(508) 888-1711. Open Monday-Saturday 10 to 5, Sunday 1 to 5, mid-June to mid-October. Adults, $1.50 each property. Combination ticket, $2.50.

Sandwich Plankwalk. The best way to sense the beauty of the area's marshlands and to get to the beach is to traverse the new boardwalk starting at the foot of Harbor Street on the northern edge of the village. Originally built in 1875 and rebuilt many times, it was destroyed by two storms in 1991 and reconstructed by townspeople in 1992 in what a plaque notes was "a labor of love" after a hurried fundraising campaign. "Welcome A-board," says the first plank of thousands, each donated by a public-spirited citizen, family or institution and duly inscribed. They make for interesting reading ("the MacLeod Clan," "In Memory of Mum and Dad," "East Sandwich Post Office") on your way out to the beach. Don't expect to find some you missed on the way back – they'll be upside down.

Shopping. Most of Sandwich's treasures are in its museums, as you might deduce when you note the signs at the principal Main and Jarves street intersection identifying the Boston Organ & Piano Co. and Sandwich Chiropractic. No Gap or Benetton here. Old houses harbor treats like the **Weather Store,** with everything from tiny compasses to big weather vanes and CDs about the weather, and **Madden & Co.** with gourmet foods, antiques and "gatherings for the country home." The **Sandwich Antiques Center** shows the wares of about 150 dealers, with glass a principal commodity. The Old King's Highway (Route 6-A east of Sandwich) offers unexpected discoveries of the antiques and gift variety, plus the **Glass Studio,** about the only place locally where you can still see a glass blower at work.

Extra-Special ————————————

Giving Tree Gallery & Sculpture Garden, 550 Route 6A, East Sandwich.
"Where Art and Nature Meet" is the theme of Judith Smith's nifty indoor-outdoor collection of American crafts, all with a peg to nature. Doing basically everything herself, this Renaissance woman has transformed a dilapidated summer cottage and grounds into two floors of exhibit space, sculpture gardens, a nature preserve and even a coffeehouse. Enter the little cottage in front and view the stylish crafts, including some great jewelry and pottery, of some of the 200 artists represented. Go downstairs to the art gallery to view some mighty good Cape landscapes. Classical music plays as you head out to the mysterious and mystical sculpture garden in a 200-year-old bamboo grove. Here sculptures on pedestals, in trees and on the ground interplay randomly with nature. Follow a path decorated with crushed glass through an open iron pyramid where you might want to sit on a bench and meditate for an hour or so. Then there's a rickety, makeshift boardwalk through the bamboo forest to the edge of a wide-open marsh and wildlife sanctuary, two more revolving sculptures and a changing landscape that is the essence of beauty. Continue on across the 50-foot rope suspension bridge that Judith and a friend built – open to "one person at a time" and not for the fearful, although it isn't very far off the ground. Look back and see a little Stonehenge in a clearing. You return into another space full of sculptures: fish hanging on trees, a girl on a swing, reptiles on the grass. Coffee, soup, light lunches, biscotti and cookies are for sale in the coffee house with tables outside for taking in the whole experience.
(508) 888-5446. Open daily 10 to 5, April-December; rest of year by appointment.

Chatham, Mass.
Serenity Beside the Sea

Of all Cape Cod's towns, we are fondest of Chatham, a sophisticated, sedate and serene enclave of affluence beside the sea. This is the elbow of the Cape, where the hubbub of much of the Cape's south shore yields to treed tranquility before the land veers north to face the open Atlantic and form the dunes of the National Seashore.

Known originally as "The First Stop of the East Wind," Chatham is one of the Cape's oldest towns (settled in 1656) and one of its most residential. Hidden in the trees and along the meandering waterfront are large homes and estates.

Explore a bit and you may see the gorgeous hydrangea walk leading up to a Shore Road mansion. Across from a windmill in a field of yellow wildflowers sparkling against a backdrop of blue ocean, it's the essence of Cape Cod. Or you may follow Mooncusser's Lane and find that the road ends abruptly at the water. Admire the view from the drawbridge on Bridge Street as well as the classic views of the Chatham Light.

Because it's so residential, Chatham has escaped the overt commercialism and tourism of much of the Cape. It does not cater to transients. Some inns and motels encourage long stays, and many accommodations are in cottages or rented houses.

The summer social scene revolves around private clubs and parties. But almost everyone turns out for the Friday evening band concerts in Kate Gould Park.

Although Main Street, which winds through the center of town, seems filled with pedestrians and shoppers, chances are they're residents or regulars. Perhaps its air of stability and tradition is what makes Chatham so special.

Inn Spots

The Captain's House Inn of Chatham, 369-377 Old Harbor Road (Route 28), Chatham 02633.

There's more than a touch of England amid all the Americana of this supremely

elegant and comfortable inn that originated in Captain Hiram Harding's restored 1839 home, set on shaded lawns screened by high hedges in a sedate residential section north of the village.

Their predecessors built this into one of the few small AAA four-diamond inns in New England. Through attention to detail and an uncanny knack for knowing what the luxury market wants, Jan and David McMaster have taken it to a higher level.

Dave, former CEO of a computer company he founded in California, continued to

The Captain's House Inn of Chatham occupies residential site north of village.

upgrade, expanding the dining porch, adding a few jacuzzi tubs and building four deluxe rooms with fireplaces. He also developed new English perennial gardens with a three-tiered fountain pond in a rear corner of the two-acre property.

Jan, a proper Brit from Bournemouth, injected her heritage into an inn whose staff already imparted an English accent. For some years, the Captain's House had hired hotel students from the University of Bournemouth in Jan's hometown, a striking coincidence, and the McMasters were happy to continue the tradition. Jan serves an elaborate and true English tea in the afternoon. She also has expanded the breakfast offerings to include smoked salmon corncakes with broiled tomatoes and cheese, waffles with strawberries or blueberries, quiches and apple crêpes to supplement the traditional fresh fruit, breads and muffins, all served at individual tables in the sunny breakfast porch.

Said breakfast area is a beauty in white and dusky rose. An addition projects eight feet out into the gardens with floor-to-ceiling windows. The floor is tiled and trailing wisteria is stenciled on the walls. Two fancy serving areas along the sides simplify breakfast service.

The entrance hall and living room retain the original pumpkin pine floors and are furnished with antiques, fine rugs and period wallpapers.

All nineteen guest accommodations have private baths. Thirteen now have fireplaces and five have TV/VCR combinations, refrigerators and coffee makers. Fine antiques are evident throughout. The eight rooms in the main Greek Revival house have a variety of furnishings, including four-poster beds with pineapple finials, lacy white fishnet canopies, white eyelet-edged curtains, colorful sheets and comforters, thick oversize towels, braided rugs and soft velvet wing chairs for reading. Special French soaps are provided in the bathrooms.

Five deluxe rooms, a couple with beamed and peaked ceilings, are found in a rear carriage house. Also coveted is the Captain's Cottage, where the sumptuous Captain Hiram Harding suite looks like a library with dark walnut paneling and beamed ceiling, fine oriental rugs on the wide-plank floor, large fireplace, plush sofa and side chairs, and lace-canopied kingsize four-poster bed. A jacuzzi tub has been added here, as well as in the newly enlarged Lady Mariah Room adjacent. In the latter, an old kitchen was converted into what Jan calls a "fantasy bathroom," a smashing space with a double whirlpool flanked by four pillars and two wicker chairs facing a corner fireplace. The fireplace is also on view from the extra-high, step-up kingsize bed.

Historic Eben Ryder House is centerpiece of Wequassett Inn.

Top of the line are three jacuzzi accommodations in the Stables, a new building behind the cottage. The upstairs suite has fireplaces in both living room and bedroom, a kingsize bed and french doors leading to a full-length balcony. Each of the two downstairs rooms has a queen canopy bed, fireplace and a private deck, and a TV/VCR is hidden in an 1875 chest or the armoire.

Next on the agenda was the conversion of the two smallest rooms in the main inn into a two-room suite.

Poland Spring water is in each guest room. Turndown service is available, and guests find an evening snack.

(508) 945-0127 or (800) 315-0728. Fax (508) 315-0728. Seventeen rooms and two suites with private baths. Mid-May through October: doubles $135 to $275, suites $275 to $325. Rest of year: doubles $135 to $215, suites $215 to $250. Three-night minimum in season. Children over 12. No smoking.

Wequassett Inn, Pleasant Bay, Chatham 02633.

Blessed with a fine location above its private beach and peninsula separating Round Cove from Pleasant Bay, this inn reflects its Indian name for "crescent on the water." The new blends quite nicely with the old in a resort compound with structures dating back more than 200 years. Eighteen Cape Cod-style cottages, motel buildings and condo-type facilities totaling 104 rooms are distributed across 22 rolling, beautifully landscaped acres amid colorful flowers of the season and huge old pines.

Large guest rooms and suites are furnished traditionally with cheery colors, patterned fabrics, pine furniture, quilted bedspreads, duck-print wall hangings and needlepoint rugs. We like best the 37 waterview rooms, with windows onto the bay and decks for outdoor lounging. Others are partial to the tennis villas, many with cathedral ceilings and private balconies overlooking the woods or courts. Rooms have cable TV, clock radios, mini-refrigerators, phones, air-conditioning and Crabtree & Evelyn toiletries. Amenities like these helped the Wequassett earn membership in the Preferred Hotels association of luxury resorts. It was the first New England inn so honored.

At the disposal of guests are five tennis courts with a resident pro, sailboats and canoes, a large swimming pool with a bar where one can order a light lunch, a half-mile-long beach and a small health and fitness center, newly ensconced in what had been a game room. A boat shuttles swimmers to the barrier beach that protects Pleasant Bay. Afternoon coffee and pastries are available in the Pleasant Bay Espresso Cafe on the lower level of the new, two-tiered veranda off the lounge, a delightful place from which to observe the bay goings-on.

The public may join inn guests for meals in the historic "square top" Eben Ryder House, a restored 18th-century sea captain's mansion with smashing bay views. Floor-to-ceiling windows on three sides is about all the decor you need in the main dining room, recently redone in dusty rose and pink with candles flickering in hurricane lamps and a pianist entertaining in the background.

Longtime chef Frank McMullen is partial to fresh seafood and continental cuisine. For starters, we liked his escargots with pinenuts in puff pastry, Thai mussels steamed in lobster broth and curry, and a green salad topped with grilled chicken and wild mushrooms. Standouts among main courses were Norwegian salmon baked on a cedar plank, served on ancho chile beurre blanc, and twin beef tenderloins on a bed of simmered lentils and prosciutto. Key lime pie and a strawberry tart were refreshing desserts.

(508) 432-5400 or (800) 225-7125. Fax (508) 432-5032. Ninety-three rooms and eleven suites with private baths. Rates EP. Late June to Labor Day: doubles $255 to $490, suites $510. Late spring and early fall: doubles $175 to $395, suites $375 to $400. April and November: doubles $100 to $200, suites $225. Closed December-March.

Entrées, $18.25 to $22.75. Lunch daily, 11:30 to 2. Dinner, 6 to 10.

Chatham Bars Inn, Shore Road, Chatham 02633.

The colorful new landscaping with luxuriant flowers, gas lanterns and brick steps tiered up the hillside toward the main entrance of this venerable inn/resort "make a statement," in the words of its management. So do the beautifully refurbished Victorian foyer and South Parlor, the front veranda awash in wicker, and the redecorated dining room and tavern.

Such statements signal the changes since Carl Lindner, the Ohio big-business entrepreneur who's lately into hotels, acquired the property in 1993. His vision is to restore the hotel to its original grandeur, circa 1914.

The Chatham Bars complex of an imposing inn and charming oceanfront houses and cottages existed virtually as a private club from its beginnings as a hunting lodge in 1914. One of the last great oceanfront resorts, it's perched on a bluff with half a mile of shoreline overlooking Pleasant Bay and the barrier beach separating it from the Atlantic. The 172 rooms run the gamut from 50 of the traditional type in the main inn to sumptuous suites in 27 cottages, many of them really houses containing two to eight guest rooms and common living rooms with fireplaces. We enjoyed watching the surf pummeling the now-famous breach in the barrier beach from the balcony off the plush sitting room of our cottage suite, which was suavely decorated in shades of mauve and rose.

Our guide, who had been here for twenty years under several owners, was "very excited about the recent changes at this special place."

He pointed with pride to the sunny new library at the end of the South Parlor, a cozy haven with leather loveseats, oriental rugs and a pressed brass ceiling. "It looks turn of the century," he noted. "But it's not at all domineering or depressing Victorian." He showed three newly renovated side cottages. Variously outfitted with tiled fireplaces, built-in TVs, lighted closets, handpainted cabinets, window seats, oversize beds and even a grandfather's clock, they are the ultimate in taste, comfort and low-key luxury. The desk in one has an old writing box bearing a picture of the old hotel. The base of a lamp in another is laminated with hotel postcards from days gone by. They make a statement of tradition, but also signify change. All the cottages are to be refurbished in similar style over the next five years. Newly opened at the north end of the main hotel are two master suites. One of 1,300 square feet on the second floor has two bedrooms, a parlor and a living room with decks on all sides.

For meals, the resort has a stately Main Dining Room in which a new chef blends the creative with the traditional, jackets are requested for dinner and dinner dances have been launched lately on summer Saturday nights. There's a more casual North Beach Tavern and Grill in space formerly known as the Inner Bar. Lunch, continental breakfast with an omelet bar and special events take place at the inviting Beach House Grill at water's edge, where the pool area has been enlarged and croquet lawns added. Guests enjoy an adjacent nine-hole golf course, five tennis courts and a sandy beach.

Although the theme is understated luxury, the resort is distinguished by its mix of accommodations. You can mingle and make merry in the main inn, or get away from it all in a house by the sea.

(508) 945-0096 or (800) 527-4884. Fax (508) 945-5491. One hundred forty-one rooms and 31 suites with private baths. Rates EP. Mid-June to mid-September: doubles $190 to $380, suites $405 to $1,100. Spring and fall: doubles $140 to $310 weekends, $120 to $290 midweek; suites $285 to $1,000 weekends, $265 to $950 midweek. December-March: doubles $120 to $190 weekends, $100 to $170 midweek; suites $200 to $550 weekends, $180 to $500 midweek. Five-night minimum in July; seven-night minimum in August; two-night minimum weekends rest of year.

Chatham Wayside Inn, 512 Main St., Box 685, Chatham 02633.

When we first vacationed in Chatham three decades ago, the Wayside seemed the quintessential New England inn – located in the heart of town and containing a lively tavern that was perfect for an after-dinner drink. If the food was mediocre and the accommodations somewhat threadbare, no matter. It had a captive audience.

But tradition carries an inn only so far. Upscale newcomers lured away its business, and the Wayside fell upon hard times. The 1860 landmark was rescued from foreclosure in 1993 by local businessmen David Oppenheim and Grant Wilson. They closed for a total rehab and reopened in 1994 with a new look, a new entry and layout, and 24 upstairs guest rooms. Ready in 1995 were 32 more guest rooms in a new three-story annex out back, occupying the site of four razed cottages. These parkside units have patios and balconies for front-row seats for the Friday night band concerts in Kate Gould Park.

Rooms in the main inn are nicely furnished with an abundance of chintz, vivid fabrics and Waverly prints. They come in three styles: Colonial, European traditional and country pine. All have king or queensize beds and thick carpeting, five have private balconies or terraces and two claim jacuzzis. TVs are ensconced in highboys or on chests facing the beds, and Lord & Mayfair toiletries await in the bathrooms. A writing desk is tucked into one of the nooks and crannies of a dormered third-floor room. "Everything looks and feels old," general manager Suki Scofield said as she showed us around, "but you can be assured it's new."

Three meals a day are served in the inn's spacious restaurant and tavern. The shady front courtyard facing the passing Chatham street scene is the place to see

Restored Chatham Wayside Inn attracts diners as well as overnight guests.

and be seen in season. It proved so popular that an expansive canopied deck was added in 1997. We still faced a considerable wait at 2 o'clock on a July weekday to snag an outside table for lunch. The wait was worth it for the setting and a superior grilled chicken salad on mixed greens, loaded with raisins and sundried cranberries. The dinner menu covers all the bases, from fish and chips to rack of lamb.

(508) 945-5550 or (800) 391-5734. Fax (508) 945-3407. Fifty-six rooms with private baths. Rates EP. Late June through Labor Day: doubles, $150 to $325. Late spring and early fall: $125 to $275. Mid-October to Memorial Day: $95 to $215. Two-night minimum in summer, two-night minimum weekends late spring and early fall.

Entrées, $12.95 to $21.95. Breakfast daily, 8 to 11. Lunch, 11:30 to 4. Dinner, 5 to 10, to 9 in winter.

The Bradford Inn, 26 Cross St., Box 750, Chatham 02633.

An attractive, 26-room inn complex evolving from a motel, this venerable establishment is well situated in a residential section just off Chatham's Main Street. For years we had admired its cheery exterior with yellow awnings, as well as the gardens with flowers of every hue. The interior, we found, is just as nice.

Five large rooms are in the Bradford House in front, which we found cozy with the fireplace in our room ablaze on a fall evening. Four are in the Carriage House near the pool. The most deluxe are four with king and queensize canopy beds, fireplaces, Federal period furnishings and thick carpeting in the newly built Jonathan Gray House.

Eleven more are in the original L-shaped motel building in back. All individually decorated, five have kitchens and some are suites. A corner of the motel was gutted to produce a two-room suite with ceiling moldings, poster bed, ceramic tub, wet bar and two TV sets.

Ever expanding and refining, innkeepers Audrey and William Gray added the fireplaced Lion's Den game room and lounge, and opened a two-bedroom house with kitchen, dining room and living room as the **Captain's Hideaway.** They restored the **Mulberry Inn** at 44 Cross St. into an elegant B&B with a fireplaced suite on the main floor and two luxurious rooms upstairs.

Recently they vacated their quarters upstairs in the 1860 Captain Elijah Smith House, which also serves as the inn's reception area and restaurant. The move freed up space for a deluxe suite with a large living room with TV/VCR, a jacuzzi bath, a private rooftop deck and an enormous rear bedroom with beamed ceiling, a kingsize four-poster bed and raised-hearth fireplace, with two swivel club chairs facing another TV in an armoire.

The Grays moved to a cupola-topped 1789 sea captain's house they call the **Azubah Atwood Inn** at 177 Cross St. Here they offer three more rooms with private baths, queen beds and TV.

Exotic small fish flash colorfully in a couple of aquariums in the lobby of the main house. The Garden Room at the rear is where a full complimentary breakfast (guests choose from a large menu) is served. The apricot pancakes are so good that they draw the public as well. In season, many prefer to breakfast outside on the shady entry patio beside trickling fountains and the small pool, savoring the extravagant roses and watching the birds feed.

Inn guests and the public enjoy dinner in **Champlain's Restaurant,** named for explorer Samuel de Champlain, who sailed into Chatham's Stage Harbor in 1606. The names of dishes – Chatham lobster crumb pie, duck caribbean, chicken madras, veal holstein and Alsatian sampler mixed grill – give an idea of the chef's range.

(508) 945-1030 or (800) 242-8426. Fax (508) 945-9652. www.bradfordinn.com. Twenty-six rooms and suites with private baths. Summer: doubles, $139 to $249. Spring and fall: $119 to $219. Mid-October to Memorial Day: $89 to $189. Children over 7.

Entrées, $19.95 to $24.95. Breakfast, 8 to 11. Dinner in summer, nightly except Monday 5:30 to 9.

The Cranberry Inn at Chatham, 359 Main St., Chatham 02633.

Once named the Traveler's Home and later the Monomoy House, this pale yellow frame inn dating from the 1830s is Chatham's oldest inn. It was grandly renovated and expanded by Richard Morris and Peggy DeHan, two innkeepers who cut their teeth on smaller Chatham B&Bs that they launched and later sold.

The Cranberry was acquired in 1994 by retired Boston hotel developer Jim Bradley and his wife Debbie, who were busy taking the eighteen-room inn "to the next level." Rates are significantly higher, and the inn now is open year-round. Jim said they had spent $180,000 on upgrades in their first nine months.

The results are evident in the common rooms. Jim showed proudly the entry/ reception room that has become more formal with fine oriental carpets, "significant" art, a baby grand piano and rare tables with board games. The bar/lounge has been glamorized and made more authentic with beamed ceiling, expensive oriental art and old hotel registers found in the attic from a century ago. The redecorated dining room is a picture of elegance in showy navy and cranberry, with fabric-covered wood chairs and a remarkable, conversation-piece dollhouse. Jim advises that it is a replica of their home in Hingham and was a 25th-anniversary gift from their children. The Bradleys also landscaped the inn, adding English gardens ("done by a British couple") and a new nature trail leading to a cranberry bog, the old Mill Pond and out to the ocean.

Back inside, the beds have been triple-sheeted, the pillows converted to down feathers, the towels are now 100 percent cotton Dundee, the TVs are remote-controlled and the windows outfitted with vinyl blackout shades. Most beds are queensize four-posters. Crystal cranberry glasses are in each room, and the ice buckets are vinyl-coated in cranberry color. The previous owners had doubled the fourteen original guest rooms in size, thanks to an addition on the east end. All have new private baths, telephones and television. They also added four fireplaced suites, each with comfortable sitting areas and a couple with private balconies.

Breakfast is now "a full hot and cold breakfast buffet" in the formal dining room. Expect a fruit bowl "with a bit of everything," assorted cereals, cheddar cheese, pastries, broccoli quiche, eggs and pancakes. Afternoon tea brings scones and croissants with raspberry jam. Complimentary popcorn is served in the bar. The owners have turned over day-to-day operations to resident innkeepers.

(508) 945-9232 or (800) 332-4667. Fax (508) 945-3769. Eighteen rooms with private baths. Late June to Labor Day: doubles $140 to $255. Spring and fall: $120 to $235. December to early May: $85 to $175. Children over 8. No smoking.

The Cyrus Kent House Inn, 63 Cross St., Chatham 02633.

Restored into one of Chatham's first B&B's in 1985 by Richard Morris, this 1877 sea captain's home was acquired in 1993 by Sharon Swan, who had lived in Chatham for fourteen years, "had watched Richard restoring the place and never dreamed that I'd ever own it." She has kept the place much as it was.

Antiques, original art and fresh flowers from the inn's gardens decorate the seven guest rooms in the main house, all with private baths, queensize four-poster beds, wing chairs, televisions, clock-radios and telephones. Some add fireplaces and decks. The comforters are coordinated with the window treatments.

The rear carriage house harbors a couple of deluxe suites. One on the main floor with a beamed ceiling and a fireplace in the center is furnished in Shaker country style with a four-poster queen bed. The upstairs suite is larger and more formal with a vaulted ceiling. A palladian window with balloon curtains is the focal point of its elegant living room.

A continental breakfast of fresh fruit compote, granola, yogurt and homemade muffins is served in the dining room at individual tables with lace runners, silver and china. Afternoon tea is offered in the off-season in the spacious living room. Guests also enjoy a front porch.

(508) 945-9104 or (800) 338-5368. Seven rooms and two suites with private baths. Doubles, $135 to $155. Suites, $250, mid-June to mid-October; $110 to $200, mid-April to mid-June; $95 to $180, rest of year. Smoking restricted.

Carriage House Inn, 407 Old Harbor Road, Chatham 02633.

"Sadie and Lucy, our friendly golden retrievers, will keep you company," advises the brochure for this relaxed and cozy B&B.

Indeed. The retrievers proved so friendly that they snuggled up against the passenger's seat of our car and wouldn't let us close the car door to leave until innkeeper Pam Patton came to the rescue.

Pam and her husband Tom – as well as Sadie and Lucy – offer six guest rooms with oversize showers in the private baths and queensize beds, dressed in chintz and floral fabrics. Three are on the second floor of the main Cape Cod-style house at the busy corner of Old Harbor and Shore roads. The side master bedroom appeals here, as does a rear room done in wicker.

The choicest accommodations are in the renovated rear carriage house, away from the road. Each has an arched window beneath a vaulted ceiling, a corner fireplace and, a boon in summer, a private flower-bedecked sitting area outside.

Guests gather by the fireplace or grand piano in the main house. Breakfast is served at a table for six in the chandeliered dining room, or at three glass tables for two on an adjacent sun porch. Cantaloupe and blueberry pancakes were offered the day of our visit. On tap the next day were mixed fruit, an egg casserole and banana bread. The sunporch holds a guest refrigerator stocked with iced tea or lemonade and a jar of chocolate-chip cookies for afternoon snacks.

(508) 945-4688 or (800) 355-8868. Six rooms with private baths. May-October: doubles, $140 to $175 weekends, $85 to $110 midweek. Rest of year: $100 to $125 weekends, $85 to $110 midweek. Two-night minimum in season. Children over 14.

Moses Nickerson House, 364 Old Harbor Road, Chatham 02633.

Located across the street from the Captain's House Inn of Chatham, this elongated, 1839 whaling captain's house is remarkable for its narrow width and extreme depth. The main house is one room wide so rooms have windows on both sides. A newer section adds a lovely solarium breakfast room, outfitted with white wrought-iron furniture on a brick floor, and two large guest rooms.

The house is decorated with flair, and the delicate, handpainted designs on the doors are a trademark. The English parlor is pretty in rose and cream with an Aubusson rug and a collection of Sandwich glass. Off the parlor is the front Emily Dickinson Room, which has a handpainted poster bed and a painted armoire amid tons of lace; some of the author's works are on the fireplace mantel. Six more spacious rooms with private baths, queensize beds and sitting areas are in one section above the living room, up steep ship's stairs from the dining room or in the newer rear section. Three have fireplaces.

Climb those ship's stairs if you can to see a room with a great window seat full of pillows, a fishnet canopy four-poster bed and a stenciled bathroom. Once here, you may have difficulty leaving – one lanky fellow had to back down the stairs.

A fox in a hunting costume sits on the mantel of the Ralph Lauren room, all dark and masculine with a leather chair and paisley linens on a four-poster bed. It's quite in contrast to the room above, summery in wicker with deep green towels; an old blouse, a pair of high-button shoes and a handbag hanging on a hook above the bed lend a nostalgic touch.

A collection of pewter lines a high shelf in the skylit breakfast solarium, which looks onto an arbor and a fish pond outside. Here is where Linda Watts, innkeeper with her husband George, serves a full breakfast. The main event could be a Canadian bacon soufflé one day and stuffed french toast the next.

The grounds attract with nice touches like statues, bird feeders and a wooden seagull perched in the crook of an old tree.

(508) 945-5859 or (800) 628-6972. Fax (508) 945-7087. Seven rooms with private baths. Memorial Day to Columbus Day: doubles $129 to $169. Rest of year: $95 to $135. Two-night minimum in season. Children over 14. No smoking.

The Old Harbor Inn, 22 Old Harbor Road, Chatham 02633.

For a change of pace, consider this newer home built for a physician who delivered half the babies in Chatham, according to the former innkeepers. Judy and Ray Braz from nearby Brockton saw its for-sale ad in the Boston Globe and, although

Comfortable home of former town physician is now The Old Harbor Inn.

they had rarely traveled to the Cape, bought the place in 1996. Built in a very different style than the Cape Cod norm, it had just been expanded and retains the residential flavor. It's nicely decorated and comfortable in a contemporary kind of way.

The stage is set in the fireplaced living room, all cream and green with lots of chintz. To the rear is a new skylit breakfast sunroom with lots of wicker, leading onto an attractive deck.

The eight guest rooms, all with full baths, are appointed in an English country look and bear the different names the town was called before it became Chatham. Largest of the four upstairs in the main house is the secluded honeymoon hideaway with wicker chairs, dhurrie rugs, balloon curtains and a wicker queen bedstead.

Two more guest rooms occupy the first floor of a rear wing. They are equally light, bright and airy, and contain the thick rugs, designer fabrics, candy and assorted amenities featured in the rest of the house. A second floor was added atop this wing to produce two deluxe guest rooms, each with private bath, gas fireplace and skylit, vaulted ceiling. The North Beach with king bed is decorated more formally. Judy's favorite is the more casual South Beach with queen bed, pocket doors and built-in cabinets.

A continental-plus buffet breakfast of fruits, cereals, and homemade breads and muffins is served in the morning.

(508) 945-4434 or (800) 942-4434. Fax (508) 945-7665. Eight rooms with private baths. Summer: doubles $145 to $195. Spring and fall: $105 to $185. Winter: $105 to $155. Children over 14. No smoking.

Port Fortune Inn, 201 Main St., Chatham 02633.

Formerly the Inn Among Friends with a changing restaurant in front, this ocean-view establishment was renovated in 1997 by new owners Mike and Renée Kahl. They converted the restaurant building into three guest rooms, a reception room and a breakfast room for house guests as well as enlarging and refurbishing nine rooms in the main Cape Cod house in the rear.

All rooms now have updated bathrooms, telephones and queensize beds, some with two beds. The rooms are simple but serviceable, and color-coordinated from

Shingled Cape Cod-style structure is home of The Impudent Oyster.

window treatments to wastebaskets (Renée wrapped the basket rims in curtain fabric). She also planted the colorful gardens that flank the hillside in front of the main inn.

Two large bedrooms upstairs in the front building over the former restaurant yield water views. So do a couple upstairs in the main house, where guests also have access to a large sitting room. Renée bakes the pastries for the continental-plus breakfast buffet in the refurbished restaurant.

(508) 945-0792 or (800) 750-0792. Twelve rooms with private baths. Mid-June to mid-September: doubles, $130 to $170. Spring and fall: $110 to $155. November-April: $85 to $110, November-April. Two-night minimum weekends in season. Children over 8. No smoking.

Dining Spots

The Impudent Oyster, 15 Chatham Bars Ave., Chatham.

With a name like that and an innovative menu, how could this place miss? Always jammed and noisy, patrons crowd together at small glass-covered tables under a cathedral ceiling, with plants in straw baskets balanced overhead on the beams. A huge mirror on the side wall makes the place seem bigger.

Owner Peter Barnard's international menu, based on local seafood, is an intriguing blend of regional, Chinese, Mexican, Indian, Greek and Italian cuisines, among others. For dinner, we couldn't resist starting with the drunken mussels, shelled and served chilled in an intense marinade of tamari, fresh ginger, Szechuan peppercorns and sake, with a side portion of snow peas and red peppers. The Mexican chicken, chile and lime soup, one of the best we've tasted, was spicy and full of interesting flavors. Also delicious were the spinach and mushroom salads with either creamy mustard or anchovy dressings.

Main dishes range from scallops San Cristobal with avocado and cilantro to the house specialty, bouillabaisse. We liked the feta and fennel scrod, a Greek dish touched with ouzo, and the swordfish with sundried tomato and basil sauce. A plate of several ice creams made with fresh fruit was a cooling finale.

The menu changes frequently, and is supplemented by nightly specials. It's the kind of cuisine of which we never tire, although we would prefer to have it in a quieter setting.

(508) 945-3545. Entrées, $16.95 to $23.95. Lunch daily, 11;30 to 3. Dinner, 5:30 to 10.

Christian's, 443 Main St., Chatham.

For a good meal, a raw bar, cocktails and dining on an upper deck or nightly entertainment in the classic English bar, Christian's has been a favorite among locals for more than a decade. It was even more popular after **Upstairs at Christian's** began serving lunch and a casual evening menu.

So it was with some skepticism that fans learned that the owners of the Chatham Wayside Inn were purchasing Christian's in early 1997 and that chef Christian Schwartz was moving to North Carolina to pursue his burgeoning sweet potato-chip business. The new owners followed through on their pledge to retain the same menu and staff, and summer visitors found that little had changed.

Although originally Christian's offered fine dining in two formal downstairs dining rooms and casual dining upstairs, before he sold Christian had combined the fare into one basic menu serving all. It follows the cutesy cinema theme of the upstairs, with every item named for a movie. The garlicky shrimp with fettuccine and parmesan that we remember from earlier days is now called, inexplicably, "Divorce Italian Style," and the medallions of veal sautéed with shrimp, garlic, lemon and white wine, a memorable presentation at the time, is "Two for the Road." You can order basic (roasted chicken over buttermilk biscuits with gravy and mashed potatoes) or exotic (lobster, shrimp and scallops tossed with scallions, garlic, artichoke hearts, mushrooms and sundried tomatoes over penne).

Clams casino, cod cakes on a red pepper mayonnaise, and fiery crab and corn fritters are among the appetizers. Caesar salads can be topped with chicken, shrimp, scallops or poached salmon to make a light meal.

(508) 945-3362. Entrées, $9.50 to $16.50. Lunch upstairs in summer, 11:30 to 3. Dinner nightly, 5 to 10, upstairs and down. Downstairs closed Columbus Day to May. Upstairs closed a couple of days a week in winter.

Vining's Bistro, 595 Main St., Chatham.

We've had lobster in myriad forms, but never before wrapped in a flour tortilla with spinach and jalapeño jack cheese, and here called a warm lobster taco. With crème fraîche and homemade two-tomato salsa sparked with cilantro, it is an appetizer fixture on the multi-ethnic menu. That and the warm roasted scallop salad with grilled eggplant and yogurt dressing, served on wilted bok choy, made us vow to return.

The bistro is run by chef-owner Steve Vining, who used to have La Grand Rue in Harwichport. It's upstairs in a retail complex called the Galleria, with beamed cathedral ceilings and big windows onto Main Street. Vining's is a casual and friendly place where a large stuffed bear was seated at the bar at a recent visit. Many of the dishes are done on the open grill, using woods like cherry, apple and hickory. The menu items are categorized as pastas, grains and roasts.

For an autumn dinner, we were tempted by the grilled bouillabaisse as well as the grilled salmon with stir-fried watercress, ginger and sesame and the Thai fire pot with chicken, sausage and seafood in a hot and sour lemongrass broth. One of us enjoyed the clam and mussel stew, served with arugula, tomatoes and sausage over fettuccine. The other made a meal of a couple of appetizers, the warm lobster taco (again) and Thai chicken satay, plus a bistro salad with feta cheese and kalamata olives. Portions were huge and the food assertive, prompting a faint-hearted couple of our acquaintance to shun the place as "too spicy." They wouldn't even think of trying the pasta from hell, made with Scotch bonnet peppers and incorporating smoked chicken, hot sausage and banana-guava ketchup.

There's a small and sophisticated wine list, plus a long list of beers (some imported from Kenya, China and Thailand) to go with. End your meal with maple-pecan bread pudding or chocolate pudding cake.

(508) 945-5033. Entrées, $13.75 to $21.50. Dinner nightly, 5:30 to 9 or 10.

The Chatham Squire Restaurant, 483 Main St., Chatham.
Once little more than a bar and still a hangout for summering collegians, the Squire has soared lately with its food, to the point where on recent visits everyone was mentioning it as one of the best in town. It's the place of choice among those who find Vining's Bistro too spicy, although it shares with the bistro a commitment to interesting food, especially the long list of daily specials. The atmosphere is perky, the decor old Cape Cod, with murals of local scenes and the bar decked out with old license plates and sailing flags. Regulars like to sit at the bar, which faces Main Street, and watch the passing parade as they slurp a hearty fish chowder or peel their own shrimp from Chatham's only raw bar.

At lunch, burgers are served with those yummy Cape Cod potato chips. We enjoyed a thick and clammy clam chowder with a blue cheeseburger, and the day's blue-plate special, a platter of fish cakes and beans, served with coleslaw and brown bread for $4.95. The grasshopper mousse torte was great for dessert.

Dinner entrées range from baked codfish to grilled sirloin with madeira sauce and mushrooms. Nightly specials might include grilled ocean perch with a cilantro and smoked tomato cream sauce, codfish cheek jambalaya, gulf shrimp sautéed with artichoke hearts and leeks, and roast Long Island duckling with grapefruit and dark rum sauce. Start with the whistling oysters or Cape Codder pâté with sundried cranberries, walnuts and bartlett pears. Finish with coconut cream pie or blueberry cobbler à la mode.

(508) 945-0945. Entrées, $11.95 to $18.95. Lunch daily, 11:30 to 5. Dinner nightly, 5 to 11; shorter hours in winter.

Campari's, 352 Main St., Chatham.
Chef Bob Chiappetta cooks in an open kitchen in this Italian bistro at the Dolphin of Chatham inn and motel. By day it's the **Bittersweet Cafe,** serving breakfast and spilling outdoors onto a covered patio area that becomes Alfresco's for cocktails in the evening. At night it turns cozy and intimate as patrons gather at tables topped with red-checked cloths amid candles in chianti bottles, hanging plants, an aquarium and two working fireplaces. Italian opera music plays as guests sip the bottled San Pellegrino water from Italy.

The kitchen resembles the household kitchen it once was, open to the dining room and imparting tantalizing aromas throughout. The five entrées from the short, changing menu come with soup (often a complex Veneto onion soup), salad and pasta. Starters could be crab cakes parmigiana, herb flavored and with a subtle tomato sauce, or calamari sautéed with prosciutto and flamed with vodka. Main courses might be scampi with mussels over cappellini, swordfish siciliana, chicken tuscano, and veal with sundried tomatoes and mushrooms.

Bob's wife Lisa does the baking, perhaps a honey-nut pie. She oversees the short, reasonably priced Italian wine list as well.

The couple also own **Carmine's,** a good pizza, espresso and gelato parlor at 595 Main St. in the Galleria.

(508) 945-9123. Entrées, $17 to $25. Breakfast daily from 8. Dinner nightly except Monday, from 6; off-season, Wednesday-Saturday from 6.

Diversions

From Chatham's choice location at the elbow of Cape Cod, all the attractions of the Cape are at your beck and call. People who appreciate Chatham tend not to head west toward Hyannis but rather north to Orleans, Wellfleet and the Truros, if they leave Chatham at all.

Beaches. Chatham has more beach area and shoreline than any other Cape Cod town, but much of it is privately owned or not easily accessible, and a lot of it suffered a beating in a 1991 storm. Those with boats like the seclusion of the offshore sandbar at the southern tip of the Cape Cod National Seashore, a barrier beach that sheltered Chatham from the open Atlantic until it was breached in an infamous 1987 winter storm. Swimming is available by permit at such town beaches as Harding Beach on Nantucket Sound or the sheltered "Children's Beach" at Oyster Pond. Those who want surf and open ocean head for Orleans and the state beaches to the north.

Monomoy National Wildlife Refuge. Accessible by a short boat trip from Morris Island, this wilderness island stretching south into the Atlantic is a haven for birds – 285 species, at latest count. The 2,500-acre refuge encompasses islands, dunes, saltmarsh, tidal flats, freshwater ponds and seaside thickets that are a natural habitat for nesting gulls, terns, herons and other shore birds. It's also a major stopping point for migratory waterfowl along what ornithologists call the Atlantic Flyway.

Chatham Fish Pier. The fish pier down the slope off Shore Road is popular with sightseers who want to see the real thing. Boats make their run to the fishing grounds ten to one hundred miles into the Atlantic and return with their catch to the pier starting in the early afternoon, depending on tides. Visitors may watch from an observation balcony. Harbor tours also are available here.

Museums. The **Old Atwood House** (1752) at 345 Stage Harbor Road, owned and maintained by the Chatham Historical Society, is one of the town's oldest houses. Upwards of 2,000 antiques are shown in its fourteen display rooms. Among its offerings are seashells, Sandwich glass and the nationally known murals of Alice Stallknecht Wight, "Portrait of a New England Town." Changing exhibits illustrate Chatham life through photos, paintings and artifacts. The museum is open Tuesday-Friday from 1 to 4, mid-June through September; adults, $3. Also open Tuesday-Saturday 10 to 4 in summer is the 38-year-old **Chatham Railroad Museum,** the former town depot now filled with more than 8,000 models, relics and photos, plus a 1910 caboose. Other historic sites are the **Mayo House** on Main Street, the old **Chatham Grist Mill,** and the **Chatham Light.**

Shopping. Some of Cape Cod's finest shops are located along tree-lined Main Street, and more seem to open every year, encroaching on the residential section to the east. A MacKenzie-Childs table caught our eye at **Lion's Paw** at 403 Main, a branch of the outstanding Nantucket gift shop. Across the street, a red English phone booth at the entry drew us inside **Uniques Ltd.,** three floors of interesting gifts and accessories, from the basement golf room to cedar doormats and a stenciled "Welcome to the Lake" sign. Wooden mermaids line the entry walk at **Mermaids on Main,** and inside are the most colorful items with mermaid and fish themes. **Tale of the Cod** at 450 Main is a ramble of rooms filled with gifts and furniture. **The Artful Hand Gallery** shows especially nice American crafts and contemporary art, and the jewelry appealed at the **Dolli Llama. Mark, Fore & Strike** has classic apparel for men and women. Specialty clothing, unusual jewelry, gallery items and home accessories are featured at **Pentimento.**

Monomoy Coffee Co. at 447 Main is the place for espresso and pastries. We never can resist a stop at **Chatham Cookware** at 524 Main, a fine kitchen store and food shop. Check the linens from France and the colorful pottery from Fitz and Floyd; we especially like the tureens. Take your pineapple scone or your cream of zucchini and almond soup and curried chicken salad to the small outside deck.

The Wayside Inn's new **Gallery/Gift Shop** is a joy to pop into. Owner Helene Wilson, wife of the inn's co-owner, seeks fun and frivolous things. "I'm from New York and look for something different," says she. "If it doesn't make me smile, I don't buy it." The stock in her large shop made us smile from start to finish. Especially intriguing was the lifesize man made of dryer lint with a pocket watch on a chain and a sign saying "please don't touch the grandfather clock – it makes him cranky!" The clock quickly sold for a cool $1,200. Less esoteric but still fun were a table handpainted with bunnies and a rug shaped like a cow.

West of town on Route 28 is **The Cornfield Marketplace,** a special shopping area of interest to those who like culinary excursions. **Fancy's Farm Market** has good vegetables and meat. We like to stop at the **Pampered Palate** to pick up a picnic lunch of sandwiches and salads. It has many specialty foods, too. Upstairs is **Chatham Winery,** with a wide array of fruit wines from cranberry mead to hibiscus flower (the dry blush is issued in a lobster bottle). **Chatham Fish and Lobster** is here as well, so you have all the makings for a picnic or a party at one stop.

Extra-Special _____

Town Band Concerts. It's hard to imagine in sophisticated Chatham, but upwards of 6,000 people turn out for the Friday evening band concerts, a town tradition every July and August, in Kate Gould Park. Brightly colored balloons bob festively overhead as Whit Tileston, band director since 1946, waves his baton and the band plays on. The 40 instrumentalists, most of them townspeople who rehearse weekly during winter, are joined by the multitudes for rousing singalongs. The natural amphitheater is good both for listening and for watching the children (and often their elders) dance to the music. Before the concerts' 8 p.m. start, St. Christopher's Episcopal Church offers chowder suppers, First United Methodist Church serves lobster roll suppers and the Lions Club runs a hot dog stand in front of the Wayside Inn.

Architecturally rich Nantucket holds treasures like this, now the Jared Coffin House inn.

Nantucket, Mass.
Island of History and Romance

Stepping onto Steamboat Wharf after a two-and-a-half-hour ferry ride twenty miles into the Atlantic is a bit like stepping onto another land in another time.

"This is the island that time forgot," announces one of Nantucket's visitor guides. "Steeped in tradition, romance, legend and history, she is a refuge from modernity."

Flanked by brick sidewalks, towering shade trees and gas lamps, the cobblestone streets lead you past more fine old sea captains' homes still standing from Nantucket's days as the nation's leading whaling port than most people see in a lifetime. The 400-plus structures from the late 1700s and early 1800s that make up the historic district represent the greatest concentration in America, evoking the town's description as "an architectural jewel."

So much for the island that time forgot. The island's romance draws thousands of well-heeled visitors to a sophisticated side of Nantucket that is uniquely chic and contemporary. More distant than other islands from the mainland and yet readily accessible to the affluent, Nantucket is all the more exclusive.

That's the way island businessman-benefactor Walter Beinecke Jr. planned it when he created the Nantucket Historical Trust in 1957 and later co-founded the Nantucket Conservation Trust. His efforts led to the preservation of 6,100 acres of open space – one-fifth of the island's land total. Through his historic and real-estate interests, the village has been transformed into what the late New England Monthly magazine termed "a perfect oasis – neat, tidy and relentlessly quaint – for upscale vacationers."

It's a bit precious and pricey for some tastes, this town in which whaling fortunes were amassed and which now is predicated on tourism for the elite. (Once you get away from Nantucket village and Siasconset, you'll find the folks on the south beaches and the west side of the island let their hair down). The week our family roughed it, so to speak, in a friend's cottage near the beach at Surfside was far different from the fall weekends starting a decade later when we returned, as so many couples do, for getaways in Nantucket village, 'Sconset or Wauwinet.

Nantucket is perfect for an escape – away from the mainland and into a dream combining Yankee history and the *Preppy Handbook.* You don't have to wear Nantucket pink trousers or dine at Le Chantecleer, although many do. Simply explore the village's treasures, participate in its activities, or relax and watch a select world go by.

Inn Spots

The Wauwinet, 120 Wauwinet Road, Box 2580, Nantucket 02554.

Grandly restored in 1988, this understated "country inn by the sea" is the most elegant on Nantucket and among the most deluxe in New England. Developers Stephen and Jill Karp, longtime Nantucket summer home owners, spared no expense in turning the weathered old Wauwinet House into the ultimate in taste and comfort.

The Wauwinet holds a fond place in the memories of the island's gentry, which helps explain the success of its restaurant and the number of sightseers who have oohed and aahed over the intricacies of its transformation. Certainly the location is unmatched – a private, parkland/residential area on a spit of land with the Atlantic surf beyond the dunes across the road in front, the waters at the head of Nantucket Harbor lapping at the lawns in back.

Twenty-six rooms are available in the inn. Our bay view room in the inn was not large but was nicely located on a third-floor corner facing the harbor so that we were able to watch spectacular sunsets every night. Fresh and pretty, it had a queensize bed with a striped dust ruffle and lace-trimmed pillows, wicker and upholstered armchairs, and a painted armoire topped with a wooden swan and two hat boxes (one of the inn's decorating signatures). The modern bathroom contained a multitude of thick white towels and a basket of Crabtree & Evelyn amenities. During turndown service, the towels were replenished and mints were placed by the bed.

VT. | N.H.
Massachusetts
Boston
R.I.
Hartford
Conn.
Nantucket
New York

All the rooms we saw had different, striking stenciled borders (some turning up in the most ingenious places), interesting artworks and sculptures, ceiling fans and such fillips as clouds painted on the ceiling. The deluxe rooms with kingsize or two queen beds included bigger sitting areas, but many did not seem to be as well located as ours was. Every room holds a TV/VCR, tapes for which may be ordered from a selection of 450, along with a bowl of gourmet popcorn.

Wicker-furnished back porch looks onto harbor at The Wauwinet.

Five courtyard cottages across the road contain seven more rooms and two suites, each with bedroom and sitting room. One is a four-bedroom cottage with kitchenette and fireplace.

The inn's main floor harbors a lovely living room and library done in floral chintz, a back veranda full of wicker that you sink into, a couple of guest rooms, a restaurant and a small, classy lounge. Outside, chairs are lined up strategically on the back lawn, a croquet game is set up, drinks and snacks are available at a small beachside grill, and a resident pro gives lessons on two tennis courts tucked away in the woods. You can swim from a dock or a not particularly inspiring beach along the harbor, or walk a couple of minutes from the hotel through the dunes to the most gorgeous, endless and unoccupied strand we've seen on the Atlantic coast. Sailboat rentals are complimentary.

Friendly service is provided by a staff of 110, an unusually high ratio for the maximum of 80 guests, according to general manager Russell Cleveland. A van transports guests back and forth to town for shopping or to catch the ferryboat. Sherry and cheese are served house guests every afternoon in the library.

Three meals a day are available in the spacious Topper's (see Dining Spots) and an adjacent patio facing the harbor. A full breakfast is included in the room rate. Guests may order any item from strawberry and rhubarb pancakes to eggwhite omelet with spa cheese and fresh vegetables.

(508) 228-0145 or (800) 426-8718. Fax (508) 228-7135. Thirty-three rooms and two cottage suites with private baths. Mid-June to mid-September: doubles $310 to $750, suites $570 to $1,350. Rest of year: doubles, $190 to $590, suites $330 to $1,090. Four-night minimum in summer. Children accepted. No smoking. Closed November to early May.

Jared Coffin House, 29 Broad St., Box 1580, Nantucket 02554.
One of New England's grand old inns, the famed Jared Coffin House is handsomely furnished with museum-quality pieces. It's also active and busy –

like a train station 24 hours a day, some islanders say, in something of an exaggeration.

The public rooms, restaurant, tap room with entertainment and outdoor patio are busy, that is, for this is a center for Nantucket life and a must visit for tourists, if only for a drink or to sample one of the restaurant's brunches or buffets.

The restoration of the island's earliest three-story house was accomplished by Walter Beinecke Jr. and the Nantucket Historical Trust, which acquired it in 1961 for $10,000, renovated and furnished it, and finally sold it in 1975 to innkeeper-owners Phil and Peg Read for more than $750,000 – an early example of the gentrification of Nantucket.

The 60 guest rooms are scattered in six buildings, two of which are connected to the main 1845 Jared Coffin House. Three are in houses 30 feet on either side of the main complex. All have private baths and telephones and most have television. Thirty rooms have a queen-size canopy bed. Singles, twins, and doubles are also available. Rates include a full breakfast.

Some guests prefer the seven twin and double rooms upstairs in Jared's former home, each furnished with period antiques, artworks and island-woven fabrics. Others covet one of the three large rooms with queensize canopy beds and sitting areas in the 1700s Swain House attached to the main building or, across the street, one of the eighteen queensize canopy rooms in the 1821 Henry Coffin House and the Greek Revival Harrison Gray House.

The public areas are a sight to behold, the living room and library furnished in priceless Chippendale and Sheraton antiques.

Breakfast, included in the rates, offers such choices as eggs florentine, grand marnier french toast and belgian waffles.

Jared's, the inn's large, hotel-style main dining room where jackets are required, features a mix of creative and classic American cuisine. Less formal dinners and a "light bite" menu are available in the beamed, pine-paneled **Tap Room** downstairs. Lunch here or on the patio might be the "Pride of New England," a choice of frankfurter or deep-fried codfish cake with baked beans, brown bread and coleslaw.

(508) 228-2405 or (800) 248-2405. Fax (508) 228-8549. Sixty rooms with private baths. Early May through October: doubles, $150 to $200. Rest of year: doubles, $85 to $145. Children and pets accepted. Smoking restricted.

Entrées in Jared's, $18 to $30.95, dinner nightly in summer, 5 to 9, closed Monday and Tuesday in off-season and November–April. Entrées in Tap Room, $11.75 to $18.75, lunch and dinner daily.

Centerboard Guest House, 8 Chester St., Box 456, Nantucket 02554.

Possibly the most elegant – and certainly the most romantic – of Nantucket's small inns is this winner of a restoration at the edge of the historic district. It was established by Long Island artist and interior designer Marcia Wasserman, who called it the fulfillment of a fantasy. She bought the guest house in 1985 and finally reopened it in 1987 after renovations took seven times longer and cost three times more than planned.

There's a big window seat in the living room, outfitted with a TV and stereo, and the floors bear a pickled finish. Adjacent is a casually formal dining room, with cane chairs around a handful of tables, where "the largest continental breakfast you could imagine is served," according to the innkeeper. A big bowl of fruit (from kiwi to blueberries), granola and cereals, assorted muffins (blueberry-cranberry and mandarin orange-chocolate chip, at our latest visit) and Portuguese breads are the fare.

A two-room suite on the first floor was inspired by a masculine sitting room in an English manor house. It has a library-style living room in dark woods and hunter green, a bedroom with a queensize canopy feather bed with down comforters, and a glamorous bathroom in deep green marble, with a jacuzzi in one section, a large marble-tiled shower in another, and the sink and w.c. in still another. The suite has two TVs and plush furnishings, and no fewer than six bouquets of fresh and dried flowers were scattered about when we stayed.

Upstairs, "the theme is romantic – one of Victorian elegance and charm," in the owner's words. All with private baths, telephones, TVs and refrigerators stocked with soft drinks, the four guest rooms here are bright, airy and decorated in soft pastels. Three have queen beds and one has two double beds. They come with ceiling fans, iron and brass bedsteads, lacy pillows, bathrooms with baskets of Gilchrist & Soames toiletries, and even a couple of murals painted by Martha's Vineyard artist Richard Immarrino. A studio apartment in the basement has built-in double beds and a tiny kitchen. All the rooms are air-conditioned.

As this edition went to press, sale of the property was pending. The buyer, Debbie Wasil from Cape Cod, said she would continue the operation as in the past.

(508) 228-9696. Five rooms, one studio and one suite with private baths. Mid-June through Columbus Day and peak weekends: doubles and studio $185, suite $325. Rest of year: doubles and studio $110, suite $185. Two-night minimum in season. No smoking. Closed January to mid-April.

Cliff Lodge, 9 Cliff Road, Nantucket 02554.

In a residential neighborhood overlooking town and harbor, the eleven guest rooms in this 1771 sea captain's house are more comfortable and have more flair than many in Nantucket. And there are all kinds of neat places to sit, inside and out.

John and Debby Bennett bought the establishment in 1996 and immediately enhanced the gardens, a talent he learned from his father, a landscaper. A Nantucket native, he met his wife-to-be at the local hospital, where both were employed.

Debby serves a buffet breakfast in one of the main-floor sitting rooms, each with a fireplace. Guests can eat here or adjourn to the patio, where the hostess matches the tablecloths with the flowers that are in bloom. Fresh fruit, cereal, muffins and Portuguese toasting bread are typical fare. In the afternoon, Debby offers hot or iced tea and snacks.

Bedrooms are notable for spatter-painted floors, Laura Ashley wallpapers, frilly bedding, fresh flowers and antiques. Many boast kingsize beds and fireplaces, and all have private baths, telephones and TVs nicely built into the walls or concealed in armoires. Room 6 on the third floor yields a view of the ocean, and two others offer harbor views. A second-floor apartment comes with a fireplaced sitting room, kingsize bedroom, kitchen and private deck.

Few B&Bs have so many neat places to sit and relax, inside or out. There are five sitting rooms on three floors, a rooftop deck with a view of the harbor, reading porches and a couple of brick patios beside the lovely gardens.

(508) 228-9480. Eleven rooms and one apartment with private baths. Mid-June through September and special weekends: doubles $125 to $165, apartment $225 (weekly, $1,450). November to mid-April: doubles, $65 to $85, apartment $135. Rest of year: doubles, $85 to $125, apartment $165. Children over 12. No smoking.

Union Street Inn, 7 Union St., Nantucket 02554.

This restored 1770 house, converted from a guest house into a luxury B&B by previous owners, is conveniently situated just off Main Street. Its twelve spacious guest quarters come with private baths (all but one with shower only), antique furnishings, air conditioning and cable TV. Six have working fireplaces with their original mantelpieces. Many have canopy or four-poster beds, and scatter rugs dot the original wide-plank pine floors.

A second-floor suite offers a sitting room with a loveseat and telephone and a bedroom with queen canopy bed, fireplace, VCR, refrigerator and wet bar. The popular main-floor Captain's Room also comes with a fireplace, a kingsize poster bed and two arm chairs.

New owners Ken Withrow, a former hotel manager, and his wife Deborah have given the inn the professional, in-residence care it needed.

Because of its location (and zoning), the Union Street can offer more than Nantucket's highly regulated continental breakfasts. The Withrows serve things like scrambled eggs and bacon, blueberry pancakes, french toast and, every fourth day, eggs benedict. These are in addition to a cold buffet that includes a fresh fruit platter, cereals and muffins. The repast is taken in a large dining room or at three handsome garden tables on the side patio beneath an ivy-covered hillside.

"Debbie cooks and I'm the bus boy," says Ken, who had been manager of the Hyatt UN Plaza Hotel in New York and the Ambassador East Hotel in Chicago. They wanted their own business and a family life for their young son, and found both here.

(508) 228-9222 or (800) 225-5116. Fax (508) 325-0848. Eleven rooms and one suite with private baths. Mid-June through mid-September: doubles $140 to $205, suite $240. Rest of year: doubles $80 to $130, suite $190. Two-night minimum in season. Children over 5. No smoking.

Cobblestone Inn, 5 Ash St., Nantucket 02554.

A collection of wooden lighthouses lines the stairs, typical of the thoughtful touches offered at this B&B by Robin Hammer-Yankow, a former Chamber of Commerce president and young mother, and her husband Keith, a local attorney. Their 1725 house along a cobblestoned street is nicely furnished with period pieces.

All five guest accommodations have private baths and queensize canopy beds, except for one with a double bed. Televisions and telephones were added to each guest room in the air-conditioned house as the Cobblestone underwent an upgrade in 1997. Among the decorative touches are painted Colonial windows and beams, oriental rugs and swag curtains that match the canopies. A sense of history in some rooms is imparted by tilted doorways, wide-plank floors and narrow closets.

The third-floor bedroom, formerly the smallest, was transformed into the accommodation of choice. Now a suite, it has a living room with a view of the harbor and a bedroom with a queensize bed and view of the Congregational Church steeple. The main-floor sunporch was converted into a small guest room with a detached private bath. Robin designed it for the budget-minded or single traveler. Along the side and rear of the main floor, the former kitchen and office were converted into two guest rooms, one with a private deck.

Given its in-town location and the cobblestones on the street outside, we were surprised to find our second-floor room so utterly quiet – at least until the church bells tolled at 7 a.m., as they're prone to do in old New England seaside towns. We arose to prepare for Robin's continental breakfast, served family style at a long table in the dining area behind the living room. Fresh fruit, orange juice, homemade granola, cereals and melt-in-the-mouth pumpkin and zucchini breads provided plenty of sustenance for the day ahead. A new guest pantry contains a microwave, wet bar and complimentary sodas and setups.

Guests have room to spread out in the living room with fireplace and a brick patio overlooking the garden.

(508) 228-1987. Four rooms and one suite with private baths. Doubles, $130 to $175. Suite, $250. Off-season: $50 to $130. Three-night minimum encouraged. No smoking.

Ships Inn, 13 Fair St., Nantucket 02554.

Built in 1831 by whaling captain Obed Starbuck, this house occupies the site where Martha Coffin Mott, the first woman abolitionist, was born in 1793. Nicely

restored in 1991 by chef-owner Mark Gottwald and his wife Ellie, it now claims some of Nantucket's most comfortable accommodations as well as a small restaurant of distinction (see Dining Spots).

Named after ships that Starbuck commanded, the ten guest rooms contain many of the original furnishings and most have queen beds, although bed configurations vary. They have been refurbished with new wallpapers and tiled baths and come with interesting window treatments, Neutrogena toiletries and mini-fridges in cabinets beneath the TV sets. Most have reading chairs and half have desks. All but two tiny single rooms are more spacious than most Nantucket bedrooms.

Guests enjoy afternoon tea with coffeecake and cookies in the large living room. Innkeeper Meghan Moore sets out

Double stairway provides entry to Ships Inn.

a continental-plus breakfast of fruit, cereal, scones and muffins.

(508) 228-0040. Ten rooms with private baths. Doubles, $150. Three-night minimum in season. Children over 10. No smoking. Closed Columbus Day to Memorial Day.

Westmoor Inn, Cliff Road, Nantucket 02554.

The secluded hilltop location at the edge of town is one of the drawing cards at this substantial inn, which has fourteen guest rooms on the second and third floors, all with private baths and some quite spacious by Nantucket standards. Other draws are the continental breakfasts in the cheery solarium dining room, the nightly wine and hors d'oeuvres offered in the elegant living room, the small library/TV room dressed in wicker, and the inviting rear patio and gardens.

Guest rooms and a suite vary in size, but all are lavishly furnished with a mix of modern and antique furnishings and have telephones. Most contain king or queen beds and one suite has a jacuzzi. We liked Room 206 with a kingsize bed and a fireplace. The bathroom in its neighbor is as big as the bedroom, but surprisingly, most have showers only rather than tubs (a pattern repeated at many local B&Bs).

Innkeeper Nancy Walsh attends the wine and cheese party, which runs from 6 to 7 and "becomes a real gathering," she says. Also special is the breakfast, beautifully served on tables with white cloths and decorative overlays in the skylit solarium, where three walls of windows afford a panoramic view. It's apt to include fresh fruit, wild blueberries, cereals, yogurt and an elaborate spread of croissants, muffins, breads and scones, and two kinds of fruit muffins.

"This house is unique here because of its large open public rooms and its grand scale," says Nancy.

(508) 228-0877. Fourteen rooms with private baths. Late May to mid-October: doubles, $135 to $255. Rest of year: doubles $105 to $185. Two- or three-night minimum in season. Children over 12. No smoking. Closed early December to late April.

The Pineapple Inn, 10 Hussey St., Nantucket 02554.

Local restaurateurs Caroline and Bob Taylor spent nearly $1 million in 1997 to transform an 1838 whaling ship captain's house into one of Nantucket's more comfortable B&Bs.

Taking the name from the Colonial symbol of hospitality, the Taylors offer twelve air-conditioned guest rooms with private white marble baths. Each has a king or queen bed topped with goose down comforters, cable television and a telephone with modem. Handmade Eldred Wheeler four-poster canopy beds are featured, along with handmade oriental carpets, reproduction furniture and 19th-century antiques and artworks.

"We set out to create the highest lodging standard for the island's historic inns," Bob said. The Taylors were known for their breakfasts during the fifteen years they owned and operated the Quaker House Inn and Restaurant here before they turned their attention to the Pineapple.

They had to scale down breakfasts to continental, but claim some of the best homemade pastries in town. The pastries – accompanied by fresh orange juice, a fresh fruit plate, pastries and cappuccino – get the day off to a good start. The meal is served at a table for ten in the chandeliered dining room or outside beneath umbrella-covered tables beside a fountain on a bricked garden courtyard.

Two tapestry sofas face each other in front of the fireplace in the side parlor, painted burnished yellow with mauve accents.

(508) 228-9992. Fax (508) 325-6051. Twelve rooms with private baths. Mid-June to mid-September and special events: doubles $175 to $250. Late spring and early fall: $125 to $175. Mid-October to mid-May: doubles $75 to $125. No children. No smoking.

The Sherburne Inn, 10 Gay St., Nantucket 02554.

The first time Pittsburgh corporate types Dale Hamilton III and Susan Gasparich traveled to Nantucket, they took their bicycles off the ferry, pedaled a couple of blocks and decided, "this was the place," in Dale's words. He didn't really have to convince his partner, both of whom had been considering a career change. Thirty days later, they were back on the island negotiating the purchase of the Sherburne (née The House at 10 Gay) Inn. By 1994, Dale had sold his construction companies in Pennsylvania and the pair were in residence in the structure, which was built as the Atlantic Silk Factory, but has served as a lodging establishment for most of its 160 years.

Dale and Susan continued the renovating and redecorating launched by the previous owner. They offer eight guest rooms, now all with private baths and king or queen beds. Four are on the main floor and four on the second; a beautiful winding staircase connects the two. Interestingly, there's a fireplaced parlor with

television on each floor. The bedrooms, bright and cheery, are decorated to the Federal period. They contain canopy and poster beds, oriental rugs and fine artworks. We liked No. 8 upstairs in the rear with a king bed, clawfoot tub with shower and a private balcony overlooking the side and rear yards. Another room holds a small library and a mini-refrigerator.

Susan bakes blueberry or rhubarb muffins to supplement the natural breads, bagels and English muffins served for continental breakfast. Fresh fruit and juice accompany. The meal is taken in the main-floor parlor, on a deck on one side of the house or in the yard surrounded by gardens and a privet hedge

Balcony view from The Sherburne Inn.

on the other side. Tea or wine and cheese may be served in the afternoon.

(508) 228-4425. Eight rooms with private baths. Mid-June to mid-October: doubles, $125 to $200. Rest of year: doubles, $65 to $135. Children over 6. Two- or three-night minimum most periods. No smoking.

Martin House Inn, 61 Centre St., Box 743, Nantucket 02554.

A broad range of accommodations and prices awaits visitors at this inn, recently transformed by new owners "and getting better by the second," in the words of an admiring colleague. This 1803 mariner's home had been a guest house since the 1920s and was rather monastic and short of creature comforts. No more.

Exceptionally pretty are the large open front foyer and the long front parlor and dining area, with sponged royal blue walls and lovely oriental rugs. The dining-room table is set for breakfast for eight, although some prefer to eat on a tray at one of the wicker chairs on the side veranda. An expanded continental breakfast of two fresh fruits, two cereals, granola, Nantucket breads and muffins is the fare.

The Martin House offers thirteen guest rooms, nine with private baths and most with queensize beds. We saw a couple of spacious rooms with canopy beds, fireplaces, cherry dressers and either a loveseat or two plush club chairs. Especially popular is Room 21 with a canopied queen and its own porch. Four rooms on the third floor share baths. One room with two double beds can accommodate four people, and two single rooms are offered at $50 a night.

As this edition went to press, the sale of the inn was pending. The prospective buyer, Debbie Wasil, who worked for thirteen years at the New Seabury resort on Cape Cod, also was buying the Centerboard Guest House next door. She said she would live at the Martin House, hire an innkeeper for the Centerboard, and would keep the properties "separate and distinct."

(508) 228-0678. Fax (508) 325-4798. Nine rooms with private baths and four with shared baths. June-October: doubles, $80 to $170 with private bath, $55 to $60 shared. November-May: $70 to $135 private, $50 shared. Two- or three-night minimum in season. Children over 5. No smoking.

Seven Sea Street, 7 Sea St., Nantucket 02554.

This guest house of post and beam construction was built in 1987 on the last vacant lot in town by the Parker family, who also run the Tuckernuck Inn and the Parker Guest House. Matthew Parker and his wife Mary oversee this B&B, where guests enter via the dining room. This is where Matthew serves the blueberry and cranberry muffins he bakes for continental breakfast, as well as coffee cake and fresh fruit, nicely presented on Villeroy & Boch china.

The accommodations include nine guest rooms with queensize fishnet canopy beds, TVs, phones and painted furniture Matthew assembled himself. All contain small refrigerators and modern baths with a vanity outside. Also available are two suites, one billed as a deluxe suite/apartment.

Guests have use of a couple of small common rooms on the second floor, the widow's walk deck with a view of the harbor, an indoor hot tub and a pleasant brick patio edged by gardens and hedges.

(508) 228-3577. Fax (508) 228-3578. Nine rooms and two suites with private baths. Late June to Labor Day: doubles $155 to $195, suite $235, apartment $265. Spring and fall: doubles $105 to $155, suite $165 to $195, apartment $195 to $235. January to late April: $75 to $95, suite $125, apartment $165. No smoking.

76 Main Street, 76 Main St., Nantucket 02554.

This B&B in a restored 1883 sea captain's home is the only one on central Main Street, a residential section of stately 19th-century mansions.

Innkeeper Shirley Peters, who arrived in Nantucket by way of Wellesley, Japan and England, and her late husband restored the original cherry, oak and walnut floors that had been covered by rugs and papered the walls hidden behind layers of paint. They added private baths for the eleven guest rooms, each furnished with queensize beds, upholstered chairs and antiques.

The large front corner room on the main floor with a canopied four-poster bed and Victorian furnishings is the showplace. Besides the other guest rooms on the second and third floors are six family units with TV and refrigerator in a motel-style annex.

Off a grand entry hall are a formal Victorian parlor for reading and the kitchen with dining area, where a continental breakfast of fruits, granola, and homemade muffins and breads is served. Outside are a sheltered courtyard and shady patio with a peach tree in the middle.

(508) 228-2533. Eleven rooms with private baths. Doubles, $135 to $155; off-season, $65 to $95. No smoking.

Dining Spots

21 Federal, 21 Federal St., Nantucket.

One of Nantucket's larger and higher-profile restaurants (founding chef Bob Kinkead opened another restaurant of the same name – now Kinkead's – in Washington, D.C.), 21 Federal is on two floors of a sand-colored house with white trim, designated by a brass plaque and elegantly decorated in Williamsburg style. There are six small dining rooms of museum-quality, Federal period decor, some with their white-linened tables rather too close together for privacy.

Our latest lunch in a small room next to the convivial bar produced a smashing pasta – spaghettini with two sauces, one thyme-saffron and one smoked tomato, topped with crabmeat-stuffed shrimp – and a grilled shrimp salad with Greek olives,

Dining rooms are decorated in Williamsburg style at 21 Federal.

feta cheese, pinenuts and spinach. Three varieties of breads came with, and a tropical fruit sorbet was a refreshing ending.

Even more memorable was a summer lunch in the courtyard, where white-linened tables create an elegant setting. The pheasant and wild rice soup of the day and a linguini salad with shrimp and pinenuts were out of this world.

Proprietor Chick Walsh and his chef change the short dinner menu weekly. Expect main courses like sautéed arctic char with lentils and baby fennel, charred leg of lamb with roasted eggplant and, from the grill, aged sirloin steak or veal loin chop with a creamy gratin of potatoes and leeks.

For starters, how about salmon tartare with cucumber salad or a signature parma ham with tomatoes, mozzarella and pesto vinaigrette? Finish with chocolate-hazelnut torte or one of the great homemade ice creams and sorbets.

This is Nantucket dining at its best, not as pretentious or as pricey as some and more exciting than many.

(508) 228-2121. Entrées, $19 to $30. Lunch, Wednesday-Saturday 11:30 to 2:30. Dinner nightly, 6 to 10; closed Sunday in spring. Closed mid-October to mid-April.

Topper's at the Wauwinet, Wauwinet Road, Nantucket

Named for their dog, whose portrait is in one of the dining rooms, Topper's succeeded beyond its owners' dreams and the kitchen had to be quickly expanded. Dining is leisurely in two elegantly appointed, side-by-side rooms with large windows. Upholstered chairs in blue and white are comfortable, tables are well-spaced (or screened from their neighbors), and masses of flowers are all around.

Chef Christopher Freeman joined the Wauwinet in 1997 from the Mayflower Inn in Connecticut, where he was known for high-caliber regional cuisine, a style he has refined here. Among appetizers, we were impressed with the signature lobster crab cakes with smoked corn, jalapeño olives and a divine mustard sauce, and the coriander-seared yellowfin tuna sashimi with soba noodles and pickled vegetables, served on handmade sushi boards of purple heart wood.

Every main course we've had here has been superior. Included were roast rack of lamb with potato-fennel brandade and grilled veal chop with wild grape compote, both accompanied by baby vegetables (tiny pattypan squash and carrots about a big as a fingernail) and a wedge of potatoes. The hearty Nantucket lobster stew – incorporating nearly three pounds of lobster, salsify, leeks, island tomatoes and tomalley croutons – is the latest hit. The caramelized sea scallops with french green lentils and seared foie gras vinaigrette is a close second.

Desserts include a signature chocolate marquise with raspberries and grand marnier and a new "ABC tart" comprised of almonds, rum-soaked bananas and chocolate that's to die for.

The sparkling Wauwinet Water pours freely from antique cobalt blue bottles, the breadsticks and French baguettes are crusty, salt and pepper are served only on request, and the Wine Spectator grand award wine list is strong in American and French vintages from a selection of more than 500.

The Wauwinet Lady, a 26-passenger water launch, offers complimentary round-trip excursions from town to Topper's for lunch or dinner in season. Lunch features a tasting selection of tapas – three to five small courses in the $9 to $27 range. There's also a three-course, prix-fixe Sunday brunch for $32.

(508) 228-8768 or (800) 426-8718. Entrées, $32 to $42. Lunch, Monday-Saturday noon to 2. Dinner nightly, 6 to 9:30, jackets requested. Sunday brunch, 10:30 to 2. Closed November to early May.

Oran Mor, 1 South Beach St., Nantucket.
Our old-favorite Second Story restaurant had slipped and finally gave way in 1997 to a highly rated successor. Peter Wallace, whose food we had enjoyed at the Wauwinet where he was executive chef for six years, and his wife Kathleen renamed the place for a Gaelic phrase meaning "Great Song." She's Irish and he's of Scottish descent and "we thought it sounded nice," he said.

They took over a summery, second-story space with windows toward the harbor and did a major reconfiguration. The front room holds a couple of booths and a neat small, semi-circular bar fashioned from the portico of the local electric company, which they rescued on its way to the dump. Three small, off-white dining rooms with seafoam green trim are dressed with paintings by local artists.

Peter calls it a soothing backdrop for international cuisine that is at the cutting edge. "I'm taking a few more risks," he said, than a hotel dining room would allow. For starters, we were mighty impressed with Peter's champagne risotto with sweetbreads and wild mushrooms, and his Asian fried quail with sticky rice. Expect other choices like beef tartare with truffle oil and tuna sashimi with nori rolls and a salad of soft-shell crab over field greens. Main courses vary from grilled halibut topped with sundried tomatoes, olives and mussels to grilled duck breast with barbecued plum confit and roast loin of lamb with potato-eggplant roesti. We liked the seared tuna with shallot jus and fresh spinach, and grilled swordfish with orange and black sesame seed butter.

Kathleen's desserts include a brûléed rice pudding, fresh fruit croustade in a tulipe, quenelles of chocolate mousse topped with pralines and molten chocolate cake with a trio of ice creams.

A nightly tasting menu is offered for $50 ($80 with selected wines). Peter was planning to offer Sunday brunch in spring and fall.

(508) 228-8655. Entrées, $18 to $32. Dinner nightly in season, 6 to 10. Sunday brunch in off-season. Closed Sunday night and Monday in off-season and January-March.

The Boarding House, 12 Federal St., Nantucket.
The Boarding House provided our first great meal on Nantucket during its inaugural summer of 1973. It since has moved around the corner to considerably larger quarters, and several owners (and chefs) have come and gone. Lately taken over by Seth and Angela Raynor (he a former sous chef at 21 Federal and both veterans of the famed Chanticleer in Siasconset), it's better than ever.

A cathedral-ceilinged Victorian lounge with small faux-marble tables on a flagstone floor opens into a sunken dining room. The latter is striking as can be in rich cream and pink, with a curved banquette at the far end in front of a mural of Vernazzia. The Raynors own the originals but sell lithographs of the exclusive Nantucket series "Streets of Paris," which hang on the walls. Villeroy & Boch china of the Florida pattern graces the nicely spaced tables, which allow for one of Nantucket's more pleasant dining situations.

Equal to the setting is the cooking of Seth, one of 30 chefs chosen to appear on the Great Chefs of the East television series. We were impressed with our latest dinner here: mellow sautéed crab cakes with scallion crème fraîche and grilled quail with crisp fried onion rings and baby mixed greens, for starters, and main courses of pan-roasted salmon with Thai curried cream and crispy rice noodles and a spicy Asian seafood stew with lobster, shrimp and scallops. Coffee ice cream with chocolate sauce and a dense chocolate-kahlua terrine were worthy endings.

We'd happily return to try other signature dishes, including rare yellowfin tuna with wasabi aioli and soy ginger glaze, grilled lobster tails with sticky rice and ginger cream, and black angus tenderloin with wild mushrooms and a creamy potato gratin.

The outdoor terrace appeals for a bistro lunch or supper. It's also a felicitous setting for an after-dinner liqueur while watching the late-night strollers pass by.

(508) 228-9622. Entrées, $23 to $32. Lunch daily in season, noon to 2. Dinner nightly, 6 to 10, Thursday-Sunday in winter. No smoking.

American Seasons, 80 Centre St., Nantucket.
A simple square room with whimsical decor, eclectic American food and moderate prices make this one of Nantucket's restaurant hits. New owners made Michael Getter, formerly of 21 Federal, a partner and chef. They also retained the concept and decor of their predecessors.

The 50-seat dining room is notable for high-backed banquettes serving as room dividers and polyurethaned tables whose tops are game boards. A local artist painted the table tops as well as a stunning wall mural of a vine-covered Willamette Valley hillside in Oregon.

Interestingly, the menu is categorized by regions – Pacific Coast, Wild West, New England and Down South – each with two or three appetizers and entrées. You're supposed to mix and match, pairing, say, a Florida rock shrimp gumbo with andouille sausage, okra and biscuits with a lobster and corn enchilada in a blue cornmeal crêpe. Those and a lentil salad with goat cheese, frisée and grilled leeks made a memorable meal. Or you could start with salmon tartare with buckwheat blinis and cucumber salad and move on to a main course of leg of lamb with flageolet beans, a roasted eggplant and tomato compote and sautéed chard.

Chef Michael says he "cranked up the menu a notch" in terms of sophistication. Typical entrées now are seared rare yellowfin tuna with green peppercorn sauce, roasted halibut with grilled shiitakes in a red wine fish reduction, herb-rubbed quail with creamy goat cheese polenta, and breast of duck with root vegetable risotto and fried celeriac.

We shared a raspberry-mango shortcake with raspberry coulis, presented artistically with fresh fruit on a square plate decorated with squiggles of chocolate and crème anglaise. The all-American wine list has been cited by Wine Spectator.

(508) 228-7111. Entrées, $19 to $26.50. Dinner nightly in summer, 6 to 10, fewer nights in off-season. Closed January-March.

Le Languedoc, 24 Broad St., Nantucket.

Although the Grennan family offer guest rooms in four buildings, their attractive white building with blue shutters across from the Jared Coffin House complex is noted most for its dining.

Downstairs is an intimate cafe with checkered cloths. Upstairs are four small dining rooms with peach walls and white trim, windows covered with peach draperies and valances, and changing art from a local gallery. Windsor chairs are at nicely spaced tables bearing hurricane chimneys with thick candles and vases, each containing one lovely salmon-hued rose.

Among appetizers, smoked Nantucket pheasant with cranberry relish was very good and very colorful with red cabbage and slices of apples and oranges on a bed of lettuce. One of us sampled chef Neal Grennan's noisettes of lamb with artichokes in a rosemary sauce. The other had sautéed sweetbreads and lobster in puff pastry, in a sauce that included shiitake mushrooms, cognac and shallots. Nicely presented on piping hot oval white plates, they were accompanied by snow peas, broccoli, pureed turnips, yellow peppers, sweet potato and peach slices. Other interesting choices include cedar-planked salmon with lobster mashed potatoes, grilled rare tuna with seaweed salad and truffled loin of rabbit with sundried cherries.

For dessert, we passed up strawberry pie and pears poached in a reduction of port to share a dense chocolate hazelnut torte spiked with grand marnier.

You can dine less expensively but quite well in the cafe. Lunch is available here and on a canopied sidewalk terrace.

(508) 228-2552. Entrées, $19.75 to $35. Lunch seasonally, noon to 2. Dinner nightly, 6 to 10, Thursday-Sunday in off-season. Closed mid-December to mid-May.

Ships Inn, 13 Fair St., Nantucket.

Dinners here have received considerable attention since chef-owner Mark Gottwald and his wife Ellie took over. Mark, who trained at Le Cirque in New York and at Spago in Los Angeles, oversees the cooking duties with a sizable kitchen staff, some of whom accompany the couple in the winter to Florida, where they run the acclaimed Ellie's in Vero Beach.

The dining room on the ground level here is attractive with apricot walls over white wainscoting, exposed beams, a white fireplace in the center of the room, candles in the many-paned windows, and white-linened tables dressed with candles and fresh flowers. There also are tables for eating in the adjacent Dory Bar.

Among entrées, you might find stuffed prawns with lobster-tamarind sauce, broiled cod with creamed spinach and tapenade sauce, crispy salmon with cabernet sauce and niçoise vegetables, roast duck with foie gras and plum wine, and steak au poivre with braised endive and haricots verts. Or consider a pasta, perhaps lamb lasagna with creamed spinach and goat cheese. Start with fried calamari with ponzu sauce or chive scrambled eggs with sevruga caviar. Finish with raspberry sorbet or chocolate-soufflé cake. A well-chosen wine list starts in the twenties.

(508) 228-0040. Entrées. $19 to $24. Dinner nightly except Tuesday, 5:30 to 9:15. Closed Columbus Day to Memorial Day.

Black-Eyed Susan's, 10 India St., Nantucket.

A recent entrant on Nantucket's dining scene, this small storefront that formerly was a breakfast diner is run by Susan Handy and Jeff Worster, both with long backgrounds in local restaurants. They still serve breakfast, featuring things like sourdough french toast with orange Jack Daniels butter and pecans and a spicy Thai curry scramble with broccoli and new potatoes. Most dishes come with a choice of hash browns or black-eyed peas.

Jeff, a chef-taught chef, obtained a lot of his cross-cultural culinary ideas while cooking in Beverly Hills. From his open kitchen behind the dining counter come such pasta dishes as wild-mushroom ravioli on carrot-ginger puree with organic greens and romano cheese. Fontina-stuffed pork with sweet pea-mashed potatoes, grilled halibut with salsa verde and oyster gumbo were a few of the intriguing dishes on his fall dinner menu. Lighter eaters could order a huge hearts of romaine salad with caesar dressing for $8. There's one dessert a night, perhaps a cobbler or bread pudding.

The atmosphere is social as in a European cafe at dinner, and singles love to eat at the long counter. Summer diners often face long waits for a table.

(508) 325-0308. Entrées, $16 to $19.50. Breakfast daily, 7 to 1. Dinner, 6 to 10. No smoking. No credit cards. BYOB. Closed November-March.

Diversions

Nantucket's attractions run the gamut from beaches to history to architecture to art and antiques. Except for the beaches, almost everything the visitor needs or wants to do is right in Nantucket village, and easily reached on foot or by bicycle or moped. A number of pamphlets detail interesting walking tours.

Fourteen buildings and exhibits of special interest are maintained by the Nantucket Historical Association, which offers a combination pass to eleven for $10. Among them:

The Whaling Museum, the largest complex and one most visitors pass just after they leave the ferry, is considered the nation's best after the New Bedford Whaling Museum. Originally a candle factory, it contains an original beam press still poised to render whale spermaceti into candles and oil. Rooms are devoted to scrimshaw, whaling equipment and objects brought home by seamen from the South Seas. A whale jaw with teeth, the skeleton of a 43-foot whale and whalecraft shops – a sail loft, cooperage, shipsmith and such – are among the attractions.

Fair Street Museum and Quaker Meeting House. Nantucket's art museum records the lives of early citizens in portraits. An upstairs gallery houses more recent works and special exhibitions. The adjoining Meeting House was built in 1838.

Farther from the center of town are the **Oldest House** (1686), the **Old Mill** (1746) and the **Old Gaol** (1805). Numerous other structures are under Historical Association auspices, but if you simply walk any of the streets fanning out from the center you'll stumble onto your own finds. Don't miss central Main Street, particularly the three handsome Georgian mansions known as **The Three Bricks.**

Walking Tours. The best of several is that led by Roger Young (228-1062), former town selectman and an energetic semi-retiree, who goes "where the buses don't," through hidden alleys and byways, all the while spinning tales of Nantucket lore. Well worthwhile, the two-hour tours leave daily at 9:30; adults, $10.

Art Galleries and Antiques Shops. Besides beaches and good food, it's said that visitors are attracted to Nantucket by all the galleries and antiques shops. They certainly have a wide choice: one brochure is devoted to antiquing on Nantucket, and one of summer's big events is the annual antiques show in early August. Such Nantucket scenes as cobblestoned streets, deserted moors and rose-covered cottages in Siasconset appeal to artists, whose works hang in galleries all along the wharves. **Erica Wilson Needle Works** is a local attraction.

Shopping. Nantucket is a shopper's paradise and, were it not for the cobblestoned streets and salt air, you could as easily picture yourself in Newburyport or New Canaan. Specialty stores with names like **Nobby Clothes, Beautiful People** and **Cashmere Nantucket** compete with the more traditional like **Murray's Toggery Shop** and **Mitchell's Book Corner,** all across the several square blocks of "downtown" Nantucket. We love the **Lion's Paw,** an exceptional gift shop full of cheerful pottery; check out the animal's tea party. Other standouts are **Zero Main** for suave women's clothing, **Seldom Scene** for eclectic accessories, the **Forager House Collection** of folk art and accessories and **Nantucket Looms** with beautiful, whimsical woven items and a sweater in the window for "only $750."

Majolica offers colorful handpainted Italian ceramics. **The Spectrum** is good for arts and crafts. **The Complete Kitchen** is one of the better kitchenware stores we've seen. **Chanticleer to Go** is the in-town gourmet takeout shop where locals and tourists splurge when they can't get out to its namesake restaurant in 'Sconset.

Extra-Special _____

Nantucket Lightship Baskets. The lightships that protected boats from the treacherous shoal waters off the south and east end of the island in the mid-18th century spawned a cottage industry indigenous to Nantucket. The crews of the South Shoal Lightship turned to basket-weaving to while away their hours on duty. Their duty ended, the seamen continued to make baskets ashore – first primitive and heavy-duty types for carrying laundry or groceries, later more beautiful handbags appealing to visitors. The latter were inspired by the Sayle family, who continue the tradition at their shop at 112 Washington St. Today, Nantucket's famed baskets come in all shapes and sizes (including 14-karat gold miniatures) and seem to be ubiquitous in the shops and on tanned arms. The handbags have ivory carvings on top and carry hefty price tags.

Edgartown, Mass.
Fall for the Vineyard

One of the best things about visiting an island is the ferry ride over from the mainland. The ringing of ships' bells, the deep blast as you depart, the hustle and bustle of getting cars on and off – all add to the anticipation of what is to come.

Even though the trip to Martha's Vineyard from Wood's Hole takes less than an hour, that's time enough to listen to the buoys clanking, and to watch one shore fade in the distance and another grow closer.

It's time enough also for a transition – to leave mainland cares behind, before arriving at Vineyard Haven or Oak Bluffs on the Steamship Authority lines and stepping into a different milieu. You also can arrive directly into Edgartown now via the Pied Piper, a little-known passenger-only ferry operation running six trips daily in summer from Falmouth Marina in Falmouth, (508) 548-9400.

The Vineyard is nothing if not varied. Oak Bluffs, where the many-splendored gingerbread cottages around the tabernacle present a rainbow of hues, was founded as a Methodist campground. It's also a Victorian beach resort and summer home

Daggett House inn backs up to Edgartown Harbor.

to many upper-class African Americans. At the other end of the island are the Indian-owned restaurants and shops atop windswept Gay Head, its cliffs a mosaic of colors and an Eastern mini-version of the Big Sur. In the interior of West Tisbury and Chilmark, the landscape is such that you might not think you were on an island.

Then there's Edgartown, as up-to-date as a resort town can be while still reflecting a heritage back to 1642. It's a prosperous seaport village, which boomed during the whaling days of the 19th century and became a yachting center in the 20th century. It's been in the news lately during summer visits by President Clinton and entourage.

Long a retreat for the rich and famous as well as the rich and not-so-famous, Edgartown is best appreciated in the off-season. The crowds are gone, but the charm remains as benign autumn weather lingers through Thanksgiving. The beaches are deserted except for strollers. The waters are left for fishermen and a few hardy wind-surfers. Cottages and condos are battened down for the winter.

Autumn is the season that islanders and knowing visitors look forward to, particularly in Edgartown, a year-round haven for retirees and escapees from the mainland. Many inns and restaurants remain open most of the year, but prices are reduced. You can be near the ocean in a moderate clime, and immerse yourself in a delightful community.

"Fall for Martha's Vineyard," the magazine ads entice in trying to boost autumn trade. It's hard to imagine how anyone wouldn't.

Inn Spots

The Charlotte Inn, 27 South Summer St., Edgartown 02539.

You register at a front desk so ornate that it is pictured in the centerfold of an Architectural Digest inn book. At one side of the main floor is a two-room art gallery and across the street a gift shop, both destinations in themselves. Behind is a small, deluxe restaurant in which you dine romantically in an indoor-outdoor garden reminiscent of New Orleans or Europe. You relax beforehand on the side porch running the depth of the Summer House, rejoicing in the fountains and flowers and a scent resembling eucalyptus; the ice for your drinks comes in a green leather bucket. And later you retire in one of 25 guest accommodations that are so lavishly and tastefully furnished as to defy expectation.

The Charlotte Inn compound, which Gery and Paula Conover have developed from a private home he acquired in 1971, is nothing short of a masterpiece. It carries the aura of moneyed elegance that's the hallmark of Relais & Châteaux properties. But it's also a very personal place, a reflection of Gery's desire to have an art gallery (he runs a restoration and real estate business as well) and of Paula's flair with flowers, decorating and stitchery. She made many of the pillows and comforters that enhance each guest room.

Rooms are in the main two-story 1860 house, a rear carriage house that Gery built without blueprints in 1980, the 1705 Garden House (so called because of its lovely English garden in back) across the street, the 1840 Summer House next door, and the Coach House Suite.

The much-photographed deluxe suite upstairs in the Carriage House has an English hunting feel to it: a queensize bed with brass bedstead, a mahogany sleigh bed redecorated as a sofa, a working marble fireplace, a beamed cathedral ceiling, thick beige carpeting, walls covered in hunter green or red and green stripes, a TV

and stereo hidden away in a chest, and a treasury of bric-a-brac from a gentleman's riding boots to one of the earliest cameras perched on a tripod in the corner. Even more to our liking is the Coach House Suite, bigger and less masculine, outfitted like a well-planned house. The bed is covered with lace, there's a tiny balcony with wicker chairs, and the living room, with its easy chairs and hassocks, is exquisite. The walk-in dressing room/closet is a fantasy of hats, fans and hat boxes. Downstairs is what general manager Carol Read calls the garage; it would be a museum anywhere else. Here – amid so many museum-quality treasures – it goes relatively unnoticed

by all but the Coach House occupants, who have their own museum for the duration upstairs. The suites command top dollar, and Gery says they're booked nearly every night.

After seeing these and a sampling of other opulent rooms, we wondered about ours (the last available and at the other end of the price scale). No. 18 in the Summer House had a private entrance off the wicker-filled side porch (we happened to be its only users on a couple of mild October days and nights). Although relatively small, it was luxuriously comfortable, with a four-poster bed, two wingback chairs and many antiques that are typical throughout. Even the hallways are decorated just so with fine paintings and antiques. Most rooms come with television and telephones.

The compound is a landscaper's dream, full of exotic greenery, vivid flowers, trickling fountains and trellised arbors.

Coach House Suite at The Charlotte Inn.

Gery laid the spacious courtyard in front of the Coach House Suite brick by brick, and tends to the flowers with old watering cans from one of his diverse collections.

Continental breakfast is served in the conservatory dining room and terrace that houses the inn's restaurant, **L'Étoile** (see Dining Spots). Classical music and a splashing fountain are the backdrop for fresh orange juice, tea or coffee and breads (perhaps raisin or cranberry) and muffins (walnut-sour cream, cheese, cranberry and apple) served with raspberry preserves and marmalade. More substantial breakfasts are available at extra cost, a choice of raspberry waffles or a sour cream and asparagus omelet, preceded by broiled grapefruit, at our visit.

Dinners at L'Étoile, whose space is leased by chef-owner Michael Brisson, are considered the priciest and most elegant on the island. After dinner, you can wander around the art gallery, watch television or play games in the small fireplaced living room of the Garden House, or simply relax on the wicker rockers on the porch of the Summer House, taking in the sights of the illuminated Charlotte Inn complex and the sounds of the fountains and the church bells on the hour.

(508) 627-4751. Fax (508) 627-4652. Twenty-three rooms and two suites with private baths. June-October and weekends in May: doubles $275 to $450, suites $495 and $750. November-April weekends and midweek in May: doubles, $175 to $395, suites $395 to $550. November-April midweek: doubles $165 to $350, suites $350 to $450. Two-night minimum weekends Children over 14. Smoking restricted.

Tuscany Inn, 22 N. Water St., Box 2428, Edgartown 02539.
Gorgeous annuals line the walkway to this showy inn, renovated and redecorated from head to toe from its rooming-house days as the old Captain Fisher House.

Laura Sbrana-Scheuer, a native of Pisa who was schooled in Florence, and her retired IBM husband, Rusty Scheuer, moved here from Potomac, Md., to create her vision of an eight-room Tuscan inn on a New England island.

"Everything you see here has been restored," said Rusty, whose wife obviously spared no expense to promote authenticity and style. It took two workmen four months just to strip the stairway and newel posts back to their original chestnut sheen. The first floor of the Italianate Victorian house is devoted to common space as the Scheuers "try to make guests feel at home." They're at home very nicely in the stunning parlor, light and airy with yellow-sponged walls, warm red sofas and chairs, and splashy art all around. In the clubby library, a table discreetly displays the Scheuers' stack of snapshots of President Clinton playing the saxophone at a local reception and of Laura whispering in his ear. The formal, white-linened dining room that's now part of the inn's restaurant holds an impressive collection of blue plates. The remarkable breakfast room reminds Laura of home. It's a work of art, with an archway onto the semi-open commercial kitchen, distressed wood trim, shelves of cookbooks and four tables dressed in blue and white checked cloths and topped with pots of flowers.

Here is where Laura combines her twin passions: interior design (she was a decorator in New York for twenty years) and cooking. She teaches Tuscan cooking weekends in the spring and fall and takes culinary trips to her home area in Tuscany in October. Her son Marco is chef at their new restaurant, **La Cucina** (see Dining Spots).

Overnight guests are treated to sumptuous fare in the breakfast room or on the side patio beside the cutting gardens. In season, Laura gets the day off to a good start with fresh juices and fruits, homemade breads and one of her specialties: frittatas, buttermilk blueberry pancakes or french toast made from baguettes.

Upstairs on two floors are eight guest rooms with private baths, three with marble whirlpool tubs. TVs are available in some. Lovely in blue and white, the honeymoon room offers a view of the harbor, a kingsize bed with a fabric-covered headboard, two halogen reading lights beside the bed, a couple of wing chairs and Lord & Mayfair toiletries. The tiny La Bohème, its twin beds tucked into the gable, has a semi-open bathtub with hand-held shower beneath a skylight. A loveseat facing the window of the second-floor front room takes full advantage of the harbor view. The curving stairway to the third floor passes a niche where a spotlight illuminates the Japanese-style flower arrangement. With an obvious eye for what goes with what, Laura has decorated the rooms with great taste to showcase acquisitions from the couple's travels.

Besides the interior of the house, guests enjoy a side gazebo on the small wrap-around porch and a back yard that's uncommonly large for a location in the center of town.

(508) 627-5999. Fax (508) 627-6605. Eight rooms with private baths. Doubles, $200 to $325, mid-June through August; $150 to $245, late spring and early fall; $90 to $145, November to mid-May. Closed January to mid-March. Children over 8. No smoking.

The Inn at 148 Main St., 148 Main St., Box 1203, Edgartown 02539.

An abandoned restaurant-turned-lodging house was transformed in 1996 into a sumptuous yet welcoming B&B. David Drinan, who had enjoyed restoring his family's homes in the Boston area, undertook his biggest task with an 1840s landmark structure at what he calls the gateway to downtown Edgartown.

The Inn at 148 Main St. has been transformed from abandoned house.

Gutting the old Horn of Plenty restaurant so that only the studs were left standing, David and his subcontractors built a spacious, all-new main house plus a rear addition for the family and a deluxe suite in a new carriage house. He rag-rolled and sponge-painted the walls, scattered oriental and dhurrie rugs and runners on the floors, spent a small fortune on Domain furniture and thought of every creature comfort. The result is three guest rooms and a suite of distinction, plus stylish common rooms and a lavishly landscaped property that focuses on a new swimming pool and spa.

Guests know they are onto something special when they arrive in the brick driveway, walk along the side veranda and enter the foyer, where the pool is on view straight ahead. To the left is a living room with big windows on three sides, jutting out toward the rear patio and pool. It's fancifully furnished in grays and creams with plush Domain sofas and chairs that live up to their Shabby Chic name. Beyond is a dining room with a wet bar, also with a pool view. The main floor also holds a large guest room with king bed, a loveseat and chair facing the TV and entertainment center, and a jacuzzi tub in the bathroom.

Upstairs in front are two guest rooms with queensize wrought-iron beds and private baths, their TVs hidden inside cozies fashioned from the curtain fabrics. The decor is spiffy in cream colors with green accents. The free-standing fireplace hearth in one room has been turned ingeniously toward the bed and sofa, and a private porch overlooks the pool area.

The crowning touch is the upstairs suite in the carriage house, a dramatic, 26-by-26-foot space notable for the peaks and valleys of its vaulted ceiling. A queen sleigh bed is angled from one corner, and an oversize jacuzzi tub holds forth beneath the side windows, outside the skylit bathroom. David said he designed the space so that guests could soak in the tub and watch the fireplace while reading the New York Times. The fireplace also is on view from two splashy floral club chairs with an ottoman, a comfortable place for lounging with a drink from the wet bar. Breakfast can be enjoyed beside the french doors opening onto a small balcony.

That breakfast can be continental or full, according to guests' preference. David will prepare french toast, blueberry pancakes or a soufflé on request, and will serve it in the guests' room, dining room or on the poolside patio. Says he: "I want people to feel as if they're visiting me in my home" – which they are. After spending twenty summers here, he's now the fulltime innkeeper, who also spends considerable time on local fund-raising efforts and benefits. His wife Helen, a banker in Boston, joins him on weekends.

(508) 627-7248. Fax (508) 627-9505. Three rooms and one suite with private baths. Mid-June through September; doubles $185 to $270, suite $350. May to mid-June and October to mid-December: doubles $145 to $225, suite $300. Winter: doubles $120 to $185, suite $250. Two-night minimum weekends in season. Children over 10. No smoking.

Hob Knob Inn, 128 Main St., Box 239, Edgartown 02539.

The old Governor Bradford Inn was upgraded from "kind of a vanilla box" in 1997 into a summery, sophisticated inn reflecting the tastes of owner Margaret White. A Colorado commercial property manager, she was looking for a new life on the Vineyard where she had summered with her parents. Her realtor pointed out the Governor Bradford and asked if she'd ever thought of running an inn. "I said, 'show me the numbers' – and here I am."

She took over the comfortable but rather charmless Gothic Revival structure in 1996, ran the inn for a season to determine guests' needs, and closed it in the winter of 1997 for three months of renovations. She redecorated every room with taste and flair, added guest services and hired a fulltime breakfast chef. She reopened the inn as the Hob Knob, named for the bygone country estate in Ohio of her grandparents from Cleveland. "All it takes is attention to detail and guest services," says she.

The sixteen rooms on three floors come with kingsize beds (except for two with twins), updated private baths, chintz fabrics, TVs and telephones. The rooms we saw were nicely appointed in crisp country English style. Down pillows and comforters, all-cotton sheets, and Caswell-Massey toiletries are the rule. Pastel-colored walls in each room are dotted with lineups of antique plates. The plates are the signature of Margaret's cousin, an interior designer, who acquired them at estate sales in Cleveland.

Common rooms include a library with fireplace, a dining room overlooking Main Street and a compact health center and mini-spa in the basement. Lemonade and afternoon tea with Neiman-Marcus cookies and finger sandwiches are served on the side porch. Breakfast, cooked to order offers a choice of omelets, eggs benedict, frittatas, waffles, pancakes and such.

(508) 627-9510 or (800) 696-2723. Fax (508) 627-4560. Sixteen rooms with private baths. Memorial Day through October: doubles, $185 to $375. Rest of year: $125 to $250. Children over 12. No smoking.

The Victorian Inn, 24 South Water St., Edgartown 02539.

Masses of impatiens brighten the striking facade of this inn, nicely located across from the famous Pagoda Tree in an area of ship's captain's homes. It's as Victorian as can be, well deserving of its listing in the National Register. It's also generally as luxurious as can be, from its elegantly furnished rooms to the gourmet breakfasts served in the English garden backing up to the Charlotte Inn compound in the rear.

Innkeepers Stephen and Karyn Caliri from Plymouth happened to be staying here when they learned the inn was being sold at auction. They put in the winning bid and set about a five-year upgrading plan, promising the inn would be "pretty spiffy when we're done." To start, they restored the fireplaces in the parlor and breakfast room to working order and redecorated the dining room in shades of rich reds and pink. They since have enhanced all fourteen guest rooms, all with updated bathrooms (only two with tubs) and some with inviting sitting areas.

Karyn's favorite is the large and elegant Room 9 with king poster bed, Empire chest and sofa in the bay window. It and another deluxe room at the rear have porches with deck chairs and loungers overlooking the English garden and the carriage house of the Charlotte Inn. Stephen is partial to the third-floor Room 10, with queen canopy bed, dusty rose carpeting and two balconies, one facing the harbor. He also likes Room 14 with kingsize plantation bed and trundle beneath, white sofa and green armchairs and a deck beyond. Rooms vary considerably in size and appeal, as the range in rates suggests. Deep, rich shades of rose, green and blue are the prevailing colors, and some of the sheets and shower curtains are patterned with roses. Decanters of sherry and bowls of apples are put out in the Victorian parlor, where tea or lemonade are offered in the afternoon.

Karyn and a chef share the cooking chores for the four-course breakfast, which also is available to the public by reservation from 8 to 10 a.m. for $12.50. Fresh fruits, five kinds of juices and a pastry basket filled with assorted muffins (from orange to banana) and croissants start the repast. Main courses could be pumpkin pancakes, eggs benedict, fish cakes topped with poached eggs and creamed spinach, or Mexican eggs with cheese, corn and chilies. In summer, breakfast is served outside at white tables on a delightful brick patio amid the greenery and flowers of the English garden.

(508) 627-4784. Fourteen rooms with private baths. Memorial Day to Columbus Day: doubles, $145 to $285. Rest of year: $70 to $165. No smoking.

The Shiverick Inn, Pent Lane at Pease's Point Way, Box 640, Edgartown 02539. Built in 1840 for the town physician, this mansion was restored in 1984 by Philadelphia descendants of the Shiverick line and opened as the Dr. Shiverick House, a fancy if somewhat austere-feeling inn. Subsequent owners Denise and Marty Turmelle have warmed up an antiques-filled masterpiece that some had found intimidating. Warmth is a hallmark of the lady of the house, an effusive type who goes by the name Denny and calls everybody honey or darling.

The theme, as described in the inn's brochure, is still a "grandly romantic sequence of visual pleasures and physical comforts purposely designed to enchant the senses and enrich the spirit." Inside the oak double-door entry is a high-ceilinged entrance hall with the original mahogany staircase and a remarkable showpiece spool cabinet.

Ahead is a formal parlor/dining room, notable for gorgeous rugs over random-width floorboards restored from a barn in Vermont. A crystal chandelier hangs over the dining table, and porcelain figures line the mantel. Balloon draperies frame the parlor's windows onto a spacious garden room, which has a long sofa along one wall, wrought-iron furniture with ivy-patterned seats, and a long tiled counter (painted with ivy) for breakfast or cocktail service. Beyond is a delightful patio and garden colorful with pink and white flowers, which are also on view from an upstairs porch. A sunny library is made for relaxing.

The inn has ten guest rooms and suites on the first and second floors. Each has a full bath and six have working fireplaces. They are sumptuously furnished with four-poster or canopy beds, a variety of art objects and antiques, oriental rugs, and rich wallpapers and fabrics. The Turmelles have changed two twin-bedded rooms to kings and queens "to go along with the theme of romance."

A continental-plus breakfast starts with fresh fruit, cereal, yogurt and granola.

The main event involves three kinds of homemade pastries (at our visit, carrot and banana breads and orange-walnut coffeecake), plus English muffin toasting bread that Denny makes every day. In the afternoon, she offers tea or lemonade, depending on season.

The Turmelles moved here from management jobs in New Hampshire when their three sons left the nest. They occupy the inn's third floor and are hands-on innkeepers.

(508) 627-3797 or (800) 723-4292. Fax (508) 627-8441. Eight rooms and two suites with private baths. July-September: doubles $205 to $260, suites $280. May-June and October: doubles $150 to $185, suites $195 to $225. November-April: doubles $125 to $150, suites $185. Three-night minimum in season. Children over 12. No smoking.

Point Way Inn, Main Street at Pease's Point Way, Box 5255, Edgartown 02539.

Remodeled from a 150-year-old whaling captain's house, this fifteen-room inn offers a variety of comfortable accommodations and personality galore. Ben and Linda Smith, who landed in Edgartown Harbor after a 4,000-mile sailing cruise in 1979, spent that winter turning the house into an inn reflecting family interests through and through.

You'll enjoy the pictures of their 38-foot ketch, the Point Way, as well as the memorabilia of the Edgartown Mallet Club, a croquet group that ex-lawyer Ben formed to play on the inn's lawn, all the yachting and golfing trophies, the photos of the Yale Whiffenpoofs of which Ben was a member, and the paintings by his aunt, who was of the Boston School of Impressionists and studied with Monet.

Each of the guest rooms, grouped off various stairways in separate sections of the house, has a private bath and ten contain fireplaces. Canopy and four-poster beds, colorful quilts, wing chairs, wicker or tweedy sofas, a couple of tiny porches and a large deck – it's a delightful mishmash that's comfortable as can be. Each room also bears nice touches like decanters of sherry, stamped envelopes, pin cushions and taffy. Six rooms have french doors opening onto private balconies or terraces. The star of the show is a two-room suite with deck and fireplace.

The cozy living room comes with a fireplace, games, a spectacular 500-piece wood jigsaw puzzle and a well-stocked honor bar. Assorted sailing trophies hold fresh flowers. Flags that Ben used on his boats are under the glass-covered tables in the breakfast room, in which fresh orange juice, cereals, granola, popovers, coffeecake, muffins and breads are served buffet style on dishes and mugs emblazoned with birds.

Tea or lemonade and cookies (oatmeal, just like our mothers used to make, at our last visit) plus clams – if guests have been successful on claming expeditions – are an afternoon highlight in the ivy-covered outdoor gazebo, which is part of the mallet club. Guests as well as members may play croquet if they wish.

And, typical of these hospitable innkeepers, they offer to do guests' laundry and loan them the inn car.

(508) 627-8633 or (800) 942-9569. Fax (508) 627-8579. Fourteen rooms and one suite with private baths. July and August: doubles $150 to $250, suite $285. Interim: doubles $100 to $175, suite $165 to $190. November-March: $90 to $125, suite $145.

The Jonathan Munroe House, 100 Main St., Box 5084, Edgartown 02539.

His family used to run the Darien Inn in Vermont's Northeast Kingdom, so Chip Yerkes comes by his new sideline naturally. A building contractor on the Vineyard,

Croquet court is ready for play alongside Point Way Inn.

he applied his carpentry talents in 1994 to his unassuming house built in 1840 and created a comfortable B&B with eight bedrooms and a cottage.

Guests check in at a corner cabinet in the small front parlor. Beyond are a larger, fireplaced parlor and a rear dining porch, where personable Chip and his assistants serve a continental-plus breakfast of fresh fruits, baked goods and cereals.

All bedrooms have private baths. Four with marble fireplaces come with jacuzzi tubs. The rooms are furnished simply but comfortably with king or queen beds and floral comforters with matching curtains.

We were among Chip's first paying guests in his rear garden cottage. Snug and modern, it has a living room with a plush sofa and a wicker chair facing a brick fireplace, an old wood chest for a coffee table, an antique wood desk bearing a diary in which the previous guests waxed ecstatic, and a kitchenette with a ceramic sink, microwave, pottery dishes and an antique side-by-side dining table set for two. A whirlpool tub is ensconced beside votive candles and sconces on the second-floor landing. The queensize bed is situated beneath a vaulted ceiling in the bedroom. The cottage's screened porch may well be the best place in town to enjoy the carillon hymns played nightly from the nearby St. Andrew's Episcopal Church.

(508) 627-5536. Eight rooms and one cottage with private baths. Mid-June through September: doubles $165 to $200, cottage $250. Spring and fall: doubles $145 to $175, cottage $200. Winter: doubles $110 to $145, cottage $150. No smoking.

The Edgartown Inn, 56 North Water St., Box 1211, Edgartown 02539.

The plaque on the side of this weathered 1798 whaling captain's residence notes that Daniel Webster, Charles Sumner and Nathaniel Hawthorne once were guests here. The place fairly oozes history and character, so we did not expect to find such comfortable, nicely furnished rooms at prices that represent good value.

The twenty rooms in the main inn, the rear garden house and "Le Barn" vary from three simple rooms with sinks in the room and a shared bath to the spacious King's Room with double beds at either end and a fabric loveseat in the center, facing the bow window and the harbor. The large Nathaniel Hawthorne Room, pretty in Williamsburg blue-green trim and floral wallpapers, comes with kingsize bed and two wicker chairs. Quite idyllic with its own balcony is the skylit Dogwood Room, one of two large and quiet rooms in the rear Garden House overlooking the garden courtyard. It has a kingsize wicker bed, pretty floral wallpaper and draperies, and television. Most rooms are carpeted and nicely refurbished by longtime owner Earle Radford, a Kansas City artist who now lives on Chappaquiddick and whose paintings adorn the inn's hallways and small front TV/common room.

The inn claims "the best breakfast on the island." If it's the best, heaven help us, but it certainly is colorful and full of character. The meal is served on the rear garden courtyard or in a small, convivial dining room where every inch of wall and shelf space is covered with bric-a-brac. The focal point is Henry King, for 52 years the inn's handyman and man Friday, who was outfitted in a bright red uniform with matching bow tie at our visit (he changes his colors daily, we're told, and donned a tuxedo for a formal state dinner honoring his dedication and commitment to the hospitality industry in 1996). He served us juice, coffee and a plate of carrot cake before taking orders for poached eggs on the inn's famous cheese toast and scrambled eggs with oatmeal toast. The eggs, nothing out of the ordinary, came with three slices of crisp bacon and only one of toast, but the character of the place more than compensated.

(508) 627-4794. Rates EP. Memorial Day through September: doubles, $80 to $180; $75 to $130 midweek in June and September. April to Memorial Day and October: $50 to $120. Closed November-March.

Breakfast daily, for the public: $4.25 continental, $7 full.

The Daggett House, 59 North Water St., Edgartown 02539.

For a waterfront location, this bed-and-breakfast inn with 31 guest rooms and suites in three houses and a cottage is unsurpassed in Edgartown. The long, narrow rear lawn with flowers, benches and umbrellaed tables slopes down to the water and a private pier next to the Chappaquiddick Ferry landing.

Guest rooms, all with private baths, are in the main 1750 Daggett House with its Colonial tavern downstairs, the newer (early 1800s Greek Revival) and larger Captain Warren House across Water Street, and the seaside Garden Cottage, which has three double rooms. The newest acquisition is the Thomas House up a lane across the street. Six junior suites were being readied for opening in 1998, each with queen bedroom, living room with sofabed and a kitchenette.

Generally quite spacious, most rooms are furnished with oversize canopy and four-poster beds, artworks and antiques. Until the Thomas House came along, those of most recent vintage were two suites. The Chappaquiddick in the main house offers a bedroom and bath with whirlpool tub downstairs, an enclosed patio with jacuzzi and a spiral staircase leading up to a living room, kitchen area and private deck overlooking the harbor. Television and telephones are offered here and in the Widow's Walk Suite, atop the Captain Warren House. It has two bedrooms, two baths, a living room with sofabed and a private jacuzzi atop the widow's walk with a panoramic view of the harbor.

After the inn's location, the next best thing is the historic tavern room, which dates from the 1660s and above which the house was later built. The island's first tavern, it looks the way an early tavern should look, with its unusual beehive fireplace chimney, dark beams, wide pine hardwood flooring, old tools and bare wood communal tables for six, where conviviality is the norm. A local artist who illustrates summer resident Carly Simon's books painted the stunning Daggett House mural that now graces one wall.

Breakfast – with wonderful toast made from bread from the recipe of the late Lucille Chirgwin, who with her husband Fred owned the inn for 40 years – costs $6 to $7.95 (for a fine eggs benedict). Breakfast is available to the public as well, and the ambiance is such that people gladly wait for a table while sipping coffee served on the rear terrace. Dinners also are available for guests and the public. Hidden near the fireplace in the tavern room is a secret staircase that provides steep, low-ceilinged access to an upstairs guest room with kingsize bed, gold wallpaper and a view of the harbor.

Off the entrance to the main inn is a small living room with sofas, wing chairs and a television set. Among the fourteen rooms in the Warren House are several efficiencies. The Chirgwin sons have turned over innkeeping duties to a manager.

(508) 627-4600 or (800) 946-3400. Fax (508) 627-4611. Twenty-three rooms and two suites with private baths. Rates EP. Mid-May to mid-October: doubles $150 to $225, junior suites $155, suites $250 to $550. Rest of year: doubles $80 to $115, junior suites $80, suites $115 to $275. Two-night minimum in season, weekends in off-season. Children accepted. No smoking. Main house and Thomas House open all year; Captain Warren House and Garden Cottage open April to November.

Entrées, $18.50 to $23. Breakfast, daily 7:30 to 11, Sunday 8 to 1. Dinner, Tuesday-Sunday 5:30 to 9.

Dining Spots

L'Étoile, South Summer Street, Edgartown.

Ensconced at the rear of the Charlotte Inn, this bow-windowed conservatory-dining room is utterly charming. It's furnished with white bentwood and cane chairs, brick walls, skylights, paintings, lush ferns and a blooming hibiscus tree.

Chef-owner Michael Brisson and his wife, Joan Parzanese, are known for exquisite food and artistic presentation, altogether worthy of the inn's Relais & Châteaux designation. The chef, who cooked for four years at the acclaimed L'Espalier in Boston, takes special pride in his treatment of game, lamb and native seafood. He also is partial to the understated place settings of white, gold-edged Villeroy & Boch china, the Reed & Barton silverplate and fluted crystal wine glasses at white-linened tables seating 45 inside. Another twenty or so can be accommodated on an outdoor patio beside a trickling fountain.

Dinner is prix-fixe for three courses, with some items carrying substantial surcharges. You can tell there's a master in the kitchen from some of the appetizers: a chilled soup of sweet yellow banana peppers and golden tomatoes with cucumber and crabmeat salsa; sautéed duck foie gras on snap pea tendrils with white peaches, muscat and leek sauce, or pastrami-smoked salmon and grilled shrimp on mesclun greens with avocado and belgian endive, caviar croustades, and a roasted white corn and molasses vinaigrette.

A homemade sorbet clears the palate for the main course. Among the six choices could be grilled wild striped bass fillet on shaved fennel with a roasted corn and smoked shrimp relish, roasted pheasant with a mushroom and mustard green ravioli and grilled figs, and filet mignon with black truffle, cabernet and oregano sauce.

Desserts include chocolate marquis, crème courvoisier with peach coulis, and caramelized macadamia ice cream with Bailey's crème anglaise.

The wine list starts with many champagnes, since for many this is special-occasion dining. But it offers good French and California choices at affordable prices.

(508) 627-5187. Prix-fixe, $62. Dinner nightly in summer, 6:30 to 9:45; Tuesday-Sunday in off-season, weekends in winter. Sunday brunch, 10:30 to 12:30. Closed January to mid-February.

Savoir Fare, 14 Church St., Edgartown

What began as basically a gourmet takeout shop has expanded into "a garden of epicurean delights" – a small but full-fledged, inside-outside restaurant that made its name serving the best lunches in town. Lunch has since been discontinued, as owners Scott and Charlotte Caskey have concentrated on dinner. Chef Scott, who used to cook in Vail, works in an open kitchen at one end of the compact restaurant, which is a picture of pristine white from its intimate, white-linened tables to the lights on a ficus tree. There's a counter with four chairs, but most of the action is outside at tables on a deck overlooking Post Office Square.

The short, changing menu touts exotic contemporary cuisine. A typical summer dinner might begin with appetizers like caramelized vidalia onion and potato ravioli with black summer truffles and a salad of grilled asparagus and Jonah crab. Main dishes could be cornmeal-dusted soft-shell crabs over creamy lemon risotto, grilled rare tuna with fried sweetbreads over a white bean and celery root puree, and a classic Italian veal rib chop with toasted garlic tuna sauce. You want lobster? Try it Caskey style sautéed with potato ravioli, English peas, sweet corn and apple-smoked bacon, an ethereal treat.

Banana cream pie with mascarpone and chocolate ganache, lemon tart with crème anglaise, and tirami su are among the desserts.

(508) 627-9864. Entrées, $27 to $33. Dinner nightly, 6 to 10; shorter hours in off-season. Closed mid-October to mid-March.

La Cucina, 22 North Water St., Edgartown.

The owners of the Tuscany Inn finally got town approval to open their long-dreamed-of restaurant in 1996, and what a dream it is. A small formal dining room in white and a more casual, café-style side room in blue and white open onto the showy, arched Tuscan country kitchen in which Laura Sbrana-Scheuer teaches her weekend cooking classes in the off-season. In summer, she turns the kitchen over to her son Marco, who recently was promoted from sous chef to evening chef at the noted Gramercy Tavern in New York.

From the kitchen come such Tuscan treats as pan-seared halibut with a summer truffle vinaigrette and seared veal chop with sherry sauce, each with a different assortment of exotic vegetables and risottos. Starters could be pepper-seared tuna with Tuscan bread salad or a Vineyard salad of arugula, tomatoes and grilled shrimp. Desserts include the obligatory tirami su.

Nearly half the 56 seats are on the side patio, an idyllic place to be unless it rains – in which case, you may go hungry, as the tables inside are apt to be fully booked and there's no provision for overflow. Such is the mixed blessing of a small, choice establishment that takes reservations but cannot control the weather.

The new raw bar features three kinds of oysters, sevruga caviar and a glass of Perrier Jouet for $19.95. The beer and wine lists are short but select.

(508) 627-8161. Entrées, $24.50 to $32. Dinner nightly except Tuesday, 6 to 9, mid-May through Columbus Day.

Tuscany Inn features cooking of Laura Sbrana-Scheuer and her son Marco.

Lattanzi's, Old Post Office Square, Edgartown.

Our longtime favorite Warriner's restaurant has given way to Lattanzi's, the Italian showplace for chef-owner Albert Lattanzi, who had been chef for years up the street at the former Andrea's. Here, he lightened up the walls of the elegant library room at Warriner's to produce a Mediterranean look, and topped the white linened tables with white butcher paper for an Italian bistro feeling.

The atmosphere is refined and the food so abundant that some complain the portions are much too big. The manager advises that almost everyone takes the leftovers home in a Lattanzi basket, and many phone to say how much they enjoyed them the next day. Albert makes his pastas by hand, cooks his meats on a hardwood grill and buys his seafood from fishermen right from the boat.

The pasta dishes are highly rated, especially the arrabbiata with spicy pork sausage and tomato and the fettuccine picante with anchovies, hot cherry peppers and garlic. Main courses range from calamari fra diavolo to porterhouse steak alla florentina. The mixed grill with lamb, hot Italian sausage, pork and spicy peach chutney and the grilled pork loin with apricots and pinenuts appealed the night we were there.

Appetizers here are good but superfluous. Save room instead for a stellar tirami su, the chocolate-hazelnut cake, the fresh fruit tarts or, at the very least, a cheese plate. The wine list focuses on Italian vintages.

The new **La Galleria** is open until midnight in season for brick-oven pizzas, cappuccino, desserts and drinks.

(508) 627-8854. Entrées, $18.50 to $32. Dinner nightly from 6, June-September; rest of year, Wednesday-Sunday from 5.

The Seafood Shanty, 31 Dock St., Edgartown.

This contemporary, three-level spot is anything but a shanty. Edgartown's best harbor view for dining is from the recently expanded upstairs deck with a raw bar above a glass-enclosed porch with water on three sides. Plastic chairs with deep blue mesh frames, bare tables with blue and white mats and bare wood walls add up to an attractive nautical setting.

You pay for the location, right next to Edgartown's Memorial Wharf. Our lunch for two came to $40 for a cup of clam chowder and a spinach salad, plus a pasta salad loaded with seafood. The sunny Indian summer setting was such, we admit, that we lingered over a second beer.

The seafood dinner entrées are fairly traditional and simple, from baked scrod to mixed seafood grill. The Cuttyhunk stir-fry tosses shrimp and a touch of lobster with vegetables. Rolls and vegetable, potato or rice accompany. After all this, who needs the desserts, which are standard anyway?

Light fare is served upstairs in the Shanty Lounge and Deck.

(508) 627-8622. Entrées, $13.95 to $22.95. Lunch daily, 11:45 to 3. Dinner, 5 to 10:30. Open May-October.

Mad Martha's, 7 North Water St., Edgartown.

One of a group of ice-cream parlors around the island, this offers an amazing variety of flavors (we loved the Bailey's Irish cream overflowing from its crackly cone, $2.25) and concoctions, from walkaway waffle sundae to oreo cookie nookie. The most outrageous is the pig's delight ($18): a dozen scoops of ice cream topped with the usual banana-split trimmings. "Order by saying `oink,'" advises the sign at the door, and some do.

Diversions

Edgartown is an eminently walkable town and everything (except some of the beaches) is within walking distance. That's fortunate, for in summer the place tends to be wall-to-walk people, bicycles and cars. The shops, restaurants and inns are compressed into a maze of narrow streets leading from or paralleling the harbor. Interspersed with them and along side streets that live up to the description "quaint" are stately large white whaling captain's homes, neatly separated from the brick sidewalks by picket fences and colorful gardens. Here you see and sense the history of a seaport village preserved from the 19th century.

Walk around. Don't miss the churches: The Old Whaling Church, the tall-columned Greek Revival structure that doubles as the Performing Arts Center, the little St. Andrew's Episcopal Church with its beautiful stained-glass windows, a cheery interior and a carillon that tolls quite a concert across town in the late afternoon; the imposing First Federated Church with old box pews and a steeple visible far at sea. Other highlights are the newspaper offices of the revered Vineyard Gazette in a 1764 house across from the Charlotte Inn, the towering Pagoda Tree brought from China as a seedling in a flower pot early in the 19th century and now spreading over South Water Street to shade the Victorian and Harborside inns, the Old Sculpin Art Gallery showing works of various artists, and all the august sea captain's homes of diverse architectural eras along Water and Summer streets.

Martha's Vineyard Historical Society/Vineyard Museum, 59 School St.

Here is a block-size museum complex worth a visit. The twelve rooms of the 1765 Thomas Cooke House are filled with early island memorabilia. You're apt to see historians at work in the Gale Huntington Library of History, through which you pass to get to the Francis Foster Museum, which has a small maritime and island collection. Outside is a boat shed containing a whaleboat, fire engine and old wagon, plus the original Fresnel lens from the old Gay Head Lighthouse, mounted in a replica of the lighthouse lantern and watch room, still lighted at night.

(508) 627-4441. Open Tuesday-Saturday 10 to 5, mid-June to mid-October; Thursday-Friday 1 to 5 and Saturday 10 to 5, rest of year. Adults, $5.

The Vincent House Museum, Main and Church streets.

The Vineyard's oldest house (1672) contains most of its original woodwork, glass and hardware. During recent restoration, some of the walls of the unfurnished house were left exposed to demonstrate the types of construction used. The museum offers tours of the nearby Dr. Daniel Fisher House (1840), an imposing Federal presence on Main Street, and the Old Whaling Church (1843), where summer resident André Previn and Friends were about to give a benefit concert at our latest visit. Hour-long walking tours of Edgartown leave the Vincent House daily at 3.

(508) 627-8017. Museum open Monday-Saturday 10:30 to 3 in summer. Admission $3, museum and tour $6.

Felix Neck Wildlife Sanctuary, off Edgartown-Vineyard Haven Road.

With blinds on Sengekontacket Pond, this is a favorite spot for birders, but we know locals who try to walk portions of the six miles of marked nature trails every day. The sanctuary embraces 350 acres of beach, marsh, fields and woodlands. The executive director has been instrumental in bringing back the endangered osprey to the island. Naturalists offer bird walks, canoeing, stargazing and snorkeling, among special activities. A visitor center in a renovated barn has freshwater and saltwater tanks containing local species.

(508) 627-4850. Grounds open daily, 8 to 7. Adults, $3.

Beaches. Katama Beach, the public part of the seemingly endless South Beach along the open shore three miles south of Edgartown, has excellent surf swimming, a tricky undertow, shifting dunes and a protected salt pond inhabited by crabs and scallops. A shuttle bus runs from Edgartown in summer. Non-surf swimming is available at picturesque Joseph A. Sylvia State Beach, a narrow, two-mile-long strip between Edgartown and Oak Bluffs. Back toward Edgartown is Bend-of-the-Road Beach; its shallow waters are good for children. In town is Lighthouse Beach at Starbuck's Neck, on the harbor at the end of Fuller Street and seldom crowded.

Chappaquiddick Island. Reached by a five-minute ride on the On Time ferry from Edgartown, it has a public beach facing the Edgartown Harbor at Chappy Point, plus the Cape Pogue Wildlife Refuge and Wasque Reservation beaches. These are remote and secluded, three miles from the ferry – best reached by car as bicyclists may find it difficult negotiating some of the sandy roads (but parking is limited). On the way you'll pass the forested My Toi Preserve, a surprising Zen-like oasis of Japanese gardens, and the Chappaquiddick General Store and gasoline station, surrounded by abandoned cars and the only commercial enterprise of size on the island. The sponsoring Trustees of Reservations, which continues to buy up open land here, offers countless hiking trails as well as a variety of activities on Chappaquiddick, from fishing trips to natural history tours – three-hour guided expeditions over ten miles of remote barrier beaches (reservations, 627-3599).

Shopping. Main Street and adjacent streets are crammed with interesting stores. **The Fligors'** (billed as the Vineyard's most delightful store for 38 years) is an intriguing maze of rooms and levels that make it almost a department store. Suave gifts, Claire Murray rugs, dolls, resort clothing (fabulous handknit sweaters for every holiday imaginable), toys, Christmas shop, a basement sale room – you name it, Carol and Richard Fligor probably have it. They also offer The Fligor Apartments at 69 North Summer St., 627-4745, four newly renovated one-room efficiency cottages done in a colorful grape motif – a find for $150 a night.

We enjoy popping into the **Vermont Shop,** the idea for which was thought up in one snow-less winter by Robin Burke, who has a ski house there. It has expanded to the point that 40 percent of the merchandise mix comes from elsewhere, but you'll find Woody Jackson cows, Vermont pottery and foods like common crackers and cheeses. We liked the ceramic steamers and came out with an interesting pair of titanium earrings. Nevin Square is a conglomeration of nice shops behind the Colonial Inn. Also of interest are the fine arts at the enlarged **Christina's Gallery** and at **Willoughby's,** the handpainted furniture and accessories at **Once in a Blue Moon,** the colorful ceramics at **Designs Gallery,** the clothing and folk art at **Chica,** the antiques and gifts at **Past and Presents,** and the jewelry at **The Golden Basket** and **Sine Qua Non, Ltd.** All manner of unusual wooden things from spoons to birdhouses to a $1,200 rocking horse intrigue at the unique **In the Woods.**

More one-of-a-kind items are shown by Sue Cooper-Street at **The Elegant Crow,** a posh wedding studio, gift shop and fine art gallery. We were struck there by the wonderful paintings and murals by her husband, famed artist Thom Street, as well as furniture and lamps made from musical instruments.

Women's clothing is shown at **Saffron** and sweaters from Australia are featured at **Island Pursuit.** Pick up your foul-weather gear at **Sundog,** which has the correct kind of Vineyard apparel – as do **Vineyard Gear** and **Very Vineyard,** even more so.

Extra-Special

Chicama Vineyards, Stoney Hill Road, West Tisbury.

The wild grapes that gave Martha's Vineyard its name are now being cultivated by ex-Californians George and Catherine Matheisen and daughter Lynn Hoeft, who make "the kinds of wines we like to drink," Catherine says. They specialize

in dry viniferas, among them a robust red zinfandel, a Summer Island red that's meant to be drunk young, and the first Martha's Vineyard-appellation merlot. Much of the winemaking operation is outside and rather primitive, as you might expect after negotiating Stoney Hill Road, a long mile of bumps and dirt that we'd rename Stoney Hole. Several hundred people make the trek on a busy summer day and relish the shop's choice of wine or herbal vinegars, dressings and jams, all neatly displayed in gift baskets and glass cases lit from behind so the herbs show through. In the fall, the Christmas shop also offers festive foods, wreaths and hot mulled wine.

(508) 693-0309. Open daily 11 to 5, Sunday 1 to 5.

Vinegars on display at Chicama Vineyards.

Newport waterfront is on view from restaurant deck on Bannister's Wharf.

Newport, R.I.

A Many-Splendored Place

For the visitor, there are perhaps five Newports.

One is the harborfront, the busy commercial and entertainment area along the wharves and Thames Street. This is the heart of Newport, the place from which the Tall Ships and America's Cup winners sailed, the area to which tourists gravitate.

Another Newport is a world apart. It's up on fabled Bellevue Avenue among the mansions from the Gilded Age. Here the Astors, Vanderbilts, Morgans and others of America's 400 built their summer "cottages," palatial showplaces designed by the nation's leading architects. Here near the Casino at the turn of the century was a society summer resort unrivaled for glitter and opulence.

A third Newport is its quaint Point and Historic Hill sections, which date back to the 17th and 18th centuries when Newport was an early maritime center. Here are located more Colonial houses than any other place in the country, and some of the oldest public and religious edifices as well.

A fourth Newport is the windswept, open land around Ocean Drive, where the surf crashes against the rocky shore amid latter-day mansions and contemporary showplaces. This is the New England version of California's Pebble Beach and Seventeen-Mile Drive.

And then there's the rest of Newport, a bustling, Navy-dominated city that sprawls south along Aquidneck Island, away from the ocean and the other Newports.

Join these diverse Newports as history and geography have. The result is New England's international resort, a wondrous mix of water and wealth, of architecture and history, of romance and entertainment.

You can concentrate on one Newport and have more than enough to see and do, or try to savor a bit of them all. But likely as not, you won't get your fill. Newport will merely whet your appetite, its powerful allure beckoning you back.

Inn Spots

Newport has at least 200 inns and B&Bs, more than any other place in the country, according to local officials. They vary widely, and many of the more advertised ones lack the personal touch conveyed by owners who are also in residence as innkeepers. Of recent vintage are some excellent inns whose owners lavish TLC on their guests as well as their properties.

Cliffside Inn, 2 Seaview Ave., Newport 02840.

What a stunner of a place is this extravagant inn that seems to have everything. Owner Winthrop Baker of Wilton, Conn., has lavished big bucks and great taste in an effort to turn his first East Coast inn into one of the nation's best.

A former Westinghouse broadcasting executive and film producer, he caught the inn bug while building from scratch an oceanfront B&B in Princeton-by-the-Sea, Cal. Here, a block from the ocean, he took over a small B&B that had been built as a summer villa in 1880 by the governor of Maryland. Redoing the inn from top to bottom, he added nine luxury rooms and suites that, he opines, are "clearly room for room the best in Newport."

For starters, he turned the former innkeeper's quarters into the Governor's Suite, which has a huge bed/sitting room clad in dark green and white floral wallpapers and swags. A two-sided fireplace faces both the kingsize bed and the double jacuzzi tub in the bathroom, which comes equipped with an antique steam shower, a rare back-to-back double vanity, thick green robes and, for good measure, a TV and a telephone. Above that is The Attic in which he literally raised the roof for a cathedral ceiling, a skylit bath with jacuzzi, a bedroom with a matching armoire, kingsize bedstead and dressing table from Singapore, and two plush floral chairs. An old favorite, Miss Beatrice's Room, was transformed into a majestic area around a Lincoln-style queen bed, with a mound of pillows along a full-length Victorian window seat across the front and an enormous bathroom of marble, antique paneling and an oval whirlpool bath in the bay window.

The third-floor Turner Suite, elaborately outfitted in white and blue Laura Ashley fabrics, offers a half-tester queensize bed designed for the room, a sitting room with a loveseat and chair in deep green, and a skylit bathroom with jacuzzi. It

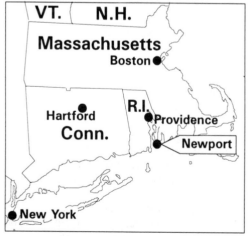

made the adjacent TV room look drab, so Win turned it and a bedroom into the Seascape Suite, harboring a cozy parlor with a cast-iron Victorian stove in the fireplace, a queensize bed, a whirlpool bath and more skylights. Next came the new Tower Suite, a two-story "labor of love" complete with a decorative, six-sided Victorian tower. The entire lower floor is devoted to the bathroom, including whirlpool tub and bidet. Upstairs is a bed-sitting room beneath an octagonal

Self-portrait of Beatrice Turner overlooks breakfast table at Cliffside Inn.

cathedral ceiling, with fireplace and bay window. Besides representing the most interesting space in the inn, Win says, the tower has an esthetic purpose. "It finishes off the front of the building to complete the Victorian look."

No room in the house has escaped his touch, whether it be the main-floor Victorian Room with a new whirlpool bath plus a dresser and a queensize four-poster bed bearing a shell headboard that he acquired at a Woolworth estate auction in Connecticut. Or the newly enlarged Garden Suite, a great summer space with a bay window off the front porch and a 28-foot-long "habitat bathroom" beneath, so-called "because you can live in it," what with a Victorian book nook at one end and french doors at the other opening onto a private courtyard.

The newest accommodations are in the Seaview Cottage, a onetime ranch house at the foot of the property. It was transformed into two suites, the Atlantic with a massive native stone fireplace and half-vaulted ceiling and the Cliff, a two-room affair with full vaulted ceiling and a two-sided "see-through" fireplace visible from the kingsize plantation bed and the plush living room.

Starting with no working fireplaces, the Cliffside now has twelve, plus eleven whirlpool tubs. All fifteen guest accommodations blend rich Victoriana with airy Laura Ashley freshness, air conditioning, telephones and TV sets (many with VCRs), as Win turns the bedrooms of his Victorian inn into places in which to linger – not from which to escape, as often we find is the case.

There are fine gathering places as well. The large fireplaced parlor is cheerfully redecorated in shades of orange-coral and moss green; the faille draperies are a sight to behold. Classical music and opera play in the background in the afternoon as guests enjoy hot apple cider, lemonade or iced tea, depending on the season, with treats like duck liver pâté, shrimp in puff pastry and brie with crackers. They help themselves to a cabinet stocked with juices, sodas and the like. They also relax on the wide front veranda, which yields glimpses of the ocean down the street.

The guest's every need is fulfilled by a pampering staff headed by resident innkeeper Stephen Nicolas, a Johnson & Wales University hospitality graduate whose experienced demeanor belies his youth. The 26-year-old son of a French chef and cookbook author, he prepares not only the afternoon canapés but a memorable breakfast. In our case it began with orange juice, two kinds of muffins and a remarkable (for winter) array of raspberries, blackberries and strawberries to lather upon homemade granola or mix with yogurt. The pièce de résistance was eggs benedict with a subtle hollandaise sauce.

There's food for the soul at Cliffside as well. During the renovations, Win became fascinated by the works of reclusive Newport artist Beatrice Turner, onetime owner of the house. He gathered many of her paintings from hither and yon to mount a fascinating retrospective exhibit that drew wide attention for the inn. In 1997 he published a book detailing her paintings and sad story. More than 100 images of her art, including a haunting self-portrait above the breakfast credenza, remain on permanent display. They add still another dimension to a luxurious inn of distinction.

(401) 847-1811 or (800) 845-1811. Fax (401) 848-5850. www.cliffsideinn.com. Eight rooms and seven suites with private baths. Doubles, $185 to $285. Suites, $285 to $350. Add $25 for weekends, May-October. Children over 13. No smoking.

Elm Tree Cottage, 336 Gibbs Ave., Newport 02840.

Large and lovely common rooms, comfortable and elegant bedrooms, enthusiastic and personable hosts. What more could you ask? You get them all at this extra-special "cottage" not far from the water. In 1990, Priscilla and Tom Malone and their three daughters took over the cottage, built in 1882 and later owned by Mrs. Crawford Hill, the Pennsylvania Railroad heiress and member of Newport's 400.

With an eye to getting the most mileage for their money, they have furnished the huge house with their own furniture and acquisitions from auctions and estate sales. "Our entire house fit into this living room," Priscilla noted of their move from Long Island. There's an 87-foot sweep from dining room to parlor, which ends at a curved wall of windows overlooking Easton's Pond and First Beach. Chintz sofas and a grand piano welcome guests to a living room that could be pictured in a design magazine. To the side are a morning garden room, great for lounging, and a handsome bar room furnished in wicker. Here the Malones put out snacks for guests who BYOB and sit at the great old bar with 1921 silver dollars embedded in its top and pictures of the former owner's Pekinese and a lion reverse-painted on the mirror behind.

Three tables in the enormous dining room are where Priscilla serves an elaborate breakfast: perhaps pear-stuffed crêpes, heart-shaped waffles, Portuguese sweet bread french toast, or apple crêpes in the shape of calla lilies. At our autumn visit, breakfast opened with juice and homemade oatmeal (the dish arrived on a saucer decorated with five varieties of dried leaves). The main event was pumpkin waffles. The day's calligraphed menu went home as a souvenir.

We'd happily stay in any of the five large guest rooms, four with fireplaces, on the second floor. The master suite, all 23 by 37 feet of it, is pretty in salmon and seafoam green. It contains a Louis XV kingsize bed with a crown canopy, two sitting areas (one in front of the fireplace) and a huge bath with a dressing table

Louis XV kingsize bed with crown canopy is feature of master suite at Elm Tree Cottage.

and Austrian crystal legs on the porcelain washstand. Country French and English linens and antiques dress this and the other four rooms, which pale only modestly in comparison. The newer library bedroom on a corner of the main floor, handsome in wine and teal colors, is outfitted in an English hunt theme and comes with a fireplace and TV. Constantly upgrading, the Malones are adding more kingsize crown canopy beds and redid the corner Easton Room in a "city French look" complete with a double soaking tub and coral-colored marble from Turkey.

In all the rooms, bottles of Poland Spring water await guests. The bedding and pillows are so extravagant that it takes Priscilla many minutes to turn down the beds at night and leave mints on the pillows. She has "fluffed up" the rooms with such touches as dried flowers, racks with old hats and individual stained-glass pieces. Tom's background in interior design and Priscilla's in fine arts and wood-working stood them in good stead for the inn's refurbishing as well as for the stained-glass business they run along with innkeeping and child-raising duties.

(401) 849-1610 or (888) 356-8733. Fax (401) 849-2084. www.elmtreebnb.com. Six rooms with private baths. July-October: doubles, $185 to $350. May-June: $185 to $350 weekends, $150 to $275 midweek. November-April: $165 to $295 weekends, $135 to $235 midweek. Three-night minimum weekends, July-October and holidays; two-night minimum other weekends. Children over 14. No smoking.

The Francis Malbone House, 392 Thames St., Newport 02840.
Elegant decor, an abundance of flowering plants and a rear courtyard retreat make this a favorite with those who like to be in the thick of things along Lower Thames Street. Five partners acquired the imposing residence in 1990 and converted it into one beautiful inn.

The downstairs common rooms are uncommonly inviting, the burgundy, pale pink and blue striped upholstery on some of the sofas and chairs in two high-ceilinged parlors matching the handsome draperies. In the rear library, the colors are also coordinated with the oriental carpet. All three rooms have fireplaces, and there's a TV/VCR in the library. At our spring visit, the rooms abounded with a profusion of colorful house plants, from African violets to hydrangeas to an hibiscus that had burst into bloom in a sunny window that morning.

Upstairs off a center hall are eight corner rooms on two floors, all with private bathrooms (two with tubs) and six with fireplaces. The front rooms are bigger and afford harbor views. Each is exquisitely furnished with antique queensize beds covered by monogrammed duvet covers in white. Baskets of Gilchrist & Soames toiletries are in each bathroom and interesting magazines are in the bedrooms.

On the main floor, a side hallway with a shelf of cobalt blue glass leads past the library to the sunken Counting House Suite (built as an office by the physician who once owned the house) with a private entry, a queensize four-poster bed facing the TV, a sitting area with a sofabed and two chairs, and a large bath with an oversize marble shower and a corner jacuzzi for two.

Although still the premium accommodation, the suite has competition from the nine new courtyard rooms in the rear, all with kingsize poster beds and jacuzzi tubs, writing desks, fireplaces and TVs hidden in recessed bookshelves. Bigger, more private and quiet because they're away from the street traffic, they encompass all the nuances that "we couldn't have in the original house and wanted here," in the words of innkeeper Will Dewey. A couple open onto private courtyards with wrought-iron furniture. The courtyard suite adds a wet bar and a sitting area. Oriental rugs, rich appointments, down comforters and duvet covers monogrammed in white are the rule.

A spectacular new dining room goes off a corridor walled with glass and Portuguese tiles leading to the courtyard wing. It's a beauty in pale yellow and gray with a domed ceiling, four round tables and two tall shelves displaying Will's collection of blue and white English china.

Will, a culinary graduate of Johnson & Wales University in Providence, and his attentive staff go the extra mile to pamper guests. They prepare a full breakfast, starting with fresh fruits, breads, muffins and perhaps raspberry croissants or cinnamon-raisin strudels. The main course possibilities range from eggs benedict or a variety of quiches to belgian waffles. Homemade cookies and beverages are offered in the afternoon.

(401) 846-0392 or (800) 846-0392. Fax (401) 848-5956. Sixteen rooms and two suites with private baths. May-October: doubles $175 to $255, suites $295 and $355. Rest of year: doubles $145 to $175, suites, $195 and $275. No smoking.

The Inn at Old Beach, 19 Old Beach Road, Newport 02840.

Unusual touches prevail in this romantic, intimate B&B opened in 1989 by Luke and Cyndi Murray. One is the anchor embedded in the third-story turret of the home built as the Anchorage in 1879. Another is the ornate wedding bed with lace draped in the center in the Forget-Me-Not bedroom. How about the palladian arch leading into the jacuzzi bathroom off the Ivy Room, handsome in dark green and burgundy with a faux book case along one wall and an antique woodburning fireplace?

The Murrays offer seven guest rooms with private baths. Cyndi favors "a lot of different styles." They are reflected in the English country decor in the rooms,

Interesting angles dominate exterior of 1879 structure housing The Inn at Old Beach.

named after flowers and full of whimsical touches. In the Rose Room, a pencil-post canopy bed angles from the corner beneath a ceiling beamed in black bamboo. Done up in black and pink, it has a fireplace, a handpainted dresser with hand-carved rose drawer pulls and even the white toilet seat cover is sculpted like a rose. Little antique dresses hang from the walls and rabbits are scattered here and there in the Lily Room. Check out the bishop-sleeve draperies with valances in the first-floor Wisteria Room. Cyndi decorates for the season, especially at Christmas, but the front hall's original stained-glass window representing the four seasons shines at all times.

Ever upgrading, the Murrays added two rooms with separate entrances in the rear carriage house, part of which they converted into quarters for themselves and their young sons. These have TVs and a more contemporary air. The Sunflower, lovely in pale yellow and burgundy, has a queensize wicker sleigh bed, a wicker loveseat and two chairs. A sunflower motif prevails, from the lamps on a nightstand to a handpainted shelf.

Guests gather in a small front parlor or a larger Victorian living room made available when the Murrays moved out back. Here, two plush chairs and a couch face a glass cocktail table resting on four bunnies. The room holds a rabbit fashioned from moss, a tiled fireplace and a copper bar in the corner.

The Murrays serve continental breakfast at four tables in the dining room or outside on the porch or a brick patio overlooking a pleasant back yard with a gazebo and lily pond. It usually involves juice, fruit and pastries like muffins, croissants and coffeecake.

(401) 849-3479 or (888) 303-5033. Fax (401) 847-1236. www.oldbeachinn.com. Seven rooms with private baths. May-October: doubles, $135 to $165. Rest of year: $85 to $125. Three-night minimum weekends in season. Children over 12. No smoking.

The Victorian Ladies, 63 Memorial Blvd., Newport 02840.

All is light and airy in these two Victorian beauties, one behind the other and separated by a lovely brick courtyard with a gazebo, birdbath, wicker furniture and tempered-glass tables, surrounded by colorful flower boxes. Innkeepers Helene and Donald O'Neill gutted and renovated the houses, opening the first of Newport's more comfortable and inviting B&Bs in 1987.

Eleven guest rooms, all with private baths, are decorated in a Victorian theme with a light touch. One of the nicest has a queensize bed and sitting area; it is fresh and feminine with dhurrie rugs and rose carpeting, puffy curtains, down comforters, eyelet ruffles, thick pink and blue towels, potpourri and vials of dried flowers on the doors.

Although Helene had never decorated before, she did a gorgeous job throughout. The small pink and blue parlor has a crystal chandelier and crystal sconces on the mantel; the fireplace was ablaze the chilly October morning we first visited. Balloon curtains adorn the parlor and the adjacent dining room, where an enormous 1740 hutch-sideboard of English pine displays plates and country knickknacks.

The O'Neills added two deluxe suites upstairs above their quarters in the rear caretaker's cottage. Both contain lavender carpeting with which Helene paired a pale yellow color scheme in one suite and red and dark green in the other. One has a wicker loveseat and a corner writing desk. Both have telephones in addition to the television sets common to all rooms.

Don, a contractor, built the gazebo and the courtyard, and his green thumb shows in a profusion of flowers in the gardens. Lately he installed a Japanese koi pond and garden. He's also responsible for the colorful paint job on the main house.

Helene serves up a marvelous breakfast, from all kinds of muffins to grand marnier french toast, eggs benedict, or an egg and spinach casserole. "She loves to cook and keeps expanding her repertoire," says Don. "I'm the dishwasher."

(401) 849-9960. Eleven rooms with private baths. May to early November: doubles, $145 to $185. Rest of year: $95 to $125. Two-night minimum weekends. Children over 10.

Rhode Island House, 77 Rhode Island Ave., Newport 02840.

Fountains and gardens out front hint of some of the treats to come inside this elegant B&B opened by cooking instructor Michael Dupré. Trained at La Varenne in Paris, the former private chef for the Auchincloss family offers culinary weekends in winter and serves breakfasts to remember in a dining room with Chinese Chippendale chairs at tables for four.

"I like to experiment," says Michael of his breakfasts, in something of an understatement. He presents a written menu, which changes daily. The meal starts with a buffet on the sideboard. Fresh orange juice, a medley of fresh fruit, homemade granola, whole-grain cereals, scones, muffins, grapefruit custard, rice pudding and jonnycakes are mere preliminaries to the main event, perhaps a soufflé omelet, grand marnier french toast, fruit crêpes or eggs benedict. These emanate from a well-designed professional kitchen, where Michael caters and gives cooking lessons, including wintertime "culinary escape weekend" classes in which everyone participates and then sits down to partake of a themed, five-course dinner.

Michael, an avid collector, has furnished the house with taste and flair, in both common rooms and bedrooms. The great hall/foyer is notable for yellow faux-marble walls. Off one side is an airy sunroom. In front is a cozy library. On the other side is a living room with a remarkable set of elaborate arched windows.

Upstairs are five guest rooms with queensize beds, chaise lounges and private baths. Four have working fireplaces. The bath in the small Mary Kay Room occupies a sun porch and retains the original pink and gray fixtures. The antique headboard on the bed matches the chest of drawers in the creamy white and floral green front Garden Room, where an ivy motif coordinates curtains, comforters and pillows. The Auchincloss Room is "dainty, lovely and nice – just like her," Michael says of the late Mrs. Auchincloss, his favorite grande dame. It has a full bath with an enormous jacuzzi, as does the rear Hunter Room, masculine in hunter green and complete with lounge chairs on a private balcony overlooking the back yard. All the rooms have large windows and are bright and airy, which is unusual for Victorian houses of the period.

(401) 848-7787. Five rooms with private baths. May-October: doubles, $145 to $225. Rest of year: $95 to $175. Two-night minimum weekends. Children over 12. No smoking.

Hydrangea House, 16 Bellevue Ave., Newport 02840.
Two antiques dealers opened this B&B in 1988 in former office space above a Bellevue Avenue storefront, now transformed into a Victorian townhouse with a colorful, deep purple facade. So you expect it to be decorated to the hilt, and it is. The furnishings came from the antiques shop owned by Dennis Blair, partner in the B&B venture with innkeeper Grant Edmondson. Now immersed in innkeeping, they haven't had time to continue their antiques business but run the Hydrangea House Art Gallery on the main floor of the B&B.

A section of the gallery became an elegant common room in 1994 with a fireplace and stenciled moldings. The rest of the gallery doubles as a breakfast room, providing a colorful backdrop for the morning repasts cooked up by Grant. He offers fresh orange juice, granola, homemade breads and perhaps raspberry pancakes or seasoned scrambled eggs. In summer, the venue moves to a spacious second-story veranda, a 16-by-30-foot deck filled with plants, where afternoon tea is offered. It lends a more residential, verdant feeling than you'd suspect from the building's front.

Four second-floor guest rooms go off a wide second-floor hallway with stippled gold walls painted with a pastry brush to look like marble. Each has a small private bath and is decorated with splashy draperies and wallpapers that match; the fabrics may be repeated on the bed headboards or, in one case, a valance over the shower. The third-floor Linen Garden Room, named for the linen fabric that adorns its walls, contains a mahogany bed, dresser and desk in the Regency style. It adjoins a sundeck formed by the roof for the veranda below.

The premier accommodation is the new Hydrangea Suite on the third floor. Furnished with Edwardian antiques, it has a kingsize canopy bed, a fireplace, a skylit double whirlpool tub encased in Italian marble in the room, a steam bath in the bathroom, and a TV/VCR and stereo system. Another suite was in the works.

(401) 846-4435 or (800) 945-4667. Fax (401) 846-6602. Five rooms and one suite with private baths. May-October: doubles $125 to $165, suite $280. Rest of year: doubles $95 to $125, suite $195. Two-night minimum weekends. No smoking.

Mill Street Inn, 75 Mill St., Newport 02840
Inn purists might find this inn austere, but we rather like its European atmosphere. A 19th-century brick mill restored in 1985 and now listed on the National Register of Historic Places, it has 23 guest suites.

The vast expanses of white walls are fine backdrops for contemporary paintings and posters, modern sofas and chairs, industrial gray carpeting, vases filled with fresh flowers, wet bars and television sets. In a few rooms, original brick walls and beams tone down some of the white. Beds are queensize, fans whir on the ceilings, and baths are gleamingly white-tiled with pedestal sinks.

Eight duplex townhouses on the second floor have living room down and bedroom above, opening onto decks raised just enough so you can sit on the chairs and still see the distant water and the Jamestown bridge.

Beds here have been upgraded to kingsize and built-in natural wood credenzas and desks have been added.

General manager Tom Petot, who came here from the famed Inn at Little Washington in Virginia, has gradually replaced the high-tech look with something more colorful and luxurious. The rooftop deck has been made into a great spot where guests can enjoy continental breakfast on summer mornings, along with a view of the harbor. Tea is available in the afternoon here, or in a charming basement breakfast room. Chocolates are put out at nightly turndown.

(401) 849-95/00 or (800) 392-1316. Fax (401) 848-5131. Twenty-three suites with private baths. Memorial Day through August: doubles, $115 to $325. May and September-October: $95 to $255. Rest of year: $65 to $185.

Castle Hill Inn & Resort, Ocean Drive, Newport 02840.

Gnarled trees on a hillside, reminding us of the olive groves in Portugal, make the approach to this reborn inn a bit mysterious as well as picturesque. When you reach the brown shingled landmark at the crest of the hill, the view of Narragansett Bay and the Atlantic is breathtaking.

The locally owned Newport Harbor Corp. has reassumed control and started fulfilling the oceanside Victorian mansion's potential. After refurbishing the main-floor restaurant (see Dining Spots), the new management upgraded some of the accommodations.

First on the agenda were the six outlying Harbor House units, which were winterized and given kingsize beds, whirlpool baths, televisions, fireplaces and french doors onto private decks overlooking Narragansett Bay. Also refurbished was what the management considered the shabbiest of seven Victorian upstairs guest rooms (all with private baths) and a suite in the main inn.

Enhancement of the rest and the three small rooms sharing baths in the former servant quarters awaited completion of refurbishing in 1998 of the side Swiss-style Chalet, former laboratory of original owner Alexander Agassiz, the Harvard naturalist. Kingsize beds and private baths with whirlpool tubs were in the works for its main-floor suite and three upstairs bedrooms that had shared baths.

No changes were planned for the spartan little efficiency cottages beside the beach that are rented by the week for $800 to $900. A complimentary continental breakfast is served to inn guests.

(401) 849-3800 or (888) 466-1355. Fax (401) 849-3838. Fifteen rooms and two suites with private baths; three rooms with shared bath. Mid-June to mid-September: doubles, $145 to $250 weekends, $125 to $225 midweek; suites, $275 to $325 weekends, $250 to $295 midweek. Spring and fall: doubles, $125 to $250 weekends, $85 to $155 midweek; suites, $175 to $325 weekends, $145 to $185 midweek. January to mid-March: doubles, $95 to $135 weekends, $65 to $95 midweek. Two-night minimum weekends. Children over 12.

Vanderbilt Hall, 41 Mary St., Box 840, Newport 02840.

With surprisingly little fanfare, this deluxe "mansion house hotel" emerged in 1997 to mixed reviews in a former YMCA building in the heart of Newport's Historic Hill district. Partners in the $10 million venture were a management team

that opened the opulent Inn at Perry Cabin in Maryland and Keswick Hall in Virginia and a Providence investor, who was familiar with the property. Built in 1909 by Alfred Vanderbilt to be granted to the town for a YMCA in memory of his father, Cornelius, it had been unoccupied since 1975.

The red-brick hotel's 52 guest accommodations, including 28 on the second and third floors of the restored hall and the rest in a new wing, are divided into five categories, from four "cozy house rooms" to a couple of 700-square-foot suites. Twenty-eight are "state rooms" that turned out not

Vanderbilt Hall is new mansion house hotel.

as large as expected. Ten of the more unusual on the third floor are classified as "executive studies," with spiral staircases leading to skylit lofts with office equipment. All are appointed with period furnishings and rich wallpapers, fabrics and linens in the style we've experienced at Perry Cabin and Keswick. The king and queen bed canopies and treatments are distinctive here; a couple of rooms have kingsize beds in the center draped in fabric. Heated towel warmers and makeup mirrors are among the amenities.

The main floor is a ramble of rooms with fireplaces, polished hardwood floors and showy furniture. Tea and cookies were offered in the main lobby as a young pianist played (somewhat errantly, we must say – or was she simply practicing? – the Friday afternoon we were there). The stately living room has countless overstuffed chairs and a rolling cart laden with fine brandies. A game room and a cheery reading room go off the living room at the far end.

Downstairs are a clubby billiards room, a spa and fitness center and the Y's restored, marble-decked indoor pool with a mural of a clipper ship at one end. Indeed, art is a major theme, from the ever-so-realistic trompe-l'oeil painting on a doorway to murals in the elevator to fine art hung on the corridor walls.

Graceful arches off the lobby lead to a bright and airy garden conservatory full of wicker and tropical plants and an outdoor courtyard with terrace and herb garden. The conservatory-terrace menu that afternoon offered a handful of treats priced from $7 for a ham and cheese sandwich to $21 for chilled tenderloin of beef with potato salad.

The paneled, richly appointed main dining room in hunter green and mauve has the finest table appointments. It's flanked by three smaller private rooms: a wine-tasting room with bottles in racks along the walls, a cigar room with humidors and a club-like "en famille" room for single diners to join a common table.

Executive chef Scott Hoyland offered upscale contemporary international cuisine. Dinner is available prix-fixe ($40) with several choices for each of four courses or $50 for a five-course tasting menu. Fillet of Georges Banks cod with roasted cauliflower and a raisin-caper emulsion, roast breast of capon with pancetta and turnip puree and noisettes of free-range veal with herbed polenta and a tian of fine beans were choices the night we were there. Lunch also is prix-fixe, two courses for $17.50 and three courses for $24.50. The breakfast menu carries prices that would make even a Vanderbilt blanch.

In keeping with the "grand house" experience, Vanderbilt Hall operates on a non-tipping policy. Instead, a "discretionary service charge" of 18 percent is added to the bill.

401) 846-6200 or (888) 826-4255. Fax (401) 846-0701. Forty-five rooms and seven suites with private baths. Rates EP. Memorial Day to mid-October: doubles, $195 to $375; studios and suites, $445 to $695. Early spring and late fall: doubles $145 to $285, studios and suites, $335 to $525. January-March: doubles $95 to $185, studios and suites. $225 to $345. Two-night minimum peak weekends. Children over 12. Smoking restricted.
Prix-fixe, $40 or $50. Breakfast daily, 7:30 to 10. Lunch, noon to 2:30. Dinner, 6 to 9:30.

Dining Spots

The Black Pearl, Bannister's Wharf, Newport.
Our favorite all-around restaurant in Newport – and that of many others, judging from the crowds day and night – is the informal tavern, the fancy Commodore's Room and the deck with umbrella-topped tables that comprise the Black Pearl.

Up to 1,500 meals a day are served in summer, the more remarkable considering it has what the manager calls "the world's smallest kitchen." Waitresses vie with patrons for space in the narrow hall that runs the length of the building; white-hatted chefs and busboys run across the wharf, even in winter, to fetch fresh produce and fish – sometimes champagne – from the refrigerators in an outbuilding.

It's all quite colorful, congenial in spirit and creative in cuisine.

You can sit outside under the Cinzano umbrellas on Bannister's Wharf and watch the world go by while you enjoy some of the best clam chowder ever, thick and dill-laced. You also can enjoy a pearlburger, served with mint salad in pita bread and good fries, plus a variety of other sandwiches, salads and desserts. Inside, the tavern is cozy, dark and noisy, usually with a line of people waiting for seats, and the fare is basically the same as outside, with a few heartier entrées available at lunch or dinner. Desserts are delectable, especially the Black Pearl cheesecake followed by cappuccino laced with kahlua and courvoisier.

Candlelight dinners in the dressy Commodore Room are lovely, the lights of the waterfront twinkling through small paned windows. The beamed sloped ceilings, dark walls and tables set with white linen topped with vases of freesia make an attractive dining room.

Chef Daniel Knerr uses light sauces and stresses vegetables and side dishes in his contemporary fare. Expect entrées like sautéed soft-shell crabs, gray sole meunière, salmon fillet with mustard-dill hollandaise, roast duckling with green peppercorn sauce, rack of lamb and dry-aged T-bone steaks obtained from a New York butcher..

(401) 846-5264. Entrées, $17.50 to $26. Tavern, daily from 11. Dinner in Commodore Room, 6 to 11, jackets required. Closed six weeks in winter.

Framed vaudeville curtain on wall is a decorative focal point at The Place.

The Place, 28 Washington Sq., Newport.

The Place, a wine bar and grill, is the au-courant adjunct of Yesterday's, a pubby Washington Square institution. It's the place for what many consider the most exciting food in Newport.

Yesterday's owners Maria and Richard Korn built the room as a showcase for their chef of sixteen years, Alex Daglis. Alex moved to a separate kitchen, put together a different staff and devised a contemporary American menu with a European flair that, Richard says, "expands and challenges your tastes."

We'd gladly order anything on his changing dinner menu. Folks rave about the changing entrées, from the pork tenderloin with jalapeño-peach salsa to the grilled tenderloin stuffed with goat cheese. But we never got beyond the appetizers, so tempting that we shared and made a meal of five. The shrimp and corn tamales, the exquisite scallops with cranberries and ginger, the gratin of wild mushrooms, and raviolis of smoked chicken and goat cheese were mere warmups for a salad of smoked pheasant with poached pears and hazelnuts. Each was gorgeously presented on black octagonal plates. An apple crêpe with apple sorbet was a crowning finale

To accompany, many wines are served by the glass. You also can get "flights" of wine (four samples of reds or whites for $13) or "schooners" of microbrews (four seven-ounce pilsener glasses ensconced in a handmade wooden schooner for $6).

The long, narrow dining room on two levels is elegant with white linens, brass rails, oil lamps, Victorian lights and sconces. An incredible vaudeville curtain from New Bedford, framed and back lit on one wall, provides quite a conversation piece.

More casual fare is served day and night in Yesterday's, recently rechristened an Ale House to differentiate it from the wine bar and grill.

(401) 847-0116. Entrées, $17.95 to $23.95. Dinner nightly, 5:30 to 10 or 11.

White Horse Tavern, Marlborough and Farewell Streets, Newport.

This imposing burgundy structure is the oldest operating tavern in the country, built as a residence in 1673 and serving as a tavern since 1687. Inside is a warren of small rooms with wide-board floors, exposed beams, small-paned windows and big fireplaces on two floors.

To some, its elegant atmosphere symbolizes Newport. We find the historic charms of the White Horse particularly appealing in the off-season, when the fireplaces are lit. They made a pleasant backdrop for a lunch that included an interesting yogurt-cucumber-walnut soup, baked marinated montrachet cheese, halibut in a brandy-grapefruit sauce and an somewhat bland chicken salad resting in half an avocado.

At night, the tuxedoed staff offers a fancy menu and prices to match. Expect main courses like an oriental sauté of shrimp and scallops, baked Atlantic salmon, grilled duck breast and confit, individual beef wellington or châteaubriand for two. Starters could be baked oysters or peking raviolis. For most, this is special-occasion dining, topped off by such masterful desserts as a three-cherry tart on a chocolate crust in a pool of vanilla cream sauce or triple silk torte on a bed of raspberry melba.

(401) 846-3600. Entrées, $23 to $33. Lunch, daily except Tuesday noon to 3. Dinner nightly, 6 to 10, jackets required. Sunday champagne brunch, noon to 3.

Restaurant Bouchard, 505 Thames St., Newport.

After training in France and sixteen years as executive chef at the famed Le Chateau in New York's Westchester County, Albert J. Bouchard III decided in 1995 it was time to be on his own. He and his wife sought out a small establishment where he could exercise "total artistic control," which turned out to be the former tea room at the new Hammett House Inn.

The restaurant is a beauty in cream and mauve, with well spaced tables dressed in floor-length cloths. Four shelves of demi-tasse cups and saucers, part of his father's collection, add interest.

The food is classic French with contemporary nuances in the style of his former domain. Entrées run from sautéed cod garnished with crab and asparagus to lobster cardinale stuffed with cognac-truffle sauce and gruyère cheese. Dover sole, salmon persille, magret of duck with spicy currant brown sauce, medallions of lamb with herb and garlic red wine sauce, and pheasant with truffle sauce are among the possibilities.

Starters like oyster ravioli with champagne sauce and confit of duck with oriental sauce earn acclaim. So do the chocolate crêpes and individual soufflés for dessert. The Bouchards landscaped a rear brick patio for drinks and hors d'oeuvres in summer, and had an option to buy the five-room B&B operation upstairs.

(401) 846-0123. Entrées, $18.75 to $26. Dinner nightly except Tuesday, 6 to 9:30 or 10. Sunday brunch, 11 to 2.

Castle Hill Inn & Resort, Ocean Drive, Newport.

The new management has upgraded the dining experience here. They renewed the richly paneled lobby, the inner Castle Hill dining room, our favorite Sunset Room with expansive windows jutting out toward the water, and the smaller Agazzi and Newport dining rooms. Only the elegant, romantic bar – long a popular hangout for the in crowd – remained untouched.

Ex-Providence chef Wayne Gibson features Northeastern regional cuisine with indigenous ingredients from Maine to the Chesapeake Bay – "you won't find artichokes here," advised general manager Leonard Panaggio.

Instead find dinner appetizers like crispy sautéed sweetbreads with red onion relish on toast, a sauté of lobster and "found mushrooms" with Sakonnet Vineyards vidal beurre blanc, and seared foie gras with fried green apples on calvados french toast. Main courses could be as basic as flat-iron chicken with buttermilk gravy or as exotic as sautéed lobster with pappardelle, truffle butter and chives. Desserts include a pecan-walnut-pignoli tart or a baked chocolate terrine with a white chocolate grid.

Lunch items range from a house-smoked turkey baguette sandwich to petite grilled angus sirloin with garlic butter. Castle Hill's long-popular Sunday brunch, served inside, is followed by drinks, jazz and a barbecue on the lawn.

(401) 849-3800 or (888) 466-1355. Entrées, $17 to $30. Lunch, Monday-Saturday 11 to 3. Dinner, Monday-Saturday 6 to 9 or 10. Sunday, brunch 11:30 to 3:30, afternoon barbecue with jazz on the lawn 2 to 8.

Asterix & Obelix, 599 Lower Thames St., Newport.
Armed with worldly talents, youthful bravado and Danish good looks, John Bach-Sorenson alighted in 1995 at age 33 in Newport – "it reminded me of home" – and looked for a restaurant site. This scion of a family of Copenhagen restaurateurs found it in a working auto-repair garage.

Three whirlwind months of sweat equity later, he had transformed it into an airy, high-ceilinged and colorful space with a part-open rear kitchen, a remarkable handcrafted bar along one side and mismatched chairs at white-linened tables dressed with votive candles and vases of alstroemeria. Two front garage doors open to the street for a European sidewalk cafe atmosphere in summer.

John calls his fare Mediterranean-Asian. The dinner menu runs the gamut from mussels in tomato broth over linguini to filet mignon à la milanaise. Among the possibilities: tandoori chicken with naan bread, sautéed swordfish in a Thai curry lobster sauce and rack of lamb with a Lebanese couscous. You might start with firecracker spring rolls with peanut dipping sauce or a salad of arugula and celery root with portobello mushroom. Finish with key lime pie or chocolate mousse.

An exotic and quite lengthy lunch menu ranges from burgers to grilled swordfish. Brunch items play a stronger role in summer.

A rack of newspapers for reading and an energetic young staff contribute to a laid-back, brasserie atmosphere. Oh yes, the place is named for John's two favorite French comic-strip characters, known for fighting the bureaucracy, which he had to do to win a wine and beer license.

(401) 841-8833. Entrées, $14 to $25. Open daily, 11 a.m. to 11 p.m. or midnight. Closed Tuesday and Wednesday in winter.

Pronto, 464 Thames St., Newport.
Pricey or prudent? The choice may depend on whether you stick to the menu or go for the specials in this dark and cozy cocoon of Victorian romance that Newporters consider expensive. The problem is that, although the pastas are quite adequate, the dinner specials emanating from the semi-open kitchen are really tempting. Consider the pan-seared red snapper with a ginger-jasmine sauce, grilled ahi tuna with orzo pilaf and mango chutney, adobo barbecued duck breast with

wild rice ravioli, and grilled angus ribeye steak with asparagus, smoky ketchup, fried shallots and stuffed red bliss potatoes.

You could, of course, stick to some wonderful and reasonable pastas like orecchiette with smoked bacon, mushrooms, peas and pecorino romano or farfalle with shiitake mushrooms, calamata olives, spinach, roasted red peppers, pinenuts and chèvre – all the currently "in" things in one superb dish. With a starter of carpaccio of beef with arugula, shaved reggiano and white truffle oil and a dessert of key lime pie, you'll hardly leave hungry.

Soft jazz played as we lunched one winter weekday on a hearty vegetable soup and a tasty wild mushroom crostini. The chicken breast encrusted in pistachios and walnuts, served on a bed of many greens with red and yellow pepper vinaigrette, was so good we asked the chef for the recipe. A masterful apple tart with praline ice cream finished a meal to remember.

Also memorable is the vintage decor: an intimate melange of gilt mirrors, heavy dark draperies, potted palms, crystal chandeliers, pressed-tin walls and ceiling, and oriental rugs on the floors.

(401) 847-5251. Entrées, $19.50 to $28.50. Breakfast daily in summer, 9 to 3. Lunch rest of year, 11:30 to 4. Dinner nightly, 5 to 10 or 11.

The Mooring, Sayer's Wharf, Newport.

The Mooring has enclosed its upstairs deck, increasing the interior dining space by 50 percent. Happily, there's still plenty of outside dining on the downstairs brick patio, brightened by colorful geraniums and hailed by its owners for the best al fresco dining east of the Mississippi.

The Mooring has about the best water location downtown, thanks to its former incarnation as the New York Yacht Club station. The inside is all blue and nautical, with a fireplace ablaze in the off-season.

The lines for meals can get long (a very spicy bloody mary served in a pilsener glass may help). Or you could stop in during off-hours for a gin and tonic, a bowl of prize-winning clam chowder, or coffee and a piece of orange ambrosia pie. Our party of four had to wait only ten minutes for a table on the breezy patio as we eyed the "glacial" salads and hefty sandwiches passing by. We sampled the warm salmon salad, the seafood quiche with coleslaw, steamed mussels with garlic bread and a terrific scallop chowder we deemed even better than the Mooring's award-winning clam chowder.

Dinner choices include seafood paella, oriental fish stew, shrimp and scallops diablo, loin lamb chops and filet mignon with lobster tail.

The **Smokehouse Cafe,** a new seasonal annex, attracts the family trade for its pulled pork sandwiches and "real barbecues."

(401) 846-2260. Entrées, $10.25 to $26. Lunch and dinner daily, from 11:30 or noon. Closed Monday and Tuesday in winter.

La Petite Auberge, 19 Charles St., Newport.

Chef Roger Putier opened Newport's first classic French restaurant with classic French service in 1975 in the historic Stephen Decatur house. Smack against the sidewalk, the severity of the dark green exterior is warmed by roses climbing fences and trellises beside a small outdoor courtyard favored for dining in summer.

The inside seems indeed petite, many people never getting beyond the two intimate and elegant main-floor dining rooms, one with five tables and the other

Classic French cooking of La Petite Auberge emanates from historic Stephen Decatur house.

with four. But up some of the steepest stairs we've climbed are three more dining rooms, available for overflow or private parties. Out back is a little-known tavern, where regulars might linger over brandy and chat with Roger.

Chef Putier's handwritten French menu is so extensive and his specials so numerous that the choice is difficult. His sauces are heavenly – from the escargots with cèpes, a house specialty (the heavily garlicked sauce demanding to be soaked up by the hot and crusty French bread), to our entrées of veal with morels and cream sauce and two tender lamb chops, also with cèpes and an intense brown sauce.

Entrées range from frog's legs provençal to beef wellington. Most dishes are finished at tableside, even the tossed salad with choice of dressings. Vegetables at our visit were green beans and creamy sliced potatoes topped with cheese.

Desserts are classic as well. We enjoyed strawberries romanoff, but regretted that the café filtre listed on the menu was really espresso. The excellent wine list is nicely priced.

(401) 849-6669. Entrées, $19.95 to $25.75. Dinner, Monday-Saturday 6 to 10, courtyard to 11. Sunday 5 to 9.

Scales and Shells, 527 Thames St., Newport.
Plain and exotic seafood items are simply but assertively prepared in what retired sea captain Andy Ackerman bills as Newport's only "only fish" restaurant. The well-spaced tables are covered with black and white checked cloths, the floors are bare and, but for a few models of fish on the walls, the decor is stark. A second-floor addition called **Upscales,** a smaller and quieter room open, is open from May-September.

The food is foremost here. The blackboard menu offers an enormous range of seafood, and you've got to walk up front and face it head-on to take everything in. Monkfish, scallops, shrimp, swordfish, snapper, scrod – you name it, it comes in many variations, wood-grilled, broiled or tossed with pasta. Shrimp fra diavolo and clams fra diavolo are served right in their own steaming-hot pans.

You can pick and choose from a raw bar near the front entrance. There also are appetizers like calamari salad, grilled clam pizza and Sicilian mussels. Desserts include Italian gelatos and tarts.

The short list of Italian and California wines is affordably priced.

(401) 846-3474. Entrées, $10.95 to $19.95. Dinner, Monday-Saturday 5 to 9 or 10, Sunday 4 to 9. No credit cards.

Le Bistro, Bowen's Wharf, Newport.
Creative cuisine and a beamed, elegant second-floor dining room with a glimpse of the harbor commend this contemporary French bistro, lately acquired by the owner of the Wharf Deli below. The convivial third-floor wine bar is done in shades of hunter green with French pencil sketches framed in gold on the walls.

We've enjoyed a fine salade niçoise, an oysters sauté with sundried tomatoes and leeks, a classic bouillabaisse and a grilled pizza with prosciutto and chèvre from a luncheon menu on which everything looks good.

On a winter's night, the atmosphere is enchanting as you gaze from a window table onto the wharf, its historic buildings shining under street lights as passersby stroll from restaurant to restaurant. Hot oysters with golden caviar and a special pheasant pâté were tasty appetizers. Dinner entrées run the gamut from burgundian sausage with hot potato salad burgundian sausages with hot potato salad to lobster sauté with tomato and basil. We liked the veal kidneys in port and mushroom sauce and a hefty plate of roast duck in a red cream sauce with endives.

A dessert tart of green grapes in puff pastry with whipped cream was a fine ending, as was Irish coffee. Creole bread pudding with bourbon sauce is always on the dessert menu, and you might find Ivory Coast cake, a rum-flavored chocolate cake with chocolate chantilly cream.

(401) 849-7778. Entrées, $9.95 to $29.95. Lunch daily, 11:30 to 5. Dinner nightly, 5 to 11. Sunday brunch, 11:30 to 2.

Elizabeth's, 404 Thames St., Newport.
Newport, her adopted hometown, seems to have a love-hate relationship with this interesting restaurant that's the reflection of Elizabeth Burley, a Welsh-born film producer from New York. Smitten by the town (which, on a winter vacation, reminded her of home), she decided to move to Newport to open a tea room "and play restaurant." Her "restaurant" is an idiosyncratic, somewhat theatrical experience. You either like it or you don't, locals advise.

It's "like dining in my home," says Elizabeth, a self-described "achieving woman." Her restaurant was saved by a guardian angel in 1997 after she was evicted from quarters on a nearby wharf. The decor is a cross between Victorian living room and dining room, with antique furnishings, mismatched plates and assorted candles.

Elizabeth's unusual culinary concept is prix-fixe "platters," $49.95 for two and no variations. The first course is always a salad platter and herbed toast, served family style. The main course usually involves a choice of things like bouillabaisse, lobster paella, chicken and sausage parmesan, scallop and shrimp parmesan, shrimp and piselli, barbecue feast and stuffed chicken breast marsala. The platters are huge and rather unusual. Her signature bouillabaisse, for instance, combines scallops, shrimp, mussels and steamers, browned with mozzarella cheese and placed in a loaf of sourdough bread, served with sides of sausage, grilled zucchini, mushrooms, steamed broccoli and stuffed vegetable-cheese-garlic bread.

Elizabeth does the prepping and cooking, although assistants prepare the orders while she works the dining room and sings jazz or opera upon whim or request.

(401) 846-6862. Prix-fixe, $49.95 for two. Lunch, Tuesday-Sunday noon to 3:30. Dinner, Tuesday-Sunday 5 to 10. BYOB.

Diversions

The Mansions. Nowhere else can you see such a concentration of palatial mansions, and nine are open to the public under individual or the collective auspices of the Preservation Society of Newport County. If you can see only one, make it Cornelius Vanderbilt's opulent 72-room **The Breakers,** although romantic **Rosecliff** of "The Great Gatsby" fame and the museum-like **Elms** would be other choices. If you've seen them all, you may find refreshing the Victorian **Kingscote,** which looks lived-in and eminently livable. Schedules and prices vary, but all are open daily at least from May through October; some are open weekends in winter.

Historic Sites. Newport has more than 400 structures dating from the Colonial era. **Touro Synagogue** (1768), the oldest place of Jewish worship in the country, offers fascinating though limited guided tours. **Trinity Church** (1726) at the head of Queen Anne Square has the only remaining central pulpit and the second oldest organ in the country. The **Quaker Meeting House** (1699) is the oldest public building in Newport. **St. Mary's Church** (1848), where Jacqueline Bouvier was married to John F. Kennedy, is the oldest Catholic parish in Rhode Island. The **Redwood Library** (1748) is the nation's oldest library building in continuous service. The **Old Colony House** (1739) is the nation's third oldest capitol building and is still used for public ceremonies. The **Hunter House** (1748) is considered one of the ten finest Colonial homes in America, while the **Wanton-Lyman-Hazard House** (1690) is the oldest house still on its original site. The **Samuel Whitehorne House** (1811) is a Federal showplace. The **Old Stone Mill** may have been built as early as 1100 by the Vikings. The military is represented in the Revolutionary fortification at **Fort Adams State Park** and the **Artillery Company of Newport** museum, as well as the **Naval War College** museum.

Water Sites. Ocean Drive winds along Newport's spectacular rocky shoreline, between Bailey's Beach where the 400 swam (and still do) and Brenton Point State Park, past weathered clapboard estates and contemporary homes. The Cliff Walk is a must for a more intimate look at the crashing surf and the backs of the mansions. Narragansett Bay is visible along the nine-mile trip run by the Old Colony & Newport Railway to Portsmouth. King Park along Wellington Avenue has a sheltered beach with a view of the Newport waterfront; the ocean surf rolls in at Easton's Beach.

Sports Sites. Yachting reigns across the Newport waterfront. The **Museum of Yachting** and the wharves off Thames Street and America's Cup Avenue appeal to sailing interests. In the landmark Newport Casino is the **International Tennis Hall of Fame,** housing the world's largest collection of tennis memorabilia and the Davis Cup Theater, where old tennis films are shown. Outside are thirteen grass courts for tournaments and public use.

Shopping. Innumerable and oft-changing shops line Thames Street, the Brick Market Place, Bannister's and Bowen's Wharves, Spring Street and, uptown, fashionable Bellevue Avenue.

Occupying a corner location at the entrance to Bowen's Wharf is the **Museum Store** of the Preservation Society of Newport County; here you'll find everything from cards to throws, from china dogs to nautical memorabilia. Of special interest along Lower Thames Street are places like **Edna Mae's Millinery Store,** which carries unique hats made exclusively for the owner, and **Tea & Herb Essence,** which offers a little of everything from passionfruit teas to herbal remedies and handmade soaps. At **Thames Glass,** you can watch owner Matthew Buechner and his fellow glass blowers at work in their fascinating studio. For sale in his adjacent shop are some of his creations, including fabulous fish, flowers, vases and ornaments. Potter-in-residence Bridget Butlin shapes wonderful stoneware at **Thames Street Pottery.** We were particularly taken by all the fish-shaped clocks and dinner plates.

Other favorites are the **Spectrum,** representing American artisans and craftsmen, and **Rue de France** for French country decor and accessories. The banners and wind socks are colorful at **Flying Colors Ltd.** Sweet pillows, quilts and prints are among the offerings at **Sarah Elizabeth's.** Toys for all ages are offered at **The Gentle Jungle. Irish Imports** carries gorgeous wool things. **Tropical Gangsters** has ties we wonder if anyone would wear. We like the shells and fishy things at **Operculum. Marblehead Handprints** offers wonderfully colorful jogging suits; actually they are too nice to wear for jogging – make that a sedate stroll instead.

Up on Bellevue Avenue, check out **Cabbages & Kings** for gifts and accessories that appeal to those who still live in Newport's "cottages." **Runcible Spoon,** an outstanding kitchen shop, displays gaily colored pottery amid the lobster platters and garlic salsas. **Cadeaux du Monde** bills itself as a museum where all the exhibits (art and handicrafts) are for sale. Peter and Paul Crowley offer home furnishings and accessories at **On the Avenue,** a store opening off their La Forge Casino restaurant. A rear hallway showcases golf and tennis memorabilia and gifts for the sportsmen.

Extra-Special _____

Green Animals, Cory Lane off Route 114, Portsmouth.

It's worth the drive north of town to see the incredible topiary gardens that live up to their name, Green Animals. Run by the Preservation Society of Newport County, the property displays 80 trees and shrubs sculpted into shapes of a camel, giraffe, lion and elephant at the corners of the original garden, plus a donkey, ostrich, bear, horse and rider, dogs, birds and more. The animals are formed of California privet, while the geometric figures and ornamental designs are of golden and American boxwoods. Willed to the society in 1972 by Alice Brayton, one of its stalwart members, the delightful small country estate sloping toward Narragansett Bay also has espaliered fruit trees, a grape arbor, dahlia and vegetable gardens, and a gift and garden shop where you can buy forms to make your own topiary. Ten rooms in the Brayton House contain original furnishings and Victorian toy collections.

(401) 847-1000. Open late April through October, daily 10 to 5; also weekends in December and Christmas week. Adults, $6.50.

Old Lighthouse Museum is landmark in Stonington.

Watch Hill and Stonington
Vestiges of the 19th Century

They face each other across Little Narragansett Bay from different states, these two venerable communities so different from one another.

Watch Hill, a moneyed seaside resort of the old school and something of a mini-version of Newport, occupies a point at the southwesternmost tip of Rhode Island. "Still echoing with the elegance of past years" (according to the brochure of the Inn at Watch Hill), the resort has enjoyed better days, although the large brown shingled "cottages" remain lived in, the shops fashionable and the atmosphere clubby. It is here that sheltered Long Island Sound gives way to Block Island Sound and the Atlantic, opening up the surf beaches for which Rhode Island's South County is known.

Stonington, on the other hand, is a peninsula cut off from the rest of southeastern Connecticut. Quietly billing itself as "a place apart," it's an historic fishing village and an arts colony. Old houses hug the streets and each other. The Portuguese fishing fleet adds an earthy flavor to an increasingly tony community. Better than any other town along the Connecticut shore, the Borough of Stonington and its rural township of North Stonington let you sense times gone by.

These two choice vestiges of the 19th century are linked – in terms of geography – by the small Rhode Island city of Westerly, through which you drive from one to the other, unless you go by boat.

In recent times, Watch Hill and Stonington have been upstaged by Newport and Mystic and, more recently, by the Mashantucket Pequot Indians' wildly successful Foxwoods Resort Casino complex in nearby Ledyard. They have been bypassed by many of the trappings of tourism, particularly in terms of overnight accommodations. Neither town wants – nor can handle – crowds. Each in its own way clings to its past, and is the better for it.

Inn Spots

Weekapaug Inn, 25 Spring Ave., Weekapaug, R.I. 02891.

Dating to 1889, this grand seaside resort of the old school is venerable, refined and ever-so-Yankee. Located just east of Watch Hill, it has been run like a club all these years by four generations of one family.

The guests tend to be repeat and long-term. Many of the friendly young staff came here as children with their families. Owners Bob and Sydney Buffum, whose winters are spent running the Manasota Beach Club in Englewood, Fla., got to know most of their guests – a trait being continued by their son Jim and his wife, the current innkeepers.

The inn's chatty weekly newsletter, Innsights, details the events of the week ahead, reports the winners of tournaments past, and lists the week's "arrivals."

The rambling, weathered-gray, three-story hotel doesn't look quite as you'd expect, perhaps because its reincarnation is a product of the late 1930s when it was rebuilt after the original was destroyed by a hurricane. But there are few waterfront inn sites to rival it on the southern New England Coast: on its own peninsula, with a saltwater pond in back, the ocean to the front and starboard, and lawns, a yachting basin, tennis courts and a mile and a half of private beach in between.

The 60 guest rooms and suites, all with twin beds (some placed together to form kingsize) and old-fashioned baths, are simple but immaculate. A few small rooms have been joined to make larger rooms, and six are suites with a sitting area and two baths. One guest's room is painted just the way she likes it; after all, she stays the whole season. She and her neighbors occupy the nicest wing, which the staff calls "The Gold Coast."

The common areas are larger and more distinctive than in

Swans in pond entertain guests arriving at Weekapaug Inn.

most similar resorts. On the ground floor, a summery dining room has floor-to-ceiling windows onto the wildflowers outside. Above it on the second floor are the front desk and a lobby full of games and books. Off it is the large and comfy Sea Room, a living room also used for games, bingo and movies. In front is a card room which is all windows on three sides.

Then there's the paneled and beamed Pond Room in which guests pour their own drinks from bottles they have stashed in their cubbyholes, and warm their tootsies by the fire.

A full breakfast is served, and a nicely presented buffet lunch is served every day but Sunday. Lobster is often among the eight or so choices on the dinner menu, which, to the public, is $30 prix-fixe for six courses.

(401) 322-0301. Sixty rooms and suites with private baths. Rates AP. Doubles, $330 to $370. Three-night minimum. Children accepted. No credit cards. Open late-June through Labor Day.

Prix-fixe, $30. Buffet lunch daily, 12:30 to 1:30. Dinner nightly by reservation, 6:30 to 8; jackets required. BYOB.

Shelter Harbor Inn, 10 Wagner Road, Westerly, R.I. 02891.

The Watch Hill area's best choice for both lodging and dining is this expanded farmhouse dating to the early 1800s, set back from Route 1 and off by itself not far from the edge of Quonochontaug Pond.

The original three-story main house contains a fine restaurant (see Dining Spots), a sun porch with a bar, a small library with the original fireplace and nine guest rooms, plus a rooftop deck with a hot tub and a water view that you must see to believe. Suffice to say that it's a scene straight out of California. The barn next door has been renovated with ten more guest rooms, plus a large central living room on the upper level opening onto a spacious redwood deck.

Newest accommodations are in the front Coach House, which has four deluxe rooms with fireplaces, upholstered chairs and telephones.

All rooms have private baths, many have queensize beds, and about half have color TV. As innkeeper Jim Dey continues to upgrade and expand with a contemporary flair, his most select rooms may be those renovated or added upstairs in the main house. Three on the second floor offer fireplaces and decks with a view of Block Island Sound in the distance. One particularly nice room comes a with brick fireplace, brass screen, rose carpet and a terrace.

Out front are two paddle tennis courts and a professionally maintained croquet court that's also used for bocci. In summer, the inn's van transports guests to and from a private beach that Jim calls the finest along the Rhode Island shore.

A full breakfast, including perhaps banana-bread french toast or ginger-blueberry pancakes, is included in the rates and is available to the public.

(401) 322-8883 or (800) 468-8883. Fax (401) 322-7907. Twenty-three rooms with private baths. Summer: doubles $102 to $136. Late spring and early fall: $102 to $136 weekends, $92 to $126 midweek. November-April, $82 to $126 weekends, $72 to $106 midweek. Two-night minimum weekends. Children accepted.

Randall's Ordinary, Route 2, Box 243, North Stonington, Conn. 06359.

A dirt road lined with stone walls leads to this remote ordinary (British definition: a tavern or eating house serving regular meals). It's anything but ordinary, from its hearth-cooked meals (see Dining Spots) to its overnight accommodations in a rural farmhouse dating to 1685 or in a restored barn that, in comparison, seems rather contemporary. Not to mention the fact that the new owner, the Mashantucket Pequot Tribal Nation of Foxwoods casino fame, was adding 30 to 40 more rooms in a barn being moved to the property in 1998.

First the accommodations. Anyone cherishing the past would enjoy the three rooms upstairs in the main house with queensize beds and handloomed coverlets, working fireplaces, air-conditioning and private baths with whirlpool tubs. They are spacious and, except for modern comforts, look much as they would have in the 18th century.

Twelve newer-feeling rooms and suites are located at the rear in a restored 1819 barn, which was dismantled and moved from Richmondville, N.Y. It's attached to a milking shed and a silo, which has been converted into the enormous Silo Suite, complete with domed jacuzzi loft above a circular silo bedroom, a skylit loft living room and a master bedroom with rustic Adirondack queen bed. Designed in what might be called a rustic contemporary style, all the rooms here retain original beams, barn siding and bare floors. They have queensize canopy (and occasionally trundle) beds, private baths with whirlpool tubs and heat lamps, TVs and telephones. Three are loft suites with sitting areas in the lofts; in one, a circular staircase leads up to a platform with a built-in sofa nestled under a skylight.

Bill Foakes, hands-on manager for the owner, warmed up the rooms with stenciling and carpeting and made the lobby area more welcoming.

In 1998, a 1759 barn was being moved to the site. Here Bill envisioned a silo with an elevator, a bigger lobby with shops and a harpist playing on weekends, and guest rooms of various configurations on three floors. Some rooms were to have king beds and some two doubles. Fireplaces, sitting rooms and jacuzzi tubs were planned for some.

Guests are served a continental breakfast of fresh fruit and muffins in the new barn. More substantial breakfasts, including such period treats as maple toast with fried apples and Shaker apple salad, venison sausage, codfish cakes with baked

Hearthside cooking is featured in 1685 farmhouse called Randall's Ordinary.

beans and biscuits, and chipped beef on biscuits are available for an extra charge ($3 to $8.50) and to the public in the main house.

Animals are on view in the barns as the Pequots seek to expand the 28-acre property into a mini-Sturbridge complex to draw the family trade.

(860) 599-4540. Fax (860) 599-3308. About 50 rooms and suites with private baths. Doubles, $95 to $115. Suites, $135 and $195.

Stonecroft, 515 Pumpkin Hill Road, Ledyard 06339.

Ten deluxe guest rooms and a promising dining room are attributes of this new inn created by a much-traveled Chase Manhattan international banker, his counselor wife and his son, a chef. Lyn and Joan Egy opened their inn in phases, first renovating the handsome yellow 1807 Georgian Colonial residence that had stood empty for five years. In 1998 they were finishing off a rear three-story barn with a fieldstone tavern and dining room on the ground floor and six deluxe guest rooms upstairs.

Country French furnishings lend a comfortable, elegant look to the four downstairs common rooms of the main house – from the Snuggery library that once was a "borning" room to a luxurious rear great room with nine-foot-wide fireplace to the fireplaced dining room in which breakfast is served by candlelight on Villeroy & Boch china. To the rear of the great room is the Buttery, smallest of the guest rooms with a beamed ceiling, queen bed, full bath and its own terrace.

An artist-friend of the Egys painted the mural of a hot-air balloon scene along the front staircase to be "cheerful and uplifting, as in the inngoing experience," said Joan. Her counseling background and interest in psychosynthesis as a way of life seem attuned for innkeeping. The stairway leads to two front corner bedrooms, one with queen bed and one with king. All are equipped with top-of-the-line mattresses and bath amenities that include inflatable tub pillows and aromatherapy bath salts for relaxation.

Up a steep rear stairway reached through an unusual cut-out door is the premier Stonecroft Room with kingsize four-poster bed, loveseat and 22-inch-wide chestnut floorboards ("the 24-inch boards were reserved for the king," Joan advised). The walls above the wainscoting bear the young artist's wraparound mural depicting a day in the life of Stonecroft about 1820.

The six new rooms in the barn were designed to be even more luxe. Kingsize beds, working fireplaces and whirlpool tubs are the norm here.

Terrycloth robes, bath sheets rather than towels, Crabtree & Evelyn toiletries and soft music throughout the common areas help Joan provide a serene, therapeutic stay. Guests respond with their thoughts in words and sketches in the room diaries.

Breakfast is a four-course event. Juice and Lynn's baked bananas, pineapples and mangos in a lemon-rum sauce might precede buttermilk waffles with strawberries and whipped cream, herbed scrambled eggs with turkey bacon or a cloud (so-called because it's four inches high) omelet layered with smoked salmon or cheese. The final course might be ginger scones or strawberry-rhubarb crisp.

The Egys host a wine and cheese mixer for weekend guests, and offer wine upon arrival.

With the completion of their barn in spring 1998, they planned to offer weekend dinners to inn guests by reservation. Son Drew, who has been sous chef at the Water Street Café in Stonington, envisioned prix-fixe meals in a new dining room opening onto a fieldstone terrace and a grape arbor pergola.

The six-acre rural property is surrounded by 300 acres of Conservancy woodlands and stone walls.

(860) 572-0771. Fax (860) 572-9161. www.stonecroft.com. Ten rooms with private baths. Memorial Day through October: doubles, $130 to $250. Midweek and off-season: $110 to $200. Two-night minimum weekends. No children. No smoking.

Antiques & Accommodations, 32 Main St., North Stonington, Conn. 06359.

An attractive yellow house, built in 1861 with the gingerbread trim of its era, has been turned into a Victorian B&B by Ann and Thomas Gray. The name is appropriate, for the Grays are antiques dealers who sell many of the furnishings in their showplace home in the center of the quaint hamlet of North Stonington.

Memories of traveling in England inspired the Grays to furnish their home in the Georgian manner with formal antique furniture and accessories. Six rooms and suites, all with private baths and canopied beds, are named after English towns where their favorite B&Bs are, among them Broadway and Tetbury. All have fresh flowers and evening sherry.

Besides a parlor with TV, the main house offers a downstairs bedroom with a working fireplace and a stereo system. Upstairs are another guest room with wing and side chairs, and a bridal room filled with photographs of honeymooners who have stayed there. It connects through the bathroom to a single, making it a family suite on occasion.

Families and couples traveling together also go for suites in the 1820 Garden Cottage, a two-story affair beyond landscaped gardens in back. Rooms here contain some remarkable stenciling, sponge-painted furniture, marbleized dressers and floral curtains, along with the antiques that characterize the rest of the establishment,

Antiques & Accommodations is based in attractive house dating to 1861.

most of them early American and country and all for sale. "You can sleep in a canopy bed and take it home," advises Ann.

The lower-floor suite contains three bedrooms, one with a fireplace, TV, and a wicker loveseat and rockers. It also has a large living room, a complete kitchen and a bathroom off a smaller bedroom. Upstairs is a more self-contained two-bedroom suite, each bedroom with private bath and a gas fireplace, and a common room with a fireplace.

The Grays, who are into cooking, almost enrolled in the Johnson & Wales culinary program but decided to open a B&B instead. They serve a four-course breakfast by candlelight at 8:30 or 9:30 in the formal dining room or on the flower-bedecked front porch. It always includes fresh fruit in an antique crystal bowl, perhaps melon with a yogurt, honey and mint sauce or hot plum applesauce. Main courses could be eggs benedict, quiche, strata or an apple-rum puff garnished with strawberries.

"Breakfast goes on for hours," says Ann. "Last Sunday, the last people got up from the table at 12:30." These hospitable hosts also have been known to dispense wine late into the evening while everyone lingers on the front patio.

Besides food and antiques, another draw here is the exotic gardens, mostly herbs and greens in meticulous quadrants. For 1998 the Grays were adding a cook's garden with edible flowers.

(860) 535-1736 or (800) 554-7829. Fax (860) 535-2613. Three rooms and two suites with private baths. Doubles, $169 to $199. Suites, $229. December-April midweek: doubles $99 to $149; suites $169. No smoking.

House of 1833, 72 North Stonington Road, Mystic 06355.
Carol and Matt Nolan spent two years and toured 36 states to find the perfect place to run a B&B before settling on this pillared, Greek Revival mansion on three hillside acres in Old Mystic. Built by banker Elias Brown in 1833, it must have been the most imposing house in town. Or so it's depicted by an artist in a

stunning mural that wraps around the curving staircase to the second floor and shows the way the hamlet looked at the time.

The Nolans moved East from San Francisco, purchased the private residence and undertook renovations to create a luxurious B&B. They gutted the bathrooms, which had been modernized, and redid them to the period. They installed a Har-Tru tennis court next to the swimming pool, and produced an assistant innkeeper, bright-eyed infant son Alexander, a year after opening in 1994.

Theirs is one gorgeous house, from the formal dining room that dwarfs a long breakfast table set for ten, to the five large guest bedrooms, all with queen beds, fireplaces and private baths, some of them quite spacious and unusual. The front part of the double parlor, outfitted in Greek Revival, opens into a Victorian section notable for a crystal chandelier, a grand piano and an antique pump organ. A heavy door off the front parlor leads to the Peach Room, the former library. Here's a guest room with a mahogany canopy bed draped in peach fabric, a plush settee with matching chair on an oriental rug, a private wicker porch facing the pool, and a bathroom with a walk-in shower through which one passes to get to the double whirlpool tub.

The second floor has three more guest rooms with thick carpeting and fine fabrics. Carol calls one room in the middle the Oak Room because of its furniture rather than its prevailing rose color because "every B&B has a Rose Room." Its bathroom across the hall contains a luxurious soaking tub. The Ivy Room in front, named for its Waverly wallpaper and fabrics, has a bathroom fashioned from two closets, with a vanity in the room.

Although Carol oversaw most of the decorating, she and Matt each picked one room to bear a personal imprint. She did the rear Verandah Room in cream and celadon green with a light pine queen bed enclosed in wispy sheer curtains, a lady slipper clawfoot tub on a platform beside the fireplace and a little wicker balcony. Matt designed the third-floor Cupola Room, masculine in plum and gold with a four-poster bed draped from the ceiling, a potbelly stove and a double whirlpool tub. The stairs rise to a cupola, with two seats from which to observe the sunset.

Breakfast begins with Matt's decorative fresh fruit plates ("he gets very creative," says Carol). His artistry continues as he plays light contemporary music on the grand piano during the main course, perhaps baked custard french toast, eggs florentine in puff pastry with honey-mustard sauce or a specialty quiche with eggs, cottage cheese and corn chips.

Chocolate-chip cookies and tea or lemonade greet guests upon arrival.

(860) 536-6325 or (800) 367-1833. Five rooms with private baths. Memorial Day to mid-November: $155 to $225 weekends, $115 to $165 midweek. Rest of year: $115 to $165 weekends, $95 to $135 midweek. Two-night minimum on weekends. Children accepted midweek. No smoking.

The John York House, 1 Clarks Falls Road, North Stonington 06359.

Antiquity reigns in this 1741 Colonial house, one of the oldest in the area. It was in rough shape when newlyweds Leea and David Grote bought it in 1996. But it had never before been renovated or restored, so much of the interior is original. That includes the king's board around the fireplace in the living room – the extra-wide boards that the King of England ordered returned to the commonwealth during the Revolution, but weren't. Also original are the bedroom door latches, the wide plank floors, the occasional sloping ceilings and a child's handprint in the plaster wall of a rear bedroom. Not to mention the reflector and bake ovens in the keeping room in which the Grotes cooked their first Thanksgiving dinner.

Doing most of the work themselves, with the assistance of family and friends, they have created a warm and welcoming – and authentic – historic experience for B&B guests in four large bedrooms with working fireplaces. That is not to say primitive. The bathrooms are private and are new or updated, the beds are queensize and TVs are available upon request.

The original living room was converted into a bedroom when the Grotes found a prized cherry four-poster bed couldn't be fit up the stairwell. So now they have it angled in the corner, facing the king's board fireplace. Upstairs is a room done in yellow French provincial – "not the way we want it eventually," Leea says, "but our most popular." Another room with its original beams has a hand-carved four-poster bed of solid mahogany from Indonesia. The bed was David's engagement gift to Leea, "so at least we had one bed for the B&B," he says. Otherwise they had no furnishings and everything was picked up at auctions, which accounted for a somewhat spare look to start. But what they have is genuine and serviceable, including a walnut sleigh bed in the rear bedroom and an arm chair with a lamp.

Downstairs is a pleasant library/parlor with one of the structure's seven working fireplaces, where tea is offered in the afternoon. The rear keeping room is centered by a rustic dining table with a top of pine boards from Home Depot and legs of newel posts. "We tell any children to bang the table with their forks to make it antique," quips Leea. The table is the setting for an extravagant breakfast: juice and fresh fruit, banana bread or scones, and perhaps eggs benedict or sourdough waffles. The rich coffee is her own blend.

Outside on eight rural acres are a spring-fed pond full of catfish, meandering trails through white pine forests, stone walls and a ridge with a view. Across the street the treat is a state-stocked trout stream.

(860) 599-3075. Four rooms with private baths. Weekends: doubles, $145 in summer, $110 winter. Midweek: $50. Two-night minimum weekends. Children over 4. No smoking.

Arbor House, 75 Chester Maine Road, North Stonington 06359.

A family farm-stay experience – with a winery accent – is offered by Allen and Michelle Kruger at what's locally known as the Old Maine Farm built by dairy farmer Chester Maine. Now reduced to a few of its original 400 acres, the property contains a four-bedroom B&B in the late Victorian farmhouse, chickens and sheep in the barn and the fledgling Kruger's Old Maine Farm Winery in the state-of-the-art facility once known as Crosswoods Vineyards.

The Krugers, who have two young daughters of their own, know what families like. Youngsters can visit the chickens, goats and horses and fish in the pond while their parents sip chardonnay or pinot gris on the side veranda, cooled by the breeze, in an utterly rural setting.

Inside the house, guests enjoy their own living room and family room with a potbelly stove and a small upstairs sitting room from which they can see the lights of Long Island's North Fork and the flashing Montauk Light at night.

The accommodations are up-to-date and stylish in pastel colors. On the second floor are a bedroom with private bath and a two-room suite also with private bath. The skylit attic has two more bedrooms that open onto a common room with a sofabed and a shared bath. All the beds are queensize, the floors carpeted and the window treatments spiffy. Each room has a TV.

Michelle serves a full farm breakfast: at our visit, a fruit kabob, blueberry coffee cake and belgian waffles with sausage and homefries. "Nobody leaves hungry," she says.

Allen, a Coast Guard Academy engineer by trade, is an amateur winemaker who planned to start limited production of varietals. His first Kruger-Maine Farm product in 1997 was Chester's hard cider. The label, Michelle says, depicts "the spirit of our mentor, the hard-working, cider-drinking American farmer."

(860) 535-4221. Fax (860) 535-8545. www.visitmystic.com/arbor. One room and two suites with private baths. Doubles, $90 to $125. Suites, $120 to $200. Children encouraged. No smoking.

The Inn at Watch Hill, 118 Bay St., Watch Hill, R.I. 02891.

Something of a misnomer, this strip of motel-type units above the shops along Bay Street was totally renovated in 1982 from what had been a ramshackle rooming house with 32 rooms.

You enter from a hilltop parking lot at the rear, register at a tiny shingled house that serves as an office, and descend to one of sixteen spacious rooms, each with contemporary furnishings and sliding doors opening onto small balconies above the street, with the municipal parking lot and harbor beyond.

Rooms have bare wood floors, white brick walls and queensize beds. They're plain but pleasant, all with full baths and TV, and certainly are located in the midst of Watch Hill activity.

Most have a sink, microwave and refrigerator (but no dishes), and prices vary accordingly.

(401) 596-0665. Fax (401) 348-0860. Sixteen rooms with private baths. Rates EP. Summer: doubles, $175 to $200 weekends, $147 to $169 midweek. Off-season: $95 to $108 weekends, $69 to $91 midweek. Closed November-April.

Watch Hill Inn, 38 Bay St., Watch Hill, R.I. 02891.

This large, unassuming white wood structure with waterfront terrace and dining room has been renovated and upgraded under new ownership.

Four guest rooms were eliminated to make space for private baths for all sixteen rooms on the second and third floors. Two of the sixteen rooms are "junior suites," with a sofabed that accommodates an extra guest.

Formerly advertised as rustic and quaint, the inn is now billed as "charming," with rooms "decorated in the warm New England seacoast style." Although only a few in front have water views, all are carpeted and have double or twin beds with frilly spreads and pillows, lacy curtains, telephones, fans, and clawfoot tubs or showers. They look a lot more comfortable than they used to.

That said, we wish we could be more positive about this inn, but it's really more of a hotel-motel – complete with a makeshift front office/porch with about as much personality as a 1950s motel counter. There are no welcoming common rooms. Instead there may be lots of coming and going from the 200-seat Positano Room, a banquet facility that caters to weddings and functions, and the **Deck Bar & Grill.**

A short, casual menu (pizzas, pastas, grilled cajun chicken, lobster in the rough) is featured in the Deck, a mirrored, two-level facility that would be at home in Atlantic City. The outdoor deck is where the action is on a summer day, and the views of the sunset here are spectacular.

A continental breakfast of bottled grapefruit juice, boxed cereal, a bagel and a muffin is served in the bar-lounge.

(401) 348-8912 or (800) 356-9314. Fourteen rooms and two suites with private baths. Summer: doubles $170 weekends, $100 midweek; suites, $190 weekends, $120 midweek. Off-season: doubles $75 to $115 weekends, $50 to $75 midweek; suites, $90 to $135 weekends, $65 to $90 midweek. Two-night minimum weekends. Closed January-March.

Dining Spots

Three Fish, 37 Main St., Westerly, R.I.

Westerly, which has not been known for good restaurants, got a winner in 1997 when this stylish establishment opened along the Pawcatuck River at the edge of downtown.

All is brick and hunter green in the casual River Pub and two main-floor dining rooms with large windows overlooking the water. Full-length windows grace the slightly more formal, skylit upstairs room, where well spaced tables are dressed in beige and green and the artworks and antiques are for sale. European travelers say that at night as you look out on the river and downtown Westerly, the scene reminds them of Venice – minus the gondolas. And who knows? They could be next, given the thought that went into the design of the restored woolen mill and the menu offerings.

The name derives from the Westerly town crest, which depicts three salmon. The seasonal menus feature seafood, with a decidedly contemporary twist. You'll find such dinner dishes as pan-seared Stonington sea scallops with Thai curry sauce, finnan haddie ravioli with diced tomato, and roasted monkfish with portobello mushroom broth. Others on the winter menu included pepper-seared chicken breast over lobster homefries, house-smoked pork loin with sour dried cherry sauce and red flannel hash, and grilled filet mignon with wild mushroom ragoût.

Start with a California lobster roll, crab and seafood cakes with rémoulade sauce or crispy calamari salad with frisée, radicchio and wasabi vinaigrette. The fulltime pastry chef prepares stupendous desserts: among them an apple-cranberry napoleon, banana-milk chocolate pudding pie, a chocolate sampler and a gingerbread ice cream sandwich with poached apricots.

The wine, coffee and cognac lists indicate this is an establishment whose customers savor the best

(401) 348-9700. Entrées, $14 to $19. Lunch, Monday-Friday 11:30 to 2:30. Dinner nightly, 5:30 to 9 or 10:30.

Shelter Harbor Inn, Route 1, 10 Wagner Road, Westerly, R.I.

The restaurant at the Shelter Harbor Inn is one of the area's finest. The original dining room with stone fireplace has bare floors, country curtains and bentwood chairs at white-linened tables topped with hurricane lamps. Beyond is a newer two-level dining room, which has rough wood beams and posts, brick walls and comfortable chairs with curved backs. It overlooks a flagstone terrace with white tables and chairs.

The food is worthy of the setting. At Sunday brunch, we liked two of the day's specials, baked oysters and lamb shanks with rice pilaf. Although the former was smallish and the latter too large, we managed by sharing the two as well as feasting on the "surprise salad" of greens, radicchio, orange slices, cantaloupe, kiwi and strawberries with a creamy poppyseed dressing.

Dining room has views onto rear lawn at Shelter Harbor Inn.

At dinner, be sure to try the Rhode Island johnnycakes with maple butter ($2.95) and, among appetizers, the crab and salmon cakes or the steamed mussels with fennel, cream and pepper toasts. Entrées run from sautéed calves liver to grilled lamb chops and black angus sirloin. Choices are as diverse as grilled tuna with ginger and soy, finnan haddie, seafood capellini and pan-blackened tenderloin.

Desserts include an award-winning sour cream apple pie, chocolate mousse cake, Indian pudding and chocolate-peanut butter torte.

The interesting wine list, honored by Wine Spectator, offers good values.

(401) 322-8883 or (800) 468-8883. Entrées, $13.95 to $21.95. Breakfast daily, 7:30 to 10:30. Lunch, 11:30 to 3. Dinner, 5 to 10.

Water Street Café, 142 Water St., Stonington, Conn.

The dining fortunes in the tony borough of Stonington were elevated a notch by Walter Houlihan, former chef at the UN Plaza Hotel in New York. He and his wife Stephanie, who runs the front of the house, upscaled the small storefront space previously occupied by Kitchen Little and, with the acclaim of locals, took over the Water Street Market across the street.

Their success prompted them to be invited to take over the bankrupt Harborview restaurant operation at 60 Water St. in 1997. They moved their café into the much larger Harborview quarters and thrived, until the building was destroyed by fire six months after their move. They returned to their original quarters and bided their time until the Harborview owner could rebuild, at which time both parties expected Water Street Café to be back, this time in slightly smaller quarters.

The menu and the style – "new world American cuisine" – are the same in either location, according to Walter, who retained some of his key kitchen staff following the fire. The original café is simply far smaller and more basic and intimate.

Typical starters are tuna tartare with ginger ponzu sauce, goat cheese tartlet in a portobello shell, escargot pot pie and poached pear salad with blue cheese and endive. Main courses could be sesame-ginger roasted salmon with sake beurre blanc, five-spice roasted chicken in a bowl of noodles and vegetables, grilled hangar steak with a red wine and blue cheese sauce, and almond-crusted rack of lamb with mint sauce. Desserts vary from warm coconut-walnut wafer cake to crème brûlée to poached pears with ginger ice cream.

Now Walter's fans can get some of his prepared foods, pot pies, breads and salads to take home from the Water Street Market. The blackboard lists wonderful sandwiches in the $4.25 to $5.75 range, and we found a loaf of his boule (peasant bread) to be exceptional.

(860) 535-2122. Entrées, $13.95 to $18.95. Dinner nightly except Tuesday, 5:30 to 9 or 10.

Randall's Ordinary, Route 2, North Stonington, Conn.

Colonial-style food, cooked as of 200 years ago and served by waitresses in period garb. That's the formula for success created by this unusual restaurant's founder and continued by the same kitchen team under the new ownership of the Mashantucket Pequot Indians, best known for their nearby Foxwoods Resort Casino.

Up to 75 dinner patrons gather at 7 o'clock in a small taproom where they pick up a drink, popcorn, crackers and cheese before they tour the farmhouse dating to 1685. Then they watch cooks preparing their meals in antique iron pots and reflector ovens in an immense open hearth in the old keeping room.

Dinner is served prix-fixe in three atmospheric but spartan dining rooms. There's a choice of up to five entrées, perhaps roast capon with wild rice stuffing, roast ribeye beef, roast pork loin, hearth-grilled salmon and Nantucket scallops with scallions and butter. The meal includes soup (often onion or Shaker herb), anadama or spider corn bread, squash or corn pudding, a conserve of red cabbage and apples, and desserts like apple crisp, Thomas Jefferson's bread pudding or pumpkin cake.

Lunch, with similar food but less fanfare, is à la carte and considered great value by local innkeepers. Entrées are $5.95 to $8.50 for the likes of hearth-roasted chicken sandwich with maple mustard, beefsteak pudding, New England cod cakes and broiled lamb chops with boiled red potatoes and cranberry conserve.

Don't worry about that flaming hearthside heat in the summer. The structure is air conditioned.

(860) 599-4540. Prix-fixe, $30. Breakfast daily, 7 to 11. Lunch, noon to 3. Dinner, Sunday-Friday at 7, Saturday at 5 and 7:30.

The Boatyard Cafe, 194 Water St., Stonington, Conn.

This nautical waterside establishment near the viaduct continues to be expanded and upgraded by Deborah Jensen, who had the Pie in the Sky restaurant in New York for eight years and taught at the Culinary School at the New School, and an old school chum, Wendy Whitall. They became reacquainted at their 25th class reunion at St. Margaret's School in Waterbury; this space was available in Wendy's hometown, and "the opportunity was too delicious for me to resist," said Deborah. They quickly expanded with a large waterfront deck and lately enclosed it for all-weather dining. They open the windows to catch summer's breezes and planned a relocated waterfront patio for 1998.

At lunchtime, we were impressed with the chef's sampler, taken at an umbrellaed table on the outdoor deck beside the harbor. The sampler ($7.95) changes with every plate, our waitress advised. This one yielded tastes of chicken-tarragon and tuna salads, a mellow pâté, spinach-mushroom quiche, roast turkey, bacon sprinkled with gorgonzola cheese, potato salad, cucumber salad and marinated red bell peppers. "The sampler is truly whimsical," the chef agreed afterward. "Some people order it every day, so we have to keep it changing." Other lunch possibilities range from a basic burger or a BLT to a platter of flounder or scallops. The smoked salmon sandwich, the oyster po'boy and Soho omelet with goat cheese and sundried tomatoes hold particular appeal.

The dinner menu ranges from Stonington flounder and chicken dijon to lobster sauté or seafood medley over pasta. Start with goat cheese and sundried tomatoes or smoked salmon and capers. Finish with carrot cake or pear-ginger pie.

(860) 535-1381. Entrées, $11.95 to $19.95. Breakfast and lunch, 8 to 2:30. Dinner, 5:30 to 9. Closed Tuesday.

Noah's, 113 Water St., Stonington, Conn.

This hip, casual restaurant in two rooms with a service bar is known locally for refreshingly moderate prices and good, unpretentious food. With a bowl of clam chowder and half a BLT plus a bacon-gouda quiche and a side salad, two of us had a fine lunch for not much more than $10.

The blackboard specials are as appealing as the regular menu: blackfish stew at lunch, regional and ethnic specialties nightly. Such luncheon salads as Greek country or sliced breast of chicken are masterpieces. Except for filet mignon, everything at night is under $12.25, including cod Portuguese and grilled chicken. Save room for the chocolate yogurt cake, bourbon bread pudding or what one customer volunteered was the best dessert he'd ever had: fresh strawberries with Italian cream made from cream cheese, eggs and kirsch.

Owners Dorothy and John Papp have decorated their two-section storefront restaurant colorfully with pastel linen tablecloths and fresh flowers beneath a pressed-tin ceiling. They have a full liquor license, with most wines priced in the teens.

(860) 535-3925. Entrées, $10 to $15. Breakfast, 7 to 11. Lunch, 11:15 to 2:30. Dinner, 6 to 9 or 9:30. Closed Monday.

The Skipper's Dock, 66 Water St., Stonington, Conn.

Originally part of the Harborview restaurant operation, this split up under the new Harborview property ownership. The main restaurant was leased to the Water Street Café until it was destroyed by fire in 1997. The more casual place on the fishing pier, including two interior dining rooms and a smashing outdoor deck right over the water, was leased to John Hewes, owner of the popular Seahorse Tavern in nearby Noank.

Here on a sunny mid-autumn day we sat beside the harbor and reveled in a lunch of Portuguese fishermen's stew and a lobster club sandwich. The bloody mary was huge, the loaf of hot bread so good we asked for seconds, and the main portions ample enough that we couldn't face dessert.

At night, you might start with steamed mussels, garlic shrimp or clams on the half shell. Main courses cover the bases from fish and chips and rotisserie chicken to grilled swordfish, seafood fra diavolo over linguini and roast duck. Key lime pie, chocolate cake and snickers pie are among the desserts.

(860) 535-8544. Entrées, $9.99 to $18.95. Lunch, daily 11:30 to 4. Dinner from 4. Closed November-April.

The Olympia Tea Room, Bay Street, Watch Hill, R.I.

This melange of booths and tables on a checkered black and white floor looks much as it must have when it opened in 1916. Until lately, waitresses in black and white tea-room outfits straight out of Schrafft's scurried around serving iced tea and desserts like Hartford cream pie.

Upscaled recently, the menu offers something for everyone, and everyone always seems to be partaking, inside the atmospheric room with a soda fountain at one end and out front at tables on the sidewalk. You can snack on smoked bluefish pâté, nachos with homemade guacamole, hummus, steamed mussels or pizza, or order a fried fish sandwich or a turkey waldorf plate. More substantial offerings range from fish and chips to mixed seafood over fettuccine alfredo, seafood casserole and filet mignon. Between meals, stop in for Darjeeling teas, cappuccino, a glass of beer or wine, a frappe or an ice-cream sundae.

(401) 348-8211. Entrées, $8.95 to $17.95. Open daily, 8 a.m. to 10 p.m., May-October.

St. Clair Annex, 6-10 Bay St., Watch Hill, R.I.

Another Watch Hill institution – as much a part of summer here as the Flying Horse Carousel – is the ice cream from an enterprise now in its second century. Besides the 28 flavors and frozen yogurts like fresh peach and maple walnut, there are interesting ice cream concoctions: fresh banana shake, cantaloupe royale, hot fudge brownie delight, turtle sundae and peach shortcake.

The ice cream parlor melds into the sandwich shop, where you'll find sandwiches and salad plates in the $3 to $6 range. An old-fashioned popcorn popper beckons passersby out front.

(401) 348-8407. Open daily in summer.

Ocean House Marine Deck, 2 Bluff Ave., Watch Hill, R.I.

The 59-room Ocean House, a seasonal resort hotel dating to 1868, is still operating, rather amazingly. Although the yellow hulk of a hotel has seen better days, there's no more picturesque place around for lunch than on its outdoor patio, hidden from view far below the street and overlooking the open ocean and the surf crashing on the beach.

Assorted faded umbrellas shade the tables as you choose from a variety of sandwiches and salads. The lobster salad roll is billed as "the traditional favorite on a torpedo roll." With a salubrious setting like this, even the most pedestrian food tastes great. At least at lunch.

(401) 348-8161. Lunch daily, noon to 4. Dinner, 6 to 8 or 9. Open late June through Labor Day.

Diversions

Watch Hill and Stonington are small, choice and relatively private places off the beaten path. The crowds head east to Rhode Island's South County beaches, particularly the vast Misquamicut State Beach where the surf thunders in, or west to Mystic, where Mystic Seaport and the Mystic Marinelife Aquarium combine with the Foxwoods Resort Casino and the new Mohegan Sun Casino to make the area Connecticut's busiest tourist destination.

Stonington Borough. We can't imagine anyone not falling for the historic charms of this once-thriving seaport, founded in 1649 and not all that changed since the 19th century. The last commercial fishing fleet in Connecticut is manned by the resident Portuguese, who stage a colorful Blessing of the Fleet ceremony every mid-July. To savor fully the flavor, walk the two narrow streets through the borough.

Monuments and relics testify to the past at Cannon Square in Stonington.

They and their cross streets are lined with historic homes, many of them marked by the Stonington Historical Society and some once occupied by the likes of John Updike, Eve Merriam, Peter Benchley and L. Patrick Gray. The house where artist James McNeill Whistler painted Whistler's Mother later was home for Stephen Vincent Benet. Edgar Allen Poe and Capt. Nathaniel Brown, who discovered Antarctica, also lived here.

Palmer House, 40 Palmer St., Stonington. The majestic, sixteen-room Victorian mansion that Capt. Nathaniel Palmer and his seafaring brother Alexander built in 1852 was saved by the historical society from demolition in 1994 and opened to the public as a fine example of a prosperous sea captain's home. Several rooms contain memorabilia from the brothers' adventures, family portraits and local artifacts. The piano in the parlor is the only original piece remaining in the house, but rooms are furnished with period pieces. The craftsmanship completed by local shipwrights is evident in the sweeping staircases and built-in cabinetry. The cupola yields a view of the surrounding countryside and sea.

(860) 535-8445. Open daily except Tuesday, 10 to 4, May-October. Adults $4.

Old Lighthouse Museum, 7 Water St., Stonington.
The first lighthouse in Connecticut is perched on a rise above Stonington Point, where the villagers turned back the British. Opened by the historical society in 1927, this museum is a tiny storehouse of Stonington memorabilia. Whaling and fishing gear, portraits of the town's founding fathers, a bench dating back to 1674, articles from the Orient trade and an exquisite dollhouse are included in the six small rooms. You can climb up circular iron stairs of the tower to obtain a view in all directions.

(860) 535-1440. Open Tuesday-Sunday 10 to 5, May-October; by appointment rest of year. Adults $4.

Watch Hill. This staid, storied resort community protects its privacy (parking is limited and prices are high), but things get busy on summer weekends. The lineups of low, weathered shingled shops and storefronts here could only be in Watch Hill. Youngsters line up at the entrance to the Watch Hill Beach for $1 rides on the **Flying Horse Carousel** (1867), thought to be the oldest merry-go-round in the country. The horses on this National Historic Landmark, suspended from a center frame, swing out when in motion. Each horse is hand-carved from a single piece of wood and they bear real tails and manes, leather saddles and agate eyes.

Napatree Point. If you can find a place to park, hike out to Napatree Point, a privately owned conservation area extending half a mile beyond the Watch Hill parking lot. The walk on the sandy spit to the ruins of a Spanish-American War fort at the far end opposite Stonington can take an hour or a day, depending on one's beachcombing and bird-watching interests.

Shopping. On your way into or out of Stonington on Route 1A, stop at **Comina,** which offers exceedingly colorful international furnishings, gifts and accessories. Along Water Street in Stonington are several special shops, with more opening every year. Fine antiques are the specialty at such places as **Grand & Water** and **Boat House Antiques.** At the **Hungry Palette,** silk-screened and handprinted fabrics can be purchased by the yard or already made up into long skirts, wrap skirts, sundresses and colorful accessories like Bermuda bags. **Oddities** has everything from stuffed animals and cards to ceramics and straw hats. **Findings** offers fine home furnishings and accessories. We enjoyed the lifelike little beach people sunning on sand, the brass fish and the flying sculptures at **Anguilla Gallery.**

In Watch Hill, **Coppola's of Watch Hill, R.W. Richins** and **Wilson's of Wickford** specialize in clothing and resort wear. The Feather Bed & Breakfast birdhouse appealed among the gifty things at the **Country Store of Watch Hill.** Unique American crafts and gifts are featured at **Puffins,** where we admired the handcrafted jewelry, aluminum sandcast pieces and pottery birdhouses from Tennessee. Sporting goods, outerwear and unusual decorator items for boat or cottage are stocked at one of the area's more unusual stores, **Watch Hill Fly Fishing Co.,** opened by Jack and Marcia Felber of the Olympia Tea Room.

Between expeditions, stop in Stonington at **Stonington Vineyards,** Taugwonk Road, where Nick and Happy Smith run a growing winery operation. Among their premium vinifera wines are a fine chardonnay and an estate-bottled pinot noir. The less expensive Seaport white and blush wines reflect the winery's proximity to the historic Stonington and Mystic Seaport areas.

Extra-Special _____

Quimper Faience, 141 Water St., Stonington.

Bet you didn't know that the world headquarters of the famed handpainted French dinnerware and decorative pottery is located along the main street of downtown Stonington. It seems that Paul and Sarah Janssens, Stonington residents who had imported and distributed the ware through their Quimper retail store here since 1979, helped save the 300-year-old Quimper factory from bankruptcy in 1984. They and several investors purchased the faiencerie (the second oldest company in France), continued its operations and turned their storefront and an upstairs apartment here into the retail and mail-order headquarters. This is the flagship store, and Quimper/Stonington now has three company stores (one in Paris) and wholesales to others. Quimperware, best known for its colorful Breton peasant motifs and always handpainted and signed by the artist, is still produced at the factory in Brittany. Fifty-eight artists paint the patterns on the pieces, no two of which are the same.

(860) 535-1712. Open Monday-Saturday 10 to 5.

Northeast Connecticut
The Quiet, Gilded Corner

Few people realize that Connecticut's oft-overlooked "Quiet Corner" once was a fashionable summer resort of the Lenox-Newport ilk.

Starting in the late 1870s, it was known as "Newport without the water." During its gilded days, wealthy New Yorkers and Bostonians summered in Pomfret and Woodstock on vast country estates with dreamlike names like Gwyn Careg, Courtlands and Glen Elsinore.

John Addison Porter, a Hartford newspaper editor and Pomfret resident, wrote in 1896 that his town was "one of the natural garden spots of the state – the ideal peaceful New England landscape. It bears on its face the unmistakable signs of being the abode of people of culture. No town of its size in Connecticut represents more wealth, but this is used unostentatiously and is in perfectly good taste."

The Depression and post-war priorities took their toll on the wealth, as did the move to the South of the textile mills upon which the local economy had been based. "The quiet corner was the neglected corner," says Nini Davis, regional tourism director, whose husband is the area's state senator. "When the mills closed, many people here gave up."

But not for long. Area officials and the National Park Service turned their efforts toward forming a National Heritage Corridor to preserve a region called "the last green valley" in the crowded megalopolis between Boston and Washington, D.C. President Clinton signed the bill so designating most of the area in 1994.

Meanwhile, sleepy Putnam, once the area's leading mill town, rapidly turned into the antiques center of New England. The change stimulated both the locale's economy and its psyche.

When Herb and Terry Kinsman moved back East from California to open the area's first B&B, "everybody thought we were crazy." Now there are more than 30 B&Bs and two inns.

Adds restaurateur Jimmie Booth, who moved long ago from New York to her husband's family farm and launched the renowned Golden Lamb Buttery: "Everything's changing out here. We're not the quiet corner any more. The developers are building in all the woods around."

Developers indeed are at work, but the change everyone talks about locally is relative. Northeast Connecticut remains the state's least-developed area. "The Street" in Pomfret carries much of the grace of a century ago. A low-key sophistication is lent by Pomfret, the Rectory, Hyde and Marianapolis

Prudence Crandall House in Canterbury is among historic structures in Northeast Corner.

preparatory schools and the headquarters of firms like Crabtree & Evelyn, one of the area's largest employers.

The visitor has a rare opportunity to share in the good life here. You can stay in restored inns that once were the homes of the rich and famous. You can have bed and breakfast with the aristocracy in houses filled with family treasures. Your host may be an artist, a furniture maker, a pediatrician, a music lover, a marketing consultant or a carpenter. In no other area have we found the innkeepers and their facilities as a group so understated and so fascinating.

You'll feel as if you're a character in a Currier & Ives etching in this area of rambling stone walls, rolling hills and fertile farmlands, languishing mill towns and tranquil villages. But get yourself going. As the antiquers have discovered, the Quiet Corner won't be quiet forever.

Inn Spots

Lord Thompson Manor, Route 200, Box 428, Thompson 06277.

A half-mile-long driveway leads to a classic English manor house set on 42 secluded acres, built as a summer home in 1917 by the owner of Gladding's, the late Providence department store. The 30-room manor had been a novitiate for 55 years when it was converted by Jackie Silverston into an elegant B&B and conference center, starting in 1989 with two guest rooms.

The main-floor common rooms are grand, as are some of the suites. 'Tis a pity that some of the bedrooms are the size of servants' quarters and play second fiddle to the rest of the house, whose grandeur makes it a favorite site for weddings and business meetings.

French doors lead from room to room, and you almost can see from one end of the main floor to the other. The 33-by-20-foot drawing room is richly paneled in gumwood, with moldings worthy of its Georgian heritage and a plush seating area facing a fireplace framed in imported marble with a hearth of ceramic tiles. Running the length of the rear of the house is a new conservatory formed by enclosing the outdoor patio. At one end of the house is an enormous sun porch with tile floors, outfitted in wicker and chintz in peach colors, perfect for whiling away the hours.

Beyond a living room and a dining room at the other end of the house is a breakfast porch with two walls of french doors to the outside. It's a dramatic space that Jackie decorates with flair. At our latest visit it was quite a sight in purple and gold. The walls had been painted aubergine and strung with grapevines, the tables were set with gold fabric cloths over aubergine skirting, ivory napkins stood tall in the purple stemware, and some of the gold chairs held purple pillows. Here's where guests are served a full breakfast, from fresh orange juice to house-ground coffee. Expect Finnish or cinnamon-apple pancakes or waffles. Past a couple of butler's pantries and anterooms is a cook's dream kitchen, thoroughly up-to-date and brightened with scores of colorful ceramic dishes shaped like vegetables and fruits. Guests have kitchen privileges here and help themselves to juice, sodas, homemade cookies and such. Jackie has been known to cook popcorn twice a day for snacks and to serve with drinks from a bar in the manorial living room.

Downstairs is a billiards room with a sitting area in front of a large fireplace and a big-screen TV. Jackie says it's an indestructible party room for the groups that frequent the place.

Upstairs are four rooms and suites with fireplaces and a wing with two small bedrooms sharing a bath. The suites, most with a horse and hunt theme, are in keeping with the downstairs. Top of the line is the Thoroughbred 1, the master suite in deep burgundy and hunter green with a queensize poster bed, fireplace, desk and a wing chair. Hunting paraphernalia, boots and saddles are placed here and there. Its bathroom includes the original full-body needle shower favored by arthritis sufferers. The suite connects with a second bedroom that shares the bath.

In striking contrast is the Morgan Suite, light and feminine in ivory and lace, with poofed curtains, Federal cherry furniture and a bathroom stocked with fine shampoos and lotions. (An alcove in the hallway displays every possible toiletry that guests might have forgotten – an example of the unassuming way that the inn plays the perfect host.) Two other rooms with queen beds and fireplaces are large enough to be called suites. Two rooms off the institutional hallway are pleasantly decorated but small and monkish in comparison. They have double beds and share a bath. The Arabian Room on the front of the main floor contains a double bed and a half-bath.

Innkeeper Jackie, whose decorating talents and fondness for Ralph Lauren wallpapers and fabrics are manifest throughout, makes a personable and lively hostess. This is one manor house without pretension and with a quirky, laid-back air that can spell good value. In 1997, Jackie and her husband Andrew acquired the nearby Vernon Stiles Inn and transformed its historic restaurant facing the Thompson common into the White Horse Inn at Vernon Stiles (see Dining Spots).

(860) 923-3886. Fax (860) 923-9310. One room with private half bath, two rooms with shared bath; three suites with private bath, one suite with shared bath. Doubles, $90 to $100. Suites, $110 to $160.

The Inn at Woodstock Hill, 94 Plaine Hill Road, Box 98, Woodstock 06267.
The 1816 Christopher Wren-style home of Henry Bowen, whose landmark shocking-pink summer cottage is up the road, was willed in 1981 to the University of Connecticut, which had no use for it. Enter a group of investors who restored the house with great taste and opened in 1987 with more ambition than the locale

Enclosed conservatory along back of Lord Thompson Manor looks onto broad lawn.

could immediately afford. The inn has stabilized nicely since the arrival in 1989 of innkeeper Sheila Becks and her partner, chef Richard Naumann.

The atmosphere of an English manor house pervades the inn's spacious and attractive common rooms, restaurant and 22 guest rooms. The main living room, a library, the morning/TV room and a small dining room in particular are a kaleidoscope of chintz fabrics, fine paintings, plush oriental rugs and tiled fireplaces.

More Waverly floral chintz accents the prevailing peach, pink and blue color scheme in the guest rooms. All are sleek and comfortable with reproduction antiques and wicker furniture, chairs and loveseats, thick carpeting and modern baths, some with double marble sinks. Television, telephones and air-conditioning come with. Six rooms have fireplaces and four-poster beds. Quiet rooms with rear views look across the valley. One room has a beamed cathedral ceiling, and a large cedar closet off another room on the third floor has been converted into a bathroom.

An outside entrance leads to a cozy lounge, where colorful wine labels under glass top the bar. Here in a wing connected to a barn are two dining rooms that form the heart of the inn's elegant restaurant (see Dining Spots).

Back in the main inn, a continental-plus breakfast is served in the morning room or the dining room. An assortment of fresh fruits, juices and cereals accompany muffins, croissants, coffeecake, and sometimes brioches and sticky buns. Warm mulled cider or lemonade and a decanter of sherry await arriving guests in the afternoon.

(860) 928-0528. Fax (860) 928-3236. Twenty-two rooms with private baths. Doubles, $85 to $150 May-October, $75 to $140 rest of year.

Friendship Valley, Route 169, Box 845, Brooklyn 06234.

Classical music soothes and Southern hospitality is dispensed at this delightful B&B. Prudence Crandall, the Canterbury educator who was hounded out of town for teaching young women of color in her academy in the 1830s, named this 18th-century, Georgian-style country house when it was occupied by one of her

B&B in 18th-century house lives up to its historic name, Friendship Valley.

benefactors. Abolitionist William Lloyd Garrison, who was married here in the 1830s, wrote of Friendship Valley: "this place that I love more than anywhere."

The name fits, for Charles and Beverly Yates, run a very friendly B&B in a bucolic valley of twelve wooded acres and wetlands near what passes for the center of tiny Brooklyn. Recently transplanted Texans, Charles commutes weekdays to Boston to continue his architectural practice. Beverly, a former high school counselor in Houston, is the perfect hostess. She quickly became head of the area's B&B association and extols the area's virtues to one and all.

The couple took over what had been a two-room B&B, added more bathrooms and now offer five guest rooms and a suite. Rooms are named for the five previous owners of the house, which is listed on the National Register. The prime accommodation is the new Prince Suite, transformed from a wood shed at the rear of the main floor, with a beamed and vaulted ceiling, queen mahogany rice poster bed, a jacuzzi tub and a private entrance. Upstairs in the main house are four more bedrooms, one combinable into a two-bedroom suite, plus an attic suite. All have private baths and three have working fireplaces. They convey a decidedly historic but comfortable air, from the step-up queensize four-poster in the Benson Room to the antique twin beds from France in the Wendel. Annabelle's Attic, named for the resident calico cat, includes two double beds, two twin beds and a sitting room with TV beneath cathedral ceilings.

The entire house is handsomely appointed with period furnishings, prized antiques and well-worn oriental rugs. Guests enjoy two small front parlors, one a library and the other a fireplaced living room with cable TV hidden in a cabinet. Beyond are a formal dining room (in which the fireplace mantel came from the home of the founder of Cleveland, Ohio) and a lovely sunporch overlooking the gardens. These are the settings for a breakfast of juice, fruit plate and main course, served with fine china, silver and linens. Quiche, pancakes and baked french toast could be the fare. "I cook," advises Beverly, "but Rusty says he's the juice and fruit chef."

She also offers tea and dessert in the afternoon or evening.

(860) 779-9696. Fax (860) 779-9844. Four rooms and two suites with private baths. Doubles, $85 to $125. Family suite, $195. Children over seven. No smoking.

Taylor's Corner Bed & Breakfast, 880 Route 171, Woodstock 06281.

The inside of this restored 18th-century center-chimney Colonial is ever so historic, but the five acres outside are positively awesome. Walk out the rear of what once was the front of the house and you're greeted by stunning perennial gardens – more plots that one person can take care of – and even a pet cow.

"I never gardened in my life," says Peggy Tracy, innkeeper with her husband Doug, both Northeast Corner natives. She learned fast after the couple purchased the residence in 1996 and converted it into a B&B. "These perennials popped out of the ground that first spring" and she and a helper have been gardening ever since. The gardens were started by a former owner who ran an herbary. The Tracys added Jessie Brown, a Scotch Highland cow, for guests to pet as she grazes in the back yard, and were looking to get her "a friend."

Inside the house, which is listed on the National Register of Historic Places, are eight working fireplaces and two beehive ovens. One of the latter is the first sight guests see as they enter the front keeping room. Beyond is a formal parlor with TV; on a wall the Tracys have framed a mysterious confession found hidden between bricks in the chimney and written by someone seeking forgiveness in 1795. Across the hall is a large, fireplaced dining room with hooked rugs on the floors and Hitchcock chairs at a table for six. Here Peggy serves breakfast on her collection of fine Danish porcelain – continental on weekdays, supplemented by entrées like oven omelets, french toast or Finnish pancakes on weekends.

Up creaky stairs are two spacious rear bedrooms with queensize beds angled from the corners. A front bedroom has twin beds, and all have private baths. Stuffed animals are on each bed, and colorful comforters, antique chairs, bedside candies and fresh flowers are the norm. Downstairs off the keeping room is a single bedroom, the original borning room, with a twin bed.

(860) 974-0490. Fax (860) 974-0498. Three rooms with private baths. Doubles, $80.

Cobbscroft, 349 Pomfret St., Pomfret 06258.

This rambling white house almost up against the road is home to Janet and Tom McCobb as well as a gallery for the works of watercolorist Tom, who has a studio in the rear barn, and those of artist-friends.

Guests are received in a library with a gorgeous needlepoint rug and deep shelves full of books and a TV. Beyond is a large gallery/living room hung with a variety of art, all for sale and all very enticing. Off the library are a double and single guest room joined by a bathroom, rented as a family suite. Upstairs are three more guest rooms with baths. One with twin beds has lacy white spreads and curtains, a sofa and knickknacks including little dolls. A front corner room has charming stenciling done by Janet, a four-poster bed, chaise lounge and oriental rug. Its bathroom has gold-plated fixtures and an oval, clawfoot tub like none we've seen; Janet said it's a birthday tub and was able to hold her four granddaughters at once. Over the living room is what the McCobbs call the bridal suite, a wondrous affair with windows on three sides, a working fireplace, a loveseat, dressing table and a bed covered in frilly white linens.

Breakfast is served at a long table in the dining room, full of country touches like a collection of lambs. The table is flanked by Queen Anne chairs and topped by two wooden chickens and eggs as a centerpiece. In her extra B&B kitchen (away from the family quarters), Janet prepares hot apple crisp or melon in season, croissants, scrambled eggs, quiche or strata. In the afternoon, she serves tea with cinnamon toast or fruit bread and offers a drink. Guests can help themselves to brandy in the living room after dinner.

(860) 928-5560. Three rooms with private baths and a two-room family suite. Doubles, $65. Suite, $80. Children over 12. No smoking.

Grosvenor Place, 321 Deerfield Road (Route 97), Pomfret 06258.

When Garfield W. Danenhower III completed his Army service as a physician in Thailand in 1973, he and his wife Sylvia, Southerners both, bought this lovely beige Colonial 1720 house sight unseen. It was built by her great-grandmother ten times removed and had been in the family ever since, so the Danenhowers knew something of what they were getting.

Their B&B guests know they are in for great comfort and Southern hospitality. A focal point of this elegant home is the spacious dining room filled with silver, portraits, chairs with needlepoint seats and oriental rugs. The living room is done with flair in reds and off-whites and a collection of family pictures. Indian shutters in the windows protect a study full of books, a piano and a jigsaw puzzle in progress.

A large guest room with private bath and fireplace occupies a front corner of the first floor. It has a half-canopy bed with crewel draperies, a sofa, plants and a deep-hued oriental rug atop a wide-plank floor.

Up some very steep stairs is another large guest room with a four-poster bed that belonged to Sylvia's grandmother in Boston. This room is unusually warm in peach tones with a taupe rug and period antiques. An adjacent single room ("good for bringing a child to school," says Sylvia) is between it and the modern bathroom.

Sylvia offers her guests tea or sherry upon arrival. She and her pediatrician-husband Woody (for Woodruff, his middle name) serve a breakfast of homemade muffins and rolls, supplemented on weekends by french toast from a recipe they acquired in Malaysia. They grind their own coffee beans and set out exotic teas.

(860) 928-4633. Three bedrooms, two with private baths. Doubles, $75.

The Felshaw Tavern, Five Mile River Road, Putnam Heights 06260.

"Welcome to Yesterday," proclaims the brochure for this inviting B&B in a pre-Revolutionary tavern dating to 1742. Terry and Herb Kinsman, he a homesick Yankee, moved into the house from California, restored it to the hilt and opened it in 1982 as the area's first B&B.

Herb, a woodworker of note, did most of the restoration himself. The results are evident everywhere, but nowhere more so than in the keeping room/library, where the remarkable ceilings are made of stained pine, and in the adjacent living room full of oriental rugs. He also put together the grandfather clock and the lowboy of black walnut in the formal dining room, and most recently built an addition off the library.

Upstairs past colorful birds in stained glass on the landing are two large guest rooms, each with fireplace and bath. One with a queensize Mississippi rice-carved four-poster is full of fine French furniture, including a Louis XIV chest and a Napoleonic chair. The other has a queensize four-poster, an Empire sofa, a 1790 bowfront dresser and a remarkable Connecticut highboy that Herb built of cherry. Guests can watch TV in an upstairs sitting room paneled in wood.

In a sunny, cathedral-ceilinged breakfast room that Herb built from scratch, he serves a full meal of scrambled eggs with sausage and bran or corn muffins. He offers tea or sherry in the afternoon. Guests may lounge on the European-looking little terrace or in a four-season garden with a fountain out back.

(860) 928-3467. Two rooms with private baths. Doubles, $80. No smoking. No credit cards.

Clark Cottage at Wintergreen, 354 Pomfret St., Pomfret 06258.

A substantial gray Victorian house at the end of a long driveway turns out to have been built for the superintendent of the old Clark estate. It's now a B&B, and innkeeper Doris Geary points out other structures still on the vast property, which affords a view across the valley.

Doris and her husband Stan, business manager at the Rectory School, offer four light and airy guest rooms (two with private baths and the other two adjoining as a family suite). Most coveted is the front corner room, which has striking green painted Italian furniture, including an incredible bedstead with an oval mirror in the headboard. The furnishings, nicely set off against peach walls, can be admired from a mushroom velvet loveseat. Plush beige carpeting enhances a rear room with a sofa, twin beds and a porch for taking in the valley view. It forms a suite with an adjoining room with a brass bed and a wood stove in the fireplace. A fourth room has a queensize bed with a quilted headboard and stuffed dolls amid the pillows.

On the main floor is a colorful entry hall with window seats and turn-of-the-century spool banisters framing the stairway. Guests enjoy a formal, fireplaced parlor and a dining room with another fireplace and a long polished table.

The Gearys serve a full breakfast of fresh fruit and a main dish like pancakes or french toast stuffed with cream cheese and nuts. "We ask our guests the night before what they'd like and cater to their wishes," says Doris, reflecting a theme that prevails at many of the area's B&Bs. She also provides tea or a drink upon arrival.

(860) 928-5741. Two rooms with private bath and a two-room family suite. Doubles, $65 to $80.

Chickadee Cottage, 375 Wright's Crossing Road, Box 110, Pomfret Center 06259.

The chickadees that descend on the bird feeders in the gardens outside this rural house inspired the name for this B&B. Transferred here from the Philadelphia area, Sandy and Tom Spackman got the idea for a B&B from their neighbors, who operated the adjacent Golden Hill Farm for a spell.

The Spackmans share their stylish house, which is more than a cottage, with guests in two bedrooms furnished with family heirlooms and antiques. One on the main floor is a hideaway with private bath, canopied double four-poster bed, a sofabed, and a wall of books in built-in shelves. The other is upstairs and larger with windows on three sides, a queensize bed, antique Italian marble-top end tables and a full bathroom shared with the owners.

The open country kitchen is the heart of the house. Guests often look no farther than the tall stools surrounding the circular island for breakfast, a hearty continental-plus affair of fresh fruit, cereals and baked goods, served in the warm glow of a fire in the family-room hearth. That is, when the meal isn't taken at the big farm table in the solarium sunporch, with its terra cotta tiled floor and plants spilling from shelves. Or when it's served at a wrought-iron table on the extra-deep screened porch open to the breeze on three sides. Or when it's served outside on the terrace beside the rear gardens.

"People always are amazed how peaceful this setting is," says Sandy. And why not? The house is set well back from the road on ten rural acres, bordered on either side by large estates and across the road from a little-known, 600-acre Audubon Society nature sanctuary with walking and nature trails.

Besides the outdoors, guests enjoy the porch, the family room with TV and a comfortable living room. They could even sit at the English hunt table in the dining room. But, with so many other places to eat in this peaceful yet convivial setting, the question of dining there never seems to arise.

(860) 963-0587. Fax (860) 963-0594. One room with private bath and one room with shared bath. Doubles, $80 to $95 in summer, $70 to $85 in winter. Children over 4. No smoking. No credit cards.

Dining Spots

The Golden Lamb Buttery, Hillandale Farm, Bush Hill Road, Brooklyn.

For more years than we care to remember, Golden Lamb Buttery has been our most cherished restaurant. We love it for summer lunches, when the surrounding fields and hills look like a Constable painting. We love it for summer evenings, when we have cocktails on a hay wagon driven by a tractor through the fields and listen to Susan Smith Lamb's pure voice as she sings and plays guitar. We love the picnic suppers followed by, perhaps, dancing to an eighteen-piece band playing songs from the '40s and '50s, or maybe a musical done by a local theater company on occasional Wednesday and Thursday nights in summer. And we love fall lunches and dinners ensconced beside the glowing fireplace. We especially love the Elizabethan madrigal dinners served in December, when a group of renaissance singers carol through the rooms and pork tenderloin is a festive main course. And everyone

Pond is on view from Golden Lamb Buttery.

loves Jimmie and Bob Booth, the remarkable owners of the farm on which the restaurant stands – she the wonderful chef and he the affable host.

You can tell as you enter through the barn, where a 1953 Jaguar convertible is displayed among such eclectic items as a totem pole and a telephone booth, that you are in for an unusual treat. Step out on the back deck and gaze over the picturesque scene as waitresses in long pink gingham skirts show the blackboard menu ($60 prix fixe) and take your order. After you are seated following the hayride, the table is yours for the evening.

Appetizers consist mostly of soups, and Jimmie makes some knockouts. Using herbs from her garden – especially lovage, her favorite – she might concoct country cottage, minestrone mother earth, cabbage soup made with duck stock or, in summer, a cold soup like raspberry puree or cucumber.

There is usually a choice of four entrées, always duck and often salmon, châteaubriand and lamb. These are accompanied by six to eight vegetables, served family style and to us almost the best part of the meal. Marinated mushrooms are always among them and, depending on the season and what's in the garden, you might find celery braised with fennel, carrots with orange rind and raisins, tomatoes with basil and lime juice or a casserole of zucchini and summer squash with mornay sauce. Jimmie cooks without preservatives or salt, and believes strongly in fresh and healthful food. Desserts might include a chocolate roll made with Belgian chocolate, coffee or grand marnier mousse, or butter cake with fresh berries.

This unfoldment takes place in dining rooms in the barn or the attached building with a loft that was once a studio used by writers. The old wood of the walls and raftered ceilings glows with the patina of age, as do the polished wood tables in the flickering candlelight. Colored glass bottles shine in the windows, and the whole place is filled with barny things like decoys, deacons' benches, pillows, bowls of apples and rag rugs. Add classical music or Susan Lamb's folksongs and a bottle from Bob's well-chosen wine list, and you will likely find yourself in the middle of a midsummer night's dream.

For lunch, entrées in the $13 to $18 range could include pasta parmesan, seafood crêpes, salmon quiche, the delicious Hillandale hash and Londonderry pork stew.

(860) 774-4423. Prix-fixe, $60. Lunch, Tuesday-Saturday noon to 2:30. Dinner, Friday and Saturday, one seating from 7. Dinner reservations required far in advance. Closed January-May. No credit cards.

The Harvest, 37 Putnam St., Pomfret.
A longtime local favorite, The Harvest at Bald Hill, reopened in large and stylish new quarters in 1997 at a prime Pomfret location and turned out to be better than ever. Peter Cooper, former chef at the Brown University faculty club in Providence, took over the Lemuel Grosvenor House (circa 1765) and built a substantial addition.

The new establishment focuses on an open lounge with a cherry wood bar and several dining tables in the center, a semi-open kitchen and a floor-to-ceiling wall of wines showcasing the Harvest's award-winning wine cellar at the entry. Around the periphery are a grill room with a fireplace, a couple of handsome fireplaced dining rooms, two dining porches, a cocktail terrace and a banquet facility. Decor is elegant country in burgundy and green, with local artworks on the walls and the oil lamps in hurricane chimneys illuminated even at noon

The menus change seasonally to reflect the harvest and are similar in style to those at Bald Hill and its subsequent location, the Harvest at Wells Farm in Southbridge, Mass.

At lunch, three of us enjoyed good french bread, a shared appetizer of gyoza (tasty Japanese dumplings), sautéed scrod with winter vegetables and two superb – and abundant – salads, caesar with Thai chicken and grilled salmon with citrus wasabi vinaigrette. These were so filling we couldn't begin to think of such delectable desserts as mascarpone cheesecake, white chocolate raspberry truffle, peach bourbon upside-down cake or cardamom crème brulée.

The dinner menu appeals as well. Main courses vary widely from plank-seared salmon with lemon-miso butter and bouillabaisse to roast duckling with red currant sauce, grilled lamb with rosemary and garlic, veal marsala au gratin and seven versions of steaks and chops. The emphasis on the harvest shows up spectacularly in the vegetable and bean sauté, the Pacific Rim vegetable grill and the roasted vegetable roulade Santa Fe. The Black Cat Bistro menu offers light fare from a Tuscan lamb sandwich to a duck and asparagus crêpe.

(860) 928-0008. Entrées. $13.95 to $24.95. Lunch, Monday-Friday 11:30 to 2. Bistro from 2. Dinner, Monday-Saturday 5:30 to 8:30 or 9; jackets requested. Sunday, brunch 11 to 2, dinner 2:30 to 7:30. No smoking.

The Inn at Woodstock Hill, 94 Plaine Hill Road, Woodstock.

This glamorous restaurant spreads across three rooms of an equally glamorous inn. It has earned its spurs over the years under German chef Richard Naumann, partner with innkeeper Sheila Becks.

The setting is elegant, whether in the main inn, a small dining room with banquettes draped in chintz in the carriage house or, beyond, the long, narrow main dining room with windows onto fields and forest. Blue armchairs are at tables set with Villeroy & Boch china and pink napkins stashed in big wine glasses.

For a springtime lunch, we were seated in the small, pretty peach and blue dining room in the carriage house, the armchairs a bit too low (the banquettes are the right height) and the atmosphere a bit too hushed until some more lunchers trickled in. Most of the menu struck us as more appropriate for dinner, with main courses ranging from oriental chicken stir-fry to filet mignon "hunter style." The menu listed three tempting sandwiches (chicken dijon, beef tips or grilled shrimp), appetizers of the dinner variety, a couple of soups and two salads, one of mixed greens and the other the house version of a chef's salad. Chosen to follow an excellent baked french onion soup, it turned out to be a rather strange concoction lacking the advertised boiled egg and topped with salami, turkey and cheese. It did come with a super mint-apple dressing, however. One of us ordered the day's pasta off the appetizer list, a fine dish of ravioli stuffed with mushrooms and a sundried tomato sauce that was almost a salsa. Another sampled the chicken dijon sandwich topped with bacon and melted swiss cheese, served with potato chips and chunks of fruit, too much to finish.

Based on our almost-dinner lunch, we would expect dinner here to be fine. The extensive continental/American menu features dishes like baked mahi-mahi with creole sauce, grilled jumbo shrimp with spicy peanut-ginger sauce, Long Island duckling with maple syrup, sautéed veal steak with portobello mushrooms, and grilled pepper-crusted lamb loin with sherry wine sauce. Most of the desserts at our visit were chocolate-based.

(860) 928-0528. Entrées, $16 to $25. Lunch, Tuesday-Saturday 11 to 2. Dinner Monday-Saturday 5 to 9. Sunday, brunch 11 to 2, dinner 3:30 to 7:30.

White Horse Inn at Vernon Stiles, Route 193, Thompson Hill.

After two whirlwind months of renovations, this 1814 stagecoach tavern reopened in 1997 with new owners and a new look. Jackie and Andrew Silverston of Lord Thompson Manor added a venerable restaurant to their holdings. They retained the name of Vernon Stiles, one of the establishment's early and more colorful landlords, who claimed that more stage passengers dined there every day than at any other house in New England.

Otherwise, the look in two dining rooms and a rear porch is all new. The dark walls and beamed ceilings were repainted white. All is now "milky hues," said

Former Bowen home and carriage house are now The Inn at Woodstock Hill.

Jackie, who was restoring the places to the era "when everything was white." Her goal was a feeling of romance, enhanced by the warmth of nine fireplaces.

The establishment also has a bakery and gift shop dispensing baked goods and blended coffees, as well as a reception parlor with comfortable sofas and chairs and a baby grand piano.

Chef Kim Reynolds, a Culinary Institute of America graduate who was married at Lord Thompson Manor, left the Mohegan Sun casino restaurant in Montville to head the kitchen here.

Her menu features "New England comfort food with an Italian accent," according to Jackie. Starters include five-onion soup au gratin, escargots in puff pastry and beef satay. Typical main courses are oven-roasted scrod, shrimp scampi, grilled swordfish with lemon-dill butter, Tuscan chicken, peppercorn-glazed pork loin and charbroiled sirloin steak with peppercorn-cognac cream sauce.

The new owners also planned to continue a popular tradition at the Vernon Stiles, the weekly Stew and Story session on Wednesday evenings. Cocktails and a supper of stew (perhaps lamb or beef) precede a fireside story told by local actors or professors in the parlor.

(860) 923-9571. Entrées, $13.95 to $19.95. Lunch daily in bakery, 10:30 to 6. Dinner nightly except Tuesday from 5. Sunday brunch, 11 to 2.

The Vine Bistro, 85 Main St., Putnam.

The antiques district in up-and-coming downtown Putnam is enlivened by a good little contemporary American bistro. Lisa Cassettari and Kim Kirker operate a stark white space accented with blond tables (dressed with white linens at night) and large, colorful paintings done by a local artist. The name reflects their aim to serve fresh fare, as in the vineyard proverb: "The grape is most delightful when first picked from the vine."

At lunch, things get off to a good start when the ice water is poured with a slice of lemon into an oversize brandy glass. Plates puddled with olive oil, garlic and rosemary arrive for soaking up the good, crusty bread. There is quite a selection of soups, sandwiches and salads, including an unusual caesar salad served with Maryland crab cakes. A specialty is vodka rigatoni, which one of us tried and pronounced successful. Others in our party sampled an appetizer of portobello mushrooms sautéed with spinach, roasted peppers, tomatoes, garlic and olive oil, and a generous sandwich of turkey, swiss and whole berry cranberry sauce. A sensational finale was tangerine sorbet, served in a frozen tangerine on a big white plate squiggled with raspberry puree. Pumpkin cheesecake laced with cognac was another winner.

Much the same fare is available at dinner, minus the sandwiches and plus half a dozen specials. Expect treats like vodka rigatoni with jumbo shrimp, broiled salmon with a velvety dill sauce, "chicken d'vine" with artichoke hearts, veal marsala and locally raised duckling.

(860) 928-1660. Entrées, $12.95 to $16.95. Lunch daily, 11 to 3. Dinner, Wednesday-Sunday, 5 to 9. Wine and beer license. No smoking.

The Vanilla Bean Cafe, 450 Deerfield Road (Junction of Routes 169, 44 and 97), Pomfret.

This popular little café in a 150-year-old barn is run by Barry Jessurun and siblings Eileen (Bean) and Brian, with occasional appearances by the rest of the family.

Here is a true place, where the turkey sandwich is "not that awful turkey roll," says the blackboard menu, but "the real thing, roasted here at the Bean." Ditto for the albacore tuna sandwich, the house-smoked meats, the spicy lentil or falafel burgers, the award-winning chili and the hearty soups (ham and bean, fish chowder, chicken gumbo). The dinner menu includes a large bean burrito, beef stew, chicken teriyaki with vegetables, smoked mozzarella and basil ravioli, plus specials.

Diners partake at tables beneath an eighteen-foot-high ceiling in one room containing the food counter and an aquarium or in a larger side room with a piano for musical entertainment on weekends. The entertainment proved so popular that the Bean added a third room beyond with sofas and overstuffed chairs. Beer and wine, espresso and cappuccino are featured.

(860) 928-1562. Entrées, $5.25 to $11. Open Monday and Tuesday 7 to 3, Wednesday-Friday 7 to 8, weekends 8 to 8, later on music nights and in summer.

Fox Hunt Farms Gourmet & Cafe, 292 Route 169, South Woodstock.

Starting with a gourmet deli par excellence, Linda Colangelo, Laura Crosetti and Lisa Evripidou have expanded into a cafe with an espresso bar and an outlying building housing an ice cream and sweets shop. Any number of fancy sandwiches are available in the $5.50 to $6.50 range, served on a variety of fresh breads. We've made good lunches of the goat cheese and sundried tomato sandwich, the smooth duck pâté on French bread, a cup of gazpacho with half a honey ham and boursin sandwich on sourdough, and a warm croissant filled with chicken and red peppers. There's seating inside and on a spacious outdoor deck.

Next door is **The Fox's Fancy,** a seasonal, old-fashioned ice cream parlor featuring gourmet gifts, homemade fudge, chocolates and ice cream. Chocolate candies are served with ice creams, and sundaes may be served over fresh melons.

(860) 928-0714. Open Tuesday-Sunday 10 to 5:30.

Diversions

Heritage Corridor. President Clinton signed the bill designating much of the Quiet Corner a National Heritage Corridor in 1994. The area's 25 hill and mill towns are cooperating with the National Park Service to promote regional greenways and preserve the rural quality of life from encroaching development. On the annual Walking Weekend each Columbus Day Weekend, experts in their fields guide upwards of 3,000 people on a total of 45 walks, visiting towns, farms, forests, parks and more.

A booklet called "Hill Towns and Mill Villages," prepared by the Association of Northeastern Connecticut Historical Societies, is a helpful adjunct for touring rural Woodstock, Pomfret, Brooklyn and Canterbury as well as the nearby mill towns of Thompson, Putnam, Killingly and Plainfield. We particularly enjoy "The Street" lined with academic buildings, churches and gracious homes in Pomfret, the Woodstock Hill green with a three-state view available behind Woodstock Academy, and the stunning Thompson Hill common.

Other little treasures are the spireless **Old Trinity Church** in Brooklyn, the oldest Episcopal church now standing in the oldest diocese in the country (open some summer afternoons but used only once a year on All Saints Day); the one-room law office of Daniel Putnam Tyler in Brooklyn, and the brick one-room **Quassett School** in Woodstock. The Brooklyn and Woodstock fairs are among the nation's oldest.

A favorite driving tour follows Scenic Route 169 which slices north-south through the heart of this region. Buildings and land along both sides have been placed on the National Register. The 32-mile stretch is the longest officially designated scenic road in Connecticut and one of the nation's ten most scenic as designated by Scenic America.

Roseland Cottage, 556 Route 169, Woodstock.

Roses and the Fourth of July were the twin passions of Woodstock native Henry C. Bowen, a New York merchant and publisher who planted a rose garden outside his summer house, upholstered much of its furniture in pink and named it Roseland Cottage. To his wild pink Gothic Revival mansion trimmed in gingerbread for his famous Independence Day celebrations came the day's luminaries, among them Ulysses S. Grant, Benjamin Harrison, Rutherford B. Hayes and William McKinley. The house, its furnishings and pink parterre garden remain much as they were in the 19th century. In the rear barn is the oldest extant bowling alley in a private residence; balls of varying sizes line the chute.

(860) 28-4074. Open Wednesday-Sunday 11 to 5, June through mid-October. Adults, $4.

Prudence Crandall Museum, Routes 14 and 169, Canterbury.

The site of New England's first black female academy has a fascinating history to reveal. Asked to educate their children, Prudence Crandall ran afoul of towns-people when she admitted a black girl in 1833. They withdrew their children, so she ran a boarding school for "young ladies and misses of color" until she was hounded out of town. Now a museum, the house is interesting for its architecture and exhibits on 19th-century Canterbury, blacks and Miss Crandall.

(860) 546-9916. Open Wednesday-Sunday 10 to 4:30, February to mid-December. Adults, $2.

For seasonal local color, visit Mervin Whipple's annual **Christmas Wonderland** of 100,000-plus lights, mechanized scenes, outdoor displays and a chapel – surely the biggest extravaganza of its kind. Much of it is gaudy but much is tasteful, including animated figures that once were in window displays in New York department stores. Signs point the way for the 50,000 visitors who come from miles around to see the nightly spectacle each December along Pineville Road in the Ballouville section of Killingly.

Shopping. Until lately, shopping for many has begun and ended in South Woodstock. **Scranton's Shops,** a ramble of rooms in an 1878 blacksmith shop, is full of country wares from more than 90 local artisans. The array is mind-boggling, and we defy anyone to get out without a purchase.

Nearby, **The Livery Shops** and **Garden Gate Florist** offer more small rooms given over to floral arrangements and local artisans who show their wares on consignment. At one visit, the impressive, one-of-a-kind items included an amusing picnic dish set with flies and ants painted on, the striking dishes of Majilly Designs, and the watercolors of Tom McCobb, one of which inspired a surprised "hey, that's my house" from our tour guide.

Other shoppers like **Resourceful Judith** for garden ornaments, **Brunarhans Designworks** for wood furnishings, the **Woodstock Orchards Apple Barn** and the **Christmas Barn,** all scattered about Woodstock.

In Pomfret in a cottage behind The Harvest restaurant is **Wilson Campbell Ltd.,** where Carol Perkins and Jo Vickers carry distinctive home accessories, crafts and gifts. Up the street is **Martha's Herbary,** featuring herbal gifts and garden accessories.

Pomfret also has a fledgling winery, **Sharpe Hill Vineyard,** Wade Road, (860) 974-3549. The first of seven acres of grapes were planted in 1992 and turned up in bottlings of three varieties, including chardonnay. The winery, furnished with 18th-century antiques, is patterned after a taproom of the 1700s. Wine tastings, Friday-Sunday 11 to 5.

Extra Special

The Putnam Antiques District. A major antiques district, with more than 450 dealers and seventeen shops, has emerged in downtown Putnam. It started in 1991 when Jere Cohen restored the old C.D. Bugby department store at Main and Front streets into the **Antiques Marketplace,** renting space to 250 dealers on three floors and producing the largest group showroom in Connecticut. More than a dozen antiques stores quickly followed. Word spread that here was the antiques capital of New England, if not the entire Northeast, stocking an incredible array of goods from tag-sale trinkets to fine furniture. The entire scene draws noted collectors and designers as well as dealers and common folk. On one floor of the 22,000-square-foot marketplace, Jere Cohen shows the largest selection of antique Stickley furniture in New England at his **Mission Oak Shop.** Down the street, the 30,000-square-foot **Putnam Antique Exchange** features architectural antiques, furniture, salvage items and other major pieces in a variety of period rooms. A former drug store has been turned into **Jeremiah's,** a large multi-dealer shop, now full of odds and ends. A former bank building has been transformed into the suave **Brighton Antiques,** purveyor of quality furniture and accessories, some at rather substantial prices. British antiques and books, along with such hard-to-find foods as haggis, bridies and salad cream, turn up at **Mrs. Bridges' Pantry,** which operates a tea room Thursday through Sunday. Poke around and you'll find your own discoveries.

Oliver Cromwell warship was launched in Revolution from what is now Steamboat Dock.

Essex and Old Lyme, Conn.
River Towns, Arts and Charm

Nearing the sea after lazing 400 miles through four states, the Connecticut River wends and weaves between forested hillsides and sandy shores. Finally it pauses, almost delta-like, in the sheltered coves and harbors of Essex and Old Lyme before emptying into Long Island Sound.

A sand bar blocked the kind of development that has urbanized other rivers where they meet the ocean. Indeed, the Connecticut is the nation's biggest without a major city at its mouth.

It is in this tranquil setting that Essex was settled in 1635, its harbor a haven for shipbuilding in the past and for yachting in modern times.. From Essex the first American warship, the Oliver Cromwell, was launched in time for the Revolution. From Essex, leading yachtsmen sail the Atlantic today.

Touted by the New Yorker magazine as "a mint-condition 18th century town," Essex relives its past in the Connecticut River Museum at Steamboat Dock, in the boatworks and yacht clubs along its harbor, in the lively Tap Room at the Griswold Inn, in the lovely old homes along Main Street and River Road.

Across the river from Essex is Old Lyme, which has less of a river feel but exudes a charm of its own. In a pastoral area that is now part of an historic district, artists gathered at the turn of the century in the mansion of Florence Griswold, daughter of a boat captain. The American Impressionist movement was the result, and the arts are celebrated and flourish here to this day.

Just inland from historic Essex along the Falls River are Centerbrook and

Ivoryton. They and Old Lyme provide a setting in which fine inns and restaurants thrive. Up river are Deep River, Chester, Hadlyme and East Haddam, unspoiled towns steeped in history.

You still have to drive the long way around to get from one side of the river to the other, unless you take the tiny ferry that has been plying between Chester and Hadlyme for 200 years. The Valley Railroad's steam train and riverboat link the towns as in the past, offering visitors scenic ways to see both river and shore.

Inn Spots

Old Lyme Inn, 85 Lyme St., Box 787 B, Old Lyme 06371.

With eight sumptuous guest suites, an addition transformed what was basically an acclaimed restaurant into a full-service inn of distinction.

The north wing was so tastefully added that the casual passerby in Old Lyme's carefully preserved historic district wouldn't suspect it was newer. On two floors, the rooms are individually decorated in a plush Empire and Victorian theme – canopy and four-poster queensize beds with Marblehead mints perched atop their oversize pillows, comfortable sofas or chairs grouped around marble topped-tables, cable TVs, telephones and large, gleaming white bathrooms outfitted with Dickinson's Witch Hazel (made in Essex) and herbal shampoos. These rooms are so attractive they make the five smaller rooms in the original 1850s farmhouse pale in comparison.

Innkeeper Diana Atwood-Johnson has furnished guest rooms and public areas alike with choice Empire and Victorian pieces acquired at auctions, tag sales and antiques shows. The mirror over the fireplace in the bar was purchased at an auction for $5 – no one else wanted it, says Diana. The marble mantels in the bar and parlor came from a Wethersfield woman who had saved them as her family's home was being razed. Many of the inn's notable collection of paintings represent the Old Lyme School of artists who were based at the Florence Griswold House across the street.

Guests have use of Sassafras's Library (named for the inn's late cat), which has a marble-topped fireplace and television. The Victorian bar dispenses drinks, shellfish from a raw bar, light snacks, special coffees and dessert pastries. Diana,

a self-described "serious fan of professional croquet," urges guests to try their hand on the inn's backyard layout.

Homemade croissants and granola are served for continental breakfast in the Rose Room. Lunch and dinner are available daily in three formal dining rooms (see Dining Spots).

(860) 434-2600 or (800) 434-5352. Fax (860) 434-5352. Thirteen rooms with private baths. Weekends: doubles, $120 to $150 May-December, $110 to $140 rest of year. Midweek: $99 to $130. Children and pets accepted.

Addition blends into original structure and expands lodging capacity at Old Lyme Inn.

Copper Beech Inn, 46 Main St., Ivoryton 06442.

Long rated highly as a restaurant (see Dining Spots), the Copper Beech has catered to the luxury market in lodging since it opened nine guest rooms in a restored carriage house behind an imposing mansion shaded by the oldest copper beech tree in Connecticut.

Eldon and Sally Senner from Washington, D.C., he a banker and she an interior decorator, purchased the inn and enhanced it with their extensive collection of fine antiques, marine paintings and oriental porcelains. They also restored the dining experience to levels it had not matched since the restaurant's early glory days in the 1970s under founders Jo and Robert McKenzie.

The newer deluxe guest rooms are furnished in "French country chic," with canopy and four-poster beds, comfortable sitting areas, TV sets and telephones. Each offers a jacuzzi bathtub and French doors that open onto an outdoor deck or balcony overlooking landscaped gardens. Second-floor rooms feature cathedral ceilings with exposed beams. The Senners keep adding more antiques and have hung their own botanical prints on the walls.

The four period bedrooms in the main inn are attractive as well. Nicely decorated in rich shades of blue, the master suite has a striking floor-to-ceiling fabric canopy enveloping a kingsize bed, a loveseat in front of a decorative fireplace, a chaise lounge across the room and a large table for two in the front dormer window. Another room is bright and cheery with wicker furniture and a brass bed. All the rooms hold good-looking furnishings and antiques, as befits a mansion once occupied by an ivory comb and keyboard manufacturer.

There's a sitting area upstairs in the spacious hall, and a small gallery in which the Senners show fine oriental porcelain by appointment. Guests gather in a delightful, plant-filled Victorian conservatory that wraps around the front and side of the inn. It's a quiet and relaxing refuge year-round. In restoring the gardens around the inn, the Senners have planted thousands of spring bulbs, and are adding terraces of annuals and perennials.

Bee and Thistle Inn welcomes guests for dining as well as lodging.

Guests enjoy a continental-plus breakfast buffet in the clubby Copper Beech Room, a handsome dining room with a view of the great tree for which the inn is named, blue oriental carpets on the floor and tables spaced well apart. Fresh fruits, cereals, a toaster for raisin bread and English muffins, and at least a couple of French pastries like croissants, brioches and puff pastry turnovers are typical.

(860) 767-0330. Thirteen rooms with private baths. Doubles, $105 to $175. Two-night minimum weekends. Children over 10. No smoking.

Bee and Thistle Inn, 100 Lyme St., Old Lyme 06371.

Stately trees, gardens all around and a flower-bedecked entrance welcome visitors to this cheery yellow inn, set on five acres bordering the Lieutenant River in the historic district of Old Lyme. Built in 1756 with subsequent additions and remodeling, the structure is a delightful ramble of parlors and porches, dining rooms and guest rooms.

It is this scene that attracted Bob and Penny Nelson. Wishing to leave the corporate life in northern New Jersey in 1982, they were looking to buy a traditional New England inn. A broker told them of one they weren't familiar with along the Connecticut shore. "It was only two hours from home so we said we'd go look," Bob Nelson recalls. "We walked in the front door, saw the center entrance hall and graceful staircase and said, 'This is it.'"

With sofas to sink into and fireplaces ablaze, the parlors on either side are inviting. On sunny days, the enclosed porches beyond are great for lingering over breakfast or lunch. The Nelsons, now joined in the operation by son Jeff and daughter Lori, have refurbished most of the inn's public spaces and guest rooms, added a cottage and upgraded the restaurant (see Dining Spots), which is often cited as the most romantic in Connecticut.

Eleven guest rooms upstairs come with private baths, fresh flowers and period country furnishings. They vary in size from small with double or twin beds to large with queensize canopy beds and loveseats. Four-poster, fishnet canopy and spool beds are covered with quilts or afghans. Some rooms have wing chairs and ruffled curtains, and one even has a washstand full of flowers. Nooks are full of games and old books are all around.

The premier accommodation is in the riverside cottage. A deck off the queensize bedroom wraps around a fireplaced reading room, a TV room and a kitchen. Continental breakfast is included in its rates.

A winter feature is afternoon tea. Served Monday, Wednesday and Thursday from 3:30 to 5 for $12.95, it's generally booked solid. Scones, tea sandwiches and a dessert of the day accompany the beverages.

Breakfast is available for an extra charge on the sunny dining porches, a great place to start the day. Breakfast in bed may be ordered the night before. The Bee and Thistle popover filled with scrambled eggs, bacon and cheese draws the public as well as overnighters.

(860) 434-1667 or (800) 622-4946. Fax (860) 434-3402. Eleven rooms and one cottage with private baths. Rates EP. Doubles, $75 to $155. Cottage, $210. Children over 12. No smoking.

Riverwind, 209 Main St., Deep River 06417.

Innkeeper Barbara Barlow found a dilapidated 1850 house and spent a year restoring it into a B&B, doing most of the work herself. Contractor Bob Bucknall didn't blanch when she told him a few years later she wanted to build an addition 150 years older than her existing inn. The result is a skillful blend of old and new, from eight guest rooms with private baths to an equal number of common rooms affording space for mingling or privacy, plus a marriage made during construction. You guessed it, the innkeeper married the contractor and they became joint innkeepers.

This is a cozy inn crammed full of antiques and folk art, with a noteworthy collection of pigs in all guises, all over the house. Barbara, who grew up in Smithfield, Va., and whose dad was a hog farmer there, serves up slices of the red, salty Smithfield ham for breakfast every morning to her guests. The hams hang from the ceiling in her kitchen, where cupboards are made of wood from a gristmill in upstate New York and the counter is a 200-year-old piece of hemlock. Guests eat breakfast by candlelight at a table for twelve in the new dining room and at a smaller table in the adjacent room. Coffee cake, real Southern biscuits in the shape of pigs, egg dishes (perhaps sliced hard-boiled eggs with artichoke hearts and mushrooms in a cheese sauce), fresh fruit in summer and hot curried fruit in winter, and her homemade jams and preserves are the fare.

There's a twelve-foot stone cooking fireplace in the "new" 18th-century keeping room. We're always attracted to the original fireplaced parlor loaded with antiques and nifty touches. Quilts, hooked and woven rugs, a set of blocks shaped like houses spelling "welcome," a wonderful lighting fixture of wooden animals holding candles and a piano topped with all kinds of sheet music make for an exceptionally welcoming room. A decanter of sherry is always out for guests. Games in the trophy room include an antique checkerboard, and upstairs is a library with a fireplace. The long narrow porch in front, set with white wicker furniture, looks as if it were made for Scarlett O'Hara.

Up steep stairs, lined with old preserve jars filled with dried flowers, are the original guest rooms. The Smithfield Room, all red, white and blue, has bluebirds stenciled around the walls and a high rope maple bed with a chamber pot underneath. A stenciled floor and her grandmother's carved oak hall tree and headboard give Zelda's Suite a decidedly Gatsby flavor. Flowers on the bedroom wallpaper, hearts on the bathroom wallpaper and a heart-filled stained-glass window are featured in the Hearts and Flowers Room. The ultimate is the Champagne and Roses Room with a private balcony, a bathroom with a Japanese steeping tub, a bottle of champagne awaiting on a table between two wing chairs, and a fishnet canopy bed too frilly for words.

Is it any wonder that Barbara bills Riverwind as a place for romance? She knows from experience, and has become a justice of the peace so that she can perform weddings. Her classic Bentley limousine parked out front intensifies the aura.

(860) 526-2014. Eight rooms with private baths. Doubles, $105 to $175. Two-night minimum weekends in season. Children over 12.

Griswold Inn, 36 Main St., Essex 06426.

The Griswold Inn has historic appeal matched by few inns in this country. There's the requisite taproom containing a steamboat-Gothic bar, potbelly stove and antique popcorn machine – Lucius Beebe called it probably the most handsome barroom in America. Copious meals and a celebrated hunt breakfast are served in four dining rooms that are a kaleidoscope of Americana. And the floors in some of the guest rooms list to port or starboard, as you might expect of an inn dating to 1776.

Commandeered by the British during the War of 1812, the inn was found to be long on charm but short on facilities. Today, all 30 guest rooms in the main inn, the annex and in houses across the street come with private baths, air-conditioning, telephones and – a new one for us – piped-in classical music that plays from 7 a.m. to 11 p.m., but can be turned down or off at will. This last fillip seems ironic, considering that there's no television other than in a small common lounge in the Hayden House.

Fifteen standard rooms in the inn and annex are unabashedly simple and old-fashioned, though most have been enhanced cosmetically of late. One upstairs front room facing the street has a beamed ceiling and sloping floor, twin beds, marble-topped table and a small bath with shower. A cut above are petite suites, somewhat larger rooms with double beds and pleasant sitting areas. Two luxury suites harboring large sitting rooms with franklin stoves and four-poster beds in the bedrooms were erected above the Steamboat Room during a massive kitchen renovation in 1989. They and four suites across the street in a retail complex known as Griswold Square are the most deluxe, in a comfortable and historic way. Two above the Red Pepper shop each have a bedroom and a sitting room with gas fireplace. The Garden Suite is a two-story house involving a large room upstairs with two double beds and, downstairs, a living room with sofabed, wet bar, dining table and a bathroom. It served as the honeymoon suite until 1994, when the Fenwick Suite opened next door. The Fenwick's main room is equipped with a kingsize bed, a brick fireplace and two wing chairs in opposite corners. An intimate sitting room with sofa and club chair leads to a large bath with clawfoot tub and separate shower. Now, owner Douglas Paul says, the bridal party tends to reserve the Garden Suite for the wedding preliminaries and the bride and groom book the Fenwick for the wedding night.

A continental breakfast buffet of juice, coffee and danish pastry is put out in the Steamboat Room section of the restaurant.

The "Gris," as it's known to neighbors and travelers from near and far, serves hundreds of meals a day (see Dining Spots), and the Sunday hunt breakfast is an institution. Before and after dinner, the Tap Room is a happy hubbub of banjo players, a singalong pianist and sea chantey singers, depending on the night. You can snack from the raw bar, sample popcorn from the old red machine, hoist a few brews and readily imagine you've been transported 200 years into the past.

(860) 767-1776. Fax (860) 767-0481. Fifteen rooms and fifteen suites with private baths. Doubles, $90. Suites, $105 to $185. Children and pets welcome.

Hidden Meadow, 40 Blood St., Lyme 06371.

When the family homestead gradually emptied as her four daughters went off to college, Karen Brossard opened this country house of a B&B. It's a beauty of a home on four rural acres, dating to 1760. Subsequent additions (some by Broadway actor Henry Hull in the mid-1930s) produced a rambling, pale yellow Colonial Revival with circular driveway, Georgian entry, a number of stone terraces, iron railings and a reflecting pool.

The Brossards offer three guest rooms with private baths. Each is nicely outfitted with family furnishings and queensize or king/twin beds. Guests enjoy a living room with fireplace and original beehive oven, a library with TV and a fireplaced dining room with a table set for eight ("we sometimes have extra visitors for breakfast," explains Karen, an engaging hostess who enjoys a good party). Breakfast in summer is served on an unusual curved slate porch overlooking the reflecting pool. Beyond are a large swimming pool, a raspberry patch, stables and riding trails. Karen keeps two horses, and used to teach her pony club here three days a week. Now she teaches paddle tennis as the pro at Old Lyme Country Club.

Breakfast is an event. The fare might be baked eggs with brie, basil and heavy cream; orange-flavored french toast with brandy, or gingerbread pancakes with lemon sauce. Fruits, homemade muffins and zucchini bread accompany.

(860) 434-8360. Three rooms with private baths. May-December and holidays: doubles $95 to $135. Rest of year: $90 to $125. Two-night minimum weekends in season. Children over 10. No smoking.

Dining Spots

Steve's Centerbrook Cafe, 78 Main St., Centerbrook.

What a difference a change in name and concept can make. Master chef Steve Wilkinson found out when he decided it was time to lighten up the interior of his small French restaurant, Fine Bouche, a culinary beacon in the area for fifteen years. One thing led to another and, next we knew, Fine Bouche was out and Steve's Centerbrook Cafe was in. A major change? Yes – and no. As the owner puts it, "we didn't want to throw out the baby with the bath water."

The interior, even lightened up, still resembles the old Fine Bouche. The menu, although more varied and appearing more affordable, retains some traditional specialties. And, nice touch, fifteen quality wines are available for $15, although the full, 250-selection wine list especially strong in Bordeaux retains the Wine Spectator award of excellence.

So, for happy diners now packing the place, it's the best of both possible worlds. They enjoy Steve's culinary expertise in a casual yet elegant setting.

You could start with the chef's selection of appetizers, which changes daily. Or, on a winter's evening, specify the duck soup, the wild mushroom risotto or the Thai shrimp roll. Salads and pastas come in small and large sizes. A salad of endive, bosc pear, chèvre and roasted walnuts could be teamed with a butternut squash gnocchi with smoked mozzarella or rigatoni with shrimp, white beans and broccoli.

Main dishes are categorized under pastas, grills and fish, and odd lots and stews. The offerings range from grilled chicken diablo to rack of lamb with pesto bread pudding and merlot-rosemary sauce. Consider the grilled salmon fillet with lime and mango sauce, bouillabaisse, cassoulet or grilled veal chop with rosemary jus.

Save room for dessert, a Wilkinson strong point. Expect a classic marjolaine, a pear and walnut tarte tatin, pumpkin swirl cheesecake and crème brûlée (the flavor changes daily). Or chill out on a selection of homemade ice creams (amaretto and crystallized ginger) and sorbets (passion fruit, kiwi and raspberry).

(860) 767-1277. Entrées, $13.50 to $18.95. Dinner, Tuesday-Sunday 5:30 to 9.

Bee and Thistle Inn, 100 Lyme St., Old Lyme.

Head chef Francis Brooke-Smith, who trained at the Ritz in London, delights in innovative touches and stylish presentations at this highly regarded dining room. Among them are edible flowers for garnishes and fresh herbs he grows hydroponically year-round. He has help in the kitchen now from Jeff Nelson, son of the innkeepers, a Culinary Institute of America grad who trained at the Ritz-Carlton in Boston. They present sophisticated fare that won ten awards, more than any other restaurant, in Connecticut magazine's annual readers' choice poll two years in a row. "Romantic dining" and "best desserts" are their hallmarks.

Dining on the enclosed side porches overlooking the lawns is a treat. Ladderback chairs are at tables with blue and rose cloths or mats. Windows open to let in the breeze. Baskets hang from the ceiling in one. Hanging plants thrive in the other.

Luncheon choices are of the brunch and dinner variety: smoked salmon-stuffed blini, shrimp and mozzarella tart, shepherd's pie, Maryland crab cakes with mango chutney, petite filet mignon and lamb chops. The only salad might be goat cheese on warm greens; the only sandwich, homemade sausage with swiss cheese and roasted red peppers on French bread.

Candlelight dinners are served on the porches or in a small rear dining room, where a guitar-playing couple sings love songs on Friday nights and a harpist plays in a corner on Saturdays.

Regulars like to start with cocktails in the living room as they peruse the menu. Entrées range widely from pan-seared salmon to roasted rack of lamb. The crab cakes with saffron aioli and the filet mignon here are sensational, their simple names failing to do justice to the complexities of their preparation or that of their accompaniments. We also enjoyed the thin-sliced, rare breast of duck served on a passionfruit puree with a spiced pear beggar's purse.

Start with the salmon carpaccio with a chiffonade of mixed peppers and basil, the smoked trout mousse napoleon, the smooth duck liver pâté with pickle relish and melba toast or a mustard crème fraîche or goat cheese french toast. Finish with apricot bread pudding with brandied caramel sauce, banana flan over mango puree, a silky port chocolate truffle or a fresh fruit sorbet. Bob Nelson, who studied wines at the Cornell University Hotel School, put together the wine list with an eye for reasonable prices.

(860) 434-1667 or (800) 622-4946. Entrées, $19.95 to $28.95. Lunch, daily except Tuesday 11:30 to 2. Dinner nightly except Tuesday from 6. Sunday brunch, 11 to 2.

Steve's Centerbrook Cafe is new incarnation of French restaurant known as Fine Bouche.

Copper Beech Inn, 46 Main St., Ivoryton.

The level of dining at the Copper Beech has been elevated to its original heights by innkeepers Sally and Eldon Senner. They credit their chef, Robert Chiovoloni, a Culinary Institute of America grad who was executive sous chef at the famed Montpelier Room of Washington's Madison Hotel, which the Senners considered the city's best restaurant when they lived there. Together, their success prompted the AAA to upgrade its dining rating from three to four diamonds in 1998.

The main Georgian Room is elegant indeed, with three chandeliers, wall sconces, subdued floral wallpaper and crisp white napkins standing in twin peaks in the water glasses. The paneled Comstock Room with beamed ceiling looks a bit like the old billiards parlor that it was, lately enhanced by the Senners' paintings. Nearby is a charming little garden dining porch, its four tables for two spaced well apart amid the plants. Windows in the clubby blue Copper Beech Room afford views of the great tree outside. In each dining room, tables are centered by a perfect red rose.

The menu is printed in French with English translations. The ten hors d'oeuvres start with pâté of pheasant and truffles and top off with ossetra caviar with blinis. Typical of the dozen or so entrées are roasted sea scallops with a lemongrass-wine sauce on a bed of diced tomatoes and herbs, veal sweetbreads with a shiitake mushroom and sundried tomato sauce and beef wellington with fresh foie gras wrapped by the inn's own pastry.

Desserts might be tarte tatin, chocolate mousse with grand marnier, and mango and coconut sorbets with a compote of grilled pineapple. Finish with one of the fancy liqueured coffees, dessert wines or fine brandies for an occasion to remember.

(860) 767-0330. Entrées, $21.75 to $26.75. Dinner, Tuesday-Saturday 5:30 to 8:30 or 9, Sunday 1 to 8. Closed Tuesday in winter. No smoking.

Old Lyme Inn, 85 Lyme St., Old Lyme.

Thrice given a three-star rating by the New York Times and its desserts featured in successive issues of Bon Appétit magazine, the Old Lyme Inn has been a mecca for traveling gourmands since Diana Atwood-Johnson took it over in 1976.

The food is inventive and the setting is formal in three large dining rooms, all regally furbished in gold and blue. Tables in the long, high-ceilinged main dining room are angled in strict formation, a vase with one perfect rose atop each. Beyond are two more dining rooms, one with an intimate windowed alcove containing a table for four.

Chef Stuart London oversees an ambitious menu. At lunchtime, look for interesting salads (local lamb over romaine leaves, chicken and sweet peppers), a smoked salmon reuben, omelets, pasta and grilled pizza. Our latest visit produced a dish called wild American meatloaf, blending wild boar and buffalo and served with mashed potatoes and mushroom gravy. Earlier, we liked the curried cream of squash soup, a special of Niantic scallops and the sweetbread fritters with tomato coulis.

For dinner, appetizers could be Irish smoked salmon, escargots wrapped in pancetta, Maine shrimp fritters served with a chipotle lime aioli, and beef and asparagus negamaki with a Japanese sesame sauce.

Entrées include planked salmon with a johnnycake, grilled Jamaican swordfish, sautéed sweetbreads with artichoke hearts over a bed of spinach, and ballotine of Connecticut pheasant with a green peppercorn and port sauce.

The inn's raspberry cheesecake Japonnaise was pictured on the cover of Bon Appétit, and its entries won the Ultimate Chocolate Dessert Award in a Hartford contest three years in a row. We can vouch for a fruit tart with an apricot glaze and kiwi and strawberries on top and a chocolate truffle cake with mandarin-flavored pastry cream topped with a layer of sponge cake soaked in cointreau.

The wine list is choice and pricey. Cafe Diana with chambord and chocolate liqueur is a worthy finale. A light supper menu is available in the grill room.

(860) 434-2600 or (800) 434-5352. Entrées, $20.95 to $32. Lunch, Monday-Saturday noon to 2. Dinner, Monday-Saturday 6 to 9. Sunday, brunch 11 to 3, dinner 4 to 9.

Griswold Inn, 36 Main St., Essex.

Even when its kitchen was closed for nearly a year as a new one was built, the famed "Gris" kept going with an abbreviated menu. You'd expect no less from an institution that since its founding in 1776 had served "precisely 3.1416 times the number of meals which had been cumulatively prepared in all the steamships of the Cunard Line, the dirigibles Graf Zeppelin and Hindenburg, and the Orient Express," as a statement to customers noted.

A meal at the Gris, whether prepared in old kitchen or new, is an experience in Americana. There's much to see in a variety of dining rooms: the important collection of Antonio Jacobsen marine oils in the dark paneled Library, the Currier and Ives steamboat prints in the Covered Bridge Room (actually fashioned from a New Hampshire covered bridge), the riverboat memorabilia in the Steamboat Room, the musket-filled Gun Room with 55 pieces dating to the 15th century. Together, they rank as one of the outstanding marine art collections in America.

The atmosphere is the match for the food, which is country New England, fresh and abundant. "We have no pretenses," says the informative Innkeeper's Log. "Our menu is printed in English. We call fish fish and beef beef." The menu is a mixed bag of seafood, fish and game. Fried oysters, broiled scrod, baked stuffed shrimp, prime rib and grilled lamb steak are typical offerings.

Three versions of the inn's patented 1776 sausages are served as a mixed grill with sauerkraut and German potato salad at dinner. They're in even more demand for lunch, when you also can get eggs benedict or Welsh rarebit, duck salad or

Historic Griswold Inn in Essex, as viewed from Griswold Square complex across street.

yankee pot roast. At our latest lunch, a wicker swan full of packaged crackers helped sustain us as we waited (and waited) for our orders of crostini and shepherd's pie. The oil lamps were lit at noon, the place was hopping and the atmosphere was cheery on a dank November day. That we remember, more than the food.

The ever-popular Sunday hunt breakfast ($12.95) is an enormous buffet of dishes ranging from baby cod and creamed chipped beef to scrambled eggs and a soufflé of grits and cheddar cheese.

(860) 767-1776. Entrées, $17.95 to $20.95. Lunch, Monday-Saturday 11:45 to 3. Dinner, 5:30 to 9 or 10. Sunday, hunt breakfast 11 to 2:30, dinner 4:30 to 9.

The Black Seal, 15 Main St., Essex.

The legendary Tumbledown's Cafe gave way to this casual and appealingly nautical place. All the stuff to look at along the walls of the front tavern and in the rear dining room could distract one from the food, of which there's something for everyone day and night.

Basically the same fare is offered at lunch and dinner, though lunch brings more sandwiches and dinner more entrées. Graze on things like chili nachos, fire-pot chili, stuffed potato skins, cajun shrimp, Rhode Island clam chowder, California burgers, and cobb and hunter salads anytime.

At night, entrées run from mussels marinara, baked scrod dijon or wok of the day to steak au poivre or "Seals Delight" – mussels, clams, scallops, shrimp and calamari in red clam sauce over pasta. Grilled tuna with caper-shallot sauce and whitefish baked in parchment paper with wine, cream and chives were specials at one visit. Desserts include chocolate mousse terrine, pumpkin-praline torte, chocolate-raspberry cake and apple crumb pie.

(860) 767-0233. Entrées, $12.95 to $16.95. Lunch, daily 11:30 to 3:30, weekends to 4. Dinner, 5 to 9:30 or 10. Sunday brunch, 11:30 to 2.

Oliver's Taverne, Plains Road (Route 153), Essex.

Named for Essex's first ship, the Oliver Cromwell, this casual spot occupies a breathtakingly high space in a former Hitchcock furniture store. The decor is mostly wood with a massive stone fireplace and a three-story window with large hanging panels of stained glass to catch the light. Ladders, wheels and parts of old car bodies accent the soaring walls. The vast upstairs loft holds a long oak and mahogany bar from Cicero, Ill., at which Al Capone once drank, lounge areas (one with 1950s-den-style sofas and chairs) and a game room with two pool tables.

Huge sandwiches served with french fries, burgers and a few entrées like quiche, crêpes or teriyaki sirloin are featured at lunch. Snacky things like nachos, potato skins, fried calamari, light fare and fajitas are also offered at night, when entrées range from yankee pot roast to sirloin steak. The barbecued pork ribs are praised by those in the know. Bailey's Irish Cream mousse cake and chocolate chip cookie pie are popular desserts.

(860) 767-2633. Entrées, $9.95 to $16.95. Lunch, Monday-Saturday 11:30 to 4:30. Dinner, 4:30 to 10:30 or 11. Sunday brunch, 11:30 to 4.

Diversions

The Essex Waterfront. As a living and working yachting and shipbuilding town, the Essex waterfront is a center of activity. For yachtsmen, it holds some of the same cachet as Marblehead, Mass., or Oxford, Md.

Connecticut River Museum, 67 Main St., Essex.
Restored in 1975 from an 1878 steamboat warehouse, this interesting structure at Steamboat Dock is a living memorial to the Connecticut River Valley in an area from which the first American warship was launched. The main floor has changing exhibits. Upstairs, where windows on three sides afford sweeping views of the river, the permanent shipbuilding exhibit shows a full-size replica of David Bushnell's first submarine, the strange-looking American Turtle, plus a model of a Dutch explorer ship that sailed up the river in 1614.

(860) 767-8269. Open Tuesday-Sunday, 10 to 5. Adults, $4.

The foundation property also includes a small waterfront park with benches and the 1813 Hayden Chandlery, now the Thomas A. Stevens maritime research library. Just to the south off Novelty Lane are the historic Dauntless Club, the Essex Corinthian Yacht Club and the Essex Yacht Club. The historic structures here and elsewhere in town are detailed in a walking map, available at the museum.

Uptown Essex. Besides the waterfront area, Methodist Hill at the other end of Main Street has a cluster of historic structures. Facing tiny Champlin Square is the imposing white **Pratt House** (circa 1648), restored and operated by the Essex Historical Society to show Essex as it was in yesteryear (open June-Labor Day, weekends 1 to 4, $2). The period gardens in the rear are planted with herbs and flowers typical of the 18th century. The society also operates the adjacent **Hill's Academy Museum** (1833), an early boarding school that now displays historical collections of old Essex. Next door in the academy's former dormitory is the Catholic Church and, next to it, the Baptist Church, one of only two Egyptian Revival structures in this country.

Old Lyme. One of Connecticut's prettiest towns has a long main street lined with gracious homes from the 18th and 19th centuries, including one we think is particularly handsome called Lyme Regis, the English summer resort after which the town was named. Lyme Street, over the years the home of governors and chief justices, is a National Historic District.

Florence Griswold Museum was once the retreat of the Old Lyme artists.

Florence Griswold Museum, 96 Lyme St., Old Lyme.

This is the pillared 1817 landmark in which the daughter of a boat captain ran a finishing school for girls and later an artists' retreat, with most of the rooms converted into bedrooms and studios in the barns by the river. Now run as a museum by the Lyme Historical Society, it has unique painted panels in every room, but especially prized is the dining room with panels on all sides given over to the work of the Old Lyme artists, who included Childe Hassam. Across the mantel the artists painted a delightful caricature of themselves for posterity. The arts colony thrived for twenty years and its works are exhibited in the second-floor galleries.

(860) 434-5542. Open Tuesday-Saturday 10 to 5 and Sunday 1 to 5, June-October, and Wednesday-Sunday 1 to 5, November-May. Adults, $4.

The **Lyme Art G**allery, next door to the Florence Griswold Museum, is head-quarters of the Lyme Art Association, founded in 1902 and the oldest summer art group in the nation. It exhibits six major shows each season (Tuesday-Sunday noon to 4:30, late April to late September). Nearby at 84 Lyme St. is the handsome, Federal-style **Lyme Academy of Fine Arts,** with changing exhibits and workshops (Tuesday-Saturday 10 to 4 and Sunday 1 to 4). The works of Lyme's American Impressionists also are hung in the Town Hall, and the public library often has exhibits.

Deep River, just above Essex and reached most rewardingly via the River Road, is a sleepy river town best known for its annual ancient muster of fife and drum corps. Portrayed lately by the New York Times as on the verge of chic between Essex and Chester, its downtown has a couple of good shops – **Celebrations** for neat cards and paper goods, as well as jewelry, children's clothes and toys and wonderful papier-mâché cats, and, next door, **Pasta Unlimited.** Here pasta of all shapes and flavors (we liked the tomato-basil and the black peppercorn) is made in the front window. Goodies like broccoli-almond salad with fusilli pasta, "not your

Mom's" macaroni and cheese, and key lime mousse are available for takeout. Try one of the sandwiches in pita and a slice of pumpkin cognac cheesecake for a picnic. Up river are the delightful town of **Chester,** an up-and-coming area of restaurants and shops; the restored **Goodspeed Opera House** at East Haddam, where lively musicals are staged in a Victorian structure beside the river, and actor William Gillette's eccentric stone **Gillette Castle** on a hilltop above the river at Hadlyme. All are well worth a visit.

Shopping. Most visitors are impressed by the quality of shopping in Essex, some of it nautically oriented. The **Talbots** store confronting visitors head-on as they enter the downtown section sets the tone. Also fashionable in different ways are **Classical Rags, Silkworm, J. Alden Clothier** and a colorful newcomer called **Equator.** The **Clipper Ship Bookstore** specializes in nautical volumes, and **Surfset Flagmakers** sells great flags across the street. Pillows and tableware are featured among home accessories at **Portabella.** Another concentration of stores is farther down Main Street at Griswold and Essex squares. **Red Balloon** offers precious clothes for precious children. At **Red Pepper,** we saw items we had never seen anywhere else, among them interesting glasses and goblets in all kinds of colors made in Upstate New York, and cat pins by a woman who lives on a farm with seven cats. The shop carries clothing from small designers, almost all made in this country – which is unusual these days.

The smell of fresh fudge nearly overpowered at **Sweet Martha's,** where you can find ice cream in 27 flavors; try caramel-almond-praline or a cappuccino frozen yogurt. Next door is **Ken's Coffeehouse,** which grinds twenty kinds of coffees from around the world, sells pastries to go with your cappuccino or latte, and offers live music on weekend nights. Genial owner Peter Charbonnier has fun with the place. He says Ken is "the guy in the coffee cup" on his logo, a fictional genie of sorts. Nearby is **Olive Oyl's** for carry-out cuisine and specialty foods. Sandwiches range from peanut butter and jelly to the French connection: pâté, brie and mustard on French bread. Or how about the liverachi: liverwurst, swiss, dijon mustard and red onion? Soups, salads, chowder and chili also are available.

Extra-Special

The Valley Railroad, Exit 3 off Route 9, Essex.

Its whistle tooting and smokestack spewing, the marvelous old steam train runs from the old depot in the Centerbrook section of Essex through woods and meadows to the Connecticut River landing at Deep River. There it connects with a riverboat for an hour's cruise past Gillette Castle to the Goodspeed Opera House and back. The two-hour trip into the past is rewarding for young and old alike.

Recently associated with the Valley Railroad is the **North Cove Express,** (800) 398-7427, a dinner train using the same tracks but its own restored dining cars. It offers dinner excursions Friday and Saturday for $29.95, periodic barbershop quartet dinner trips as well as train robbery and murder mystery excursions. Every Thursday night in summer is the new rail-to-river rendezvous. With an elegant dinner on the train and a moonlight cruise followed by dessert on the train, it's great fun.

(860) 767-0103. Trips run daily in summer, mainly weekends in spring and fall and at Christmas. Adults, $15 train and riverboat; $10 train only.

Stanley-Whitman House dating to 1660 is home of Farmington Museum.

Farmington Valley, Conn.

The Best of Both Worlds

A long mountain range separates the Hartford area from its outlying western suburbs. The Talcott Mountain range – "the mountain," as it's called locally – shields the Farmington River valley from the capital city and creates a place apart.

It is a special place of bucolic landscapes, meandering streams, venerable structures and lingering history. It's the place where their founders established no fewer than five private preparatory schools, where an industrialist's daughter gave her home as a prized museum, and where many executives of corporate Hartford today make their homes.

The "valley," as it's known locally, expands or contracts, depending on who is doing the defining. It always includes historic Farmington, home of the exclusive Miss Porter's School and some of the area's finest estates as well as office parks and corporate headquarters. Here you find a country club occupying one of the prime four corners in the center of town.

It includes Avon, a forested expanse of newer houses that command the region's highest prices. It includes Simsbury, a suburb that has lost more of its obvious 17th-century heritage than has Farmington but has retained more sense of community than Avon. For these purposes, the valley does not include Canton, Granby Burlington, Harwinton or, for that matter, our hometown of West Hartford, which is the largest town in the Farmington Valley Visitors Association but does not consider itself part of the valley at all.

The valley is a place more for seeing and doing than for contemplation. Hot-air ballooning, hang-gliding, horseback riding, river tubing and kayaking are the activities of note after tennis and golf. The International Skating Center of Connecticut adds another dynamic. There are museums to explore, countless shops (from boutiques to art galleries), interesting restaurants, rural byways and, recently, a handful of inns and B&Bs that qualify the valley as an inn spot as well as a special place.

Although this is suburbia, don't expect to see tract houses or many commercial strips. Most of the houses are tucked away on large lots off winding roads in the woods. Except along busy Route 44, the shops are in old houses and new clusters.

Stray from the mainstream, which is easy to do in the valley. You won't believe that a "suburb" is just around the corner, or that a city is just over the looming mountain. Partake of suburban and rural pleasures, but know that the diverse offerings of Hartford are only a dozen miles away.

"We have the best of both worlds," say leaders of the Farmington Valley Visitors Association. They have much to promote and increasingly receptive takers.

Inn Spots

Merrywood Bed & Breakfast, 100 Hartford Road (Route 185), Simsbury. 06070.

Michael Marti, a high-powered Pratt & Whitney manager, and his German-born wife Gerlinde had traveled the world, so they knew exactly what they wanted when they decided to open the valley's first professional, fulltime B&B. They found it in the old Glover estate, a 1939 Colonial Revival brick mansion hidden in five acres of an evergreen forest on the side of Avon Mountain.

They offer common areas unusual in both decor and number on the main floor, plus a second floor with two air-conditioned bedrooms and a suite, all with private baths and the creature comforts typical of a deluxe hotel, from sitting areas with TV/VCRs and a collection of old black and white movies to mini-refrigerators and whirlpool tub, sauna and steam shower.

Enter the impressive foyer and find a living room that is, well, unique. The furnishing are all antiques from the Continent, but most startling is the large display on the wall of spread-out Indian robes, hats from the Far East and, on the floor beneath, a lineup of at least twenty pairs of children's wooden shoes, mostly Dutch. Gerlinde collects textiles and is a dealer in antiques, and both are displayed liberally throughout the house. Off the living room is a large enclosed sunporch. Behind the living room is a sunny, well-stocked library of particular interest to travelers.

Breakfast may be served here or in a formal, somewhat formidable dining room outfitted in ornate Jacobean carved furniture that originated, Michael thinks, in a church in Germany or Italy. From a butler's pantry and adjacent kitchen comes the morning's meal, a wide selection from belgian waffles to german pancakes to eggs hussard, the choices checked off by the guest the night before. The Martis serve afternoon tea with finger sandwiches. They also will prepare four-course

Colonial Revival mansion is now Merrywood Bed & Breakfast.

dinners ($50 for two, including wine), served by candlelight in front of the fireplace in the living room.

Upstairs are the rear Empire Room (all American Empire antiques) with kingsize poster bed and the front Victorian Room, frilly and feminine with a queen bed draped from head to ceiling to foot in twenty feet of an antique lace tablecloth, with a wicker loveseat and two chairs nearby. The Continental Suite harbors a small queensize bedroom, an exotic bathroom with a sauna in a closet, and an enormous living room with two sitting areas, a Louis XV writing desk and, in one section, a full kitchenette used by long-term business guests who stay here.

Light opera or new-age music plays on a sound system throughout the house. Outside are walking paths and gardens.

The Martis bill theirs as "a bed and breakfast adventure." Responsive guests would agree.

(860) 651-1785. Fax (860) 651-8273. Two rooms and one suite with private baths. Doubles, $120. Suite, $145.

The Linden House, 288 Hopmeadow St., Simsbury 06070.

A circular stairway suspended in the turret is one of the remarkable architectural details in this Victorian B&B scheduled to open in 1998.

The stairway was installed once and then removed and rebuilt farther back from the windows. It was part of a lengthy and total renovation of the 1860 structure that formerly held railroad apartments and only got plumbing and heating in the 1950s. Julia and Myles McCabe from Westchester County bought it as a retirement project. The renovation turned out to be much more extensive than they anticipated. "We could have built three houses for what this is costing," Julia rued in her Irish accent as she and her husband were readying the finishing touches for a June opening. Only an old staircase to the couple's private quarters and the seven fireplace mantels were left from the original structure.

Beige with green trim, the structure is handsome and ornate on the outside with the landmark turret and a side porch. The interior has spacious rooms, but normal-height ceilings as opposed to the high ceilings of most Victorian houses.

The couple created five bedrooms, all with private baths and working fireplaces. Beds are king or queensize, except for one with two twins. A main-floor guest room in front of the side living room has a tiled bathroom with a jacuzzi tub. The upstairs bedrooms have clawfoot tubs, and one on the third floor comes with a refrigerator/microwave area. Julie planned a chaise lounge for every room, along with plush down comforters and duvets. "We have a house full of beautiful furniture and accessories collected over the years," she said, longing for the day when the construction work ended and the rooms took shape.

The dining room is large enough to hold a round table in one part and a long table in the middle. Here, Julia planned to serve a continental-plus breakfast of fruit, cheese, cereals and homemade breads. Tea or wine and cheese were on tap for the afternoon.

The B&B takes its name from a spreading linden tree in the front yard. The property stretches well back from Route 10 to the Farmington River, and the McCabes planned to exercise their love for gardening once they fnished the interior.

(860) 408-1321. Five rooms with private baths. Doubles, $85 to $95.

Simsbury 1820 House, 731 Hopmeadow St., Simsbury 06070.

Listed on the National Register of Historic Places, this country manor on a gentle rise above Simsbury's main street was restored by some of Hartford's movers and shakers, among them a corporate leader, a decorator and a restaurateur.

A veranda full of wicker, luncheon tables and baskets of hanging flowers greets guests at the entrance of the imposing gray building, reopened as an inn in 1986 and since taken over by the local group known as Classic Hotels of Connecticut. The entry and the public rooms retain the remarkable wainscoting, carved molding and leaded-glass windows of the original structure; all the gilt-framed oil paintings are reproductions. The living room, sun room and dining room are furnished in the manner of a country estate, although they appear quite business-like when used by day for meetings and functions.

Reproduction and English antiques grace the twenty guest rooms on the inn's three floors. King and queensize four-poster beds, wing chairs, chintz curtains, and shades of mauves and blues predominate. Most of the private baths have windows and have been tucked ingeniously into the nooks and crannies with which the house fascinates (one bathroom goes around a corner and is almost bigger than its bedroom). Most rooms have comfortable sitting areas for reading but not for watching television – the TVs are entrenched in front of the beds.

Across the side lawn designed by Frederick Law Olmsted, the Carriage House offers eleven more rooms and a suite, some of them on two or three levels and decorated in dark and masculine tones, a couple with an equine theme. Particularly interesting is the "executive suite" with its own garden terrace, a sitting room like a men's club and, up a couple of stairs, a room with a kingsize four-poster bed and an armoire. Beyond is a bathroom with a jacuzzi tub big enough for two, a separate shower, and his and her sinks. "European romance in Southern New England" is how one guest described a stay here.

A continental breakfast of fruits, juices, granola, cereal, muffins and breads is taken in the inn's sunroom. The inn's downstairs restaurant closed in early 1998.

(860) 658-7658 or (800) 879-1820. Fax (860) 651-0724. Thirty-one rooms and one suite with private baths. May-October: doubles, $125 to $185. Rest of year: $115 to $175. Suite, $145. Two-night minimum peak weekends.

Historic manor has been converted into Simsbury 1820 House.

The Barney House, 11 Mountain Spring Road, Farmington 06032.

You can live as the Farmington gentry do in this stately 1832 mansion, situated amid formal gardens on a winding street of secluded estates. It was donated by the family of the head of the Hartford Electric Light Co. to the University of Connecticut Foundation, which turned it into a low-key educational conference center and a B&B of character.

Business magazines and conference accoutrements are evident in the main-floor rooms, among them two dining rooms, a great hall lit by crystal chandeliers, a fireplaced library, and spacious porches framed with wisteria and awash with wicker. They give way on the second and third floors to six unusually spacious guest rooms with private baths. Only the fact that four have twin beds hints at the conference-center use; two have kingsize beds. The one in the third floor's Yale Room "is for the honeymooners," our guide pointed out. The smallest room in the house with lots of angles and ells, it's big enough to accommodate a twin bed as well.

Each room is distinguished by high ceilings, tall windows fronted by free-standing plants, well-worn oriental rugs and period furniture. Each has a small TV set and a phone. The rear Farmington Room is especially appealing, with huge closets, an enormous bath with separate shower and tub, and a pink chaise lounge for enjoying the many books. Through the window you can watch the sun set over a pond.

Guests enjoy the grounds, particularly the open side lawn, the formal gardens with a Victorian greenhouse whose lettuce and herbs later turn up in the dining room, and the long, deep swimming pool and tennis court. They also enjoy a continental breakfast of juice, cereal and a basket of fresh fruits, muffins and breads in the roomy second-floor hall where a sunny window seat is heaped with pillows. A small refrigerator in the third-floor hall contains sodas and tonic water, and a hot pot is at the ready for tea or coffee.

If they're lucky, overnight guests may happen onto a conference and enjoy a fine luncheon buffet or a dinner of highly regarded new American cuisine (prices vary, depending on the fare). Two chefs prepare meals for the conferences and private parties, and overnight guests are welcome to eat by prior arrangement.

(860) 674-2796. Fax (860) 677-7259. Six rooms with private baths. Doubles, $89.

The Simsbury Inn, 397 Hopmeadow St., Simsbury 06089.

New in 1988 and stylish as can be, this is really a sleek, gracious hotel with 98 rooms and suites. A fireplace warms the soaring lobby with its parquet floors that lead to the Nutmeg Cafe and the reception desk. Upstairs past a stunning antique chandelier is Twigs, a fireside lounge with a semi-circular bar. Guests pass a wine cellar along the hallway to Evergreens, the inn's pleasant restaurant. An indoor pool opens to the outside in summer and adjoins an exercise room with whirlpool and sauna.

Up the elevators are curving hallways leading to the light and pleasant guest rooms on three floors. Pineapples top the headboards of the beds, each covered with custom-designed pastel spreads. Lace curtains or draperies, antique clocks, remote-control TVs, work desks, closets with removable coat hangers and two double beds or one kingsize are standard. Bathrooms have superior lighting, solid brass fixtures, mini-refrigerators, built-in hair dryers and a basket of the inn's own amenities, including a small sewing kit. Beds are turned down on request and fresh towels are added to the ample supply on hand.

Four mini-suites have sitting areas, some with fireplaces. Two larger suites each have a living room attractive in Colonial Williamsburg style with a chintz sofa, an oriental rug over deep blue carpeting, a round table circled by four Queen Anne chairs and a TV with VCR hidden in an armoire. Another TV and a kingsize four-poster on a raised platform are in the adjoining bedroom. Extra touches like electric shoe polishers set the inn apart.

Breakfast is available in the snack bar or dining room. Dinner in Evergreens is from a changing menu of contemporary American/continental fare, ranging from pastas and grilled sea bass in a lime vinaigrette to veal loin and filet mignon with a choron sauce.

The inn is part of the locally based Classic Hotels of Connecticut.

(860) 651-5700 or (800) 634-2719. Fax (860) 651-8024. Ninety-two rooms, four mini-suites and two suites with private baths. Doubles, $149 EP. Suites, $200 to $275. Entrées, $16 to $24. Dinner, Tuesday-Saturday 5:30 to 9 or 10. Sunday brunch.

Avon Old Farms Hotel, Routes 10 and 44, Box 961, Avon 06001.

What started long ago as an ordinary motel has grown like topsy up and around a hill through two major additions and many levels into first an inn and now a hotel. The enterprising Brighenti family have parlayed it into something of a local lodging empire, recently acquiring the financially troubled Simsbury Inn, then the Farmington Inn and lately the Simsbury 1820 House. The group is now called Classic Hotels of Connecticut.

The original 24-room Avon motel with exterior doorways remains opposite the main entrance and the large, homey lobby where coffee is put out all day near the fireplace. Above the lobby, a second floor curves uphill to become the main floor. Eventually the visitor enters the grand new wing, a soaring spectacle of three marble floors with an open lobby, curving staircases and an elevator.

The 160 rooms and suites have kingsize or two double beds or a queensize bed with pullout sofa. They are distinguished by handsome watercolors of Farmington Valley scenes – more than 400 originals in all – and the current month of the Travelers Insurance Cos. calendars of Currier & Ives etchings framed on the walls.

Rooms increase in size and price as they wind up the hill. Those in the new Georgian-style wing adopt a luxury-hotel style with kingsize pencil-post beds,

Gazebo frames front view of The Simsbury Inn.

stenciled borders matching the fabrics, remote-control TVs and bathroom scales. Many yield woodland views. Two mini-suites have sofas and Queen Anne chairs.

There are an exercise room and sauna, and the twenty acres of grounds include a stream and a pool.

Three meals a day are served in the hotel's **Seasons Restaurant** (see Dining Spots), a glass-enclosed dining room overlooking woods and stream, with a handsome new pub beside. Continental breakfast is included in the rates.

(860) 677-1651 or (800) 836-4000. Fax (860) 677-0364. One hundred fifty-eight rooms and two mini-suites with private baths. Doubles, $119 to $159. Mini-suites, $225.

The Farmington Inn, 827 Farmington Ave., Farmington 06032.

Totally gutted and refurbished in 1988, the old Farmington Motor Inn was transformed into an inn of taste and value. We barely recognize the place where we stayed during a house-hunting trip nearly three decades ago.

More than most refurbished motels, this seems like an inn, from its lovely reception area with a fireplace, a couple of comfortable seating groupings and a basket of shiny red apples and a platter of cookies, to the jaunty second-floor dining area. A continental-plus breakfast with cereals and pastries is served here.

Seventeen artists were commissioned in 1997 to paint 150 local landmarks and landscapes to complement the decor as well as pique guests' interest in the Farmington Valley, according to Michael Brighenti, spokesman for the family owners.

Seventy-two rooms and "junior suites" go off interior hallways. Each has a recessed door beneath an overhead spotlight and bears a brass nameplate – "like entering your own home or apartment," as the manager put it. Rooms have king, queen or two double beds and are decorated in country or traditional style. The country involves light pine furniture and overstuffed club chairs. The traditional means dark cherry furniture, teal carpeting and mauve Queen Anne wing chairs. Bathrooms have lucite fixtures, separate vanities and baskets of toiletries.

The TVs are hidden in armoires in the junior suites, far from the bed and at an awkward angle from the sofas in the oversize rooms. With swagged draperies and substantial furnishings in teal and pink decor, the suites represent good value.

(860) 677-2861 or (800) 648-9804. Fax (860) 677-8332. Fifty-nine rooms and thirteen junior suites with private baths. Doubles, $99 to $119. Suites, $109 to $159.

Dining Spots

Apricots, 1591 Farmington Ave., Farmington.

Outside on the jaunty terrace beside the Farmington River. Inside on the enclosed porch, its windows taking full advantage of the view, its white walls painted whimsically with branches of apricots. Beyond in a more formal dining room of brick and oak. Or downstairs in a cozy pub with exposed pipes painted with more apricots. These are the varied settings offered by one of the Hartford area's more popular and enduring restaurants.

The food is usually equal to the setting, thanks to the inspiration of Ann Howard, a Farmington resident first known for her cooking lessons and later the Ann Howard Cookery, from which she and her staff cater some of the best parties in town. In 1982 she reopened an abandoned French restaurant in an old trolley barn sandwiched between Route 4 and the river, calling it Apricots, "a juicy pub." Expansion was planned in 1998.

We know folks who eat dinner at least once a week in the cozy, convivial pub, which offers items like grilled salmon, chicken pot pie and venison stew. We prefer the upstairs porch with its view of the passing river. For lunch, we've enjoyed the spinach and strawberry as well as the cobb salads, the specialty chicken pot pie, a vegetarian focaccia pie with romaine and radish salad, a creamy fettuccine with crabmeat and mushrooms, grilled lime chicken and wonderful mussels.

At night, when the dining room turns serene, entrées run from roast chicken stuffed with chestnuts and wild mushrooms to rack of spring lamb. Seasonal favorites are ginger-rubbed salmon with a soy-wasabi vinaigrette, crispy duck confit and grilled pork chops with chipotle pepper sauce. Start with sautéed lobster with truffle butter over orecchiette pasta, a grilled portobello napoleon or wilted spinach and lamb with feta cheese and pancetta vinaigrette. Finish with apricot gelato, tirami su or one of the heavenly cakes – marquis au chocolate, charlotte russe, New York cheesecake with strawberry puree and lemon roulade. Or indulge in the Ann Howard ice cream sandwich: chocolate biscuits with almonds and white chocolate chunks held together with praline ice cream and set atop strawberry sauce with a white chocolate lace.

The staff, some of whom have been at Apricots for years, treats customers like the old friends that many of them are.

(860) 673-5405. Entrées, $17.50 to $26; pub, $7.95 to $11.95. Lunch, Monday-Saturday 11:30 to 2:30. Dinner nightly, 6 to 10; pub from 2:30. Sunday, brunch 11:30 to 2:30, dinner 5:30 to 9.

Max-A-Mia, 70 East Main St., Avon.

A fabulously successful offshoot of Hartford's inspired Max Downtown, this suburban hot spot is hot. Hot as in trendy, hot in value and hot in popularity. Folks are lined up day and night and waits of an hour or more are not uncommon.

And why not, when you can dine well and happily on a variety of thin-crusted pizzas called stone pies, assertive pastas (some baked al forno in the wood-fired

Apricot stenciling adorns porch dining room overlooking Farmington River at Apricots.

oven) and a few grills at wallet-pleasing prices. The formula works, for the place expanded in 1998 into an adjacent storefront.

A birthday lunch became quite festive here when four of us sampled the sautéed chicken livers (served elaborately with white beans, roasted shallots, arugula, plum tomatoes, porcini mushrooms and fresh herbs), the sautéed catfish topped with a cucumber salad and served over a roasted plum tomato and lavender coulis, the PLT (prosciutto, arugula, roma tomatoes and fresh mozzarella served on focaccia), and a di Bella Luna stone pie with white clams, sweet roasted peppers, pancetta and parmigiana. An order of bruschetta and a $14 bottle of pinot grigio from the all-Italian wine list accompanied. Tirami su, ricotta cheesecake with amarone cherries, chocolate polenta cake with cappuccino sauce and chocolate-hazelnut gelato were better than any birthday cake.

As if the wide-ranging menu weren't enough to draw regulars back, the daily specials here are really special. The food takes precedence over the decor, which is sleek but simple in yellow and brown with wood trim, track lighting and a mix of tables and booths. A bottle of olive oil and a container of impossibly tall and thin breadsticks are the centerpiece on each. The lively crowd provides the rest of the color. And, we should warn you, this place can be so noisy that you can't hear yourself think.

(860) 677-6299. Entrées, $13.95 to $17.95. Open daily, 11:30 to 10 or 11. Sunday, brunch 11 to 2:30, dinner 4 to 9.

Métro bis, 928 Hopmeadow St., Simsbury.
You might think the name for this 60-seat charmer is short for Metropolitan Bistro, which in a sense it is. But it's really a dual meaning, says Kathleen Schwartz, partner with French chef-caterer Claude Maurice of the former Métro Kitchen in Granby. Bis is the French word for once again, and this encore to the Granby operation is furnished in part with subway benches, doors and other paraphernalia from the Paris métro that Claude's family was involved in renovating.

The long, narrow room is ever-so-sophisticated and inviting, with cut lace curtains along the side windows, crystal chandeliers, fascinating art on every available inch of wall space, copper pans, marble-top tables and, beside the entrance, entire regiments of lead soldiers in a glass case. And we like the spirit of the contemporary French fare. At a winter lunch, we sampled an outstanding tomato-pasta-pesto soup with chunks of nuts floating therein, samplers of exotic salads, and the best crêpes we have ever tasted, the delicate pancakes filled with large shrimp and scallops with a lovely sauce. We also liked the black forest mousse and the cappuccino.

At dinner, you might begin with escargots, duck breast and lentil gâteau with raspberry vinaigrette or a country pâté of veal, pork and ham with a caramelized onion, red wine and cassis confit. Entrées could be pan-seared salmon with leek-chardonnay sauce, roast tenderloin of pork with mustard-sage cream sauce, and tournedos with a stellar marchand de vin sauce. There are always interesting specials, and we hear good things about the cocoa dacquoise, the kahlua praline coupe de glace and the crêpes chantilly with strawberries or chocolate ganache. We can vouch for the ginger tuile flower filled with grand marnier pastry cream, kiwi-strawberry compote and raspberry puree.

A breakfast menu is served on weekends, including many flavors of croissants. Métro french toast made with oatmeal bread, cream cheese and warm berry sauce sounds wonderful.

(860) 651-1908. Entrées, $16.95 to $21.95. Lunch, Tuesday-Friday 11 to 2. Breakfast and lunch, weekends 9 to 2. Dinner, Tuesday-Saturday 5:30 to 9 or 10, Sunday 5 to 8.

Piccolo Arancio, 819 Farmington Ave., Farmington.
Of all the contemporary Italian restaurants sprouting like topsy, this is one of the more warm and inviting. Brothers Salvatore and Dino Cialfi, owners of Hartford's acclaimed Peppercorns Grill, branched out with "as authentic-looking a trattoria as you'll ever see in Connecticut," in Dino's words, "because it's like the ones where we lived in Italy."

They converted the ground floor of a former office building next to the Farmington Inn into a couple of dining rooms done up in Mediterranean earth tones, with rich mahogany trim and a ceiling of light blue to give the impression of being outside. A tape of an Italian singer provides background music.

From a wood oven, wood grill and rotisserie in the semi-open kitchen, chef Sal serves what he calls rustic, simple fare. That translates to robust pizzas, quite a selection of homemade pastas and basic grills. More complex are such entrées as roasted red snapper on a bed of sautéed fennel, sautéed chicken with rock shrimp in a cognac cream sauce, osso buco and grilled filet mignon with a pink peppercorn sauce. A Tuscan-style pot roast hits the spot on a winter night.

Start with a classic carpaccio, seafood seviche, grilled shrimp with crispy gnocchi or a choice of bruschettas. Crème caramel, tirami su, chocolate mousse and an ethereal eggless custard are typical desserts.

(860) 674-1224. Entrées, $15.95 to $20.95. Lunch, Monday-Friday 11:30 to 2:30. Dinner, Monday-Saturday 5 to 10 or 11.

The Grist Mill, Mill Lane, Farmington.
The 1650 grist mill beside the Farmington River was reopened in 1994 as a cafe and restaurant by veteran restaurateur Mario Zacco (of Farmington's late Corner House and New York Restaurant Associates fame). The site had been the home of

an antiques shop and of our favorite Reading Room restaurant, but had been empty for some years.

Mario kept the decor of the historic building as authentic as possible, with exposed beams and rustic walls, a grist mill wheel in the dining room and mill chains hanging from the ceiling. Mirrors and angles add dimension, and there's a river view from most tables.

The kitchen is on full display through big windows to the outside as you enter. Its focal point is a rotisserie turning natural-grain chicken, roasts of beef, pork and lamb, game in season and even roasted lobster. Other main courses on the French/ Italian menu include pastas, seafood from saltwater shellfish to fresh trout from the mill's own tank, and such "traditions" as dover sole meunière, veal piccata, lamb chops and filet mignon with sauce bercy. Quail, partridge, squab and rabbit are prepared with advance notice.

Expect such starters as house-smoked salmon, duck liver pâté and lobster, shrimp and avocado salad. Desserts include Italian ice creams that Mario makes himself, crêpes filled with apples and raisins, amaretto cheesecake, fresh fruit tortes and gelati.

(860) 676-8855. Entrées, $13.95 to $22.50. Lunch, Monday-Saturday 11:30 to 2:30. Dinner, 5:30 to 9 or 10, Sunday 11:30 to 8.

Avon Old Farms Inn, 1 Nod Road, Avon.

The sign inside the old entry identifies this as one of the twenty oldest restaurants in the country. The sign serves a purpose, for the huge new banquet and conference facility, a focal point in back, conveys quite another impression.

Established in 1757, this is strictly a restaurant and function house (a hotel of similar name but separate ownership is across the busy intersection of Route 44 and Route 10). The heart of this endearing place has always been the seven dining rooms that sprawl through a series of additions hugging the old Albany Turnpike in front. The choicest is the Forge Room, far at the end of the old building. A splendid tavern atmosphere is this, with rough dark stone walls, flagstone floors, cozy booths made from old horse stalls, and lots of equestrian accessories hanging from dark beams. Bright red tablecloths and red leather chairs add color to the room, which is one of the most atmospheric around.

The Sunday champagne brunch has been voted best in the state for eighteen years by Connecticut magazine readers. Set up in the main dining room, the spread is dished out by twenty servers at two long banquet tables, then taken to one of the six other rooms, which have enough nooks and crannies to offer privacy. Up to 700 people may be served at three seatings.

New American cuisine in a quintessential Yankee setting is featured at lunch and dinner, when service is personal and each dining room functions almost as its own restaurant. The extensive dinner menu opens with treats like lobster bisque, watercress and beet salad, smoked salmon roll and crispy shrimp with pineapple-ginger sauce. Traditional favorites like baked stuffed shrimp and prime rib have been augmented lately by cutting-edge fare: pan-seared sea bass with banana mashed sweet potatoes, stone-broiled swordfish with pear-tomato salsa and rack of lamb with plum-wine sauce and goat cheese-mashed potatoes. The English trifle is still a masterpiece among desserts.

(860) 677-2818. Entrées, $16.95 to $27.95. Lunch, Monday-Saturday noon to 2:30. Dinner, 5:30 to 9:30 or 10:30. Sunday, brunch 10 to 2:30, dinner 5:30 to 8:30.

Fat Cat Cafe, 136 Simsbury Road, Riverdale Farms, Avon.

Talented chef Glenn Thomas left the nearby Seasons Restaurant (see below) in 1997 to open his own place in a nearby Riverdale Farms property that has had a succession of short-lived restaurants. The name is obscure – "fine dining, no whining" is the logo. But the food is typically Thomas, that is to say innovative and reflective of the seasons. Robust food and affordable prices have packed in the crowds.

We sampled the fare at lunch, when a pasta special of roasted chicken with portobellos and adobo sauce over penne – a rather small portion for so big a bowl – and the house antipasto with prosciutto, roasted peppers, mozzarella and salad greens hit the spot. The antipasto was too much for one; the other filled up on good, crusty sourdough bread.

For a winter's night, the menu trotted out Thomas trademarks like rotisserie chicken topped with "our grandmother-style" pan sauce and roasted garlic, thick-cut mahi-mahi steak with grilled fruit relish, pan-seared shrimp and pancetta over braised escarole, and cassoulet of duck confit, pork and lamb shank with country-style beans and garlic sausage. Start with shrimp and crab gumbo or chicken liver terrine with brandied fruit relish. Finish with a warm apple-cranberry crisp or white chocolate crème brûlée.

(860) 674-1310. Entrées, $14.95 to $17.95. Lunch, Tuesday-Saturday 11 to 2. Dinner, Tuesday-Saturday 5 to 9 or 10.

Seasons Restaurant, Avon Old Farms Hotel, Routes 10 and 44, Avon.

Off an atrium in the hotel's new wing is a glass-enclosed restaurant, upgraded from a cafe and known for outstanding regional American cuisine. Chef Charles Williams carried on the tradition launched by founding chef Glenn Thomas.

The semi-circular back room looks out onto the trees and changing seasons. It is colorful in pink, green and white with balloon curtains framing the view and green beams on the ceiling. Piano music and monthly art shows provide entertainment, and there's a stylish new pub with a casual menu at the side.

The fare changes with the seasons. At our winter visit, we were tempted by entrées like sea bass baked in white wine, a classic bouillabaisse, herb-roasted chicken with velouté sauce and grilled veal chop with exotic mushrooms. Smoked cream of chicken soup, tangy crab fritters and sweet potato pierogi with basil cream sauce make good starters. Among desserts are chocolate mousse cake, raspberry linzer torte and homemade sorbets.

(860) 677-6352. Entrées, $18 to $22. Lunch, Monday-Friday 11:30 to 2. Dinner, Monday-Saturday 5 to 9; Sunday brunch, 11 to 1.

Newport Blues Cafe, 51 East Main St., Avon.

Local business-sports tycoon Brian Foley took over the old theme-park Airstream's Roadside Cafe in 1997, transforming it into an encore of his successful blues cafe in Newport, R.I.

Here he toned down the old dining venue to a neon blue dining room and bar with a stage at one end. He added a more casual sports dining room in back with big-screen TVs to satisfy sports fans, and renovated the outdoor deck to provide a Tuscan-style grill.

Live jazz and blues are offered Thursday-Saturday nights and proved an instant hit. The cafe sponsors a gospel brunch on Sundays.

Lest skeptics think the entertainment takes precedence, Brian hired French chef Serges Backes – who had opened several of his own Avon restaurants – to oversee the kitchen. The menu speaks with a contemporary French accent, as in grilled tuna with sesame-soy vinaigrette, Cajun swordfish, shellfish savannah, saffron risotto, braised lamb shanks provençal, venison tenderloin and grilled sirloin steak with wild mushrooms and béarnaise sauce.

Dessert, after-dinner drinks and blues were becoming addictive, according to weekend regulars.

(860) 676-2583. Entrées, $16 to $22. Lunch, Tuesday-Sunday 11 to 3. Dinner, Tuesday-Saturday 5 to 10 or 11.

Diversions

Stanley-Whitman House, 37 High St., Farmington.

The most painstakingly accurate restoration said to have been undertaken in a New England house preceded the reopening of this 1660 structure that houses the Farmington Museum, one of the best examples of a 17th-century frame overhang house in New England. With rare diamond-paned windows, it is furnished with early American pieces, many the gifts of local residents. It offers a fascinating glimpse into the life and conditions enjoyed – or endured – by the early colonists. The grounds reflect the utilitarian uses of a Colonial dooryard garden with culinary, medicinal and herbal plantings.

(860) 677-9222. Open May-October, Wednesday-Sunday noon to 4; rest of year, Sunday noon to 4. Adults, $5.

Massacoh Plantation, 800 Hopmeadow St., Simsbury.

Three centuries of Simsbury history dating to Indian days are recreated in this little complex of buildings most interesting for its reproduction of a 1683 meeting house, nicely hedged and screened from a nondescript shopping plaza. The adjacent 1771 Elisha Phelps House shows the furnishings of an early tavern and canal hotel. The low-key complex also has a 1740 school house, a pastor's cottage, sheds full of Victorian carriages and, surprise, a gallery of contemporary art and sculpture.

(860) 658-2500. Open May-October, daily 1 to 4. Adults, $5.

Heublein Tower, Talcott Mountain State Park, Route 185, Simsbury.

A national historic site, the landmark, 165-foot-high tower built as part of a summer home by the Gilbert Heublein family (of Heublein liquor fame) atop Talcott Mountain is open to the public as an observation tower and small museum. The four-state view from the top is smashing during fall foliage, but worth the 1.2-mile climb from the parking lot at any time. Along the ridge you may see members of the Connecticut Hang Gliding Association soaring from the cliffside trail that's considered one of the best gliding spots anywhere.

(860) 677-0662. Open April 15 to Labor Day, Monday-Friday 10 to 5; Labor Day to early November, daily 10 to 5. Free.

Arts and Crafts. Of special interest is the **Farmington Valley Arts Center,** 25 Arts Center Lane, Avon, 678-1867. A park-like setting of century-old factory buildings in Avon Park North off Route 44 contains a complex of studios for more than 40 artists, who open at their whim but often can be seen at work on weekends. The Fisher Gallery Shop is open all year, Wednesday-Saturday 10 to 5, Sunday noon to 4; extended hours in November-December. The Center's annual Christmas show and sale is a great place to pick up holiday gifts.

The **Farmington Crafts Common,** 248 Main St. (Route 10), Farmington, 674-9295, is a co-op where more than 2000 artists and crafters show under one roof. A coffee and sandwich shop is part of the complex. Almost across the street is **Farmington Lodge Antiques,** a large group antiques shop housed in a 1763 mansion where each room is furnished to a different theme.

Outdoor Activities. The **Farmington River** is popular with canoeists and bird-watchers. Hikers can walk along sections of its banks in Farmington, Avon and Simsbury. Water-skiers may be seen jumping in the Collinsville section of Canton. A popular activity is **tubing.** Young and old alike enjoy riding double-inflatable tubes down the river from Satan's Kingdom State Recreation Area in New Hartford to Canton. Tubes may be rented at Satan's Kingdom for $9 a ride. The newest activity is **kayaking.** Rentals are available from Collinsville Canoe & Kayak along Route 179 in Collinsville, which claims to be New England's biggest such outfitter.

For reasons best known to those involved, the same mountain and valley that are so good for hang-gliding are also favorable for **hot-air ballooning.** No fewer than six outfits now float over the area in season, presenting a colorful spectacle at dawn and sometimes at dusk. The hour's ride is quite an event, which explains the price ($175 to $200 per person). KAT Balloons Inc. leaves from the "balloon farm" at 40 Meadow Lane, Farmington, 678-7921. Reservations are required long in advance.

International Skating Center of Connecticut, 1375 Hopmeadow St., Simsbury, 651-5400. Olympic champions Oksana Baiul, Viktor Petrenko and Ekaterina Gordeeva were among those in early residence at this eye-popping center, which emerged quickly from concept to reality in 1994. Up-and-coming skaters from across the world make Simsbury their temporary home as they work their way into the international spotlight. Two side-by-side indoor rinks are busy day and night with Olympic training sessions, hockey games, skating lessons and public skating hours (mostly on weekends). Also here are a skate shop, the Sk8ters Cafe and even a video arcade featuring hockey games.

Shopping. This sophisticated suburban area provides a variety of shopping opportunities, from the upscale stores (Lord & Taylor, Nordstrom, Brooks Brothers and Abercrombie's) at **Westfarms** mall on the Farmington-West Hartford border to free-standing shops throughout the valley.

Historic atmosphere pervades the site and shops of Old Avon Village along Route 44. Browsers like the setting and such stores as the **Little Silver Shop.** Gifts and garden things are offered at **Ribbons & Roses,** while **Country at Heart** stocks rag rugs, handpainted pottery and lots of dolls.

The shops get tonier as Old Avon Village melds into the Shops at River Park. You'll find everything for bird feeding and watching at the **Wild Bird Center** and every with-it children's outfit at **Little Darlings.** A branch of **The Secret Garden of Martha's Vineyard** carries gifts, paper goods and toiletries. **The Pampered Bath** speaks for itself. For distinctive paper goods and stationery, there's no better place than **Lettres.**

Nearby is Avon's Riverdale Farms, which advertises "today's shopping amid yesterday's charms." Some buildings have been converted from barns from a 19th-century dairy farm, while others are newly built (the latest looks barn-like from the outside but plants cascade down a two-story atrium inside its handsome interior). The tenant mix changes frequently.

Fine Colonial Revival country house is home of prized Hill-Stead Museum.

The Simsburytown Shops are the most interesting in Simsbury. **The Work Shoppe** offers gifts and accessories of timeless tradition (though we thought their bird "lunch stations" were hardly traditional). **Finula's** stocks women's sportswear and **La Grande Pantrie,** cheeses, specialty foods and kitchen accessories.

Extra-Special _____

Hill-Stead Museum, 35 Mountain Road, Farmington.

This exceptional cultural treasure is important on three fronts: art, architecture and furnishings. The 29-room white clapboard house with rambling wings and a Mount Vernon facade is considered one of the finest Colonial Revival country houses in America. Willed as a museum by its designer and last occupant, architect Theodate Pope Riddle, it's a pleasantly personal masterpiece of a mansion that remains as she left it. Hung on its walls is the matchless collection of one of the earliest American collectors of Impressionist paintings before they became fashionable – what Henry James in 1907 called "wondrous examples of Manet, of Degas, of Claude Monet, of Whistler." The furnishings include remarkable mementos of an early 20th-century family, from Corinthian pottery and Chinese porcelain to a first edition of Samuel Johnson's *Dictionary* and a handwritten letter from Franklin D. Roosevelt. As you are guided on an hour-long tour, it is "as if the owners, having to be away for the afternoon, nevertheless invited you to stop for a time to delight in their house and collection," as a museum guide puts it. The 150-acre property's elaborate sunken gardens, designed by landscape architect Beatrix Farrand, have been reconstructed to their pre-1925 state.

(860) 677-4787. Open Tuesday-Sunday 10 to 5, May-October; Tuesday-Sunday 11 to 4, rest of year. Adults, $6.

Lake Waramaug provides backdrop for wines at Hopkins Vineyard.

Litchfield/Lake Waramaug
Connecticut's Colonial Country

Nestled in the hills of Northwest Connecticut, picturesque Lake Waramaug boasts an alpine setting that appeals enough to an Austrian innkeeper to call it home. Nearby is Litchfield, the quintessential Colonial Connecticut town preserved not as a restoration in the tradition of Williamsburg, with which it has been compared, but as a living museum community.

The lake and the town, ten miles apart, represent the heart of the Litchfield Hills, a chic yet sedate area of prep schools and foxhunts, of church spires and town greens. The landed gentry who call this never-never land home are joined by celebrity New Yorkers who savor its low-key lifestyle.

Hills rise sharply above the boomerang-shaped Lake Waramaug. Its sylvan shore is flanked by a state park, substantial summer homes, and four country inns. With little commercialism, it's enveloped in a country feeling, away from it all.

Litchfield, a small county seat whose importance long has transcended its borders, is perched atop the crest of a ridge. Its beautiful North and South streets are lined with gracious homes and exude history (George Washington slept here, Harriet Beecher Stowe was born here, Ethan Allen lived here, the nation's first law school and its first academy for girls were founded here). The village is so preserved and prized that only in recent years has it attracted the inns, restaurants and the kind of shops that affluence demands.

Between the hills and lakes are fine natural and low-key attractions –

Connecticut's largest nature sanctuary, a world-famous garden center, two farm wineries, state parks and forests. Connecticut's entire Northwest Corner has much to commend it, but there's no more choice a slice than Litchfield and Lake Waramaug.

Inn Spots

Mayflower Inn, Route 47, Box 1288, Washington 06793.

It's long been hidden away on 28 hilly, wooded acres overlooking the campus of The Gunnery, the private school that used to own and operate it. But a $15 million renovation and expansion has cast this venerable inn into the limelight as one of the premier English-style country hotels in America.

"Stately" is the word to describe the entire place as styled in 1992 by New York owners Robert and Adriana Mnuchin and steered since by general manager John Trevenen. The Mnuchins – he a Goldman Sachs whiz for 30 years and she a retailer and born-to-shop collector – have a weekend home here and, with an obsession for detail, dedicated themselves to putting the up-and-down Mayflower Inn of the past on the up path forever.

No expense was spared in producing 25 guest rooms and suites that are the ultimate in good taste. A staff of 85 adds to the feeling of pampered luxury. Fifteen rooms are upstairs on the second and third floors of the expanded main inn. Ten more are in two guest houses astride a hill beside a magnificent tiered rose garden leading up to a heated swimming pool and a tennis court.

Fine British, French and American antiques and accessories, prized artworks and elegant touches of whimsy – like four old trunks stashed in a corner of the second-floor hallway – dignify public and private rooms alike. Opening off the lobby, an intimate parlor with plush leather sofa and chairs leads into the ever-so-British gentleman's library. It possesses one of the largest collections of mystery novels in Connecticut, Playbills from the 1930s and the complete works of Wharton and James, plus a curved bay window looking across the side veranda to manicured lawns. Across the back of the inn are three dining rooms (see Dining Spots), and along one side is an English-style bar. Downstairs is a state-of-the-art fitness center that would do many a private club proud. The outlying Teahouse is a tranquil,

Adirondack-style lodge that's the ultimate meeting facility. Opposite the front desk is a gift shop offering small antiques, Italian leather goods, cashmere sweaters, jewelry and such of appeal to Adriana's New York set (the first guests to book a suite were Mike Nichols and Diane Sawyer, who were at the inn for Stephen Sondheim's birthday party).

Suite or no, each guest room is a sight to behold and some are almost unbelievably glamorous. Room 24 offers a kingsize canopy four-poster feather bed awash in pillows, embroidered Frette linens, a feather duvet and a chenille throw. An angled loveseat faces the fireplace, and oversize wicker rockers await on the balcony. Books and magazines are spread out on the coffee table, the armoire contains a TV and there's a walk-in closet. The paneled bathroom, bigger than most bedrooms, has marble floors, a double vanity opposite a glistening tub, a separate w.c. area and a walk-in shower big enough for an army. Even all that didn't prepare us for a second-floor corner suite with a large living room straight out of Country Life magazine, a dining-conference room, a lavatory, a bedroom with a kingsize canopied four-poster and a second bathroom, plus a porch over-looking the sylvan scene.

And so it goes, room after room of great comfort and élan – each full of surprises and "everything with a story behind it," according to our guide. Fancy toiletries and fresh orchids and nosegays of roses (Adriana's favorite flowers) are much in evidence. The rear balconies and decks off the rooms in the guest houses face the woods and are particularly private.

The outside is equally magnificent, from the acres of lawns shimmering in emerald green to the exotic specimen trees strategically placed all around. The 28 acres of horticultural Eden include terraced Shakespeare, rose and cutting gardens. The Mnuchins had a hiking trail blazed to the top of the big hill they renamed Mayflower Mountain, where a ring of stones is now "Meditation Circle."

Breakfast, available from a full menu, is a pricey extravagance that's likely to add $25 to $40 more to an overnight bill for two. The oversize Limoges breakfast cups were custom-designed for the Mayflower based on what the Mnuchins enjoyed during whirlwind travels to Europe as they planned their inn.

From the beguiling botanical and canine prints in the hallways to the weeping Alaskan blue atlas cedar and boxwood gardens outside, the place is a treasure for those who appreciate the finest.

Recently, the Mayflower became the first Connecticut property to become associated with the Paris-based Relais & Châteaux hotel group. It also recorded a stunning 80-plus percent annual occupancy rate. Said manager Trevenen, with a trace of Australian accent: "We've reached the niche where we want to be."

(860) 868-9466. Fax (860) 868-1497. Seventeen rooms and eight suites with private baths. Rates EP. Doubles, $250 to $415. Suites, $430 to $630. Two-night minimum weekends. Children over 12. Smoking restricted.

The Boulders Inn, Route 45, New Preston 06777.

Its setting just across the road from Lake Waramaug, its handsome and comfortable living room, its deluxe guest houses and carriage house, and its fine kitchen make this an appealing inn. Built as a private home in 1895, it has been a small inn since about 1950. Kees and Ulla Adema of Fairfield, he a ship's broker from Holland and she born in Germany, took it over in 1988 as a retirement venture. "We were thinking of a three-room B&B," recalls Ulla. "Instead, we bought an inn with a restaurant and now we seem to be running a restaurant with an inn."

The food operation (see Dining Spots) keeps them busy, but the Ademas have made fine improvements to the three guest rooms and two suites in the inn as well as the eight more contemporary rooms in four outlying duplex guest houses. They also added a rear carriage house with three choice guest rooms with plush chintz seating in front of stone fireplaces.

Rooms upstairs in the main house come with thick carpeting, comfortable sofas

Library at Mayflower Inn is dressed in finest British style.

or chairs, and king or queensize beds, most covered with handsome quilts. Period antiques, American folk art and Ulla's intricate cut-paper lampshades are the norm. Three rooms facing the lake offer large, cushioned window seats to take in the view, and a corner suite has its own balcony. All come with private baths, as do the eight rooms in the duplexes scattered along the hillside behind the inn. Renovated and upgraded with four-poster beds, air conditioning and fireplaces, guest houses have new decks in front and back facing woods and lake, and four have whirlpool tubs. The fireplaces and whirlpools make them especially popular with the New Yorkers who comprise the bulk of the Boulders clientele.

Back in the inn, a basement game room offers ping-pong and skittles, and a library has been added to a small den with a color TV. The paneled living room, its picture windows overlooking the lake (binoculars are provided), is a lovely mix of antiques and groupings of sofas and wing chairs in reds, blues and chintz. In one corner are book shelves and a stereo with many tapes. A Russian samovar may dispense tea in winter months, and guests also enjoy cocktails here.

In summer, swimming, sailing and canoeing are favorite pastimes. If you feel lazy, just sit in the beach house's wicker swing and watch the changing moods of the lake.

A full breakfast is served by the windows in the six-sided Lake Dining Room. A help-yourself cold buffet is set up with fresh fruit and juices, cereals and coffee cake. Eggs any style, omelets, french toast and pecan, apple or blueberry pancakes with bacon, sausage or ham can be ordered and are accompanied by English muffins or homemade whole wheat toast.

(860) 868-0541 or (800) 552-6853. Fax (860) 868-1925. Six rooms, two suites and eight guest houses with private baths. May-October and all weekends: doubles, $200 B&B, $250 MAP. Suites and guest houses, $200 to $250 B&B, $250 to $300. Memorial Day-October weekends: $50 more. November-April midweek: $50 less. Three-night minimum on summer weekends.

Toll Gate Hill, Route 202, Litchfield 06759.

The rural 1745 landmark home near the Torrington town line in which Captain William Bull once took in travelers on the Hartford-Albany stage route was handsomely restored and reopened as a small inn and a good restaurant in 1983. Inviting it is, situated back from the road in a stand of trees, its red frame exterior dimly illuminated at night and appearing to the traveler much as it must have more than two centuries ago.

Such was the demand for the six original rooms that innkeeper Fritz Zivic opened four more rooms and suites in the adjacent "school house." A new building with ten more rooms and suites and a much-needed lobby/reception area has since been added toward the rear of the property.

Although the main inn with the restaurant is listed on the National Register of Historic Places, the most choice guest rooms are those in the outbuildings. They're splashily decorated with comfort in mind, and an emphasis on coordinated Hinson and Schumacher fabrics, bright colors, queensize canopy beds, and upholstered chairs and loveseats.

Fireplaces are attractions in three rooms and five suites. The latter also have minibars stocked with a split of wine and Perrier. The bathrooms are outfitted with Gucci colognes. The bedspreads are coordinated to match the shower curtains, and in the soaring two-story lobby, the paisley print on the walls is repeated in the chairs and curtains. Balconies overlooking the woods off rooms in the new building hold chairs and a small table.

The nicest rooms in the main inn are three larger ones on the second floor, each with a working fireplace. A small parlor for house guests is located on the second-floor landing next to the ballroom.

A continental breakfast of fresh juice and homemade breads and rolls is served on trays in the guest rooms or in the restaurant (see Dining Spots).

(860) 567-4545 or (800) 445-3903. Fax (860) 567-8397. Fifteen rooms and five suites with private baths. Mid-May through December and all weekends: doubles $110 to $140, suites $175. January to mid-May, midweek: doubles $90 to $115, suites $150. Two-night minimum weekends. Children and pets welcome.

The Hopkins Inn, 22 Hopkins Road, New Preston 06777.

This landmark yellow inn astride a hill above Lake Waramaug is known far and wide for its European cuisine (see Dining Spots), and we often recommend it when asked where to take visitors for lunch in the country. Its reputation was built by Swiss-born innkeepers and has been continued since the late 1970s by Austrian Franz Schober and his wife Beth.

Built in 1847 as a summer guest house, the Federal structure with several additions was converted from a boarding house into an inn in 1945, and the guest rooms have been considerably enhanced by the Schobers. Warmed only by small heating units (thus used only from late March through December), the eleven guest rooms and an apartment on the second and third floors have been sparingly but comfortably furnished with brass or wood bedsteads, thick carpeting, floral wallpapers, chests of drawers and the odd loveseat or rocker. Nine rooms have private baths. A new two-bedroom apartment has been added in an annex.

Guests share a couple of small main-floor parlors with restaurant patrons, and may use the inn's private beach on the lake. There's no better vantage point for lake-watching than the expansive outdoor dining terrace, shaded by a giant horse

Landmark 19th-century hilltop structure above Lake Waramaug houses Hopkins Inn.

chestnut tree and distinguished by striking copper and wrought-iron chandeliers and lanterns. Breakfast is available for house guests.

(860) 868-7295. Fax (860) 868-7464. Doubles, $63 to $73, EP. Apartments, $80 and $140 EP. Two-night minimum weekends. Closed January to late March.

The Birches Inn, 233 West Shore Road, New Preston 06777.

A trucker from nearby Middlebury poured big bucks into a total renovation of this venerable inn on Lake Waramaug in 1996. He found innkeeping was not his forte, so he leased the property in 1997 to Nancy Conant, owner of the venerable Inn on Lake Waramaug across the lake. She promptly installed talented French chef Frederic Faveau and his wife, Karen Hamilton, as innkeepers in residence.

The result is fortuitous for all. The guest rooms and the inn experience are much improved, and the meals are sensational (see Dining Spots).

The inn's second floor has been renovated and reconfigured to produce five handsome guest rooms with private baths. Room 7, the largest, claims the best lake view. It has a king bed, two armchairs, an impressive armoire and handpainted bureau. The bathroom with a double vanity comes with the terry robes, hair dryer and Caswell-Massey toiletries common to all. Room 8, with queen poster bed and a sofabed beneath skylights, opens onto a rear balcony shared with guests in two other rooms.

The most coveted rooms are the three in the Lake House. They're smaller but share an extended deck beside the water, and the views are spectacular. "You can almost fish from the porch," Frederic said wistfully as he led a tour. One has a king bed with a brass headboard, a loveseat, a wicker rocker and the inn's only jacuzzi. The other two have queen beds.

Back in the main inn, classical music wafts through the public areas, including a small parlor with a fireplace, where wine and cheese are put out in the afternoon. Breakfast is served in a sunny room overlooking the front deck. In the French

Lake Waramaug is on view from window of front room at The Birches Inn.

style, it's a meal to remember. Frederic makes his own saucisson, which he hangs for eight weeks, and bakes his croissants and brioches. They and a fresh fruit salad precede the main event, perhaps poached eggs with arugula and a potato pancake.

The Inn at Lake Waramaug, incidentally, closed suddenly in early 1998. The buyer planned to raze the lodging facility and reopen the main building eventually as a restaurant.

(860) 868-1735 or (888) 590-7945. Fax (860) 868-1815. Eight rooms with private baths. May-October: doubles, $175 to $300 weekends, $125 to $225 midweek. Rest of year: doubles, $150 to $225 weekends, $95 to $175 midweek. Two-night minimum weekends in season. Children over 12. No smoking. Closed midweek in January and February.

Litchfield Inn, Route 202, Litchfield 06759.

Set back from the road west of the village on a vast expanse of lawn in need of more landscaping, local entrepreneur James Irwin's Litchfield Inn is a relatively new (1982) white Colonial-style inn with modern accoutrements, 30 guest rooms and a couple of suites, restaurant and a banquet facility. More seedlings, a pond and a fountain were in evidence at our latest visit.

Furnished with early American reproduction pieces, the rooms are air-conditioned and include a single double bed or two double beds, modern baths, color TV and telephones, and some have wet bars. Commanding top dollar are eight "theme rooms," ranging from the Sherlock Holmes to the Western Room to the Lady Agnew Suite. The Lace Room, all white and lacy with canopy bed and swagged draperies, is billed for honeymooners. The Presidential Quarters commemorates past presidents with mounted coin displays and wall hangings.

Ever-changing in an effort to find a niche, the restaurant operation was leased to John Roller of the acclaimed Bistro Cafe in New Milford. He lightened up the menu for what he called **The Bistro East,** housed in the large and formal Benjamin

Talmade Room, with a contemporary menu from pan-seared catfish to gorgonzola-crusted strip steak. Lunch in the Terrace Room and lounge is more casual.

(860) 567-4503 or (800) 499-3444. Fax (860) 567-5358. Thirty rooms and two suites with private baths. Doubles, $105 to $175, April-December; $90 to $150, rest of year. Entrées, $13.95 to $17.95. Lunch daily, 11:30 to 2:30. Dinner, 5:30 to 9:30. Sunday brunch, 11:30 to 2:30.

Dining Spots

The Birches Inn, 233 West Shore Road, New Preston 06777.

Young French chef Frederic Faveau has elevated the dining experience at this renovated inn to unprecedented heights. Lured by the opportunity, he and his wife, Karen Hamilton, who handles the front of the house, moved here in 1997 from the West Street Grill.

Painted coral with eucalyptus green trim, the serene dining room seats 70 at well spaced tables draped in white over floral undercloths. Big windows look down the lawn toward Lake Waramaug. "The view is beautiful and so is the food," says Frederic, not immodestly. He and two assistants do all the cooking for dinner, and Frederic, who lives on the property, prepares breakfast in the morning.

Frederic's food, which we experienced at the West Street Grill, has earned rave reviews. His short menu might list five entrées. Their simple descriptions – penne pasta and grilled Atlantic salmon, grilled chicken, grilled pork loin and grilled leg of lamb, each with different accompaniments – do not do justice to the subtleties of taste and complexities of presentation.

Appetizers demand attention, perhaps the house hickory-smoked salmon with a potato and scallion pancake and red tobiko crème fraîche, or grilled black tiger shrimp with Asian slaw, mizuna salad and red miso vinaigrette. The herbed potato galette with sautéed wild mushrooms, watercress and cognac demi-glace is a specialty.

The dessert tray illustrates his French heritage: fresh berry tart with almond paste, crème brûlée, chocolate marquise with homemade candied orange and a plum clafouti from Burgundy.

The wine list is select and fairly priced, and a number are available by the glass.

Frederic and Karen spent their winter vacation in Thailand in 1998, so expect more Pacific Rim accents on the fare.

(860) 868-1735 or (888) 590-7945. Entrées, $16 to $20. Dinner, Thursday-Monday 5:30 to 9. Closed January-February.

West Street Grill, 43 West St., Litchfield.

The food here is the subject of raves from food reviewers and the perfect foil for the trendoids who make this their own at lunch and dinner seven days a week. The two rooms were full the winter Saturday we first lunched here, and the host rattled off the names of half a dozen celebrities who had reserved for that evening.

The grill is the kind of place weekending New Yorkers love. It's sleek in black and white, with a row of low booths up the middle, tables and mirrors on either side, and a back room with stunning trompe-l'oeil curtains on the walls. The only color comes from the artworks on a side brick wall and from the power clientele.

The kitchen has maintained its culinary high through a succession of talented chefs, thanks to owner James O'Shea's magic touch. Our first lunch here began with a rich butternut squash and pumpkin bisque and the signature grilled peasant bread with parmesan aioli. Main dishes were an appetizer of grilled country bread with a brandade of white beans and marinated artichokes and a special of grilled smoked pork tenderloin with spicy Christmas limas. Among the highly touted desserts, we succumbed to an ethereal crème brûlée and an intense key lime tart that was really tart. With two generous glasses of wine, the total lunch bill for two came to a rather New Yorkish $50.

Memorable as it was, lunch was nothing compared with a special tasting dinner showcasing a summer menu. That extravaganza began with beet-green soup, grilled peasant bread with roasted tomato and goat cheese, corn cakes with crème fraîche and chives, roasted-beet and goat-cheese napoleons with a composed salad, and nori-wrapped salmon with marinated daikon, cucumbers and seaweed. A passionfruit sorbet followed. By then we felt that we had already dined well, but no, on came the entrées: tasting portions – which we shared back and forth – of pan-seared halibut with a beet pappardelle, spicy shrimp cake with ragoût of black beans and corn, grilled ginger chicken with polenta and ginger chips, and grilled leg of lamb with a ragoût of lentils, spicy curried vegetables and fried greens, including flat-leaf spinach. A little bit here, a little there, and next we knew emerged a parade of desserts: a plum tart in a pastry so tender as not to be believed, a frozen passionfruit soufflé, a hazelnut torte with caramel ice cream and a sampling of sorbets (raspberry, white peach and blackberry).

Both meals testified amply to West Street's incredible culinary prowess.

(860) 567-3885. Entrées, $17.95 to $23.95. Lunch daily, 11:30 to 3, weekends to 4. Dinner, 5:30 to 9:30 or 10:30.

Mayflower Inn, Route 47, Washington.

The three dining rooms along the back of the house are as stately as the rest of this grandly refurbished inn. They're appointed in English country-house style with upholstered high-back chairs at tables covered with white linens over dark green patterned skirts that match the draperies. Tapestries and wrought-iron furniture decorate the garden room. The bar room is English-looking in hunter green.

The chef changes the menu daily. Our latest autumn visit produced such treats as potato-crusted grouper fillet with tomato-basil relish, grilled swordfish with ossetra caviar cream, stuffed veal chop with wild mushroom fricassee and grilled peppered New York strip steak with caramelized vidalia onions. Starters included house-smoked salmon and salmon torte with roesti potatoes and lavash, lobster and sweet pepper stew with leeks and sherry peppers, and Alaskan crab cake with Thai curry sauce.

Desserts are to die for, from caramel roasted pears served over a warm semolina terrine to blueberry and raspberry crème brûlée. Two pages of fine wines are available by the glass from a wine list honored by Wine Spectator.

Some of the dinner appetizers and pastas turn up on the lunch menu. The outdoor terrace with its view of manicured lawns and imported specimen trees is an idyllic setting in season.

(860) 868-9466. Entrées, $18 to $30. Lunch daily, noon to 2. Dinner nightly, 6 to 9. Bar menu daily, 11:30 to 3 and 5 to midnight.

The Boulders Inn, Route 45, New Preston.

Boulders are a good part of the decor at this inn, jutting out from the walls of the intimate inner dining room as well as in part of the smashing six-sided addition,

Wall of boulders at Boulders Inn.   **Mirrored dining room at West Street Grill.**

where, through large wraparound windows, almost every diner has a view of Lake Waramaug across the road. Three levels of a spacious outside deck/terrace are the delightful setting for cocktails and dinner during the warmer months.

Inside, chandeliers with pierced lampshades made by innkeeper Ulla Adema hang from the ceilings. Tables are covered with white cloths over forest green.

The scene is rustically elegant, and the food quite sophisticated. Over the years we've trekked here for memorable meals in a magical setting.

One recent night's main courses included fillet of monkfish baked in radicchio with hot bacon vinaigrette, sesame-seared yellowfin tuna with ginger cream sauce, grilled whisky-marinated pork chop with caramelized apples, and grilled chipotle-marinated venison with sweet blueberry sauce.

Among appetizers were spicy shrimp egg rolls with soy peanut dipping sauce, aged goat cheese baked in brioche with mesclun greens and basil vinaigrette, and smoked pheasant quesadilla with grilled red pepper salsa. Desserts were an ethereal cheesecake with candied ginger crust and white and dark chocolate mousse in a tuile cup.

(860) 868-0541 or (800) 552-6853. Entrées, $18 to $27. Dinner nightly except Tuesday in summer, 6 to 8 or 9, Sunday 4 to 8. Thursday-Sunday in winter.

Hopkins Inn, Hopkins Road, New Preston.

On a warm summer day or evening, few dining spots are more inviting than the large outdoor terrace under the giant horse chestnut tree at the entrance to the Hopkins Inn.

With the waters of Lake Waramaug shimmering below and a bottle of wine from the Hopkins Vineyard next door, you could imagine yourself in the Alps. No wonder Austrian chef-owner Franz Schober feels right at home.

Dining inside this 1847 Federal structure is rewarding as well. Two dining rooms stretch around the lakeview side of the inn; the overflow goes to a paneled Colonial-style taproom up a few stairs. One dining room is Victorian, while the other is rustic with barnsiding and ships' figureheads on the walls.

The menu reflects the Austrian and Swiss dishes of the chef's heritage. You might start with pâté maison, eggs à la russe, escargots or bundnerteller. Dinner entrées include specialties like wiener schnitzel and sweetbreads Viennese that we remember fondly from years past. Chicken cordon bleu, loin lamb chops and filet mignon with béarnaise sauce appeal to traditional palates. In spring, you can get shad roe; Beth Schrober says her husband's roast pheasant with red cabbage and spaetzle is especially popular in fall. Vegetables are special, especially unusual things like braised romaine lettuce.

Regulars cherish the frozen grand marnier soufflé glacé and strawberries romanoff. The varied wine list offers half a dozen from Switzerland as well as several from Hopkins Vineyard. Finish with a flourish with cappuccino or liqueured coffees.

The luncheon menu offers many of the same specialties at lower prices. Entrées like lamb curry and sirloin steak are in the $8 to $10 range. Little wonder the place is so popular.

(860) 868-7295. Entrées, $16.50 to $19.75 Lunch, Tuesday-Saturday noon to 2. Dinner 6 to 9 or 10. Sunday 12:30 to 8:30. No lunch in April, November and December. Closed January-March.

Le Bon Coin, Route 202, Woodville.

The small white dormered house along the road from Litchfield to New Preston is home for classic French cuisine, lovingly tendered by chef-owner William Janega, who moved from Le Parisien in Stamford with his wife and sons to take over a very personal country establishment. He describes his cooking as "classic French, flavorful but light."

The dark, cozy barroom has copies of French Impressionist paintings on the walls and Hitchcock chairs at half a dozen small tables. On the other side of the foyer is a dining room, barely larger but brighter in country French style. Colorful La Fleur china tops the double sets of heavy white linen cloths at each table, and the rooms are most welcoming.

Dinners might begin with pâté of pork and duck, extra-garlicky escargots, vol-au-vent or Maryland crab cakes. The onion soup and the robust lobster bisque are classics, and the salad with gorgonzola is extravagant.

Entrées include dover sole with mushrooms and artichokes, frog's legs provençale, sweetbreads du jour, lamb sauté, pepper steak and scallops of veal with basil and tomatoes. Desserts include a plate of assorted ice creams and sorbets, floating island, poached pear with raspberry sauce, chocolate rice soufflé and crème caramel.

Chef Janega is proud of his wine list – mostly French – and of his front entry, decorated with wine casks, spigots and crate labels plus some handsome stained-glass windows.

(860) 868-7763. Entrées, $12.75 to $19. Lunch, Monday and Thursday-Saturday noon to 2. Dinner, 6 to 9, Sunday 5 to 9. Closed Tuesday.

Toll Gate Hill, Route 202, Litchfield.

Innkeeper Fritz Zivic, who founded the late Black Dog Tavern steakhouse chain in the Hartford area in the 1960s, features a changing menu of what he calls "light, unencumbered food" in two small, charming dining areas on the inn's main floor and upstairs in a ballroom complete with a fiddler's loft for piano and other musical entertainment on occasion.

The original dining rooms took on a new look recently, when tall booths were added to the old tavern with its dark wood and wide-plank floors. The more formal room, dressed with peach linens and Villeroy & Boch china, was enhanced by wall murals of 18th-century Litchfield painted by a local artist.

The menu changes seasonally. The dinner fare ranges from roasted cod with horseradish crust to the signature shell-fish pie in puff pastry, about which we've heard raves. Other favorites are poached salmon with sundried tomato sauce and New York strip steak with roasted garlic.

The wine list is choice and reasonably priced, the soups (like clam chowder with green chiles and tomatoes) are creative and our summer dinners a few years ago of shrimp in beer batter and sautéed sea scallops with sweet butter and braised leeks were outstanding. The English hunt brunch is good value for $12.95.

Corner table at Toll Gate Hill.

(860) 567-4545 or (800) 445-3903. Entrées, $18 to $24. Lunch daily, noon to 3. Dinner, 5:30 to 9:30 or 10:30. Sunday brunch, 11:30 to 3:30. Closed Tuesday and Wednesday in off-season.

Grappa, 26 Commons Drive (off Route 202), Litchfield Commons, Litchfield.

This is the Italian offshoot of the West Street Grill, housed at the rear of a shopping complex. Here all is convivial and intimate (make that very) with rich wood tables cheek-by-jowl in two dining areas and a solarium. Mirrors are positioned to make the place look bigger. It manages to seat 100 inside and 44 more outside on a courtyard in season.

Warm, warm, warm is the sunny southern exposure in the solarium, partially shaded by billowing curtain-type affairs on the ceiling. That and the adjacent 650-degree wood-burning oven, with walls of brick and a floor of lava from Mount St. Helen's, must produce quite an air-conditioning bill (or perhaps save on heating in winter). From the oven, which is open to the bar area, come exotic thin-crust pizzas ($8.95 to $13.95), a dozen or more versions from clam and pancetta to calamari fra diavolo.

The kitchen also is strong on novel starters, of which we'd gladly make an entire meal. There are about eight pastas and eight entrées of the day. Expect things like cappellini with rock shrimp and shallots, grilled salmon on a bed of spinach, flank steak rubbed with chile and garlic, and Tuscan veal stew with crimini mushrooms and madeira.

Predictable desserts include white chocolate cheesecake, apple turnover and tirami su. Co-owner Charles Kafferman installed an ice-cream machine for frozen drinks and sundaes to attract the family trade.

(860) 567-1616. Entrées, $14.95 to $17.95. Dinner, Tuesday-Sunday 5 to 9:30 or 10:30.

G.W. Tavern, 20 Bee Brook Road, Washington Depot.

This restaurant of many changing names has seen several big-bucks renovations over the years. But none more so than the latest that transformed the late Bee Brook, a highly rated fine-dining establishment, into a downscaled pub and tavern with an unlikely name.

The conversion by New York restaurateurs Reggie Young, the host, and Robert Margolis, the chef, has been done with style and an eye to a market niche. The main dining room with vaulted skylight is now a tavern with an upscale Colonial look, oriental carpets on the floors and wonderful murals of surrounding towns on the walls. The rear porch beside the stream has been enclosed for year-round casual dining. The outdoor terraces are popular in summer.

The chef features "good, simple pub food." At our latest autumn visit, the changing menu started with black bean and pork soup, chicken liver pâté with red onion relish and steamed mussels with garlic and white wine. Main courses ranged from a burger and fish and chips to grilled mahi-mahi with dijon cream sauce, chicken pot pie and roast beef with yorkshire pudding. Desserts included "Reggie's mom's pumpkin pie," blueberry cobbler and triple chocolate cake.

The initials on the name stand for George Washington, whose hatchet is carved in the sign out front. This is, after all, another of those towns named for the first president.

(860) 868-6633. Entrées, $7.50 to $16.50. Lunch, Monday-Friday 11:30 to 2:30, weekends to 3. Dinner nightly, 5:30 to 10 or 11.

La Tienda Cafe, Sports Village, Route 202, Litchfield.

A green neon cactus beckons in the window of this two-room Mexican cafe with a bar in the rear. Glass tops the cloths of wide, bright stripes and a cactus in a small pot may be on each table. Colorful prints and rugs adorn the walls.

Crispy homemade tortilla chips and a fairly hot salsa are served. We found a lunch of Mexican pizza almost more than one could handle: a flour tortilla topped with ground beef, cheese, lettuce, tomato, chiles, guacamole and sour cream. One half had hot peppers, the other mild. An order of burritos, one stuffed with cheese and scallions and one with chicken, was also delicious and hearty.

Both lunch and dinner menus include "north of the border" dishes, but who would come here for a BLT or strip steak? Black bean soup, flautas, Arizona-style nachos (topped with ground beef) and seafood quesadilla are some of the starters, and there's even a Mexican egg roll. Dinners include Mexican rice and refried beans or salad, and range from folded tacos to seafood chimichanga. Lime pie is the favored desert, but flan and sopaipilla also are popular.

Margaritas, piña coladas and daiquiris are offered by the carafe.

(860) 567-8778. Entrées, $7.95 to $14.25. Lunch, Tuesday-Saturday 11:30 to 2:30. Dinner, Monday-Saturday 4:30 to 9 or 10, Sunday noon to 9.

Spinell's Litchfield Food Company, On the Green, Litchfield.

Rick Spinell, pastry chef at New York's famed River Cafe, answered a for-sale ad "for that expensive takeout place in Litchfield" and ended up owning it. He thought running a specialty-foods shop, bakery and deli with a handful of tables would be easier than a full restaurant, but found that he had to become jack of so many trades that he's rarely in the kitchen. While he's out front, several chefs and bakers work behind scenes to prepare baked goods from scratch, delectable salads and soups of the day (perhaps tomato-bean-rosemary and mushroom-brie-onion). Rick lowered the prices charged by his high-profile predecessors and added breakfast items every day but Wednesday. The focaccia sandwich with sundried tomatoes, goat cheese, roasted peppers, oil and vinegar and a three-salad combination plate made a stellar lunch for two.

(860) 567-3113. Open daily, 8:30 to 6, Saturday to 7.

The County Seat, 3 West St., Litchfield.

This new coffee house and cafe quickly became the county seat, so to speak – a favorite gathering spot day and night. Occupying a prime corner space facing the green, it's a veritable living room of sofas and banquettes, potted palms, a soda-fountain counter and a variety of tables for enjoying soups and salads, pizza and pasta, in addition to specialty coffees. Fruit smoothies are dispensed from the ice cream bar. The dinner menu has been expanded lately, and people bring their own beer or wine to enjoy with musical entertainment afterward. Gifts, confections and poetry readings are among the attractions.

(860) 567-8069. Open Sunday-Wednesday 7 a.m. to 9 p.m., Thursday to 10, weekends to midnight. BYOB.

Diversions

Lakes and Parks. Lake Waramaug State Park at the west end of the lake is a wonderfully scenic site, its picnic tables scattered well apart along the tree-lined shore, right beside the water. The lake's Indian name means "good fishing place." It's also good for swimming and boating, and is blessedly uncrowded. On the north and east sides of the lake are the forested Above All and Mount Bushnell state parks. Not far from Lake Waramaug on the road to Litchfield (Route 202) is **Mount Tom State Park.** It has a 60-acre spring-fed pond for swimming and again picnic tables are poised at shore's edge. A mile-long trail rises to a tower atop Mount Tom.

White Memorial Foundation and Conservation Center, Route 202, Litchfield.

Just west of Litchfield are 4,000 acres of nature sanctuary bordering Bantam Lake. Thirty-five miles of woodland and marsh trails are popular with hikers, horseback riders and cross-country skiers. This is a great place for observing wildlife, birds and plants in a variety of habitats. The Conservation Center in a 19th-century mansion contains a natural history museum with good collections of Indian artifacts, butterflies, live and stuffed animals, and an excellent nature library.

(860) 567-0857. Grounds open free year-round. Museum, Monday-Saturday 9 to 5, Sunday noon to 5, April-October; Monday-Saturday 8:30 to 4:30, Sunday noon to 4, rest of year. Adults, $2.

White Flower Farm, Route 63, Litchfield.

This institution three miles south of Litchfield is a don't-miss spot for anyone with a green thumb. In fact, people come from across the country to see the place made famous by its catalog, wittily written by the owner under the pen name of Amos Pettingill. Ten acres of exotic display gardens are at peak bloom in late spring; twenty acres of growing fields reach their height in late summer. Greenhouses with indoor plants, including spectacular giant tuberous begonias, are pretty all the time.

(860) 567-8789. Shop and grounds open daily 9 to 6, April-October; 10 to 5, rest of year.

Litchfield Historic Sites. The Litchfield Historic District is clustered along the long, wide green and out North and South streets (Route 63). The seasonal infor-

Litchfield Congregational Church.

mation center on the green has maps for walking tours, which are the best way to experience Litchfield. Note the bank and the jail with a common wall at North and West streets. Along North Street are Sheldon's Tavern, where George Washington slept, plus the birthplace of Harriet Beecher Stowe and the Pierce Academy, the first academy for girls. South Street is a broad, half-mile-long avenue where two U.S. senators, six Congressmen, three governors and five chief justices have lived. Here too is the **Tapping Reeve House and Law School** (1773), the first law school in the country. The house with its handsome furnishings and the tiny school with handwritten ledgers of students long gone are open Tuesday-Saturday 11 to 5 and Sunday 1 to 5, May-October, $3. The fee includes admission to the **Litchfield Historical Society Museum,** which has four galleries of early American paintings, decorative arts, furniture and local history exhibits.

Wineries. Two of New England's premier wineries occupy hilltop sites overlooking the beauty of Litchfield and Lake Waramaug. **Haight Vineyard,** Connecticut's first farm winery just east of Litchfield, occupies an English Tudor-style building with a large tasting room and gift shop across Chestnut Hill Road from its original barn. Guided winery tours on the hour and a fifteen-minute vineyard walk are among the attractions. You can pick up a bottle of award-winning covertside white or chardonnay plus a pink T-shirt ("Never bite the foot that stomps your grapes"), wine accessories and such. Open Monday-Saturday 10:30 to 5, Sunday noon to 5.

Hopkins Vineyard, Hopkins Road, New Preston. A hillside location with a good view of Lake Waramaug marks this family operation run by Bill and Judy Hopkins, dairy farmers turned winemakers, and their offspring. The rustic red barn provides a quick, self-guided tour from an upstairs vantage point, an attractive showroom and tasting area, and the country-sophisticated **Hayloft Wine Bar** upstairs, where you can order a cheese and pâté board and wines by the glass and savor a view of the lake. The gift shop sells wine-related items like baskets, grapevine wreaths and stemware, even handmade linen towels. The winery's cat may be snoozing near the wood stove, upon which a pot of mulled wine simmers on chilly days. On nice days, you can sip a superior seyval blanc or an estate chardonnay in a small picnic area overlooking the lake. Open Monday-Saturday 10 to 5, Sunday 11 to 5, May-December; Wednesday-Sunday in March and April, Friday-Sunday rest of year.

Shopping. Good shops have sprung up in the center of Litchfield and its western environs. In quaint Cobble Court downtown, check out **The Litchfield Exchange,** where practically everything is handmade, including lovely clothes for children, **Wildlife Landing** (a nature lover's gift store, from figurines and jewelry to bird feeders) and the **Kitchenworks.** On the green is **Workshop Inc.,** a boutique with updated women's apparel and accessories; downstairs is a gallery of home furnishings, from wicker furniture to pillows and dhurries to unusual placemats. **Barnidge & McEnroe,** a good book store, has an espresso bar up front. **Hayseed** stocks a great selection of cards along with jewelry, sweaters and clothes. **R. Derwin Clothiers** outfits men and women.

Litchfield Commons, a cluster of changing shops in an attractive grouping around a brick walk, is worth a stop as you traverse Route 202 west of town. Beyond is **House in the Country Ltd.,** where new homeowners can furnish their digs.

New Preston, a mountain hamlet just down the hillside from Lake Waramaug, is experiencing a flurry of shop openings. We never can leave **J. Seitz & Co.** without wishing we could make a purchase. In a converted garage overlooking a waterfall, Joanna Seitz shows clothing, antiques and accessories from around the world, with a decided emphasis on the American Southwest. The coats made of old Pendleton Indian blankets for $425 are unique, as are the baby jackets made of Southwest blankets ($125) and the handpainted furniture. Other shops worth browsing are **City House/Country House, Lou Marotta Inc.** for painted furniture, **Ray Boas, Antiquarian Bookseller, Jonathan Peters** for fine linens and lacy things, **The Trumpeter** for antiques and autographs, and **Black Swan Antiques.**

Extra-Special ——————————————

The Pantry, Titus Road, Washington Depot.

One of our favorite places for lunch and shopping is this upscale gourmet shop lovingly run by Michael and Nancy Ackerman. A counter displays the day's offerings from an extensive repertoire. The fare is innovative, with especially good soups, salads, sandwiches and desserts. A spring visit brought forth soups like celery-leek and curried cauliflower. Among entrées were fresh tuna and swordfish niçoise with tarragon carrots, torta rustica, salmon cakes with mixed green salad and a vegetarian chili with watercress cabbage slaw. Continental breakfast is served from 10 to 11:30; a huge sticky bun and cappuccino would make a good break from nipping around Washington Depot's shops. In summer, poached salmon is a favorite, more salads are offered, and soups like gazpacho teem with fresh vegetables. For dessert, chocolate indulgence, mayan torte and pecan tart with ginger ice cream are worth the calories. Tables, decorated perhaps with lilies in flat bowls, are set amidst high-tech shelves on which are just about every exotic chutney, mustard, vinegar, extra-virgin olive oil and the like that you could imagine, as well as kitchenware and tableware, baskets and pottery.

(860) 868-0258. Entrées, $6.50 to $8.95. Open Tuesday-Saturday 10 to 6. Lunch from 11:30 to 3:30. Tea 3:30 to 5.

Index